NOT BORED!
Anthology
1983-2010

Colossal Books
Cincinnati, Ohio

Published February 2011

Colossal Books
P.O. Box 20201
Cincinnati, OH 45220

Copyright 2011 by William J. Brown. All rights reserved.

www.notbored.org

Cover design: Susan J Hull.
NOT BORED! logo: Orrin Pava 1996.

ISBN: 978-0-578-07654-6
Printed and bound in the USA.

Dedicated to my readers, past, present and future

Contents

Preface (1996)	i
Preface (2010)	vi

Local interventions
    Nectarine Ballroom (Ann Arbor)   1
    Against Ondine/Warhol (Ann Arbor)   2
    The UB Graffiti Scandal (Buffalo)   4
    Bulletin From Rewrite (NYC)   28
    Squatted Buildings (NYC)   28
    Squats Evicted (NYC)   40
    Unabomber for President (NYC)   43
    A Unabomber for President Banner (NYC)   45
    Fucking Ugly Buildings (NYC)   47
    Decrees of the NYPA (NYC)   49
    Pedestrian Barricades (NYC)   50
    Drifting with the NYPA (NYC)   53
    Yuppie Go Home (NYC)   58
    Debord Film Screening (NYC)   70
    Turning Over a New Leaf (NYC)   72

Internecine Polemics
    The Pro-Situs   74
    Situationist Films   80
    Guy Debord's Films   83
    Keith Sanborn's Bootlegs   91
    Stewart Home   95
    Bob Black   100
    Retort   102
    An Expose of Bob Black   114

The Situationist International
    An Intro to the SI   120
    Guy Debord's *Comments*   131
    Charles Radcliffe's *Heatwave*   133
    At Dusk: The Situationist Movement   136
    Yet Another Intro to the SI   140

The English Situationists	150
Pierre Guillaume	155
50th anniversary of the SI's Founding	160
The Virtual Spectacle	169
Dispensing with Clausewitz	197
Professor Galloway's Latest Stupidities	201
To Guy Debord in Hell	206
Guy Debord in 2009	211
Re: Wayne Spencer's Proposal	215

Book reviews

TJ Clark, *The Painting of Modern Life*	219
Greil Marcus, *Lipstick Traces On a Cigarette*	225
Henri Lefebvre, *Introduction to Modernity*	228
Raoul Vaneigem, *Movement of the Free Spirit*	234
Unabomber, *Industrial Society and Its Future*	238
Dennis Rodman, *As Bad As I Wanna Be*	244
Cornelius Castoriadis, *Political and Social Writings, Vol. I*	248
Thomas F. McDonough, *Guy Debord and the SI*	258
Len Bracken, *Guy Debord: Revolutionary*	261
Jamie Reid, *Peace is Tough*	264
Angelo Quattrochhi, *The Beginning of the End*	266
Gianfranco Sanguinetti, *Veritable Report on the Last Chance*	274
Simon Sadler, *The Situationist City*	281
Jacques Attali, *Noise*	296
Cornelius Castoriadis, *Political and Social Writings, Vol. II*	304
Norman Cohn, *Pursuit of the Millennium*	312
Henri Lefebvre, *The Production of Space*	318
TJ Clark, *The End of an Idea*	329
Cornelius Castoriadis, *Political and Social Writings, Vol. III*	363
Michael Perlman, *The Invention of Capitalism*	374
Thomas Pynchon, *Vineland*	382
Jean-Michel Mension, *The Tribe*	393
Georges Bataille, *The Accursed Share*	397
Allan Antliff, *Anarchist Modernism*	403
Lester Bangs, *Mainlines, Blood Feasts and Bad Taste*	406
Kurt Cobain, *Journals*	408
Paul Virilio, *The Strategy of Deception*	410
Paco Ignacio Taibo, *'68*	414

Greil Marcus, *Like A Rolling Stone* 418
Paul Virilio, *Art and Fear* 424
Paul Virilio, *Popular Defense & Ecological Struggles* 431
Tom McDonough, *Guy Debord and the SI* 433
Elizabeth Byrne Ferm, *Freedom in Education* 437
Giorgio Agamben, *Homo Sacer* 444
Henri Lefebvre, *Writing on Cities* 451
Ken Knabb, *Situationist International Anthology* 461
Raoul Vaneigem, *A Declaration of the Rights* 464
Eyal Weizman, *Hollow Land* 473
Guy Debord, *Correspondence (June 1957-August 1960)* 489
Greil Marcus, *When That Rough God Goes Riding* 491

Musicians
  David Bowie 500
  Gang of Four 502
  Radio Noriega 505
  Sinead O'Connor 507
  "Rough Music" 509
  Gang of Four Return 513
  Os Mutantes 517
  Pete Townshend 521
  Lou Reed 525
  The Cure 528
  Led Zeppelin 529
  Kurt Cobain 532

Miscellaneous
  41 Curses, Crises & Conspiracies of Everyday Life 546
  United Auto Workers on Strike 553
  The Violence in Seattle 554
  Rebuilding the World Trade Center 557
  The Relevance of Antonio Negri 561
  Foucault's *Discipline and Punish* 570
  A Critique of Neo-Anarchism 573
  Cynical Proposals for the Advertising Industry 575
  Text About Guy Dauve Censored 578

Index 583

Preface 1996
Preface to *Tract Record:*
NOT BORED! 1983 to the present

NOT BORED! was first published in Ann Arbor, Michigan, in July 1983. At the time I was 24 years old; I'd finally graduated from college, but wasn't really using my degree. I was working full-time as a cook in a restaurant and writing a weekly column as well as freelancing articles on pop music for *The Ann Arbor News*. I was also doing a lot of reading: every article on rock 'n' roll in *The Village Voice* and *Musician*; anything by Greil Marcus or Lester Bangs, my favorite rock critics; all of Tom Wolfe's books, early Susan Sontag, and eventually, through her, Roland Barthes and contemporary French theory. I was beginning to have trouble getting my increasingly informed and self-conscious stuff by my new editor. It all came to a head, so to speak, when I saw David Bowie for the first time, in Detroit's Joe Louis Arena, in the summer of 1983. (You'd think I'd remember the exact date, but I don't.)[1]

Bowie was out on yet another "comeback" tour; his new touring show was, yet again, "his best since Ziggy Stardust." Dressed in a white suit, white shoes and a blue shirt – his hair a natural-seeming blond – the man I had listened to, learned from and adored for a decade emerged from a tall clear tube and sang "Space Oddity," his first major hit single. As I remember it today, when the tune was done, Bowie took off his white jacket, raised his acoustic guitar and for a few spectacular, flashbulb-popping moments, rested his head on it – striking the exact pose and wearing the same colors as Picasso's *Man with a Guitar*! It was an absolutely brilliant touch, easily managing to suggest where Bowie's music would fit in to the history of modern art, or, if you please, where modern art (specifically painting) would fit in to the spiraling history of Bowie's musical development. But what really struck me was the possibility that I might have been the only one attending the concert that night who caught the allusion.

There were, of course, several more truly remarkable moments in Bowie's show. It was easily the best rock 'n' roll show I'd ever seen. But it was also terribly alienating. By the end of the show, I was alarmed by the possibility that a great majority of the audience was completely missing the overall drift of Bowie's allusions and quotations, not to mention the individual allusions and quotations themselves. As was clearly demonstrated by the staging of "Modern Love," the last song in the show and Bowie's current hit single, the overall drift of Bowie's contrapuntal performance was towards fascism. "Modern Love" is both an ironic commentary on the institution of marriage and an opportunity for Bowie to explain the nature of the romance between himself and his fans: the line "It's not really

---
[1] It was 30 July 1983. See "Introduction and Acknowledgements" in Bill Brown, *You Should've Heard Just What I Seen: Collected Newspaper Articles 1981-1984* (Colossal Books, 2010).

Preface 1996

work/It's just the power to charm" is designed to fit both marriage and pop superstardom. To sing this song, Bowie arranged his musicians and backup singers (all of whom were men) to form a huge pyramid, with Bowie himself at the very top of the hierarchy. When it came around, the line "Modern love/Tests my faith in God and Man" chilled me to the bone, for I caught a glimpse of a society that was strong and faithful precisely because there were no women in it at all.

I made the perfectly understandable, indeed, perfectly logical decision to try to express what I'd seen and experienced at the Bowie concert in a review to be published in *The Ann Arbor News*. But the article wasn't rejected; it was published over the strenuous objections of my new editor. I'd successfully appealed "my case" for publishing it to my old editor. When the article drew letters to the editor that protested its presumption to speak about Bowie's attitudes towards women and politics in a mere concert review, I began to see that it was time for me to move on. Eventually, my movements would carry me out of Ann Arbor and into Buffalo, New York, where I started going to graduate school in January 1985 to study American Literature. But my first movement was away from daily newspapers such as *The Ann Arbor News*, despite the fact that they had a certain immediacy: what I wrote at 2 in the morning was published at 2 in the afternoon of the very same day.

Every July, various parties in Ann Arbor come together to present the "Ann Arbor Art Fair," a several-day-long event in which several of the town's most important streets are turned over to pedestrians and to the artists, craftspeople and vendors who would sell them their products. I decided that at this particular "Art Fair" (as a present to myself) I would give away as many copies as I could of "my new magazine," which was actually an excuse or opportunity for me to write about and make known exactly what was troubling me about David Bowie and the pop psychology of fascism. In other words, the article "David Bowie: Friend or Foe?" came first and the magazine it was eventually published in came second. After I'd surrounded the article with various unrelated bits (an article on Ann Arbor skate-kids that was rejected by *The Ann Arbor Observer*; a short story; a couple of adverts for things done by friends, etc.), there was "enough" to be a magazine of some kind. In total, about 100 copies of this photocopied magazine were given away free.

Perhaps the easiest part of putting out the first issue was coming up with a name for the magazine. As both a fan and a rock critic, I had been struck by the accuracy of a description I came across in the journalism of Tom Wolfe, who referred to the look, style and attitude of musicians such as David Bowie, the Rolling Stones and Elvis, as "gloriously bored." These musicians were so rebellious that they were bored with the very idea of it; they were such connoisseurs of the exotic that they could find a perverse pleasure in their own boredom. In a word, I wanted musicians who were not bored. Personally, I wanted to be *not* bored, to be excited by the idea of rebellion or even rebelliousness, to be naive enough to hate being bored and all of its subtleties, nuances and reputed

Preface 1996

compensations. And so that was the title of the first issue of my little photocopied vanity magazine: *NOT BORED!*

It is somehow appropriate, given the fact that the establishment of the magazine came after the creation of the centerpiece of the first issue, that it wasn't until the second issue of *NOT BORED!* that I realized what the purpose of the magazine was, once the Bowie piece had been published. Sometime after the publication of NB!#1, two related things caught my attention: 1) the importance of the Sex Pistols, a punk band I loved, to Greil Marcus's *Village Voice* book review of *The Situationist International Anthology* (Bureau of Public Secrets, 1982); and 2) the importance of the situationist concept of detournement to a local anti-military research group whose style I very much admired. I purchased and began reading (devouring would be a better word) everything by the situationists that was available in English: the *Anthology*, Guy Debord's *The Society of the Spectacle* (originally 1967; translated in 1983) and Raoul Vaneigem's *The Revolution of Everyday Life* (originally 1967; translated in 1983). By the second issue, which came out in January 1984, *NOT BORED!* had become a "situationist fanzine." It has remained one ever since.

What does this mean, "a situationist fanzine"? It means that the magazine has been devoted to reviewing recently published or recently translated texts – as well as public exhibitions of artistic works – by or about the (ex-)situationists. A handful of obscure situationist texts have also been reprinted or translated and published for the first time in its pages. *NOT BORED!* is a "situationist fanzine" to the extent that the content of the magazine has been concerned with relatively sophisticated topics (such as the nature of capitalist society, the value of good works of popular art, and the role of the intellectual in modern America), while the form of the magazine has remained amateurish, rudimentary, even crude. The tension or disparity between the sophistication of the content and the crudity of the form used to express that content can obviously be quite productive. It can, for example, suggest "Anyone could do something like this" as well as "More people should do something like this." The disparity between the development of the content and that of the form can also call attention to the fact that, in most if not all "mainstream" publications, the disparity works the other way: the form of these publications is relatively sophisticated, even impressive, while their content is deeply impoverished. And so the "structural" reversal at work in *NOT BORED!* is thus a kind of critique-in-acts of what is possible in the spectacularly overdeveloped publishing "world," of what could be possible in this "world" if it wasn't organized as it currently is.

As "a situationist fanzine" – perhaps that should be, So as to be "a situationist fanzine" – *NOT BORED!* has also included in every issue since the second one a section that deals with what is really happening in the town or city in which I happen to live. While I was living in Ann Arbor, that section was entitled "What's Happening in Ann Arbor?" After I moved to Buffalo, its title became "What's Happening in Buffalo?" What I have meant by these questions is, "What

Preface 1996

am I, as the principal writer/editor/publisher of a situationist zine, actually doing in the real world to make things less boring?" And so each issue has contained descriptions and self-evaluations of such actions or projects as graffiti campaigns, flyers and pamphlets that have been given out, posters that have been put up, meetings that have been held, experiments that have been made, adventures that have been lived, and battles that have been fought (and won or lost). As a result, *NOT BORED!* has been and continues to be a very personal magazine: it is my diary as I navigate my way through space, time, ideas, and states of mind. And yet *NOT BORED!* has never been what *Factsheet Five* calls a "personal zine": it has included the work of other writers and artists (mostly friends of mine); furthermore, one can find the magazine interesting without knowing me personally or even knowing my identity (my name and my "real" job). Indeed, ever since 1987 or so, the magazine has been published anonymously.

But I get ahead of myself. In the summer of 1984, I noticed increasingly sophisticated references to the situationists in music-related publications (especially those that specialized in punk and hardcore). It was clear that the publication of *The Situationist Anthology* and the resulting discussions of the situationists' influence on and importance to the Sex Pistols had turned a lot of people on. And so I took upon myself the burden of researching and writing "An Intro to the S.I." that would be suitable for a 1980s "punk audience," in particular, for publication in the November 1984 issue punk fanzine *Maximum Rock'n'Roll*. To fully master what I'd been teaching myself, I had to try to teach it to others. Only then would I be able to move on to producing "authentic" situationist theories and actions of and on my own. Because the writing, publication of and responses to "An Intro to the S.I." roughly coincided with my December 1984 move from Ann Arbor (and my "job" as a freelancer) to Buffalo (and my graduate-level studies), the history of *NOT BORED!* contains at least two periods: the Ann Arbor period and the Buffalo period.

If the height, so to speak, of the Ann Arbor period was a text ("An Intro to the S.I."), then the height of the Buffalo period was an action (persistently writing poetico-political graffiti in a cold, all-concrete tunnel at the State University of New York at Buffalo campus that was to be "officially" decorated sometime in the future). Both the text and the action generated small, but intense controversies in which I was an active participant, not a spectator. In both instances, I was treated to healthy doses of the commentary and criticism of other people; I had to take a stand and then defend and answer for it. But in the latter instance, I was also treated to warm praise as well as to stern critique: Greil Marcus wrote a review of *NB!*#11 (January 1987) in his "Real Life Top Ten" column, then published in *The Village Voice*. In his review, Greil called attention to the fact that "Our Methods & Goals in the UB Graffiti Scandal" (NB!#11, 1987) harkened back to the situationists' "Our Methods & Goals in the Strasbourg Scandal," which appeared in *Internationale Situationniste* #11, 1967. "The serendipity of numbers," Greil asked, referring to 11 and 1967/1987, "or the numbers of serendipity?"

Preface 1996

I must say that, though the review was a dream come true for me, it made me more self-conscious about putting out *NOT BORED!* than I'd ever been. Especially as the graffiti scandal grew and grew – it finally petered out in 1989, three years after it began – I became more and more self-conscious about my own "importance as a revolutionary." As you might imagine, this mental state was not at all conducive to producing an intentionally marginal, self-avowedly amateurish magazine that came out in quantities of 100 or less per issue. After the publication of the 13th issue, which came out in December 1987, I was too confused to go on, but I wasn't willing to dissolve the magazine itself. My solution was that, thenceforth, I would only produce supplements to the 13th issue: there would be no more "new" issues; there would only be issues that supplemented or replaced earlier issues of *NOT BORED!*

As artificial as it might sound, this strategy worked for a year or so. A total of three full-length supplements to "the last issue" were published, all of them in Buffalo. Perhaps it was as a result of this very self-conscious process of mourning – in combination with moving back and forth between Buffalo and Ann Arbor as I wrote my doctoral dissertation – that I eventually got back in touch with the impulses that originally led me to write, edit and publish *NOT BORED!* In any event, a 14th issue finally did come out in February 1989, but it was a "special," transitional issue devoted almost entirely to detourned comic strips. The 15th issue of *NOT BORED!* (April 1989) saw the decisive return of its "original," situationist format; this issue also included the last report on the UB graffiti scandal.

At this writing, the most recent issue is #24 (September 1995); #25 will be published in June 1996. Much happened between the 15th and 24th issues: in particular, I moved twice, from Buffalo to Providence, Rhode Island, and then from Providence to New York City, the place of my birth. I have the sense that I have come full circle, and am now preparing to go for another round. It is therefore to the future that this *Tract Record* is dedicated.

NOT BORED! #25, June 1996

Preface (2010)

My years in New York City were very productive. It was there that I co-founded the Surveillance Camera Players, a situationist-inspired street-theatre group. With a slightly different group of people, I co-founded the New York Psychogeographical Association, which executed a number of actions, including a very successful anti-Yuppie graffiti campaign in Williamsburg, Brooklyn. And, with a different group of people, I participated in efforts to both document and defend the community gardens and squatted buildings in the lower east side of Manhattan, which were then under sustained attack from the Giuliani Administration.

While in New York, and with help from friends (chiefly Orrin Pava), I established an on-line "presence," as one used to say, for *NOT BORED!* In addition to materials drawn from the printed copies of the magazine (scans of various covers and the texts of my favorite articles), www.notbored.org has also been the repository for a huge archive of materials produced by or otherwise related to the Situationist International: scans of paintings and photographs; texts in translation that were published in various books, most of them copyright-protected; and lists of the group's sections and members. In time, as I became proficient in translating from French into English, the website also became an archive for texts that were newly published and/or had never been translated before, especially the hundreds of letters Guy Debord wrote between 1957 and 1994. Because of the website's long and interrupted success in hosting "infringements" of copyrighted material, it has also been used to help other publishers, authors and translators (Jean-Francois Martos, Michel Bounan, and David Ames Curtis, among them) who have had their respective projects blocked by various self-righteous copyright-owners.

In March 2008, I left New York City and moved to Cincinnati, Ohio, so as to be with a woman whom I thought I loved. Two issues of *NOT BORED!* were published in this new location: #40 (November 2008) and #41 (November 2009). While the former is a "traditional" sort of issue (it is letter-sized, stapled together and includes a local intervention section), the latter is not. It is a small, perfect-bound volume that consists of translations and polemics, and doesn't contain any local interventions. One might say that, as a result, it really isn't a "proper" issue of *NOT BORED!* To date, I haven't been able to produce any material that might be included in a *NOT BORED!* #42.

But I have not been unproductive during the last two-and-a-half years. I have (finally!) brought to fruition two major projects. The first is a scholarly effort that existed alongside *NOT BORED!* for a great many years: a history of the invention of the mechanized grain elevator, which was published in March 2009 by Colossal Books under the title *American Colossus: the Grain Elevator 1843-1943*. The second is the material I published before, during and after the founding of *NOT*

Preface 2010

BORED! An anthology entitled *You Should've Heard Just What I Seen: Collected Newspaper Articles 1981-1984*, it was published by Colossal Books in October 2010. With the publication of this, my third "colossal book," I have finally caught up with myself, with my past, with the work that I produced long ago and have been carrying around with me ever since.

This book is not a complete anthology of all the texts and images I published in *NOT BORED!*, but a collection of my favorites. It also includes texts that were posted on-line, but never published in a printed edition. Due to the tragic loss of many of my belongings in 1998, I do not have any printed copies of seven back issues (#7, #12, #13, Appendix to #13 Vol. III, #15, #20, and #24). In the production of this anthology, I have had to make do with scans of the copies held in the Labadie Collection at the University of Michigan (many thanks to Julie Herrada).

My apologies to all those who contributed essays and/or illustrations to *NOT BORED!*, but whose work is not included in this anthology: Ben Agger, Jean-Pierre Baudet, Joe Brennan, Michael Carter, Lydia Eccles, Erick Heroux, Terry Laban, Robert Lederman, Curtis Leung, Lyn Lifshin, Jean-Francois Martos, Mark Murrell, Orrin Pava, Beverly Sanford, Stuart Schrader, Seth Tobocman, John Ulrich, and Nicole Williams. Apologies also go to those who think that *Tract Record* was a great name.

Though somewhat arbitrary, the various sections in the book have been created for the purposes of clarity and thematic unity. Each section is organized chronologically. The contents of the first section, "Local interventions," are either reports about actions I personally undertook or reprints of the texts that were distributed during them. The illustrations are divided into three unpaginated blocks, and they follow the sections ("Local interventions," "The Situationist International," and "Miscellaneous") to which they generally correspond.

In the interests of style and readability, I have corrected typos, standardized some of the usages, and added obviously missing words or phrases. On occasion, I have deleted passages to avoid repetition (long quotations from prior issues, etc.). Otherwise, nothing – nothing of any substance – has been changed, removed or added. All endnotes were part of the original versions. All footnotes were added in the course of compiling this anthology, and have been used sparingly.

Bill Brown
Cincinnati
January 2011

Part I:

Local interventions

Local interventions

The Nectarine Ballroom Means
CLASS WAR DECLARED!

The assault of the classical workers' movement against the totality of the old world was completely finished after the failure of the Spanish Revolution of 1936. Ever since then, conventional wisdom has ridiculed the possibility of a new revolutionary proletariat arising. In this widely accepted view, the proletariat of the 20th century won major concessions from the dominant class and is now fully integrated into and satisfied with modern capitalist production.

Yet RIGHT NOW, RIGHT HERE, in Ann Arbor, there is concrete evidence that the great class struggles of the 19th and early 20th centuries are reasserting themselves after a long hiatus. Under the title, "Second Chance to be transformed into a more subdued music scene," the *Ann Arbor Observer* has reported that,

> On April 30 the often raucous Second Chance rock music club at 516 East Liberty will close its doors for good. One month later The Nectarine Ballroom will emerge in its place, a high-fashion dance club with disc jockeys, video screens, top-quality liquor, and a new dance floor and sound system.
>
> Second Chance owner John Carver says the new club will have "a friendly, high-tech look." The heavy wooden front doors will be replaced with more inviting glass doors, topped with polished aluminum. The inside will be radically changed with a new bar, neon decoration, and new woodwork and drywall.
>
> There will be no live music at the new club except for one or two concerts a month by nationally known artists. This essentially means Ann Arbor will lose its premier rock 'n' roll venue, a move that some observers see as another sign of the deterioration of the local live music scene. The attraction of live music seems to be waning throughout the Ann Arbor-Detroit area. Many bar owners blame the video rock boom. As one observer put it, "Why pay to see a local band do top forty when you can watch the real thing at home on MTV?"
>
> Carver seems eager to attract a new type of clientele to the new club, which some see as his effort to reverse Second Chance's downward slide. When the 600-person club opened in 1974, Carver said it would cater to college students. But in recent years, the college crowd has been replaced by younger audiences from Detroit's western suburbs. This clientele, described by some as "seedy," is more unruly. Some potential customers are uncomfortable in the rowdy atmosphere [...]

Local interventions

Carver is also looking for a new crowd with more money to spend. "Ann Arbor's got a lot of fancy clothing stores," he says. "We want to give the people who shop there a chance to strut their stuff."

Carver says he wasn't forced to change his club for financial reasons. "It's not like business is terrible, but the time seems right to make the change," he says. "We've got to follow that baby boom. But who knows? It may be the stupidest thing we've ever done."

Amid all the self-contradictions here, an important insight becomes clear: the ideological spectacle of the Second Chance must change, no matter what or why; furthermore, it must change not in accordance with objective changes in the conditions of the local live music scene (which happens to be thriving), but in accordance with subjective changes in the dominant spectacle (the "Baby Boom" generation). The current ideology is "against" seedy audiences and unruly punk bands, and so ruling class lackeys like John Carver have got to realize – and convince everybody else – that "this is 1984, not 1974," even if all indications are to the contrary.

We note that the vanguard of these new class struggles are members of the dominant class, and not, as one might expect or hope for, members of a modern cultural avant-garde; we note that the dominant class has chosen to locate its newest battles against the working class (here figured by the youths who live in the western suburbs of Detroit) in a cultural milieu, rather than a political or economic one. This is because there is no longer a distinction between the two, between "culture" and political economy. They have both been turned into self-justifying spectacle-commodities.

NOT BORED! #3, May 1984

WE ARE ALL PROLETARIANS NOW: WHAT IS TO BE DONE?
Action in Ann Arbor Against Ondine/Warholism

On April 6, the night of the only showing of Andy Warhol's *Chelsea Girls* (brought to Ann Arbor by Ondine, the owner of and an actor in the film), we distributed copies of the following statement to the audience:

> To Ondine, this gathering is just one more boring event in his boring life. We, on the other hand, see this assemblage as anything but boring. It may be appalling: for here is an over-the-hill "actor," who,

by sole virtue of his association with that proto-fascist swine Warhol, is able to help himself to the unanimous, servile enthusiasm of several hundred University of Michigan students too young to know anything about Warhol. Tonight's assembly may also be potentially liberatory, because here is an opportunity – not to celebrate our own freedom, nor to observe someone else as he or she exercises his or her own freedom – to exercise the most urgent form of freedom, which is the destruction of idols, especially those idols (Ondine, for example) who present themselves in the name of freedom. Tonight will be anything but boring.

One need not be a film or art critic to realize that Warhol's "revolutionary" aesthetic of the 1960s was a complete failure in that it didn't unseat the dominant political and social conditions, which is at least what it pretended that it wanted to do. But, when viewed from the perspective of the interests of the dominant class, Warhol's "revolution" was a resounding success. As any reader of Warhol's *Interview* will attest, it now proposes and ratifies the bourgeois credo *What is good exists, and what exists is good.* And yet here is Ondine, in the middle of an unsavory campaign to transform Warholism into a recognized institution of the dominant society, for which it has always been a loyal watchdog. When pressed to justify himself and his dogma, Warhol – and, no doubt, Ondine as well – will resort to the specious defense that Warholism, unlike Fill-in-the-Blankism, defended certain aspects of the old world that are supposedly dear to all.

We call upon the students of the University of Michigan to reject this phony, this apologist for the old world. YOU HAVE ALREADY COMPROMISED YOURSELVES by being mixed up with *Chelsea Girls*, an immense compendium of mediocrities. Look at the person sitting next to you: you have practically nothing in common with him or her. This film and the Question and Answer session to follow are nothing but false encounters. The time has come to make them real. Let's decide something.

Several important things happened over the course of the evening, the most obvious of which was Ondine's statement that Warhol was indeed a fascist and "that he makes no bones about it." This remark wasn't greeted by a storm of protest and indignation: except for the 20-odd people who walked out of the screening, no doubt due to boredom, the students in question fully lived up to the "unanimous, servile enthusiasm" of which we had accused them. Ondine then went on to attempt to excuse Warhol's politics with the unsupported and surely unsupportable claim that Warhol is a "genius, " as if that might make a difference one way or the other. Ondine's attachment to the reigning spectacle was elaborated further when he claimed that *Chelsea Girls* represents "the apex" of the 1960s, that it captured better than anything else that era's style, mood and content. If this is true, then the "history" of the 1960s has little relevance to what's going on today. Who would even want to live in the society depicted by *Chelsea Girls*?

NOT BORED! #3, May 1984

Our Methods and Goals in the UB Graffiti Scandal

At the beginning of the fall semester 1986, we began an intense graffiti campaign on and against our campus, which is the State University of New York at Buffalo (commonly called the University of Buffalo or UB). Our first targets were the elevators servicing Clemens Hall, the location of the English department. At least five different people – Bill B, Bill McB, Beverly, John and Joe (all grad students in English) – were involved in the campaign. Our graffiti included phrases taken from songs by the Mekons, the Birthday Party, or Parliament/Funkadelic, lines copied out of theory books, and stuff we made up ourselves (such as Bl@h, such stood for "Bop Like Adorno & Horkheimer").

The effect wasn't immediate, but it was what we were looking for. On 7 November 1986, the following letter to the editor ran in *The Spectrum*, UB's student newspaper. Entitled "Some people mistake building for subway," it was written by Emily Tall, who was identified as an Associate Professor of Russian.

> I am appalled at the way some students keep writing on the walls of the Clemens Hall elevators! What is this, a zoo? The New York City subway system? What are these people trying to prove – that they are above the norms of public behavior? Or don't they even know that there are any? Whoever you are, I hope you realize that your scribblings are offensive.
>
> While I am at it, I would like to express my anger at the person who ripped off all the notices and pictures from the bulletin board outside my office. All that information was for your fellow students; you were depriving them of part of their education.
>
> I guess I'm still naive; I expected more of you.

Our responses were to write even more graffiti in the Clemens Hall elevators (some of the graffiti was in Russian and mockingly repeated Professor Tall's rhetorical questions) and to take the graffiti campaign to the entire campus. Calling ourselves "the Bomb Squad," we would wander around the campus, writing graffiti everywhere we thought it would offend people like Professor Tall. Eventually, we read about and visited the ghastly walkway between the Student Activities Center and Knox Hall. Because there were official plans to decorate this awful place, we concentrated our efforts there. We weren't alone; there were others – some of them more traditionally "political" in their graffiti than we were – who relentlessly bombed the SAC walkway.

On 10 December 1986, the following letter to the editor ran in *The Spectrum*. Entitled "Bad poets spoil hallway's progress," it was written by one Michael Zekser, who was identified as the coordinator of Kappa Sigma's "Make A Difference Committee."

> I want to talk about the walkway between the SAC and Knox Hall. Since January, I have worked very hard to change this undecorated, institutional hallway that is so characteristic of UB.
>
> Much to my surprise the administration actually liked the idea and wanted to help, not just give permission; they wanted to share in the planning. I found myself forming The Make A Difference Committee to find a path through SUNY red tape. Believe it or not, the administration hates the red tape as much as we do.
>
> At any rate, this is the first project of its type on the Amherst campus. Sixteen years without students doing anything about the environment we all complain about. My philosophy has always been: Don't complain about something if you aren't willing to work to change it. So I worked, some SUNY administrators worked, and some of my fraternity brothers worked.
>
> Well, designs were submitted, funds were dug up, and plans finalized. The University then primed the walls of the walkway – what came next? The winning design? Wrong. Graffiti. Whoever did the graffiti could have submitted a design like others did.
>
> Instead some anarchists, anti-Nicaraguans and bad poets made their statements. To me, this shows they don't know what's going on at this University and that they don't care about others. Predictable. There must be a better way to get political.
>
> I hope I don't see anyone in the walkway with an uncapped marker. I would definitely do something.

With this letter, the graffiti scandal at UB began.

Working as fast as possible and yet well prepared for our task, we wrote the following response to Zekser, photocopied it on bright yellow paper, and posted it all over campus. Entitled "An Open Letter to Michael Zekser, Coordinator of the 'Make A Difference Committee,' Kappa Sigma, Dated 11 December 1986," our single-page response was wedged between the handwritten phrases "WARNING!" and "THROW THIS AWAY."

Local interventions

There is much in your letter to the editor of *The Spectrum* (10 Dec 86) that I, as one of the "anarchists, anti-Nicaraguans and bad poets" who tried to write all over your beloved walkway between the SAC and Knox Hall, can agree with. We agree that the "undecorated institutional walkway" is, unfortunately, "so characteristic of UB." We agree that for the last sixteen years, students haven't been doing anything about "the environment we all complain about." We agree that a good rule of thumb is "Don't complain about something if you aren't willing to work to change it." Finally, we agree that "there must be a better way [than writing graffiti] to get political." It seems that those "better ways" are inaccessible to us at this moment in time, and so the "political" graffiti will have to act as our Northwest Passage.

What we disagree on is the role of the UB administration – the very people who leave undecorated all of the "institutional" stairwells, hallways and classrooms at this university – in all this. You were surprised that "the administration actually liked the idea and wanted to share in the planning." Your reaction is understandable, given that you don't understand that you are doing the Administration a favor, not the other way around! Even if the official "Make A Difference Committee" chose the most "political" design imaginable, the completed design would be little more than a caption that insists that the overseers of the still-institutional SAC hallway are really great people who act in our interests. With the same idea in mind, we note that the officially sanctioned designs in the Norton and Talbert Cafeterias depict the very food that is sold there. How literal-minded can you get? Your red-tape cutting administration is more than happy to provide the leninist Graduate Group in Marxist Studies with adequate funding, because it knows that the GGMS can be used to obscure the fact that this university community is in fact reactionary and closed in on itself.

You are right to say that "whoever did the graffiti could have submitted a design like others did." But we chose not to, because we don't want decoration; we want communication, communication that is outside of the marketing mentality of the university community. We chose to drop the Bomb on the SAC/Knox Hall walkway precisely because it was to be officially painted; we wanted to test the strength of the desire here for radical communication, for refusing the silence of a community that only wants to advertise itself. The result of that test, as you are obviously aware, is that the desire for radical communication is stronger than anyone thought, ourselves included! You say that "anarchists, anti-Nicaraguans and bad poets made their statement." But there were more of us than that! There were pro-

Local interventions

Nicaraguans, anti-Iranians, undefinables, situationists, Marxists and good poets. It was as a result of the Make A Difference Committee's futile efforts to humanize the walkway that all these writers became aware of their membership in an unorganized organization. We are now working to weed out the anti-Nicaraguans and other reactionaries, so as to attack the present marketing-society with even greater force.

I should like to take this opportunity to respond to Emily Tall, who complained about the graffiti in the Clemens Hall elevators in a recent letter to the editor of *The Spectrum*. She asked if we thought that UB was a "zoo" or "a NYC subway." She also asked if we had crippled one of the elevator's doors. Yes, we think UB is a zoo and is like the NYC subways, and we are happy to respond to the name "Monkey Nigger," which is what these two places, taken together, must signify for a woman as limited and fearful as Professor Tall. We want to destroy everything you apparently hold dear. The Clemens Hall elevators and the SAC/Knox Hall walkway are just the beginning. We're coming to your town and we drive a trashcan.

Entitled "To: Anarchists, Bad Poets, Anti-Nicaraguans," Zekser's hilarious response to our open letter was posted all over campus a day or two latter. Significantly, it attempted to imitate exactly the form and style of our open letter, as if these things, which were actually quite contingent, constituted some sort of established practice that we ourselves were obliged to follow. Printed on colored paper, Zekser's response was wedged between the phrases "WARNING!" and "DON'T THROW THIS AWAY." All this proved our point, namely that "this university community is reactionary and closed in on itself." If it is true that "the only way to change a system is to get inside it," as Zekser claims, this is because the system cannot tolerate the idea that something exists outside of it. For people like Zekser, negation, which is quite asymmetrical, can only be tolerated if it is reduced to a "No" that neatly corresponds to a "Yes." Thus Zekser changes "THROW THIS AWAY" to "DON'T THROW THIS AWAY," and demonstrates a fetish for permanence and a hostility to ephemerality.

Zekser wrote:

> [To: Anarchists, Bad Poets, Anti-Nicaraguans] or whoever else does graffiti unjustifiably. I will justify unjustifiably soon. First I am glad that you replied so quickly. Must be nice to be a philosophy or poly sci major with access to printing equipment. However, trashman, it was very predictable that you and your group didn't sign your flyer. You wouldn't want to be bound to your current beliefs after graduation when most of you will swing to the right, get haircuts, new wardrobes and maybe marketing mentality jobs.

Local interventions

You say better ways of expressing yourselves are inaccessible to you. The flyers you put up Thursday makes you a blatant liar. Also, ever hear of the Alternative News Collective. It used to be a school-funded newspaper for people with viewpoints very similar to yours. Too bad radical liberals didn't want to do the work involved in airing the views they pretended to live by. The paper could always be restarted, but that would mean work.

Next, SUNY-Central in Albany are the people responsible for the institutional look – not U.B.'s administration.

Next, I chose the judges. I chose open-minded administrators and students who represented organizations who got involved.

Next, ever hear of AIA. They are here because faculty are biased in your direction.

Next, you don't want decoration either. Neither does SUNY-Central. Maybe you guys work for SUNY-Central. You want communication. Remember the ANC? How about getting a speaker to come here? How about a rally?

Next, the great radical purge is going on now, huh? Three other purges come to mind: The Ayatollah's, MacCarthy, and, of course, the inquisition. Great idea.

In closing, thanks for the reply. By the way, it's a common fact that the only way to change a system is to get inside it. Good luck on the outside.

More than anything else, Zekser's letter is an indictment of what passes for a university-level education in this society. In this hastily, poorly written and poorly argued response, the all-too-familiar and already impoverished "First, second, third, fourth and finally" structure is further degraded into a "First, next, next, next and in-closing" format. The whole thing is short on things to say; even its insults and threats are lame. This guy is a student leader, ready to graduate and assume his position in the world at large? At the risk of wasting time, we'd like to make a few specific comments about the contents of his response.

Zekser has a real and quite comic problem with names and correctly identifying people. Though we clearly stated that we would respond to the name "Monkey Nigger," Zekser insists on calling us "trashman" (as if there could only be one of us, and as if this person could only be a man!). This proves the value of the name "Monkey Nigger" to us: it cannot be uttered, by anyone, without causing a scandal, and so it is forgotten as quickly as possible.

Quite obviously, Zekser's uninformed decision to dump the "anti-Nicaraguans" (who are presumably anti-Sandinista) in with the anarchists and bad poets was a glaring, stupid mistake. Others have already caught it: we saw one of Zekser's flyers with the phrase "anti-Nicaraguans" circled and the words "Fuck Head" written on it. Perhaps it is only a matter of time before one of Zekser's cronies will ask, "Hey, Mikey! Ain't we the anti-Nicaraguans?" How will Zekser be able to unravel that one? Answer: he won't. And a fine thing that will be, too, for Zekser is obviously a self-important know-it-all. Note that his response to our open letter, unlike his letter to the editor, does not identify him as a member of Kappa Sigma. As a result, when he writes, "I chose the judges," etc. etc., it sounds as if he thinks he's King. But who chose him to make the choices?

According to King Zekser, "radical liberals" such as ourselves hate hard work: we are too lazy to work hard at anything, even "radical liberal" causes such as the Alternative News Collective. And yet, when the time comes, most of us will not find a way of staying out of the workforce; we will apply ourselves and will get the haircuts, wardrobes and mind-sets necessary to get jobs. To insulate himself against the idea that "radical liberals" will shortly be invading the job market and changing it from the inside, Zekser says that we are only pretending to be radicals. But we are not pretending. We are really fucking lazy, and we don't give a damn that our hair, clothes and beliefs will keep us from getting the type of job someone like Zekser would do anything to get.

Let's conclude this piece by making some general comments on the architecture here at SUNY at Buffalo and its effects on the preconditions for radical political action, for these are the issues foregrounded by writing graffiti in places such as the SAC/Knox Hall walkway. Radical political action in the 1960s, which sought to destroy all of the separations that keep people apart from each other and from themselves, was made possible by the existence of public spaces big enough to accommodate large-scale rallies, demonstrations and protests. It seemed clear that without these spaces, radical political action would have nowhere to be born, grow and thrive. And so, at the end of the 1960s, SUNY administrators began the construction of a second, "satellite" UB campus in Amherst, New York, and began the long-term process of moving all of UB from the old campus to the new one. The new campus – a polycentered maze of aboveground tunnels and easily separable buildings – had and still has absolutely no place big enough for a rally, demonstration or protest. As a result, once student protest died in the 1970s, it was unable to revive itself in the 1980s.

Throughout this period, the goal of radical political action has remained the same: the elimination of separation. But many student radicals still adhere to the idea that, to protest against something in an effective way, you've got to hold a mass demonstration. As a result, they come to the conclusion that it is impossible to protest at UB, at which no mass demonstrations can be held. But this conclusion is false: protest is still possible, but it must be done in manners appropriate to the changed physical environment. UB's architecture may prohibit macro-political actions, but it is a rich field for action on the micro-political level. Most people, but especially administrators and security forces, never imagine that a virulent student politics might be born in a stairwell or a walkway. And so small, out-of-the-way areas of campus can be liberated from control, but without the administration or security knowing anything about it (until it is too late). Though not as spectacular as a mass demonstration, a network of liberated pockets can be far more potent in its effects, for it possesses the element of surprise. If or when the administrators and security forces do learn of the liberated areas, and bring them back under their control, student radicals need not be concerned that their whole movement will die if one of these areas is re-claimed. The radicals can simply move on to another out-of-the-way place that no one thought was vulnerable. In this way, their movement won't easily be defeated, for it will be small, mobile and intelligent.

NOT BORED! #11, January 1987

Our Methods and Goals in the U.B. Graffiti Scandal, pt. II

23 January 1987

Well, the attempts to foment a graffiti scandal here, which we started to tell y'all about last time, go on! During winter recess, the Student Activities Center walkway was cleaned up, so we felt compelled, upon returning to campus, to write stuff like "WAKE UP, KING INK!" "MAGIC MARKER," and "GRAFFITI SCANDAL ROCKS U.B.!" in various places in the walkway. We noted that there were some other things written there by other people.

In another development, we discovered that a portion of the hallway leading to Talbert Cafeteria was being reserved for the fraternities and sororities to publicize themselves underneath huge plagues bearing their names. Now dig it: Kappa Sigma's contribution – one of the very first – was a painting of a NYC subway car with graffiti on it! We could not believe the nerve of those idiots! We were really hot to deface the thing by recalling the memory of Michael Stewart, the 25-year-old NYC man who was beaten to death by transit cops (later acquitted on all charges) for doing precisely the thing Kappa Sigma so cynically appropriated for their own uses. When we returned to Talbert later in the day, the painting had been removed. We never got a chance to touch it.

26 January 1987

There is this great letter to the editor about the SAC Walkway in today's *Spectrum*, a student newspaper.

> SAC Hallway is forum of expression
> Editor:
> In a letter on December 10, Michael Zekser wrote that he was upset that people are expressing themselves on the walls of the walkway between SAC and Knox Hall. He is upset because they are

changing their environment in a way that creates a forum of free expression. He is upset because free expression ruins his plans to paint railroad tracks on the floor, and to "change this undecorated, institutional hallway" into a display case for UB paraphernalia, as well as club and Greek activities.

Is there anything more "institutional" than that? This graffiti represents political, emotional, and conscious thought, a rarity on this campus. It is not profane or vulgar, but represents a discourse between students. This is a benefit to UB that has been lacking since the hallway between Harriman and the late Squire Union was painted over. It is something of value in this factory of conformity. As Emma Goldman said, "The strongest bulwark of authority is uniformity; the least divergence from it is the greatest crime." If you, Mr. Zekser, should happen to catch me diverging from conformity, and feel compelled to "do something," go ahead. Make my day.

Peter J. Kalshoven
Graduate student

We looked up Kalshoven's telephone number and gave him a call. He seemed hesitant to talk to us and would only exchange phone numbers or make any concrete plans to get together until he had been sent and had time to read *NOT BORED!* #11, which came out a few weeks ago. We could understand his hesitancy to talk – for all he knew, we could've been Zekser's boys setting him up for a bust. We'll see what he has to say in a week or two.

30 January 1987

Just like last time, Zekser has wasted no time in responding to his critics. And, once again like last time, the speed with which he worked has undermined his efforts – this thing is a mess.

Playing within the rules
Editor [of *The Spectrum*]:

Upset? Me? Nah. Maybe you're upset that you missed out on entering a design. Putting up a board or something for malcontents to scribble on would have been a good idea. But then again, you would probably write it next to such a space. You want a forum of free expression, I gave you the opportunity.

Everybody knows the University will erase your ink. Why not find a way to get your ideas across by working within the system? That's the only way to change the status quo. All you are doing is giving the University more reasons to restrict the creativity of the individual.

Look at it this way – you and I both want to change the walkway. The University eradicates what you do but is helping me. That's the difference between wisdom and ignorance, success and failure.

The Squire hallway? Ever see pictures of it in its last months? Nazism, antisemiticism, and some offensive stuff. I'm all for free expression, it helps me develop my own thoughts. But there is a difference between making a lasting contribution to changing the system and immature actions without a real plan of action.

Michael Zekser
Kappa Sigma

Whoa! It seems Mikey – in his haste to contain the damage inflicted by Kalshoven's letter – forgot that 15,000 other people would read his own letter to the editor and that many of them would not know the context for his patronizing remarks. In the absence of some kind of reference to Kalshoven's letter, it appears that Zekser is railing against some hallucinated, invisible being that is vexing him and his royal plans for free expression. In his delirium, Zekser (once again) unintentionally affirms those things that have been said about him negatively. Affecting the tone of a King about to be martyred by the screaming hordes, "You want a forum of free expression, I gave you the opportunity." Attempting to sound like a true liberal pluralist, the King says, "I'm all for free expressions," but demonstrates that free expression is only valuable insofar as it "helps me develop my own thoughts." But, best of all, he shows just how deep and lasting an impression the supposedly "erasable" and "eradicable" ink of the graffiti in the old Harriman/Squire Union hallway made on him!

2 February 1987

It looks like Zekser got tired of taking on all of the "malcontents" by himself; he's brought in one of the Kappa Sigma brothers to help out. Help!

SAC hallway is not for drawing
Editor [of *The Spectrum*]:

I'd like to respond to Mr. Kalshoven's letter about graffiti on the walls and how desirable it is to a healthy society.

The best way to present my case is to tell you of a personal misadventure. When I was younger, I was punished by my heartily enraged mother. What, you may ask, was my crime? I had, in a joyous attempt at expression, crayoned on the wall. In time I was to learn the error of my ways and restricted my creative urges and statements on

Local interventions

society to better, less controversial places.

The point of my story is this; there are appropriate and inappropriate places, times and mediums of expression. In fact, in this society there are literally hundred of creative ways to tell people your views without offending others or defacing public property. Thus, Mr. Kalshoven, I might suggest you put down your crayons and encourage other, more enlightened forms of expression.

If, on the other hand, you do not appreciate this view, I'd like to ask that you contact me with the intent of giving me your address. You see, my friends and I have always wanted to "express" ourselves on someone's house and we feel yours would certainly be the best place to start.

Michael J. Rotundo
University student

Under the name Mark Freeman (a graduate student who is on leave this semester), we have already written and sent a letter to the editor in answer to this one. (We'll include it here, in one form or another.) Today we also saw some graffiti in the SAC Walkway that said "SAGA" with the letter "As" circled. The anarchy reference we get, but what or who the fuck is SAGA? Not that awful band!? Not the organization that produces and serves "food" at university cafeterias!?

6 February 1987

Wow, that was fast! All of a sudden, graffiti is an issue – something that the editorial staff of *The Spectrum* thinks that it should take a position on. Well, maybe it's not such a sudden development . . . there has been a lot of graffiti in the SAC walkway for at least a solid month or two. . . . Anyway, there's a lot in this editorial that is really confused.

DISTASTEFUL ART AT UB

Without doubt freedom is one of this country's greatest gifts, but like everything, there is a place and forum to express that privilege. Yet there are those that indiscriminately choose to express their thoughts on some of the most conspicuous and ill-suited places around campus: walls of buildings and the walkway between the Student Activities Center and Knox Hall.

Graffiti does have a place and at times may be useful as a form of social demonstration. But when the declarations amount to pure scribble, then there is something wrong. Granted, the walls around campus are bland; however spraying useless words and phrases is only an eyesore and blemishes the surroundings.

Local interventions

There have been plans for some time to constructively decorate the SAC Walkway. In fact, a winning design was selected last semester, but that plan is for the time being on hold. Perhaps frustrated UB students just decided to design a little bit every day and fill in the space.

The markers and paints used to do the spontaneous art not only pervert a sense of aesthetics, but they also drain UB's custodial staff who must scrub away for long stretches of time, only serving to clean the unofficial canvas for later use.

Stop writing on and defacing the walls. If students have something to say, how about a letter to the editor?

Freedom is not a privilege, not something that can be given to and taken from human beings, but an "inalienable right" that is irrevocable.

(We are graduate students: can you imagine what it is like to try to *teach* these kids?)

The Spectrum's editorial condemning the emerging graffiti scandal at UB was accompanied by a cartoon ("the Dented View of A Day in the SAC Walkway") drawn by a staff member, one P. Dent. The cartoon depicts two small, identical-looking boys, both facing a wall upon which right-wing slogans (?!) such as "OUT OF IRAN!!!" and "END SOVIET OPPRESSION" have been written. The boy on the right has evidently just finished writing phrases that he's apparently taken from the book that is lying open at his feet: "HAIL TO FREEDOM OF EXPRESSION" and "REAGONOMICS [sic] SUCKS!!!" (It's as if the cartoonist just cannot believe or admit to himself that the essence of writing graffiti is spontaneity; it responds directly to the site itself, and not to some subject or thing located elsewhere.) The boy on the left, brush and rag in hand, is cleaning the wall of graffiti. Get it? One hand doesn't know what the other is doing. If we could only put our hands together. . . .

We met with Kalshoven today. He called and said that he'd like to get together for a chat. He's a nice guy, but we didn't feel it would be productive to remain in serious contact with him about these matters. Though he quoted Emma Goldman, he personally isn't an anarchist or anything like that. He likes the free forum of expression in the SAC walkway, but he doesn't want it spilling over into the hallways that he walks through everyday. It doesn't appear that he read much of our zine.

9 February 1987

Today an open letter, signed by a group calling itself "Students Against Growing Apathy" (or SAGA), appeared in *The Spectrum*.

SAGA Trying to Wake Students
By SAGA

Local interventions

SAGA, students against growing apathy, is a name you may have seen around campus lately. SAGA is a group of students attempting to bring some life to this sterile, antiseptic University, a cold, impersonal place, with little indication of a student population (especially one of UB's considerable size).

We, the members of SAGA, are not attempting to destroy, defile, deface, or vandalize the "University." Our attempts at colorization have been exercised with restraint, in places where, if the administration is so inclined (and it has been already), the letters can be removed. We hope that this will not always be the case.

SAGA is simply trying to express our anger and disgust at any administration which deprives us of our student union, which stifles the voice of the student body, which names buildings after men whose only contribution to the University (and mankind) is monetary.

The students against growing apathy encourage more students to colorize and add like to [sic] the University. UB may be a corporation, but with some work, we (and only we, the students and faculty) can make a difference, and turn our school into a forum for the expression of our ideas, not the ideas of an administration which seems to consider a green triangle on a blue background "art" (see Clemens [Hall]!).

Get a marker and put your mind to work! This is your school, your money pays for it. We are more than just able bodies and minds to do the menial or "dirty" work on their grants, grants for SDI (Star Wars) which is a significant amount of UB's population is opposed to, to begin with. Show that students are what UB is all about. When you leave here, will anyone knew you existed? The right to express yourself is in your hands.

Students Against Growing Apathy

We have a general idea of who these students are: several weeks ago, we hung out with and distributed copies of *NOT BORED!* #11 to a group of leftist undergraduate students. Despite our differences in age and "cultural orientation" (many of these kids are neo-hippies), everyone agreed that writing graffiti was the thing to do and that the time to do it was right now. They didn't tell us about plans to form a group; perhaps they made the decision to do so later.

The problem with what became SAGA's interest in things "political" is that the end result is graffiti that has neither style nor poetry. Hectoring against the "apathy" of others just isn't creative – it isn't even interesting – especially if it is adorned with the trappings of anarchism. By definition, SAGA's dubious "restraint" in the exercise of "colorization" (an awful expression, given its

Local interventions

connotations with the abusive "restoration" of black and white films) precludes graffiti that is site-specific, graffiti that is a spontaneous expression of passion and that is, consequently, attentive to the possible construction of situations at that very site. Who wants to wander around this already awful campus, thinking about the absence of a student union (we'd just write graffiti on it anyway!) or the presence of Star Wars research money? Those things are givens. We prefer to wander around in a daze, writing on the walls whatever it is that comes into our music-soaked heads, not looking for answers but for the right questions to ask.

Our objection to SAGA is that, if we are going to form small groups, we should give ourselves a name that is a scandal in its own right. Despite the circled As, there is nothing scandalous about the name SAGA, especially when it is compared to the now long-forgotten names "monkey nigger" (used in our open letter to Zekser) and "trashman" (used in Zekser's response to our open letter). It is also unfortunate that this first "pro-graffiti" group has defined itself negatively, as being "against apathy" rather than for something really cool sounding (like "comparative vandalism" or somesuch). There is something self-defeating in undergraduate student "radicalism" that is always eager to rush headlong into action – into single-issue graffiti campaigns, letters to the editor from newly and rather ill-formed groups, sit-ins, marches and so forth – without having first come to some kind of coherent critique or diagnosis of the forces against which it desires to fight. As a result, when pressed to reveal something of its programme, SAGA (especially in the sentence that begins "UB may be a corporation, but with some work"), sounds just like Zekser and his "Make A Difference Committee." We need to revive what the situationists called "the organizational question," and "the minimum definitions of a revolutionary organization." In the meantime, SAGA SUCKS. SAGA has attempted to appropriate the emerging graffiti scandal for itself, and has thereby made itself a target for that scandal.

10 February 1987

Today another open letter from SAGA was published, this time in *Generation*, the weekly student-run magazine.

> *Editor's Note: We are printing this letter, although it is anonymous, because it would explain some of the graffiti appearing around the University. We do not advocate graffiti, but this person (or group of persons) has something to say.*

Editor:

This is an open letter to all students, faculty, and administration. Our name is SAGA – Students Against Growing Apathy. Our purpose is for change at UB. We hope to provoke this student body into action. Our university is stifling the students. We have no central location for socializing (such as a student union), thus the expression of ideas is stifled. We are caught up in the advancement of a "super university" without consideration for the social needs of a community. Buildings continue to rise and student population continues to grow (it is predicted to surpass 60,000), yet we still have the reality [of] split campuses and a lifeless student body. Part of the blame is on us students. We have, in fact, become apathetic. However, we feel students do have opinions which are afforded no method of expression. Do you, the administration, really feel upgrading sports is the sole mechanism for generating school spirit? Do you, the students, feel the Student Activities Center serves a purpose even remotely close to the student union past students enjoyed and fought so hard to keep?

We need the support of the University community in our efforts. The name SAGA is appearing rapidly on the walls of this institution. Much of it is also being washed off. This is part of our plan. We realize our name and slogans will be washed off and painted over, but we do not intend to let this cease our action. We believe our ideas will provoke the community into action. We are not the sole producers of graffiti on this campus. Many students have obviously felt the need to write on the walls of their campus. It seems to be the only way to express ideas to such a divided student body. We have no one place to congregate and share ideas. Different social groups have niches here and there, but is this unity or is this division of a student body?

We intend to remain underground using the school publications as our medium for more lengthy explanations of our purpose. We intend to continue to express our ideas on the walls in an attempt to provoke this University into thought and action. The circled A's in our name symbolize anarchy. We do not intend to imply destruction of our campus. We merely intend to show we mean business.

We want a better campus for future students, but passivity has moved this student body into apathy. We have been made to believe we are helpless. Research grants have taken precedence over student needs. It is time to change this environment. This is only the beginning.

SAGA
Students Against Growing Apathy

These SAGA kids certainly have the abilities to think and write clearly. But there is something down right terroristic about the logic they use and, in particular, their idea that "anarchy" means "we mean business." Very reductive, even simplistic:

there is only one real issue and that is the absence of a student union; the "provocations" (graffiti attacks, but they could just as easily be kidnappings or bombings of uninhabited buildings) are designed to bring about the construction of a real student union; presumably, the "provocations" will stop when "the administration" builds that student union, the one all of us need so desperately. But the contradiction between the "unity" of the student body and the "division" of it into "niches" is a false one, or, rather, it can be set into motion and superseded only by the appropriation or detournement of the "trivial" spaces (stairwells, hallways, walkways, and so forth), the spaces that are literally not suited for "unity" (a student union) nor for "division" (the metaphorical "niches"). Might as well call themselves Shameless Hippies in The Streets, or SHITS. . . .

11 February 1987

Hello! Better late than never, *The Spectrum* has published Mark Freeman's letter to the editor concerning Michael Rotundo's letter to the editor about Peter Kalshoven's letter to the editor concerning Michael Zekser's letter to the editor. (Got that?)

> Mr. Rotundo should stop drawing on walls
> Editor:
>
> According to Mr. Rotundo's February 2 letter to the editor, he was punished by his Mommy, when he was younger, for crayoning in the walls of his room. As a result, he became able, or so he claims, to distinguish "appropriate" from "inappropriate" behavior, and "enlightened" from presumably childish forms of expression. Now an adult, he suggests that Peter Kalshoven also grow up by "putting down your crayons and encouraging other, more enlightened forms of expression" because "there are literally hundred of creative ways to tell people your views without offending others or defacing public property."
>
> It is altogether remarkable that Mr. Rotundo offers to punish Mr. Kalshoven, just like Mommy did to him, if he doesn't "appreciate this view." The mode of punishment: defacement of Mr. Kalshoven's own personal house. Apparently, Mr. Rotundo's Mommy didn't learn her son too good: he is unable to distinguish public property (like the SAC Walkway) from private property (Mr. Kalshoven's house), and he still harbors an unreconstructed desire to "express myself on someone's house."
>
> What do you think: should Mr. Rotundo be returned to his Mommy for further punishment or should he be encouraged to think of the SAC hallway as private property and thus an "appropriate" place for his self-expression?

Local interventions

Mark Freeman
Graduate student

I wonder if anyone will respond to it.

On another page of today's *Spectrum* there is an untitled comic strip (by a student named Blenk) about graffiti in the SAC Walkway. In it, an irate man with a paintbrush in his hand is running down the walkway, in the direction of two graffiti-writers (a boy and a girl) he's caught "red-handed." Here the graffiti in question is little more than the "pure scribble" *The Spectrum* itself had railed against: tic tac toe games, stick figures with no faces, a heart with an arrow through it, the year "87," etc. As for the couple of graffiti-writers, they look like parodies of Sid Vicious and Nancy Spungen as they appear in *Sid and Nancy* (in local movie theatres starting this week). As he stands spraying what appears to be more pure scribble from a paint can, Sid is literally two-faced: he is depicted looking at the wall in front of him and back towards the running, irate man at the same time. As she bolts from the walkway, spray-paint can in hand, Nancy looks like she would be more likely to use the paint to color her lips than to write graffiti. Pesky little domesticated graffiti-writing punks!

On the same page is a bit of good news, which arrives under the headline, "Time Track Project is Still Derailed."

> The hallway between the Student Activities Center and Knox Hall remains cold, colorless and lifeless. Except for a few students, most people that traverse the walkway seem indifferent to the bland surroundings. But it was not supposed to be like that. At one time there were plans by the University to put eye-catching designs in the hallway. Now graffiti mars the whitewashed walls and water leakages cause the ink to stream from the markings in crooked lines to the floor.
>
> Last semester Kappa Sigma Fraternity in conjunction with Student Affairs launched the "Make A Difference Program," a project to spruce up the stark passageway. The organizations held a design competition to choose a theme for bedecking the walkway and "Time Tracks" won. The plans featured railroad tracks painted across the walls, fitted with wooden showcases laden with UB memorabilia; a journey through the school's past aboard the "UB Express."
>
> The project's coordinators set the end of last semester as the hallway's expected finish date. But work has not yet begun. Mike Zekser, vice president of Kappa Sigma, attributed the delay to the winter temperatures. "It is now too cold to paint," he said. But even preliminary work remains undone. The technical measurements, such as the spacing between the tracks and the supports needed to fit the

display cases, have not been incorporated into the design sketches.

Diane Diehl, one of the Time Tracks designers, complained that "the workload came as a surprise." She criticized the organizers for failing to explain that the winner would also be responsible for the technical measurements, in addition to the design concepts they submitted.

Steve Fort, another of the Time Tracks designers, admitted that none of the organizers has contacted him since the middle of last semester. "No one has been in touch," he said. Jim Gruber, director of Student Unions, expressed a more positive outlook on the project's coordination and leadership. "Mike deserves a lot of credit for following through and staying with the project."

He [Gruber] was unaware of any of the complaints cited by the designers and blamed any delay on the detailed safety requirements demanded by the University, which he said were stringent, but absolutely necessary. Zekser himself claimed that the "SUNY guidelines are ridiculous" and that bureaucratic red tape has held the project back. "SUNY likes things done gradually," he added.

Zekser graduates this spring, however, and time is growing short. If attention is not soon given to organizing the designers and completing the technical measurements, there may never be enough time to work on the hallway's new, more spirited, face.

As John Lydon sings on the first PiL record: "Attack!"

17 February 1987

Today one of the Voices of Reason made itself heard in the form of a letter to the editor of *Generation*.

> Editor:
>
> I am responding to a letter written by an anonymous "pro-student" group that calls itself SAGA that was in your February 10 issue.
>
> While I admire and support the cause that SAGA claims to be fighting for, I can hardly believe that a can of spray paint is going to obtain much support among University students. Granted, the graffiti will get attention, but for the most part it will be unfavorable. While many students disapprove of the UB administration, destruction of the campus doesn't make us feel any better or stronger about our identity as a group.
>
> When I first spotted the SAGA sign written over one of the posts in the Baldy lobby, I was disgusted. Several of my friends also expressed disapproval of the signs. For every defilement of our

campus, the University must make the effort of cleaning it up. The more mess, the more time and money spent removing it. This doesn't sound like an effective method of preventing apathy, or promoting a sensed of brotherhood among students. All this senseless graffiti does is amuse most, and annoy many members of this community.

It is a given that this University acts as an impersonal institution, and it is another given that the students themselves lack a voice and/or a common goal. But graffiti won't eradicate widespread passivity, and neither will vague, slipshod letters that make sweeping claims lacking in supportive evidence and concrete plans of action.

Have I a better solution? No one has absolute answers, but I suggest you come out of the closet and answer three questions: Who are you? What are your specific goals? How do you intend to achieve them? I believe you should set up an office, hold a general meeting to answer students' questions, and make a public stand. If your beliefs are so strong, then the possibility of public disapproval shouldn't phase you.

You mentioned in your letter that in spite of actions taken to erase your signs, you will continue to put them up. What about students' opinions of these signs? If they disapprove of them, you aren't listening; you aren't even giving us a forum to express our opinions. Ironic, isn't it, since you claim to be a group geared towards students?

If you are sick of apathy and want to fight it, you've got to communicate with students face to face. A meaningless sign in a wall won't help your cause in the long run.

Anna DeLeon
University student

The problem here is of SAGA's own making, for it was SAGA itself that rather self-consciously used graffiti to frame "larger" and "reasonable" questions about such highly specialized areas as political apathy, student unions and military research on campus, while all the time ignoring the fact that graffiti can be – and continues to be – used to embody its own content, that is to say, "small," general, and unreasonably totality-conscious questions about everyday life. Thus SAGA left itself open to valid objections of this sort: How can you use an "unreasonable" (or impoverished) method such as graffiti, if your intent is to raise and eventually answer eminently reasonable (and specialized) questions? How can you aspire to unite the student community when your tactics quite clearly divide it?

No doubt, SAGA will not respond. This will be a missed opportunity, for there much in DeLeon's letter deserving of comment. We would draw your attention to a couple of items, both of which concern the infantilism of the persistent association of writing graffiti with childishness and immaturity. 1). For DeLeon, graffiti is a dirty, disgusting mess: writing graffiti is a form of playing with feces. 2). It is therefore shameful in enjoying writing graffiti, especially anonymous graffiti – which is a "defilement" done "in the closet" and subject to "public disapproval." It is instructive to remember, in this context, *The Spectrum*'s reference to graffiti's status as a "perversion" of aesthetics.

It is also instructive to open Deleuze & Guattari's *Anti-Oedipus* to pages 62-63, which discusses the Freudian theory of the "death instinct." In the graffiti scandal currently rocking UB, there is a fissure developing between those who hypostatize an eternal social order (i.e., DeLeon's "givens") and then define, position and engage in "pleasure" as the activities of defending and, if need be, dying for that social order, and those who recognize the mortality of supposedly "eternal" social orders and then define, position and engage in "pleasure" as the playful re-articulations ("detournement") of these social orders. Without shattering the blind faith in the "eternal" social order, it will not be possible for revolutionaries to use concepts or discourse to convince the reactionaries that writing graffiti is fun, intellectually healthy and a surefire defense against apathy.

Today we saw some interesting reactions to the "SAGA SUCKS" slogans. In the stairwell of Clemens Hall, for example, someone has written beneath one of them "YOU WRITE, WE WIN." A good response, that: it uses a pun to suggest that "YOU'RE RIGHT, BUT WE WIN" or to suggest that, by the very fact that we wrote graffiti in response to their graffiti, SAGA doesn't suck. But the central problem remains: here "points" (for or against SAGA) accrue to the simulacrum of a revolutionary organization, and not a real one.

18 February 1987

Couple of relevant letters to the editor in today's *Spectrum*.

No reason for graffiti on campus
Editor:

I agree 100 percent with your editorial of February 6 ("Distasteful Art at UB"). Please reprint it many times.

Simply stated, it's just not professional to write on walls, regardless of the message being conveyed. It shows a lack of pride in our University and definitely gives the wrong signal to visitors, prospective students, parents, and those of us who work and study here every day.

In my opinion, there is absolutely no justification for any graffiti in the SAC tunnel or any place on campus.

David R. Rhoads
Director, Physical Plant, North Campus

Local interventions

SAGA should abandon crayons
Editor:

    According to Webster's *New World Dictionary* the word "saga" means "any long story relating heroic deeds." For some strange reason I fail to see how this definition fits the group of sophomoric marauders who call themselves SAGA (Sorry about not having the clever neo-anarchist circles around the A's!). Maybe a name like story or tale would be more appropriate since it describes what they're telling the students of UB . . . since the beginning of time people have accomplished great gains by vandalizing their surroundings . . . this is obviously and laughably not true.

    SAGA would lead us to believe that their method of cretin expression will get the students of UB a new student union. I suppose we could get a whole new luxury dorm complex if we just colored half of the town of Amherst with lovely SAGA's.

    SAGA places the blame of our lack of school spirit and a Student Union on the Administration. To call this a misconception would be vague. It was the former Administration that performed the act of pulling the plug on our Student Union and segmenting the University population through the design of the dorm complexes. It was SAGA's predecessors from the 1960's and 1970's, however, that precipitated this dramatic Administration action. Groups like SAGA are an ominous threat to our personal freedoms and further discourage the formation of a plan for a new Student Union.

    The members (or members) of SAGA have displayed that they are literate (or someone they know is) from the articles that have appeared in *The Spectrum* and *Generation*. Since they appear to have the ability to communicate their views through the available media[,] why is it necessary for them to trash our collective property with their spray paint, pens and Crayolas?

    The Student Association and its various branches are designed to provide a forum for student opinion, and membership in it is unrestricted. If one of SAGA's goals is student unity, as they claim, then they should get involved. If they are really serious about the ideas they wish to encourage then they should come up with a saner method of promoting them. Until then, they should stick to their coloring books!

Shane P. Connolly
Student Assemblyman

Local interventions

The latter of these two letters is, needless to say, the one that calls for comment.

This "student assemblyman" is evidently a politician-in-the-making: only a politician could accuse a group of people of telling a "[tall] tale" that "is obviously and laughably not true," and then go on to assert in a prophetic tone that these same people "are an ominous threat to our personal freedoms." Only a politician could feel threatened by the way SAGA's name alludes to the act of literary creation, which – as a matter of fact – does in fact document the "great gains" people have accomplished "by vandalizing their surroundings," especially since the French Revolution. Only a politician could admit the truth of his adversary's central position – in this case, that the UB's "cold, impersonal" north campus was deliberately designed to prevent or at least help defeat-in-advance student protest of the sort that SAGA clearly wishes to revive – and then use it as a means of undermining his adversary's credibility and good faith.

23 February 1987

Today we realized that the members of SAGA have come to the realization that we have been the ones placing the word "SUCKS" underneath every appearance of the SAGA tag. Evidently, they are not happy. They appear to have taken it rather personally, for they are now attacking us personally, or, rather, by name. Referring to our slogan "No Fun" (a reference to the Stooges' song), someone has written in the Clemens Hall stairwell "IF YOU ARE HAVING NO FUN, WHY ARE YOU NOT BORED?" Because not having fun (or finding that there is no fun to be had) is not the same thing as being bored; because being NOT BORED (a magazine that said on its most recent cover that it wants to suck the readers' blood) is not the same thing as "having fun." Elsewhere, we've seen the word "REACTIONARY!" thrown at (attached to) our alterations of SAGA's signs so that they say SAGA SUCKS. In comparison with us, is SAGA "progressive" or even "revolutionary"? We've been told, "YOU ARE A HYPOCRITICAL ELITIST – THINK ABOUT IT." We have not betrayed SAGA or any of the specific positions it has taken on certain issues, precisely because we have never been part of SAGA nor have we ever entered into any kind of agreement with SAGA concerning our commonly shared goals or principles. All we ever "agreed upon" was the "idea" that graffiti is fun to write, especially in the SAC walkway.

24 February 1987

Today's *Generation* has an article (actually it is a column by "Bitter Twisted") about the graffiti scandal. Entitled "Write & Wrong," it says the following about "the SAGA phenomenon."

> I would refer to it as the "SAGA people" or "the SAGA project," but despite the alarming rate the marker virus is spreading, you can't really tell how many people are involved.
>
> I know people who have enough time on their hands to while

away a few days making their mark on the university. It would be tough on one person, though. It must get on your nerves, waiting for the time that someone finally walks in while you are busy. Then there's the oversized SAGA spraypainted on the nuke center at [the] Main Street [campus] . . . gads. It could be catching on. (Pinch your nose shut, then say, "Look, Martha, a fad. How gauche.")

Whoever's doing it must be pleased by the attention and sustained fire their brainchild has drawn on campus. Due in part to the SAGA manifesto being published in the campus papers, letter-writers have been foaming at the mouth for weeks.

One pinhead, possibly disoriented by the vast blankness of his stationary, lurched far past the borders of the extreme by laying the blame for Squire Union's closing on "SAGA's predecessors." When I read "Groups like SAGA are an ominous threat to our personal freedoms," I could see the writer had pitched his tent where he was and decided to stay for a while.

Graffiti is an issue now. There has been at least one editorial already (summary: graffiti is writing on walls/writing on walls is bad/graffiti is bad), so somebody must be thinking about it, I guess. It's one of those safe issues everybody likes to address because, like a Mobius strip, there's only one side.

It must have been those circled A's that started the cerebral fluid perking overtime. They mean anarchy, and there's nothing like a little anarchy for bringing critics charging out of hiding to mend the fabric of society and make the world safe for law and order. People tee off so hard they hurt themselves.

Using the term "anarchy" to describe UB should be grounds for suspending someone's poetic license. If there were [real] anarchists here, we'd know it. Life would get hairy. Someone would dump 500 gallons of Coke into the main computer the day before Drop/Add. One winter night, the Amherst Campus electrical substation would go up in a shower of sparks, eliminating heat, light, water, and elevators on the Amherst Campus (don't get any ideas, or Public Safety will have my kidneys barbacueing slowly on a spit somewhere in Bissell Hall.)

The authors of the manifesto knew what vapors of anarchy would do to some people. They must have been hysterical when they read the response. I hope they didn't hurt themselves laughing. These anarchists, you know, they get carried away.

I sympathize with the janitors, but you have to admit that the walls of the Knox-SAC tunnel do look a teensy-weensy bit like they're asking to be defaced. Okay, maybe they're begging for it.

If enough grey cells in the administration got enough oxygen for once in their anemic lives, the university could give it a coat of the washable paint used in NYC subway cars and give everyone permission to express themselves all over it.

That would be one clean tunnel. No more "Graffiti Scandal Rocks UB." This, however, would seem to be the logical thing to do. Around here, that can be a fatal flaw.

Speaking as the writers of the graffito "Graffiti Scandal Rocks UB," we must disagree with the "self-evident truth" of these remarks and say in advance that they would not apply to us. Prior to our intervention, graffiti at UB had been largely confined to bathrooms; precisely because they were indeed covered with layers on washable paint, these bathrooms were already a de facto location for permitted graffiti. We moved graffiti out of the bathrooms because graffiti had grown decadent in the space that had been allotted for it to lead an impoverished existence. It was as a result of this action, and not as a result of the subsequent appearance of SAGA, that "graffiti [as such] is an issue now." The simple fact is that, if the Knox Hall-SAC tunnel is painted with washable paint and allowed to become a field for tolerated creativity, we will move on to another place and try to create another scandal. And we will not move on rashly; we will pick our target with the care that originally led us to the Knox-SAC tunnel.

25 February 1987

Today *The Spectrum* ran its first pro-graffiti op-ed piece.

UB Graffiti Important for Remembering Tragic Past
By Patrick Fogarty

In regard to your recent article about graffiti on the wall between Knox and the Student Activities Center, I too believe that useless scribble is an eyesore, however there is some purpose and nostalgia behind graffiti at UB. When we had a union, oh so long ago, the tunnel between Squire and Harriman Halls was covered with little sayings of yesterday. Before reading them we could only know through movies what students went through during the turbulent times of the late sixties and early seventies.

Here the walls in the tunnel gave us a first hand account. The writing was something permanent so that we would never forget.

I find this the central concept behind the importance of graffiti, and necessary to battle a tragic quality in most human beings. People have a habit to forget about the past, to joke about what has not had a serious effect on their lives. Let us see people laugh about the Holocaust if they lost their family. I doubt they would or do. Yet it is unfortunate that even this can be and is taken lightly if you do it the right way. There is no way to take the death of six million Jews in jest. Listen to all the Ethiopian jokes. I wonder what we would look like if Buffalo did not get precipitation for 11 years . . . which is more likely than UB getting a [student] union.

The wall should be our book to write so our children don't make or ALLOW our mistakes to happen again. In 50 years when my best friend's son is president, maybe he'll be smart enough not to sell arms to Iran or at least not get caught.

One can argue that we have classes to teach us about these things. However, I find that a wall written on by your parents' generation makes more of an impression on you than a book required by a history class that was written by someone who now drives a Porsche. The different things in life are what stand out. It took Peter Gabriel to make people sit up and take note of Stephen Bikko.

Also, in light of the fact that SAC is to be a sort of "pseudo-union," it seems appropriate that an adjacent hallway become the new writing place. It is not to say that we should stop going to classes and just write all over walls, but seeing it makes me stop and think about next time.

As for the vulgarity, there are other, more diplomatic ways of writing a potent statement or idea. Doonesbury does it every day on a national scale, not just one wall.

Patrick Fogarty is a University student.

This is, in some ways, the best analysis of graffiti we've yet had in our public discussion. For Fogarty – and, we should mention, for historians of everyday life – graffiti is a better indication of or introduction to life as it was really lived than "a book required by a history class." And that's because graffiti from the "tragic past" is "first hand": it is a writing within history, not a writing about history. The problem comes when Fogarty turns his attention to the importance of today's graffiti, which for him will only be significant when the future (50 years from now) gives it a retrospective look. But today's graffiti can be a door to the history of our own present, as well as the future's door to the history of the past. To his credit, Fogarty seems to realize that crossing over the threshold of the door to the history of our own present involves a decision to "stop going to classes and just write all over the walls [all day, every day]." We've got to encourage people like him to go all the way the "next time," instead of simply stopping and thinking about it.

NOT BORED! #12, May 1987

Local interventions
BULLETIN FROM REWRITE
Re: William S. Burroughs

Calling partisans of all nations – Writer William Burroughs captured by The Powers – Nike spokesman onscreen talking – "Technology should not confuse the mind but should serve the body" – Are we going to stand still for a routine such as this? – Traitor to all souls everywhere – Serve the body?! – So-called technology even a fucking pair of sneakers should free the mind *from* the body – We are here to go not be "served" you dumb hick – Not confuse the mind?! – The Powers want us clear and just so clear enough to choose from a selection of paltry dry goods but not so clear we see through – Shift linguals – Cut word lines – Vibrate tourists – Disorder the senses Rimbaud – Writer captured must be – Got to him at – "The reality film has now become an instrument and weapon of control – The full weight of the film is directed against anyone who calls the film into question with particular attention to writers and artists – Work for the reality studio or else – Or else you will find out how it feels to be *outside the film* – You will readily understand why people will go to any length to get in the film to cover themselves with any old film scrap – Anything to avoid the hopeless dead-end horror of being just who and where you all are: dying animals on a doomed planet" – quoted from *The Ticket That Exploded*, Evergreen paperback 1987 page 151 – Irony of tipping his hat at the – "Just an old show man is all" – Either he accepts a Rewrite job or he is condemned to live eternally in the conditions imposed on this copy planet by The Powers – Too valuable to leave in enemy hands – Too useful as a trophy –

NOT BORED! #23, January 1995

SQUAT THE WORLD!

This report is being distributed for a variety of reasons: to celebrate the summer of 1995 in NYC, to assist in the general demolition of spectacular separation and to open a dialogue on key issues and situations. This report was not written by a squatter, but by someone who lives in the traditional bourgeois fashion, that is, rents an apartment (on E. 14th St.) from someone who has proper title to it. And so this report can't help but miss the mark to some extent: it was written by someone with no first-hand experience of the events that have taken place at the squats on E. 13th St. since May 25 1995. First-hand experience is, of course, essential in all matters, this one being no exception. And so, from the start, we're aware that this report can't help but have certain inevitable weaknesses and limitations that could only be overcome if the writer had actually squatted a building in the East Village this past summer. But these facts are not reasons enough to delay the writing and distribution of a report through these channels. It's a mistake to assume that someone who isn't currently a squatter is automatically an "outsider" with respect to the lives of people who are currently squatting buildings. Such assumptions always distort and mislead: to be an "outsider" (to even have an "outside"), there have to be "insiders" and an "inside"; there has to be a stable dividing line, a wall, separation. But how did it get there? Despite appearances, both sides are deceived: the outsiders could produce or discover their own "inside scene" at any time, but do not realize it; the insiders depend upon the outside to gauge the effect they are having and to determine the direction of future actions, but what they know about it is fed to them by compromised sources. And so, where there was once a crowd capable of recognizing itself, there are now actors and spectators, the same tired old show in which no one really knows what they want. In the case of squatting, such a situation is especially self-defeating: the significance or meaning of squatting – getting inside of and living in a formerly sealed and unused place – would seem to be the simple fact that it makes walls and separations seem as unnatural as they really are.

> The ultimate in disposing one's troops is to be without ascertainable shape. Then the most penetrating spies cannot pry in nor can the wise lay plans against you. – Sun Tzu, *The Art of War*

Squatting is an immediate and practical solution to an immediate and concrete problem: you need a place to stay and you don't have one. After it has been located, unsealed, entered and rendered relatively habitable, a formerly abandoned ("squatted") building solves the problem. Thereafter, other problems – both abstract and concrete – present themselves and need to be solved. Indeed, squatting a building allows you to more easily solve those secondary and tertiary problems. Squatting rather than renting a place to stay allows you to save whatever money you have for food and clothing, or – if you have enough – for "luxuries."

There is nothing inherently "spectacular" about squatting. It has been done in New York City, indeed, in this very neighborhood, for more than 130 years – that is, ever since the 1860s, when urban development became an observable, cyclical process (of construction, inhabitation and use, abandonment, dereliction and destruction) that repeated itself every 30 years or so. Squatting, as either an individual act or as a "movement" of some kind, drew very little, if any, attention in the world of surveillance. In a certain sense, squatting – in the strict sense of acquiring title to a portion of public land, under the regulation of the government – had for a long time been official federal policy in the western territories. Under the Homestead Act of 1863, people who had "settled" – that is, squatted – portions of the public lands, without first securing the right or title to do so, were entitled to the opportunity to secure ownership of those portions through purchase at prices set by the government. The general similarity to the legal concept of adverse possession, which is another method of acquiring complete title to land (as against all others, including the record owner), is clear. Adverse possession differs from homesteading in that the former presupposes the uninterrupted failure of the owner to utilize his or her property and to prevent others from utilizing it, while the latter presupposes the desire of the owner to see the property developed and used as soon as possible. But the core of the two concepts is nearly identical: if you live in and work on it in a uninterrupted fashion, you have the right to own it. It matters little if you are squatting an abandoned building in a city or land "abandoned" by the Native Americans: in either case the property has come into the possession of the government, that is to say, the taxpayer-voters, and goes undeveloped or unused. Tolerance of squatting was also the de facto housing policy of the City of New York during the height of immigration to the United States from Europe in the early 20th century. The squatters were tolerated because 1) if it meant living in America, they were willing to live in derelict buildings, which saved the City from the expenses of demolishing unsafe old buildings and constructing new tenement blocks; and 2) they were alerted to and helped into these derelict buildings by family and friends who had already settled in the neighborhood, and were thus not likely to be "rootless," that is, much less likely to eventually need assistance of some kind from the city or state governments as they became employed and otherwise socialized to life in America.

Beyond this, the squatting of buildings in the heart of New York City was not a spectacle for the reason that the squatters and the media/police apparatus (itself barely out of its infancy) were mutually uninterested in each other: the locus of class struggle was on the job, not in the home. The squatters – and everyone else, for that matter – did not see the way they lived as a "something" that begged for generalized attention. There may have been nourishingly strong familial and interfamilial bonds, and a rich appreciation of the promise of a new life in America, in the partly squatted tenement buildings, but there wasn't the external impression or the internal pretense that there were a group of people within the buildings and the neighborhood who had discovered or established some kind of unusual social protest or alternative lifestyle called squatting. No one was an "insider" or an "outsider" to "the scene" because there was no scene to be "inside" or "outside" of. Strictly speaking, if you had a place to stay of any kind, you were "inside"; only the homeless were "outside," and this wasn't a metaphor.

I would not pretend to be able to divine when the activity of squatting in New York City became a spectacle. But I can say with certainty that squatting could only become spectacular after several historical conditions had been met: 1). when the locus of class war had been expanded into the home and the entire realm of everyday life, as well as into the workplace (a condition met in the 1930s and '40s); 2). when squatting had become an effective socio-political negation of and attack on modern urbanism and the colonialization of everyday life, as well as a practical solution to a concrete problem (met in the 1950s and '60s); 3). when the media/police apparatus had developed to the point that both its functionaries and squatters discovered the value of constantly updated information on each other's tactical positions, both in the city itself and in the abstract space of "public opinion" (the 1970s and '80s); and 4). when a sufficient number of buildings in the same neighborhood had been abandoned – as the result of both irresponsible property speculation and default on property taxes – for the beginnings of a real "squatter's community" to form in and around them (also in the 1970s and '80s).

One observes that the meeting of these historical conditions has coincided with the internationalization of the images of both squatters and squatting. In his introduction to a recent Autonomedia translation of *Cracking the Movement,* a book about squatting in Holland in the 1980s, Steve Englander reports that,

> Throughout the 1980s the squatters' movement in Northern Europe exerted a powerful attraction and fascination for squatters in New York and other American cities, for those familiar and interested in that milieu, and for activists predisposed to autonomous political action. . . . To hear or read about the spectacular actions perpetrated by European squatters was for many in North America, and in particular, New York, an encounter with their own desires and fantasies realized in distant parts; it reinforced their own pride through feelings of solidarity, as well as their own righteous certainty: 'if it happened there it can happen here. . .'

The element that was apparently lacking – riots and other direct confrontations with the media/police apparatus – was supplied in the summer of 1991, when the NYPD rioted during its city-mandated evictions of homeless people from Tompkins Square Park, injuring a number of people and generating many complaints about police brutality. By and large, the only people who supported the homeless people who were forcibly evicted were the squatters and activists who lived in nearby tenement buildings. As a result, the situation in the East Village has been increasingly spectacular ever since: the squatters fear, distrust and dislike the cops, and the cops fear, distrust and dislike the squatters. Both groups mythologize and, no doubt, derive some ideological satisfaction from recalling the events that took place in the Park, because "that was when the shit went down." But the events of the last four months or so have produced a public show so visible and noisy that all of New York no doubt has heard the words and has some feelings about "the squatters," just as the squatters must have strong feelings about "the police" and "the media." In such a situation, it is quite understandable that "the squatters" are suspicious of reports about their activities and conditions (no doubt police/media spies are everywhere these days), even or especially one written by an activist predisposed towards autonomous action. This may not in fact be the time for "autonomy," but for "solidarity."

Local interventions

Precisely because they do not constitute a "movement" nor a "subculture" of some kind, the squatters of the East Village – there is no point in singling out those on E. 13th Street – radiate out conflicting messages on these subjects. The rhetoric of "DEFEND THE SQUATS" – a slogan that has been spray-painted all over the East Village – implies that one knows which squats are "the squats," that both squatters and bourgeois renters alike are called upon to defend them, and that no explanation for why one should "defend" the squats (as opposed to squatting in general) need be given, because "we all know why." And yet the creation and maintenance of a specialized, relatively-easily identifiable "squatter lifestyle" – which is more than just a decision about where and how to secure shelter, and encompasses such largely irrelevant matters as choice of clothing, style of dress, public behavior, and ideological-cultural commodity preferences – , though far from being enforced or universally practiced, are common enough to discourage day-to-day contact with squatters when an "action" isn't taking place, and thus to warrant some attention on the part of individual squatters.

Certainly the internationalization of the images of both squatters and squatting in general has, ironically, contributed to the homogenization of the "squatter look" in the East Village, just as it did in the 1980s in Holland, Switzerland and Germany, where there is still a disquieting conformity (a form of isolation) among squatters. A dead-end is certainly reached when New Yorkers, in an attempt to look "authentic," adopt the gesture of wearing Palestinian scarves in mimicry of Amsterdam squatters who adopted the gesture of wearing Palestinian scarves, which were originally worn for practical reasons, as a symbol of their own struggles against conformity and isolation. But this dead-end isn't simply aesthetic or theoretical in nature. What works on the practical level in Amsterdam may not work on the practical level in New York City, precisely because the two cities are located in two very different legal cultures.

Under Dutch law, one is successful in proving adverse possession of a squatted building if the uninterrupted period of "illegal" occupancy has been a quiet one in which no one – especially the property's owners – has noticed, much less objected to your presence. But under American law, adverse possession is proven if, during the period of uninterrupted occupancy, the "illegal" possession has been visible, open, "notorious" and "hostile" (as prescribed by statute). Some of the implications of this difference should be immediately clear. The American system encourages, perhaps even necessitates a turn towards the "public eye" and the general spectacle, while the Dutch system nearly rewards turning away from them. Given the fact that abstractions such as the "public eye," "public opinion" and the spectacle of "consensus" are obviously manufactured falsehoods, the American system effectively traps squatters, while the Dutch system allows a certain margin for escape. In America, you are either "out of the public eye" (and thus not entitled to squat with the expectation that the property will become yours if you inhabit it without interruption) or you are "in the public eye" (and thus constrained to live by its inhuman rules, despite the fact that you have, by squatting, presumably freed yourself from one of society's most powerful constraints on living).

Ironically, a solution to the American problem can be found in the controlled use of tactics tried out and found to be effective in Amsterdam and other European cities. The solution begins with the insight that both the police and "the media" (considered as a bloc) deliberately and continuously say what they know to be absolutely ridiculous things about particular groups of squatters and squatting in general, with the intent of doing two things at once: fixing distorted images of squatters and squatting in the "public eye" (thereby defeating in advance their attempts to construct positives images of themselves); and summoning, daring, even provoking the squatters to produce "the truth" about themselves and squatting in general. Too much attention has been focused on the first goal, and too little on the second, which is in many ways the most important of the two. If squatters take the bait, and try to define (for themselves and for the consumption of others) "the truth" about themselves and squatting in general, they automatically do damage to the essence of who they are and what they are doing – whether or not "the truth" they produce and relay for mass consumption is spectacular or "mediagenic" enough for "the media" to recognize, accept and broadcast. For the squatters have begun to conceive of themselves and their activities in ideological ("expert") terms: this and that won't be reported by "the media" and therefore won't help us gain the support and approval of "the public"; consequently, those "things" must be de-emphasized, while these "things" here – which will help us gain control of "public opinion" – must be brought to the foreground. On this stage, one abstract monolith ("the squatters" or the "squat community") meets and faces off against another abstract monolith ("the media," "the police" or "the public"). Whatever happens, the category of the abstract monolith wins. In the meantime and inevitably, the things that have been temporarily de-emphasized (i.e., certain concrete particularities, unique to squatting and to squatting on, say, E. 13th Street) – because they are "just not what we need right now" – are on their way to being completely forgotten. Conversely, that which has been temporarily foregrounded (i.e., actions, images and rhetoric intended for mass consumption) is, in the meantime and inevitably, on its way to becoming "second nature."

If "the truth" squatters have produced for mass consumption is in fact spectacular enough for the media to recognize and accept, they will find that they have inadvertently assisted the general spectacle in keeping in motion the dizzying – and ultimately counter-revolutionary – enterprise of continually fixing, circulating and condemning "newly improved" distorted images of people who are hostile to the way life is currently organized and lived day to day; they will find that they have provided this enterprise with more cannon fodder, and have done nothing substantial to help their own tactical positions. As for the general spectacle, it has – by being given the opportunity to present "the public" with a deliberately distorted image of the squatters' careful correction of "the media's" first distorted image of squatting – once again (two times in a row) prevented the squatters from constructing a positive image that "the public" can understand and sympathize with. And yet the spectacle has, by allotting the squatters a place (any place) on its stage, given them a false reason to believe that next time "the media" will get it right and allow them to finally clear their names, let "the truth" be known, and win the "support" of "the public," which was "really" on their side all along (only they were deceived and didn't know it).

Quite obviously, there are great temporary rhetorical advantages to entering the spectacle at precise times and places. But any gains made from such contact can be quickly reversed into long-term losses if one doesn't enter the spectacle (at a precise time and place) as a clear enemy of the spectacle itself. There are examples, I'm afraid. Though "Bear" is no doubt not a spokesperson for anyone other than himself, he has felt free to conduct himself in a fashion that has ultimately (and rather quickly) had effects on the images of each and every East Village squatter. Though "Bear" makes the gesture of masking his face when he is giving TV and press interviews, he is obviously no enemy of the spectacle. User of a pseudonym or not, "Bear" has made a name for himself and has consequently satisfied the spectacle's need for an image, indeed, any image, of an East Village squatter. As will be discussed in the chronology that follows, his decision on the night of 4 July 1995 to grant a live television interview with WCBS-TV reporter Rose Arce and anchorperson John Johnson may have been ill considered. But it was certainly a serious tactical mistake for him to grant both television and print interviews with reporters on the night in September 1995 that the NYPD raided a beer party in La Plaza Cultural (9th Street and Avenue C) and ended up fighting with and arresting 25 people (to whom the news media referred as "punk rockers," "skinheads" and "anarchists," without the slightest concern that these names have nothing in common with each other and have very little to do with the people at whom they were thrown). "Bear's" presence in the spectacle – whatever his original intentions – was obviously used to say something along the lines of, "These skin-headed, anarchistic punks are so bad even the squatters don't like them and we all know how much we don't like those good-for-nothin' rent-stealing squatters, don't we?" But his presence did more than that. It showed that "the squatters" must not really be so bad; after all, they don't like those skin-headed, anarchistic punks either. The damage is two-fold: distorted images have been fixed and distributed for both "the squatters" (bad, but not the worst) and "the punks" (the worst); a spectacular separation has been imposed between "the squatters" and "the skins/punks/anarchists," though there might actually be instances of and room for more genuine contact between them.

BACKGROUND

In November 1994 the State Supreme Court slapped the Guiliani Administration with a restraining order intended to prevent the city from going forward with its illogical and vindictive plans to try to evict – rather than grant adverse possession to – over 100 squatters from buildings on East 13th Street between Avenues A and B (537, 539, 541 and 545 E. 13th Street). Some of these squatters had been uninterruptedly occupying these tenements for as long as 10 years. They had accomplished a lot in that time: the immediate neighborhood was and is no longer a market for drugs nor a place to use them. The squatters had clearly indicated their willingness to fit into the neighborhood, as well as their desire to eventually gain adverse possession of some of its buildings, by obtaining permits to have water and electrical services installed or repaired, and by paying Sanitation and Fire Department-issued fines against them (just like they were any other group of residents).

The Guiliani Administration has changed its official reasons for evicting these people as the situation (political expediency) has called for. In November 1994 it was still advancing the claim that the squatters were preventing the City from renovating the tenement buildings and turning them into 41 low-income (below $24,500 a year) apartments, thirty percent of which were to be reserved for people currently housed in the city's homeless shelters. But it is clear that the real reason for the Guiliani Administration's determination to evict the squatters has been a very personal and wounded desire for revenge against the very people (or at least their friends and sympathizers) who were beaten up in the Tompkins Square Park police riot and had the nerve to file lawsuits against the City (most of which – thanks to "amateur videos" recorded during the riot – stood a very good chance of being settled in the plaintiffs' favor if they went to trial). The City has no doubt determined that the squatters were and are a source of continuing "instability" in the neighborhood, largely on the basis of exaggerated claims from the neighborhood Community Board, which has been generally unsupportive of the squats. In April 1995 the City manufactured what it took to be a great reason for the immediate eviction of the squatters in at least two buildings, 541 and 545 East 13th Street: they were in danger of imminent collapse. On 20 April, the City issued the squatters an illegal eviction order. State Supreme Court Justice Wilk knew a piece of illegal bullshit when it was thrust in front of him – how could the same buildings the city wanted to turn into apartments only a few weeks ago now be in danger of imminent collapse? – and ruled against the City, which appealed to the federal Court of Appeals. On 25 May, the appellate court stated that it would rule on the city's claims about the buildings' safety in September 1995; in the meantime, the restraining order against the City was lifted. An attempted eviction was sure to follow. Rather than simply abandoning the buildings, the majority of squatters decided to stay and to prepare to fight against any attempt to evict them. The precise date and time of the intended eviction was leaked by the police in an attempt to intimidate the squatters. It seems to have failed miserably. The cops realized this, and took appropriate steps.

31 MAY 1995

The prior evening and throughout the early morning of 31 May 1995, a number of very creative measures were taken by the squatters to slow the police's passage through the streets immediately surrounding the area, including the placement of an overturned car on the East 13th Street. At around 4 am or so, and in the style of the Amsterdam squatters, an eviction tape was played really loud and the squatters' neighbors, friends, fellow squatters and other supporters turned out to attempt to fill the street with bodies, dancing, noise and a generally festive atmosphere. Before the police moved in, they (the cops) made sure to gather and hold together in one place ("the pen") all the journalists, reporters and TV crews who'd come down to cover the eviction. As a result of this very effective post-Gulf War tactic, the police were able to get and maintain a chokehold on the flows of information in and out of the area. There were also free to, once again, commit brutality and other criminal and civil violations with impunity.

The police certainly came prepared, as prepared as any army. Their primary attack force consisted of 250 fully-clad riot police; a 25-ton armored vehicle – reputedly called "Anytime, Baby" – that saw action in Korea, presumably against the Communists; three police helicopters; and assorted police vans and squad cars. Because the pretense that the "crumbling" (*New York Post*) buildings were in danger of imminent collapse had to be maintained – even as that pretense was completely undermined by the rumblings of the tank –, the primary attack force was accompanied by fire engines, sanitation trucks and other "emergency service vehicles." (Ostensibly, the police were there to accompany and ensure the safety of the officials from the Buildings Department, but it was obvious that the Buildings people were there to accompany and justify the presence of the police.)

Perhaps most importantly, the police also arrived with their own camera crews and videotape recorders. They filmed everything and everybody, not only to have the means to answer and disprove allegations that they were guilty of police brutality, but also to have the means to identify anyone who might elude arrest or do something illegal (like resist arrest). But the squatters intended to be nonviolent in their resistance to the eviction, and they succeeded in not being provoked by the police into a pointless and no doubt violent confrontation. The centerpiece of their plans was the creation of a human chain around "their" buildings. The tactical advantage of the chain was that it (further) delayed the police's efforts to arrest the protesters. In the end, 31 people were pulled away from the chain, roughly handled, and taken to the 9th Precinct as arrestees. Most of those arrested were not from the evicted squats, but from the surrounding buildings. This suggests that it is much easier to "defend the squats" on an abstract level (those situations in which it is not "your" squat but someone else's that is threatened), than it is on a concrete one (those situations in which the most important thing is to save your ass first and then worry about everything and everyone else later). The concrete defense of a squat requires people acting directly on their own behalves: violence may be inevitable, given the stakes.

The local newspapers, of course, weren't the least bit fair or kind to the squatters in their treatments of what happened. Making a point it would repeat again and again over the course of the summer, *The New York Times* ranted:

Unlike the poor immigrants who have taken over city-owned buildings in the Bronx and elsewhere as an alternative to homeless shelters, most of the squatters on E.13th Street are artists, musicians and poets whose stance against the city is as much about politics as about the need for housing. Most are white, most have jobs and, over the years, they have carved comfortable spaces out of the dilapidated properties that the city owns because the previous owners defaulted on taxes.

Though this passage relates a few basic facts, its tone is outraged. It is not describing reality, it is objecting to it! In particular, it is objecting to the simple but apparently inconceivable and unacceptable facts that, in the words of Community Board member Lisa Kaplan, "these are younger people living in a very free-wheeling style with other economic choices." In other words, the spectacle of squatting in the heart of Manhattan (as opposed to any other borough of New York City) is not about obstacles to the building of low-income housing developments or finding places for "real" homeless people, but about the "economic choices" made by these "middle-class misfits" (to quote a *New York Post* editorial). The damage done by the squatters is not to the buildings, the neighborhood nor the tax revenues of the City of New York, but to this whole society's image of what "happiness" is. That's right: here are young people from middle-class (code for "white") backgrounds who have soundly rejected all the things that being young, middle-class and white in America entitle you to! Mayor Guiliani knows very well the threat these kids pose, not only to other young, white, middle-class kids (who might also "drop out"), but to all those poor immigrants and working-class stiffs out there who think that the most important thing in life is getting exactly what all those young, white, middle-class kids have already got, because those are the only things that can bring true happiness in America, right? Wrong, say the squatters. "This world was made for them, not me: let them keep it!"

4 JULY 1995

Approximately one month after squatters launched a failed attempt to re-take (or re-squat) 541 E.13th Street, another attempt was launched on the 4th of July, commonly called Independence Day. No doubt the first attempt failed in part because the police had taken steps to "secure" E. 13th Street and turn it into an armed camp (a "restricted zone" into which only "respectable citizens" with a damn good reason for being there could enter). News reports in June contended that at least three press photographers and one radio reporter who had tried to enter this "zone" were relieved of their press credentials by police officers who were no doubt concerned about their personal safety. But by July – and especially during the July 4th weekend, when hundreds of thousands of people were descending on the lower East Side of Manhattan to watch Macy's annual fireworks "spectacular"

– the police's grip on the neighborhood was forced to loosen up a bit. The squatters' collective sense of timing was brilliant.

At 10 pm – that is, as the meaningless fireworks display was ending, sending thousands of people meandering through the East Village's streets – the squatters began to re-take 541 E.13th by kicking through the barred and closed windows. By midnight, they had destroyed the security system put in by the cops, re-taken the entire building, booby-trapped its floors with tar so as to slow up and fuck with the officers who would later get into it, unfurled a series of very mildly worded banners – "OUR HOME," "FREEDOM," and "*ESTAMOS, QUEDAMOS*" (Spanish for "WE ARE HERE, WE STAY") – and ascended to the roof, from which they yelled to their supporters, who'd collected across the street, and yelled at the riot police and police helicopters circling around them. The police had been completely caught off guard, and could do nothing to stop the squatters. But that wasn't all, as they discovered when they finally broke down the door and entered the building. There was no one there, no one at all: they had been completely out-foxed.

All the police could do was beat the shit out of or arrest anyone and everyone who didn't run away in response to their raised clubs and "protective" shields. Significantly, the police eventually arrested only 18 people, a mere 5 of whom they claim they can prove were in the building just before they arrived and found no one there. The police were evidently more interested in beating the heads of sympathetic protesters across the street, uncooperative neighbors in adjoining buildings and, of course, innocent bystanders (wherever they were) than in making arrests and getting convictions – despite the fact that there were rumors they were going to charge those squatters who threw things from the roof with attempted murder. But the police weren't the only ones completely out-foxed by the squatters: so were "the media." All of the local TV stations had sent their live crews to the East Side for the fireworks display, which began at 9:15 pm. The strategy of their 11 O'clock news reports was obviously going to be their tried-and-true one: rely on pre-taped segments on the general spectacle of "the Fourth of July" and then, for a bang-up closer, go to scenes from the "spectacular" itself and get a quick live report. The re-squat ruined these plans with little trouble. By 11 pm, the competing and very compelling spectacle of the re-squatted squat was in full swing: it was news! More than that, it was news with a hook: you know, the independence thing. The local TV stations had no choice but to interrupt a spectacle of their own making for a spectacle of someone else's making. Instability must have broken out in boardrooms all across the city. To interrupt or not to interrupt? Which spectacle is the most spectacular? Think of it: to interrupt themselves, the TV stations had to re-locate their live TV crews or send out a second set to cover "the late-breaking developments on the troubled lower East Side of Manhattan." In either case, it meant confining their "award-winning news teams" in "the pen" that the police once again created and maintained by force and intimidation. In the meantime – tick, tick, tick: time is money – valuable advertising revenues might be lost; indeed, the advertisers might not be happy that the stations decided to cover the re-squat at all. But if they didn't cover the re-squat, their competitors might have ate them alive. Oh! what to do? what to do?

It is at a time like this that you don't let someone as earnest as Peter Spagnuolo get on a cellular phone and talk to the Associated Press.[1] For the same reason you would like to escape at the last minute and leave the police all alone in an empty building, you would like to maintain total "radio silence" until something big is set into motion. If you are going to let your actions do the talking for you (and this was a brilliantly eloquent action), keep your fucking mouth shut. If you are going to put banners up that use lackluster phrases, don't bore everyone to sleep by paraphrasing them aloud on the telephone. (If *The Daily News* is content to say that the squatters "also unfurled a banner, although police would not say what it said," go ahead and let them.) If you are going to say anything at all, you might as well say the most irresponsible things you can think of. Say that the prisoners are being murdered in the prisons! Call for a permanent universal rent strike! Call for a general wildcat strike! Declare that people should never work! Yell out, "Come on over, baby, we got shakin' goin' on!" It is quite conceivable that, in their confused state, the media will broadcast these messages, precisely because they irresponsible. "Be reasonable: demand the impossible." But don't let someone like Peter tell the world reasonable rubbish such as "we've done this to re-establish our homes." Though the strategy (we've got to show the people we love HOME as much as anyone else) may seem sound, the tactical position required by it is untenable: if you act like you don't want to be a "rootless" squatter (that you do not want to be kicked out of "your" squatted home), you completely undermine the idea that you are, in fact, a squatter. Explanations are required: it seems that revolutionary squatters would only symbolically return to buildings they had once squatted and been evicted from; that they would find another building in which to stay and re-establish "the squat," even if they were involved in litigious efforts to return to the old building on the grounds that adverse possession had been attained before the eviction took place. But maybe I'm wrong. Who am I talking to, anyway?

NOT BORED! #24, September 1995
Translated into Dutch and published in *Mba-Kajere*, issue #1, Spring 1996

[1] On-line notice dated 22 February 1997: in point of fact, Peter Spagnuolo *did not* have a telephone conversation with the AP during the 4 July action, and so did not say the things that I criticize him for saying. The Associated Press fabricated the remarks that were attributed to him.

Local interventions
Squatters Evicted from E. 13th Street

On 8 August, 1996, an Appellate Court reversed an injunction issued by State Supreme Court Judge Eliot Wilk that barred the City of New York from evicting squatters in several buildings on East 13th Street between Avenues A and B. The reversal was issued because the squatters were not able to prove to the court's satisfaction that their occupation of these abandoned, city-owned buildings – just a handful out of over 900 (!) such buildings in New York City – was continuous over the course of the last 10 years. (Some of these buildings have in fact been continuously squatted for as many as 12 years.) Had continuous occupation been proved, the court would have no choice but to grant the squatters the legal right, under the concept of "adverse possession," to own the buildings they have occupied, renovated and lived in.

In the very early morning of 13 August 1996, with the San Diego Republican Convention about to start, the City of New York – through its attack force, the New York Police Department – carried out eviction orders at 535, 537, and 539 East 13th Street. A total of 80 people were forced out of these buildings and immediately made homeless. (These evictions came about 15 months after the City successfully evicted squatters from two other buildings on East 13th Street, a series of events we attempted to document in our pamphlet *Squat the World!*) After completely sealing off the area, the City's armed forces proceeded to completely gut all the affected buildings, thus rendering them completely uninhabitable, once and for all. At this writing [October 21, 1996], the police are still occupying 13th Street between Avenues A and B.

Also on 13 August, the City sent its Fire Marshals to intimidate, search and confiscate certain "dangerous" items from the 7th Street squat.

In the evening of 14 August 1996, a large group of people assembled peacefully in Tompkins Square Park to protest the evictions of the 13th Street squatters. Invoking a clearly unconstitutional park rule that forbids the assembly of groups numbering more than 20 people, the NYPD moved in and roughly arrested 31 people, including artist Eric Drooker, who was grabbed by the throat for singing "Dem Bones." To protest these arrests and the evictions, squatters unsealed "Glass House," a formerly squatted, now once-again abandoned building on 10th Street and Avenue D. (In 1994, when the City evicted the residents of the Glass House, it claimed it was going to use the former glass factory as housing for people afflicted with AIDS, which it did not do.) There were 29 arrests at the Glass House action, which was cheered on by several hundred people. But a rally and march called for 25 August 1996 drew only 50 or 60.

Though we are not squatters, we have several friends who are currently squatting buildings in Manhattan and Brooklyn. But even if we did not have such brave and creative friends, we would be outraged at the policies and actions of the

Local interventions

City of New York, and would be fully committed to doing whatever we could do to help NYC's squatters. In part because former federal prosecutor and current Mayor Guiliani still has the reactionary mindset of a prosecutor, in part because the gentrification of the East Village is a top priority of the City's ruling classes, and in part because the squatters have been so successful for so long at finding, unsealing, re-furbishing and maintaining these "urban homesteads" – without any help or money from anybody – in the very heart of the capitalist theatre of operations, the City is moving against all of the squats in the East Village and the Lower East Side. Other squats that are in immediate danger of eviction include the one located at 537/539 East Fifth Street, and ABC No Rio, the squat on Rivington that since 1980 has housed a well-known gallery/performance space, a garden and an artist's studio, as well as living spaces for untold numbers of people.

Of course we believe that the City's campaign against the squats is (among many other bad things) disinformative, misdirected, counter-productive, short-sighted, authoritarian, unnecessarily violent, unconstitutional, probably illegal, vindictive, cynical, callous, condescending, self-righteous, and wasteful of the taxpayers' money and the resources of the NYPD, both of which are said to be in short supply these days. But we also believe that the squats are beautiful, creative, courageous, constructive, directly democratic, autonomous, lively, environmentally-conscious, and highly valuable to the surrounding community for a variety of reasons (the squats, in addition to keeping the housing stock from deteriorating so quickly, tend to discourage the dealing of drugs, the dumping of trash and other "quality of life" offenses).

Far more so than any group of self-avowed "revolutionaries" active in the NYC area, the squatters are setting precisely the type of example that no one in power – neither the politicians nor the bureaucrats, neither the landlords nor the real estate "developers," neither the community groups nor the local educators – want anyone else to follow. The squatters are demonstrating – neither in words nor in speeches, but in acts – exactly how much is possible for small autonomous groups of people to accomplish outside of the dominant institutions, the most basic of which is landlordism. The squats are laboratories for the revolution of everyday life: within them, people learn to teach themselves and each other such "specialized" skills as carpentry, masonry and electrical engineering; within them, people learn to discover, develop and refine real desires, and to organize themselves in such a fashion that the realization of everyone's desire is possible, if not likely; within them, people learn to experiment with "free" time, because not having to pay rent means not having to have a steady job, and because not having a steady job means having the freedom to "spend" time as is desired. By contrast, the meeting rooms of the city's anarcho-syndicalists, federated anarchists and revolutionary socialists are morgues for the corpses of defeated revolutions.

And so we have done what we can to help the squatters: during the eviction of the East 13th Street squats, we provided distribution and unlimited, free photocopying of flyers produced by squatters and their supporters. We appeared on the pirate radio station Steal This Radio (88.7 FM) between 6 and 7 pm on 14 August 1996 – during the very height of the protests – to state and explain the reasons for our support of the squatters. We lent our physical presence to and carried signs at the various spontaneous protests against the evictions that broke out across the street from where the squats had been, at the action at Glass House, and at the 25 August rally and march. (Our sign proclaiming LONG LIVE THE REVOLUTION OF EVERYDAY LIFE was photographed by the *Village Voice* and appeared in the edition dated August 27, 1996.) We wish we could have done more.

Perhaps it would be helpful if we framed two questions that might clarify what needs to be done in the coming months and future struggles:

1). It was claimed in the 15 August 1996 edition of *The New York Post* that "it's noteworthy that the squatters are now virtually without sympathizers." In the handout entitled "Some Facts About Squatters and The Evictions," an anonymous squatter pointed out that

> Squatter's and community activists were joined by over 200 Lower East Side (L.E.S.) residents, mostly of the public housing units across from Glass House, the site of the protest that took place on Wednesday the 14th over the previous day's violent evictions of 80+ tenants from their homes on 13th street. More than 350 people took to the streets in support of the squatter's [sic] and the larger issues facing the community: gentrification, outrageous rent increases that are forcing long time residents out of the community and unchecked police violence and racism. There were 29 arrests.

Note the confusion here: were there 200 or 350 sympathizers on hand? This inconsistency seems to signal the presence of a deeper, unresolved problem: Were these people really there to "support" the squatters, or were they there as spectators? And how does one tell the difference between supporters and spectators, without personally interviewing each person? It would be an inadequate response to say, "It hardly matters whether there were 200 people or 350 people, or if they were there as supporters or spectators – what matters is that they were there." Such a response would overlook the fact that the squatters' rights movement as a whole is isolated, without a broad base of popular support, and currently being decimated by the City of New York, despite the presence of what could very well have been 350 hard-core supporters at the (completely symbolic) Glass House action.

2). In the 15 August *New York Post* piece, it was claimed that "most of the 13th Street squatters are would-be bohemians and pseudo-anarchists who simply enjoyed living rent-free." The answer contained in "Some Facts about Squatters and the Evictions" was in part as follows:

Local interventions

[The 13th Street squatters] are politically diverse and come from all walks of life. Many squatters are activists who are working towards building community structures that encourage self-determination and run counter to the prevailing forms of impersonal, capitalist-oriented living that result in forcing people to give half of their pay over to shamelessly wealthy slumlords for housing.

In other less imprecise words, the squatters *are* real bohemians and anarchists who (of course!) enjoy living rent-free. There is no point in denying that squatters are lifestyle anarchists, people whose very way of organizing their domestic life is a direct action against both capitalism and the State. Indeed, it is because they are lifestyle anarchists that the squatters inspire such so much admiration among militant workers, radical intellectuals and, of course, social anarchists such as the folks at *NOT BORED!* But coming to grips with and mastering these facts is difficult, and difficult for at least two reasons: A). It will require a renewed awareness of the necessity of theoretical analysis (even after the squatters have "come out" as lifestyle anarchists, the spectacular media will no doubt continue to maintain that the squatters aren't "real" anarchists and/or deny that it is even possible for anyone to be an anarchist in NYC in 1996); and B). It will require a renewed awareness of the necessity of organizational innovation (to prove that not only is anarchism "possible," but also that the squatters themselves are "real" anarchists, it would be highly desirable to create a directly democratic council or federation that brings together delegates from all the squats in the East Village/Lower East Side, which are otherwise "represented" by a group of spectacular militants who continually rely on such utterly stale forms of protest as rallies, marches and speeches). But if anyone can overcome these difficulties, it is the squatters.

NOT BORED! #26, November 1996
Modified and translated into Dutch by Freek Kallenburg, and published in *Mba-Kajere* (Winter 1997)

Unabomber for President
Political Action Committee, New York City

The Unabomber for President Campaign was launched in Boston in September 1995 by Lydia and Chris. In February 1996, the UNAPACK (the Unabomber for President Political Action Committee) attracted the interest of one Radio Free Al, who went on to write several stories about it in *The Boston Phoenix*. It was Radio Free Al who, while visiting NYC in July 1996, introduced us to the UNAPACK, its delightful array of bumper stickers and fliers, and its website, which has been up since March 1996 and updated many times since then (the last update took place on 23 Sept 1996). *NOT BORED!* opened a New York City office of UNAPACK in early August 1996. Since then, UNPACK NYC has been very active:

1. It hath caused to be printed and distributed more than 5,000 copies of the flyer headlined CRASH THE PARTIES, which announced the opening of its office. Most of these fliers were stuffed into unsuspecting copies of *The Village Voice* and *The New York Free Press*, both of which are distributed for free in Manhattan.

2. It hath caused to be printed and distributed approximately 1,000 copies of the flyer headlined WHY WE ARE NOT VOTING GREEN OR SOCIALIST, which was designed for Little Billy not de Bored's appearance at the "progressive" forum at the NY Society for Ethical Culture (held 26 Sept 1996), which featured remarks by Green Party presidential candidate Ralph Nader.

3. It hath raised a 6-foot-wide and 60-foot-long banner proclaiming UNABOMBER FOR PRESIDENT (in international day-glo orange!) on the top of the abandoned grain elevator in Red Hook, Brooklyn. This banner remained in place for four days.

4. It hath caused to be printed and distributed 200 copies of the clandestine bilingual pamphlet entitled "WHAT WE HAVE DONE AND WHY," translated into Spanish by R. Buono, which was designed to explain the choice of the grain elevator as the place for the banner.

5. It hath with intent to sow confusion among the general public mixed its fliers (as well as the fliers issued by UNAPACK Boston) in among the rest at such respectable gatherings as: "Madison Avenue vs. Mass Society," *Baffler* editor Tom Frank's 22 Oct 96 lecture on liberation marketing techniques (sponsored by New York University School of Education's Media, Power, Culture lecture series); "Looking Past the Elections: A Talk with Todd Gitlin, Ellen Willis and Manning Marable" held on 23 Oct 96 at NYU (sponsored by the Democratic Socialists of America); and the panel discussion "Campaign '96: Its Impact on NYC" (moderated by former Mayor Dinkins and held at the New School for Social Research on 28 Oct 96), among many other events.

6. It hath disturbed the peace at numerous events in the NYC area, including two appearances at the Roseland Ballroom by the muscle-rock group Rage Against the Machine (17 and 18 Aug 1996) and an on-Broadway performance of Douglas McGrath's play *Political Animal* (12 Oct 1996), as well as the aforementioned appearance by Ralph Nader on 26 Sept 1996. (When contacted by a caller to the 16 Oct 1996 edition of Brian Lehrer's daily program for WNYC-FM called "On the Line," Douglas McGrath indicated that UNAPACK's campaign was far too "cynical" for him and that UNAPACK NYC's stunt outside of his show not at all funny.)

7. It hath repeatedly used the silk-screened, red-white-and-blue bumper

Local interventions

stickers generated by UNAPACK Boston to deface the property of the Metropolitan Transportation Authority, the City of New York, the Mr. Softie Corporation, and Pathfinder Books (a Trotskyist bookstore) in Brooklyn, among others too numerous to mention.

8. It hath crossed state lines to appear *en masse* outside and inside of the Hartford Civic Center during the first Presidential debate, held in Hartford on 6 Oct 1996. At this non-event, members from both UNAPACK NYC and UNAPACK Boston distributed fliers, spoke to passersby and the curious, and were interviewed by over a dozen reporters from such upstanding enterprises as WABC-AM in New York, Trinity College's radio station and newspaper, Brandeis University's radio station and newspaper, and ZDF Television (Germany).

9. Little Billy not de Bored, director of UNAPACK NYC, has been interviewed by the *San Francisco Examiner* (24 Sept 96); by the Manhattan cable access TV shows *Anarchist Forum* (channel 69 on 2 Oct 96, 9 Oct 96, 23 Oct 96, 30 Oct 96 and 2 Nov 96) and *The Anarchist Propaganda & Variety Show* (channel 17 on 23 Oct 96); by WABC 770 AM (Oct 7 96); and by Joey Manley on the World Wide Web site freespeech.org (Activism 101 for the week 3 Oct to 9 Oct 1996), among others. A transcript of the interview with Joey Manley is reproduced elsewhere. As-of-yet unpublished interviews have been conducted with Jim Ciment and Steve Wilson.

Though the presidential election on 5 November 96 will mark the official end of the 1996 campaign, UNAPACK will continue to exist as a national organization, with regional offices in Boston, New York, Chicago, North Carolina and Arizona; it will immediately introduce and popularize the slogan DON'T BLAME ME, I VOTED FOR THE UNABOMBER; it will meet in Boston on 15 November 96 to publicize, celebrate and evaluate our candidate's strong performance in the election; it will thenceforth campaign against the spectacle of the year 2000, by which time UNAPACK hopes to have induced the rupture that will inaugurate the rapturous beginning of the perpetual revolution of everyday life.

NOT BORED! #26, November 1996

We put a UNABOMBER FOR PRESIDENT banner on the huge, abandoned grain warehouse in Red Hook, Brooklyn . . .

We put a UNABOMBER FOR PRESIDENT banner on the huge, abandoned grain warehouse in Red Hook, Brooklyn, because 1). we want to publicize our campaign to convince registered voters to write the name Unabomber in on their ballots in the presidential election to be held November 6, 1996, and 2). we want to call attention to the fact that, for more than 30 years, modern American industrial society just can't figure out a single thing to do with Red Hook's strange and beautiful grain warehouse, other than let it become a depressing, isolated ruin.[1] These two reasons have a lot in common.

For poor and working-class Americans, there is so little difference between the candidates for President in 1996 that it doesn't really matter which one you or I vote for. No matter who we vote for – either for President Bill Clinton, Republican Bob Dole or third party candidate Ross Perot – the result will be the same: another rich, white male who doesn't care about you or me will be elected president. We have so little to say about how things are run in Washington, D.C. – the politicians who run the government care so little about how things are going in places like Red Hook – that you and I might just as well vote for the Unabomber, that is, if we vote at all! The Unabomber has just as much chance of getting elected President as we have a chance of electing a President who really represents and cares about the interests of the American people today!

It is true that the Unabomber is a terrorist and that he killed some people and tried to kill several more. But these facts shouldn't keep him from being President. Republican candidate Bob Dole is a World War II veteran; 50 years ago he killed some people and tried to kill several more. But no one is saying that this disqualifies him for office, or that this means that the people who want him to be President are "sick." Republican speechmaker Colin Powell is a Gulf War veteran; just 5 years ago he helped kill hundreds of thousands of Iraqis and tried to kill many more. But no one is saying that he is a "violent madman," a "sociopathic genius" or forever "unfit" to be President of the United States. The only thing the Unabomber did wrong was break the federal government's monopoly on violence. All the Unabomber did was take the tool of violence into his own hands, without the government telling him that, under these special circumstances, it is OK to kill innocent people.

Unlike Bob Dole, Colin Powell, Bill Clinton and the rest of them, the Unabomber doesn't want politics to be the business of making the organization of the brutal, exploiting society under which we are forced to live "better" than it is. Unlike the professional politicians, the Unabomber isn't interested in the symptoms of what is wrong. In his manifesto, called "Industrial Society and Its Future," the Unabomber said he wanted politics to be the making of a new and better society, a society that is not brutal and exploitative. He said that he wanted to get to the underlying cause of what is wrong with America today. And this is what is wrong: American industrial society puts profits before people. It doesn't value you as a person; it values you for the money you make for it. Everybody who

---

[1] This warehouse is written about at some length in William J. Brown, *American Colossus: the Grain Elevator 1843-1943* (Colossal Books, 2009).

Local interventions

lives here for even a short time knows what this means: the moment you are not making any money for American capitalism, you are worse than "useless" – you have become a "burden" to society, even though you helped build that very society! And when you are "useless" or "a burden to society" in modern America, you are left alone to die and rot, just like the abandoned grain warehouse in Red Hook, just like Red Hook itself. But we refuse to be abandoned, we refuse to die, we refuse to rot! Join us.

NOT BORED! #26, November 1996

NO MORE FUCKING UGLY BUILDINGS

People come to and fall in love with Manhattan because they find here a unique atmosphere, an urban environment unlike any other, one that makes them feel and act differently than if they were anywhere else in the world. The enduring appeal of New York City, the source of what makes Manhattan Island "so New York," is easy to locate: it's the beauty of the buildings, the charm of the streets, both wide and narrow, along which the buildings rise, and the varied ambiances of the neighborhoods, all the Greenwich Villages, China Towns and Little Italys that are crammed onto one huge island. Despite the incredible distances and differences that exist between these areas, a certain fragile unity of atmosphere – a certain "New Yorkness" – can be perceived and enjoyed, no matter where you go in Manhattan. It is to the preservation and enrichment of this psychogeographical spirit of New York that we are resolutely dedicated.

Fucking ugly buildings such as the huge United Artists theater complex that is being erected at Broadway and 14th Street are destroying the charm of our city's streets and the ambiances of our city's neighborhoods. We should be fighting against fucking ugly buildings as vigorously as we are fighting against terrorist bombings of the World Trade Center and other city landmarks, for these architectural monstrosities are horrible explosions in reverse, disasters that spring up, rather than fall down. Fucking ugly buildings are the neutron bombs of urban planning: they kill the spirit – the love of beauty – of the people who have to experience them day after day, while leaving their bodies intact. Because fucking ugly buildings are the same anywhere you go – what makes them fucking ugly in the first place is that they all look alike, each one has the same square-headed, blank, glassy-eyed expression – their construction in Manhattan is destroying its uniqueness, fragmenting its unity, and threatening its very spirit.

We think that it is telling that this particular fucking ugly building will eventually house the city's biggest movie theater complex and a Virgin Records megastore. Why can't the building itself be as creative, interesting and satisfying as the commodities that are sold inside are supposed to be? These commodities (the movie spectaculars, the junk food, the consumer electronics, and the pre-recorded bits of entertainment) will change all the time, but the fucking ugly building will remain there, day in, day out. Why should we be stuck with it? We are the ones who, through our state taxes, are helping to finance its construction. If Union Square needs anything, it needs affordable public housing, which is what was supposed to be constructed, that is, until Antonio Pagan's crew got involved. A huge theater complex such as this one belongs in Times Square (if anywhere), but most definitely not in Union Square, which has traditionally been home to the city's printing presses. We fear for Times Square (which has been invaded, occupied and destroyed by such distinctly un-New York corporations as Disney), but not nearly as much as we fear for Union Square, which has recently suffered the construction of such fucking ugly buildings as the Beth Israel Medical Center and Bradlees Toys, which is what the statue of George Washington, mounted on his horse in Union Square Park, has to look at every day for the rest of his monumental life. Union Square is near death; there is even a TV show named after and set in it. We must do something now.

Rally around the cause of beautiful buildings, lively streets and unified neighborhood ambiances! Enjoy your city for what you can experience and the people you can meet by traveling through and in it, not by what you can buy in it! Join the New York Psychogeographical Association, or, better yet, form your own!

NOT BORED! #28, December 1997

On-line notice dated 9 January 2000: *The New York Post* published the findings of a panel of architectural experts who'd been asked to vote on "The City's Ugliest Buildings." Completed in 1999, the fucking ugly building at One Union Square South was a shoo-in. In the words of *The Post,*

> This new high-rise with the bizarre, fog-belching sculpture called "Metronome" on its face is a grotesque modern nightmare, the panel concluded. "Now, one of the great urban vistas – Park Avenue South, from Grand Central to Union Square – ends with a building so mediocre, so poorly built, so uninteresting technologically as to make it almost nothing at all," Elliot said. He complained that the building's harsh "supermarket lighting" and personality-free design makes no attempt to fit in with the look or history of Union Square. "What were they smoking?" asked Tihany. So wonders Raymond Gonzalez, a security officer at the Virgin Megastore that occupies the building's ground floor. "The sculpture is really dumb, he said. "Yeah, it's ugly."

Local interventions

Decrees of the New York Psychogeographical Association

All private automobiles will be banned from Manhattan. The only automobiles allowed to operate during the day will be taxicabs, buses, and emergency vehicles such as fire trucks. Commercial trucks and tourist buses will be allowed on the streets between 2 and 6 a.m. only.

All mass transportation systems (buses, subways and commuter rails) will be modernized and expanded.

Bicycle lanes will be created on every city street; more and more people will choose to use bicycles, skateboards and roller skates to get around.

Pedestrian zones will be created throughout the city. In Greenwich Village, no cars (except for emergency vehicles) will be allowed in the areas east of the West Side Highway, west of Avenue of the Americas, north of Houston Street, and south of 14th Street. In downtown Manhattan, all cars except emergency vehicles will be banned from the areas south of the Brooklyn Bridge and west of Broadway.

There will be an indefinite ban on the construction of new buildings. All "construction" projects will become the renovation of already existing buildings.

The following will be eliminated and cleared out, with their sites allowed to grow wild: public and private parks, monuments, churches, cemeteries and parking lots.

Any building deemed to be really fucking ugly by majority vote of the people living in Manhattan will be demolished. Depending on the will of the people, the building will either be left in ruins or cleared out, with its site allowed to grow wild.

Any street or avenue that is currently referred to by number (i.e., Eighth Avenue or 14th Street) will be given a proper name. These names will of course reflect the streets' ambiance or mood, and thus may change over the course of time.

Marijuana and hashish will be de-criminalized, and people will be able to purchase and smoke it within any number of "coffee houses."

Museums will be abolished, their buildings put to other purposes, and their masterpieces will be distributed among the city's coffee houses and bars.

All other "crackpot" notions will be entertained.[2]

---

[2] Since this text was written, two of these decrees have been adopted in New York City (bike lanes and pedestrian zones), and marijuana has been de-criminalized in California, Michigan, and several other states.

Local interventions

NOT BORED! #28, December 1997

The Ride of the Midnight Marauder

Superbowl Sunday night, while most of New York City was at home watching TV, Little Billy not de Bored (a.k.a. Bill Brown, publisher of the situationist fanzine *NOT BORED!*) was arrested by the NYPD for allegedly spray-painting graffiti that denounced the outrageous pedestrian barricades that Mayor Giuliani and Police Commissioner Safir have installed at every intersection along 49th and 50th Streets between Fifth and Lexington Avenues in Manhattan. Little Billy is now facing felony criminal mischief charges, despite the fact that writing graffiti is a Class A Misdemeanor under New York State Penal Law.

Originally installed in December 1997 as a "holiday season" experiment, the barricades – despite intense criticism of them by the public, the press and even the cops themselves – have been stubbornly defended by the Mayor's Office and have not been removed. Designed to allow motor vehicles to make turns onto one-way streets without having to contend with pedestrians, the barricades must be guarded by police officers, who are supposed to see to it that pedestrians obey the signs that tell them not to cross the street between the hours of 9 am and 9 pm, despite the plainly visible "WALK" signal. Significantly, the barricades-and-cops "solution" to the problem of hypercongestion in midtown was not presented or approved of by the Department of Transportation, under whose jurisdiction matters such as this should fall. The idea of the barbaric barricades was hatched by top bureaucrats in the Police Department, in collaboration with the Mayor – in other words, by people totally unskilled in the areas of traffic management and urban planning, but deeply interested in advanced techniques of social control.

The intersection at Madison and 50th Street (the one at which Little Billy was apprehended) is quite obviously badly designed, like so many of our City's streets: it is the intersection of two very busy one-way streets. Bad planning such as this – combined with the super-concentration of both pedestrian and automotive traffic – is deadly, especially for pedestrians and bicyclists.

According to the Office of Safety Programs (NYC Department of Transportation), every year in New York City 15,000 pedestrians are struck and injured by automobiles. New York City leads the nation in pedestrian fatalities. Fully one-half of the people killed by cars are pedestrians, not other drivers. Contrary to the ravings of City Hall, the majority of the people killed aren't fast-

Local interventions

walking jaywalkers; forty percent of them are senior citizens.

Little Billy says that the only sensible solution to ready-made traffic jams such as the intersection of Madison and 50th is to re-route all automobiles away from this intersection and the others in the city like it.

Said Little Billy: "It makes absolutely no sense to try to keep throngs of pedestrians out of the intersections, especially in a city that is unique in the world in that you don't have to own a car to live here; you can rely on mass transportation and walking or a just a bicycle to get anywhere you want to go. To install barricades is to openly display symptoms of severe debilitation by the widespread, constantly reinforced and suicidal madness once known as the 'car craze.' Forget about the average driver's 'road rage' – the politicians and bureaucrats have 'mad car disease,' which is caused by sacrificing increasingly precious public space so that cars, polluting pieces of private property, can travel to and be parked absolutely anywhere."

Not surprisingly, the barricades – even on their own terms – are a complete failure. Studies done at the end of January 1998 by Transportation Alternatives, a bicyclist group opposed to automotive traffic, show that automobile traffic did not move any more freely because of the barricades; traffic conditions remained gridlocked. As a result, the barricades are hated by both pedestrians and by the police officers who are assigned to enforce the no-walking zones. Both groups have been vocal in their opposition to the barricades and surprisingly clear in expressions of their feelings that the Mayor has too big of an ego to admit that the barricades are a failure and an affront. Giuliani's response to these criticisms: he got the City Council to raise the jaywalking fine from $2 to $50, and now he wants to raise it again to $100.

The first big protest against the pedestrian barricades was orchestrated by Transportation Alternatives, and featured a group of people who had dressed up as cows to express their desire not to be treated like human cattle. An essentially silly protest – "Remooooooove the barricades!" was a typical slogan – it nevertheless received a great deal of media attention and placed the issue of pedestrians' rights squarely in the public eye. Dissatisfied that Transportation Alternatives did not follow-up on their first demonstration, Time's Up!, a group of radical bicycle riders, organized a second demonstration in mid-January. Though the protesters were numerous, placard-bearing and quite visible (they marched back and forth in one of the intersections, but not against the new rights-of-way), the demonstration was hardly covered at all by the mainstream media. Some protestors decided that bolder steps were needed.

The week before Mr. not de Bored's arrest, the entire area in which the barricades are installed was hit by a massive graffiti attack. According to news reports that covered the attack in depth the following day, every single no-walking sign had the word "GO" painted on it; arrows were drawn on the streets pointing right through the barricades; and the phrases THE BARRICADES SUCK and BAN ALL PRIVATE CARS FROM MANHATTAN were spraypainted on the sidewalks and on the walls of buildings. While NBC's report emphasized that writing graffiti is considered vandalism and criminal mischief, both The WB Channel and New York 1 (cable) left their viewers with the definite impression that the barricades do indeed suck, and big time.

Though the District Attorney's office has yet to establish whether Little Billy was a copycat or the perpetrator of the original graffiti hit as well as the second one, the zine publisher was arrested yellow-handed (for the color of spray paint he was using was yellow), by foot patrolman Hennington as he was writing "THE BARRICADES SUCK" – though he only got as far as "THE BARRICADES S" before he was nabbed – on the sidewalk.

Handcuffed and thoroughly searched, though not informed that he was under arrest or given his Miranda warning, Mr. not de Bored was taken to the 18th precinct at around 10:30 pm. He was held for several hours in a holding cell before being formally arrested, finally Mirandized, and interrogated at length by two detectives who'd watched too many episodes of *NYPD Blue*. It wasn't until 7:00 am that he was taken from the 18th Precinct to Central Booking. But – because the arresting officer had found a bottle of prescription medication in Mr. not de Bored's possession – he was refused by Central Booking, and sent to Bellevue Hospital for a psychiatric examination. Several hours later, handcuffed to a wheelchair and in the middle of a day room in the hospital, Mr. not de Bored was quickly judged to be sane, though he could have just as easily been judged a danger to himself and others, and detained for up to 72 hours for "observation," had the examining doctor been inclined or under orders to do so.

Returned to and finally accepted by Central Booking at around noon, Little Billy was held in the Tombs until his arraignment, which took place after the sun had gone down. At around 9 pm, he was finally released on his own recognizance and made his way home in the cold, without his gloves, hat or winter coat, all of which had been seized as evidence by the cops. *The New York Post* – not known for its populist stances on controversial issues – wrote up Bill's arrest under the headline MIDNIGHT MARAUDER NABBED DEFACING HATED BARRICADES. Once again, it is to the hated barricades that one's attention is drawn. They are hated; and for damn good reason. They suck.

In the weeks since LB's arrest, the barricades have remained in the news, thanks in part to activists such as Robert Lederman, who got arrested on a disorderly conduct charge at an anti-barricade protest in early February. He was wearing a sign that says it all in a nutshell: "GIULIANI=POLICE STATE."

Activist criminal defense attorney Stanley Cohen has agreed to represent LB as he tries to get these absurdly trumped-up felony charges dismissed. If you would like to help out, write NOT BORED! Donations should be made payable to "Stanley Cohen."

If you want to show moral support, Little Billy's next court date is 27 July

Local interventions
1998, at 100 Centre Street, Part F, at 9:30 AM.[3]

Published in *The Shadow* #43 (Dec 1997-June 1998) and attributed to Mildred Pierce
Reprinted in *NOT BORED!* #29, July 1998

Drifting with the NYPA

In the middle of the afternoon of Wednesday 10 June 1998, Little Billy not de Bored made his second visit to the former site of the Brooklyn Eastern District Terminal (a huge stretch of abandoned waterfront property in Williamsburg, Brooklyn), in preparation for the second meeting of the New York Psychogeographical Association (NYPA), scheduled to take place there on Saturday 13 June.

(Let it be noted that the first meeting of the NYPA, which took place in Blackout Books on 1 February 1998, was *a total disaster*. Little Billy [LB] was an hour late in coming to the meeting; and so, when he finally got there, everyone – a total of ten people – had already left. Using the list of names and e-mail addresses that these people had thoughtfully left behind, LB contacted them all, apologized for his lateness, and expressed his desire to try again some time soon – that is, to arrange a "meeting" at which the only order of business was to explore a particular place in the city. To a person, those who responded to LB's message indicated that they were more interested in exploring virtual or cyber space than real space; that is to say, they took the word "psychogeography" – which appeared in the announcement of the meeting that appeared on the Blackout Books' internet events calendar – to mean the drifting through and mapping of a computer-generated representation of "space." Shit: even an imbecile such as Simon Sadler knows that "cyberspace represent[s] a retreat into a virtual rather than a real space, and, therefore, an impoverishment of situationist aspiration"! Still, LB was disappointed that he missed the opportunity to meet these people, as both individuals and as a group, face-to-face.)

Entering from the east, through the unlocked and open gates to the property at North 10th Street and Kent Avenue, LB proceeded westerly on his bicycle, towards the water.

The circumstances of his coming to explore this particular part of Williamsburg are worth mentioning. Almost as soon as he moved to this working-class neighborhood in Brooklyn in April 1998, LB had heard about an important upcoming public hearing about the State of New York's plans to permit the construction of a huge garbage-processing plant on a large slice of abandoned

---

[3] All charges were eventually dropped.

waterfront property in Williamsburg that had originally been ear-marked for the creation of a park. There is only *one* place in the entire Greenpoint/Williamsburg area – it is the former landing point for the Grand Street Ferry (service to Houston Street in Manhattan from 1800 to 1918), just three blocks from the factory basement in which LB lives, if you *must* know – at which it is permitted to walk down to the water, that is, to the banks of the East River, and contemplate the awesome spectacle of Manhattan, laid out along the western horizon. Think of the sunsets, of the bruised light pushing its way through the heavy, polluted air! Unfortunately, this one bit of public space – ironically wedged between a sweet-smelling sugar warehouse on the south and a fugly battery of steel storage tanks on the north – is tiny. To make matters worse, Brooklyn already has more garbage dumps than any other borough in the city. Quite obviously, the answer here is *more parks, fewer dumps.* Or is it?

Little Billy and several activist friends went to the public hearing, which was attended by over a thousand loud, angry, slogan-shouting, sign-holding protesters, all of them "from around the neighborhood." It was an incredibly inspiring experience to be part of that huge, unruly crowd: there was so much energy – so much noise – in that high school auditorium! But it was also an incredibly dispiriting experience to find that – despite the overwhelming evidence of consensus on the part of the people of Williamsburg that a garbage-processing plant should not be constructed along Kent Avenue between N 7th and N13th Streets – the business of the "public" hearing went on *as if the people had not spoken with one voice.* That is to say, the representatives from USA Waste, as well as a whole slew of slimy politicians, bureaucrats, and officials – none of whom actually live in Greenpoint or Williamsburg – were allowed to speak, to "state their case," to *demonstrate their utter contempt for the people in the room.* The decision about the future of the abandoned property was deferred until later, when only USA Waste's representatives and the politicians, bureaucrats, and officials would be in attendance. It was intolerable: it seemed that the only sensible thing for the crowd to do was to get some gasoline and burn down the offices of USA Waste. But this was not likely to happen, despite the anger of the crowd; and so LB left – but not without promising himself that he and his friends would explore and utilize the abandoned property in Williamsburg as thoroughly as he and they had the abandoned grain elevator in Red Hook, Brooklyn, during the summer and fall of 1996.

On his first trip to the site, Little Billy – riding a white bicycle – had quickly but thoroughly covered the entire place. The overall atmosphere – despite the fact that the site had evidently been abandoned and left to deteriorate a long time ago (back in 1982, in fact) – was inviting, even pleasant. The place reminded LB of a meadow: it was open, flat and very green in spots. The sight of the wide and active East River – it's actually an estuary and not a river, for the current flows both ways – was both stirring and calming. And there was, of course, the totally unobstructed and truly *spectacular* view of Manhattan, the city that stands tall atop an island of

Local interventions

granite; the only city in the world in which one's eyes are always drawn upwards, ever higher, toward the blinding sun. One is never alone in New Babylon! There were fishermen at the end of the long-ruined peers that extend into the East River. Small but diverse groups of people – older Poles, young Latinos, middle-aged black women, white kids in couples, even tourists in cars – all babbling away in different languages, were wandering around, exploring the place for themselves, unafraid to nod "Hello" or say "Hi" when confronted by a fellow wanderer.

On his first trip to the site, LB's attention had been drawn, among other places, to a large single-storey building. On the inside of this huge and burned out shed, on all four of its walls, were a great many large, very colorful and very imaginative spray-painted murals. As with some of the murals LB had seen on the exterior part of a different building at the site, these murals were highly abstract and very "lettrist" in their way: they formed their complex images out of letters, not out of pictures. To turn this abandoned building into an open, public art gallery, all one would have to do is sweep the floor clean and find some way of illuminating the place at night. The art is already installed, already ready for viewing! The idea was such a good one that Little Billy, during his first visit to the site, set a tentative date for its realization: Friday, 31 July 1998. But there were concerns: in the building adjacent to the potential art gallery, there was a sign that said, "Not a hangout, for Family only," which LB took as a clear indication that a gang had already laid claim to it. The question was: Had they also laid claim to the art gallery next door as well? It would therefore be necessary for LB to scout the place out several times – and, if possible, to talk to members of the "Family" at least once – before the exhibit's "opening" on 31 July.

After going about 200 feet towards the west and the water, Little Billy stopped and sketched a map of what he had passed so far: the art gallery was on his left (south) side; some more incredible graffiti was on the exterior of one of the buildings on his right (north) side. But as soon as he was done with the sketch, he realized that it wouldn't do: to get the whole site on one piece of paper, he would have to begin again, and start on a much smaller scale than before. And so the map was discarded. Continuing along the path in the middle until the row of buildings on the left side came to an end, LB turned left. Once he had gone a few yards in this direction, he saw a group of men standing around and drinking on a kind of plateau. Since this plateau had caught his attention – and imagination! – during his first visit, LB decided to approach them and see if they were friendly.

The plateau on which the men were standing was very unusual. It was totally swept clean and there were upon it benches that someone had made, with great care, out of boards and bricks. The whole arrangement created the impression of an outdoor school. (It turns out that this area was originally designed as part of an outdoor cinema, with the movies being projected onto a huge white spot painted on a nearby building.) Evidently, the men spent a great deal of time on this spot. Their tolerance for the presence and activities of the NYPA – especially the gallery show scheduled for 31 July – would be crucial to its success.

Local interventions

After he approached and introduced himself to the group as a whole, LB found himself in conversation with a large bearish man named Charles. The two men hit it off immediately, despite huge differences between them when it came to attitudes about women, minorities, Jews and foreigners. Charles, like the other men in the group – which they called The Patrol – seemed like the type of man who might have belonged to a militia or some other right-wing group. He could have been a veteran of the illegal war in Vietnam: he said he spends a lot of his time playing the video game called *Panzer General*, in which he tries to take over the world from the side of the Nazi Germany. In any case, LB was smart enough to steer away from certain potentially explosive topics and to remain focused on his goal.

He and Charles had plenty of other things in common: a taste for conversation; pleasure taken in smoking marijuana with a new friend; questions of strategy and tactics in games like chess; and, most importantly, a hatred of work. Like LB himself, Charles and the other men out on the plateau that afternoon were not homeless; they rented apartments in nearby buildings; they did not work, and got their money from unemployment or disability benefits; they spent their time totally at their leisure. Every day, they came to this spot, hung out, looked at Manhattan, which Charles said they rarely visit, and called it "Ratland." Equipped with binoculars and a healthy sense of curiosity, they knew what was going on everywhere on the abandoned property, which they explained used to be a railroad freight depot in the 1970s. (Charles warned LB away from the building at which the "Not for hanging out; Family only" was hung: there were low-level thieves and drug dealers there, he said. All of the other buildings appeared to be squatted by poor Polish or Latino people.) On the day LB met them, they also had with them books, beer and bicycles, one of which – owned by Charles and called *The Impressionist Bike* – was painted to resemble (you got it!) an impressionist painting.

Little Billy now believed that he had sufficient information about the site, and departed.

The second meeting of the NYPA took place as scheduled, despite occasionally heavy rain, on the afternoon of Saturday 13 June 1998. In attendance were Spike, Hector Rottweiller, Jr., Laurent (a Parisian living in NYC) and Little Billy – all whom live in Brooklyn. (Little Billy is the connection between the other three people: Spike is his ex-girlfriend; Hector is someone Billy met on an internet listserv focused on the situationists; and Laurent is someone who intended to meet Billy at some point, and did so quite accidentally in Blackout Books.) Together, this group explored, talked about and photographed the entire abandoned site. They covered the ruined piers; the plateau on which the Patrol meets (though they were not there that day); the garden near the Patrol's plateau, in which someone had planted poppies; a huge concrete platform that faces Manhattan and looked like an abandoned airplane runway; a nearby wall on which incredibly complex and colorful graffiti had been created by the "Crazy Brooklyn Kids"; and the inside of

Local interventions

the building in which the "gallery exhibit" was to take place on 31 July 1998.

The group was on its way out when it encountered Eddie, a fast-talking man with a bottle of beer in one hand and a walking stick (a metal pipe) in the other. Over the course of the next hour or so, the assembled members of the NYPA learned a great deal about Eddie: that he is 35 years old, and half-Latino and half-Irish; that has only one kidney and has struggled with drug addiction; and that he is squatting a neighboring building with his girlfriend Monica (German-American), their two dogs and their two cats. Though he only talked about himself and did so uninterruptedly, Eddie was very engaging. The content of his rap was almost entirely centered on the nature and functioning of language; he was also interested in mysticism and spiritual contemplation. He played question-and-answer with Hector, much as Charles of the Patrol had played the same game with Little Billy when the two of them first met. Eddie was also an excellent tour-guide and host: he showed us where he, Monica and their pets had lived previously (a building upon which a previous resident, a rock 'n' roller, had spray-painted an exquisite and very large Egyptian-style talisman), and where they lived now. Though all four members of the NYPA were a little uncomfortable with Eddie – eventually he asked each of them for some money, which was forthcoming – they all found sufficient grounding in Monica, in their pets, or in the experience of taking photographs together to stay awhile and make friends.

Later that day, in a nearby Thai restaurant, the members of the NYPA ate, drank and discussed at great length their experiences, focusing on Eddie and what they had each made of him. It was the perfect way to end the drift.

The following Monday, Little Billy and Hector were to meet and pass on to Eddie and Monica the pictures they had taken, but the pictures weren't developed in time, and thus the meeting didn't come off as planned. It wasn't until Friday that LB, without Hector (who couldn't make it that day), bicycled to the site in an attempt to find Eddie and give him the pictures. For the first time in LB's experience, the gates to the site were locked. Alarmed, LB tried to find Eddie, but could not. After bicycling around the area for several minutes, LB finally caught sight of Eddie entering a building with which LB didn't associate him. When LB caught up with him, Eddie – uncharacteristically laconic and rushed – explained that the police had ordered him to vacate the property; he was only going inside to get identification. LB sped off to get the people and tools necessary to break the chain and open the doors to the site. Within two hours, he and his roommate John were back at the site. They had seen the thick black smoke on their way there. The building immediately next to Eddie's was completely engulfed in flames; the place was surrounded by police cars and fire trucks. LB and John tried to tell any cop or fireman who would listen that there were people and pets in there, but no one listened to them. Eddie and Monica were nowhere to be found.

NOT BORED! #29, July 1998

Local interventions

TO THE WORKING CLASS OF WILLIAMSBURG
Re: The Garbage Dump

The State of New York owns a large strip of waterfront property in Williamsburg, Brooklyn. What should be put on this property: a garbage-processing facility or a park? Well, which one does Williamsburg really need and want?

The Governor of New York, the bureaucrats in Albany and the capitalists at USA Waste all believe that the construction of a garbage-processing facility on Kent Avenue will provide jobs and stimulate the local economy. No doubt they are correct. However, though everyone agrees that creating jobs and helping the local economy are good things, opponents of the plan believe that it is shortsighted.

With the long-term in mind, they believe that what Williamsburg really needs is green space. The children of Williamsburg need parks to play and grow up in, precisely because there are already so many garbage dumps and so few parks in the area. Even the parents, many of whom need jobs far more than they need parks, see the urgent need for green space. Besides, garbage dumps are unpleasant and parks are nice . . . . So this one is, like, ya know, a no-brainer: dump the dump and put in a park!

NOT SO FAST.

Just as a garbage dump would only be good for the politicians, bureaucrats and capitalists who would make money from it, a park would only be good for the children of those people who could continue to afford to live in Williamsburg after the opening of the park. Make no mistake about it, you "green" do-gooders: if they put a park on Kent Avenue, the rents in this area will start skyrocketing (just as they are skyrocketing all over Manhattan, but especially in such traditionally working-class areas as SoHo, TriBeCa and the Lower East Side). Poor and working-class people will be forced out of their homes to make way for new buildings and parking lots. Older buildings – some, but not all of them abandoned – will be hastily demolished and new ones constructed in their places for the sole reason that their owners want to get around New York State's already weakened rent stabilization and control laws. The only people who will be able to live in "trendy" Williamsburg will be members of the middle- and upper-classes, most of which are racially "white" and in favor of using the police and the prisons to punish the poor.

Williamsburg has traditionally been an industrial area of the City, a literal dumping ground for the heavy industries and commercial operations that the bourgeoisie and its government did not want in Manhattan. And so Williamsburg has long been a place in which poor and working-class people have been able to find affordable housing, precisely because the members of the bourgeoisie have traditionally been loathe to live among "their" factories and the pollution "their" factories produce. Because immigrants are often poor, and because racism and religious intolerance are among the most effective tools by which class society maintains itself, isolated Williamsburg has also been an ethnically diverse area. There are large and vibrant communities of Poles, Hassids, Puerto Ricans, African-Americans and Dominicans living in this area. Despite being politically powerless and economically poor, Williamsburg has long been rich *socially*.

It is only been recently, since the gentrification of the working-class districts in Manhattan, that Williamsburg has become a haven for disaffected members of the bourgeoisie, for "creative" types, for musicians, painters, and photographers, for young members of the bourgeoisie who are so confident that the economy works *for them* that they, unlike the truly poor and disadvantaged, can tattoo, dye and pierce themselves to their hearts' content, but without fear of rendering themselves unemployable or of permanently consigning themselves to the ranks of the working-class – in short, for people in search of cheap rent who are willing and able to live among factories and industrial pollution. (Worry not, dear bourgeois of Williamsburg, about the health risks of this particular garbage-processing plant: you are already poisoned.)

Everybody wants cheap rent, but for some people "cheap rent" is $800 a month, while for others it is $400 a month. If you are middle-class – in plain English, if you make more than $30,000 a year – the difference between $800 and $400 is not critical: you can afford the former, but you'd rather pay the latter. But if you are a worker, a senior citizen or a person collecting government benefits (someone who makes less than $15,000 a year), the difference between $800 and $400 is make-or-break. You can just barely pay the latter, while the former is completely out of the question; if confronted with the disappearance of truly cheap rent, you will have no choice but to move somewhere else.

And so we – the members of the New York Psychogeographical Association – say BETTER POOR AND INCLUSIVE THAN RICH AND EXCLUSIVE.

MORE GARBAGE, FEWER YUPPIES!
FEWER YUPPIES, CHEAPER RENT!

Posters in English, Spanish, Polish, French and German, 25-27 July 1998
NOT BORED! #30, February 1999

Local interventions

Yuppies Can't Go Home

"At home he feels like a tourist." – Gang of Four

Graffiti has appeared around Bedford Avenue that proclaims YUPPIE GO HOME. While we sympathize with what we assume to be the author's (or authors') motivations for spray-painting this phrase in several locations in our rapidly gentrifying neighborhood, we must say that we don't believe that yuppies can be told to "go home" – not because it is rude to do so, nor because they are already at home in Williamsburg – but because Young, Upwardly-mobile Professionals have no home to go back to, no matter where they sleep and store their stuff. To be a yuppie is to be at home nowhere and to be a tourist everywhere.

Yuppies aspire to be members of the elite, to be among those super-privileged few who have real wealth and who hold real power, to rise to the top, to make it their home. But the top has become just as uninhabitable as the bottom. Everyone knows that it is impossible to continue to pretend that capitalist industrialization – or digitization, its contemporary equivalent – will slowly elevate everyone to the level of the elite. Industrialization has so thoroughly ravaged and poisoned the entire planet that everyone – even the elite – has been lowered to the level of common women and men. But this is not to say that common women and men have it pretty good these days, though most everyone seems to think so. We are all in the shit, and really fucking deep.

Everything that a real elite would love – well-educated and stimulating conversation; good wine and food; beautiful, well-preserved old buildings, extensive libraries, and great works of art and literature – all this is in fact fast disappearing everywhere and being replaced by inferior copies. Having $40 to spend on a single Cuban cigar is just not the same thing as having the power to prevent acid rain from irreparably damaging the soil in Cuba's tobacco fields. No one is immune to the effects of toxic pollutants in the air, water and soil. Though the members of the elite will have the money to treat their cancers, while everyone else will not, we will all die of cancer, unless global capitalism is overthrown and replaced with a superior form of social organization.

No one denies that the once-remote suburbs now closely resemble the gritty cities more and more, or that the countryside is deteriorating everywhere. The wilderness? Where is that, exactly? Montana?! There is nowhere on Earth the members of the elite can go and enjoy their privileges in peace, quiet and good health. The entire planet is a becoming nightmare, not only for poor shits and sinners like you and me, but also for dear "saints" such as Lady Di, the Dead Princess of Wales.

Wherever you go, there is either incredible poverty, famine, and disease, or cell phones that irradiate the brain with deadly microwaves, "second homes" shabbily constructed by corrupt builders, automobiles stuck in traffic and spewing poisonous gases, and supermarkets well-stocked with frozen meats that need to be recalled and burned.

No one denies there is something ridiculous about all politicians, but especially those at the top. What child grows up wanting to be President some day? Though everyone wants to be as rich and powerful as Bill Gates, no one denies that the man is a social idiot, bereft of any culture whatsoever, not to mention a culture that a member of the real ruling class would deserve to have and enjoy.

And so – YUPPIE GO HOME? No, impossible. YUPPIE OUT OF WILLIAMSBURG, maybe. REVOLUTION OR DEATH, even better – that is, of course, if you really have tospraypaint a slogan about gentrification on buildings in the neighborhood.

Poster dated 2 September 1998
Published in *The Williamsburg Observer* #2, 1998
Reprinted in *NOT BORED!* #30, February 1999

Miscellaneous texts related to the "Yuppie" affair

"The Scene" by Jason Grote, *Waterfront Week,* Volume 8.19, Oct. 8-21, 1998

> A funny aside: I met the guy who's been plastering the "YUPPIE GO HOME" stencils everywhere. I'm not going to give his name because a) the ethics of the situation are kind of sketchy, and b) I can't remember it. You'll all be relieved to know, however, that it's the work of a single wing-nut rather than some kind of organized movement. I met the guy at Blackout Books, the anarchist bookstore on Avenue B, just south of Tompkins Square. He's a middle-aged guy and he's wearing a T-shirt with a picture of Lenin on it. He seemed proud of his handiwork. To give you an example of his thinking, he described this publication as "corporate." "Corporate?" I replied, "The whole operation's run by these two women who live on the Southside. I mean, it's more of a traditional community paper. It's geared toward people who have lived in the neighborhood for a while." "That's what I mean," he said. So if he thinks the old Slavic ladies who read *Waterfront Week* are yuppies, God know [sic] who he considers yuppies. Is it just me, or are guys like him: white, hyperpolitical, obsessed with a "fringe-dweller" pose, even more obnoxious than yuppies? I mean, okay, gentrification sucks, but this whole "politics of self-expression" crap failed in the L.E.S. and it's doomed to fail here.

Local interventions

While guys with persecution complexes jump up and down and point fingers at any neighbor with a regular adult job, politicians and real-estate developers write off whole communities and snap up all our land. It's like treating a car-crash victim for a vitamin deficiency (say, you're hurt pretty bad, mister – have some Wheaties!). Whew! Yes, I feel much better, thanks [...]

"Yuppie Go Home?" by Kevin Kosar (cover story)
The Williamsburg Observer **October 15 1998**

It was all of six weeks or so ago when the spray-painted words, "Yuppie Go Home" began appearing all over the Northside. I recall asking myself, "What the hell is that all about?" Over the next week I made it a point to ask folks in the bars and shops I frequent whether they knew what this was all about. The answer I got was uniform: Williamsburg, and especially the Northside, is changing. It used to be a real dump and now there are a lot of people who can't afford to live in the Village coming over here looking for places to live. Sounds right to me.

Well, shortly after the graffiti appeared, manifestoes written by the New York Psychogepgraphical Association were slapped up everywhere on the Northside – on business windows, on mailboxes, phone polls – EVERYWHERE. Upon reading these one gets the feeling that Armageddon cometh, that it's time to board up the windows, arm yourself to the teeth, and get ready to do battle with the fiends who are infiltrating our idyllic town. The invaders' aim is nothing short of evil: to eradicate the low-income residents, to drive out *les miserables*, to create an all-white and wealthy Aryan kingdom.

Who then, are these devils? Why they're yuppies! The young urban professionals! And why are they aiming to do this? Well, quite simply, says the New York Psychogeographical Association, because they are mean, elitist, racist people. I won't bother to take up the very debatable assertion that yuppies are by definition racists and elitists. Instead, I'll let that one lie and ask a more fundamental question: is Williamsburg being overrun by yuppies?

To answer this, why not take a moment to get a grip on what we mean by the term "yuppie." As I understand it, a yuppie is a nouveau riche or soon to be wealthy young, white person who possesses a college education which has enabled him or her to obtain a high-paying, white collar position, often in the financial services. The direct descendants of George Babbit (Babbitt: a type of conventional

Local interventions

American businessman, ambitious in his business, but otherwise provincial, mediocre, and smug, named after the title character in Sinclair Lewis' 1922 novel, *Babbit*), they are nervous around non-whites, they have crude tastes, and they enjoy spending money on trendy consumer goods. The picture that comes to mind is of a guy named Skip and a gal named Peaches, wearing matching college sweatshirts, wearing Gucci shoes, gabbing loudly on cell phones to friends named Chet and Allie, and driving about in their $30,000 sports utility vehicle.

The taxonomy delineated, now let us ask ourselves a basic question: do we see these people in Williamsburg? If so, are there lots of them? In my experience, and from the experience of those who I've chatted with, nobody knows anyone of this description who lives in Williamsburg. Moreover, only on the rarest occasion has anyone spotted a yuppie. Indeed, I myself have even gone looking for yuppies in the place you would think they would most likely frequent: the streets and subways during weekday rush hours. My findings: NO YUPPIES. There are lots of people of different ages and races who appear to be schlepping off to Manhattan for low-paying jobs, nose-ring-sporting artists, and immigrants of all stripes – but NOBODY wearing suits, or even ties, and certainly nobody carrying briefcases or screaming into cell phones, "sell, sell, sell!"

In short, what we have here is non-existent yuppies being called the moral equivalents of Hitler and being told to go home or just go away from Williamsburg (NIMBY?) Most strange. As for the talk of the evils the yuppies are wreaking, well, it's hard to see how their dastardly plots can be hatched if they aren't here.

Now, in light of this empirical fact, one wonders, "Why are non-existent yuppies being blamed for problems they haven't caused, or perhaps, problems that don't exist?" Perhaps it's a case of what Nietzsche called ressentiment, the habit of those who feel helpless about their situation to cook up phantasms to explain them and to strike moral poses against them (See *Beyond Good & Evil* and *The Antichrist*). Who knows.

I can hear the voices already clamoring, "But it is a fact that rents are rising!" Yes, yes indeed, it is a brute fact that rents are going up dramatically. However, this is not BECAUSE of yuppies. It is quite simply a matter of increased demand for apartments being recognized by Williamsburg's landlords. More clearly, there are lots of folks like me (young, making over $15,000 a year – barely) who want to live in Williamsburg. Neither I nor they are yuppies, far from it. However, by virtue of our demand and landlord recognizing that we are willing and able to pay $700 or $900 for places they used to rent for $300, rents rise. Indeed, if there is anyone to demonize, it is the landlords who have decided that because they CAN charge higher rents, they SHALL.

That said, one can only hope that all the "yuppie go home" hubbub and the desecration of private and public property by the self-appointed defenders of the neighborhood will end. Their hearts are in the right place, but they've misconstrued the shift in the market for apartments as a hostile invasion. And from what I hear from chats with my neighbors, it's not much appreciated by Williamsburg denizens, old and new.

Letter to the Editor
The Williamsburg Observer, **October 15, 1998**

As an urban professional, who happens to be young, I resent the bias against me exhibited in the streets of Williamsburg (ie the "yuppies go home" graffiti) and especially in the pages of your paper. Could somebody tell me just what is wrong with being a successful young professional? Ever since the mid-1980s, when the term "yuppie" was first coined, people like myself have lived under a cloud of suspicion and hostility, as though we were lepers or infected with some kind of horrible infectious disease. It's just not fair, and it's time we spoke up for our rights.

Let's face it: what all this anti-yuppie sentiment boils down to is envy. It's as if having a well-paying job, and being able to afford the better things in life – good clothing, expensive wines, fine food, exotic vacations – it's as if this were a moral offense, like pedophilia or cannibalism. But let's face it, this is America and anyone who wants to earn a good living can; people should stop whining about their lots in life and do something about it. Nobody is stopping you from making $75,000-$100,000 a year but yourself. Go out and get a good job, for Christ's sake; sitting home, slacking off, and moaning about it does nothing for your self-esteem.

A poisonous atmosphere has been created by certain elements in this society who want to condemn all those who are successful, and I am beginning to think that graffiti like "yuppies go home" should qualify as a hate crime, just like the Nazi insignia painted on a synagogue, or "go back to Africa" painted on a Negro home. Why can't we all live together in harmony? Why does my money make me different? I am still human and deserving of respect. Young urban professionals are people, too, dammit.

This hateful and divisive anti-yuppie rhetoric must stop, or we shall soon find ourselves, as a society, engaged in the kind of class-warfare that Karl Marx predicted, where the working-class sees no common interest with the middle and upper classes. Yes, as an undergrad I thought that Marx was kind of cool; but when you look at Russia now you can see that capitalism rules. Everybody in the world wants to be a capitalist, and who can blame them? It's the only game there is.

Grow up, *Williamsburg Observer*, and take a bite of reality.

Sincerely,
Anonymous

"Multi-Kulti Willhelsmburg," by Eric Redlinger
The Williamsburg Observer, October 15, 1998

When WBO [*Williamsburg Observer*] contributor Bill-Not-Bored plastered his original pseudo-philosophical discourse on the essentially homeless ontology of "yuppiedom," YUPPIES CAN'T GO HOME (see *WBO* issue #2), on myriad flat surfaces of Williamsburg, he cannot possibly have anticipated the overwhelming multi-cultural response his oeuvre would subsequently provoke. In fact, the development has been as amusing as it has been revealing:

First, there was the expected version in Spanish presumably posted at the same time as the English original or shortly thereafter. Since the Latino community of Williamsburg represents the largest single ethnic group to be directly effected by the current gentrifying push this was a logical extension. Hot on the heels of the Spanish edition, however, was the Polish version, posted with similar tenacity to the copious boarded-up storefronts and construction fences which pepper the Bedford northside. Some areas sported all three versions side by side, along with accompanying commentaries added by numerous sidewalk critics.

Last week, while schlepping my bike up the miles of recently added stairs on the Williamsburg Bridge, I was surprised to see two further additions to this increasingly multinational debate: translations in both French ("*Yuppies ne peuvent pas renrer chez eux*") and German ("*Yuppies koennen nicht nach Hause gehen*")! Now, let's stop to consider this for a moment: translation is a time-consuming and onerous task. Yet someone felt the need to invest his/her valuable time in the clarifying service of a message that was itself a work of satire for the sole consumption of hitherto unknown cultural niches.

Moral: next time you write your Brooklyn address on a mailing list or post card consider including alternatives such as "Chateau Guillaume" or "Willhelmsburg." You never know who you might be in/excluding....

Addendum: rumor whispers of a Yiddish version of YUPPIES CAN'T GO HOME which the editorial staff has as of yet been unable to track down. Anyone who had the foresight to grab one of these and is willing to mail it to us will earn our sincere thanks. -ed.

Letter To the Editor
Waterfront Week, Oct 22 - Nov 4 (Volume 8.20)

In past issues of *Waterfront Week,* texts have been printed about the New York Psychogeographical Association's interventions in Williamsburg, Brooklyn. In the September 10 - September 23 issue, a letter to the editor from Annette La Matto, a local businesswoman, remarked upon the "dangerous current" that "is flowing through Williamsburg – 'yuppie go home' graffiti, lamppost fliers, and the like." In the October 8 - October 21 issue, columnist Jason Grote proclaims that he "met the guy who's been plastering the 'YUPPIE GO HOME' stencils everywhere." It is possible that the September 24 - October 7 issue also contains something on the subject: we don't know, because we missed that issue.

Our questions are simple: back in late July 1998, why didn't *Waterfront Week* print – or even acknowledge receipt of both printed and e-mailed copies of – our address "To the working class of Williamsburg"? Since it is clear you believe that your readers are interested in what's happening in Williamsburg, are you now prepared to publish our original address – or our subsequent one, "Yuppies Can't Go Home" – in your publication?

The New York Psychogeographical Association

The following text, attributed to "Editor," was printed below our letter to the editor.

Where, oh where to begin: first of all, Annette La Matto is not a local "businesswoman" – she is a community activist and Executive Director of a local non-profit organization.

I have carefully read both circulars and believe that their sole purpose is to pit part of the community (working class men and women) against another part of the community ("Yuppies"). While the Association has the right to publish its views, I reserve the right not to print messages that I believe are discriminatory. Instead of

Local interventions

trying to divide the community into "us" and "them," the Association would be more effective if it attempted to find some real solutions to the myriad problems which plague this community.

"The Scene" by Jason Grote
Waterfront Week, **Volume 8.21, November 5, 1998**

It's been a mad, busy couple of weeks for your intrepid reporter, what with 'Get Out of Hell Day' on S6th Street, another 'Poetry-A-Go-Go' at the Charleston, the WAH Center Symposium, 'The Utopians' at Galapagos and the hilarious sequel to the Reclaim the Streets party, the 'Lower East Side Tea Party'. Whew! I'm starting to think my fingerprints are on, like, everything. If I didn't have a hand in it, you can bet I know someone who did.

Speaking of which, I noticed that I was mentioned in a letter to the editor from the New York Psychogeographical Association last issue. I'd actually like to issue a mea culpa for coming down so hard on Bill Not Bored (I've decided it's okay to release his nom du whatever) for his 'YUPPIE GO HOME' graffiti. My opinion of his work hasn't changed, but I've run into him a few more times and he's actually a pretty good guy. Besides, it's just some stupid graffiti. There's no point in jumping up and down about it. Look at it this way: when I see racist or homophobic scrawlings in men's rooms I don't see it as a sign of an impending Nazi takeover – I see it as the work of a drunken moron. Oh, and if I may offer the NYPA my humble opinion as to why the editor of this magazine won't print your manifesto: you're nuts!

This prompted the following letter to the editor from us.

In a published letter to the editor, we protested that this magazine continues to print texts about us, and yet – in an attempt to be politically correct – refuses to print texts by us. Because this pattern has been again repeated in the November 5 issue, we must protest again, but this time about a serious and glaring factual error.

In Jason Grote's self-serving comments about one of our members (Grote has in fact written about the New York Psychogeographical Association twice, both times with a cavalier disregard for basic facts), he writes: "I'd actually like to issue a mea culpa for coming down so hard on Bill Not Bored (I've decided it's okay to release his nom du whatever) for his 'YUPPIE GO HOME' graffiti. My opinion of his work hasn't changed, but I've run into him a few more times and he's actually a pretty good guy."

Local interventions

For the record: to Bill's knowledge, he has only met Grote once. That experience was so completely disagreeable – for on that occasion Grote *pretended* to be sympathetic to the graffiti, and deceitfully used this pretense to gain information that would not otherwise have been forthcoming – that Bill promised never to speak to Grote again. If he has "run into Bill a few more times," Grote has done so without Bill's knowledge. Has Grote again used deceitful means to garner information for publication in this magazine?

If so, this warning must be given. If this columnist – who arrogantly thinks that he knows exactly who is writing the graffiti, but in fact does not – is allowed to speculate in print about Bill Not Bored's real name, a defamation of character lawsuit wouldn't be out of the question.

The New York Psychogeographical Association

To the Editor,
***The Williamsburg Observer*, 15 December, 1998**

In the *Williamsburg Observer* of October 15th there was a letter to the editor by an anonymous yuppie who "fights back" against what he/she must feel as personal aggression: the "Yuppie Go Home" spray-painted on the walls of the Northside. This letter cannot go unanswered.

You want to be respected as a human being which is a legitimate and noble right. To be a human being, however, is to be conscious of the human reality you create through the values you choose to incarnate and the full responsibility you take for your actions. You should not assume that the content and form of a human being always move as one.

There is nothing wrong with money in itself. But it has been proven that finance as the ultimate aim and only means to get "the best things in life" comes with its always predictable consequences of blindness, coldness, enslavement, and destruction. If "the best things in life" are for you gourmet food and Honolulu sunburns, I guess you've forgotten what money can't buy.

You imagine that "Yuppie Go Home" is written by some jealous Losers. When thinking about what will bring your life toward its fullness, can't you conceive of choices not based on some sort of consumerism, choices not entirely dependent on the appropriation of some material goods? Can't you conceive of choices based on the freedom to refuse to give your working time to a company that invests in ways that overlook human health or dignity?

Local interventions

Furthermore, you dare to compare yourself to the Jews persecuted during WWII and killed in concentration camps, and to the "Negroes" that I am sure your ancestors exploited on the plantations. You dare ask that the author of "Yuppie Go Home" be punished for crimes against humanity as a handful of Nazis have been.

To compare the scope of these atrocities to the petty discomfort you feel from these three words points one more time to the emptiness of your mind and feelings. Indeed, turning ideas and values around to your advantage is a well-known strategy of your kind.

To become a Master of Confusion – is that what it means to be a yuppie?

[Signed]
Sylie Menta

Letter To the Editor,
The Brooklyn Bridge, **March 1999**

The journal [*The Brooklyn Bridge*] erred in portraying the situation in Williamsburg as a matter of yuppie wars ("There Goes the Neighborhood," January 1999). There are no wealthy white folks over-running the area in Pathfinders. I dare anyone to spend time in the bars, streets and subway stations of the area and find a yuppie. Rents are rising because landlords have recognized the increased demand for housing. Had your reporters chatted with more newcomers, they would have found that people here aren't "young professionals from Wall Street and the computer industry," but folks who simply cannot afford Manhattan because they make $25,000 a year. Instead you chose to frame the situation in terms that there are these evil yuppies invading this helpless neighborhood, maliciously displacing the obviously superior artists and ethnics. Please! Go back to Economics 101 and you'll see that if the demand for a product increases, product suppliers usually raise the price. The debate over what to do about this problem transcends puerile acts like painting stencils on property and moves toward consideration of rational, sensible solutions, like limiting landlords' rights to raise rents.

[signed]
Kevin R. Kosar, via e-mail

Local interventions

The Very First North American Screening of All Six Films Made by Guy Debord

It was an almost-complete disaster. Only 10 people came to a place that could accommodate 70 people; and they came, not all at once, but dispersed over a nine-hour-long period (5 pm to 2 am). We, the sponsors of the event, got soaked: we expended more than $500, and recouped only $100. Quite a *potlatch,* eh?

Consider, if you will, the following: 1) the name "Guy Debord" is pretty well-known, especially (only?) in New York City, which is the home of such situ-sympathetic publications/publishing houses as *October,* Verso, and Autonomedia; 2) three of the six films being screened had *never* been screened outside of France, where they had only been screened a few times, and the remaining three films had only circulated as bootlegged videotapes; 3) the event was held on 42d Street in Manhattan (very easy to get to); 4) it was listed in *Time Out New York,* which is the best and perhaps the most-often-used weekly guide to events in New York City, though the preview itself was idiotic and error-ridden:

> The midtown theater [Chashama] presents all six films directed by France's radical leader of the Situationists, prophets of the global impact of advertising and the commodification of everyday life. Starting Sun 5pm with 1952's *Howlings in Favor of de Sade* (which no doubt involves howls, Sade and some kind of narration), and extending through the rest of the evening with Debord's definitive *The Society of the Spectacle* (1973) and four other works, it's an event for those who like to wear their thinking caps. Also bring your command of the French language; none of these prints have English subtitles. Chashama will be providing translated synopses to help you get, erm, situated. (*Time Out New York,* 2-6 March 2006, p. 102).

5) the screening was announced two months in advance; 6) the press release was sent, as either an email or a snail-mail or both, to *The Village Voice,* to "radical" professors at NYU, the Graduate Center at CCNY, Columbia University and Princeton University, and to a variety of "independent" on-line news sources; and – last but not least – 7) the press release somehow came to the attention of "Alice Debord" (also known as Alice Becker-Ho, Guy's widow, heiress and executrix) or, rather, we received an email from the Intertalent Agency that *claimed* that Alice Debord had learned of the event and, presumably on her behalf, wanted to know who, if anyone, had granted us the rights to exhibit Guy Debord's films (or, rather, Gaumont's three-disk DVD set, released in France November 2005).

All of this boded well, *very* well, it seemed, for the Guy Debord Film Retrospective at Chashama, 217 East 42d Street, on Sunday 5 March 2006, the 22d anniversary of the assassination of Gerard Lebovici.

But what happened with Intertalent, you ask? We responded quite simply that we had not secured any rights from anyone, which triggered the following email on 6 February 2006 from a Julien Messenmackers:

> "You make money with Guy DEBORD's work but please don't call you situationist or something like this, better small traders. Poor guys of you ... So long disneyland's sad clowns!"

Yeah, whatever, buddy: you've realized that you don't have the authority to order a cease-and-desist letter or that doing so wouldn't be worth the time and trouble. And so we are free to do what we want with the DVDs we bought. *By the way*: when you want to insult an American, but especially a New Yorker, you *must* use one of the following words or phrases: asshole, bitch, doody-head or short-dicked motherfucker.

We dreamed of 400 people coming to the screening, prepared for 100, would have settled for 70, never expected less than 30. That day, we attempted to create an atmosphere: romantic scented candles; good music (Argentinean tangos, lettrist sound-poetry, Miles, Erik Satie, African Juju and PiL); fresh water, lemons, good wine (red and white, both Australian) and liquor (tequila and scotch whiskey); and programs, translations, and other relevant texts. Kava was at the door; Bill cued and played the DVDs; Lisa came to volunteer, but wasn't really needed. Like the others, she saw a couple of the films, enjoyed the absurdity of the event itself, and left after a while.

There was, of course, a *blogger* in attendance: one Andrew Potter. His commentary for 7 March 2006 was typical of bloggers (the "meme" is me me me), but caught something worth reporting, nevertheless:

> New York is the most populous city in the United States. The Debord screening was advertised in *Time Out*. I don't even want to think about what it says about me that I was one of five people in the city who thought this worth attending.

Something is exhausted: either it's the New York pro-situationist milieu; or the interest among the movie-going public (mainstream and/or underground) in the *very* obscure films of Guy Debord and/or French avant-garde films in general; or it's NOT BORED!'s reputation for putting on a good show. Could it *really* be that people who would "normally" have come to such an event were distracted/diverted by the Academy Awards, that is to say, by its host, cute little Jon Stewart, who was on TeeVee that very night?

NOT BORED! #38, October 2006

Local interventions

A New Leaf

In issue #24 of *Green Anarchy* (Spring/Summer 2007, p. 9), there's a short text called "A New Leaf" and attributed to John Zerzan. In it, one is offered a reassuringly simple opposition between what's bad ("what the dominant culture is trying to sell us," "an ever more insistently estranging, oppressive reality") and what's good ("visions that take on mass society and domesticated non-life," "something different, challenging the very nature of what we're stuck in and offering liberatory perspectives on all that should no longer be taken for granted").

I must say that I was quite amused to see – listed among the various dire and depressing indications that "the Left has no answers to what is overtaking us, inspires pretty much no one" and that "we are going through a transition period in which something is dying out" – an event that I organized. Zerzan refers to it as "a curious non-event last spring in New York" and says that the indications just mentioned "very possibly" explain it. The event was a screening of Guy Debord's six films, which a few months previously had been released on DVD. It was held on 5 March 2006, that is to say, the 22d anniversary of the assassination of Gerard Lebovici, who had been Debord's publisher, film producer and friend. To quote Zerzan again, "hundreds were expected" and yet "to this much-publicized occasion five people showed up."

Yes, it was a disaster: I lost hundreds of dollars. But Zerzan is quite wrong about what went wrong on that night, which also happened to be the night of the live telecast of the Academy Awards, hosted by Jon Stewart.

I bring this up – not because I want to argue the obvious (Guy Debord was certainly not a "Leftist," nor a part of "the dominant culture") – but because it neatly highlights a real problem with Zerzan's entire paradigm: what does one do with the millions and millions of people who simply do not care that "ecocide plunges forward throughout the world" or that "the other side of the coin of the enveloping crisis, the social and personal, seems to be equally threatening"? That is to say, what does one do with all those people who do not respond to Zerzan's brand of moralism (this is good, that is bad, people should do this, people should not do that)?

These questions do not concern the quantity of publicity that is given to Zerzan's moral condemnations of "civilization." The publication of more issues of *Green Anarchy* or more books like Steve Jones' *Against Technology*, Victor Li's *The Neo-Primitivist Turn* and Kirkpatrick Sales' *After Eden* – all mentioned and praised by Zerzan in this short text – are not likely to affect the people who prefer tee-vee to films and the Academy Awards to *The Society of the Spectacle*. Nor will they be affected by the intensification of the moralizing extremism (or the extreme moralizing) of the green anarchist movement. These people are obviously making the conscious decision not to listen to this movement (and others like it) or they are so deeply conditioned by this society that they cannot hear what this movement is saying. Either way, yelling at them louder and/or using more violent rhetoric ("we are not only against capitalism, we are against civilization") is not going to work. What will work? *This* is where the "new leaf" must be turned over.

NOT BORED! #40, May 2008

Second to last page, *NOT BORED!* #4, July 1984.

Flyer for *NOT BORED!* #9, January 1986.

Cover, *NOT BORED!* #12, May 1987.

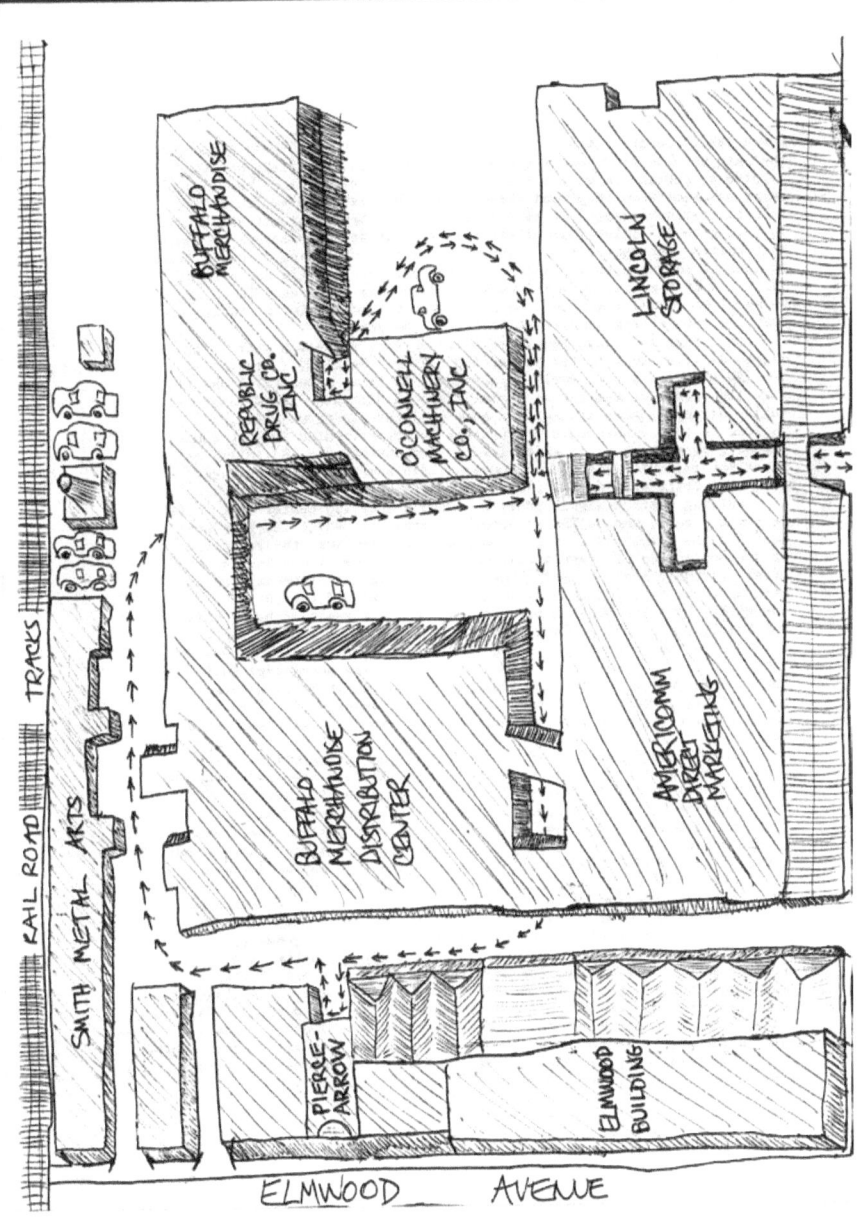

Drawing of Pierce-Arrow Complex, Buffalo, NY.
NOT BORED! #16, December 1989.

Newspaper photo, Anti-European Union Rally, Copenhagen
(circle added)
NOT BORED! #22, August 1993.

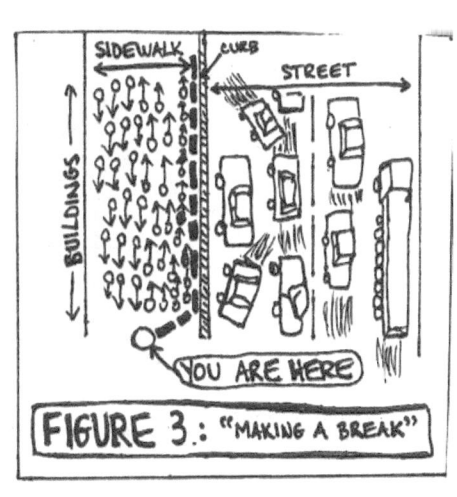

Urban games
NOT BORED! #25, September 1995.

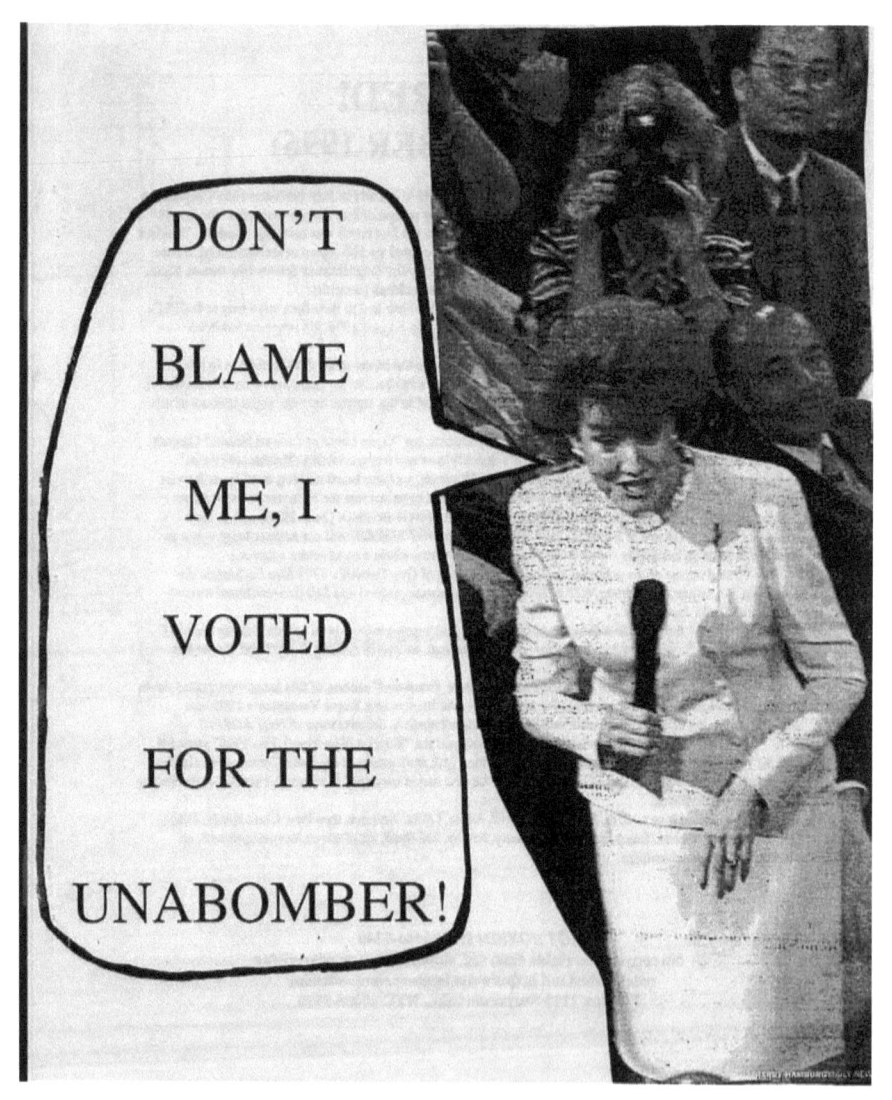

Cover, *NOT BORED!* #26, November 1996.

Defaced Lufthansa advertisement
NOT BORED! #26, November 1996.

Defaced Forbes advertisement
NOT BORED! #26, November 1996.

Flyer distributed in front of main Nike store, New York City
Back cover, *NOT BORED!* #27, May 1997.

Pathfinder Bookstore
59 4th Ave.
Brooklyn NY 11215

November 7 1996

To Whom It May Concern,

It has come to our attention that some time before Election day -- no doubt in a desperate, last ditch, 11th-hour effort to bolster the flagging appeal of the "socialist" presidential candidates to whom you pledged your support -- you spray-painted the phrase UNABOMBER FOR PRESIDENT '96 on the metal shield that protects your store when it is closed. While we are flattered by your recognition that the Unabomber's texts and actions have received far more serious attention in the press and amongst the general public than any texts or actions attributed to the candidates to whom you have pledged your support, we are very concerned that the Unabomber's reputation will be sullied by association with Trotskyism or any other "revolutionary" ideology. *And so we demand that you remove this graffiti immediately.*
Thank you for understanding.

Sincerely yours,
UNAPACK (The Unabomber for President Political Action Committee)

NOT BORED! #27, May 1997.

Flyer for event
NOT BORED! #27, May 1997.

if modernization appears to you, as it does to us, to be historically necessary,

we should counsel you to carry your enthusiasm into areas more urgently in need of it,

that is to say, to your political and moral institutions.

Text from Henri Lefebvre
NOT BORED! #28, December 1997.

Original image by Seth Tobocman
NOT BORED! #28, December 1997.

Midnight marauder nabbed defacing hated barricades

By FRANKIE EDOZIEN and DAREH GREGORIAN

A disgruntled pedestrian was busted in Midtown last night for defacing signs for the city's new much-maligned pedestrian barricades with neon-yellow paint, police said.

William Brown, 38, was caught yellow-handed by a beat cop on patrol at 50th Street and Madison Avenue, who witnessed him spray painting "the barricades suck" on one side of the no-crossing sign and "go" on the other, officials said.

Brown allegedly scrawled the same message on the sidewalk, and cops believe he did the same thing to another sign on 50th and 5th.

Officer Matthew Harrington arrested him, yellow paint in hand, and took him to the W. 54th Street station house, police said. Charges were pending.

Cops are investigating whether Brown, of W. 127th Street, is responsible for other similar graffitti that has plagued the signs since the barricades went up unexpectedly on Dec. 23, much to the chagrin of Christmas shoppers.

Despite pedestrians' outrage over the metal barriers, which were installed along congested 49th and 50th Streets between Lexington and Sixth Avenues as an experiment, Mayor Giuliani and Police Commissioner Howard Safir have said they're here to stay.

Extra cops have been assigned to patrol the barriers, but the recent graffitti attacks have all happened at night, most after midnight, when pedestrians are legally allowed to ignore the signs.

New York Post, January 26, 1998
NOT BORED! #29, July 1998.

Exhibit of photographs
of the murals and "Fort Chico Mendez,"
destroyed by real estate developer
Donald Cappocia

OPENING RECEPTION: 7 pm, Friday 30 January 1998.
BLACKOUT BOOKS: 50 Avenue B, bet 3rd and 4th Streets.

Flyer for exhibition of photos by Bill Not Bored, NYC
NOT BORED! #29, July 1998.

Collaboration with Susan J Hull
Back cover, *NOT BORED!* #30, February 1999.

Capital Project BED-767
Brooklyn, NY

Department of Design & Construction

June 2001

Deconstruction Newsletter
SACKETT STREET AREA PROJECT

Project Description

As you know, the New York City Department of Design & Construction has contracted Tully Construction to build sewer and water mains in the Sackett area. What you may not know is the fact that *this multi-million dollar project is not being undertaken to provide better service to existing residents, but to provide water for new residents, who will be moving into this neighborhood after luxury housing units have been constructed on the empty lots on Sackett Street near Fourth Avenue.*

In the meantime, current residents and small businesses will be forced to spend almost two years dealing with heavy machinery, gangs of construction workers, constant noise, piles of dust and debris, exhaust fumes, torn-up and nearly impassable streets and sidewalks, water-service interruptions, altered bus routes, problems with garbage collection, no wheelchair access, no parking, etc etc. *If current residents and/or businesses find these conditions intolerable, they can do themselves a favor and move out now, before rising rents and property values eventually price them out.*

Construction Status

Sackett Street: Everything's back to normal now. Don't worry about the rats. They'll go away if you leave them alone.

5th Avenue: Garbage collection has been suspended indefinitely. Residents should try to dump their garbage somewhere where the rats won't get it.

Union Street: Some of the power lines that Tully "re-located" for Con Edison are hanging from poles and laid out along sidewalks. Though they aren't labeled with warning signs, these power lines are active. It's your responsibility to stay away from them! Otherwise, you might get electrocuted.

A Message from the NYPD

What with all the construction and the re-routing of the bus lines that used to run on Fifth Avenue and Union Street, traffic conditions in the neighborhood have gotten pretty bad, haven't they? Especially for pedestrians, bicyclists, people confined to wheel-chairs, stuff like that. Must be tough.

Now, even though there are several traffic cops regularly assigned to the neighborhood, *puh-leeze!* don't ask any of them to do anything about the many dangerous driving conditions and traffic violations that are taking place right in front of their eyes. These officers are *not* there to serve and protect the public. Thank you!

Key Project Personnel

Tully Construction has sure come a long way since the 1990s, when the City of New York repeatedly found it to be a "non-responsible bidder" on city construction contracts because of Tully's stunning record of environmental violations, tax problems and alleged ties to organized crime. But thanks to an agreement signed in 1996 -- right around the time that Mayor Ghouliani established the DDC -- Tully adopted a Code of Business Ethics, agreed to be monitored by an independent "Private Sector Inspector General," and won $86 million in contracts with the City of New York. Ever since then, business has been great!

Hours of Operation

Though the permit restricts Tully's work to the hours between 7 AM and 6 PM, the company will consistently start work at 6 AM, so that the construction workers can go home at exactly 3 PM. This allows Tully to avoid potentially nasty problems with the labor union.

Lies, Lies, Lies!

If you lodge a complaint about any aspect of this project with the self-avowed "community construction liaison" (one Paul Kidder at 739 Union Street and 718 857-8674), you'll quickly discover that *no one* is looking out for the real interests of the community. The City has structured things so that it isn't involved, and Tully is only interested in money. You are on your own, people.

Others to contact if you like *big heaping piles of bullshit* are the members of Community Board #6 (643-3027), the DDC's Sybil Dobson (391-2347), the NYC Department of Buildings (212-312-8000) and the Mayor's Troubled Orifice, of course (212-788-9600).

Rudolph W Ghouliani, Mayor   Kenneth Holden, BureaucrRAT

Collaboration with Susan J Hull
NOT BORED! #33, September 2001.

Cover, *NOT BORED!* #40, November 2008.

Bill Brown

Reception: Thursday, November 20, 6-8 PM

The rallying cry of NOT BORED! was first heard in 1983, when Bill Brown, a newspaper writer and amateur punk musician, then living in Ann Arbor, MI, started a handmade, cut-and-paste, photocopied "zine". Reproduced in small quantities (200 copies per issue), NOT BORED! hasn't been distributed or sold in bookstores (it is given away to friends, advertised by word of mouth, and sold through the mail). Over the years, Brown's zine became devoted to documenting, translating and expanding upon the creations of the Situationist International, an art and politics group, active in Europe between 1957 and 1972, which had a profound and largely secret influence upon the Sex Pistols, Gang of Four, Stone Temple Pilots, and other punks.

Images courtesy the artist

Gallery Exhibition, University of Cincinnati, 2008.

Program for performances at the opening
Gallery Exhibition, University of Cincinnati, 2008.

Part II:

Internecine polemics

Internecine polemics
Situating the Pro-Situs

In his "Translator's Notes" to the *Situationist International Anthology,* Ken Knabb writes: "pro-situ: pejorative term referring to followers (passive or active) of the SI." In the words of the SI itself, a pro-situ is one who lacks "cohabitation with their own practice" (Debord, "Remarks on the SI Today") and who has not applied his or her own theory "in the very activity of the formulation of that theory or in the general conditions of its struggle" (Debord, "Untitled Text"). Elsewhere (in his "Remarks on Contradiction and Its Failure"), Knabb writes: "There is hardly a thesis in the Debord-Sanguinetti portrait of the pro-situ where I do not recognize myself – in the past and far too much right now!" I think this is an extraordinarily honest remark. *Anybody* who reads the texts the situationists left behind and is inspired to attempt something similar – and this (of course) includes myself – starts out as a pro-situ. The serious attempt to "do something similar" to what the SI did must start out with the recognition of this starting point before it can proceed. My criticisms of the Feederz, Bob Black of the Last International and Dan Todd of AntiAuthoritarian Anonymous are based on the belief that these men have repressed the fact that they are pro-situs. Their misogyny, hostility to students, and total refusal to take seriously any criticisms of them flows from this basic repression.

Sometime earlier this year, I received a copy of *Popular Reality* (Number 6, April-May 1985), in which there was a reprint of the cover of *NOT BORED!* #4. I was pleased this particular graphic of mine had been reprinted, because it is one of the few that addresses itself to the problem of sexual oppression, an issue about which the situationists had very little to say. It depicted a nude, 10-year-old Brooke Shields saying "Love must be freed from its myths, images and spectacular categories" and "To approach someone in any exhibitionistic way is to condemn oneself to a reified relationship from the very first." What displeased me greatly was that this graphic of mine was included in a publication that also included three highly offensive remarks about women (two of them by pro-situs). I wrote each of the three offending parties a letter, indicating my displeasure and the reasons for it.

1) In an article reprinted from *The Free Beer Press* (POB 1513, Kalamazoo MI 49005), an unidentified writer announced, without the slightest touch of sarcasm, "I'll back you up in anything you attempt, be it shows, ads, or (especially) killing Madonna." And this immediately after claiming that "I don't need to slice up my 'friends' *or* my enemies to make myself feel complete"! In a world in which women are routinely beaten, raped and killed, I see nothing funny about a proposal to kill Madonna, even if it was made sarcastically and Madonna *is* terribly annoying. Kill power, I said, not people.

2) In an article explaining and defending Bob Black's campaign against the San Franciscan magazine *Processed World,* an unidentified member of

AntiAuthoritarians Anonymous [obsolete addressed deleted] who later identified himself as Dan Todd felt compelled to describe the situation in the following manner: "Those familiar with CHRLA (the Council for Human Rights in Latin America) will appreciate the similarity to the *PW* (*Processed World*) operation. At the center of both groups one finds a dominatrix with money, surrounded by a core of loyal executants, depending on a large group of volunteers doing the shit work and largely kept in the dark." My objection was that it was unnecessary (and no doubt inaccurate) to call these women dominatrixes. A "dominatrix" is a slang expression referring to women who are sexually dominant. Given that the women in question dominate their followers by means *other than* the sexual, Dan Todd's use of the word "dominatrix" in this context was metaphorical. My suggestion was that Todd should refrain from such metaphors, because they are of a piece with the radical Right to the extent that they encourage people to define women (solely) by their sexuality. Once they are defined by their sexuality, women can be controlled by the (male) administrators of sexuality – the doctors, the psychoanalysts and the rapists.

3) In "The Correct Line," its parody of dogmatism, The Last International (later identified as Bob Black) lined up two columns of "Incorrect" and "correct." But all (except one) of the 33 items in the "Correct" list were Sadean, situationist or Reichian catchphrases: sedition (not sedation), after-hours parties (not vanguard parties); playing (not praying); sex (not sects); erotics (not neurotics), etc. Thus Black's piece ended up reinforcing dogmatism rather than negating it. Significantly, the only item in the "Correct" list that wasn't "correct" concerned female sexuality: whores (not wars). My objection was that prostitution and those whose job it is, unlike sedition, after-hours-parties, playing, etc., are thoroughly imbued with commodity relations. The concept of "whores" is unreconstructed (or undeconstructed) and thus cannot be translated as is into the corpus of Sadean, situationist, Reichian discourse.

I have not yet received a reply from *The Free Beer Press,* and I do not expect to in the near future. Dan Todd and I, and Bob Black and I, have exchanged three letters each. At the time of this writing, I've gotten the last laugh in both instances (whatever that's worth).

Dan Todd's reaction to my criticism of him was as follows:

> Your point is not well-taken re: our use of the word 'dominatrix,' meaning a woman who aspires to dominate or does so in fact. Why does this choice of words offend your sensibilities? The only pertinent question here is: do Link and Manning [CHRLA and *PW*, respectively] in fact dominate their milieus and willing subjects? Since you indicate no first-hand knowledge of either of them, you must assume in the abstract that to call a woman a 'dominatrix' is a slur of some sort. What sort of half-assed sub-liberal feminism is this? Don't you accept that women – given the opportunity and inclination

– have shown equal aptitude in dominating those they can? For someone who presumes to write about Sade, it seems to me you've missed one of the essential truths: women can be just as cruel as men.

It was obvious that Todd still didn't understand that the word dominatrix was coined within the subculture of S&M sexual practices, and that in fact it was a poor description, a *misleading* description, of the state of affairs at CHRLA and *PW*. If Todd wanted to say that these women dominated their milieus and willing subjects, why didn't he say it just like that, without bringing sexual metaphors into it? I pointed out to him that he and Bob Black, both pro-situs, manifested a similar insensitivity to language, to the workings of language. "As previously happened with surrealism, the internal development of the Situationist International shows that when the crisis of language and poetry is pushed beyond certain limits it ends up putting in question the very structure of society" ("La Tour de Feu," quoted in Knabb's *Anthology*).

I didn't expect that Todd would immediately contact and join forces with Black. The second letter that the former sent me was all pumped up with Blackian bellowing. I regret that I can't quote from it, on account of the fact that I sent it back to him with my letter attached to it. I did this because this was what Todd did with my previous letter. At the top he'd written, "Go to the back of the class (struggle) Brown." His mode of attack had changed from ridiculing my "half-assed sub-liberal feminism" to ridiculing (never properly critiquing) me for attending grad school in critical theory. The level of his violence, his insults, had noticeably increased. He was on the verge of totally breaking with me because I had dared to question a remark he'd made. I called his attention to the fact that in my previous letter I had made it clear that I liked most of what he did under the name AntiAuthoritarians Anonymous and was only asking for modifications in just one area.

Todd's last letter to me runs as follows:

> You're damn right about my total rejection of you. It wasn't instantaneous, however, as you claim: it took two letters to convince me you had shit for brains, and your last letter only confirmed it. I didn't need your fucking credit to begin with, and the modifications in one area you wanted to see we dealt with *extensively* in my previous letters: namely a patient explanation of why 'dominatrix' accurately described the two people under discussion. You would whimper about the tone of my letter, since you have no substantive ground to stand anymore. You can only snivel that Manning/Link shouldn't be described in sexual terms. You're really a precious little shit!
>
> It's been fun kicking you around, but it's so easy it's starting to feel like child molesting. If you bother to write again, don't expect an answer. You can have the last word *and* the last laugh.

It seems that I did indeed get both the last word *and* the last laugh. I told him that I wasn't going to totally reject him, but that I was going to totally *embrace* him and his organization! He's now selling an anthology of his fliers from 1981 to the present. I found this out by turning over the letter he had written me. I told him that I was going to review his anthology in every spectacular magazine that would accept the review and thus sell so many of his anthologies that he wouldn't know what hit him.

Bob Black's reaction to my criticism of him was as follows:

> It's no big deal – stand 'em on their heads they all look the same – but I'd lay off hassling the whores as politically incorrect, they have enough problems, and the two I've known intimately flatly deny the feminist/*USA Today* consensus that prostitution (even from *their* point of view) "has little to do with sex." Another convenient myth bites the dust. If is agreeable to your leftist morals you can put the johns in the incorrect column, but lay off the ladies (of the night), okay? Any other move smacks of misogyny, a la the dykes and other prurient feminists who wish to suppress prostitution – but not out of any generalized opposition to commodity relations, no way! – but because, so long as there are hookers around, sometimes straight-laced feminists are mistaken for whores and this error *oppresses* them. Life is tough. As I once asked, 'Why won't these women get in bed with any man except the DA?'

Black also sent me a total of nine pages worth of various things he'd written, including a long statement about *Processed World.*

Pages of situationist-influenced writing notwithstanding, it was immediately clear that the questionable opposition of wars with whores was only the tip of the iceberg. Here was a huge, undifferentiated floating block of misogynist stupidities! Black seems incapable of admitting that there are active feminists who are not prurient (Sheila Rowbotham, for example) and that the desire to suppress prostitution isn't the same as the desire to repress sexuality, just as the desire to suppress wage-labor isn't the same as the desire to repress the human ability to mold the world. I pointed out to him that he'd misunderstood me: I wasn't hassling the whores as politically incorrect, but was hassling *him* for uncritically thinking of whores as politically correct. I maintained that the word whore defined a function, the selling of sex for money, and only secondarily referred to whores as people.

Black responded as follows:

> Why don't you send me your thing so I can go on the offensive?
> No, no, you misunderstand me on whores, to begin at start, my

text, which you persist in investing with a precision far from it, said "*whores*" (who are people) were "*correct*," not that *prostitution* (which is a social relation) was correct. I've sung your commodity-relations tune on prostitution for at least a decade, and I still know the score, but what relevance for practice it has when real whores, pimps and john sashay across the phenomenal field is not so clear.

Black also sent me more fliers about his work and his work for others.

Clearly I wasn't getting anywhere, but I continued to correspond with Black, I even sent him a copy of *NOT BORED!* #6, because the tone of his letters was friendly. In the letter just quoted, Black even went so far as to inform me that "*Semiotext(e)* is taking a leap into the unknown by doing an issue on the country most foreign to it, *America*. I have opened my marginals files to them in an effort to help; you might send them post-x material you deem pertinent if you like."[1] In the meantime, Black was contacted by Dan Todd (see above) and the experience resulted (as it did for Todd) in a rage of righteous indignation and insults.

Black's last letter to me runs as follows:

> Sonny, I'm going to tell you a thing or two before I send you to bed without supper. Your invective is puerile, stilted and above all, bookish. I know your type. You think the way to put yourself on the avant-critical map is to play king-of-the-mountain with your betters. Just a friendly word of avuncular wisdom: you're not in Ann Arbor any more, and if you don't curb your tongue, the next recipient of your learned, negativist billingsgate might not make allowance for your distinguished intellectual ancestry and might knock your teeth out.
>
> I would not be rejoining you in the sandlot but for my genuine gratitude for the bellylaugh I owe you thanks to Dan Todd sending on your exchange with him. It is the same pseudo-sit scat-scam you tried on me. See Billy write. See Billy bid defiance to the old world and all of its rules! See Billy apply hermeneutics to "The Correct Line," mistaking it for *Parmenides*. (That's a book by Plato. He was Greek.) See Billy go-by-the-book – namely, the dictionary. But see Billy flunk the test of his own devising, for, lo! "dominatrix" *is* in the dictionary: try the *OED* ("A female dominator; mistress, lady"). Go buy the book.

---

[1] I did indeed send several copies of *NOT BORED!* and a submission to Semiotext(e). When the *Semiotext(e) USA* issue finally came out in 1987, I discovered that its editors hadn't published my submission, didn't mention *NOT BORED!* among their acknowledgements, and yet had plagiarized the title of my zine for their own uses. On the back cover of *Semiotext(e) USA*, and within the covers of many other books subsequently published by Semtiotext(e), it says, "We are amazed. We are NOT BORED." When I complained, I was summarily and apparently permanently blacklisted by both Semiotext(e) and Autonomedia, its publisher.

Internecine polemics

And if it was "obsolete" a few decades ago it is all the rage today.

Laddy, I'm not very old but I haven't had to be to see your kind come and go quicker than ducks at an arcade. You're a 90 pound weakling resentful of men who can *pump irony*. I wouldn't surmise that you're pussy-whipped, but I think you'd *like to be*. At best your published tracts are Situationism 101 take-home exams, but you are rarely at your best. I regret I cannot tutor you any further, mindful as I am of Diogenes' query: "Why not beat the teacher when the pupil misbehaves?" So *beat it,* runt.

As usual, Black also sent me a flyer about how bad *Processed World* is.

I was struck by the fact that both Dan Todd and Bob Black, when pushed a little and given the opportunity to mutually reinforce their own weaknesses, easily slip into a Total War mentality. The only thing the two of them have in common is, on the one hand, their opposition to *Processed World,* and, on the other, their opposition and hostility to me. Unlike the situationists, who knew both the value of critique between like-minded individuals *and* the value of exclusions and breaks, pro-situs such as these two know only the value of exclusions and breaks, the politics of hate.

I do not think I got the last laugh on Black, but I most certainly got in the last word. I simply pointed out to him that his theory (that is to say, his macho bellowing, which proclaimed me unfit to be associated with) and his practice (of including copies of his fliers, a gesture which presumes that I or someone I might know are quite fit to be associated with) were at odds with each other. I counseled that he should make up his mind. Apparently he went with his theory. So then maybe I *did* get the last laugh on Black! *He* was always complaining that *I* was too theoretical, too bookish!

I want to *make sure* that I have the last laugh on Black. To do that it would be necessary to pursue the matter of bookishness a little further. The reader will notice that both Black and Todd consider it to be the greatest insult to someone influenced by the situationists to be called a student. They are joined in this hatred of the student milieu by the pro-situ punk band the Feederz, whose letter to the editor (*Maximum Rock 'n' Roll* #21) about my "Introduction to the Situationist International" (both *Maximum Rock 'n' Roll* #19 and *NOT BORED!* #6) contained the passage: "One must also ask if your darling little display of 'intellectual virtuosity' didn't double as a term paper for some sociology class. You proved you knew all the catchwords but *understand* SHIT. You also proved that there IS one thing worse than an intellectual – a PSEUDO-intellectual. Only a student would be capable of such stupidity."

There is no denying that, in their journals ("as anyone who can well imagine, the pitiful student milieu is of no interest to us"), as well as in their interventions (the distribution of *On the Poverty of Student Life* under the aegis and with the financial support of the Strasbourg University student government), the situationists were openly hostile to all students. On the face of it, given the fact that I'm enrolled in grad school, I should be treated with hostility by *real* situationists, who (of course!) don't go to school and don't want to return in the future. I'm nothing but a "pedantic little Marxist" (Todd).

But as I remember from Tom Ward's book review of the recent translation of Vaneigem's *The Revolution of Everyday Life* in the *Village Voice*, Debord was born in 1930 and Vaneigem in '32. That means Debord was 27 when the SI as formed in 1957 and Vaneigem was 29 when he joined in 1961. What I'm suggesting is that the reason both Debord and Vaneigem could afford to be hostile to the student milieu was because, well before the formation of the SI, they had already spent years there. Where else could Vaneigem have so fully developed his Nietzschean epigrammatic style? Where else could he have learned who Jean de Meung, La Boetie and Vanino Vanini were?

But the situationists found it expedient to cover up this part of their individual backgrounds by striking a pose. To a certain extent, then, they therefore did a disservice to the revolutionary movements that they knew full well would follow theirs and for which they claimed to be trail-blazing. But we don't have to take the SI's anti-student rhetoric too seriously. We can leave Black, Todd and the Feederz to the ignominious task of aiding the SI in the repression of its origins. The pro-situ at work.

NOT BORED! #8, July 1985

Situationist Films in New York

I went to see "Film Modernism and its discontents: a perspective from Paris," which was designed to, in the words of program organizer Keith Sanborn, "bring to light four evenings of rarely seen, seldom recognized work from the Lettristes, the Lettriste International and the Situational International," at Exit Art, 578 Broadway. In particular, I attended the screenings of Friday, November 9, at which Jens Jorgen Thorsen's *The Situationist Life* (1964-68), Bruce Conner's *A Movie* (1958), Gil J. Wolman's *L'Anticoncept* (1952), and Rene Vienet and Gerard Cohen's *La Dialectique peut-elle casser des briques?* (1972) were shown.

I thought it was going to be a real cool time. I dressed for the occasion: black sneakers that had been splattered with bleach; ripped up blue jeans with red thermals beneath; and a detourned T-shirt, on the front side of which I induced the Democracy Statute erected in Tian-am-en Square to say, "Down with statutes!" and on the back side of which I applied the slogan "NEVER WORK!" to "You Can Not Massacre An Idea," which had been the T-shirt's official slogan. I drank beer and smoked pot all the way from Providence, Rhode Island, to Manhattan

Internecine polemics

Island. I was sure that all manner of pro-situs (or would they be anti-pro-situs?) would be standing around outside the gallery, handing out scabrous attacks on this "most blatant recuperation of Lettrist/Situationist cinema." I wondered if I should've produced one of my own flyers for the event. Would my mine be anti-pro-situ? Pro-anti-pro-situ? How about anti-pro-anti-pro situ? Huh? The possibilities seemed unlimited. Shit, even if no one remembers to bring a flyer, it'll be a lotta fun simply because the place will be packed with anti-pro-anti-pro-situs just like me! Or, rather, such was my expectation.

Of course, I was disappointed. (After all, the screenings were held in New York City, the international capital of disappointment.) Not only weren't there any recuperation-denouncing, flyer-wielding, anti-pro-anti-pro-situs in attendance, but there weren't even any people in attendance who simply wanted to enjoy themselves. Paradoxically perhaps, the place was absolutely packed, "standing room only, sir." Typical Manhattanites: dressed in apparently very expensive clothes that came in two colors, black and dark brown. They all looked like they were on some sorta dinner-and-a-movie trip. No alcohol was served in the gallery itself. The mood was stone cold sober. Sanborn himself, or, rather, his introduction, was "scholarly" and tedious, very serious. Why were all these people here? I wondered. They were quite clearly far from selfish people: they had come to the gallery tonight to *give,* to *give* their precious time, to pay attention. If the members of this audience planned to *take* anything with them, it was clearly going to be the ridiculous idea that the films and what-we-all-did-here-together-this-evening is really important. Dig Sanborn: "This exhibition is offered not to embalm or to consecrate this work in the pantheon of museologically heroic dead, but to unleash what remains of its historical charge of creative destructive energy in an environment still sorely in need of demolition." Hur-rumph!

The serious people in the audience gave it up – I mean, they applauded in the commonly accepted fashion – for the videotaped copy of Jens Jorgen Thorsen's 18-minute-long film. Composed by adding a monotone voiceover about the various Situationists to a collage of footage taken from TV commercials, documentaries (one is about a sinking ship), and good old soft-core pornography, *The Situationist Life* is no longer alive. It's dead. It was probably a fun movie to make and to watch in a drunken revel with its "stars," but it struck me as pointless and boring. This isn't to say that this *Life* "hasn't aged well." I don't think it was ever intended to "age" at all. It was intended to be reborn, is all. It wasn't, and you know what they say, nothing rots like that which has not been superseded.

The serious people in the audience gave it up for Bruce Connor's 12 minute long, 16mm film, which was included here – Connor was neither a Lettrist nor a Situationist – for "context," as a "historical film antecedent/related film work produced concurrently," to quote the ever-eloquent Keith Sanborn. Though it was a little more pointed than Thorsen's film, *A Movie* was just as boring, perhaps even more boring because it was a comparatively well-produced, traditional work of avant-garde cinema.

And then . . . and then the serious people in the audience *gave up* on Gil J. Wolman's *L'Anticoncept* (60 minutes, 16mm), quite possibly the greatest film I've ever seen ("experienced" would be a better word, since the film is completely bereft of filmed images). The audience members left in droves as *L'Anticoncept* was taking place, obviously thinking that it was pointless and boring, a "little too self-indulgent." When it was over, they were only about 15 people left in the gallery, including the people who worked there. What went wrong? or, rather, Wow! How did the film construct the provocative situation that it so obviously did?

Wolman's creation needs, wants and takes nothing from its "audience"; there is nothing to give it, neither recognition nor approval. *L'Anticoncept* is a machine that produces giving; it does nothing but "give" (in all senses of the word). Upon a huge white spherical weather balloon, the film projects or casts either bright white light or nothing at all, darkness. There is nothing to look at, or, rather, nothing more to look at than a simple signaling device – perhaps a traffic signal with only two colors, or, in this case, all colors at once (black) and the total absence of all colors (white) – going On, Off, On, Off, On, Off, On, Off, On, Off etc. etc.

The voiceover is Wolman's own voice, speaking, crying, rejoicing, ranting, mumbling, singing, making noises, remaining silent. It is an absolutely virtuosic poetic performance. The text of the voiceover, which Sanborn has translated from the French (and is claiming or trying to retain copyrights upon!), is beautiful, even moving. The members of the audience who left the film while it was "showing" did so because they didn't know what to do with themselves – with their bodies (suddenly so cumbersome) – and because they had nothing to feed their eyes upon. Without a spectacle, which is in the simplest sense of the word something to look at, there was no film at all for them. And so they left.

It clearly never occurred to them – or never occurred to them as a serious possibility – that they might stop watching, get up out of their chairs and (with Wolman's voice ringing in their ears) wander around a bit, in the way that they might conduct themselves as if it was the intermission. The vast majority of the audience never "got" the concept of *L'Anticoncept*, or, perhaps more simply, they never "got" the anticoncept. And that's because the anticoncept is not something to understand, to "give" or to "get": it is something (a unique opportunity, a constructed situation, call it what you will) to take advantage of, something to seize and enjoy to the fullest. At the very least, a "showing" of *L'Anticoncept* is an opportunity to look at something other than the film when a film is being screened.

For whatever reason (abstract or concrete), I couldn't sit still during *L'Anticoncept*. Fuck! I couldn't even sit still for *The Situationist Life* or for *A Movie!* And so I walked, I paced, I wandered, I tried to drift within the confines of the gallery. One moment I was in the back of the room; another I was in the front, up where that silly fucking balloon was, in the spectacle, where people could see me. I was hoping (I almost wrote "hopping") that other people would start dancing,

dancing in the dark. But everybody (so far as I could see) kept their eyes on the ball, er, balloon. And so I danced alone. The only one to say anything to me about my little *pas de un* was some guy (Sanborn himself?) who told me to stay clear of the video-camera. Yeah, right. Here this guy is – videotaping a buncha people who, after allowing themselves to be bored by an unusually interesting film, get up and leave – and he doesn't want *me* "fucking up a perfectly good videotape"?!

There was no discussion after the screening of this film.

After a break, Rene Vienet and Gerard Cohen's *La Dialectique peut-elle casser des briques?* (*The dialectic, can it break bricks?* 90 minutes, shot on film but shown on video) was screened. Vienet was certainly one of the most talented and lucid Situationists: like Guy Debord, he was an accomplished filmmaker, theoretician of "the new forms of art" and writer. In a manner similar to *The Situationist Life*, Vienet and Cohen's film is detourned, i.e., composed by adding a voiceover to plundered footage. In the case of the latter, the appropriated footage is an entire Kung Fu movie; the premise of the detourned film is a battle between the forces of "radical subjectivity" (the good guys) and "ideology" (the bad guys). From what I gathered, I wasn't the only one who thought that Vienet and Cohen's "detournement" was empty and redundant. The themes of radical subjectivity and ideology where in the original film to begin with, in the form of an underlying conflict between the Koreans and the Chinese. This fact would seem to raise questions about the differences between uplifting, negationist "appropriation" and condescending, affirmationist cultural imperialism). Besides, Woody Allen had already done this shtick to death in *What's Up, Tiger Lily?*

There was no discussion after the screening of this film.

NOT BORED! #18, December 1990

Screening of Guy Debord's film
The Society of the Spectacle

It was scheduled to take place on Tuesday, 20 February 1996, at the State University of New York at Buffalo's recently completed, very expensive and fuckin' ugly Center for the Arts. Though this screening of Debord's first full-length film was in fact the very first in the United States, it was publicized in an ambiguous fashion. In Buffalo (i.e., in the SUNY at Buffalo milieu, which is – as we shall see – not the same thing as in Buffalo), the screening was billed as an historic event: the very first American showing of a rarely seen film by a man – famous in some circles – who'd killed himself in 1994. But in the world at large (i.e., everywhere else), it wasn't publicized at all. (That is, until *we* found out about it.) This was either as a result of incompetence or intention: either way, this sideshow could serve as a kind of trial run or dress rehearsal for one Keith Sanborn before he took the film on the road to such really important places as New York City.

(From the crowd: "Hiss! Boo! Too bad we didn't take Sanborn's picture at the showing! Then we could insert a photograph of him here so that folks could see.... !")

Sanborn gave himself two roles to play in the dress rehearsal: on the one (very visible) hand, he was the young, handsome assistant professor of film at the SUNY at Buffalo who organized the event, which was made part of the rag-tag "Magnificent Media" series sponsored by the Media Studies Department; on the other (sleight of) hand, he was the bold revolutionary and radical filmmaker who'd managed to get hold of a pirated videotape of *La Societe du Spectacle*, who'd translated the film's voiceover monologue into English, who'd cleverly inserted his translation into the "original" videotape in the form of subtitles, and who was – under the name Mr. Zero and the Ediciones La Calavera – using the World Wide Web to advertise copies of the bootlegged film that were priced at only $30 a copy!

(From the crowd: "Broken down into plain English: 'Welcome to the show, which is pa owerful anti-capitalist and anti-commodity statement; you can buy a copy of it from me for only $30!'")

It is telling that Sanborn chose to show the film on campus and as part of a university film series, rather than downtown and under the aegis of a financially independent gallery, performance space or film archive. He wanted to be in control of all aspects of the dress rehearsal – otherwise, it wouldn't be a dress rehearsal at all, it would be the real thing, and thus subject to all kinds of accidents, contingencies and unforeseen events that might damage Keith Sanborn/Mr. Zero's respective roles, reputations, aspirations and "secret identities." Preventing damage from occurring was obviously far more important to Sanborn than the golden opportunity to show his students and university chums where and what the "Buffalo art scene" is, and thereby help that scene in the long run.

We found out about Sanborn's little dress rehearsal by accident: that is, when one of our comrades at the State University of New York at Buffalo saw a notice and leaked the news to us by e-mail. Within moments, we'd contacted the *Village Voice* and found out that nobody there knew anything about the showing. We then entered into a contract with the *Voice*: we would hand in a 600-word preview of the film, and it would run in the issue appearing the week before the screening.

Our next step was to e-mail Keith Sanborn. We obtained his e-mail address from the World Wide Web sub-page that advertises copies of "his" videocassette *The Society of the Spectacle* in the following banal way:

> The films of Guy Debord have been an occult presence. Available at first only by pilgrimage to the Rue de Cujas, they became completely inaccessible in the mid-1980s when Debord withdrew them from

circulation. In January of this year [1995], 2 older films and a new video collaboration with Brigitte Cornand were broadcast on French tv, shortly after Debord's suicide. The vcrs were running. Through the machinations of Ediciones La Calavera, Debord's film version of *The Society of the Spectacle* is now available in an English-subtitled NTSC version on VHS video. It may now enter the arena of theory and practice in the English language world. The subtitles are by Keith Sanborn. Proceeds will go to fund further subtitling projects.

At 12:35 pm on 5 February – presuming Sanborn to be a reasonably receptive audience for our missives – we sent him the following electronic message: "Writing up screening of SoS in Buffalo (2/20) in the *Village Voice*. Deadline is tomorrow at 5 pm. Please rsvp asap." An hour-and-a-half later, we were looking at Sanborn's response, which was, "Given our previous 'encounter' I don't think you're informed enough to write intelligently on Situationist film." What exactly does this mean, "our previous 'encounter'"? Dear reader, we ourselves didn't know – and still don't know – to which event Sanborn was referring. We think his reference was to our conduct in the aftermath of Sanborn's "Film Modernism and its discontents: A Perspective from Paris," a series of screenings held between 7-10 November 1990 at Exit Art in Manhattan. Having been given a copy of Sanborn's own translation of the voiceover of Gil J Wolman's extraordinary film *L'Anticoncept* in exchange for the price of admission, we felt free to reprint it in the 18th issue of *NOT BORED!* (December 1990). The only things we did to the hand-out that might be considered objectionable were A) write the phrase "Some asshole told me that this xeroxed hand-out would be valuable 'some day' as 'a collector's item'" at the top of its first page and B) cross-out the sentence "All Translations c Keith Sanborn 1990" and write next to it, "over-ruled by order of the Council for Maintaining even the appearance of being against private property." Oh, yes! and in the accompanying essay, we referred to Sanborn's introduction to the film as "tedious and scholarly." *Mea culpa.*

And so it appears that poor little Keith Sanborn didn't like the fact that we insulted and violated his apparently faultless and eminently reasonable claim to the copyrights on his own translation of the voiceover in a stolen situationist film. (Actually, *L'Anticoncept* is a pre-situationist film, but there is no point in quibbling over relatively unimportant details.) When it came his chance to get even – even though *six years* had gone by – he hit us with his best insult. Pow! We are not "informed enough"! Only another academic could be wounded by such a remark. Our response, e-mailed at 3:50 pm on 5 February under the intentionally ominous subject heading "You just made a mistake," was as follows:

> What you think about me, how "informed" I am, or whether I can write "intelligently" on situationist cinema just isn't relevant. What

will be relevant – at least in so far as the *Voice* is concerned – is the fact that I gave you a chance to get the facts straight BEFORE I met my deadline. As for "encounters," you ain't seen nuthin' yet.

At the time, we had no specific plans for the evening of 20 February, other than the fact that we were committed to be in Buffalo for the screening of *La Societe du Spectacle* and have as much fun there as we could without getting arrested. Over the course of the next week or so, we were very busy. On 8 February, we took out and mailed to Ediciones La Calavera a United States Postal Money Order worth $30; our intention was to get a copy of the film before we traveled to Buffalo, so that we could sell copies of it, at Sanborn's showing of the film, for the far more reasonable sum of $5. (It is worth noting that Ediciones La Calavera operates out of a post office box in New York City, not in Buffalo; indeed, Sanborn's box is located in the very same Post Office station that we use.)

We wrote and sent in our 600-word piece for the *Village Voice*, even though we'd been told by its film editor that there was actually insufficient space for it to run as scheduled, and that we'd be getting a kill fee for our efforts. We also produced our own "original" edition of an English-language version of the filmscript for *La Societe du Spectacle* by bringing together into one text Richard Parry's translation of the film's camera directions, subtitles, printed boards and musical cues, and Donald Nicholson-Smith's translation of the book *La Societe du Spectacle*, from which the film's voiceover is taken. Our primary intent in producing this edition wasn't to correct problems in Richard Parry's version of the filmscript (published in *Society of the Spectacle and Other Films*, 1992) – although that version could use the work – but to have something meaningful to give out at the screening of the film in Buffalo, something that could be used to break Sanborn's effective monopoly on access to the content of the film. (We reasoned that even Keith Sanborn isn't stupid enough to make the same mistake twice and simply give out copies of his precious little translation to people he doesn't know very well; we assumed that he hadn't planned to give out any hand-outs at the showing. It turned out that these assumptions were correct; consequently we were well prepared for the "encounter.") Because we have friends in the right places, 200 copies of our edition of the filmscript were produced at no cost to ourselves, thus allowing us to give them out for free.

We also had the idea of calling The *Buffalo News* in advance of the screening, to see if its Arts & Entertainment editor was aware of it and if he had already assigned someone to write it up. Significantly, the editor had been officially informed of the screening, but had also been rudely denied access to a copy of the film by Sanborn himself, about whom the editor had heard nothing but bad things: that he was a "prima donna"; that he'd insulted and had to apologize to his department's secretary for calling her "stupid"; that the chairperson of the Media Studies department wasn't having much success in keeping Sanborn and the rest of the department in line, etc. In other words, Sanborn was being as cooperative with his university colleagues as he was with us. Especially because we'd worked with the editor in question before, it was easy for us to get a contract with *The Buffalo News* to write up the screening. Though we had lost access to the "prestigious" *Village Voice*, we had gained access the only local newspaper in all of Buffalo, which would turn out to be far more useful to us than some over-the-hill rag published in New York City.

At 1:50 pm on 14 February, we e-mailed Keith Sanborn with the intent of keeping a rattling hand on his cage. Under the intentionally vague subject heading "In an attempt to avoid making a mistake," we wrote nothing but the simple phrase, "you just made another (mistake)." The provocation worked very well, indeed. Though we did not find out about it for another week and a half, on 14 February Sanborn sent a half-hysterical e-mail message to someone – anyone – at our Internet provider, claiming that he was being "harassed" by our e-mail messages and that he was considering legal action! Concerned that this bit of infantilism ("I'm gonna tell Mommy on you!") wouldn't do enough damage to us, Sanborn also sent us the following e-mail message at 5:30 pm, 14 February: "It seems you're the one with the history of mistakes from Buffalo to Providence. I know why you left town each time." That is to say, after spending all afternoon or maybe even a solid few days digging around in the fetid pits of rumor, gossip and intentional distortion, Keith Sanborn finally had some dirt on us. But his clumsy attempt to insinuate that – employee of the State of New York or not – Keith Sanborn is not above resorting to innuendo and black-mail to "defend" himself didn't phase us in the slightest. The next day, we sent our last message to him.

> Everybody knows what you claim to know. But it doesn't stop me from doing what I want, when I want and where I want. Have you realized what your second mistake was?

But no: Sanborn didn't yet realize that he'd not only alienated The *Buffalo News*, but also that we were the ones assigned by it to write about "his" screening. He would find out eventually, of course: but by then it would be too late.

Since Ediciones La Calavera had not yet filled our order for a copy of the videocassette, there was just one more thing to do before we departed for the Queen City on the Lakes: design a suitable poster for the event that we could put up in all the places in Buffalo that we figured Sanborn would ignore. (We wanted a big turnout, so that the heavy concentration of ovine undergraduate students at the screening would be diluted.) Note the differences, not only in style, but also in content, between our poster and his: while we see ourselves throwing rocks at our enemies in the midst of a revolution, Sanborn sees himself seated comfortably in a theatre, watching a "revolutionary" movie.

Our article for *The Buffalo News* appeared the very day of the screening of the film. It's not particularly worth the effort of restoring the two or three paragraphs our friendly editor had to cut out due to a shortage of space that day, because the truly remarkable thing about the piece is that it was even printed at all, given the obscurity of its subject matter and references. But let us say that we elaborated further on the assertion that the primary purpose of *La Societe du Spectacle* was to re-edit and reinforce Debord's 1967 book of the same name in the "light" of the general wildcat strike that paralyzed France in May and June 1968 – an assertion which was amply confirmed by our subsequent viewing of the film itself.

Four of us showed up at the screening, which was attended by approximately 60 undergraduate students. Two of us were dressed as fools: one handed out our edition of the filmscript and – as baked as an Idaho potato – smiled and laughed a lot, while the other took and handed out Polaroid shots of everyone in the audience and – as roasted as a peanut – smiled and laughed a lot, too. (Ours was the only creative demonstration to take place at the showing.) All the while, glum Keith Sanborn stayed up in the projection booth, brooding and busying himself with his introductory remarks. When it came time to be nervously and rather formally introduced by Media Studies chairperson, avant-garde musician and world-famous dim bulb Tony Conrad, Sanborn literally stood at the opposite end of the stage from his boss.

We would have relished the opportunity to introduce the film, but only or precisely for the reason that at that moment Patrick Buchanan (a genuine, homegrown American fascist) was doing very well in the Republican primaries, which were then in full swing. But when it came time for Keith Sanborn to deliver his introductory remarks, all he wanted to talk about on that balmy Tuesday evening in February was us, that is to say, our *Buffalo News* article and our edition of the filmscript! He used his introduction to do nothing but go on a very defensive offensive. We almost felt bad for the poor fuck: he demonstrably had no vision, project nor personality of his own. Claiming he preferred "accuracy" to "spontaneity" – a stunning admission, given the intense commitment of the situationists to the latter – Sanborn spent about 10 or 15 solid minutes identifying and sometimes correcting all of the apparently numerous errors in the *News* article, which he referred to as part of "the cesspool of yellow journalism," or something equally clever. The people who laughed at this remark appeared to be students hoping for a better grade in the course they were currently attending.

Then Sanborn spent about 5 minutes on our edition of the filmscript, which he faulted for relying on Donald Nicholson-Smith's translation of Debord's book, which was, of course, inferior to his own translation. There was a funny moment in which Sanborn threw out some remark questioning our ability to speak French; when we called out *"Mais bien sur!"* from the exact center of the very back of the room, he just didn't know what to say or do! There was another moment in which Sanborn himself – in response to a remark from the crowd – had to admit that a truly revolutionary element of our edition of the filmscript was the fact that it was given away for free. (It was quite clear from the audience's total unfamiliarity with the film and its maker that we could have charged at least $5 for a copy of our edition and sold all of the copies we had brought with us.) We think it was shocking that Sanborn didn't say one damn thing about Mr. Zero, Ediciones La Calavera, or the fact that he was "clandestinely" selling pirated copies of the film for $30 apiece.

When he was done wasting his time on us, Keith Sanborn told us that Debord's film was meant to "change the world." That was the only thing he said about the film itself in all of his introduction. Shit, back in 1968, even the Beatles could sing, "We all want to change the world"! Who knows what Sanborn would have talked about had we not crashed "his" semi-public party!!

Then there was the film itself. Although there are some great moments in it – we have written about one of them elsewhere in this issue under the title "Walk in Space" – *La Societe du Spectacle* is a 90-minute-long bore. There is nothing to do while it is showing other than look at it. As we've mentioned in "Situationist Symphony, No. 1," there is hardly any music in it, and what music there is, is a few snippets of classical music. While it is quite true that the sound and sense of Debord's voiceover is shattering, the audience still can't look away from the spectacle of the screen (and thus at the building they are in, the people they are with, and the situation as it then-and-only-then exists) for fear of missing more than a few of the many famous stills and shots Debord-the-filmmaker has assembled. It was, in short, far too much of a film, and too little of a ploy designed to create a scandal.[2]

We don't mean to imply here any judgments of Debord's five other films, the work Debord did after the dissolution of the Situationist International in 1972, or situationist films in general. We just don't seeing any point in asserting that the "revolutionary" cinematic techniques used in *La Societe du Spectacle* (sudden cuts, quick edits and, above all else, ironic juxtapositions) are provocative or particularly significant *today*, in 1996. Furthermore, we see no point in perpetuating the myth that Guy Debord, or any situationist for that matter, could turn his talents to any medium that struck his fancy and never make a dud nor a merely interesting failure.

Upon returning to NYC, we experienced a couple of appropriately anti-climatic events. We learned, as we've mentioned, that Sanborn tried to tell Mommy on us. *The Village Voice* found that it had the space to run an article on a showing of *The Society of the Spectacle* in Manhattan. We have reprinted it elsewhere in this issue, simply because the thing is ridiculous to the point of absurdity, and thereby likely to bring mirth to even the most cynical of our readers. Note as well the one remark attributed to Keith Sanborn: Debord made this movie to "change the world." Elsewhere in NYC, Sanborn received, opened and, on 11 March 1996, sent back to us our letter and postal money order for $30, on the

---

[2] I have changed my mind, not about the film – which I continue to think is superb as a work of art, especially the last 20 minutes – but about the value of creating a scandal. In 1973, Debord didn't need to create one; the new post-1968 era required something else.

grounds that it was "Opened in error," no doubt because Sanborn realized that this particular request for a copy of *The Society of the Spectacle* originated from the same post office box that is listed as a NOT BORED! contact point in our edition of the filmscript. Perhaps Sanborn had learned of the open call we had issued on the World Wide Web to obtain, duplicate and sell for a reasonable price his subtitled-version of *The Society of the Spectacle*. Perhaps he's merely a petty, spiteful little bastard. We'll see, if (and when) he refuses to sell copies of "his" film to other people who have gotten in his face and yawned loudly and unceremoniously.

NOT BORED! #25, June 1996

Keith Sanborn responds

The following was posted to the "Frameworks" Experimental Film Discussion List by Keith Sanborn on October 03, 1996.

> So sorry to have bruised your pathetic little ego, Herr Doktor Professor Brown. But really why do persist in making your persecution manias into public wanking sessions? But then you're an expert at public wanking. Just to set the record straight about the video translation I have been selling.
> Since you obviously have no idea what it costs to put 1200 2-line subtitles on a video tape, let me just put it this way: at $30, I'm selling the tape at a loss for the production costs alone.
> Next time you do a public wank on my account, please at least take the time to inform yourself about a few of the facts. But then you're not really that good at distinguishing facts from fantasy as your post makes obvious. You must have spent a lot of time on that magnum opus of stupidity and disinformation.
> And by the way, how's your ambulance chaser father who supports your webwank?[3]
>
> love and kisses,
> Keith Sanborn

Our response was posted on October 10, 1996.

> What took you so long to respond? It took you FIVE months to

---

[3] I'm not sure where Sanborn got these notions from, but they are false. Though a lawyer, my father didn't specialize in personal injury cases, nor did he ever support any of my on-line endeavors.

Internecine polemics

come up with a handful of lame "insults"?

No matter. In the meantime, I have – among other things – broken your monopoly on distribution of copies of *The Society of the Spectacle,* and that is ALL that matters to me.

Keith Sanborn's $30 bootlegs

We see value in Keith Sanborn's production of a subtitled videocassette version of Guy Debord's 1973 film *La Societe du Spectacle*. The availability of such a videotape cannot fail to introduce Debord and the other situationists' critique of the society of the spectacle to English-speaking audiences that might not have otherwise been aware of or receptive to the significance and enduring usefulness of Debord's 1967 book (which bears the same title as the film). We also believe that Keith Sanborn should be adequately compensated for his efforts, which mostly involved the subtitling and duplication processes. (Very little new material needed to be translated, precisely because the film so closely follows Debord's book, of which good translations have been in circulation since the 1970s.)

But it is clear that Keith Sanborn is demonstrably attempting to receive more financial compensation than is appropriate for someone who claims to be interested in furthering the situationist project, and not simply making a buck off of it. In a word, we firmly believe that – in charging between $30 and $40 for copies of the subtitled tape – he is gouging. We believe this even though we know that (he claims) this admirable project cost $7,000 to bring to completion. We also believe that he should be held accountable, so to speak, for his shameless profiteering, if not financially, then at least in the eyes of his peers in the international post-situationist scene.

We must remind all concerned that Sanborn's videocassette is nothing but a pirate edition, a bootleg, an illegal duplication of a film that was originally made by a man who committed suicide in 1994 and thus cannot do anything to prevent or denounce clear abuses such as this. Sanborn's "new" translation of the film's voiceover, as well as his creation, distribution and very well-attended (and thus highly profitable) public screenings of the subtitled videocassette, are most definitely NOT authorized by the estate of Guy Debord. As Sanborn himself knows, it is only a matter of time before Alice Becker-Ho (Debord's widow) learns of what he is doing, and instructs her lawyers to ask Sanborn to cease and desist from these unauthorized and illegal activities.

In the meantime – or, rather, before the situationist shit hits the international fan – Sanborn is trying to receive more than adequate compensation for his efforts: he is clearly trying to make as much money as possible. If it cost a total of $7,000 to complete this project, why aren't copies of the tape priced at $10 each? It is clearly reasonable to expect that, over a reasonably short period of time, 1000 people would buy a copy of the tape if it were reasonably priced. At $10 a copy, Keith Sanborn would stand to get back all of his original investment and a $3,000 profit as well. But at $30 a copy, he stands to make a profit of $23,000 (again assuming 1000 people will eventually fork over the money).

Think of it this way: What other 90-minute-long minute videotape on the market costs $30 or $40? If one were to go to, say, Blockbuster Video (not known for its low prices), and discretely inquire as to what item in the store costs $30, the answer would be, "Well, the director's cut of *Natural Born Killers*, which includes one full hour of previously cut footage, as well as never-before-seen interview segments with the director himself and all the important actors, retails for $27.95." In other words, Sanborn has drastically over-estimated or deliberately ignored the relative cultural value of the subtitled bootleg he has produced. But professional bootleggers – who are not widely known or respected for keeping their greed under control – do know the relative cultural value of a bootlegged videocassette, which translates into $15 or $20 a copy, at the very most. "To live outside the law, you must be honest," Bob Dylan sang many years ago. Keith Sanborn is living outside the law, but he is not being honest.

One thinks here of Ken Knabb, and how much Keith Sanborn is different from him. In 1981, when he first published *The Situationist International Anthology*, Knabb priced it at only $10 a copy, despite the facts that it was a huge book upon which he'd spent years of his time, and that it was a book that he published himself, with his own funds. Quite obviously, Knabb – someone genuinely committed to the situationist project – knew that he was undertaking a long haul: there would be very little demand for the *Anthology* in the short-term; he wouldn't make any money (back) for several years, if at all; over the course of 10 or 15 years, he might be adequately compensated for his efforts. Hindsight shows that Ken Knabb was right. Today, copies of *The Anthology* cost $15 (still a bargain) and Ken Knabb is well-respected by nearly everyone in the post-situationist milieu. But what will people say about Keith Sanborn in 10 or 15 years? Well, what are they saying today?

When priced at $30 to $40 each, copies of Debord's film are too expensive for students, the unemployed and the working classes – in other words, for precisely the very people about and for whom Debord's film was made in the first place. Indeed, Sanborn's subtitled videotape is so expensive that even independent bookstores cannot stock it without losing money. The only "people" who can afford these ridiculously inflated prices are relatively large institutions such as libraries and film societies, and such relatively-well paid college-level teachers as Sanborn himself – in other words, the very people and things from which Debord so unequivocally and completely distanced himself during his lifetime.

We have obtained one of Sanborn's over-priced, unauthorized and subtitled reproductions of Debord's film, and have used it to generate good quality second-generation copies, which we are selling for $5 postpaid (domestic orders) and $10 postpaid (international ones), while they last. Please send cash only to [obsolete addresses deleted].

Since Sanborn is also selling unauthorized, subtitled videocassettes of Rene Vienet's 1973 film *Can Dialectics Break Bricks?* for $30 to $40 each, we would obviously be pleased if this film escaped from Sanborn's clutches in the way we have helped *La Societe du Spectacle* escape.[1]

This text may be freely reproduced and distributed, for if and when Madame Debord's lawyers contact us, they will be contacting both clear consciences and meager bank accounts.

On-line notice dated 16 November 1996
NOT BORED! #27, May 1997

[1] Note added 14 March 1997: we have obtained an "original" copy of Rene Vienet's *Can Dialectics Break Bricks?* and are making good, second-generation copies of it available for $5 cash (domestic orders) or $10 cash (international orders).

On the pricing of the tapes

Ever since November 1996, NOT BORED! has been selling dirt-cheap copies of two situationist films – Guy Debord's *La Societe du Spectacle* and Rene Vienet's *La Dialectique, Peut Elle Cassez les Briques?* both made in 1973 – that a filmmaker named Keith Sanborn subtitled and released as videotapes, in 1995 and 1990, respectively. As we made clear at the outset, we only got involved in making and selling second-generation copies of these tapes because of Sanborn's *cynical and manipulative greed.* Before we arrived on the scene, Sanborn had been selling his subtitled versions for $30 and up, thus keeping them out of the reach of poor people and small infoshops. (He also had been refusing to sell copies to people he deemed too stupid or uninformed to understand them, despite the fact that he had not been given permission from either Debord or Vienet to release their respective films as subtitled videotapes.) To break up Sanborn's monopoly on distribution, we priced our second-generation copies at $5 each ($10 if shipped to somewhere outside the USA). We lost no money doing this, and indeed made a little over a dollar per tape, for it costs about $2 for a blank cassette and $1.87 to mail it to an address in the USA.

Our strategy worked. Over the course of the last three years, we have sold hundreds of copies of these videotapes to people all over the world; these videotapes, despite being second-generation copies, were of sufficient quality that they themselves could be copied, which means that anyone to whom we've sold a tape could become, in his or her turn, a "distributor" of it. Indeed, we have been so successful that Sanborn himself has stopped trying (or stopped advertizing his efforts) to sell his "original" copies for $30 each. His monopoly on distribution is over. Hurrah!

And so now we feel free to raise our prices to a level more appropriate to the new situation, that is, more responsive to the fact that it is a *fucking drag* to make all these copies one-at-a-time on two VCRs. Not to mention the fact that all this copying and rewinding has worn out our VCRs and that we will shortly have to purchase new ones, thereby wiping out whatever "profits" we've made over the years. From now on, each copy of these videotapes will be priced at $10 (for domestic orders) and $15 (for international orders). Thanks for understanding.

On-line notice dated 11 March 2000

Seven Years is Enough Already!
We're no longer selling copies of Guy Debord's films

On 16 November 1996, exactly seven years ago today, we announced that we had obtained a subtitled copy of Guy Debord's 1973 film *The Society of the Spectacle,* which the subtitler (one Keith Sanborn) was selling for $30 each, and that we would be selling bootlegged second-generation copies for only $5 each. We were appalled by Sanborn's greed and concerned that the high prices would keep the film from being seen. (On 14 March 1997, we also started selling $5 bootlegged copies of Rene Vienet's 1973 film *Can the Dialectic Break Bricks?* which Sanborn had also subtitled and for which he was also charging $30 per copy.)

Three years later, on 11 March 2000, we declared that our intervention had been a success, and we announced that we were raising our prices slightly (from $5 to $10 per copy). And yet demand for the tapes, especially those by Guy Debord, remained strong; it even grew stronger. By 23 June 2003, we were *so* far behind in filling orders – mind you, these copies were made, one at a time, on a pair of battered VCRs – that we were forced to stop taking any new orders so that we could catch up with the old ones.

Today, 16 November 2003, we announce that, once we have caught up, we will not be taking any new orders for the films of Guy Debord, that is, *The Society of the Spectacle* and *Refutation of All Judgments [...] Concerning the film 'The Society of the Spectacle.'* We aren't stopping because its too expensive (without raising prices again, to pay for worn-out VCRs) or because of pressure from the Debord estate. . . . No: it's because we're just *sick and tired* of dubbing videotapes all day long. Seven years is enough. We've made our point, now it's time to move on.

Sometime in 2004, all six of Guy Debord's films – including the two we've been selling – will be officially released in subtitled versions. Prospective buyers

Internecine polemics
will have to wait until then. We don't know what the prices will be.

As for the Vienet film, *Can the Dialectic Break Bricks?* we will continue to sell it; otherwise it would be unavailable.

On-line notice dated 16 November 2003

The Assault on Greil Marcus: An Open Letter to Stewart Home

In his widely-circulated "Introduction to the Polish edition of *The Assault on Culture,*" Stewart Home writes, "While I am very pleased to see the work translated into Polish, I would write something completely different if I were to sit down again and compose a treatise on the movements that are described in the following pages." Why is that? According to Home, "the text has its faults"; however, "if I began to correct them there'd be no end to the process and I'd find myself writing a different work." In other words, *The Assault on Culture* is a piece of shit – twice in his introduction Home describes it as a "bluff your way guide" and as "a fairly painless means of getting an overview" of utopian currents since the late 1940s. He knows that the only reason his book was ever taken seriously is that it was "published in the summer of 1988, at a time when it was difficult for English readers to obtain information on groups such as the Situationists and Fluxus." Unfortunately for Home and the other bluff-your-way-through-life intellectuals for whom he writes, "there have been [since then] major retrospective exhibitions devoted to both these movements and the publication of numerous catalogues," as well as "[t]wo further monographs" that are neither bluffs nor "painless" books to read. And so, only one year after its publication, *The Assault on Culture* stood revealed as a hollow shell, a bluff that had been called. It should either be rewritten in the light of the books published in 1989 or quite simply flushed down the toilet.

Home has found a third alternative: instead of defending his book against claims that it is a bluff with nothing to back it up, he is attacking those who have written the books that called his bluff in the first place. In particular, Home has targeted his alienated anger at Greil Marcus's *Lipstick Traces: A Secret History of the Twentieth Century* (Harvard, 1989), the book that goes over much of the same ground that is covered in *The Assault on Culture*, in particular, the idea that the punk bands of the late 1970s took up the most radical positions staked out in the 1960s. In 1990, Home published no less than four negative reviews of *Lipstick Traces*; these reviews appeared in *Here and Now,* the *New Art Examiner, City Lights* and Home's own pro-situationist fanzine, *Smile.* According to Home's quite obviously less-than-impartial judgments, "With the concept of the 'voice,' a hidden authority which (dis)organizes the world, Marcus abandons any need for a rational explanation of the events he describes." Home alledges that "such a discourse has more in common with the simple faith of a priest than the considered reflections of a critic or historian."

One would think a person such as Stewart Home would be content with hurling these insults and then moving on to other things, confident in the knowledge that people cry when he puts them down. But no. Home remains so bent upon assassinating both Greil Marcus's personal character and the intellectual character of *Lipstick Traces* that the majority of his "Introduction to the Polish edition" of *The Assault on Culture* (Warsaw: Wydawnictwo Hotel Sztuki, 1993) is devoted to these twisted aims. We admit that there might well be another motive for devoting so much space to attacks on Greil Marcus: it is clear that Home knows next to nothing about revolutionary movements in Poland, the citizens of which he is supposed to be addressing. All he knows comes from bluff-your-way-through-it guides: "It was reported that during a December demonstration," he writes, that "members of the [Polish group] Orange Alternative dressed up as Father Christmas – and that this caused a great deal of confusion among representatives of the Polish authorities." It is, in Home's words, "likely" (some would say "obvious" or even "unsurprising") that "at least some Orange Alternative activists were familiar with both Debordist theory and the sixties counterculture of the West." But just in case his Polish readers misunderstand and take offense at what he will go on to say about Debord and the other situationists, Home is there to say – wearing his best poker face, one assumes – that the Polish pro-situationists "clearly developed a praxis that reflected their unique social situation."

The beginning of Home's assault on Greil Marcus seems innocuous enough. "Much of what has been written about the SI [Situationist International] simply consists of anecdotes from a mythologized history," Home writes in his introduction.

> Even the American journalist who tried to break out of this vicious circle by adopting a technique of free association, demonstrates little more than the failure of his own imagination by endlessly falling back on the key episodes of Strasbourg, May '68 etc. In *Lipstick Traces* (Secker & Warburg, London, 1989) Greil Marcus moves effortlessly from John of Leyden (religious heresies of the Middle Ages) to Johnny Lydon (who under the pseudonym Rotten sang for the Sex Pistols), not simply due to the names sounding similar but because they make up what the author perceives as a hip and radical alternative history. The result is a sanitised Situationist family tree, the more unpleasant findings that ought to turn up given Marcus's technique of free association [sic] simply don't feature in the book. For example, the Council for the Liberation of Daily Life, who went on to become the American section of the SI, operated out of Box

Internecine polemics

666, Stuyvesant Station, New York – 666 is, of course, the number of the Beast or Satan. Likewise, Sid Vicious (bass player with the Sex Pistols) murdered his girlfriend in New York's Chelsea Hotel, which many years earlier had hosted Ku Klux Klan meetings.

Let's give Home the benefit of the doubt and assume for a moment that he knows that Marcus's ironic juxtaposition (it is not a "free association") of John of Leyden with John Lydon – has an intentionally comic, playful dimension. It would then appear that Home simply doesn't think this kind of poetic license has a place in a truly useful history of the radical movements in question. Ironic or poetic juxtaposition ("free association") is as irrelevant to radical historical inquiry as the Beast or Satan is to the American section of the SI. This might be a mistaken notion, but it is at least a rational notion, presumably offered in the spirit of constructive criticism.

But one should never give the benefit of the doubt to a person who makes a career out of profiting from people naive or stupid enough to believe him when he is obviously bluffing. As if more proof were needed, there's the authoritative-sounding implication (Home's specialty) that the American section of the SI must also have "operated out of" Box 666, Stuyvesant Station. As a matter of easily checkable fact, when the Council became the American section of the SI, it rented Box 491, Cooper Station, and not Box 666, Stuyvesant Station. So who knows if Home realizes that Greil Marcus has a sense of humor as well as a penetrating mind? We don't. But we do know that Home's bluffery extends to at least two levels: he will pretend to know facts that he doesn't in fact know; and he will pretend to hold opinions that he actually doesn't hold.

That's what happening when Home – apparently quite serious, again wearing his best poker face – writes in his "Introduction" that, "There are numerous parallels to be drawn between the SI and the far-Right."

> Many reactionaries not only write in a manner similar to the specto-Situationist house style [Home goes on to say], they're also drawn towards the same themes. Taken out of context, suitable censored chunks of ultra-rightist propaganda could be passed off as Debordist texts.

Home goes on to quote "a piece of writing by the notorious anti-Semite Douglas Reed" and to claim that a quotation from "the economic crank" C.H. Douglas "sounds even more trenchantly Debordist" than the quote from Reed does. But for Home, even when the writings of the situationists are taken in context, there are "parallels" that "run far deeper" and "can't be reduced to a single issue without grossly distorting our understanding of the subject."

Bluntly stated, as always, "the SI plagiarised a number of slogans that had previously been popular among Christian heretics of the Middle Ages"; "the religious ideologies from which these epigrams sprang were virulently anti-Semitic"; therefore (?!) we have "another angle from which we can look at the Situationists' relationship to the racist right." We don't have (proof of) an actual connection between the SI and the far-right, but that isn't what is needed. What is needed is "an angle," a bluff that sounds good enough to pass, some really sticky mud to be slung at Greil Marcus. "It's extraordinary that Marcus fails to mention this," Home insists, "since he cites a work – Norman Cohn's *The Pursuit of the Millennium* (revised edition, Oxford, New York, 1970) – which deals very explicitly with the anti-Semitic content of feudal heresies."

There is a point to be made here: as a matter of fact, several – but not all – of the "heretics" of the Middle Ages who inspired the situationists were in fact as openly hostile to Judaism as they were to the Catholic Church. This fact certainly merits further study. But it isn't "extraordinary" that Marcus doesn't mention it: his book is about the Sex Pistols' "Anarchy in the U.K.," not feudal heresies nor the re-appearance of these heresies in the ideas of the situationists and other twentieth century radicals. (Even if Marcus's book were about these subjects, it would certainly not reach the conclusion that the SI and/or the individual situationists were anti-Semitic, despite the pronouncements of some of their conceptual antecedents.) But Home isn't trying to make a point here: he's clearly trying to insinuate that Greil Marcus is an anti-Semite or that Marcus's book amounts to a cover-up of the SI's anti-Semitism (take your pick, they are equally ridiculous ideas).

Does Stewart Home know – what would his twisted mind make of the fact – that Greil Marcus is Jewish? We have no idea. But, as reasonably well-informed people, we do know that Poland is governed by and filled with virulently anti-Semitic people, though it has been many years since the Nazis exterminated the vast majority of the Jews who'd been living and thriving in Poland. More to the point, as Polish Jews who have traveled in Europe, we know that it is all too likely that Polish anti-Semites will have no trouble reconciling the apparent self-contradiction in Home's insinuation that Greil Marcus, who is Jewish, is either an anti-Semite or an apologist for anti-Semites. It is all too likely that they – just like our own Reverend Louis Farrakhan – will say that rich Jewish anti-Semites (such as Greil Marcus) are the worst kind of Jews, for they will sell out everyone, including their poor brethren, just as the ancient Jews once and forever sold out Our Lord and Savior Jesus Christ to the Romans. It is all too likely that, for Stewart Home (and many other "radicals"), anti-Semitism can be played like a wild card and the world at large is a gigantic game of poker in which the stakes are incalculable.

It is quite certain that Home is aware of the risks he is taking – or, rather, the risks to which he's exposing the reputation of the SI and the person of Greil Marcus – by "playing the anti-Semitism card" in a book to be published in Poland. For as soon as he's done with Marcus's presumably suspicious "failure" to reiterate Norman Cohn's examination of the anti-Semitic tendencies of the feudal heresies, Home decides that this is the appropriate time "to return again to the technique of free association." As if his cynically intentional misuse of the technique of ironic juxtaposition were capable of nothing more than producing a few "interesting results," Home goes on to "freely" associate the situationists with such murky goings-on as Masonic lodges, the "Illuminati," esoteric traditions, shamanism, mysticism, occultism, secret societies and – in the passage that really nails it down – strong interest in "ancient cultures, the Egyptian, the Sumerian, the Central American and Jewish cultures, cultures that left traces in our memories, from magic to religion to fanaticism." (Home attributes this passage to Ettore Sottsass, Jr., "who was an integral part of the milieu that formed itself into the Situationist International" and whose "attitudes are typical of those who belonged to the SI.") Once again, the apparent self-contradiction in the claim that the anti-Semites in the Situationist International were strongly interested in and respected ancient Judaism can all too easily be papered over with the tautological prejudices that 1) occultists of any type – be they anti-Semitic occultists or Judaic occultists – keep secrets and are, therefore, probably up to no damned good, and/or 2). the worst Jews are the ones who either pretend to be anti-Semites when they are really super-secret Jewish conspirators or pretend to be Jews when they are really the children of the Beast or Satan.

We call upon Stewart Home to clarify his positions on the insinuated anti-Semitism of both Greil Marcus and the Situationist International. Furthermore, we call upon him to unequivocally denounce anti-Semitism itself, so that both the people of Poland and the people of the English-speaking world will have no cause to continue to doubt his honesty, integrity and good faith.

NOT BORED! #25, June 1996

On-line notice dated 21 September 1997: this "Open Letter to Stewart Home" has been translated into Spanish.

On-line notice dated 15 November 1997: Stewart Home's official response to our "Open Letter to Stewart Home" is "To Make Shame More Shameful Still: Will Bill Brown Come Clean About Playing the Race Card?" Dated 9 July 1996, this official response alleges that Bill Brown is "probably" the author of the "anonymous" tract entitled "Manufacturing Dissent: Stewart Home, Bill Brown and Larry O'Hara United in Phony Feuds Designed to Stifle Much Needed Critical Debate," when in fact he is not: *Stewart Home is*. Home is in fact the author of both "To Make Shame" *and* "Manufacturing Dissent." These facts go a long way toward confirming the complete accuracy of the insights and criticisms contained in the "Open Letter to Stewart Home," which the author stands by, unequivocally.

Internecine polemics
Dead Man Talking:
Bill Brown responds to Bob Black

It is quite fitting that Bob Black should write of the voiceless dead in "Brownian Motion," his review of my review of Len Bracken's lifeless book *Guy Debord: Revolutionary*. "It is just not possible at this late date," Black explains to the brain-dead idiots of the world, "to interview Washington, Lincoln, Marx, Bakunin, or Janis Joplin." Black should know: he himself has been a proverbial DEAD DUCK since 21 February 1996, when he sent a letter to the Narcotics Division of the Seattle Police Department about the personal habits of author and publisher Jim Hogshire, with whom Black had had an argument. This deadly letter (widely distributed since then) and its unapologetic author have been unequivocally condemned by almost everyone in the anarchist milieu and on the ultraleft – except for the poor schmucks at CAL Press, though they learned their lesson soon after they foolishly agreed to work with Black and publish his attack on Murray Bookchin, which is entitled *Anarchism After Leftism*. And yet Bob Black's corpse continues to stagger on, to show its awful face, to put its voiceless words into published texts about events in the world of the living.

Black's "critique" of me – one "Critic" critiques another – is literally full of ghosts, spirits that continue to haunt him, sometimes years after their putative passing. There is Bookchin, of course, who just wouldn't stay dead after Black's book came out. Ken Knabb and Michel Prigent – another wooden stake in the heart should *finally* fix the both of them! And poor Baboon Dooley – no one knows who *he* is anymore, but Black clearly cannot restrain himself from shooting the mortally wounded just one more time.

As for me, I am someone who – in the lifeless eyes of Bob Black – was dead and buried way back in the mid-1980s, when Black filled up the pages of Rev. Crowbar's *Popular Reality* with my obituary. (I had dared to question Black's glib dismissal of "feminism as fascism," and had dared to object to the degree of hostility with which Black was then attacking *Processed World*; and so Black judged me to be deserving of the ultimate penalty.) But I was neither mortally wounded by Black's attacks, nor was I inclined to give up the ghost voluntarily. I still live, and have as little fear of criticizing Debord as I have of Big Bad Bob Black coming after me, again, after all these years. (And Black says that *he* wants the evil Critics of the world to "fear" that "anyone of them . . . might be next"! Har de har har.)

The person who really seems *scared stiff* here is Bob Black. Read what he says in the heart of his article, that is, in the paragraph in which I have emphasized Black's obsessive use of the terminology of the criminal justice system (interviewees are "informants" and information is "evidence").

Internecine polemics

Bracken (complains Brown), unlike Brown's idol Greil Marcus, neglected to interview such crucial **informants** as Henri Lefebvre, Alexander Trocchi, and Gil Wolman. A sentence later, Brown hints at a possible explanation: Like Debord, these guys are now dead. This is a difficulty experienced by many biographers. It is just not possible at this late date to interview Washington, Lincoln, Marx, Bakunin, or Janis Joplin. Brown has this addled idea that the oral interview is a privileged historical source. Historians are now making a lot of use of oral history – the only way they can, like the social scientists, they *generate* **evidence**, not just find it – but they also appreciate its limitations. Oral **informants** may be forgetful, their memories may be influenced by later experiences, and they may be lying. When historians crosscheck oral history with written records, they find that oral histories are very uneven in their reliability. Not only do (often elderly) **informants** forget things that did not happen, they sometimes remember things that didn't happen, but that they heard about later. History is yet another of the practices that Brown doesn't know how to do.

When Black – *who has a law degree* – writes of "the published evidence of Guy Debord's career," it appears as if he has Debord's "career" as a criminal – the image of Guy Debord as a "career criminal" – in mind. But Black's tone is dispirited, full of despair; he hardly sounds like a confident prosecuting attorney. Indeed, he sounds like a man pleading his own case in front of a jury that he knows will convict him and sentence him to death. "Oral informants" *such as Jim Hogshire and his wife* "may be forgetful, their memories may be influenced by later memories, and they may be lying." But they might also be telling the truth. In this case, it seems quite clear that the Hogshire's oral testimony is quite accurate, and that Bob Black is both a police informant and a liar.

Just as the cultural world simply cannot be divided into Performers, Fans and Critics (as Black wishes to do), a person such as myself cannot be pigeonholed as a Critic and dismissed generically. While it is true that I am a writer of cultural criticism, I am also a performer, a creator of culture: I have created paintings, photographs, zines, websites, postcards, films, and musical recordings (I can play bass, guitar and drums). But, most importantly, to the police I am a writer of graffiti, NOT AN INFORMANT, and have been one since the Ann Arbor days, as even Officer Black must admit.

NOT BORED! #29, July 1998

Internecine polemics
An Unkind Reply to RETORT

It says here, at the end of the first footnote to an essay entitled "Afflicted Powers: The State, the Spectacle and September 11" and reprinted in the May/June 2004 issue of *New Left Review*,[1] that RETORT "is a gathering of council communists and affiliated nay-sayers, based for the past two decades in the San Francisco Bay Area." In a tell-tale use of the passive voice, this footnote goes on to say: "Involved in the writing of the present essay were Iain Boal, T. J. Clark, Joseph Matthews and Michael Watts."

Yes, dear reader, T. J. Clark: the author of that horrible book *Farewell to an Idea*, which we had such a good time demolishing several years back. As you might recall from that rather long essay, we castigated Professor Clark for adamantly refusing to discuss his subjects (modern art and socialism) in terms of the situationist concept of spectacle, preferring instead to call upon such *boring old farts* as Sigmund Freud, Paul de Man and Noam Chomsky. And yet, here is Clark, signing his name to an essay that goes on and on about Guy Debord and the Situationist International. Since Clark was once a situationist, one must take seriously – or at least give a fair hearing to – his "dissent" from the "totalizing closure" of the concept of spectacle. Or such is the underlying assumption of "Afflicted Powers."

But this assumption is completely unwarranted. In point of fact, "Afflicted Powers" is – to seize and re-direct the accusations RETORT makes about the manner in which the Bush Administration has conducted its war against Iraq[2] – dominated by blunders, gullibility, over-reach, unfathomable ignorance and wishful thinking about literally everything it attempts to shed light on. Clark and his mates can't even say an intelligent thing about pop music![3]

Blunders and Ignorance

"We start from the premise," RETORT says, "that certain concepts and descriptions put forward forty years ago by Guy Debord and the Situationist International, as part of their effort to comprehend the new forms of state control and social disintegration, still possess explanatory power – more so than ever, we suspect, in the poisonous epoch we are living through." This is a valid premise, *provided*, of course, that one actually understands and accurately summarizes those concepts. But RETORT fails to do either one of these things.

Over the course of their essay, the members of RETORT rack up a staggering array of errors. The group refers to the situationists' "hypotheses," but the Situationist International (SI) positioned their ideas as *theories,* that is, as hypotheses that had been tested and found to be valid. RETORT claims that the "original objects" of the theory of the spectacle "were the Watts Riots and the

Proletarian Cultural Revolution," but Debord said that "the modern spectacle" was invented by *Nazi Germany* and *Stalinist Russia.* RETORT claims that "spectacle" names "the submission of more and more facets of human sociability [...] to the deadly solicitations (the lifeless bright sameness) of the market" and that the situationists "were interested in the means modern societies have at their disposal to systematize and disseminate *appearances,* and to subject the texture of day-to-day living to a constant barrage of images, instructions, slogans, logos, false promises, virtual realities, [and] miniature happiness-motifs," but, for the SI, "spectacle" named *the bureaucratic state in both the "capitalist" West and the "Communist" East* and found its ultimate expression not in "appearances" but *the organization of space.*

But the worst mistakes RETORT makes are to reduce the SI to Guy Debord, to focus on what Debord wrote in the 1960s (in particular, his 1967 book *The Society of the Spectacle*), and to ignore virtually everything he wrote in the 1970s and 1980s.[4] "The version of 'spectacle' with which we operate," RETORT says,

> is minimal, pragmatic, matter of fact. No doubt the idea's original author often gave it an exultant, world-historical force. But his tone is inimitable, as all efforts to duplicate it have proved; and in any case we are convinced that the age demands a different cadence – something closer (if we are lucky) to that of the lines from *Paradise Lost* we use as our pamphlet's epigraph [and title] than anything from Lukacs or Ducasse.

But Guy Debord – who *did not* "author" the "idea" of spectacle, but "detourned" (diverted) the way this concept was used in the critical theories of Georg Lukacs, Georges Bataille, Roland Barthes and many others – *does not* designate a tone of voice or cadence. And, as we will attempt to show, "the age" *doesn't* demand "something" different; instead, our poisonous epoch would be quite well-served by Debord if it managed to actually understand what he meant.

Not surprisingly, RETORT's "version" of spectacle is flat-out wrong. Instead of being a dialectical exposition, it is a chronological narrative.

> Debord, to speak of him directly, was concerned most of all with the way the subjection of social life to the rule of appearances had led, in turn, to a distinct form of politics – of state formation and surveillance [...] We extract the following propositions from his pages. First, that slowly but surely the state in the twentieth century had been dragged into a full collaboration in the micro-management of everyday life. The market's necessity became the state's obsession. (Slowly, and in a sense against the state's better judgment, because always there existed a tension between the modern state's armoured other-directedness – its *raison d'etre* as a war machine – and capital's insistence that the

state come to its aid in the great work of internal policing and packaging [...]) This world of images had long been a structural necessity of a capitalism oriented toward the overproduction of commodities, and therefore the constant manufacture of desire for them; but by the late twentieth century it had given rise to a specific polity. The modern state [...] has adjusted to its economic master's requirement for a thinned, unobstructed social texture, made up of loosely attached consumer subjects [...]

Alas, poor State, it has been led astray – and, what's more, against its better judgment (!) – by what RETORT elsewhere calls the "shady corporate world." And so, despite its announced impatience with "classical Marxist terms, proudly unreconstructed," RETORT presents and assumes its readers will accept the vulgar Marxist notion that the "superstructure" (the State) follows what goes on in the "substructure" (the economy). But Guy Debord never had any truck with this simplistic nonsense. As much an anarchist as a Marxist, he knew that the State – long before there was such a thing as a globalized capitalist market – had been deeply involved in surveillance, internal policing, spatial deconcentration and the "micro-management" of everyday life.[5]

Gullibility, Over-Reach and Wishful Thinking

According to RETORT, the events of September 11 weren't a confirmation of the theory of the spectacle, but a demonstration of its limits. After quoting a few lines from Debord,[6] the group says,

Too many times over the past twelve months[7] these sentences, in their anger and sorrow at the present form of politics, have echoed in our minds. But ultimately we dissent from their totalizing closure. Living after September 11, we are no longer sure – and we do not believe that spectacular power is sure – that [Debord was correct when he asserted that] "there is no danger of riposte [to the spectacle], in its own space or any other." For better or worse, the precision bombings were such a riposte. And their effect on the spectacular state has been profound: the state's reply to them, we are certain, has exceeded in its crassness and futility the martyr-pilots' wildest dreams.

Note well RETORT's insistence on what's happened *since* September 11. Situationist concepts "strike us as having purchase on key aspects of what happened since September 11, 2001," they write. RETORT asks, "Are we to understand the forms of assertion of American power since September 11 [...] as a step backwards, *a historical regression* [...] to a new/old era of gunboats and book-burning?" and "How, politically and strategically, has the US state responded to [September 11]?" To RETORT, September 11 was a "defeat" suffered by the American state, and the group states that "The spectacular state is obliged, we are saying, to devise an *answer* to the defeat of September 11."

RETORT never seems to imagine – let alone think through any of the implications of the possibility – that the attacks of September 11 weren't perpetrated by "organized enemies of the US Empire," but by the US Empire itself. Apparently believing everything that the spectacle has told them about the attacks, the members of RETORT go on and on about "Islamism," "the new terrorists," the "new breed of bombers," "regimes hostile to the new world order," and the "failed states" (presumably Saudi Arabia and Afghanistan) "from which the personnel and ideology of September 11 so unmistakably arose." For RETORT, it is "common knowledge" that the events of September 11 "were trained for in Jalalabad, [and] paid for in Riyadh."

RETORT's confidence in the truth of what the spectacle has told them is so complete that its members believe that they can tell what the "new terrorists" were thinking. Veritable mindreaders – despite the thousands of miles that separate their native Berkeley from Osama bin Laden's training camps – they write:

> 'You know our demands,' said the martyr-pilots (strictly to themselves). 'And we know you cannot accede to them. We know what you will do instead. We are certain your answer will be military. We anticipate your idiot leader blurting out the word crusade. What you will do will vindicate our analysis point by point, humiliation by humiliation, and confirm the world of Islamism in its despairing strength. And you will do it because there is no answer to our image-victory, yet you (because humiliation is something in which you have no schooling) have to pretend there is one.'

A few pages later, RETORT says:

> The perpetrators knew full well that they lacked the means to spread out through the wider social fabric and bring ordinary doings to a halt. And they believed, rightly or wrongly, that in present circumstances they did not need to. What they did was designed to hold us indoors, to make us turn back and back to a moving image of capitalism screaming and exploding, to make us go on listening (in spite of ourselves) to the odious talking heads [on television] to put something, anything, in place of desolation.

This is precisely the point where RETORT's complete and total ignorance of the real value of situationist theory comes back to haunt them.[8] Had they read Gianfranco Sanguinetti's *On Terrorism and the State*,[9] or Debord's 21 April

1978 letter to Sanguinetti concerning the kidnapping of Aldo Moro, or Debord's *Preface to the 4th Italian Edition of "The Society of the Spectacle"* or even his *Considerations on the Assassination of Gerard Lebovici*, the members of RETORT would have focused on what happened *on September 11,* not during its aftermath.[10]

RETORT never thinks about what preceded the attacks (the creation, training and arming of Al Qaeda by the CIA; the surprising strength and vehemence that the "anti-globalization" movement showed in Seattle and Genoa; and the theft of the 2000 US Presidential election), never tries to get inside the heads of those who are in charge of NATO, the Pentagon or the CIA,[11] never asks the classic question, "Who benefited?" Instead, RETORT occupies itself with the "singularity" of "the present madness,"[12] as if what happened at the Reichstag, or at the Bologna train station, could never happen here. But it can; indeed, it already has.

[1] As recently as 1997, T. J. Clark and another ex-situationist, Donald Nicholson-Smith, attacked *New Left Review* for totally ignoring, and then falsifying, the contributions of the Situationist International to modern revolutionary theory.
[2] RETORT says of Bush's war against Iraq:
> We too take seriously the idea that factions within the US administration had long thought the impasse of 'sanctions' intolerable, had thirsted for oil, had dreamt of a new bridgehead in an increasingly anti-American region, and so on. But at the very least it can only be said that the manner in which these policies were finally acted upon – they had been pipedreams of the ultra-Right in Washington for more than a decade – has been a barely credible mixture of blunder, gullibility, over-reach, lip-smacking callousness (hardly bothering to disguise its lack of concern at the 'stuff happening' in the streets of Kandahar or Baghdad), unfathomable ignorance and wishful thinking, and constant entrapment in the day-to-day, hour-by-hour temporality of the sound bite and the suicide bomb.

Though the members of RETORT take "seriously" the idea that there were impatient "factions" within the US administration, they don't take seriously enough the idea that some of these factions might have conspired with, "tele-guided" or simulated Al Qaeda's operations.
[3] According to RETORT,
> The silence of so-called 'popular culture' in the face of September 11 has been deafening. (It is as if the commercial music of America in the mid-twentieth century had nothing to say about war, or race, or the Depression, or the new world of goods and appliances. It had plenty – partly because the adjective 'popular' still pointed to something real about its audiences and raw materials. That was long ago, of course:

the present total obedience of the culture industry to the protocols of the war on terror – its immediate ingestion and reproduction of the state's interdicts and paranoias – is proof positive, if any were needed, of the snuffing out of the last traces of insubordination in the studios of TimeWarner.)

Obviously the members of RETORT have never heard – or have never heard of – Bruce Springsteen's famous album *The Rising,* which was released in July 2002.

[4] It is true that the members of RETORT quote (in re-ordered fashion) a few sentences concerning "the media" from Debord's 1988 book, *Comments on the Society of the Spectacle,* but they ignore the fact that its author was at pains to point out that,

> Rather than talk of the spectacle, people often prefer to use the term 'media.' And by this they mean to describe a mere instrument, a kind of public service which with impartial 'professionalism' would facilitate the new wealth of mass communication through mass media – a form of communication which has at last attained a unilateral purity, whereby decisions already taken are presented for passive admiration. For what is communicated are *orders*; and with perfect harmony, those who give them are also those who tell us what they think of them. Spectacular power, which is so fundamentally unitary, so concentrated by the very weight of things, and entirely despotic in spirit, frequently rails at the appearance in its realm of a spectacular politics, a spectacular justice, a spectacular medicine and all the other similarly surprising examples of 'media excess.' Thus the spectacle would be merely the excesses of the media, whose nature, unquestionably good since it facilitates communication, is sometimes driven to extremes.

RETORT doesn't seem to realize that Debord's *Comments on the Society of the Spectacle* – like his *Preface to the 4th Italian Edition of "The Society of the Spectacle"* (1979) and his *Considerations on the Assassination of Gerard Lebovici* (1985) – are about *the State* and, to be more exact, its use of *terrorism* as a method of government.

[5] See the following passage from Debord's *Comments on the Society of the Spectacle*: "In *The Eighteenth Brumaire of Louis Bonaparte,* Marx described the state's encroachment upon Second Empire France, then blessed with half a million bureaucrats: '[Everything was] made a subject for governmental activity, whether it was a bridge, a schoolhouse, the communal property of a village community, or the railways, the national wealth and the national universities of France.'"

[6] See footnote [4].

[7] It would appear that the body of "Afflicted Powers" was written in September or October 2002, and that footnotes were added as late as March 2004.

[8] As Debord writes in *Comments on the Society of the Spectacle*: "We should expect, as a logical possibility, that the state's security services intend to use all the

advantages they find in the realm of the spectacle, which has indeed been organized with that in mind for some considerable time: on the contrary, *it is the difficulty of perceiving this that is astonishing, and rings false*" (emphasis added).

[9] There is a strange echo of the convoluted beginning of Sanguinetti's *On Terrorism* in RETORT's ridiculous pronouncement that "Terror as a political instrument [...] the property of the state (maybe the founding property of the state in its 'modern' manifestation), or of those thinking like a state." In his 23 February 1981 letter to Jaap Kloosterman, Debord denounces the "insolence" of Sanguinetti's attempt to "reduce to a ridiculous schemata [...] the historical and strategic question of armed struggle in general and the particular case of all terrorism as it has existed in many diverse forms throughout history."

[10] Note well that RETORT wants to keep "September 11" nice and simple: "The terror of September 11 had a handful of targets (our tendency to make it, in memory, simply 'the bombing of the Twin Towers' is not untrue to the logic of the event)." But what is "not untrue" in one "logic" is *totally false* in another. At least two of the events that also took place on that day – the explosion at the Pentagon and the collapse of World Trade Center building #7, *which wasn't attacked by the "martyr-pilots"* – are highly suspicious and suggestive of the perpetration of an "inside job."

[11] Once again, we counter RETORT with Debord's *Comments*: "But actually all established powers, despite certain genuine local rivalries, and without ever wanting to spell it out, never forgot what one of the rare German internationalists after the outbreak of the First World War managed to recall (on the side of subversion and without any great immediate success): 'The main enemy is within'."

[12] "It matters profoundly," RETORT says, "that the horrors of September 11 were designed to be visible, and that this visibility marked the bombings off from most previous campaigns of air terror, especially those sponsored by states. There were no cameras at Dresden, Hamburg, Hiroshima. The horror there had to be unseen." Quite true, but *there were plenty of cameras present when Jack Ruby shot and killed Lee Harvey Oswald.*

NOT BORED! #36, July 2004

Another Unkind Reply to RETORT

It comes labeled as "An Exchange on *Afflicted Powers: Capital and Spectacle in a New Age of War,*"[1] but in no way is it an exchange; it is more like a series of juxtaposed rhetorical flourishes. The questions ("posed by Hal Foster before the first bombings in London," that is, before 7 July 2005) are separated in both time and space from the so-called responses ("delivered by Retort in the midst of the first flooding of New Orleans," that is, on or after 29 August 2005). It is clear from these sparse explanatory notes, which were provided by *October,* and from the movement or flow of the "exchange" itself, that it was conducted by email, but without the rapid-fire back-and-forth of typical emailed exchanges, not to mention instant messaging. Hal Foster and RETORT might well have simply sent each other letters.

Both parties are responsible for the ensuing disaster. Hal Foster can't seem to ask a direct question; instead, he relies on a series of small, indirect or "leading" questions, some of which lead nowhere. He doesn't seem to have done his homework, and might even have forgotten things that he knew when he wrote *Recodings.*[2] When Foster asks, "What are the possibilities of Situationist responses to this situation?" – that is to say, the fact that "today radical invention, and not only reckless power, is most [sic] in the hands of the Right, both here and abroad" – it is clear that he has no idea that *at least three different authors* have gone beyond contemplating "possibilities" and have actually made "Situationist responses" to September 11th, and did so in the immediate aftermath of the event(s), not several months or several years later. Worse still, Foster unironically refers to situationist theory as "situationism," despite everything that has ever been said on the subject of its non-existence or its status as a tool of the situationists' enemies. But, then again, two out of the three writers published in this particular issue of *October* (half-devoted to Guy Debord) unironically refer to and comment about the existence of a "Situationism"![3]

Foster isn't totally clueless; at some level, he *gets it.* After reminding RETORT that it called September 11th "a spectacular defeat," despite the fact that September 11th "has served as the cover for both the military neoliberalism prosecuted abroad and for the political neoliberalism pursued at home" and has resulted in "an awesome burgeoning of powers," Foster asks, "with defeats like these, some in D.C. [District of Columbia] backrooms might chuckle, who needs victories?" Despite his disorganization, Foster clearly sees the obvious emptiness of RETORT's claims that the September 11th terrorists, thinking spectacularly, launched a successful attack against the spectacle; and that, as a result, the society of the spectacle was changed, the *theory* of the society of the spectacle needs to be changed, and RETORT's book is a good orientation for such a debate, such an "exchange" of ideas, "on the Left." One wants Foster to come right out and say, "No, you blatant apologists for the everything-changed-on-September-11th ideology promulgated by the Bush Administration, September 11th was a clear *victory* for spectacular power, for 'the spectacle,' and for the military/industrial/entertainment complex whose representatives meet in D.C. backrooms." One wants Foster to press the point: all this would have been *obvious* to Debord, if he had been asked about it between, say, 1969 and 1980, when spectacular terrorism was clearly being used by the Italian State (among others) to extinguish proletarian subversion. As we have already pointed out,[4] there is no need for a "new" or "changed" theory of the society of the spectacle: Debord's would suit us well enough, if we were properly informed of it and knew how to read what it says.[5]

But the primary responsibility for the disastrous "exchange" with *October* belongs to RETORT. Despite the group's announced intention to develop a "non-rejectionist" critique of modernity, RETORT refuses to refer to Hal Foster by name, instead calling him *"October,"* as if he *represents something,* something beyond or larger than himself, something ideological, like "Octoberism" (he is in fact one of the journal's editors). As a result, RETORT doesn't so much respond to the questions it is asked as respond to "the overall drift of *October*'s questions," which RETORT manages to discern after only two of them. This tactic allows RETORT to hold itself above everyone else or, at the very least, above the "Octoberists"; the "mice" who gnaw upon what RETORT in its haughty superiority labels (but does not describe or explain the details of) "a Conspiracy Hillbilly version" of the idea that September 11th was a victory for spectacular power;[6] and "the actually existing art world of the [American] Empire."[7] Needless to say, RETORT has never deigned to respond to (or even acknowledge the existence of) our "Unkind Reply," even though it was sent copies by both email and ground mail.

But this is not why we felt it necessary to respond to RETORT's "exchange" with *October*. We again reply unkindly to RETORT because of the group's continued inability to understand just what the fuck Guy Debord was on about when he wrote about "the spectacle," and because mainstream ("spectacular") publications have begun to buy into and repeat RETORT's illogical horseshit that September 11th "put [the] spectacle in doubt." It is *absolutely appalling* to read that, prior to the publication of RETORT's book, "the concept of spectacle needed to be desacralized. It needed to be applied, locally and conjuncturally – to dirty its hands with the details of politics," especially because one of the members of RETORT is T.J. Clark, who – just a few years ago – went to great pains to show that Guy Debord was a very "social animal"[8] and that Debord and the rest of the Situationist International were political animals, not uninvolved theoreticians.[9]

RETORT's worst bit of disinformation concerning Debord's theory is the idea that "the spectacle" and "the State" are two different forms of social control, whereas every reader of *The Society of the Spectacle* knows that "the spectacle" is what the modern State became during its post-Depression (1939) fusion with the capitalist economy. Thus, it is *meaningless* to refer to "the state's entrapment in the [spectacular] logic of image-control," or to imagine that "the trouble with the spectacle, from the state's point of view, is that its monadology of consumption constantly dissolves (even paranoid) distinctions and puts Don't Know in their place."[10] But the writers from RETORT do, and people praise them for it, and we think we know why. Scared by the possibly paranoid idea that Guy Debord (and Henri Lefebvre and Walter Benjamin and Theodor Adorno) were actually Right-wing in their respective critiques of the spectacle of "modernity,"[11]

RETORT seeks to protect itself by becoming less radical than Debord *et al* in its critique of the State. Despite identifying itself as "Council Communist," as "a gathering of [...] antagonists of the present order of things," RETORT never speaks of political revolution. For RETORT, the State need not be destroyed: it simply needs to free itself from the illogic of the spectacle. This margin allows the various members of RETORT to remain rooted in traditional politics: reinvigorating and strengthening "the Left" and the antiwar movement;[12] god knows what else (election to the Berkeley City Council?). To detourn Raoul Vaneigem: those such as RETORT, who talk of everyday life without mentioning revolution, have a corpse in their mouths.

[1] *October* 115, Winter 2006, pp. 3-12. RETORT's *Afflicted Powers: Capital and Spectacle in a New Age of War* was published by Verso in the summer of 2005.
[2] *Recodings: Art, Spectacle, Cultural Politics* (1985).
[3] In "Terres Inconnues," Anthony Vidler studies the influence of the 17th century *Carte de Tendre* and the aerial photography of Chombart de Lauwe (circa 1950) on the ideas and illustrations in *Internationale Situationniste,* but completely misses the importance of the *continuous illumination* of the earth's surface by military devices (night-vision goggles, searchlights, helicopters, warplanes, satellites, et al), even though he himself quotes relevant material. For example: "Le Corbusier had noted thirty years before [that] 'the bird can be dove or hawk. It became a hawk. What an unexpected gift to be able to set off *at night under the cover of darkness* and away to sow death with bombs upon sleeping towns'" (emphasis added). See instead Paul Virilio, *Cinema and War* (1989).

In "The Lessons of Guy Debord," Vincent Kaufmann tries to fashion or reinforce the image of Debord as "unilateral," "a principle of perfect autonomy, a principle of noncommunication and nonexchange," but is forced to admit *in a footnote* that "The Situationist group and more precisely the way Debord was leading it has often been described as Stalinist because of the many exclusions that occurred in its history. However, with the ongoing publication of Debord's correspondence, it becomes obvious that these exclusions had little to do with Stalinism." Indeed. And with the on-going translation of Debord's correspondence into English, one can expect an increasingly violent rejection of the ridiculous half-truths, falsehoods and outright lies told about Debord over the years by people such as Stewart Home, Len Bracken, Andrew Hussey, et al.

And, in "Guy Debord, or the Revolutionary without a Halo," Tom McDonough – about whom we've written once before, in 1997 – tries to discern "a break in Debord's work, which might be dated to the end of the 1970s, and which was marked by the deployment and consolidation of a normative – if not archaic – conception of selfhood." But such a project is doubly misguided: either one might argue (following, say, Vincent Kaufmann) that Debord's whole life was dominated by "interruption," that is to say, by a *series of breaks,* and/or one might argue that Debord first deployed and consolidated a "normative/archaic conception of

selfhood" around 1961, when he stopped calling himself Guy-Ernest Debord and started using only his voice on the soundtracks of his films; or in 1972, when Debord authored the auto-dissolution of the Situationist International, etc, etc.
[4] See "An unkind reply to RETORT" (June 2004).
[5] We do not at all mean to imply that, like sacred texts, Debord's/Sanguinetti's theories from the 1970s and 1980s can only be understood by adepts, disciples or other mystics. It is simply a matter of the availability of good translations. Preferring a work published in 1967 to one published in 1988, RETORT never accounts for Debord's *Comments on the Society of the Spectacle*. Even if RETORT did so, the best-known English translation of it is *terrible* and needed to be re-done from scratch by another translator.
[6] It appears clear that the "mice" are those who go further than timid Hal Foster and actually believe that, in addition to benefiting immensely from September 11th, the Bush Administration (the current face of the military/industrial/entertainment complex) actually perpetrated some or all of that day's events. For an account of RETORT's arrogant refusal to engage in a non-rejectionist "exchange" with these so-called conspiracy theorists, visit the on-line archives of the Portland Indymedia Center.
[7] The very last line of this text is actually an avowal of RETORT's arrogant refusal to engage in a discussion with or critique of the art world: "We shall refrain from putting alongside Mohammad Sidique Khan's last testament a brief listing of the themes and styles of this week's gallery offerings in New York and Los Angeles, or a sample of the 'ethical stances' of their reviewers."
[8] See his "Foreword" to Anselm Jappe's *Guy Debord*: "For no one was better [than Guy Debord], over the whole stretches of his life, at making himself enough of a community for the purposes of the moment; and if that community had nothing to do with the 'political' culture of Sartre, Garaudy, and de Gaulle, then so much the better. Writing was one social activity among others. The room on the Rue Saint-Jacques where *The Society of the Spectacle* got written was at once an austere cell – with nothing on the shelves, I remember, but a few crucial texts (Hegel, Pascal, Marx, Lukacs, Lautremont's *Poesies*) laid open at the relevant page – and also the entryway to Debord's miniscule apartment, through which friends and comrades continually passed. The process was meant to be seen, and interrupted. One moment the deep, ventriloqual dialogue with *History and Class Consciousness*; the next the latest bubble for a *comics detourne,* or the best insult yet to Althusser and Godard."
[9] See "Why Art Can't Kill the Situationist International," co-written with Donald Nicholson-Smith: "All the same, what we find nauseating in the received account is the implication that concern for problems of internal organization – above all a determination to find a way out of the legacy of 'democratic centralism' – is more token of these art-politicians' lack of seriousness. Anyone who actually reads what the SI wrote in 1966 and 1967 will quickly realize that it could not have issued from a group of people walled into their own factional struggles. There were such

struggles. They were thought (sometimes rightly, sometimes wrongly, in our view) to be the necessary condition of the kind of revolutionary clarity that informs the best of Situationist writing. But the Situationists never got stuck in their own turmoil, and they went on thinking, especially as things heated up in the course of 1967, about how they were to act – to 'expand' – if the capitalist State offered them an opportunity. Here, for instance, are extracts from a working document entitled 'Response aux camarades de Rennes – sur l'organization et l'autonomie.' Signed by Debord, Khayati, and Vienet, and dated 16 July 1967, this text came out of a series of discussions (and joint actions) with other small groups on the Left [...] We cite the 'Response aux camarades de Rennes' because its contents contradict the current travesty-history of the SI during this period, and not least that travesty-history's favorite *political* claim – that the Situationists were simply 'council communists' whose only answer to the practical questions of revolutionary politics was to hypostatize past experiments with workers' councils as a way of solving all problems of organization in advance."

[10] Let the reader be assured that we, too, have no idea of what is meant by this remark, which receives no further comment or explanation from RETORT.

[11] According to RETORT, "to the extent that the Left tradition inevitably did include moments when the modern condition was thought about as a whole – as of course was true of Benjamin and Adorno or, for that matter, Debord and Lefebvre – what resulted most often, it seems now in retrospect, were Right-wing motifs repeated in an ultra-Left register [...]. Modernity, says Benjamin somewhere in the *Arcades Project,* is 'the time of Hell.' The language, again, is that of the Right. It is a line from *The Pisan Cantos.* We could imagine it nowadays issuing straight from Al-Zawahiri's mouth." But RETORT refuses to acknowledge the possibilities that, in evoking Hell, Benjamin was speaking metaphorically or was *detourning* that line from *The Pisan Cantos*; that Benjamin (a Jew), Adorno (a Protestant), Al-Zawahari (a Muslim) and Debord (a former Catholic) might not have the same concept in mind when they each evoke "Hell"; or that – *whatever* the political orientations of these four men or the desire we might experience to "kill the messenger" of bad news – modernity might in fact be the time of Hell. See Debord's evocations of the Devil in his 1978 film *In girum imus nocte et consumimur igni.*

[12] Clark and Nicholson-Smith, "Why Art Can't Kill the Situationist International": "It was the Left (as opposed to, say, the art world) that the Situationists most hated in the 1960s and thought worth targeting. Whether the Left is still worth targeting we are not sure. We have tried several times to write a conclusion to these pages that did so, and have come up hard against the emptiness of the present. As usual, Debord is the best guide to this state of affairs."

NOT BORED! #38, October 2006

Internecine polemics

An Exposé of the Abuse Perpetrated by Bob Black, Written by One of his Victims

One of the worst things about abuse (physical, emotional or verbal) is that the victim can rarely be counted on to come forward, identify his or her attacker, and describe what he or she was forced to endure. The victim was originally chosen because of perceived weakness. There is shame in realizing this, as there is shame in the very fact of being abused. There are fears about being abused again. And so, many victims of abuse find it easier to suffer their abuse in silence. Unfortunately, many abusive people are aware of this all-too-human tendency, and take advantage of it. Not only do they remain unpunished; they become brazen. They know that their crimes won't be reported to the precise extent that these crimes are shameful; victims of shameful crimes are ashamed to come forward; thus their victimizers feel comfortable with attacking them again and again, for many years in some cases.

But I will not be silent any more. For several years now, I've been receiving word from people around the country that Bob Black has been barraging them with vicious, hateful lies about me. I've had enough of this self-appointed judge, this cowardly COINTELPRO-wannabe, and I'm denouncing him publicly for his latest unprovoked, scurrilous attack. On 22 November 2008, just two days after the opening of an exhibition of my work at a gallery at the University of Cincinnati, Black looked up some names on the university's Web page and sent them emails that began, "I write to report the background of bill Brown, who has an exhibit at the Reed Gallery." By way of attachments, these emails include "a chronicle of his movements," which "place[s] at your disposal everything I have on Brown."

Is Black trying to write like a police detective or is he trying to be confused with a police detective? He identifies himself as a lawyer, but his reason for writing has nothing to do with the law. He writes, "He [Brown] has often publicly insulted and libelled [sic] me in his fanzine 'Not Bored!' – the zine you are exhibiting, and quite possibly one of these libels is on display, which, technically, renders you liable as its 'publisher' as this term is used in defamation law. I have no intention, of course, of proceeding in that fashion." Absent this intention, there is no reason for Black to continue to write, indeed to write anything at all, to the people at the University of Cincinnati. As he himself has shown, if he continues to write, it is only because he is interested in *perpetrating libel,* not stopping it.

There is a sickening irony in Black lecturing strangers (people he's never met) about the very thing he is doing, elsewhere in his emails: namely, deliberately defaming someone's character, in this case, mine. Of course, the fact that Black's emails had no "publisher" (other than his ISP, which has Terms of Service that precisely forbid this kind of abuse of their services) doesn't mean that his letter isn't an instance of defamation. Furthermore, it is chilling that Black is perfectly aware of the precarious position that he has placed many publishers (real and virtual) over the years: *Anarchy Magazine,* for example, which several years ago published a letter to the editor from Black that contained obvious lies and libels about me. Of course, I threatened to sue unless a retraction was printed.[1] That's what honorable people do: when confronted with dishonorable behavior, they use honorable means.

Given Black's calculated use of defamation – either defaming others or using the claim that he's been defamed to launch a campaign of defamation – it is hard to believe that publishers, especially "anarchist" ones, continue to allow themselves to be used in this fashion. Should not "anarchist" publications be interested in targeting as their "political enemies" the people who run the government and the corporations, that is, if these publications are really anarchist? But Black is no anarchist either: he simply terrorizes people he thinks are "leftists." Who could benefit from his on-going smear campaigns? Only right-wing zealots and nutjobs who hate leftists.

What does the content of Black's "chronicle" on me reveal? It is a nauseating collection of fantasies, half-truths and outright lies: the truly unpleasant thing is that Black is utterly obsessed with me, and has been tracking me for over 20 years. I'm a terrorist, a CIA agent, a fascist, a card-carrying Communist; I'm an assimilated Jew, an anti-Semite, a neo-Nazi; I'm a baby-killer, a drug addict, a moral degenerate; I'm trying to reanimate dead bodies in the basement of my mountaintop laboratory – the particular content of Black's lies do not matter. What matters is that these lies are spectacular enough to make the reader forget that *Black has no business making them up and/or spreading them.*

Though he may cast me as a mortal threat to something that he pretends to hold dear, Bob Black has never been injured, abused or libeled by anything I've said or done. He is simply using this opportunity (a bit of success on my part) to vent his pathological hatred against someone whom he calls his "self-appointed political enemy," that is to say, a target for perpetual character assassination. If *any* of the many serious charges that Black makes were true, and if Black himself were an honorable person, he wouldn't have wasted his time filling up the in-boxes of a few people at a university: he would have gone straight to the police, the FBI, the House Un-American Activities Committee and/or the Spanish Inquisition (whichever has jurisdiction in such matters). But he didn't, because none of his charges are true; his insinuations are preposterous; he knows that the "authorities" would simply laugh at him and his bungling attempts to be a freelance COINTELPRO agent if he tried to sell them his trash.

Unfortunately, I am not the only one whom Bob Black stalks and attacks at will: he has also targeted the people at *Processed World,* Jim Hogshire, Ward Churchill, Ramsey at AK Press, and no doubt many others. We know about only a fraction of the dirty tricks that this man has played over the years. Is Bob Black keeping a file on *you*? How would you know? He didn't let *me* know that he's been "chronicling" my "misadventures" for over 20 years. If he is also keeping a file on you, to whom has he sent a copy? How would you know? I only found out about this most recent incident indirectly, four days after it happened.

The important thing, of course, is the outcome. *None* of the people to whom Black sent his emails took them seriously. In fact, they suspected that their author was actually me, trying to cause a "situationist" scandal and thus promote my own show! Yes, indeed, that would have been pathetic, but not as pathetic as the simple truth: the ranting hate-filled lunatic who signs his emails "Bob Black" is a real person, not a fiction. When the recipients of Black's emails found out that their content was a matter of defamation of character, not self-promotion, they immediately reassured me that the matter was over. Case closed. The gallery would never take down an exhibition in response to complaints, and certainly not in response to the artificially generated outrage of a dossier-compiling sociopath.

The moral of the story is simple: for predators like Bob Black to succeed, they must find, not only victims, but dupes who provide them with alibis, excuses and self-justifications. In this case, Bob Black encountered not dupes, but intelligent people interested in ascertaining the truth, and so his despicable efforts at sabotage were thwarted. May he find neither victims nor dupes, wherever he goes.

[1] Note: the following is from Black's file on me. It shows Black's utter cynicism: when he commits libel, he knows exactly what he can get any with. (Please note that, despite what follows, my father practiced *civil law,* was neither rich nor powerful, and never employed me.)

> He [Brown] caught the [*Anarchy Magazine*] project at an awkward time, with longtime editor Jason McQuinn beginning to spin off more and more editorial responsibilities onto an editorial collective forming in Berkeley, California. McQuinn quite properly involved the Berkeley collectivists in the decision how to respond, but as any legal liability would still fall on him, he made the final decision. It could have been worse.
>
> I am a lawyer admitted in New York and California and I know the law of libel a lot better than Bill Brown or probably even his dad, who is a specialist in criminal law, and lawyer specialists usually know little law outside their specialty. I explained to McQuinn that, for legal and practical reasons, Brown's threat was as hollow as he is. In the first place, truth is an absolute defense. If what I wrote was true, it was not libelous. Second, Brown has incurred no monetarily provable damages, without which his hurt feelings are irrelevant, because Dad didn't fire him and Brown cannot show any other out-of-

pocket damages either.

Third, courts are hostile to libel actions and usually find ways to dismiss these cases, either on the pleadings (i.e., for failure to use the right highly technical magic words in the complaint) or by summary judgment (i.e., there is no genuine contradiction as to the important facts and on those facts the case cannot be won so why have a trial?). Fourth, such a lawsuit lays the plaintiff open to pretrial "discovery," which is the compulsory extraction of information and evidence from the other party and anybody else. Because libel is about injury to reputation, there is nothing, absolutely nothing about the life of a libel plaintiff which cannot be coerced out of said plaintiff or anybody else. Even if all this evidence did not substantiate my statement in every detail, it would certainly elicit enough evidence to nauseate any jury into ruling against Brown. And the jurors will know his home address.

Fourth, following in part from the foregoing, Brown almost certainly could not have found a New York lawyer to take the case. Even in New York City, only a handful of plaintiff-side lawyers will accept a libel case, and only on a contingent fee basis, i.e., for a proportion of the damages won, but nothing if the case is lost. Even if Brown had a slam-dunk case, the defendants are what we lawyers call "judgment-proof," they have almost no money, collecting from me is impossible, collecting from AJODA [*Anarchy: Journal of Desire Armed*] would require slow, costly, difficult, and ultimately futile efforts. Missouri and California lawyers who do collections work will want more money up front than Brown has, which is probably more money than he could ever hope for from an award of damages.

Fifth – and it wounds my pride that this factor was not given more weight – I pointed out that AJODA (now) has a lawyer licensed to practice in New York State who is willing, indeed eager to defend, at no charge, against this claim. True, it is quite an inconvenience for me to defend a case in New York City, 150 miles away, but I have almost unlimited time and I am, to put it mildly, highly motivated. I could easily lay down procedural roadblocks it would take Brown's lawyer thousands of dollars to clear away, and he might not clear them all away.

My suspicion is that AJODA was overimpressed by the fact that Brown's Daddy is a lawyer (what am I, chopped liver?). I observed that while a father who is a criminal law expert will go to some trouble to get his son out of a criminal prosecution, there is no reason to believe that his indulgence extends so far as to sacrifice tens or (I can at least force this) hundreds of thousands of dollars in foregone income to pursue a grudge lawsuit against Sonny's obscure and penniless political enemies which Dad is not qualified to handle without foregoing more tens of thousands of dollars at least, to educate himself in an unfamiliar and esoteric field of law he will never know as well as I already do.

The AJODistas, however, fear for their project. They may have discounted my legal explanations as self-serving, which is disappointing, for they have known me for a long time and they should know me better. Some Berkeleyists want to call Brown's bluff. McQuinn probably agreed that a lawsuit a lawsuit whose very filing would disrupt the project was only a remote possibility, yet fretted that it was nonetheless too much of a risk. So what they did was publish, in AJODA #57, an apology to Bill Brown for a "gratuitous personal attack" by an unnamed letter writer. Consequently "the letters policy has been changed" to forbid "irrelevant, gratuitous personal attacks," although most readers enjoy them very much.

On-line notice dated 27 November 2008

Notice

Today, we received a letter dated 22 January 2009 and sent by the Labadie Collection at the University of Michigan in Ann Arbor, the foremost collection of anarchist literature in the USA. This letter "acknowledge[s] receipt of *Character Assassin: Bob Black's Vendetta Against Bill Brown.* We will be sure to add it to the Labadie Collection and to note its presence when we index Black's Papers." "Black's Papers" refers to the personal papers of the self-proclaimed "post-Leftist anarchist" Bob Black, which include his ludicrously inaccurate and hateful history of Brown's "misadventures" from the mid-1980s to 2004, entitled "Memories of Bill Brown." This Orwellian hatchet-job bears the legend: "Prepared as an introduction to a file on Bill Brown for inclusion in the author's papers archived in the Labadie Collection of the University of Michigan." And so we now rest assured that posterity – allowed the benefit of getting "both sides of the story" – will judge the matter appropriately.

Published in a very limited edition on 15 January 2009, *Character Assassin: Bob Black's Vendetta Against Bill Brown* is Brown's definitive account of the situation. It includes his only public statement, "Expose of the Abuses Perpetrated by Bob Black, Written by One of his Victims," which was published on-line on 27 November 2008, as well as two texts that have not and will never be published on-line: Brown's line-by-line annotation of the 62 mistakes, lies and calumnies in

Internecine polemics

Black's "Memories," and Brown's preface to *Character Assassin,* which calls attention to Black's similarity to the type of yellow journalism practiced by police specialists. If anyone is interested in reading either of these two texts, they will have to go to Ann Arbor.

On-line notice dated 30 January 2009

Part III:

The Situationist International

The Situationist International
An Introduction to the Situationist International

1
This text may be freely reproduced, translated or adapted, even without mentioning the source.

2
As recently as the 1940s, art forms which shared punk's ugliness, dissonance, and bohemian roots – dada and surrealism in the visual arts, existentialism in philosophy, and serialism in music, to name but a few – were considered scandalous and offensive by middle-class culture. Whatever notoriety these art forms attained in their day, they were suppressed for being attempts to destroy aesthetic, political and moral values. Since then, middle-class culture has come to regard these works of art as "classics," as "realistic" perspectives on society, things to be studied in the universities and copied – minus their critical edge – by the advertising industry. As a result, our generation (I am 25) has grown up with the mistaken idea that these gestures of opposition are reified monuments to a dead culture, rather than starting points in our efforts to create a world without alienation or boredom.

3
It is highly significant, therefore, that in 1976, when punk took its stand against the English socio-cultural terrain, the most powerful cultural institutions – EMI and CBS Records, *Melody Maker* and *New Musical Express* – greeted the Damned, the Sex Pistols and the Clash with open arms. With the lone exception of the Pistols, the first wave of punk bands shook, rather than bit, the hands that fed them. The Clash, in particular, have always shown a desire to help those who have rather opportunistically helped them. Eight years later, "punk rock" is a commercially successful form of expression, something that even frat boys and neo-Nazis can like without fear of being considered weird or repulsive. Mohawks, shaved heads and safety pins, not to mention the Clash or John Lydon, can now be seen with increasing frequency on MTV.

4
What has happened since the 1940s is that aesthetic production has become fully integrated into commodity production generally. Rather than merely tolerating "art for art's sake," the capitalist imperative to produce fresh waves of ever-more novel-seeming goods, at ever greater rates of turnover, now assigns an increasingly essential structural function and position to aesthetic innovation and experimentation. As a result of these changes in the cultural logic of capitalism,

changes brought about by the movement from the monopoly stage to the multinational stage of capitalism, our sense of history, both personal and collective, has been completely eroded. We now live in a perpetual present. Under such conditions, it's nearly impossible to conceive of the future; any traditional attempt to oppose society's development are now secretly disarmed and reabsorbed by that very society.

5

The intellectual adjuncts of official Western culture would have us believe that it has only been very recently that anyone has come to understand these dizzying, discomforting and historically original changes in culture, and that it will be many more years before anyone, even revolutionaries, will be able to develop a new set of oppositional tactics. From art magazines such as *Artforum* and *ZG* to the sociology departments of Yale and the University of Paris, as well as "alternative" newspapers such as *The Village Voice* and *In These Times*, one now sees a torrent of discussion and analysis of these themes, generally lumped under the rubric of "theories of postmodernism." Yet the fact of the matter is that the nature of the cultural logic of multinational capitalism, as well as the nature of the new forms of revolt, have been known for at least 30 years! Preeminent in this regard, and not solely by dint of personal talent, have been a group of extremists collectively known as the Situationist International. It is no coincidence that the recent proliferation of analyses of "postmodernism" has been accompanied, after years of silence, by growing references to the situationists. In a passage equally applicable to the sudden visibility of postmodern culture as it was to the SI's reception in the early 1960s, the situationists wrote that "many intellectuals hesitate to speak openly of the SI because to speak of it implies taking a minimum position. Many of them believe, quite mistakenly, that to feign ignorance of it in the meantime will suffice to clear them of responsibility later."

6

Originating in the Lettrist movement in Paris in the early 1950s, the Situationist International was formed in 1957 by a few European avant-garde groups. Over the next decade, the SI developed an increasingly incisive and coherent critique of Western multinational capitalism and Eastern bureaucratic capitalism, its pseudo-opposition. The new methods of agitation developed by the SI were highly influential in leading up to the May 1968 revolt in France. Since then – though the organization itself was dissolved in 1972 – situationist theses and tactics have been taken up by radical currents in dozens of countries all over the world, perhaps most notably for our purposes in the punk movement in England in the mid-1970s. In this article I will attempt to present a useful selection of excerpted situationist writings and images "detourned" by the SI, as well as to illustrate the SI's origins and development. Anyone who is serious about learning from the SI's example will want to read their writings in their entirety. Guy Debord's *The Society of the*

The Situationist International Spectacle is available for $2 from Black & Red (POB 02374, Detroit MI 48202); Raoul Vaneigem's *The Revolution of Everyday Life* is available for $7 from Left Bank Books (Box B 92 Pike Street, Seattle WA 98101); an anthology of the SI's journal, as well as various postmortem critiques, are available for $10 from Ken Knabb (POB 1044, Berkeley CA 94701); our own attempts to update situationist theory and practice can be sampled for $2 [outdated address deleted].

7

The misfortune of the situationists' theory and that to which comparable movements of revolutionary intellectuals in the past succumbed were ultimately reunited in the very nature of their failures. Just as with Marxist thought and other, later attempts at revolutionary critique, all the results of the SI's efforts wound up knowing a complete inversion of their meaning in the 1970s, so as to now constitute nothing more than a particular brand of cultural verbiage in the generalized false communication imposed on men and women by existing conditions, as much in their acceptance of these conditions as in their revolt against them. A case in point is the band the Feederz, who proclaim with great self-satisfaction that "the situationists were a big influence on us," despite the fact that the Feederz have done violence to the integrity of the situationists' theory by turning it into an ideology, into situationism. "Such people," the situationists proclaimed, "are extremely handicapped and uninteresting compared to those who may not be aware of the SI but who unflinchingly confront their own lives." One must invert the Feederz's song "Dead Bodies," itself an inversion of one of the SI's theses, to get at its real truth (i.e., that any attempt to apply an ideology to current conditions is necrophilous by definition). To pursue this line of thought (and thus clear up any misconceptions about the situationists' ideas about revolutionary violence): the real truth of the Feederz's song "Destruction Unit," once it has been inverted to correct for itself inverted perspective, is that unarmed dissatisfaction, which goes so far as refusing the false activities offered by the work-a-day "world" without being able to reinvent human activity upon other bases, is indistinguishable from capitalist advertizing and twice as odious when it is advocated by so-called revolutionaries.

8

An objection might very well be made that the writing and publication of this article will encourage spectacular, imbecilic (a la the Feederz) or otherwise inappropriate uses of the situationists' theses and example. My hope is that by intentionally nourishing these inappropriate uses of the SI, I will thus dialectically create the possibility of better uses of it. To be blunt: everyone reading this article must realize that the situationists are in the past. By extinguishing the security afforded by self-satisfied references to the SI, or to any external authority, for that matter, it is hoped that each revolutionary feels as I do: namely, that he or she has to take responsibility for his or her own thoughts and actions. This is necessarily the first step toward autonomy and the possibility of forming truly revolutionary organizations without militants, followers or sycophants.

9

"The new revolutionary theory," the situationist Mustapha Khayati wrote in 1966, "cannot advance without redefining its fundamental concepts. 'Ideas improve,' says Lautremont. 'The meaning of words participates in the movement. Plagiarism is necessary. Progress implies it. It embraces an author's phrase, makes use of his or her expressions, erases a false idea, and replaces it with the right idea.' To salvage Marx's thought it is necessary continually to make it more precise, to correct it, to reformulate it in the light of a hundred years of reinforcement of alienation and the possibilities of negating it." The situationists, in their attempts to develop a coherent critique of society as it really is, plagiarized the writings of Marx, Hegel, Fourier, Lewis Carroll, Sade, Lautremont, the surrealists, Henri Lefebvre, Georg Lukacs – in short, from anyone whose basic impulse was to theorize the totality of society. Yet, unlike nearly all of the theorists and artists from whom they plagiarized, the situationists critiqued society without the pull of allegiances or the fear of reprisals. The SI never pretended to have a monopoly on intelligence, but on its use.

10

The touchstones of Marxist-situationist theory are these: A). That all forms of capitalist society, be they corporate or bureaucratic, are in the final analysis based on the generalized and – at the level of the masses – stable division between directors and executants: those who give orders and those who carry them out. B). That subsequent to the total domination and colonialization of nature by technology (a victory that freed mankind from having to struggle to survive), the directorate, its hand forced by capitalism's need to locate and exploit new raw materials and new markets for its products, began to dominate and colonize human nature. The only other alternative was for the directorate to admit that the battle against nature had been won and that the directorate itself was no longer necessary or even desirable. C). That the domination and colonialization of human nature took the form of a consumption-based society, rather than a production-based society; this "new" society the situationists called the society of the spectacle. D). That the alienation which, in the 19th century, was rooted in economic misery had, in the 20th century, become located in false consciousness. E). That this false consciousness believes that "everyday life" (i.e., one's personally selected ensemble of commodities and ideologies) is separate from "history" (i.e., the sum total of that which is accomplished at and by work). And F). That the society of the spectacle perpetuates itself by compensating those denied the opportunity to make history with more and more commodities, all of which are fundamentally unsatisfying because the ideology of survival remains coded within them.

11

The touchstones of Marxist-situationist practice are these: A). That during the 1910 to 1925 period, in the form of Dadaism and surrealism, modern art had already revealed and, on the plane of ideas, destroyed the workings of the society of the spectacle. B). That the failure of modern art, on the plane of actions, to make good its promise to destroy spectacular society is inseparable from the failure of the workers' movement of that same era. C). That post-surrealist modern art, if it doesn't link up with the workers' movements of the current era, cannot help but be boring, sterile and openly apologetic for multinational capitalism. D). That there is most definitely a modern workers' movement; the problem is that clinging to outdated notions of who the modern proletariat is prevents everyone from seeing what it is doing. E). That the modern proletariat, which more often than not revolts out of boredom, does not yet know that it encompasses nearly everyone. And F). That, when situations are constructed (this is the derivation of the term "situationist") in which the freedom of modern art is put into practice, the modern proletariat will come to know what it truly is and will realize that it wants to live modern freedom rather than be a spectator of it.

12

One can discern three main periods in the situationists' development. In the first, which preceded the actual formation of the International in 1957, the situationists devoted themselves to derives, to drifting through the city for days, weeks, even months at a time, trying to find what the Lettrist Ivan Chtcheglov called "forgotten desires": images of play, eccentricity, secret rebellion, negation. The derives were part of a self-conscious attempt to organize a new vision of everyday life; this was a process that ordinarily took place without self-awareness. In the second period, which stretched from 1958 to 1962, the situationists experimented with the supersession of art. These experiments took four forms: 1). the imposition of additional or altered speech bubbles on pre-existing photocomics; 2). the promotion of guerilla tactics in the mass media; 3). the development of situationist comics; and 4). the production of situationist films. Accompanying this article, one will find several examples of "authentic" situationist cartoons and photocomics. (I've placed the word authentic in quotes because the whole point of situationist comics is that anyone with an understanding of what distinguishes them from mere parody or satire can produce "authentic" examples themselves.) In the third period, which extended from 1963 to 1968, the SI developed a theory and practice of the exemplary act. Citing, celebrating, analyzing and, as often as possible, lending practical support to such exemplary acts of refusal as the Watts riots of 1965, the Algerian Revolution of 1966 and the resistance of students to the Chinese Cultural Revolution in 1967, the SI made explicit their belief that the only successful revolutionary movement would be an international one. Some of these actions led nowhere; some – like the assaults the SI itself made against French cyberneticians at the University of Strasbourg in 1966, and against sociologists at the University of Nanterre in 1967 – led to May 1968, which was the first mass wildcat strike in history, and the largest general strike that ever stopped the economy of an advanced industrial society.

13

Perhaps the most revolutionary aspect of the SI was its steadfast refusal to reproduce internally the hierarchical conditions of both the "world" of the commodity and the various self-styled "workers" parties that claim to oppose it. "The SI cannot be a massive organization and it will not even accept disciples as do the conventional radical groups," wrote an unidentified situationist in 1963. "One of the classic weapons of the old world, perhaps the one most used against groups attempting to alter the organization of life, is to single out and isolate a few of the participants as 'stars.' We have to defend ourselves against this process, which has an air of being 'natural.' Those among us who aspired to the role of stars or depended on stars had to be rejected. The SI will only organize the detonation; the free explosion must escape us and any other control forever." True to their word, when the explosion came in 1968, the situationists, unlike others involved in the insurrection, didn't trade their victory for whatever rewards the momentarily defeated spectacular society offered them. Rather, the SI struggled against reformism in an attempt to define the revolt's most radical possibilities, which meant that, in the end, the situationists would leave behind the most radical definition of all that May 1968 could have been, but wasn't.

14

If the May 1968 insurrection was the realization of the Situationist International and the confirmation of its theses and tactics, then this realization was also the end of the SI. Though the situationists used their theories about the society of the spectacle as rules of thumb in the construction of their organization, they did not apply them to the very activity of theory formulation. The backlash generated by the confirmation of situationist theory threw the SI, which was generally unprepared to resist self-satisfaction, into incoherence, impotence and finally massive psychological repression of the whole experience, without their ever having asked themselves what was happening to them.[1]

15

In the aftermath of the May 1968 revolt, two things have happened which are of great importance to the readers of *Maximum Rock 'n' Roll*. The first is that revolution has moved from being an apparently marginal phenomenon to a visibly central one. The underdeveloped countries have lost their apparent monopoly on contestation; but the "Third World" revolutions haven't stopped; they have simply

---

[1] False. Between 1969 and 1971, the SI did nothing but "resist self-satisfaction" and "ask themselves what was happening to them."

become modern and more and more resemble the struggles in the advanced countries. The formerly isolated gestures of revolt against what seemed to be isolated alienation and boredom now know themselves to be international and proliferating. It is this global visibility that has once and for all shattered the ideologies that saw revolution everywhere but in the proletariat. The second aftermath of May 1968 is that this society, which proclaimed its well-being in the 1950s, is now officially in crisis. Everything that the situationists said about art, the proletariat, the spectacle, is broadcast everywhere – minus the essentials. Revolutionary theses don't appear to be what they really are (the ideas of revolutionaries), but rather appear to be images seen in unexpected outbursts of lucidity on the part of the rulers, the stars and vendors of illusions. The very fact that EMI Records, the biggest and most conservative label in England, agreed to release "Anarchy in the U.K." is confirmation of this hypothesis.

16

The genius of the Sex Pistols – the style that distinguished them from their contemporaries in the English punk movement of the mid-1970s – was their thorough understanding of society's weaknesses in the aftermath of May 1968. By making explicit reference to the MPLA, the UDA and the IRA, "Anarchy in the U.K." accomplished several things at once: it restored revolutionary ideas as the product of revolutionaries; it pointed out the visibly central nature of revolution to modern society; and, by asserting that dissatisfaction with society is either profound or it is nothing, it revealed the true desperation behind society's official proclamations that it's in a state of crisis. Like the situationists before them, the Sex Pistols didn't exchange the ground "Anarchy in the U.K." won for them for whatever rewards society offered them. Rather, the Pistols progressively upped the ante: by asserting, in "God Save the Queen," that the function of sacred thought has been taken over by ideology; by challenging, in "Pretty Vacant," the cult of the image; and finally, in "Holidays in the Sun," by demanding the right to make history now. Once again like the situationists, the Sex Pistols only organized the detonation; they – Johnny Rotten, at least – allowed the free explosion to escape them. If one can believe Malcolm McLaren, who once told *Melody Maker* that "it's wonderful to use situationism in rock 'n' roll," the connection between the Pistols and the SI is a solid one.

17

Earlier in this article I asserted that punk is dead, that it is no longer at all shocking to middle-class culture, and that it and its hallmarks can now be seen with increasing frequency on MTV. Quite obviously, the same cannot be said for the hardcore movement. Yet the hardcore movement's days may be limited if we don't act fast. Already one can detect in it the same weaknesses which crippled and ultimately destroyed punk: namely, the fact that the vast majority of the people involved in it haven't theorized their relationship to the "world" of the commodity.

In the absence of such a critique, the hardcore movement has found itself under the tutelage of a small clique of dubious leaders who have tried to maintain their visibility by developing an ideology of anarchism, a salad thrown together out of the mildewed leftovers of a feast they've never known. Since anarchism can never be more than a period of wavering between two extremes – one leading to submission and subservience (as in Jello Biafra's mayoral campaign), the other leading to permanent revolt (the Dead Kennedys' "Nazi Punks Fuck Off") – it is most definitely not the ground upon which to build a revolutionary movement. An example? East Bay Ray of the Dead Kennedys: "You'd be surprised how many people think we're serious. 'Kill the Poor' was Number 4 on the charts in Portugal. We think the government promoted it." To save itself from its external enemies as well as its internal enemies, the hardcore movement must revolt against its own leaders, which means dumping people like Frank Discussion and Ian MacKaye; it must reduce its numbers, which means de-emphasizing "scene building"; it must increase the quality of its numbers, which means that each person should be able to understand his or her own relationship to the totality of social life; and it must internationalize its reach, which means linking up with the revolutionary forces of the modern proletariat. Quickly! I have already taken up too much of your time.

NOT BORED! #6, November 1984
Maximum Rock'N' Roll #19, November 1984

Publisher's note:
Shortly after the publication of this text in *Maximum Rock'N'Roll*, the Feederz issued two public statements concerning it. The first was a letter sent to me personally.

> Bill Brown,
> Congratulations! You have managed to produce one of the most insipid collections of rubbish ever written on the subject of the Situationist International.
> One wonders whether you were purposely trying to ruin the S.I.'s good reputation or just a pathetic imbecile who would be only too happy to transform the S.I.'s ideas into an alternative religion, replete with Holy Gospel looked after by would-be priests – like yourself.
> One must also ask if your darling little display of "intellectual virtuosity" didn't double as a term paper for some sociology class. You proved you knew all the catchwords but understand SHIT. You also proved that there IS one thing worse than an intellectual – a PSEUDO-intellectual. Only a student would be capable of such stupidity.
> You attack us (Feederz) for turning situationist theory into

ideology, into SituationISM. But – WE ARE NOT SITUATIONISTS! We are heavily influenced by them, for good reason. We are not "Lewis Carrollists" just because we see no good reason why we can't create a situation where "everyone has won and we all must have prizes" (*Alice in Wonderland*), or "Bruce Leeists" because we find that to "research all experience, absorb what is useful, reject what is useless, and add what is specifically your own" is a very good method for cleaning up messes. We are guilty of mistakes – some severe – that we have rightly been crucified for. However, being ideologues is NOT one of them.

You attacked me as a "leader" to be dumped. Funny, a leader without followers – who doesn't even want followers – who would be only too happy, in fine situationist tradition, to dump MYSELF if a truly "revolutionary" (for want of a better term) situation occurred. Hey, asshole, I get my right to speak FROM MYSELF.

Finally, the truth of the matter is YOU requested assistance from US. (I have enclosed a xeroxed copy of your postcard.) You received no reply for two reasons:

1) I received your post card just two days before your stated deadline, and

2) we had no idea who you were or what you were going to write about the S.I.!

There are, after all, a lot of STUDENTS in Ann Arbor where you live. And, whenever possible, we try not to associate with idiots. Is it really too much to ask to demand to know who you are dealing with?

It turned out lucky for us. Your "article" (read: tripe) was, aside from your attacks on us, merely a fine example of how to say NOTHING while boring the greatest number of readers. The only saving graces were when you allowed the S.I. to SPEAK FOR THEMSELVES (in their cartoons, etc.). So – beware of lying 'cause the truth just might BITE YOU IN THE ASS.

Insurrection means never having to say You're sorry, Frank "nice, nice" Discussion

P.S. Try writing Guy Debord about the S.I.'s plagiarism of Lukacs and Lefebvre, I'd LOVE to see his reply.

The second response from the Feederz was the following letter to the editor of *Maximum Rock'N'Roll*, published in issue #21.

Rather than an intro to the SI, your article comes off as what you think the SI said, what you think The Feederz are saying, and what "actions" you think need to be taken to change the "hardcore movement" from whatever it is (or was, or evermore shall be) to the "revolutionary movement" in your mind. You set yourself up as some kind of authority, and like any authority (or expert), you use all the right jargon to disguise the poverty of your understanding, your charges, and your goals.

You fail miserably as an authority and as a "hardcore" thinker, not for lack of intellectualizing about the SI (you seem to spend a great deal of time, probably too much time, absorbed in situationist thought while learning nothing), but simply for lack of substance and proof. Your "touchstones" of "Marxist-situationist" (?!) theory and practice show little understanding of what the SI was and even less understanding of "theory and practice." Your allegation that the SI was Marxist or the "reformulation" of Marxism is a claim with no basis in fact and nothing to back it up. Although the SI may have redefined "revolution," it certainly was not a redefinition of Marxism. Your definition of revolution is hackneyed and without joy. Those who find love in subversion (and subversion in love) must take care not to use situationist theses and example "inappropriately," and if they do, it's good to know that they will always be brought to task by the likes of you.

So now, as your contribution to the revolutionary struggle, you bring The Feederz to task. You say that we not only misuse situationist theses and examples (a claim supported nowhere in your article), but are ideologues because we claim that the SI was a big influence on us. We make that claim not as a pledge of allegiance, but as a statement of fact. We have nothing to hide. Your claim that we have done violence to situationist theory by turning it into "Situationism" (you don't do violence to anything but your own credibility) is bullshit with, again, nothing to back it up. It's the kind of thesis one might find in a college freshman's english term paper. Here's your argument: Since The Feederz mention an influence by the SI, therefore, The Feederz are not merely the disciples of the situationists but the priests of "Situationism." Then, you pick apart our songs and without quoting a single word, spew out the most ridiculous interpretations, using lots of situationist "buzzwords" to make yourself sound like a proper authority. But mere "refutation" doesn't satisfy you. You have to call us "spectacular" and "imbecilic" relying on the reader to fill in the missing logic.

Ideologues are, like you, the first to pass judgment on how appropriately or inappropriately someone's every thought and act plugs into theory because the ideologue is compelled to plug his pet theory into his (and thus everyone else's) own thought and action. To you, only organized "revolutionary movements" (like the Revolutionary Communist Party, perhaps?) are profound enough to be truly revolutionary. You say the "hardcore movement" could be truly revolutionary, but there are a few problems that you (as a potential leader?) don't mind going into and offering some of your possible solutions. What it all has to do with the SI, I can only guess. My favorite cliché of yours is that the "hardcore movement" needs to link up with the revolutionary forces of the modern proletariat. I have my doubts as to whether any proletarian, revolutionary or otherwise, gives a shit about the "hardcore movement" that, in your fantasies, will serve as the vanguard for a struggle that you have no concept of.

If I may plagiarize a situationist term, you are a "mystifier." Your "introduction" to the SI was nothing more than heresay [sic] and misinformation. Your intent was to be an authority and your effect was to create a neutralization of your subject matter. Your document is shit. The SI can speak for itself.

Signed, MARK
FEEDERZ Office of Anti-Public Relations
San Francisco, CA 94110

P.S. We're far from being leaders. We can't even get a gig in our own fucking town!

In response to the Feederz, I published a letter to the editor in *Maximum Rock and Roll* # 22, February 1985.

STARVE A FEEDER
Dear MRR:

Before writing "An Introduction to the Situationist International," I sent a postcard to the FEEDERZ informing them that "any contributions on your part would be greatly appreciated." Frank Discussion, in his letter to me (*MRR*#21), claims it arrived "two days" before the deadline, meaning Oct. 13. Yet his own photocopy of the postcard, which he insisted on sending back to me, shows plainly that it was postmarked on Sept. 18! The only other reason Frank said the FEEDERZ had for ignoring my request was that I might've been (gasp!) A STUDENT, and thus presumably not ever capable of becoming "politically correct."

Now that this STUDENT has challenged their monopoly on the hardcore movement's access to the techniques and writings of the

Situationists, the FEEDERZ are suddenly ready to talk, or rather, to bellow insults at me.

Go back and look at the liner-notes on *Have You Ever Felt Like Killing Your Boss?* Sure, they tell you about all the great Situationist books, but they withhold the addresses of the books' publishers. You had to go through them [the FEEDERZ] to get it and if you were (gasp!) A STUDENT, maybe you wouldn't get it at all. But don't worry, those days are gone forever, the "Intro to the S.I." saw to that. It's your turn now. Bill Brown [outdated address deleted].

P.S. It is still inconceivable to me that the Situationists would, under any circumstances, ever endorse a song as reactionary as the FEEDERZ' "Love," whose narrator says he wants to respond to a woman's unwanted amorous advances by "kicking her where she pees" and "sticking a broken Coke bottle up her cunt."

Guy Debord's
Comments on the Society of the Spectacle

As late as 1979, Guy Debord could write about his 1967 book of theory, which is entitled *The Society of the Spectacle*: "There is not a word to be changed . . . . [Since 1967] the spectacle has done nothing but meet more exactly its concept. . . . In fact, it fell on spectacular society itself to add something of which this book, I think, had no need – heavier and more convincing proofs and examples." But in 1988, Debord was forced to admit that,

> in other circumstances, I think I could have considered myself altogether satisfied with my first work on this subject, and left others to consider future developments. But in the present situation, it seemed unlikely that anyone else would do it.

And so Debord, twenty-one years later, wrote a second work: *Comments on the Society of the Spectacle* (Verso, 1990; trans. Malcolm Imrie).[2] The pun in the title suggests that Debord's 1967 book and the society it discusses are virtually the same thing.

What changed between 1979 and 1988? What forced the writer's hand? Answer: the long-term spectacularization of the May 1968 revolution in France.

Except for Debord, every major "radical" thinker in the West continues to

---

[2] Finding this translation to be defective, I translated it from the French myself in August 2005. This translation is only available on-line: http://www.notbored.org/commentaires.html.

sing the praises of May 1968. Let us take as an example Felix Guattari & Antonio Negri, the authors of *Communists Like Us* (Semiotext[e] Foreign Agents Series; written in 1984 and translated in 1990). In this book, these writers say again and again, "The events of May 1968 mark the re-opening of a revolutionary cycle"; they say again and again "It is thus a world in the process of change that began its expansion in '68 and which, since then, through a process of continuous mutation, including all sorts of failures and successes, has struggled to weave a new network of alliances at the heart of the multiplicity of isolated singular components comprising it." For Guattari & Negri, who were active in the Italian struggles of the late 1970s, the revolution of 1968 was an "irreversible" success, and thus they can write about it in the present tense: 1968 is this and 1968 represents that.

But, for Debord, 1968 – though it was indeed a modern revolution – represents an exception to the rule of the society of the spectacle. "The disturbances of 1968, which in several countries lasted into the following years," he writes in his *Comments,*

> having nowhere overthrown the existing organization of the society from which it springs apparently spontaneously, the spectacle has thus continued to gather strength; that is, to spread to the furthest limits on all sides, while increasing its density in the centre. It has even learned new defensive techniques, as powers under attack always do.

As Debord will explain, the spectacle has become "the integrated spectacle." There has been a qualitative change in its nature. But, for writers such as Guattari & Negri, there has been no such change. They write, "Capitalist and/or socialist restructuring in the '70s has stitched together the old modes of production, redistributing the functions of the players, and reorganizing on a world scale the division of exploitation." While Guattari & Negri suggest a global system of domination that is merely stitched together, Debord envisions one with an increasingly organic unity, in which "diffuse" and "concentrated" spectacles are integrated.

What are the new defensive techniques the spectacle has learned in the last two decades? In other words, what is the nature of the *new* situation in which we find ourselves today? "The society whose modernization has reached the stage of the integrated spectacle is characterized by the combined effect of five principal features," Debord tells us. They are 1). incessant technological renewal; 2). integration of state and economy; 3). generalized secrecy; 4). unanswerable lies; and 5). an eternal present.

The first two features have, in Debord's words, "proved to be highly favorable to the development of spectacular domination," while the other three features are "direct effects of this domination, in its integrated stage." The purpose of the *Comments on the Society of the Spectacle* is to look at the socio-psychological effects of the spectacle – the political-economic causes having been addressed in 1967's *Society of the Spectacle*. Even more precisely: in his *Comments*, Debord has tried to 1). combat "generalized secrecy" by openly writing to and working upon the fifty or sixty people in his "network of influence" (Debord's own estimate); 2). combat "unanswerable lies" by filling his book with easily checkable truths; and 3). combat an "eternal present" by insisting that some things are definitely in the past, but especially "1968."

This is it, a thumbnail picture of the whole book:

> Our unfortunate times thus compel me, once again, to write in a new way. Some elements will be intentionally omitted; and the plan will have to remain rather unclear. Readers will encounter certain decoys, like the very hallmark of the era. As long as certain pages are interpolated here and there, the overall meaning may appear; just as secret clauses have very often been added to whatever treaties may openly stipulate; just as some chemical agents only reveal their hidden properties when they are combined with others. However, in this brief work there will be only too many things that are, alas, easy to understand.

Debord's *Comments* is not a "book": it is a text, partly written in invisible words, that must be edited by the reader before it can read (for the second time). The secret clauses must be made to manifest themselves somehow; the chemical reaction must be begun. But what is the missing ingredient?

NOT BORED! #19, June 1991

Heatwave thirty years later

This originally mimeographed magazine, published in July 1966, was reprinted as a photocopy in 1993 by Chronos Publications (BM Chronos London WC1N 3XX). Though only two issues of *Heatwave* were ever published, it remains a noteworthy publication. In their November 1966 pamphlet "On the Poverty of Student Life," the Situationist International wrote – apropos of "profoundly revolutionary tendencies in the critique of all aspects of the prevailing way of life" – "One thinks here of the excellent journal *Heatwave*, which seems to be evolving toward an increasingly rigorous radicality." In December 1966, *Heatwave's* editor Charles Radcliffe was admitted into the Situationist International as a member of its British section. But within a year, the British section no longer existed: Radcliffe resigned in November 1967, and Christopher Gray, Donald-Nicholson Smith and T.J. Clark were excluded in December 1967.

The British never did produce a review of their section of the SI – though they did write a detailed manifesto in 1967 – and so the reprinting of *Heatwave #1* furnishes us with a rare opportunity to examine and evaluate a (pre)situationist discourse that speaks to us in our native language and not in translation. (Other situationist publications originally written in English were published by the American section of the SI.)

"On May Day [1966], the first Anglo-American edition of the Chicago wobblies' *The Rebel Worker* was published here [in London] because a group of us felt there was an audience in Britain for an experimental, perhaps slightly crazed libertarian socialist journal," Radcliffe explains at the very beginning of *Heatwave #1*. "*The Rebel Worker* will continue to be published from Chicago; the London group will publish *HEATWAVE*." The Rebel Worker group in Chicago – which seems to have included Franklin and Penelope Rosemont, and Bernard Marszalek – was strongly influenced by the situationists: they rebelled against being workers. In 1965, these Chicago wobblies (that is to say, these members of the persecuted but undefeated Industrial Workers of the World) distributed copies of the situationists' reading and encouragement of the riots in Watts ("The Decline & Fall of the Spectacular Commodity Economy," first published in English and only later published in French) as well as their own pamphlets. Issue #6 of *The Rebel Worker* – "the issue that started *HEATWAVE*" and is advertized in it – contains an essay on subject matter that the situationists found interesting; furthermore, this essay bears the type of title ("The Precursors of the Theory of Total Liberation") that the SI favored in its publications.

This point of contact between the "old" form taken by the international workers' movement (as embodied by the Wobblies, founded in Chicago in 1905) and the "new" form taken by that movement (as embodied by the Situationist International) is highly unusual and very instructive. For one thing, situationist style demands that, in general, there be as few points of contact between the "new" and the "old" forms of struggle as possible. In this way, the SI attempted to prevent current struggles from clinging to spectacular fragments of the past and thus losing the ability or opportunity to construct a totally new world in part based upon what has happened since the crushing of the earlier revolutionary movements. But there have to be some points of contact between past and present, "old" and "new," for the latter to come into existence and sustain itself.

In marked contrast to the Wobbly/Heatwave group and perhaps to the British section of the SI as well, the Lettrist International and the other small European groups that came together to form the SI only found points of contact between itself and prior movements in the artistic field; none of their points of contact were in the field of the labor movement. Guy Debord's crucial June 1957 "Report on the Construction of Situations and on the International Situationist Tendency's Conditions of Organization and Action" is mostly interested in what, in 1957, was left of revolutionary surrealism, and not what was left of the socialist labor movement. And yet, from beginning to end, situationist theory relies very strongly

– perhaps even ultimately – on terms and concepts drawn not from the vocabulary of art criticism or art history, but from the vocabulary of a German 19th century economist and the international revolutionary labor movement he helped to launch.

Unfortunately, Marxism is a revolutionary philosophy of history and action that has never had an adequate appreciation for or relationship to the creative arts. Indeed, the very premise of the foundation of the Situationist International in 1957 was that it was urgent and at last possible to reconcile or realign Marxism with anti-bourgeois art, and thus begin again the proletarian assault on capitalism. But, despite its successes with re-introducing the "modern world" to revolution, the SI only transcended the contradiction between revolutionary politics and revolutionary art in its words. Significantly, the SI's most notable internal battles were fought between "artistic" situationists and "political" situationists, not between "proletarians" and "militant intellectuals," which would have been the case had the SI had been a "traditional" (i.e., Leninist, Stalinist, Communist, Trotskyist, Bordigist, or Maoist) revolutionary organization, which it obviously was not. But the SI cannot be spared from the criticisms that its members, whether they were "artists" or "politicos," were drawn from the bourgeoisie, and not from the working-classes; that the proportion of workers to nonworkers in the SI was even worse than the proportion found in the first congresses of the Russian Social-Democrat Workers Party – a proportion that is mocked by the situationist Rene Riesel in his "Preliminaries on the Councils and Councilist Organization."

The striking thing about *Heatwave #1* is that it shows aspects of the traditional, revolutionary socialist labor movement and the newly-emerging situationist project co-existing in a single, relatively coherent format. Written between July 1965 and June 1966, and presented in chronological order, the essays in *Heatwave #1* are pretty much equally divided between texts written by members of the Rebel Worker/Heatwave group and texts written by nongroup members and originally published elsewhere. Among the former group of texts are short, precise and insightful articles about income policies and the Dutch trade union movement ("Strange Adventures in Holland," by Gaby Charing); the Puerto Rican riots that took place in Chicago during June 1966 (Bernard Marszalek's "Footnote to The Long Hot Summer"); and the Dutch "Provo" movement (Charles Radcliffe's "Daytripper: A Visit to Amsterdam: June 22, 1966"). The reprinted texts include news reports on and statements issued by the Provos in Amsterdam (one such statement, entitled "What is the Provotariat?" was originally published in French in the socialist workers' publication *Informations, Correspondence Ouvriers*); a statement from a NYC group – apparently lead by one Jonathan Leake – called the Resurgence Youth Movement; and flyers (one of which is about the war in Vietnam) issued by Wobblies in Chicago. The overall feel is inclusive, nonsectarian and in-touch: the "Advertisers' Announcements" page features spots for English luddites, Belgian provos, and the Solidarity group (an English version of Socialisme ou Barbarie in France).

It is also striking that several of the articles in *Heatwave #1* are about cultural and personal subjects. Mixed in with the aforementioned essays on current events and oppositional groups – all of which are sober, well considered and detached – there are several unabashed, "slightly crazed" and still-fresh forays into pop culture. These include an addiction diary in the style of William S. Burroughs ("The Expanded Journal of Addiction," written during 1965, the year the censorship of *Naked Lunch* made it and its author international news items); a book review of Dave Wallis' Pop dystopian novel *Only Lovers Left Alive* (originally published in 1964 and reprinted the following year as a paperback); and a long piece by Charles Radcliffe (entitled "The Seeds of Social Destruction") on such "groupings of disaffected youth" as the Teddy Boys, the drag-racing Ton-up Kids, the Beats, the Ban-the-Bombers, the Ravers, the Mods and the Rockers.

The reasons for the inclusion of these articles into *Heatwave* are clear: pop culture, consumerism and subcultural "style" are phenomena that modern workers have directly experienced, have questioned deeply, and have understood at a profound level. It isn't at all relevant, important or even interesting that classical Marxism and its contemporary adherents disapprove of these phenomena as distracting, degenerate or superficial. What is truly relevant, important and interesting is the question, Toward what end will modern workers put their understanding of these phenomena? *Heatwave* answers: Toward the autonomous creation of a society without classes and exploitation. If this goal seems fantastically out-of-reach to those who pride themselves on the "fact" that they "live in the real world," *Heatwave* is not worried. "Nothing can stop me! I'm the Hulk! I'm the strongest there is!" says a comic book hero on the page Radcliffe devotes to past issues of *The Rebel Worker* and to future issues of his own zine. "Careful? Ya never get to be a comic book hero by bein' careful," says another. And, of course, he is right.

NOT BORED! #26, November 1996

Quoted at some length in Franklin Rosemont & Charles Radcliffe, *Dancin' in the Streets: Anarchists, IWWs, Surrealists, Situationists & Provos in the 1960s, as recorded in the pages of "The Rebel Worker" and "Heatwave"* (Chicago: Charles H. Kerr, 2005), pp, 325 and 355-356.

At Dusk: The Situationist Movement in Historical Perspective

At Dusk: The Situationist Movement in Historical Perspective was written and published in January 1976 by David Jacobs and Christopher Winks, members of the Berkeley-based, situationist-inspired group Perspectives (a later incarnation of Point Blank). We here at *NOT BORED!* didn't even know of this text's existence before it arrived in the mail one day in January 1997 (a gift from fans of the SI in Stuttgart, Germany). It isn't mentioned or discussed by any of the commentators who have published major essays, books or catalogues in the last 15 years, with the sole exception of Simon Ford, author of *The Realization and Suppression of the Situationist International: An Annotated Bibliography 1972- 1992*, who refers to it as a "key and extensive text" that "contains an extensive critique of Situationist concepts." And so we began distributing second-generation photocopies of *At Dusk* to people we thought would be interested in them.[3]

Perspective was one of several situationist-inspired groups active in the Berkeley area in the early 1970s. The Council for the Eruption of the Marvelous, Contradiction (of which Ken Knabb was a member) and Negation (which later became known as For Ourselves) were also based there. (It appears that the groups founded by former members of the American section of the SI – Tony Verlaan's Create Situations and Jon Horelick's Diversion – were both based in New York City, just as the short-lived American section of the SI had been.) "In the ensuing war of succession after the collapse of the SI [in late 1971]," Jacobs & Winks write, "each [of these groups] was to assert its claim to the situationist throne." There was a rash of exclusions and breaks. "However justified some of the breaks may have been," Ken Knabb writes in *Public Secrets: Collected Skirmishes of Ken Knabb: 1970 - 1997*, "the whole situ scene ended up looking pretty silly when virtually every individual disdainfully split from virtually all the others." Silly is not the word. Try inconsequential.

A good bit of *At Dusk* is devoted to critical assessment of all the pretenders to the American situationist throne, including Perspectives itself, but especially Ken Knabb and Daniel Denevert. (An honest masochist, Knabb begins the section of his new book reserved for "Selected Responses" to his work with a large but obviously heavily-edited quotation from *At Dusk*.) But the interest of Jacobs & Winks' book lies in what they have to say about the SI in the years after 1968. *At Dusk* challenges a notion that is almost universally accepted by and repeated in the official literature on the situationists: the dissolution of the SI sometime in 1971 was a triumph of self-determination, a carefully considered decision, a tactic that had an important part to play in the broader situationist strategy. To Jacobs & Winks, the SI's dissolution was an "inglorious demise," an embarrassment rather than a triumph, a collapse rather than a disbanding. Why? Because the Situationists did not disband when the getting was good, which was in 1969, after they had carefully documented, expanded upon, and evaluated the occupations and wildcat strikes of May 1968, but before they had embarked upon their disastrous "orientation debate" of 1970-71. Why should the SI have disbanded in 1969?

---

[3] We sent a copy to AK Press, hoping that they would distribute it. Without consulting us, AK reproduced that complimentary copy with a more "professional" cover, and started selling *their* copies for $15 each, which was *three times* what we were selling it for. Eventually (after several years), one of the pamphlet's authors stepped forward and an official reproduction of *At Dusk* was published.

Because that was when the split between their theory of revolution (the way things should have been going) and the revolution itself (the way things were actually going) became acute. Because the SI did not disband in 1969, but staggered on for a few more years, its sunset has been colored with bad blood, bad theories and bad reputations.

At Dusk identifies two aspects of the veritable split that destroyed the SI. The first aspect is social in nature, and concerns the situationists' personal distance from (Jacobs & Winks' words) "the class to which they ascribed fantastic powers," namely, The Proletariat. It might have been amusing and productive to define the SI as "a union of workers in an advanced sector of culture," as Guy Debord did in his 1958 text "Theses on the Cultural Revolution," but it was preposterous and obfuscatory to do so in 1969. *At Dusk* calls our attention to the fact that, "during the orientation debate of 1969-1971, a situationist could say, 'We are at the intersection point of all classes, and thus, we are no longer in any class.'" The obvious facts are these: the situationists were members of and defectors from the class known as the intelligentsia, which owes its independent existence and status to the general division of labor in capitalism; the situationist "project" or "movement," despite its fascination with society's productive sectors, was a radical intellectual current against and within the society it contested; its primary adherents were and still are drawn from the cultural, professional and educational sectors of society, and not from the industrial and manufacturing sectors.

The situationists never faced these facts, even when the facts, not to mention the end of their international revolutionary organization, were staring them right in the face. *At Dusk* points out that Debord & Sanguinetti's 1971 text "Theses on the SI and Its Time," the very last document issued in the name of the SI, is remarkable for A). its stubborn refusal to even consider the possibility of re-thinking situationist theory in light of the obvious and simple facts that students find this "proletarian theory" more alluring, provocative, inspiring and useful than workers do; and B). its patronizing tone and hostile attitude toward the efforts made by fans of the SI ("pro-situs"), who are attacked in much the same way that the effectiveness of student rebellion was ridiculed in the 1966 situationist pamphlet "On the Poverty of Student Life." The real problems confronting the SI were obviously elsewhere – either that, or the SI was doomed to collapse precisely because these were in fact its most pressing problems.

Unfortunately, ever since the publication and meek acceptance of the untenable propositions contained in "Theses on the SI and Its Time," insulting students and their "pro-situ" milieu has been an obligatory situationist gesture. Indeed, paying lip service to the masochistic proposition that "in a society that has learned to 'look' situationist, we are all pro-situs" has become *de rigueur* in certain scenes. Ken Knabb is as good an example as anyone else: "There is hardly a thesis in the Debord-Sanguinetti portrait of the pro-situ (in 'Theses on the SI and Its Time') where I do not recognize myself – in the present and far too much right now!" he gushes in "Remarks on Contradiction and Its Failure" (1973). Such guilt!

Such intense self-hatred!

Is all of that really called for? The facts say "No." In France and elsewhere in May 1968, and ever since then and all over the world (in Mexico City, in Seoul, in Belgrade, in Tianamen Square, and again in France), high school and college students have been there, fighting for freedom and justice, year after year after year – while The Proletariat has not. And, as a matter of fact, these students have not been "contesting the totality of capitalism," as the SI expected and tried to demand of all revolutionaries. These students, much like the activist members of the working classes, have been concentrating on specific demands, on issue-based actions, on local issues and grievances – in other words, on all the things the SI arrogantly dismissed as spectacular, reformist and recuperative.

And yet, though they had plenty of time for hindsight and re-evaluation, neither Guy Debord nor any of the other situationists ever considered the possibility that they were wrong when it came to what they insisted on calling the "poverty" of student rebellion. This brings us to the second aspect of the split that destroyed the SI; this aspect is theoretical, and it concerns the fundamental nature of capitalism. "The initial theses of the SI concerning the post-war period of capitalist development," Jacobs & Winks remind us, "were centered around the concept of the 'cybernetic welfare state,' which postulated that this period involved the increasing rationalization of social processes, a progressive modernization of social administration which would result in the stabilization of the capitalist order . . . [and] a continuous program of social reform: [in short,] with the elimination of 'irrational' features of the past (e.g., material and intellectual privation and overtly repressive authority), capitalism would realize an anti-Utopia based on economic prosperity." It would not really necessary to develop a new critical theory of capitalist production if one lived in a society governed by a cybernetic welfare state: a detourned version of Karl Marx's should be sufficient. It would, however, be necessary to develop of a new critical theory of capitalist consumption. And this in fact is what the theory of the spectacle is: a critical theory of consumption, but not of production.

In the analysis of Jacobs & Winks, the SI didn't imagine that the movement toward the emergence of the cybernetic welfare state might be reversible. "By taking what were then [in the 1940s, '50s and '60s] only provisional conditions of capitalist development to be in fact permanent tendencies," Jacobs & Winks point out, "the situationists converted what was at best a working hypothesis into 'theoretical' doctrine, into a perspective which appeared as absolutely conclusive." For a long time, this "situationist" perspective appeared to be as accurate as it was conclusive, and so the SI was a powerful anti-capitalist and anti-Stalinist agent at a time when there were virtually none.

The theory of the spectacle began to become obsolete in the early 1970s, when international capitalism – under pressure from its enemies and unable to manage itself – was, to quote Jacobs & Winks, "forced to reassess its expectations, and the ideology of unlimited abundance which served as a compelling incentive during its most recent expansionary cycle [was] summarily dispensed with. . . . On the command of capital, a more subdued scenario is devised: all available resources are directed towards the stabilization, through remedial actions, of the economic status quo." At least in America, the changes were decisive. Just to name two of them: the labor unions, rather than being used to integrate The Proletariat into the economic spectacle, were destroyed; and the Democratic Party, rather than being used to integrate The Proletariat into the political spectacle, was publicly sold off to Big Business. Austerity, not abundance, has ruled the day ever since. As a result, issues once thought by situationists to be of decidedly secondary importance – material poverty, wage demands, contract givebacks, rent control, and health benefits (just to name a few) – are once again of primary importance. Conversely, the importance of issues relating to social authority, spiritual poverty and commodity consumption is no longer unquestionably paramount.

In his "Preface to the third Italian edition" of his 1967 book *The Society of the Spectacle*, written in 1979, Debord himself recognized the change in capitalism's direction, but it did not mean that he had to re-formulate either the critical theory of the spectacle or his book in light of these developments. They were for him superficial developments only. Debord again showed a spectacular gift for denial in 1988, when he claimed in his *Comments* that *The Society of the Spectacle* still didn't need to be updated in light of recent events – save for the apparently painless insertion of a middle position called "the integrated spectacle" in between "the concentrated spectacle," on the one hand, and the "the diffuse spectacle," on the other. After reading *At Dusk*, you realize (again?) that this isn't "modern theory": this is bullshit. How's this for a basic banality? Fuck "reconceptualizing" situationist theory! From now on, we establish new bases for the ruthless critique of all that exists.

NOT BORED! #27, May 1997

Yet Another Introduction to the SI

Let us begin with an experiment: search the Internet for the obscure and ambiguous word "situationist." MetaCrawler reports 45 collated references. Magellan reports 47 results returned. Lycos reports the existence of 409 documents. Excite reports 792 documents found. InfoSeek reports 1,285 sites. (Thanks, folks. Love your engines!)

By any standard, there is substantial interest in the Situationist International (SI), an intentionally obscure but very influential group of avantgarde artists and ultraleftist political extremists that was formed in Italy in 1957 and dissolved in 1971 after finding that its members were becoming celebrities, despite their best efforts to the contrary.

At least four major introductions or guides to the SI have already been written and uploaded to the Internet:

1). our own "Intro to the SI" (written in 1984), which can be found at the *NOT BORED!* website. Consult this text if you are interested in Greil Marcus's 1989 book *Lipstick Traces* (without doubt the single best work on the SI written in English) and in the situationists' influence on such Anglo-American punk bands as the Sex Pistols, Gang of Four and The Feederz. This introduction to the SI is one of the very few, if not the only one written after 1981 to cause a public scandal.

2). Jamal Hannah's "About the SI," which is located at Jamal's "Egoist Communism" website. Easily the best of the four uploaded introductions, this short essay emphasizes the appeal of the SI to educated youths, students and intellectual dropouts (people who would normally have nothing at all to do with revolutionary groups and politics because they are widely perceived to be boring and repressive).

3). Shawn Wilbur's "On the Use of the SI" (1994), which is posted at Shawn's website. Written in the epigrammatic style favored by the situationists (who intended to parody Hegel's epigrams), this text emphasizes the enduring importance of such situationist practices as drifting through urban spaces as a kind of anti-tourism, and subverting advertisements and other forms of spectacular propaganda.

4). Max Anger's "Go 'Beyond the SI' in Ten Simple Steps," which is posted at the "Against Sleep And Nightmare" website. Very poorly written, riddled with mistakes and typographical errors, and nearly impossible to follow, this text presumes to definitively "critique" and thereby have done with the situationists, which it doesn't really bother to describe or explain in a sustained or fair manner. As such, this text is an excellent example of the quality of much of the writing about the SI that has been published in Anglo-American zines over the course of the last 15 years.

Quite obviously, these four texts do not account for all of the hits in a search for the word "situationist." As a matter of fact, a great many of the articles and reviews currently available on the Internet that mention the magic word concern Guy Debord, a founding member of the SI, its most prolific and influential theoretician, and one of its last remaining members in 1971. Because of Debord's enduringly central role in the development of the SI, and because of the fact that in the post-SI period Debord continued to write and publish short but very potent books, and made several feature-length situationist-influenced films, the habit of most students and amateur historians of the situationist movement is to treat the SI as a moment in Debord's life, rather than treat the SI as a group that contained 70 different people, one of whom was Guy Debord. Many overviews of or introductions to the situationists can be found tucked within reviews of Debord's books, especially his 1967 masterpiece, *La Societe du Spectacle*, his 1988 follow-up to it, entitled *Commentaires sur La Societe du Spectacle*, and his 1989 autobiography *Panegryque*.

The Situationist International

An essay such as this introduction to the Situationist International apparently needs to be (re)written and (re)published every five years or so; no definitive introduction, overview or critique of the SI seems likely to be written. Why is this? One might think it would be easy to summarize definitively a group that no longer exists, that remains fixed in the now-gone post-World War II period. But this isn't the case. It just isn't sufficient to keep reprinting the same old introductions to the SI every time someone new is interested in finding out where he or she should start in his or her own studies. One must start again, each time.

One explanation for the existence of this unusual situation – which is not necessarily a bad thing (indeed, it seems to be quite a good thing, for it prevents dogmatism) – is that, ever since the mid-1960s, publishers in the United States and England have been bringing forth waves of translations of situationist books, pamphlets, flyers, wall posters, graffiti and film-scripts. (Though there were British and American sections of the SI, the vast majority of the organization's sections were based in European countries. Since the French section contained the SI's most prolific theoreticians and writers, most of the situationist texts now translated or still awaiting translation into English were originally written in French.)

Significant waves were made in 1981, when Ken Knabb published his *Situationist International Anthology*, now in its third printing; in 1983, when the small American presses Left Bank and Black & Red reprinted or brought into print new translations of Raoul Vaneigem's 1967 book *Traite de savoir-vivre a l'usage des jeunes generations* and Debord's *La Societe du Spectacle*; in 1989, when the Institute for Contemporary Art mounted a traveling exhibition (Paris, London and Boston) of situationist works and produced an exhibition catalogue that included previously untranslated materials; in 1992, when the small English presses Pelagian and Rebel brought forth translations of the film-scripts for each of Guy Debord's six films; and in 1995, when Keith Sanborn produced a subtitled translation of Debord's most celebrated film, *La Societe du Spectacle* (Simar Films, 1973).

We learn more and more about the SI and what it did during its 14 years as time goes by. Inevitably, changes to or revisions of our most basic conceptions about the situationists have been and will no doubt continue to be necessary. There are several more important situationist books written in French that need to be translated. There are also quite a few very interesting and still untranslated situationist texts in Danish, Dutch, German, Italian and Spanish. And so there will be at least several more waves of English translations to hit these shores over the course of the next decade or so.

Another reason for writing a new introduction to the SI every few years is the fact that situationist literature, like all great art, is far too experimental, unstable and internally inconsistent to be definitely summarized by anyone, no matter the familiarity with French or with the texts themselves, at any time. Something important always manages to escape; all guides to or summarizers of the SI seem doomed to make crucial mistakes, incredible omissions, unfortunate misinterpretations, and poor or hasty judgments. As writers of two and now three introductions to the SI, we unfortunately speak from experience. (In case you're wondering, we didn't list our 1991 performance-piece "The Situationist Concept of Spectacle, Then & Now" among the existing introductions to the SI because the text of it has not yet been uploaded to the Internet.)

But it is also a distinct possibility that the "problem" of having to write new introductions does not lie with the SI or the nature of its texts. Instead, the "problem" might lie with the changing nature of the society in which we find ourselves, and our relationship to it. As we will see, the situationist project was the beginnings of an attempt to completely abolish both Western capitalism and Eastern bureaucratic communism, and institute true ("anarchist") social democracy for the first time in history. Since the dissolution of the SI, a number of unprecedented events have taken place; the world scene is quite simply no longer what it was over the course of the 1950s, '60s and '70s. In particular, the Soviet Socialist Republics (as well as all of its European satellites) have collapsed and disappeared.

Consequently, the global contrast between capitalism and bureaucratic communism – sharp during the 1957 to 1971 period – has become dull. But it has not disappeared: the most populous nation on Earth, and thus one in four people, is still governed by a totalitarian "socialist" bureaucracy. Armed conflicts seem to take place less and less in the geo-political realm and more and more in the socio-economic realm; racial and ethnic hatreds seem to be replacing ideological hatreds. But international class struggle has not disappeared: in Nigeria, in Albania, in Chiapas, in Seoul, and in Rangoon, the laboring classes are now fighting intense, all-out battles against both the military juntas that rule them and the multinational corporations that ruthlessly exploit them. In the midst of the organized confusion that is the "post-Cold War period," it seems increasingly difficult to imagine that something other than capitalism has been or will ever be possible. And yet the material preconditions for the emergence of anarchist social democracy grow riper every day.

Consequently, we feel the need to tell (again) the story of the Situationist International, a group of anarchists and artists who wished more than anything else to have a clear and accurate description of what capitalism really is and how it functions, and to have a concrete and effective programme by and through which capitalism could be completely abolished, bureaucratic communism could be avoided, and anarchist social democracy could begin.

As we mentioned, the Situationist International was founded in Italy in 1957, a year after representatives from three small but very ambitious European groups met to see what they had in common and what they could possibly do together. The three groups were the Lettrist International (founded in 1952 and based in France), the International Movement for an Imaginist Bauhaus (founded in 1953 and based in Italy), and COBRA (founded in 1948 and based in Copenhagen, Brussels and Amsterdam [thus the name of the group]). The fact that each of these groups was international in character immediately tells us a good deal about the Situationist International, which established sections in other parts of Europe (Germany and Scandinavia) within the first year of its existence.

From the start, the SI – a kind of international federation of internationalists – was intended to be completely free of ties to nations, national identity and nationalism, and therefore the most accurate representation or expression of what was really going on in the world. (Not coincidentally, what was "really going on in the world" was and still is the internationalization of certain conditions and phenomena, usually associated with advanced capitalism, that had previously been restricted to certain countries.) The fact that the three original micro-groups – as well as the macro-group that they combined to form – were intentionally kept small (never including more than a dozen members at any one time) tells us that the SI was designed to be as pure, militant and extreme an organization as it was international.

Other than their determined internationalism, the LI, the IMIB and COBRA shared a deep devotion and commitment to two things: modern art and radical politics, both of which are fundamentally utopian in nature. The problem for these groups was that, in the decade or so after the end of World War II, precious few (if any) of the existing or traditional forms of modern art and radical politics were not irretrievably lost to corruption, exhaustion or collaboration with Big Business, Nazism or Stalinism. Wherever one looked – in both pro-capitalist political parties and "socialist" alternatives to them, in both the workplace and in leisure time – elites, larger-than-life leaders and huge, impersonal bureaucracies were increasingly dominating, controlling and ruining the lives of individuals. Utopia literally was nowhere.

The solution to this daunting problem was obviously to reject mere tinkerings with existing forms, and to re-invent both modern art and radical politics from scratch. But how? By finding a way of combining them into a unified project in which art and politics could be begun again – but begun again in such a way that they would enrich and strengthen each other, rather than misunderstand, attempt to control or dogmatically deny the relevance of each other, which had happened all too often in the past.

Following the direction pointed out in the late 1940s by the Marxist sociologist Henri Lefebvre, who had been a Surrealist partisan in his youth and had not lost his feel for art, the Situationist International based their unified project in the demands and expectations associated with everyday life and the subjectivity of individuals, rather than in those demands and expectations associated with history and the objectivity of so-called Progress. For the SI, both modern art and radical politics had to be exciting, satisfying and effective immediately, in the here-and-now, in life as it is, day after day, for the majority of society – and not in some far off future, some Heaven, or some period after the Great Revolution.

Art and politics that continued to defer the delivery of satisfaction and human enrichment, while all the time making promises and proclaiming that delivery was nevertheless certain, had to be abolished. Those forms, which the situationists called "spectacular," were designed to obscure the fact that so-called Progress had long ago produced the material preconditions needed to make everyday life in the modern world a paradise on Earth, rather than a living hell. Since no one else was around or willing to do it, the SI took upon itself the burden of starting the onslaught against "the society of the spectacle" (the irrational society that intentionally perpetuates that which is outmoded, obsolete and decomposed), quite confident that others would soon join in. Slightly more than a decade after the organization's founding, it became clear that, in a word, the SI was right. Social revolution was and still is both desirable and possible.

The members of the Situationist International came up with several names and phrases that designated the new hybrid of art and politics (i.e., the new forms of social life) they visualized. The most important of these designations was the "constructed situation," which the SI would define in the first issue of its journal as "a moment of life concretely and deliberately constructed by the collective organization of a unitary ambiance and a game of events." It was from this central and yet deliberately vague notion that the name "situationist" was derived. A situationist is "one who engages in the construction of situations," who has "to do with the theory or practical activity of constructing situations," as well one who is a member of the SI.

A fundamental and thus very productive ambiguity is thus created: though there are situationists, there can be no "situationism" – in the SI's words, no "doctrine of interpretation of existing facts," no dogma to learn and repeat – precisely because situations truly worthy of the Twentieth Century had not yet been constructed. Such situations would have to be constructed *before* one could derive a dogma or doctrine of interpretation from them. Thus "there is no such thing as situationism," the SI declared in the first issue of its journal; "the notion of situationism is obviously devised by antisituationists." But if we withdraw the very idea of situationism, how can we speak of "the theory of constructing situations"? What theory can there be?

Perhaps a concrete example of a situation that was actually constructed would help clarify the issue. But this, precisely, was the SI's problem (and its greatest strength, because the problem allowed the SI to adapt to changing circumstances over the course of 15 years): though it could find a great many historical examples, the SI was never in complete agreement on what an ideal constructed situation really was. As a result, the SI could never quite agree on the precise nature of the situations its members, and the organization as a whole, should be engaged in constructing. But rather than letting this fact become an obstacle to action, the SI produced all kinds of passageways that might lead to a constructed situation, whatever that might be.

For clarity's sake, let us postulate, as others have done, that the history of the SI has three distinct stages. (Note, this postulation is rejected by Thomas F. McDonough in his article "Rereading the Situationists, Rereading Debord.") In the first stage (1957 to 1961), the members of the organization dedicated themselves to creative expressions of the new hybrid of art and politics. Over the course of these few years, they produced a staggering quantity and variety of art-based political ("synthetic") works: issues of their journal, tracts, pamphlets, scrapbooks, tape-recorded presentations and lectures, conferences, exhibitions, paintings, drawings, architectural models and plans, films, boycotts, disruptions of "spectacular" cultural events, etc. etc. In this first stage, a constructed situation was akin to what became known in the United States as a "happening" – an interactive performance that was politically radical to the extent that it was a synthesis of all available means for the sole purpose of satisfying real, human desires – though the situationists expected their happenings to encompass, fill and transform entire neighborhoods, and not just performance spaces. In other words, the construction of a situation was something that required the cooperation and participation of relatively large groups of people.

Around 1962, the membership and direction of the SI began to change, in part as a result of the organization's strict policy of excluding and breaking with people who seemed more interested in avant garde art than in radical politics, and in part as a result of the new types of people who approached the SI with the intent of joining it. Stated crudely but accurately: radically experimental artists were out and radically experimental theorists were in. The scission or break was so deep that a group of more than half a dozen excluded situationists (the so-called Nashists) constituted themselves as the Second Situationist International. Under this name, these ex-situationists continued to be active for several years, publishing *The Situationist Times* from Amsterdam. But very little attention was or has recently been given to the Second International, which incidentally was never officially disbanded.

In the second stage of the (First) Situationist International's history, which lasted from 1962 to 1967, the group's emphasis shifted from producing art-based political works to developing the critical theory of the spectacle. Consequently, the situationists' theatre of operations moved from the exhibition space to the university classroom. In 1965, the SI assisted in attacks on renowned cyberneticians who intended to speak at the University of Strasbourg. The following year, the SI wrote "On the Poverty of Student Life," the publication of which was, thanks to a group of student radicals at the University of Strasbourg, paid for by their student union (which was not amused). The culmination of this period of agitation among the academics was the nearly simultaneous publication of two books of situationist theory: Debord's *La Societe du Spectacle* and Vaneigem's *Traite de Savoir-vivre*. In these works, and in the essays published in the SI's journal during this period, the best example of what a constructed situation is became a popular insurrection such as the 1871 Commune of Paris, the Kronstadt Rebellion of 1921, or the 1956 Workers' Councils of Budapest.

It was with this orientation that the SI went forth into 1968, during which it met and participated in the festival-like Parisian occupations movement of early

May 1968, which triggered an unprecedented general wildcat strike that paralyzed all of France for several weeks and almost toppled the French government. Unlike so many others (including no doubt the members of the Second SI), the situationists weren't taken by surprise when this clearly anarchist rebellion broke out and took hold of the populace – they had been predicting the rebellion's unlikely arrival for more than a decade. As a result, the SI was able to act quickly and yet with confidence and effectiveness during the May Events; its members could plainly see the importance of the event, which so many commentators were determined to dismiss as minor, localized, even nonexistent. Conversely, because the SI's devotion to resuscitating the international revolutionary movement had been unwavering, the rebellion could not fail but to have certain distinctly situationist features (such as the Enrages' use of politico-poetic graffiti and slogans, images taken from and turned against popular culture, and demands for the radical alteration of the patterns of everyday life).

The third period of the SI (1968 to 1971) was largely taken up with accurately reporting, documenting and interpreting what had happened in Paris and elsewhere in France during May 1968. Because of the clarity and severity of their take on the rebellion, the situationists – in Rene Vienet's 1968 book *Enrages and Situationists in the Occupations Movement* and in the 12th and, as it turned out, last issue of their journal (September 1969) – produced both the most knowledgeable and the most useful accounts of it. But the SI was not sure what its own next step should be, now that "the much anticipated revolution" had arrived; indeed, its members weren't even sure if the SI could or should, in the aftermath of May, continue to exist as it had before.

The beginning of 1970 saw the organization polling itself on these questions. By the end of the year, Raoul Vaneigem had resigned and several members had been excluded for being too "contemplative," that is, being too taken with their status as stars of May 1968. In 1971, the remaining members of the SI decided to dissolve the group and pursue their respective activities as unaffiliated individuals. The following year, the group published *The Veritable Split in the International*, within which there were in-depth analyses of everything of interest – the May 1968 revolt, the situationists' spectacular visibility, the resignation of Vaneigem and the issues it raised, etc. – with the exception of the SI's quiet and unexpected decision to disband. (Note: a different interpretation of the SI's last few years and end can be found in *At Dusk*.)

Other options for the group clearly included acclimating themselves to their unwanted celebrity and learning how to use it to further their aims, or arming themselves, going underground and becoming terrorists, as several ultraleft groups in France, Germany, Italy, England and the United States did in the 1970s. But these options were no doubt rejected as absurd. The only choice left was to disappear – to return to the nowhere out of which their movement had so unexpectedly emerged – as quietly as possible. So quiet is the farewell to the SI contained in Debord's 1973 cinematic adaption of *La Societe du Spectacle* that you might miss the fact that celebrating the rise and fall of the SI is the film's *raison d'etre*.

Neither fetishizers nor deniers of their past, unsullied by both nostalgia for the 1960s and empty praise for the 1970s, the situationists managed to go out much as they had come in: e.g., masters of their own fate. Thus it seems to us now that their project can be resumed at any time and by anybody who has the ambition, the vision and the commitment to do so. And yet it's obvious and inevitable that there will be problems with any concerted attempt to apply the theory and practice of the Situationist International to contemporary struggles in America. Let us concentrate on four of the most important of them.

1). The Situationist International organized and conducted itself as an avant garde group, indeed, as if it were going to be the very last of this century's many avant garde groups. Though it was militant about maintaining the appearance of equality among the members of the group, the SI was nevertheless an elite group of revolutionaries. It sought to recruit the most promising people and to expel those who after a period of time failed to make good on their promise. The problem here is that America is a country without an avantgarde tradition. The cultural movements that do very well here are anti-elitist, inclusive and "of the times" (rather than "ahead of the times"). Little groups – no matter how grand their names and ambitious their programs – are easily, indeed routinely lost in a country the size and breadth of the USA. And so, if the example of the SI is to be brought to or adopted in America, would-be situationists must find a way of building a heterogeneous, populist movement that is not theoretically nor organizationally incoherent as a result of its inclusiveness.

2). The Situationist International emerged from a culture in which both the State and the private sector were in the business of funding, distributing and exhibiting works of modern art. Thus there were in this culture two possible agencies of what the SI called "recuperation": i.e., the turning of rebellion into money. To combat both of these agencies of recuperation, the SI found it increasingly necessary as it developed to renounce the practice of art (even the practice of such situationist art techniques as detournement, drifting and psychogeography) and to denounce those who practiced it without sufficient regard for the dangers associated with recuperation. The problem here is that, in America, the State has never really been in the modern art business; only the private sector is used to recuperate the wounding attacks and dangerous demands that are made through art. And so, if there are to be American situationists, they need to be less dogmatic than the original situationists when it comes to the production of art, but without losing awareness of the crucial function of recuperation.

3). The Situationist International emerged from a political culture that had a long tradition of anarchist struggle against both private and bureaucratic capitalism. Though European anarchism had won no decisive battles or launched any successful revolutions, in the 1957 to 1971 period it remained an active social tendency with its share of followers. As a result, the SI could use anarchism –

something from which it strove to kept its distance at all times – as something to define and clarify the SI's own position with respect to the dominant institutions of society. The problem here is that America – despite its traditional lawlessness and individualism, and despite its own an anarchist tradition (which stretches from Benjamin Tucker and William Godwin to the Industrial Workers of the World and Dwight MacDonald) – is strongly and deeply suspicious of anarchism, which it routinely confuses with terroristic violence against the State. And so would-be American situationists must define and practice anarchism in such a way that both "rugged individualists" and anti-bureaucratic anti-capitalists can feel comfortable with it.

4). The Situationist International emerged from a culture that had powerful trade unions and a strong labor movement. Though these unions were dominated by the parties of the detested Communist Left, the SI could count on two things: the members of the rank-and-file were accustomed to talk of class consciousness, class struggle and revolutionary socialism, and so could easily understand the publications of the SI; the rank-and-file members of the union, as well as the theorizing intellectuals employed by the various Communist parties, were excellent candidates for recruitment into the SI or independent manifestations of the anarchist revolutionary project. The problem here is that, though nearly all of America's major labor unions were founded by socialists, these unions are A). drastically weakened after decades of concerted anti-labor political and economic policies; and B). no longer controlled nor even fought for by organized Communist Left groups, which have themselves been in steady decline for many years. Americans who would be situationists therefore must not count on workers to be familiar or comfortable revolutionary themes and rhetoric, and must not automatically or necessarily look to the unions and the "socialist" political parties for readers, contributors, recruits or people to man the barricades, all of whom must come from elsewhere.

But to change one's expectations in these specific ways is to embrace anarchism and to admit that Marxism must not only be "detourned" (brought up-to-date), but finally dispensed with as well. One has every right to wonder what might remain of the situationist project after the changes proposed here have been made. In particular, one would be correct to ask, "What is 'situationist' about a situationist theory and practice that is no longer tightly focused on the proletariat and the ways in which the Stalinist parties prevent it from fighting effectively against both private and bureaucratic capitalism?" The answer would appear to be "Nothing other the various tactics and techniques the SI introduced to the revolutionary movement." It may turn out that, just as they claimed, the situationists were in fact much closer on the strategic level to Marxism than they were to the anarchism of Bakunin, Proudhon and Blanqui. It may also turn out that the recent global collapse of Marxism as a revolutionary theory of action took the SI down with it, and that only anarchism can help us now. But this should not dissuade us from trying to apply what the situationists did to contemporary

America. Indeed, it should encourage us, for it means that, when we are done, what we have come up with will truly fit our time, place and situation.

NOT BORED! #27, May 1997

The English Situationists

"The Revolution of Modern Art and the Modern Art of Revolution" was published as a pamphlet in October 1994 by Chronos Publications (B.M. Chronos, London WC1N 3XX). Previously unpublished, this text was written in October 1967 by four English situationists (Christopher Gray, Tim Clark, Charles Radcliffe and Donald Nicholson-Smith) for publication in the first issue of their review. Just a couple of months later, there were no more English members of the Situationist International: Radcliffe resigned in November, and the rest were excluded in December over the so-called Ben Morea affair. ("So many hasty journeys!" Guy Debord says in his last film, *In Girum Imus Nocte et Consumimur Igni*, while a picture of Nicholson-Smith appears on the screen.) The review of the English situationists never came out, and neither the four original authors, nor the SI itself, ever saw fit to publish "The Revolution" as a separate text.

When compared to the texts the continental SI was publishing at the time, "The Revolution" is something of a throwback. In it the English situationists seem to be in the process of absorbing the SI's first set of themes concerning art and culture, catching up with them, trying to make them their own. In the meantime, the central focus of the continental situationists had shifted to other matters: the "crisis" of the university system, the rise of a youth "counterculture," and the role played by the left-wing political parties that sought voters and members among students and faculty members. As Tim Clark and Donald Nicholson-Smith themselves write in "Why Art Can't Kill the Situationist International" (*October 79*, Winter 1997), "it was the Left (as opposed to, say, the art world) that the Situationists most hated in the 1960s and thought worth targeting."

Significantly, the only quotation from the review *Internationale Situationniste* that appears in the English situationists' pamphlet comes from *I.S. #1*, which was published in 1958. But one suspects this is a not reflection of the relative "immaturity" of the English situationists' theoretical development, nor a consequence of the delay in the translation and dissemination of situationist texts in England. One suspects that this is an expression of discomfort or ambivalence, an intentional distancing. Unlike situationist manifestoes – such as that issued by the Spur Group – "The Revolution of Modern Art and the Modern Art of Revolution" doesn't speak at any length or in any detail about the situationists, and doesn't encourage the reader to believe that the SI is a unique or even an interesting group. "There is *no* organization to date which would not completely betray [the new revolutionary movement]," the authors assert; "*all* previous political critiques of the repressive hierarchy engendered by the past revolutionary argument . . . have completely missed the point: they were not focused on precisely what it was that this hierarchy repressed and perverted in the form of passive militancy" (emphasis added). It is possible that the English situationists were excluded or resigned from the SI so quickly after their admission because they weren't ever really committed to being members of any type of official organization. But it is quite clear that the English situationists (especially Gray, Clark and Nicholson-Smith) were and are still deeply committed to the dissemination of situationist theory and to the undertaking of the situationist project by as many autonomous people as possible. Clark and Nicholson-Smith's efforts, as we have seen, continue to the present day.

Presented as a series of subsections that have their own (sub)titles, "The Revolution of Modern Art" is a strongly worded condemnation of what passes for human creativity in modern capitalist societies (that is, "art" and "culture"), and a call for revolutionaries to begin the recreation of the nature of creativity itself. Much like Debord's 1956 text "Preliminaries," the article by the English situationists insists on the central importance of what they call "the most radical theses of the European avant-garde during the revolutionary upheavals of 1910-1925: that art must cease to be a specialised and imaginary transformation of the world and become the real transformation of lived experience itself." Much like the founding documents of the SI, the article by the English observes that a parallel realization took place within the workers' movement during the 1910-1925 period: that class struggle must cease to be a bureaucratic transformation of the specialized world of parliamentary politics, and become the real transformation of everyday life. "Only now," the English situationists write, "with the Welfare State, with the gradual accession of the whole proletariat to hitherto 'bourgeois' standards of comfort and leisure, can the two movements [avant-garde art and radical politics] converge and lose their traditional animosity." If the artist does not recognize and move as fast as possible toward the historic, previously impossible and Utopian convergence between art and politics – that is, the continued allegiance to "phantasy erected into a systematic culture" – then the practice of art "has become Public Enemy Number One." As for the traditional cultural "philistinism" of the Left, it "is no longer just an incidental embarrassment," the English situationists assert. "It has become deadly."

In place of both traditional avant-garde art and traditional communist/socialist politics, the English situationists – in step with the continental members of the SI – propose to situate the game (more precisely, the detournement of whole cities into game-cities). "If all the factors conditioning us are co-ordinated and unified by the structure of the city," reason the English situationists, "then the question of mastering our own experience becomes one of mastering the conditioning inherent in the city and revolutionizing its use." Situationist games, which in the words of English situationists are intended to be both "the means and the end of total revolution," must be "simultaneously self expressive and socially disruptive," and are thus easily distinguishable from the socially edifying, so-called participatory art forms thrown up by the various pseudo-avant-gardes (the mass media, the avant-garde art establishment and the entertainment industry).

The social class most likely to immediately take to heart the idea of the situationist game is the intelligentsia. "While the way of life of the servile intelligentsia is the living denial of anything remotely resembling either creativity or intelligence," the English situationists declare,

> the rebel intelligentsia is becoming caught up in the reality of disaffection and revolt, refusing to work and inevitably faced, point blank, with a radical reappraisal of the relationship between creativity and everyday life. Frequenting the lumpen, they will learn to use other weapons than their imagination. One of our first moves must be to envenom the latent hostility between these two factions. It shouldn't be too difficult.

To the intelligent rebel, situationist games are deeply desirable: they will eradicate modern poverty, which is defined by the English situationists as "the inability to live, the lethargy, the boredom, the isolation, the anguish and the sense of complete meaninglessness which are eating like a cancer" through the proletariat of the 20th century, and not as the "brutal struggle to survive in the teeth of exposure, starvation and disease" that typified the experience of the proletariat in the 19th century. Situationist games only need everything – "the whole accumulated power of the productive forces" – for them to be totally satisfying for all.

A couple of things stand out here, worthy of remark. The first is this ridiculous and yet uncanny stuff about the lumpen(proletariat), the social milieu the rebel intelligentsia will "frequent" and therein learn to fight. In the "lumpen" the English situationists include rioters, juvenile delinquents, petty criminals, thrill seekers, shoplifters, members of such organized groups as the Provos and the Hell's Angels, and working-class subcultural groups as the Mods and the Rockers. To the English, the lumpen represent "the assertion of the desire to play in a situation where it is totally impossible," and "the turning point between the pure destruction of the commodity and the stage of its subversion."

> The new lumpen will probably be our most important theatre of operations. We must enter it as a power against it and precipitate its crisis. Ultimately, this can only mean to start a real movement between the lumpen and the rest of the proletariat: their conjunction will define the revolution. In terms of the lumpen itself the first thing to do is to disassociate the rank-and-file from the incredible crock of shit raised up, like a monstrance, by their leaders and ideologists.

This is a remarkable passage, and it is so for a variety of reasons.

We have said that the themes of "The Revolution of Modern Art" seem to be throwbacks to those of the great situationist texts of the 1950s. But if we compare the article by the English to, say, the SI's seminal pamphlet *On the Poverty of Student Life* (published in 1966 and translated into English by British situationist Christopher Gray as *Ten Days That Shook the University*), we find a sharp disagreement on tactics. Though situationists on both sides of the English Channel agreed with Vaneigem when he wrote that the real heirs of Dada are the juvenile delinquents, the continental SI believed that its most important theatre of operations was the rebel intelligentsia, not the lumpen. For the continental SI, the goal was to negate the separation between the intelligentsia (which includes the art world and the student milieu) and the proletariat; but for the English situationists, the goal was to negate the separation between the lumpenproletariat and the proletariat.

At first the latter goal seems far-fetched. After all, the situationists themselves were members of the rebel intelligentsia, and not the (lumpen)proletariat; therefore, they would seem more likely to have success in uniting the intelligentsia (and not the lumpen) with the proletariat. In the notes to Chronos Publications' edition of the article by the English – which Chronos mistakenly calls their "manifesto" – the eulogy on the violence of the juvenile delinquents is called "crass" and cited as an incidence of "vulgarization," presumably of the SI's lofty analyses. But the English situationists were right, or, rather, they worked diligently to help create a situation in which their analysis was proved right.

In the same way that the continental SI tried diligently to instigate and later participated in the occupations movement when it broke out in France in 1968, the English situationists tried diligently to instigate and later participated in the punk movement when it broke out in England in 1977. In addition to translating, publishing and distributing *On the Poverty of Student Life,* Christopher Gray teamed up with Jamie Reid, who'd been publishing the situationist-influenced fanzine Suburban Press since 1970, to produce *Leaving the Twentieth Century: The Incomplete Work of the Situationist International* in 1974. Designed to introduce situationist theory to a new generation of lumpen, *Leaving the Twentieth Century* was the first English-language anthology of situationist material. Eventually, Reid and his friend Malcolm McLaren found the right group of lumpen to give copies of the book to: the future members of the Sex Pistols and all their friends. Nothing if not the revolt of the lumpenproletariat, the punk movement clearly demonstrated the revolutionary power created and released when the separation between lumpen and prol is negated.

One last point. It seems necessary to say again – though we have pointed it out before (see our comments on Perspective's *At Dusk* pamphlet) – that the Welfare State may have arrived and grown tremendously powerful and far-reaching in the 1960s, but its existence since then has been far from unchallenged or permanent: indeed, it has been under sustained and increasingly deadly assault in the United States since the early 1980s, with the most serious damage coming in the last three years. The same reign of "austerity" has come to many other industrialized countries, but especially France, Italy, and Germany, and even the Scandinavian countries. Though the bourgeoisification of the whole proletariat may have appeared to be an essential, inevitable and irreversible aspect of the development of modern capitalism in the 1950s and 1960s, no one thinks so now, not even capitalism's defenders, apologists and ideologues.

In part in response to the outbreak of mass disaffection and revolt in the 1960s, capitalism simply took back in the 1970s and 1980s what it appeared to be giving in the 1950s and 1960s. The brutal struggle to survive material poverty has returned (that is, if it ever really left), and with a vengeance. "One knows very few people dying of hunger," quip the English situationists. "But everyone one knows is dying of boredom." The times have changed, moved on but also reverted back to the intensely class-divided conditions of the 1930s. Unfortunately, today "one" sees thousands of people who are homeless and dying of hunger, exposure or disease; "one" sees them everywhere these days, in the parks, on the subways, in doorways, on the sidewalks. And so here's a fuckin' basic banality, yo: what the situationists took to be permanent developments were in fact temporary. As a result, their dream of a Utopian convergence between avant-garde art and radical politics – if it is to be realized – will either have to wait for another day (when the objective economic pre-conditions are in place) or have to find another way of becoming real.

Quite obviously, we're fucking tired of waiting for reality to catch up to our dreams, and so we – as true believers in the situationists' Utopian dreams of game-cities, never working and yet still being able to feed, clothe and house ourselves, the uninterrupted revolution of everyday life – will have to find another way of making them real for ourselves and right now. But one can't help thinking that the situationists' mistaken beliefs about the future of modern capitalism are indicative of a fundamental flaw in situationist theory. The problem it isn't so much the fact that the SI was wrong about the linearity and direction of the development of capitalism, but the fact that it put so much trust in capitalism and its technology. The English situationists write:

> No project, however phantastic, can any longer be dismissed as 'Utopian.' The power of industrial productivity has grown immeasurably faster than any of the 19th century revolutionaries foresaw. The speed at which automation is being developed and applied heralds the possibility of the complete abolition of forced labour – the absolute pre-condition of real human emancipation – and, at the same time, the creation of a new, purely ludic type of free activity, whose achievement demands a critique of the alienation of

'free' creativity in the work of art.

The key word here – as it is in "Revolutionary Gamesters: S.I. Manifesto of 17 May 1960," which glibly speaks of replacing work with "the automation of production" and the "irresistible development of technology," and in Constant's "New Babylon" (1974) – is automation. Everything is up for critique here except for this automation, which is presumably the highest, if not final stage of capitalist technological development. For the situationists, automation is both a given and something absolutely indispensable. And so the paradox is this: *the situationists would rely upon automated technology that was produced by and for a capitalist society to act as the basis for the creation of a "new," workless libertarian society.* It didn't occur to a single situationist that all capitalist technology – but especially automated capitalist technology – is inherently defective to the extent that the distinctively capitalist split between decision-maker (Capital) and executor of decisions (Labor) is part of its very functioning and substance. The split between Capital and Labor in automation is total: labor only "works" when the machine breaks down. But whether it is automated capitalist technology or manually operated capitalist technology we're talking about, one thing is crystal clear. *Capitalist technology can be put to no other uses but capitalist ones.* The new libertarian society must fashion its own technology if that society is to be really new and libertarian. Following the wisdom of the expression "Socialism will arrive on a bicycle," we are confident that – from the perspective of capitalist technology – libertarian technology will be a step in a de-evolutionary direction.

NOT BORED! #28, December 1997

Pierre Guillaume's "Guy Debord"

About a year ago, in response to our "Open Letter to Stewart Home" (which in part concerns alleged anti-Semitism in the situationist milieu), a sympathetic European comrade sent us a copy of Pierre Guillaume's untranslated text "Guy Debord," which was published in *La Vieille Taupe* in Spring 1996. Though our French is not good, we were able to ascertain that the text in part questions Debord's relationship with historical revisionism. It was clear to us that – no matter the nature or truthfulness of the accusations contained therein – Guillaume's text would be of interest to our readers, and so we offered to make a copy of the untranslated French text for anyone who wished to read it. We answered about ten requests, and after a while the significance of the text faded somewhat.

Then, in September 1997, Guillaume's "Guy Debord" was recalled to our attention by a French comrade who wondered why we hadn't discussed what the text says about the situationists' interest in workers' councils, which was the theme of our piece "Workers' Councils, Cornelius Castoriadis and the Situationist International" (*NOT BORED!* #26, 1996). Our answer was simple: we hadn't discussed Guillaume's text in this context because the text remained untranslated; we didn't know what the piece said about the councils in sufficient detail to discuss it. Our French correspondent, who had prepared a rough draft of a translation of Guillaume's "Debord" into English, kindly sent it to us. Nearly unreadable due to all the mistakes and typos in it, the text had to be edited before it could be properly read. Uninvited to do so, we edited and proofread the entire translation, and then worked closely with the translator – who was pleased with our efforts – so that the final version was acceptable to both of us.

During this several-week-long process, the translator disclosed the fact that the translation had originally been prepared for publication by Serge Thion, a prominent French historical revisionist and webmaster for L'Association des Anciens Amateurs des Recits de Guerres et d'Holocaustes (the Ancient Amateurs Association of War and Holocaust Tales). This revelation did not trouble us, and has not dissuaded us from posting the translation on our site. Though we disagree with the conclusions and distrust the motives of historical revisionists such as Guillaume and Thion, we defend their right to free speech. We are categorically opposed to all forms of censorship. In posting Guillaume's text and allowing the translation to be freely circulated all over the world, we are not providing a forum for Guillaume's views, but an opportunity for understanding and discussing the issues that he raises.

It turns out that – among other things – Guillaume's "Guy Debord" supports our deductions and provides a great deal of useful background information about a variety of related subjects. According to Guillaume, who was a member of S. ou B. in the early 1960s, Debord was a member of the group in 1960, despite the SI's official policy against dual memberships. Guillaume's piece describes the S. ou B. group's chilly reception of the text "Preliminaries toward a definition of the revolutionary program," which was jointly authored by Debord and S. ou B. member Daniel Blanchard (aka Pierre Canjuers) in 1960, and which we found remarkable for its total absence of references to workers' councils. Finally, Guillaume's remembrance of Guy Debord includes a description of the circumstances of Debord's resignation from the S. ou B. group in 1961, which did not end his interest in S. ou B.'s themes and research. "From 1960 on," Guillaume writes,

> the influence of 'social-barbarian' theses and knowledge (more or less recomposed) didn't cease to grow in the situationists' publications; it appeared as a reference to the workers' movement. This incorporation was to constitute to me the main interest of the S.I. and determined the broadening of its audience in France.

To Guillaume, the SI became "heir of the best Socialisme ou Barbarie had produced," even if Guillaume himself had by 1967 abandoned the S. ou B. line, and started reading Bordiga and ridiculing the "illusions" of council communists like the SI.

Guillaume's text also includes very useful – and previously unavailable – information on the relationship between Debord and the situationists, on the one hand, and Guillaume and *La Vieille Taupe* (The Old Mole) Bookstore, on the other. Founded, named and stocked with books by Guillaume and Debord in 1965, *La Vieille Taupe* seems to have been an important source of situationist publications; indeed, for a time it may have been the only store in Paris to keep them in stock. The bookstore must also have been a hangout for situationists and other ultra-leftists. According to Guillaume, the tie between *La Vieille Taupe* and the SI was rather suddenly severed (by the later camp) in June 1966, at which time another store in Paris became the official repository for situationist publications offered for sale. Despite the stinging notice about *La Vieille Taupe* that appeared in *Internationale Situationniste* #11 (October 1967), Guillaume declares that the parting of the ways was amicable on both sides. He says that he still thinks and speaks highly of both Debord and the SI (though there are a few situationists Guillaume doesn't care for), and he takes comfort in the idea that – other than the stinging but short notice that appeared in I.S. #11 – there has not been a single published or publicly declared critique of *La Vieille Taupe* by Debord, the SI, or any individual situationist. This would seem to be cold comfort, for, after the 1966 break-up and for the rest of his life, *Debord had absolutely nothing to do with – and nothing to say or write about – Guillaume personally or any of the post-bookstore projects in which he has been active.*

If this were all there was to Guillaume's story, it would be a useful and occasionally interesting account, but ultimately sterile: the angry, paranoid and yet still devoted-to-Guy testimony of yet another worthy – another former friend and collaborator – excluded, once and for all, from the side of Guy Debord, revolutionary situationist. But there is more, much more. Guillaume seems to presume that his audience is familiar with his own post-S. ou B. activities, and so doesn't tell his readers very much about what he's been up to since 1967. But it is clear from what he does say that sometime after 1978 he – like Serge Thion – became active in the defense of the free speech rights of such historical revisionists as Robert Faurisson, and became a historical revisionist himself. The translator of Guillaume's portrait of Debord assures us that, though Guillaume is a Holocaust revisionist, this does not mean that he is either an extreme Rightist or a white supremacist. Guillaume is an ultra*leftist* historical revisionist. This makes him something of a double exception, a stereotype-buster.

One would expect someone in Guillaume's delicate position to claim that Debord "had among his close friends a few more or less consistent [historical] revisionists," and Guillaume does not disappoint us (though he doesn't name any names). One would even expect Guillaume to assert that Debord – whether he knew it or not – was at times close to positions taken by many historical revisionists. Again, no disappointment: he says of Debord's very paranoid and very oblique book *Comments on the Society of the Spectacle*: "if you replaced the word 'capitalism' by words referring to the ideology and the mono-ethnic organizational structures that pretend to be the representatives of the Jewish 'community'" – in other words, groups such as the "powerful international freemasonry" B'nai B'rith – certain passages take on their "full meaning." This is garden-variety right-wing propaganda: disingenuous, ridiculous, banal.

But Guillaume shows himself to be more than a common right-wing propagandist when he describes his own responses to Debord's post-1966 silence. "Until 1979," he writes,

> this silence could be understood by *La Vieille Taupe*'s enemies as being the consequence of mercy shown to an insignificant thing. . . . Or even as a manifestation of indifference, if not contempt. It's fairly possible. . . . But the silence of Debord since 1979 (and the public outbreak of the Faurisson affair) . . . is much less easy to understand.

It is strange that, in a text so full of details and evidence of the author's desire to be thought a reliable and reasonable source of information, Guillaume tells us absolutely nothing about the Faurisson affair and nothing about its relevance to Guillaume himself and to Debord's silence. Strictly speaking, the Faurisson affair has nothing to do with Debord's severed relationship with Guillaume. Professor Robert Faurisson of Lyon University is a French historical revisionist; the "affair" that bears his name concerns the suppression of his writings on the existence of gas chambers at the Nazi concentration camps. Perhaps because he personally was vocal in his support of Faurisson's positions and in his defense of Faurisson's right to free speech, Guillaume believed that the affair made it more likely that Debord would break his silence and say something, anything about *La Vieille Taupe*. But Debord remained silent.

"Until 1985, I couldn't exclude the idea that Debord was biding his time," Guillaume writes. He had to know: was Debord remaining silent because he secretly sympathized with the plight of the historical revisionists (but couldn't come right out and say it), or was he silent because he thought that both the revisionists and the scandal of the suppression of their writings were spectacularly inconsequential? It's a false question: Debord was silent in 1979 and 1985 (and thereafter) because of a decision he had made back in 1966; that decision was based upon Debord's impressions of Guillaume as he was then. There was no possibility of re-admittance or change of mind, no matter what had happened since then. This was Debord's rule, and it applied to Guillaume as much as anyone else.

In 1988, Guillaume thought he'd come up with the perfect way of forcing an answer to the question that was evidently driving him crazy. He would publish excerpts from Debord's newest book, *Comments on the Society of the Spectacle,* in the *Annals of Historical Revisionism*. Widely noted for treating references to him and his work as direct modes of address, Debord would have to respond to Guillaume's use of these excerpts. It would look like Debord approved of this recontextualization if he didn't. Clever trick this: it's called blackmail.

To Guillaume, the content of Debord's *Comments* "doesn't seem to be explainable without the hypothesis of an implicit reference to the Faurisson affair." The point might be better put this way: some of Debord's remarks, especially those concerning censorship, could easily and appropriately be applied to Faurisson's situation. But the principal theme of Debord's book is – to quote from the very same passages from the *Comments* that were reprinted by Guillaume – "historical knowledge *in general*," "the *totality* of events whose consequences would be lastingly apparent" (emphasis added). Guillaume and other historical revisionists – perhaps because of their simple stupidity, willful ignorance, personal prejudice or inescapable religious indoctrination – are fixated on historical knowledge of only one event. They are totalitarians to the extent that they elevate a fragment, i.e., the critique of historical knowledge about the Nazis' attempted extermination of Europe's Jews, to the level of a total critique of contemporary society. (This same totalitarian movement is repeated within the revisionists' critique of the history of WWII: i.e., if it can proved that there are reasonable doubts about the existence and widespread use of gas chambers in the camps, then the mass murder of Jews couldn't have taken place at all.)

After Guillaume published the excerpts, once again "there was no comment at all" from Debord, who clearly preferred to run the risk of being thought of as a secret supporter of historical revisionism, than to say anything at all about Pierre Guillaume and his friends. Given the way Guillaume tried to blackmail Debord, whom he praises as "impossible to tame, constrain or maneuver," Debord's silence is not only understandable: it is admirable as well. But for Guillaume, the silence was too much; and so he wrote this piece, which attempts to damn Debord posthumously. "By making a show of the way he had been persecuted and of the media's vindictiveness against him," Guillaume says of Debord, "and – at the same time, by occulting the infinitely more serious, constant and systematic persecution of the revisionists – he collaborated with the totalitarian coherence òf the spectacle." Since Debord did not "apply to the commemoration of the Holocaust and the Shoah business the principles of his critique of the spectacle," he must have been a collaborator with the spectacle, and thus – by Debord's own absolute standards – no revolutionary at all.

But Debord did not ignore nor did he miss "the central role of Auschwitz in the spectacle," as Guillaume claims. As a matter of fact, in the *Comments* Debord precisely traces the beginning of the modern spectacle to 1939 and the beginning of World War II. For Debord, Nazi Germany and Soviet Russia were the inventers of the concentrated spectacle; and the concentrated spectacle – rather than being an aberration or the polar opposite of the diffuse spectacle of American society – is the diffuse spectacle's essence and its destiny. For Debord (as well as Henri

Lefebvre and the members of the SI), the concentration camp uncannily prefigures the post-World War II housing block. "If the Nazis had known contemporary urbanists, they would have transformed their concentration camps into low-income housing," Raoul Vaneigem quips in "Comments Against Urbanism" (*Internationale Situationniste* #6, August 1961). "The final result of the process thus undertaken," Theo Frey writes (*I.S.* #10, March 1966), "henceforth appears as the modernized version of a solution that has proven itself, the concentration camp, here deconcentrated all over the planet." For the situationists, it was *the reality of the Nazis' deportation, concentration and mass murder of Europe's Jews, homosexuals, Communists, anarchists and Gypsies* – and not *the way the concentration camps have been (mis)represented* – that makes them "spectacular" and our society "the society of the spectacle" in the precise way that Debord used these terms.

"Thus it is no longer possible to believe anything about anyone that you have not learned for yourself, directly," Debord writes in one of the passages reprinted by Guillaume, who would have his readers believe that this statement strengthens the revisionists' assertion that the official history of the Holocaust is falsified, or that even if it isn't falsified, the official history of the Holocaust is only accurate to the extent that you personally have verified it. But it seems far more likely that Debord meant that conditions such as the one he described can be all-too-easily exploited by totalitarian ideologies such as historical revisionism, which can become popular by intensifying and exploiting any one (or a combination) of the deep prejudices held by segments of the population. Whereas Guillaume seems to ask his readers to acclimate and adapt themselves to these new conditions of perpetual doubt, Debord expected only half his readership to do so. The other half he expected to create a society in which it is possible to believe the word of another about historical events. This affirmative side is completely missing from Guillaume's portrait of Debord.

NOT BORED! #28, December 1997

On the 50th Anniversary of the Founding of the Situationist International

"It is vain to want to revive a Situation that was valid 45 years ago. And especially when the people who occupy themselves with this 'restoration' are only chefs who do not know how to cook." – Raoul Hausmann, letter to Guy Debord dated 5 April 1963.

"Surrealism is obviously alive. Its creators are still not dead. The new people, more and more mediocre, it is true, claim kinship with it. Surrealism is known to the public as the extreme of modernism and, on the other hand, it has become an object for university studies. It is indeed one of the things that live at the same time that we do, like Catholicism and General de Gaulle. [...] The real question is thus: what is the role of surrealism today?" – Guy Debord, "Supreme Height of the Defenders of Surrealism in Paris and the Revelation of their Real Value" (December 1958).

Exactly 50 years ago today – on 28 July 1957 – the Situationist International (SI) was founded in Cosio d'Arroscia, a small village in Italy. Is it not senseless to celebrate such an event? The SI disbanded in April 1972, and so is no longer with us. Several of its most important members (Asger Jorn, Constant, and Guy Debord) are dead. When the organization *was* in existence, it existed both in and against its era;[1] it was never intended to last beyond it.[2] To the extent that the SI's era has passed, so has the SI itself. There is no going back.

Over the course of those 15 years, the SI changed a great deal. It is commonly agreed that the organization went through three distinct stages (and so one might say that there were *three* Situationist Internationals, without considering the "Second Situationist International," which was formed in 1960 by several people who had been excluded from the "First" SI). Between 1957 and 1961, the SI both theorized and made *revolutionary art*; between 1962 and 1968, it both produced and disseminated *revolutionary theory*; and, between 1969 and 1972, it both theorized and participated in the post-1968 *revolutionary movement.* There were different, even conflicting tendencies within each of these three periods: between 1957 and 1961, there were intense debates between Jorn and Constant, that is to say, between the painters and the architects/urbanists; between 1962 and 1968, there were conflicts of style and tone that pitted Debord against Raoul Vaneigem, that is, dialectical epigrams against narrative exposition; and, between 1969 and 1972, there were splits between those who wanted to the SI to stay small or even shrink in size (most of the French section) and those who wanted it to grow (the American section).

Such was the richness of the SI. This richness – the group's incredible fertility – is why one marks and celebrates the anniversary of the organization's founding. But when one speaks of the SI, one most often has the SI of the 1962-1968 period in mind. Did not Debord himself say that "one can not speak of 'coherence' in the first years of the SI," because coherence was only achieved in "the period begun in 1962 and in large part as a project that was more or less *verified* later on"?[3] It was, of course, during the SI's "middle" period that Vaneigem wrote and published *Treatise on Living for the Younger Generations*[4] and Debord wrote and published *The Society of the Spectacle.* More so than the essays published in *Internationale Situationniste,* these are the texts – plus Mustapha Khayati's pamphlet *On the Poverty of Student Life* (written and published in 1966) – for which the SI is best known.

Each of these famous books elaborates its own theory: Vaneigem's *Treatise* elaborates the theory of "everyday life"[5] and Debord's *Spectacle* elaborates the theory of "the spectacle."[6] But the former was in fact *not* a theory, but a concept; and, furthermore, it has not changed or been developed since the early 1960s. *Everyday life* was and remains an empty "terrain" (really, a block of time) that is occupied by and with passionless, joyless and meaningless activities: primarily work and the consumption of commodities. The *revolution of everyday life* was and remains the quest *by individuals* for a certain lifestyle, for time freed from the necessity of working and for consumption freed from the necessity of buying commodities.

On the other hand, "the spectacle" was indeed a theory, and Debord changed and developed it *twice* over the course of twenty-odd years. (One must not forget that the 15 years of the SI's existence is matched by the 15 years of diligent and high-quality activity that Debord personally engaged in between 1973 and 1988.) In 1967, the spectacle – a stage of capitalist society in which super-abundant wealth is displayed and wasted instead of being used to revolutionize that society – was defined as a binary opposition (and cooperation) between *the diffuse spectacle* of the "democratic" West and *the concentrated spectacle* of the "totalitarian" East. In 1973, in Debord's film *The Society of the Spectacle,* the spectacle was shown to be a stage that could be and indeed was actually being contested all over the world, in both the West (especially France) and the East (especially Poland).[7] And, in 1988, in Debord's *Comments on the Society of the Spectacle,* the spectacle[8] was defined as an "integration" of the diffuse and concentrated brands.

And so we are confronted with a troublesome series of observations: though the theory of the spectacle began as an exclusively situationist theory (no one else elaborated it), it ended up as Guy Debord's theory.[9] Unlike both the concept of "everyday life" and the Situationist International itself, the theory of spectacle *moved beyond the 1960s* and so did not pass away with them. More than that: with the development of the theory of the integrated spectacle, "situationist theory crosses over its disintegration point."[10] That is to say, situationist theory – *purely* situationist theory, undeveloped situationist theory, situationist theory that bases itself too heavily or solely upon the revolution of everyday life – finally became spectacular, finally became "situationism."

* * *

"Is it worth the bother of saying this again? There is no 'situationism.' I am myself only a situationist due to the fact of my participation – at this moment and in certain conditions – in a community practically grouped together in view of a task, which this community will or will not know how to accomplish [...] The SI is obviously composed of very diverse individuals and even several discernable tendencies of which the relations of force have sometimes changed. Without doubt, its entire activity is only pre-situationist. We do not in any way defend 'creations' that belong to someone and still less to a single one of us: on the contrary, we find it very positive that the comrades who have joined us have already, by themselves, attained an experimental problematic that blends ours. The surest symptom of idealist delirium is, moreover, the stagnation of individuals, supporting or quarreling for years about the same values, because they are the only ones to recognize them as the rules of a poor game. The situationists leave them to their dust-ups." – Guy Debord, "Concerning Several Errors of Interpretation."[11]

Such a split – friends of Guy Debord, on the one hand, and adherents to situationism, on the other, with no situationists to be found on either side – was clearly visible during the polemic surrounding the *Encyclopedia of Nuisances*.[12] Unlike Debord and his friends, who were deeply interested in the political events taking place in Spain, Poland and Italy during the 1980s, the Encyclopedists were preoccupied with situationist texts (from the pre-1962 period!) and abstract concepts.[13] Significantly, the bone of contention between the two groups was an event: the French student movement of November-December 1986, in particular, the occupation of the Sorbonne and the erection of barricades in the Latin Quarter on 6 December. While the Encyclopedists were highly critical of these actions for reasons of "theory," Debord and his friends valued these actions for their practical boldness.[14] One *might* have expected that the reverse would have been the case: the Encyclopedists on the side of "action" and Debord *et al* on the side of "theory." But the times had changed, and so had Debord.

The same split exists today, even though Guy Debord himself is dead. There are a great many adherents to situationism and, though there are important differences between them, they share several of the preoccupations and limitations of the Encyclopedists. Here is a brief sketch, which excludes writers who do not consider themselves to be either adherents to situationism or friends of Debord and who have written texts about the SI that are openly hostile (Stewart Home, Bob Black, Simon Sadler, etc.):

Ken Knabb. This fellow has spent more than 25 years polishing his translations of the texts published in *Internationale Situationniste,* and in 2002 he offered yet another translation of Debord's 1967 book *The Society of the Spectacle* (it had previously been translated by Fredy Perlman and then by Donald Nicholson-Smith). But Knabb is completely uninterested in Debord's work after 1972: his collaboration on the "Censor" pamphlet,[15] his *Preface to the Fourth Italian Edition of "The Society of the Spectacle,"*[16] his virtually unknown 1980 intervention in favor of imprisoned libertarians in Spain,[17] his *Comments on the Society of the Spectacle,* etc. Knabb's interest in Debord's films, most of which were made and released after 1972, does not undermine the validity of our reproach: these are mostly lyrical-poetic works, redolent of the SI's first period, and not strategic interventions, redolent of its third.

Retort. This is the name taken by a group of Anglo-American academics who are utterly fixated on Debord's 1967 book, and seem to be completely uninterested in Debord's post-1972 work. As we have pointed out,[18] this bias renders their analyses of September 11th completely boring and reactionary. Despite their name, this group's members do not dialogue or "engage in polemics" with people who disagree with them.[19] Not surprisingly, Retort's politics are explicitly Leftist, not revolutionary.

Various "Anti-Conspiracy" Pro-Situationists. Like the members of Retort, these are people who – during their denunciations of what they call "conspiracy theories" concerning September 11th – demonstrate their lack of knowledge or interest in both *Preface to the Fourth Italian Edition of "The Society of the Spectacle"* and *Comments of the Society of the Spectacle*. As if the Italian section of the SI never published "Is the Reichstag Burning?," such people claim that "conspiracy theories" are either non-situationist or anti-situationist.

Various Neo-Anarchists. Here we have in mind such groups (or participants in such actions as) "Reclaim the Streets," "Carnival Against Capitalism," The Yes-Men, The Rev. Billy, *et al* – that is to say, most of what used to be called "the anti-globalization movement." These are Leftists and former-Marxists who are strongly influenced by the pre-1962 situationists, who call themselves "anti-authoritarians" because it is a good marketing strategy, and who are single-mindedly obsessed with defective or toxic commodities, evil corporations and economic globalization, and yet absolutely unconcerned with concentration camps, fascism, the "refugee crisis" and other properly political problems. They are also openly disdainful of September 11th "conspiracy theories."[20]

Jordan Levinson. This is a neo-anarchist who refers to Debord as "de Bore," who gloats about the fact that Debord "offed himself," and excoriates "the impotent rhetoric of dead fools from 40 years ago," *and yet* uses the email address situationist@email.com and insists on uploading his bad translations of situationist texts to a website that is full of advertisements and that deposits cookies and pop-up windows for commercial products on the hard-drives of the people foolish enough to access it. Levinson is an excellent example of a "Vaneigemist": full of rage and resentment, terrified of being judged or correcting himself, and content with things (virtually *anything,* of whatever quality) as long as they are free.

Raoul Vaneigem. To the casual observer, or even the moderately well-informed person, Vaneigem resigned from the SI in November 1970 and never looked back, that is to say, pursued his ideas and projects positively and progressively, not negatively or in reaction to his resignation from the group to which he belonged and derived whatever notoriety he possesses. Only those who have tracked Vaneigem's collaborations with the virulent anti-Debordist and madman Jean-Pierre Voyer – and Vaneigem's use of pseudonyms (not "Ratgeb" or

"Jules-Francois Dupuis," but "Jean-Pierre Bastid," "Pierre Bree" and "Jacques Vincent") in these collaborations[21] – would know that his resignation has both determined and ruined much of what he has written since 1970.[22] (We fear that something similar is in play where Donald Nicholson-Smith is concerned.[23])

Though the adherents to situationism are awful and awfully frustrating, it is not at all comfortable being a "friend of Debord." (Note that we realize that we are certainly not Debord's only "friends," who also include Giorgio Agamben, Jean-Francois Martos and all of the various people who wrote articles about the obviously conspiratorial aspects of September 11th from a "situationist" – that is to say, "Debordist" – perspective.) The many causes for this discomfort are not all "theoretical"; not all of them have to do with the inappropriateness or counter-revolutionary aspects of the cult of personality, hero-worship, etc., especially where this particular person is concerned. Around 1990 or so – but *not before then,* we are sure of it – Debord became seriously depressed, paranoid, moralizing and very dull. These qualities can certainly be discerned in his letter to Jean-Francois Martos dated 26 December 1990, and they quite simply ruined *Son Art et Son Temps,* the TV program he made with Brigitte Cornand in 1994, shortly before his suicide. No doubt Volume 7 (1988-1994) of his *Correspondance,* which will be published in 2008, will show that these were not isolated episodes, but typical of the man's last few years. There will be no point in denying it.

* * *

"For the moment, you must observe all the treatments or regimes that are called for, even the severe ones. We will soon come to Italy, which, I hope, will encourage you. If a culpable indifference to what you can do in the world or a deplorable sense of humor causes you to still play with the idea of suicide, you must consider other alternatives. You know that I have always allowed, with a very great facility and nearly an equal spirit, that *life* separates me from many friends and several girls whom I have loved. But I tolerate death very poorly." – Guy Debord, letter to Gianfranco Sanguinetti dated 25 September 1974.

But this does not mean that Debord's theory of the spectacle should be renounced or abandoned: far from it. Never before has it been so clear that "our" society – the one we are forced to live in and create against our will – is the society of the spectacle. And so our task should be developing a theory of the spectacle as it is today. A step has already been taken in this direction by McKenzie Wark in his book *A Hacker's Manifesto* (2004), in which the author speaks of "the vector." Adopting this term, we might speak of "the vectoral spectacle," but this is clearly inadequate: the relation of the vector (a spatial metaphor) to digital technologies is not clear. And so – drawing upon such easily comprehensible (and relevant) terms as virtual images, virtual memory and virtual reality – we propose the virtual spectacle," the spectacle at its point of virtuality.

[1] "It is necessary to make it understood how the adventure of the SI was narrowly circumscribed *in time*; and contrary to many other 'avant-gardes' with pretensions to lead several [subsequent] generations. Literally, the SI existed from 1957 to 1972. And, by counting the period of the 'origins,' it existed from 1952 to '57. And here was the profound meaning of the operation of 'dissolution' that one can say took place between the autumn of 1970 and the first months of 1972." Guy Debord, letter to Jean-Francois Martos dated 14 September 1985.
[2] One wouldn't know this from the way the SI's texts have been translated into English. Take, for example, Ken Knabb's butchery of Michele Bernstein's "No Useless Indulgences." Despite the facts that this short text was written by one of the SI's founders and published in the very first issue of the group's journal, Knabb saw fit to remove – to leave untranslated – *all* of this text's references to the people outside the SI who are held up for ridicule (Francoise Giroud, Georges Mathieu and Michel Tapie). Knabb's intentions were obvious: to present to the English-speaking world only those passages that were "timeless," that were not "tied" to France in the 1950s, even if that meant leaving *half* of this short text untranslated.
[3] See Debord's letter to Juvenal Quillet dated 11 November 1971.
[4] Better known as *The Revolution of Everyday Life.*
[5] Sources for this theory included Henri Lefebvre's *The Critique of Everyday Life, Volume I* (published in 1947) and *The Critique of Everyday Life, Volume II* (published in 1962).
[6] Sources for this theory included Georg Lukacs' *History and Class Consciousness* (1926) and Georges Bataille's "The Notion of Expenditure" (1933).
[7] In a letter to Eduardo Rothe dated 21 February 1974, Debord sketched out the differences between the pre-1968 and post-1968 periods as follows: "The epoch no longer simply demands a *vague* response to the question 'What is to be done? [...] It is now a question, if one wants *to remain in the present,* of responding to this question almost every week: '*What is happening?*' [...] The principle work that, it appears to me, one must engage in – as the complementary contrary to *The Society of the Spectacle,* which described frozen alienation (and the negation that is implicit in it) – is *the theory of historical action.* One must advance *strategic* theory in its moment, which has come. At this stage and to speak schematically, the basic theoreticians to retrieve and develop are no longer Hegel, Marx and Lautreamont, but Thucydides, Machiavelli and Clausewitz."
[8] As we have noted in our translation of the *Comments on the Society of the Spectacle,* Debord uses the word "spectacular" to designate this integrated form and to distinguish it from its constitutive parts.
[9] It is difficult to not refer here to *Debordist theory.* Surely Debord himself would have said, following Karl Marx's famous declaration "I am not a Marxist,"

that he was not a Debordist and that "Debordism" did not exist.
[10] See remark attributed to Serge Quadruppani in Jean-Francois Martos' letter to Debord, dated 11 September 1990.
[11] Published in *Internationale Situationniste* #4, June 1960. For some reason, this text remained untranslated until a few days ago, when we ourselves translated it.
[12] Founded in 1984 – in the aftermath of the assassination of Debord's publisher, film producer and friend Gerard Lebovici – by the ex-situationist Christian Sebastiani and Debord's friend Jaime Semprun, the *Encyclopedia of Nuisances* published many essays of situationist inspiration, including three by Debord himself ("Hunger-Reducer," "To Abolish" and "*Ab Irato*").
[13] Take for example the perfectly awful essay entitled "Abundance."
[14] See the essay entitled "The Encyclopedia of Powers," which was written by Jean-Francois Martos and Jean-Pierre Baudet, with help from Debord.
[15] Written by the ex-situationist Gianfranco Sanguinetti. See our translation of this important and yet often over-looked work from 1975.
[16] Written and published in 1979, and translated into English shortly thereafter.
[17] We have recently translated *Aux Libertaires* into English.
[18] See both "An Unkind Reply to Retort" and its follow-up, "Another Unkind to Retort," neither of which the group has seen fit to respond to.
[19] "I think this serious and fundamental relation between struggle and truth, the dimension in which philosophy has developed for centuries and centuries, only dramatizes itself, becomes emaciated, and loses its meaning and effectiveness in polemics within theoretical discourse. So in all of this I will therefore propose only one imperative, but it will be categorical and unconditional: Never engage in polemics." Michel Foucault, lecture notes for 11 January 1978, in *Security, Territory, Population: Lectures at the College de France, 1977-1978* (Palgrave/Macmillan, 2007), pp. 3-4.
[20] For more on this subject, see my "Critique of neo-anarchism."
[21] Cf. *Protest to the Libertarians of the present and the future on the capitulations of 1980* (1980) and *Echecs Situationnistes* (1988). In 1976, Vaneigem teamed up with Mustapha Khayati (using the pseudonym "Mustapha Martens") to denounce Gerard Lebovici for reprinting *On the Poverty of Student Life*. For a taste for their resentment and envy, read the note they wrote and falsely attributed to Lebovici.
[22] See our review of Vaneigem's truly awful book entitled *A Declaration of the Rights of Human Beings*, published in 2000.
[23] Most well-informed people will known that, in his last film, *In girum imus nocte et consumimur igni* (1978), Guy Debord included a picture of Donald Nicholson-Smith – who was excluded from the SI in December 1967 – among pictures of other ex-situationists whom he remembered fondly (Asger Jorn, Giuseppe Pinot-Gallizio and Attila Kotanyi).

In a letter to Jon Horelick and Tony Verlaan dated 28 October 1970, Debord remarked that "Certain [excluded] comrades were very simpatico and had some real capabilities. Their participation could be of great value in certain general circumstances many times described by us. I am thinking, for example, of Donald [Nicholson-Smith] and Eduardo [Rothe]: they were excluded, one and then the other, two years apart, for having totally failed to live up to an accord on a specific problem, an accord that they agreed to after very extended discussions."

In a letter to Nicholson-Smith himself dated 16 February 1978, Debord declared, "But beyond the 'organizational' plane on which this regrettable discord arose, you certainly remember that I always accorded you the greatest confidence in all the qualities that I recognized in you, and not only your intellectual talents. Of course, as everything continues, I find nothing surprising in the fact that you are still in the same historic party." The two men agreed to work together on translations of Debord's texts that would be published by Gerard Lebovici's Editions Champ Libre. After a series of exchanges concerning Nicholson-Smith's rather stiff financial requirements, Debord (and Lebovici, too) soured on the arrangement.

In a letter to Lebovici dated 27 May 1979, Debord wrote: "What you have seen in Donald appears to me to confirm the entire picture: bitter discontent at lacking so much in his life, due to my fault in a certain way. This conclusion is reinforced by his lack of eagerness to telephone me. And when he does so, I will respond that I am absent, and that the moment is not quite suitable, but there is nothing pressing. I leave it to you to manage things the best you can on the purely professional level and still remain prudent. Because he who has not known how to affirm himself by himself, over the course of twelve years, must thus *necessarily* associate with the most jealous of our enemies." It appears that "the most jealous of our enemies" is Raoul Vaneigem.

It is certainly true that, in the aftermath of this affair, Nicholson-Smith translated Vaneigem's *Treatise of Living for the Younger Generations* into English (it was published in 1983 as *The Revolution of Everyday Life*); and, in 1999, he translated Vaneigem's crappy little book *A Cavalier History of Surrealism*. In 2002, Nicholson-Smith translated a novel by Jean-Patrick Manchette, a person whom Debord *detested*. . . . It is in this light that one should remember that Nicholson-Smith's translation of Debord's *The Society of the Spectacle* (Zone Books, 1993) does not read like Debord, but like Vaneigem. That is to say, it might be an act of revenge.

Written 28 July 2007
NOT BORED! #39, September 2007

The Situationist International
The Society of the Virtual Spectacle

"The destiny of the theory of the spectacle belongs to those (...) who will individually and collectively retrieve the ideas of anti-hierarchy, coherence [and] global contestation." – Jean-Francois Martos.[1]

"May we succeed in lending a hand to those who in our dear native land are called upon to speak with authority on these matters, that we may be their guide into this field of inquiry, and excite them to make a candid examination of the subject." – Carl von Clausewitz.[2]

Part One

To begin at the roots: capitalism cannot be depended on to "correct" its own defects or fix the damage and destruction it has caused, nor can it be depended upon to collapse, on its own, due to its own internal contradictions and then leave a *tabula rasa* upon which one could build a new and truly human society. Capitalism cannot be fixed by piecemeal reforms, nor can revolution "fix" capitalism if that revolution is limited to the political, economic, technological, moral or indeed *any* particular sector. Only *social revolution,* which is total revolution, can both save humanity from capitalism's evils (war, pollution, poverty, ignorance and intolerance) and instaurate the kind of society in which humanity can truly flourish (peaceful co-existence, physical and mental health, self-fulfillment and pleasure).

Social revolutionaries must have a working theory of capitalist society: that is to say, what it really is, how it continues to exist despite its nearly fatal defects, and how it defends itself against both reformist and revolutionary actions. Here we distinguish ourselves from all those who do not believe that a theory of any kind is necessary, who believe that theory only keeps revolutionaries from acting, that "radical" action is the only theory that is needed, etc., and who form "organizations," and "federations" among these "organizations," most of which have programmatic statements that declare that their members are against a list of bad things (abstractions such as militarism, religious fundamentalism, patriarchy, racism, sexism, et al) and that they are in favor of a list of good things (abstractions such as self-organization, voluntary association, mutual aid, freedom, justice, et al).

We believe that only theory allows our actions to be strategic rather than tactical, to be effective rather than ineffective, to be precise rather than approximate. "The first business of every theory is to clear up conceptions and ideas which have been jumbled together, and, we may say, entangled and confused; and only when a right understanding is established, as to names and conceptions, can we hope to progress with clearness and facility, and be certain that author and reader will always see things from the same point of view" (Clausewitz, *On War*). But we have no illusions about the completeness of theory. As Clausewitz notes, "nothing more than a limited theory can be obtained, which only suits circumstances such as they are presented in history. But this incompleteness is unavoidable, because in any case theory must either have deduced from, or have compared with, history what it advances with respect to things. Besides, this incompleteness in every case is more theoretical than real" (*On War*).

There are, of course, many theories of modern society: psychoanalytic (institutions are created by repressive sublimation); sociological (power is held by large groups, small elites or complex networks); etc. But none of these theories were conceived or elaborated so as to overthrow modern society. Many were in fact intended to justify that society's existence. As a result, they are not perceived as scandalous or unacceptable to it; such perceptions are among the hallmarks of a truly revolutionary theory.

There are at least two major sources of truly revolutionary theory: Marxism and anarchism. Both try to explain who (or what) holds power in society, and why or how they hold it: for the Marxists, the bourgeoisie holds power because it owns and controls the means of production; for the anarchists, the State holds power due to its monopoly over coercive force (the military and the police). Each theory is revolutionary because it envisions an end to this kind of society and its replacement by another, truly humane one: Marxism envisions proletarian revolution, which abolishes all class power; and anarchism envisions a political revolution after which voluntary association will replace coercion.

But both Marxism and anarchism have degenerated a great deal over the course of the last century. Some Marxists now prefer to call themselves "libertarian communists" and have completely abandoned the idea of revolution: "Our primary focus," say the people who run libcom.org, "is always on how best to act in the here and now to better our circumstances and protect the planet." Other Marxists (such as those who produce the journal called *Aufheben*) retain the idea and goal of revolution, but – despite their announced intention to move with the times – remain trapped in the worst aspects of classical Marxist theory, in particular, a fetishism of the proletariat and "proletarian theory." There are still handfuls of Leninist, Trotskyist and Maoist sects in existence; not surprisingly, all of them are hierarchically organized, rigid and terribly dull. Though some of these groups are "behind" several large organizations (including the A.N.S.W.E.R. coalition), these "front groups" are not explicitly revolutionary and indeed simply channel revolutionary impulses back into the electoral system (typically, support for the Democratic Party).[3]

There are many small contemporary groups and movements that subscribe to "anarchism" and "anti-authoritarianism," but few of them are sources (or even readers) of revolutionary theory; mostly they eschew theory in favor of "radical" or "direct" action. For too many of them, action is taken against particular aspects of capitalist society: police brutality, the treatment of animals, biotechnology, racism, pollution, environmental degradation, the war on drugs, sexual violence against women, homophobia, neo-liberalism, etc etc. Very rarely is action taken against capitalist society or the State as a whole. The very idea of such action seems utopian, millenarian and even impossible. And, of course, some of these "anarchists" aren't anarchists at all, but Leftists or "citizenists" who have simply adopted the label because, in the aftermath of the Seattle 1999 riots, it became fashionable and even won several people TV coverage and book contracts.[4]

There are exceptions: the insurrectionary anarchists, the green anarchists, the "primitivists," those who describe themselves as anti-technology and anti-civilization, etc. (there can be a great deal of overlap between these various currents of thought). Most of these folks certainly speak about revolution, but – because they have come after a wave of extremism exemplified by the Situationist International (SI), but do not want to follow in its Marxist footsteps – they feel themselves compelled to be even more extreme than those extremists. And so, while Marx and Engels were opposed to the bourgeoisie and capital's domination of labor, and while the Situationist International was opposed to work and the spectacle's domination of everyday life, the revolutionary anarchists declare themselves to be against virtually everything: technology, industrial society, progress, rationality, and civilization itself. Some of these hyper-extremists are even against revolution, because – to them – it is the ultimate manifestation of the ideology of progress.

At least in France, there is a great deal of friction between the anti-progress ("technophobic") anarchists and the situationist-inspired revolutionaries. (There is also some conflict between these two currents in America: see issue #24 of *Green Anarchy*,[5] as well as the exchange between John Filiss and Ken Knabb.) At issue in this conflict is determining the fundamental nature of the enemy: is it industrial society or is it capitalism? Which contains the toxic element: industrial production or the commodity? Because he was a member of the SI, Rene Riesel's opinion on these questions carries some weight, at least in France. In his "Preface" to *On the progress of domestication* (2000), Riesel claims that, among "the most backwards scoffers at anti-progressivist positions" are those who claim "the heritage and exclusive use that no one disputes them, this or that radical *doxa*" (the "orthodoxy" of situationist theory). Riesel refers to the "arguments to which diverse living fossils, issued from situationism or the ultra-Left, have recourse to refute the idea that one can find more advantage in designating this society as industrial society. They find it sufficient to continue to speak of capitalist society, of capitalized society, of the society of the spectacle." These "wax figures," Riesel says, "each being free to *communicate* as he understands," "have indeed found their *adequate form*: they expect their public on the Internet, the great libertarian media in which capital works hard to spoil the creativity of the masses." Riesel has been answered, among others, by Les Amis de Nemesis: "But if one conserves a minimal amount of seriousness, one must admit that those who are opposed to the notion of 'industrial society' never defend the reality that the technophobes have labeled in this way, and that their opposition to certain terms and to a certain analysis, which appear impoverished, only aim at maintaining a more fundamental opposition to the dominant society."[6]

We believe that Guy Debord's theory of the spectacle, which is a total theory that attempts to blend or at least reconcile the best aspects of Marxism and anarchism, is the most relevant and useful revolutionary theory available to us today. As Anselm Jappe remarked in 1998, "thirty years [after May 1968], now that Althusserianism, Maoism, workerism, and Freudo-Marxism have all disappeared into historical oblivion, it is clear that the Situationists were the only people at that time to develop a theory, and to a lesser extent a practice, whose interest is not merely historiographical but retains a potential relevance today."[7] But, unlike Jappe, who is content to reiterate and critique the theory of the spectacle (he does both quite well), we wish to go even further and bring this theory up to date. After biding its time for so long, perhaps this theory is finally ready to surpass the spectacle.

Given our personal autonomy with respect to all of the existing groups and movements, we might be asked: "Why not simply start from scratch, with your own theory?" Clausewitz provides a good answer: "Theory is instituted so that each person in succession may not have to go through the same labor of clearing the ground and toiling through his subject, but may find the thing in order, and light admitted on it. It should educate the mind of the future leader (...), or rather guide him in his self-instruction, but not accompany him to the field of battle" (*On War*).

Part Two

> "For it is hard to speak properly upon a subject where it is even difficult to convince your hearers that you are speaking the truth. On the one hand, the friend who is familiar with every fact of the story may think that some point has not been set forth with that fullness which he wishes and knows it to deserve; on the other, he who is a stranger to the matter may be led by envy to suspect exaggeration if he hears anything above his own nature [...] Although I shall perhaps be no better believed than others have been when I speak upon the reality of the expedition, and although I know that those who either make or repeat statements thought not worthy of belief not only gain no converts, but are thought fools for their pains, I shall certainly not be frightened into holding my tongue when the state is in danger, and when I am persuaded that I can speak with more authority on the matter than other persons." – Thucydides, *The History of the Peloponnesian War*.

Everyone, even the capitalists and their apologists, agree that *spectacles* are increasingly central to and typical of this society. Note that we do not refer to "images." Spectacles – unusual, strange, remarkable or memorable sensory phenomena, especially visual phenomena – are more compelling and attractive than mere images. Spectacles fill up and dominate all aspects of capitalist society: war ("shock and awe"), politics (photo opportunities, televised conventions, and debates, and commercials), culture (tabloid journalism, "breaking news"), sports ("extreme" competitions), consumerism ("spectacular" sales and events), art (body-centered performance art), architecture (especially of the post-modern type) and, of course, entire cities.

And so we must be clear that *the concept* of spectacle is not the same thing as the critical or revolutionary *theory* of the spectacle. Unlike the theory, the concept of spectacle simply describes superficial phenomena, especially the omnipresence and "invasiveness" of television and the other mass media. Typically, for those who elaborate the concept of spectacle, it is something that has long or even always existed, and thus they give it no precise or localized historical existence, and no possible end. Nor do their denunciations of spectacularization (which are chiefly of a *moralizing* nature) displease or unnerve existing society: contemporary capitalist society has officially recognized itself as "spectacular," and "situationism" (everyone can or should play a role in the show) has become its official ideology. "That modern society is a society of spectacle now goes without saying," *Le Monde* said on 19 September 1987.[8]

The preface to Fran Shor's *Bush-League Spectacles: Empire, Politics and Culture in Bush-Whacked America* (2005) offers a more contemporary example. After quoting "Guy Debord, *The Society of the Spectacle*" – who/which says "The spectacle cannot be understood as a mere visual deception produced by mass-media technologies. It is a worldview that has actually been materialized" – the author proclaims,

> Spectacles have played a significant part of empires and public life throughout history. From the circuses of Rome to the Nuremberg rallies of Nazi Germany, the staging of public events for mass mobilization has served the interests of the ruling elite. However, in this era of the society of the spectacle where images dominate beyond just the media environment, the spectacle is even more integral to the functioning of society. While there are obviously efforts to manipulate spectacles for partisan purposes, spectacles become the primary vehicle through which popular discourse and opinion are channeled.

By contrast, the central thesis of Debord's theory of the spectacle – first enunciated in book form exactly forty years ago today, in the short but very thorough and dense book entitled *La Societe du Spectacle*[9] – is that the spectacle is a stage in the history of capitalism or, rather, the freezing of history itself at a particular moment. That moment can be dated sometime between 1917 and 1939, and can be described as a two-fold development: 1) capitalist abundance (the abundance of mass-produced commodities and material wealth) crossed a certain threshold and entered superabundance, and 2) because superabundance made social revolution both desirable *and* possible, the ruling classes and bureaucracies of the world found it necessary to have this superabundance systematically dissimulated or denied outright. Instead of consuming its surpluses in what Georges Bataille has called "unproductive expenditures"[10] (feasts, festivals and games), modern society – claiming that scarcity still exists – reinvests them in new cycles of production. And so, "the economy" becomes autonomous from the rest of society, and develops only for itself. And so a one-sentence-long definition of the spectacle would thus be this: the spectacle is a form by and in which social revolution is deferred. It is not simply a form of hyper-visibility (as in the concept of spectacle), but a form of invisibility, dissimulation or hiding: to the extent that the spectacle is organized, it is a conspiracy to hide, dissimulate and deny the reality of capitalism's obsolescence.

A handful of revolutionaries were able to detect these changes in society as they were happening. Some of their names are well known: Bataille, Breton, Artaud, Benjamin, Korsch, and Lukacs. But precisely because of the continuing development of the capitalist economy since 1939, these changes – as well as the desirability and possibility of social revolution – have become both even more serious and easier to discern in the last few decades. Let us address them in the form of four questions.

1) What is obsolete and can be dispensed with? First and foremost, work, that is to say, the necessity of having to work for a living. There is in fact so much accumulated wealth that, if it were evenly distributed, *no one* would ever need to work ever again (a certain amount of *labor* might be socially necessary, but the institution of work could be abolished.) By the same token, poverty, hunger and homelessness could be eradicated all over the world. And since the institution of work under capitalism involves or is limited to the production, distribution and sales of commodities, there is in fact no more need for the market, advertising and the commodity itself. Yes, people still need to eat, shelter and clothe themselves, but these needs do not have to be met through the production of commodities.

2) What can be destroyed and reinvented in complete freedom? Above all, everything that used to be done while not "at work": leisure activities, vacations, and entertainment. Rather than being pursued as ways of resting or refreshing oneself so to be able to return to work, all these activities – indeed, the very time in which they were accomplished – could be enjoyed freely and independently. People need not simply "have fun" all the time (although they could, if they wanted to): all of the forms that merely speculated on the possibility of utopia – philosophy, art in all its forms, and religion – could now be pursued directly and fully. One would not go to school to study to become a good worker or a good consumer, but a good person. All forms of morality and ethics could be completely

reinvented.

3) Who prevents these radical changes (this *social revolution*) from taking place? The owners of this world, of course, but they have a great deal of help: the people who position themselves as "representatives" and thus arbiters of who gets what (the politicians and union bosses); the people who design and construct the buildings, modes of transportation and cities that use separation and isolation to prevent the vast majority of the population from forming general assemblies or enjoying unproductive expenditures (the architects, urbanists and developers); the people who use deadly force to prevent wealth from being reappropriated (the police, private security firms, and the military); the people who continue to propagate the general myth of scarcity (the mass media), who hinder or suppress distribution so that scarcity seems to continue to exist (the various mafias), or who invent and impose new scarcities (the people in the businesses of security and safety); the people who specialize in the controlled and very limited expenditure of surpluses (the spectacular entertainers, stars and performers); and, last but not least, the suppressors of dreams and utopias (the priests, social workers and psychiatrists).

4) What happens because social revolution is continually deferred? In the words of the situationists, the autonomous capitalist economy – "one of those fragments of social power which claim to represent a coherent totality, and tend to impose themselves as a total explanation and organization" (*Critique of Urbanism*) – becomes more and more totalitarian. The autonomous economy becomes "the totalitarian dictatorship of the fragment" (*Basic Banalities*). Not surprisingly, its products become more and more noxious, to the point of toxicity, which was clearly reached with the invention and widespread use of nuclear power plants. Precisely because an autonomous economy is an economy deprived of reason, the increasing toxicity of capitalism itself and its various products seem "natural" or impossible to understand, and (in either case) unavoidable. Note well: even if the economy had not become autonomous, the commodity would still be noxious. Indeed, there were plenty of toxic products put on the market before the 1917-1939 period. The toxicity of the commodity is not accidental nor even controllable: it is part of its very structure as "value," that is to say, its internal split into use-value, which is useful by definition, into exchange-value, which is essentially indifferent, if not openly hostile to usefulness. This is precisely why revolutionaries, if they wish to live in a society without alienation, cannot simply return to the days before either capitalism or industrial society existed: the very same structure of alienation exists in the "value" of money, which is the commodity that has no use-value in itself, except for its ability to be exchanged for *any* other commodity, indeed, *all* other commodities.

To continue to develop the economy *and* yet to continue to defer social revolution, certain forms of government have been necessary, and their study was in fact Debord's central concern, not just in *The Society of the Spectacle,* but also in his *Preface to the Fourth Italian Edition of "The Society of the Spectacle"*

(1979), and his *Comments on the Society of the Spectacle* (1988).[11] Between 1967 and 1988, Debord identified three such forms: 1) the concentrated spectacle ("totalitarian" societies such as Nazi Germany and Communist Russia), 2) the diffuse spectacle ("democratic" societies such as the United States), and 3) the integrated spectacular, which resulted from the "historic compromise" between "Communism" (State bureaucratic capitalism) and "capitalism" (corporate bureaucratic capitalism) that began in the mid-1970s (in France and Italy), and culminated in the late 1980s and early 1990s as the dominant paradigm.

In many ways, the most important of these forms is the concentrated spectacle. Even though it arrived many decades after the Industrial Revolution, and arose as a spectacular alternative to free-market capitalism, the concentrated spectacle is the "first" spectacle: in its very totalitarianism, it is the closest to the essentially totalitarian nature of the commodity.[12] And, to the precise extent that it is the form taken by the capitalist State when it is in crisis, the concentrated spectacle will also be the final form it will take: "the destiny of the spectacle," Debord says near the very end of his *Comments,* "is certainly not to end in enlightened despotism."

There were and still are real differences between these three forms of the modern State: wars, both "hot" and "cold," have been fought. But what makes all three spectacular – what makes the spectacle a truly global system of government – are the facts that they have positioned themselves as balancing each other out (as in the "balance of terror") and that each one has striven to suppress working-class subversion within its borders. There have also been moments – and these are quite instructive – in which the apparently opposed or competing State-forms have collaborated on the suppression of working-class revolution: Spain in the 1930s, Hungary in the 1950s, and Italy in the 1970s.

It is indeed significant that precious little of what we have just mentioned appears in contemporary discussions of the spectacle and/or Guy Debord personally. Generally such discussions focus upon Debord's art (he was primarily a filmmaker, but also a writer, translator and book designer), or upon the early years of his involvement in the Situationist International (1957-1961) and its art-based theories of detournement, *derive* and psychogeography. Here's a good example, provided by the university professor and neo-anarchist David Graeber: "The Situationists, like many '60s radicals, wished to strike back through a strategy of direct action: creating 'situations' by creative acts of subversion that undermined the logic of the Spectacle and allowed actors to at least momentarily recapture their imaginative powers."[13] It is very infrequent that there are discussions of Debord's political theories or the middle years of the SI (1962-1968), when it was preoccupied with purely political subjects (the Watts riots in the USA, the Six Day War, the Vietnam War, the Algerian independence movement, the Czech Spring of 1968, and, of course, May 1968 in France). Furthermore, there is virtually no discussion of Debord's political activities after the SI dissolved itself in 1972: that is, no discussion of his efforts in and with revolutionaries from Italy (1973-1975), Portugal (1974-75), and Spain (1980-81).

And yet commentators of all types – on both the Right and the Left – feel compelled to speak of him. Why? "The extreme disaster in which spectacular democracy has plunged us, by confirming ever more clumsily Guy Debord's conclusions, has in large part convinced the enemy of the truth of his judgments" (Jean-Francois Martos, *Oil on Fire*). If we now briefly focus on a recent article by Henry A. Giroux – "Beyond the Spectacle of Terrorism," which derives from his book, *Beyond the Spectacle of Terrorism: Global Uncertainty and the Challenge of the New Media* (2006) – it is only because it is one of the very few to take Debord's *political* ideas (half-way) seriously and because it does so in such an inadequate fashion. In other words, it indicates just how empty the field is of serious discussion.

Following a pattern established in the 1970s by Michel Foucault[14] and Jean Baudrillard, Giroux only mentions Guy Debord and his "pioneering" theory of the society of the spectacle so as to say that, since the 1960s, the spectacle has changed so much that Debord's theory is no longer relevant. Debord and "older notions of the spectacle" could not possibly account for "the emergence of new media and image-based media technologies" such as "camcorders, cellular cameraphones, satellite television, digital recorders and the Internet" because none of it existed in 1967. Either these gadgets are so fundamentally different from radio, TV and the cinema, or the "new media" exist in such great quantities, that "a structural transformation of everyday life" has taken place: these media "have revolutionized the relationship between the specificity of an event and its public display." And while "neither the concept of the spectacle nor the practice of terrorism itself is new," there has been a new and completely unprecedented "merging of the spectacle, terrorism, war and politics." There is, in sum, "a new regime of the spectacle in which screen culture and visual politics create spectacular events just as much as they record them."

Lest we suspect that this "new" spectacle seems an awful lot like the "old" spectacle, and that is it not true that "critical discourses of the spectacle need to be revised so as to provide the theoretical tools required to fully understand how the spectacle has changed," Giroux contrasts "the terrorism of the spectacle" (the old, surpassed reality) with "the spectacle of terrorism" (the new one). While the former was based in "fascist culture and late capitalism's culture of commodification," the later is rooted in "a new notion of the subject forged in social relations largely constructed around fear and terror." And, while the former was dominated by "consensus," "a sense of unity," "solidarity," "illusion" and "depoliticization" (as if the Cold War never existed!), the later is dominated by "a theatrics of fear and shock," "politicization," and "the image added with the thrill of the real." The key idea is that "the spectacle of terrorism *undercuts the primacy of consumerism,* challenges state power and uses the image to construct a new type of politics organized around the modalities of death, hysteria, panic and violence" (emphasis added).

To dismiss Debord in this way requires two operations, neither of which is intellectually honest. First, Giroux must primarily rely upon summaries of Debord's *The Society of the Spectacle* produced by other academics, and not on a direct confrontation with the text itself. Not surprisingly, such summaries are completely inadequate and have an agenda that Giroux shares: "The image had replaced the commodity as the basic unit of capitalism; rather than arguing that commodities remained the *sine qua non* of domination, [Debord] insisted, as Eugene L. Arva points out, that in the current era, 'the system of mediation by representation (the world of the spectacle, if you wish) has come to bear more relevance than commodities themselves.'" Second, Giroux must pretend that Debord never wrote another word about the spectacle after 1967: "Debord could not have imagined either how the second media revolution would play out, with its multiple producers, distributors and consumers; or how a post-9/11 war on terrorism would shift, especially in the United States, from an emphasis on consumerism to an equally absorbing obsession with war and its politically regressive corollaries of fear, anxiety and insecurity." And so, for Giroux, neither the *Comments on the Society of the Spectacle* (and its remarks on computerized networks), nor the preface to the fourth Italian edition of *The Society of the Spectacle* (and its remarks on *the spectacle of terrorism* in Italy during the 1970s), ever existed.

With Guy Debord and his inconvenient insistence on the commodity out of the way, Giroux can get to where he wants to go (where he has always been?), which is a completely uncritical embrace of the "new" media and Leftist politics: "Radically new modes of communication and resistance based upon the new media are on full display [sic] in the global justice movements, in the emergence of bloggers holding corporate and government powers more accountable, and in the new kinds of cultural and political struggles waged by the Zapatistas, the Seattle protesters, and various new social movements held together through the informational networks provided by the Internet and the Web." Unlike Debord, obsessed as he was with social revolution, "theorists such as Thomas Keenan, Mark Poster, Douglas Kellner and Jacques Derrida are right in suggesting that new electronic technologies and media publics 'remove restrictions on the horizon of possible communications' and, in doing so, suggest new possibilities for engaging the media as a democratic force both for critique and for positive intervention and change."

Part Three

> "It is the law as in art, so in politics, that improvements ever prevail; and though fixed usages may be best for undisturbed communities, constant necessities of action must be accompanied by the constant improvement of methods." – Thucydides, *The History of the Peloponnesian War*.

If we return to Debord's theory of the spectacle today, we do not do so to simply reiterate it or defend it. Good, even great as it is, the theory of the spectacle must be improved. And this is why we offer our readers the theory of the *virtual* spectacle, which is what the global spectacle becomes as or after the integration of Communism and capitalism becomes so complete that one no longer refers to "Communism," and "capitalism" is replaced by euphemisms such "free enterprise" or "the free market." The moment of its birth can be dated fairly precisely (the first American-led attack on Iraq), as can the beginning of its maturation (September 11th, 2001).

It is our hope that our proposed extensions and improvements will increase the theory's usefulness to today's struggles. Theory, Clausewitz says, "must always remain practical." For him, and for us, "All positive results of theoretical inquiry, all principles, rules, and methods, are all the more wanting in generality and positive truth the more they become positive doctrine. They exist to offer themselves for use as required, and it must always be left for judgment to decide whether they are suitable or not."

* * *

First, a note about the manner of our exposition. In *The Society of the Spectacle,* which was partly composed of "detourned" (altered and unattributed) quotations from Hegel, Marx and other famous sources, Debord explains why he chose this unusual form of communication.

> Critical theory must be *communicated* in its own language. This is the language of contradiction, which must be dialectical in its form as in its content [...] In its very style, the exposition of dialectical theory is a scandal and an abomination according to the rules of the dominant language and for the tastes of those that it has educated because, in the positive use of existing concepts, this exposition includes both the intelligence of their retrieved *fluidity* and their necessary destruction [...] Detournement is the contrary of the quotation, of theoretical authority that is always falsified due to the sole fact that it has become quotation; a fragment torn from its context, its movement and finally from its era as a global reference and from the precise option that was inside this reference, exactly or erroneously recognized. Detournement is the fluid language of anti-ideology. It appears in communication that knows that it cannot claim to hold any guarantee in itself and definitively [...] What presents itself as *detourned* in its theoretical formulation – by denying all durable autonomy to the sphere of what is theoretically expressed, that is, by (*through this violence*) bringing about the intervention of the action that disturbs

and carries off the existing order – recalls that the existence of the theoretical is nothing in itself and can only know historical action and the *historical correction* that is its real fidelity.

But, in the 1979 *Preface* and his *Comments on the Society of the Spectacle,* Debord abandoned detournement in favor of a new or at least different method of exposition. He says in the latter work,

> This misfortune of the times thus compels me, once again, to write in a new way. Some elements will be intentionally omitted; and the plan will have to remain rather unclear. Readers will encounter certain decoys, like the very hallmark of the era. As long as other pages are interpolated here and there, the overall meaning may appear just as secret clauses have very often been added to whatever treaties may openly stipulate, just as some chemical agents only reveal their hidden properties when they are combined with others.

To the extent that *The Society of the Spectacle* was an extended detournement of Marx's *Capital* (it was published almost exactly 100 years later), the abandonment of detournement as a form of exposition corresponded with an apparent abandonment of Marxism. Unlike Marx, who focused on the workers and their relationship to the means of production, Debord's focus in the *Comments* is on consumers and their relationship to the means of distribution. There are some who allege that this movement away from Marx either weakens or ruins the *Comments,* and transforms the theory of the spectacle into a kind of "conspiracy theory." These objections do not particularly trouble us.

In 1967, it was both surprising and disturbing that Debord had "returned" to Marx: the pre-war defeat of the workers' movement and the post-war birth of the "consumer society" seemed to render much of what Marx had written on the pauperization of the working class irrelevant. Furthermore, revolutionary groups such as Socialisme ou Barbarie had begun to abandon Marx as early as 1964 or 1965. (It was in fact to counter this abandonment that Debord wrote *The Society of the Spectacle.*)[15] But one must remember that Debord's connection to Marx was neither full nor direct: it proceeded through Georg Lukacs' *History and Class Consciousness* (1924), which was not available in French until 1960, and connected back to Marxian themes that were either marginal or relatively undeveloped at the time that Marx himself was alive (the chapter of *Capital, Volume 1* that concerned commodity fetishism) or texts that weren't published until well after Marx's death (*The Economic and Philosophical Manuscripts,* which were not published in any language until 1932).

But *today,* references to Marx trigger nearly automatic reactions of laughter and dismissal from both the capitalists, who either believe that the collapse of the Soviet Union marked the definitive defeat of Marxism or believe that Marxism was one of the best things to ever happen to capitalism (!), and hostility and resentment from the anarchists, who see Marxism as their enemy. And so, we see no reason not to let the whole thing go, provided, of course, that we retain the good things that Debord got from Marx via Lukacs and remove the bad things that Debord retained from them both.

On the positive side, Debord (through Lukacs) inherited Marx's insistence on theorizing *the totality* of capitalism, not just one aspect of it. "It is not the primacy of economic motives in historical explanation that constitutes the decisive difference between Marxism and bourgeois thought," Lukacs wrote, "but the point of view of totality." The situationists echoed: "The primacy of the category of totality is the bearer of the principle of revolution in science" (*Concerning Several Errors of Interpretation*). This insistence on the totality prevented the situationists from focusing on and getting caught up in isolated facts or events, and allowed them to grasp the overarching process that included such moments. Unlike Marx, Debord was not a scientist: he did not maintain a linear view of history, nor did he put any faith in the "laws" of history. Struggle is everything, and the outcome of that struggle is neither determined nor known in advance. In *The Society of the Spectacle,* Debord declared:

> What closely tied Marx's theory to scientific thought was the rational comprehension of the forces that were really active in society. But Marx's theory is fundamentally *beyond* scientific thought, which is only conserved by being surpassed: it is a comprehension of the *struggle,* and not at all the *law.* "We only know a single science: the science of history," says *The German Ideology.*

On the negative side, Debord retained a certain ambivalence, lack of certainty or self-contradiction concerning the economy. "There are in fact two competing views to be found in Marx," says Anselm Jappe, "the one envisaging liberation *from* the economy, the other liberation *by means of* the economy; nor may the two be simply assigned to different phases of this thought, as some would like to do." This shows up in Debord in his famous graffito "Never Work!" (which he claimed in 1963 to be the "Preliminary Program to the Situationist Movement"), on the one hand, and in his insistence in *The Society of the Spectacle* that "the finally discovered political form in which the economic emancipation of work can be realized" has "in this century taken a clear form in the revolutionary Workers Councils, concentrating in themselves all the functions of decision and execution, and federating themselves by the means of delegates who are responsible to the base and revocable at any moment" (Thesis 116). The problems, of course, are that those who never work will never form workers' councils, and workers' councils must eventually put the idea "never work" into practice, which thereby undermines the very basis of their own existence.

This split concerning emancipation can be closely associated with another. Is the proletariat ("the negative at work in this society" in the words of Thesis 114 of *The Society of the Spectacle*) inevitably constituted by capitalism itself? Is the proletariat potentially or virtually "revolutionary" because of its crucial place in the production process, its internal cohesion, its concentration in the cities and its exclusion from the benefits of bourgeois society? Or, rather, is a revolutionary proletarian *anyone* (student, housewife, mid-level manager) who has no power over his or her own life, who is condemned to an existence of executing the commands of others, knows it and is willing to act on that knowledge? Anselm Jappe makes a very good point: the urban proletariat of Marx's time "was in reality nothing but a pre-capitalist relic, an 'estate' in the feudal sense, and not a direct result of capitalist development at all." Precisely due to the maturation of capitalism – that is to say, its post-1960s embrace of robots, automation and computerization – the proletariat of Marx's time has been dissolved or at least been displaced to third-world countries. In the words of Les Amis de Nemesis: "the dominant system is no longer – as in the *Ancien Regime* or the strong, national State – a centralized system that possesses a 'seat of power' against which the *jacqueries* must march, with pitchforks and scythes in hand; that there is no longer even a network of factories that the workers can blockade or appropriate, but a diffuse order of which the manifestations are everywhere, like the market values that constitute themselves through all of the moments of the economical cycle (through the production, circulation and consumption of commodities), and in which human beings vegetate without jobs and especially without income."[16]

And yet, as late as 30 June 1992, when he wrote his "Preface to the Third French Edition" of *Spectacle,* Debord believed that "everywhere gets posed the same frightening question, which has haunted the world for two centuries: how to get the poor to work, where illusion has been foiled and force has been defeated?" He does not take into consideration the people stuck in France's *banlieus,* where the poor are left completely alone, except of course, when they riot.[17] The very fact that his *Comments on the Society of the Spectacle* does not include a single word about "the proletariat" or "class struggle" does not show that Debord managed to overcome this self-contradiction, but that he was aware of it enough to try to suppress it.

* * *

To return to our main line of inquiry: *Comments on the Society of the Spectacle* is clearly an elaboration of the theory that Debord formulated in 1967. Early on in this book, he reminds his readers of the two essential features of the spectacle (that is to say, the essential features of the concentrated, diffuse and integrated spectacles): "incessant technological renewal" and "fusion of State and economy." Together, these two features match the original definition of the spectacle: it is the one-two punch that both creates and destroys the conditions for social revolution.

Debord then goes on to illustrate three new aspects of what, back in 1967, he theorized under the heading of *decomposition,* which we discussed in Part Two of this text under the heading, "What happens because social revolution is continually deferred?" He emphasizes three features:

> Generalized secrecy stands behind the spectacle, as the decisive complement of all it displays and, in the last analysis, as its most important operation.
>
> The simple fact of being without reply has given to the false an entirely new quality. At a stroke it is truth which has almost everywhere ceased to exist or, at best, has been reduced to the status of pure hypothesis that can never be demonstrated. The false without reply has succeeded in making public opinion disappear: first it found itself incapable of making itself heard and then very quickly dissolved altogether. This evidently has significant consequences for politics, the applied sciences, the justice system and artistic knowledge.
>
> The construction of a present where fashion itself, from clothes to music, has come to a halt, which wants to forget the past and no longer seems to believe in a future, is achieved by the ceaseless circular passage of information, always returning to the same short list of trivialities, passionately proclaimed as major discoveries. Meanwhile news of what is genuinely important, of what is actually changing, comes rarely, and then in fits and starts. It always concerns this world's apparent condemnation of its own existence, the stages in its programmed self-destruction.

Each one of these features continues to be, shall we say, operational. Let us take them one-by-one.

Secrecy – and here one doesn't simply mean keeping secrets, but also keeping quiet about things that should be discussed openly – has grown immensely since 1988. Perhaps the biggest secret of the last 20 years is September 11th: what *really* happened on that day? Obviously "state secrets" (the role of the secret services in the attacks or their failure to detect and prevent them), "trade secrets" (were the towers that collapsed shoddily constructed?) and questions left unanswered by the official investigation (why did Building 7 at the World Trade Center collapse, even though it wasn't struck by an airplane?) are in play. And, of course, precisely because those attacks were used as the justification for launching "the war on terrorism," all of the secrets mentioned by Debord (who was accused of being paranoid) – "the 'defense secrets' that today cover an immense domain of full extra-judicial liberty of the State," the "police and counter-espionage services, along with secret services, both State and para-State" that "each country, not to mention the numerous supranational alliances, currently possesses an undetermined number of," the "many private companies dealing in surveillance, security and investigation," and the services employed by "the large multinationals" – have become a routine part of everyday life.

Debord mentions a number of fakes in his *Comments*: art works, historical relics, and food, among them. But he also implicates revolutionary groups.

> When, for example, the new conditions of the society of the integrated spectacular have forced its critique to remain really clandestine, not because it hides itself but because it is hidden by the heavy stage-management of the thought of diversion, those who are nonetheless charged with surveilling this critique and, if necessary, denying it, can now employ traditional methods in the milieu of clandestinity: provocation, infiltrations, and various forms of elimination of authentic critique to the profit of a false one which will have been put in place for this purpose.

In our translator's footnote to this passage, which again might seem wildly paranoid, we remind the reader of the following example: "In the summer of 1968, an Italian neo-Nazi and *agent provocateur* named Mario Merlino succeeded in infiltrating Roman anarchist circles by forming the 'XXII March Group,' whose name was a close echo of the '22d March Movement,' the French group from Nanterre that included Daniel Cohn-Bendit and several *enrages* who later joined the Situationist International. One of the first actions taken by the XXII March Group was the destruction of several cars after a demonstration in front of the French Embassy in Rome. The Italian press quickly blamed the violence on the Italian Communist Party." As another example of a "false flag" operation, we might also have cited the Red Brigades, which allegedly kidnapped and murdered Aldo Moro in 1978.[18] Of course, there are people who believe that September 11th was also a "false flag" operation.

Today, the creation of *fake people* is increasingly common in advertising. In "viral marketing," which induces consumers to voluntarily disseminate propaganda amongst themselves, an advertising agency will create several imaginary people, complete with full "profiles." These "people" (or, rather, their puppet masters) will contribute blog entries on particular Web sites about a commodity, politician or idea. (Note that these things need not be real either. In fact, it is better if they, too, are fakes.) These blog entries can either be positive or negative. Other imaginary people will post comments to these entries, thereby simulating dialogue. Still other people (or the original entry writers) will create hypertext links from these blogs to a Web site that promotes or slanders the commodity, politician or idea, thereby increasing the ranking given to this Web site by prominent search engines. In an effort to prove the truthfulness of the claims made, people will post supporting (but completely fake) visual evidence on popular community web sites such as Flickr, Photobucket or YouTube. A blogger (another imaginary person) who reports on "grassroots" stories for news sites such as DIGG, the Huffington Post and/or the

Drudge Report will then "break the story" about the particular commodity, politician or idea.

It is at this point that the commodity's manufacturer, the politician's press secretary or the people who supposedly believe in the idea will speak, as if for the first time. Whoever or whatever they are, they will circulate press releases or other statements about themselves and their "values." They will either confirm or deny what the "grassroots" has been saying. The original bloggers and posters of comments will then respond, and the whole cycle of *spectacular lies* takes another turn. Inevitably – or so it would appear – people (hopefully real ones) will start protests that deny whatever has been asserted, be it praise or slander, which will once again gets the "news" cycle going again. Finally, whomever is intended to profit from this entire operation will reveal the hoax, that is to say, the actual nonexistence of the now-(in)famous commodity, politician or idea, and then will let it be known that the *real thing* (whatever it is) is spectacularly valuable, because, after all, he or she or it was smart and resourceful (and cynical?) enough to perpetrate such a successful hoax in the first place.

Since Debord mentions clothes and music in his discussion of the "perpetual present," we feel justified in reminding our readers that in, say John Lennon's peaceful "Imagine" or the Sex Pistols' apocalyptic "God Save the Queen," the denial of the future was a crucial element in the liberation of the present. But the perpetual present of the integrated spectacular is not liberated, nor is it an idyllic hippie dream. It is either a bland dream that has gone on for too long or a nightmare that we wish would end. But it doesn't: it keeps going and going and going, producing nothing more than exhaustion, which in turns strengthens the desire to sleep.

Today, almost 20 years after the publication of *Comments on the Society of the Spectacle,* incessant technological renewal has produced the "information economy," that is to say, the economy (*a whole society*) that is filled with and dominated by computers and data networks. It is here that the word "virtual" imposes itself. This word can mean three different things: 1) (*Linguistics*) almost as described, but not completely or according to strict definition; 2) (*Computing*) not physically existing as such but made by software to appear to do so; and 3) (*Optics*) relating to the points at which rays would meet if projected backwards. And so, today one speaks of virtual images, virtual memory and virtual reality. Ironically, perhaps, none of these things are "strong" (as in the Latin word *virtus*) or possessed of "moral excellence" (as in the word *virtue*): the virtual itself is weak to the extent it really doesn't exist, and is a cheat to the extent that it is "almost" what it is defined as or what it attempts to duplicate. Thus, the "virtual spectacle" fits in nicely with the regression sketched out in Thesis 17 of *The Society of the Spectacle*:

> The first phase of the domination of the economy over social life involved in the definition of all human realization an obvious

degradation of *being* into *having*. The current phase of the total occupation of social life by the accumulated results of the economy leads to a general slide from *having* into *appearing*, from which all real "having" must draw its immediate prestige and final function.

In the third phase, *appearing* has slipped into *seeming*: even the image has lost its "being," its substance. Social life or "human realization" doesn't exist: it only seems to appear to exist.

Today, the State and the economy are fused into a single, autonomous institution by a shared interest in "terrorism": on the one hand, fighting the "global war on terrorism" (GWOT), which requires tremendous investments in and reaps equally large profits for the military-industrial complex; and, on the other hand, protecting both the State and the economy from "terrorist" acts committed by the same forces against which the GWOT is fought. Because the first was or claims to be a response to the second, and because the second is in fact a response to the first (and the foreign policies that the GWOT is intended to support, justify and protect), an extremely dangerous and profitable "vicious cycle" is guaranteed. To the precise extent to which "the terrorists" fight in a spectacularly "asymmetrical" fashion, the State and the economy can justify even further research into and development of "smart" (technologically renewed) weaponry, even deeper retreats into secrecy, and even further advances into "false flag" operations.

The society modernized to the stage of the virtual spectacle is characterized by the combined effects of five new features: sonorization, torture, speed, accidents and refugee camps.

It is not just sight that is spectacularized in the society of the virtual spectacle: so is sound. This is done in two ways: first by digitizing it, then by having computers "play" it everywhere, all the time. When CDs were first introduced, they were condemned by music lovers because – during the process of transferring the music from analog to digital – what the machines defined as "noise" was removed and replaced by "clean" silence. This *ruined* many recordings made prior to the introduction of advanced studio techniques in the 1960s: they sounded dry and brittle, and lacked the excitement and vividness of the originals. But then, after the introduction of even more "advanced" studio techniques, all new recordings were made by digital equipment. The problem was worsened: all recordings now lacked excitement and vividness. And yet, when played upon the new mini-computers (cellphones, iPods and the like), they sounded "spectacular": clean and dry, as if no human beings were involved in their production. And, of course, in music that relies almost completely on synthesizers, sequencers, drum machines and other microprocessors, few human beings are in fact involved.

With the proliferation of both stationary and hand-held computers, spectacularized sound has also proliferated. Indeed, it isn't just in "unusual" places such as supermarkets and elevators that one is forced to listen to muzak: pre-recorded computerized sounds, messages, prompts and ringtones are virtually everywhere. Like analog sound before it, silence itself is disappearing. Paul Virilio has called this development "sonorization."[19] We can think of no better illustration of it than the pre-recorded messages that are regularly delivered to the riders of the new computerized subway trains that run in New York City. Clearly audible – no, loud and clear enough to intrude into or force the temporary suspension of conversation – these messages never let up: "Ladies and gentlemen: not only is it unsafe, it is a violation of the rules to walk between subway cars when the train is in motion, except in an emergency and when directed by emergency personnel. For a complete list of subway rules, please visit mta.info"; "Ladies and gentlemen: please use trash receptacles that are provided for your use on subway platforms"; "Ladies and gentlemen: riding on the outside of subway cars is dangerous. Please remain inside subways cars at all times"; "Ladies and gentlemen: backpacks and large containers are subject to random search by the police"; and "Ladies and gentlemen: this is an important message from the New York City Police Department. Keep your eyes on your belongings at all times. Protect yourself. If you see a suspicious object or activity on the train or platform, do not keep it to yourself. Tell a police officer or a MTA employee. Remain alert and have a safe day."

There are obviously a handful of themes shared by these commands: there is danger; there might be an emergency; obey the rules; respect the authority of the police; and "have a safe day." Clearly the millions of people who ride the subways of this city are being psychologically prepared for the rapidly emerging national security state, for the time when temporary emergency measures become permanent. But the maddening repetition of these messages is more than just propaganda or even brainwashing: it is torture. What are the riders supposed to do, crack under the pressure and declare (aloud, of course) that they, too, love Big Brother?

Like assassination, torture used to be practiced – secretly, illegally and with discrimination – at both the very summits of spectacular power (CIA agents) and the very nadir of the "underworld" (mafia enforcers). But today, torture is now practiced openly, legally and indiscriminately. Rather than being practiced by professional sadists for the dubious results that it might produce – the extraction of information or money from unwilling subjects – torture is now practiced by amateur sadists as a form of punishment or retribution against large groups of people.

Take for example the U.S. military's use of *loud rock 'n' roll music* against Manuel Noriega in December 1989 or the Israeli Defense Force's use of *pornography* against the besieged people of Ramallah in April 2002. Note well that, in the first instance, it wasn't punk or another "marginal" form of pop music, and that in the second instance, it was not torture-themed pornography: in both cases, just run-of-the-mill commercial product. In the words of reporter Charles Paul Freund, "The idea, apparently, is to locate a cultural form that discomfits the target, and to subject that target to an unending stream of it."[20] Here "torture" is relative: what is intensely painful to Noriega or Muslim insurgents might be pleasurable to some. While I might find working in an office with no walls or cubicles – just a big room in which we can all see and hear each other, all day – to be torture, you might find it pleasurable. But what distinguishes the 1989 episode from the 2002 one is the presence of large numbers of innocent third parties and unwilling witnesses. As Freund reported,

> Replacing Palestinian news and other programming with such material also increases the stress and frustration of the populace. Remember, Ramallah's residents were unable to leave their homes, even to buy groceries. Their need for information was intense. Israeli forces had the option of taking the TV stations off the air entirely. Instead, they left them operating, but broadcasting "replacement" imagery. The pornography may well have been even more demoralizing than no programming at all.

Today, representations of pain and painful representations are everywhere: TV shows such as *24* and *Law & Order Special Victims Unit*; movies such as *Wolf Creek* and *Hostel*; advertising campaigns for "Razr" cellphones and "Mentitas" breath mints; etc etc. Not surprisingly, so is self-inflicted torture and passionate self-abasement: *Fear Factor,* Stelarc, noise music, genital piercings, participation in reality TV shows and contests, etc. Is this not a generalized confirmation of the thesis of the "Stockholm Syndrome"? People who are kidnapped and held against their will eventually come to identify with their kidnappers. Only, today, "Stockholm" is the whole world.

Modern technologies – and here we mean both digital and industrial technologies – are technologies of speed: they all lessen the time necessary to accomplish tasks, deliver objects or messages, and travel through space. Profitability ("time is money") originally drove the need for speed, but with the invention of digital technologies and hyperspeeds, decreased time is now both expected and desired for its own sake. For example, people like to drive fast cars not to get anywhere, but simply enjoy the sensation of rapid transit.

But as the "speed of speed" has increased and approached the point of instantaneity, certain problems have emerged and worsened. Accidents that involve greater speeds tend to be more serious, more destructive to all concerned. Decision-making becomes increasingly difficult and prone to error when the time in which to make decisions shrinks; indeed, instantaneity precludes all decisions that are not pre-programmed and machine-controlled. Space – the sense of it and thus its importance – becomes dismissible and even forgettable, which in turn leads to its homogenization or destruction. And, finally, time (the only "thing" that matters) becomes spatialized, that is to say, frozen in place, frozen into a perpetual present.

None of these problems bother the spectacle, which is in fact strengthened by them. And yet, in some places, speed is not allowed to accelerate any further or to approach or attain simultaneity. Indeed, in one place in particular, speed has been "reversed" or replaced by extreme slowness: the political arena. In the United States at least, the primary season has been greatly lengthened. It is now *an entire year* before the 2008 presidential election, and yet the candidates in both parties have been at it for several months. Surely such a slow pace – a kind of torture, given the aggressive saber-rattling and warmongering of almost all of these people – guarantees increased campaign donations. But it also guarantees over-exposure and the exhaustion of the voter's interest in any or all of these candidates. One is forced to wonder: is this an accident or precisely the intention?

Incessant technological renewal accidentally creates accidents on a large scale: the invention of the automobile was also the invention of the automobile crash; the invention of the airplane was also the invention of the airplane crash, etc. Because capitalism's technological renewal is deliberate, the accident becomes easily foreseeable, even predictable; and because such renewal is incessant, the scope of the accident becomes wider and deeper. The "vector" here is clear: spectacular accidents will take place globally: not just *anywhere* in the world, but all over the world *at the same time*. Thus, there is a certain symmetry or integration between the predictable technological accident and deliberate acts of terrorism, which can be defined as the interruption of everyday life by acts of war. It will become increasingly impossible to distinguish, say, an "accidental" explosion at a nuclear power plant and a deliberate act of sabotage at such an installation. *In the society of the spectacle, terrorism and everyday life become indistinguishable.*

Let us put forward an example. Many people have wondered how it was possible for *both* towers at the World Trade Center to collapse speedily and completely – as if brought down by controlled demolitions – after each building was struck by an airplane that was deliberately crashed into it. Some have simply believed the official explanation, which says that the crashes (and/or the heat released by the explosion and immolation of the planes' fuel) were sufficient to bring the buildings down in "pancake" fashion, while others have put forward the "conspiracy" theory that bombs were detonated in these buildings at the same time of the crashes and/or immediately after them. The first theory is scientifically (physically) impossible, while the "conspiracy" theory makes it necessary to believe that either the "outsiders" (the hijackers of the planes) and the "insiders" (the placers and detonators of the bombs) were working together. It is true that the second theory offers an explanation that seems to account for what actually happened, but it requires us to believe in a super-competency that none of the potential "insiders" (Bush/Cheney, the CIA, the Mossad/Bet Shin, etc.) demonstrated before September 11, 2001 or have been able to demonstrate since then.

Drawing upon – or, rather, attempting to prove – the hypothesis that terrorism and everyday life have become indistinguishable, we can envision the following situation: there were indeed "outsiders" (terrorists) who managed to hijack several airplanes on September 11, 2001 and fly two of them directly into the twins towers at the World Trade Center, but these terrorists did not know that both of these buildings (as well as WTC 7, which also completely collapsed on that day, though not struck by an airplane) had been slated for closure and evacuation due to their failure as commercial enterprises and – because it was cheaper to do it well in advance – had already been secretly wired for demolition by experts. In other words, the towers were "accidents" waiting to happen, and the "accident" that happened was a pre-planned terrorist attack.

While right-wing politicians in France and the United States use "the immigrant question" to frighten the general population and erect literal and figurative walls around their countries to prevent any more "illegals" from entering them – all the while ignoring or worsening the destruction *from within, from the summits of spectacular power,* of what makes France "France" and America "America" (a revolutionary history and a tradition of liberty) – there is another question that goes without being posed, not to mention answered. And that is the question of the refugee, the person who, "owing to a well-founded fear of being persecuted for reasons of race, religion, nationality, membership in a particular social group, or political opinion, is outside the country of their nationality, and is unable to or, owing to such fear, is unwilling to avail him/herself of the protection of that country" (*United Nations Convention Relating to the Status of Refugees,* 1951).

According to a variety of estimates, there are at present between 15 and 20 million people who are refugees, that is, "temporary" inhabitants of refugee camps, in which – while they wait to be granted asylum in another country – they have no freedom of movement, no right to employment and no right to own property. They are simply wards of the UN and international humanitarian aid groups. All too often, they are not granted asylum, and simply live out their lives, such as they are, in these camps.

Unfortunately, the UN's definition of refugee does not cover the 20 to 30 million people who have been displaced (generally by civil war) *within* their own country, nor does it include the untold millions of people who have fled their own countries due to natural catastrophes, "man-made" accidents, market ("crop") failures, and invasions and occupations by foreign powers. And, of course, no one thinks to account for all the people who remain where they are, "undisplaced," and yet – due to alienation, embittered disgust or political opinion – are unwilling to avail themselves of the *alleged* protections of the countries of their respective nationalities. Together, are not all these people the majority of the world's population? And so we see that the vector of the virtual spectacle points to *billions* of refugees, either held in huge and always-growing camps or walking around like ghosts, strangers in their own lands, exiles on Main Street. This is not a world turned upside-down, but a world turned inside-out.

No one – certainly not the neo-anarchists, the citizenists, nor the Leftists, preoccupied as they are with multi-national corporations, neo-liberalism and strengthening ("democratizing") the State to keep these powers "honest" – has adequately theorized this vector. Not even Guy Debord, whose response to the Vaux-en-Velin riots of 1990 was unexpectedly unsupportive and moralizing, and certainly at variance with his excellent 1985 text on the "immigrant question."[21] In refugee camps, the capitalist economy (work and the consumption of commodities purchased with money earned at work) is absent; and, to the extent that such camps operate under states of exception, so is the State. Thus these camps are in great peril of being turned into concentration camps or even death camps.

According to the Office of the United Nations High Commissioner for Refugees, there are three "durable solutions": voluntary repatriation of the refugees to their respective countries of origin; local integration into the countries of intended (rejected) asylum; and resettlement to other countries. Quite obviously, none of these solutions is possible. Here as elsewhere (e.g., *favela* squatter developments in Rio de Janeiro, *gecekondu* homes in Istanbul, etc.), the only viable option is revolution and autonomous self-rule.

Part Four

> "I might, it is true, have written to you something different and more agreeable than this, but nothing certainly more useful, if it is desirable for you to know the real state of things here before taking your measures. Besides I know that it is your nature to love to be told the best side of things, and then to blame the teller if the expectations which he has raised in your minds are not answered by the result; and I therefore thought it safest to declare to you the truth." – Thucydides.

Let us now concentrate on practical or, rather, organizational matters. Revolutionaries must band together: the spectacle is predicated on isolation and separation; each revolutionary needs the support, encouragement, inspiration and friendship that only other revolutionaries can provide. But such bands must themselves be revolutionary, which means they must be constituted by *equals* and they cannot reproduce within themselves the conditions that exist in the spectacle, in particular, hierarchy, deception (of self and others), fragmentation and incoherence. In sum, revolutionary organizations cannot be collectives or, even less, federations of collectives: they must be *groups of individuals,* that is, groups that do not suppress or dissolve the individuality of their members, but retain and enrich them, and in turn are enriched by them.

Thus, we reject the concept of "multitudes" as it has been elaborated by Antonio Negri.[22] We are not philosophers, nor are we interested in establishing or elaborating ontological systems, which are better suited to academic discussions than revolutionary activity. Note well that, despite Negri's post-modern replacement of the word "individuals" with "singularities," his politics go no further than electoral politics and "radical" political parties. We also reject the text by the Situationist International entitled "Minimum Definition of Revolutionary Organizations," which rather dogmatically insists that any such organization "pursues *with consequence* the international realization of the absolute power of the Workers' Councils, such as it has been sketched out by the experience of the proletarian revolutions of this century." Oppressed workers but not members of a single class, becoming ever-more conscious of our situation but in no need of class consciousness, we seek our emancipation *outside* the economy, whether it be capitalist, socialist or communist.

It seems to us that all of the organizational tactics used by the situationists remain relevant and useful to today's struggles. Since the spectacle is a global system, revolutionary organizations must be international in composition and action, and must include members of as many countries as possible. But such members cannot be nationalists or "representatives" of their respective countries of origin: they must be internationalists. (Foreign language skills therefore are obligatory.) Since revolutionary organizations must be small, they cannot admit too many members; nor can they tolerate the presence within themselves of people who turn out to be fundamentally different from what they appeared to be before they joined. As a result, exclusions are regrettable but absolutely necessary, as are breaks with "outsiders" who are hostile to our existence, program or actions, or who continue to collaborate with third parties with whom we have broken.

Revolutionary organizations must also be *real* communities that exist in face-to-face situations: they cannot exist "online," that is, in or on list-servs, posting boards or chat rooms. Such communities must strive to produce their own food, clothing and housing; otherwise they are part of the commodity system. Such communities must constantly strive to better their personal and interpersonal communication skills, which means that individuals must be "in touch" with their true feelings and desires, and must know how to express and act upon them; otherwise, deception, hierarchies and power structures are inevitable.

To be coherent, our political "programme" must return to and derive from our definition of the spectacle. That is to say, it must insist upon the super-concentration of wealth in this society, the poor and even lethal uses to which this wealth is put (the USA spends $3 billion per week on the GWOT), and the type of society that could be constructed if this society were overthrown and its wealth was put to truly human uses. The pleasures and "happiness" that this society offers must be mercilessly critiqued as insufficient. Our programme must condemn the obsolescence and irrelevance of work, the commodity and the market; and it must ceaselessly expose and undermine those institutions, people and forces that prevent these relics from being placed squarely in the trashcan of history.

Part Five

"Citizens who carry out some undertaking in republics either in favor of liberty or of tyranny should, then, consider the basic material of their society and should judge by that the difficulty of their undertakings, because it is as difficult and as dangerous to try to liberate a people that wishes to live in slavery as it is to try to enslave a people that wishes to live in freedom [...] Those cities used to living in servitude think nothing of changing their master frequently, indeed, many times they desire to do so." (Machiavelli, *Discourses on Livy*).

Despite the optimistic reports of self-congratulatory neo-anarchists such as David Graeber,[23] we face a very difficult situation today, indeed, one that is much worse than the situation faced by the SI in 1957. Never has the spectacle been so powerful: it has succeeded in raising yet another generation molded to its laws; it has been able to accomplish its lethal program, despite the objections, critique and protests of millions and millions of people; and it aims to accomplish even more. All this is due in part to the confidence or sense of invulnerability among its leaders: as Debord wrote at the very end of his *Comments on the Society of the Spectacle*,

> We must conclude that a change is imminent and ineluctable in the co-opted cast who manage the domination and, notably, those who direct the protection of that domination. In such an affair, the novelty of course will never be displayed on the stage of the spectacle. It will only appear like lightning, which we know only when it strikes. This change, which will decisively complete the work of these spectacular times, will occur discreetly and, although it concerns those already installed in the sphere of power, conspiratorially. It will select those who will take part in it on this central requirement: that they clearly know what obstacles they have overcome, and of what they are capable.

The current success of the spectacle also derives from the failure of the various protest movements of the past decade (the anti-globalization movement and the anti-war movement, in particular) to correctly identify the roots of the problem and the best means of solving it. Instead, they have wasted time, effort and good faith by focusing on symptoms and remaining solidly within the systems of workplace and political representation. We should also not discount the role played by the passivity and apathy of the large numbers of people who are not politically active or, in other words, the continued effectiveness of the spectacle in keeping the majority of the people from turning their anger and bitterness into a desire to be politically active. Either they enjoy (are tranquilized by) their beer and TV too much, or they doubt that anything meaningful can be done to change the way things are.

The Situationist International

In our struggles, we must never forget that we are a minority within a minority: the vast majority of the contestatory movement is made up of paleo-Marxists, citizenists, Leftists and neo-anarchists. That is to say, the majority is not made up of revolutionaries, but radical reformers who are content to work on aspects of the problem, or to use the State ("democracy") to correct problems in the market. On the other hand, like the situationists in their day, we cannot expect much help from the artists, who tend to see themselves as mere questioners and habitually act unconcerned with what the answers might be: it is up to others to decide. It is crucial that we are just as persistent and merciless in our critique of these "radicals" as we are of the "conservatives" who are perfectly happy (or happy enough) with the way things are. Significantly, when they *are* critiqued, the artists respond quite differently from the activists: while the former do not respond or, after a single response, disappear, the latter become "defensive" or even go on the attack. They are indignant that *anyone* would dare to criticize them (this is especially true of activists who are actually academics), and proclaim that their "attackers" are damaging the movement itself through their "negativity" or "divisiveness." (Strangely enough, few activists will make these claims about the snitches and wannabe-COINTELPRO agents who are in their midst.) Especially if they are part of a "collective" or any other individuality-suppressing group, and feel confident in their numbers ("everyone feels as I do"), they will try to shame their "attackers" into silence or retractions. We have seen this so many times that we feel confident in making the following claim: the very fact of individuality is what is shameful to these people, and so anyone who displays his or her own individuality (autonomy) must be shamed, must be made to feel shame. But we, who have nothing to defend in the spectacle, cannot be shamed. We are in fact *shameless*.

[1] From "Oil on Fire," which was Martos' 1997 preface to his book *Correspondance avec Guy Debord*.
[2] *On War* (1832), translated from the German by Colonel J.J. Graham (Barnes & Noble, 2004).
[3] The presence of "Communist" groups in various American protest movements (against police brutality, against the war in Iraq, and against the on-going imprisonment of Mumia Abu-Jamal) is quite significant in the light of Guy Debord's comments on the roots of the "integrated spectacular."
[4] Our short text "A critique of neo-anarchism" (April 2007) denounces Leftists and other reformists who have cynically chosen to call themselves "anarchists." An anonymous text that we translated from the French called *The Citizenist Impasse* (April 2001) defines "citizenism" as "an ideology of which the principal traits are 1) the belief in democracy as something capable of opposing capitalism, 2) the project of reinforcing the State (the States) so as to put this politics in place, [and] 3) the citizen as the active basis for this politics." Many "citizenists" are active in the so-called anti-globalization and "global justice" movements.

[5] It seems significant to us that, despite its overall rejection of the theories and practice of the Situationist International (too Marxist, too enamored of technology), this issue contains a text by the ex-situationist Raoul Vaneigem entitled "Lines of Flight: To Liberate the Earth of Celestial Illusions and Their Tyranny." It is a confirmation of our thesis (advanced in our July 2007 text "On the 50th Anniversary of the Founding of the Situationist International") that there is now a significant difference between situationist theory (which is "Vaneigemist" in nature) and Debord's theory of the spectacle.

[6] All quotes in this paragraph come from the March 2007 essay by Max Vincent entitled *Du Temps que les situationnistes avaient raison*.

[7] Anselm Jappe, *Guy Debord* (originally published in Italian in 1993; translated from the 1995 French version by Donald Nicholson-Smith in 1999).

[8] Quoted in Guy Debord's *Comments on the Society of the Spectacle* (1988).

[9] Originally published by Buchet-Castel, *The Society of the Spectacle* has been translated into English by three different translators: Fredy Perlman (Red & Black, 1977); Donald Nicholson-Smith (Zone Books, 1994); and Ken Knabb (Rebel Press, 2005). Here, as elsewhere in this text, we have preferred to translate all passages from Debord and the other situationists ourselves.

[10] Georges Bataille, "The Notion of Expenditure," originally published in French in 1933; translated by Allan Stoekl and published in *Visions of Excess: Selected Writings, 1927-1939* (University of Minnesota, 1985). Note that Bataille uses the word "spectacle," but in a way that completely differs from Debord's use. For Bataille, "spectacles," "spectacular collective expenditures" and "the spectacular function" refer to the traditional obligation of the wealthy to provide or make "unproductive social expenditures" for the excitation and orgiastic satisfaction of the entire society, but especially the poor. "In so-called civilized societies," Bataille notes, "the fundamental *obligation* of wealth disappeared only in a fairly recent period (...) Today the great and free forms of unproductive social expenditure have disappeared." He goes on to say, "As the class that possess the wealth – having received with wealth the obligation of functional expenditure – the modern bourgeoisie is characterized by the refusal in principle of this obligation. It has distinguished itself from the aristocracy through the fact that it has consented only to *spend for itself,* and within itself – in other words, by hiding its expenditures as much as possible from the eyes of the other classes." It is precisely this state of affairs that Guy Debord called the society of the spectacle. For Bataille, the revolution against this society will be a *"great night* when their beautiful phrases will be drowned out by death screams in riots," which is "the bloody hope which, each day, is one with the existence of the people, and which sums up the insubordinate content of the class struggle." But for Les Amis de Nemesis, writing in "On Politics: Letter to JLD 13 October 2001": "It is not at all a question of opposing a Dionysian irrationality to an Apollonian rationality, but rather surpassing this sterile opposition and surpassing the finding of the rational where, stupidly, one does not seek it."

[11] One of the primary differences between situationist theory and Debord's theory of the spectacle (see footnote #5) is that, unlike the former, the latter was updated and reiterated several times after its first formulation in the era prior to May 1968.
[12] It is worth recalling in this context that many ancient Greeks believed that Lydia was the birthplace of both the first commodity (coined money) and political tyranny. For example, in the legend of the ring of Gyges, tyranny begins after the king is deposed by a man who wields a special, inscribed ring that allows him to become invisible at will. See Marc Shell, *The Economy of Literature* (Johns Hopkins University Press, 1978).
[13] From the essay entitled "Revolution in Reverse," which was posted to a Web site called Infoshop News. In the "Comments" section, Bill Not Bored pointed out that Graeber used a falsified quote from Raoul Vaneigem in this essay. Graeber's (non)responses to this point are typical of the neo-anarchists (see Part Five of the current text).
[14] See our essay entitled "On the flaws of Michel Foucault's *Discipline and Punish*."
[15] Debord was a member of Socialisme ou Barbarie from July 1960 to May 1961. On 5 May 1961, he addressed a very interesting letter of resignation to the participants in the national conference of *Pouvoir Ouvrier*. In a series of essays written between 1996 and 1999, we explored the relationship between Cornelius Castoriadis and Socialisme ou Barbarie, on the one hand, and Guy Debord and the Situationist International, on the other. For the role this relationship played in the writing of *The Society of the Spectacle*, see Debord's letter to Edouard Taube dated 17 October 1964.
[16] See the essay entitled "From a Supper of Ashes to Embers of Satin (On the Riots of November 2005 in France)."
[17] For good discussions of the November 2005 riots in the French *banlieus*, see the aforementioned text by Les Amis de Nemesis (footnote #16) and Max Vincent's "Remarks on the Riots of Autumn 2005 in the French Banlieus."
[18] See Guy Debord's letter to Gianfranco Sanguinetti dated 21 April 1978.
[19] See our review of Virilio's 2003 book *Art and Fear*.
[20] "Porn and Politics in Palestine," *Reason Magazine Online*, 3 April 2002.
[21] For Debord's reaction to the Vaux-en-Velin riots, see his letter to Jean-Francois Martos dated 26 December 1990. Debord's *Notes on the "immigrant question"* was written to help Mezioud Ouldamer, who was working on a book entitled *The Immigrant Nightmare in the Decomposition of France*.
[22] See Arianna Bove's translation of Negri's essay Approximations: Towards an Ontological Definition of the Multitude." For more on Negri, see our July 2001 text "The Relevance of Antonio Negri to the Anti-Globalization Movement."
[23] From the essay entitled "The Shock Of Victory," which was posted to Infoshop News. In the "Comments" section, Bill Not Bored pointed out that "there is a big difference between optimism and self-congratulatory self-deception."

Graeber's (non)responses to this point were very revealing.

NOT BORED! #40, May 2008

Gene McHugh Dispenses with Clausewitz

Once employed by the political consultancy group Devine Mulvey, and now pursuing a graduate degree at the Center for Curatorial Studies at Bard College, Gene McHugh says he is interested in "questioning the applicability of Debord's own conception of resistance (particularly *detournement*) in an age of networked, topological communication." Perhaps "Debord's strategies of resistance do not in fact jive with our version of the society of the spectacle."[1] Then why keep bringing him up? Like so many before him, McHugh needs to both cite Debord (an obligation at this point) and put Debord behind him so that he (McHugh) can continue to do what he is doing "in good faith."[2] McHugh's article on the Radical Software Group's version of Debord's cabinet game *Kriegspiel* – which drew a cease and desist letter, alleging copyright infringement, from a lawyer retained by Debord's widow, Alice Becker-Ho, in April 2008 – attacks Debord's relevance on two fronts.

First, McHugh asserts that "*detournement,* that famous cornerstone of Situationism [sic] . . . is itself, by now, a familiar concept in Internet culture [...] The second major Situationist tactic, *derive,* or the arbitrary drifting through urban space, has become a primary tool of online capitalism [...] At least some of his [Debord's] strategies of countering it [the spectacle] have been effectively incorporated into the internal logic of communications media today."

Commonly repeated though they are, these claims are largely meaningless. First, the Situationist International evolved and progressed over time, so much so that there were *three* distinct periods in its existence. Detournement and derive were important, even "cornerstone," concepts, yes, but in the SI's *first* period (1957-1961). And so, while it may be true that the spectacle of today has apparently recuperated detournement and derive, this says nothing about the status of the weapons forged and used during the SI's second period (1962-1966), when theoretical critique replaced artistic experimentation, nor during the SI's third period (1967-1971), when the SI concentrated on strictly political interventions in France and elsewhere. But has the spectacle *really* recuperated detournement and derive? McHugh refers to certain *forms* of communication that have been recuperated. But what about their *content*? It is quite clear that there has been no "incorporation" of Debord's primary themes (alienation, dispossession and decomposition) into the language of the spectacle, even at this late date.

The second move McHugh makes is to claim that Debord's *Kriegspiel,* rather than recuperated, has been revealed to be *unworthy of recuperation.* Building upon remarks made by the RSG's Alexander Galloway, who claimed in *Cabinet* magazine[3] that *Kriegspiel* had "more in common with Napoleon's 1806 Battle of Jena than Debord's own 1968 Battle of Paris," McHugh tries to call attention to "the blatant anachronism of the Clausewitzian theories underlying [Debord's game] and the accompanying lack of a substantive formal connection to the asymmetrical warfare that Debord himself experienced in May 1968 [...] The tactical apparatus of both the 'Game of War' [by the RSG] and *Kriegspiel* crumbles when viewed through the lens of postmodern military theorization." According to McHugh, Debord (and thus Galloway's version of the game) "neglects to represent how communication has in fact been used by more recent resistance groups such as guerrilla armies, terrorist cells, and hackers unleashing computer viruses." Thus, McHugh concludes, Alice Becker-Ho isn't to be criticized for exerting copyright control over a work by her husband, but for going after an infringement that actually demonstrates the "futility" of her husband's work, not its potency.

It is ludicrous to imagine that Guy Debord was the either the "Napoleon" (the military leader) or the "Clausewitz" (the military historian) of "the Battle of Paris." Debord was simply one person among many at the barricades of the rue Gay Lassac,[4] in the occupied Sorbonne and, later, in the national library occupied by the situs and Enrages. He was never "in command." Furthermore, the May 1968 movement in Paris (and elsewhere in France) was *not* some kind of military battle, i.e, an instance of "asymmetrical warfare" between cops and protestors. Such a notion both exaggerates the degree of organization that the May movement had reached (unlike the Paris Commune, it did not possess an armed guard) and trivializes the stakes of the contest (the "battlefields" of May 1968 weren't simply a few student-dominated streets in Paris, but the factories, ports and transportation systems of the entire country, as well).

It is even worse to imply on the basis of such flimsy claims that Debord himself – despite or perhaps precisely because of his very participation in the May 1968 movement – did not realize that it had little or nothing to do with classical military theory (Clausewitz) and that May 1968 was in fact an early *postmodern* instance of "nonhierarchical dispersion," "networked opposition" and "cutting-edge warfare." Perhaps this is why General Debord lost the Battle of Paris? In McHugh's hypothesis, Debord had been clueless about truly contemporary warfare ever since 1968: in 1977, when he designed *Kriegspiel,* and again in 1987, when he defended it in a book co-authored with Alice Becker-Ho. It simply took Alex Galloway's failed attempt to bring Debord's *Kriegspiel* into the age of computers to reveal the game's fatal weaknesses.

But of course Guy Debord did not live and write in the era *before* the advent of "more recent resistance groups such as guerrilla armies, terrorist cells, and hackers unleashing computer viruses." Guerrilla armies and terrorist cells were active in the 1970s, when *Kriegspiel* was created, and Debord spent a good deal of time discussing them both in his *Preface to the 4th Italian Edition of the Society of the Spectacle* (1979) and his *Comments on the Society of the Spectacle* (1988). And though he knew nothing of hackers or viruses, Debord deliberately constructed his *Comments* so that it could not be read by computers. Parts of it are, in Debord's own words, "deliberately confused."[5]

More to the point, Debord's interest in Clausewitz was neither superficial nor short-lived. As far as we can tell, it began in the early 1970s, when Gerard Lebovici showed Debord a copy of Clausewitz's book. In a letter dated 21 February 1974, and speaking with respect to the developments then taking place in Portugal, Debord – always one to move with the times – proclaimed that, "At this stage and to speak schematically, the basic theoreticians to retrieve and develop are no longer Hegel, Marx and Lautreamont, but Thucydides, Machiavelli and Clausewitz."[6] It was presumably this turn from critique to strategy that led Debord to create his *Kriegspiel* three years later. Between 1984 and 1989, Debord devoted a great deal of time and energy to helping Editions Gerard Lebovici publish Jean-Pierre Baudet's translation of Clausewitz's *Vom Kriege,* which had previously appeared in French, but never unabridged or translated well. Debord not only "recommended" the book for publication, he also fact-checked, copyedited and proofread the manuscript himself. He insisted that Baudet's translation be illustrated with maps from the time, and even went to the National Library and managed to locate seven suitable examples.[7]

McHugh and Galloway, by contrast, know nothing about Clausewitz. The former speaks of "Clausewitzian theories," as if Clausewitz were a source of theories, instead of a rare and fine example of dialectical thinking about theory; and the later speaks of the "Clausewitzian mentality" – the mentality of "resistance" – as if Clausewitz's theories [sic] were actually a mind-set that always and only sees two alternatives (attack or be defeated). Together, these two "budding anarchists"[8] reject Guy Debord (and Carl von Clausewitz, too) in favor of the well-known military theorist Roland Barthes (!), who wrote "there is only one way left to escape the alienation of present-day society: to retreat ahead of it." But won't such a "retreat" be a series of defeats, ending in a rout? No, it will be a "'hypertrophic' forward escape," says McHugh; it will "push technology into a hypertrophic state, further than it is meant to go."

What successes can this "postmodern military theorization" claim? (I mean, *in reality,* not in cyberspace or on university curriculum vitae.) Under the name "Revolution in Military Affairs," this theorization called for the single-minded use of "shock and awe," airpower, and small teams of special forces – and the rejection of such "traditional" (Clausewitzian) theories and practices such as diplomacy, ground troops and the use of overwhelming force – in America's attacks on the Taliban in Afghanistan in October 2001 and in America's second war against Iraq in March 2003. This same "postmodern" theorization was utilized in Israel's war against Hezbollah in southern Lebanon in 2006.[9] In each of these cases, "postmodern military theorization" did not lead to spectacular victories, but to humiliating defeats. And yet, here are McHugh and Galloway – claiming to be speaking in the name of effectiveness in combating the spectacle – blithely continuing to advocate this "theorization" of warfare as if it were more relevant than Debord and his "merely nostalgic" *Kriegspiel*![10] The similarity of these postmodernists to Bush, Cheney and Rumsfeld is striking: all have little or no actual knowledge of warfare, and all see "war" as an end in itself, as a "network," as something fundamentally open-ended and impossible to terminate, and not as a means to a political end.

[1] "Battle Code: Guy Debord's Game of War and the Radical Software Group," *Artforum International* (November 2008), pp. 167-168. Earlier in the year, *Book Forum* (an off-shoot of *Artforum*) published an article by Nathan Heller ("What is it good for? Guy Debord believed his war board game would be his legacy") that contains at least 50 incorrect, slanderous or otherwise objectionable statements about Guy Debord and *Kriegspiel*.
[2] Note the relevance here of the last four paragraphs of Section Two of "The Society of the Virtual Spectacle," published in our previous issue.
[3] We would like to quote from this article, but it is not available anywhere on-line.
[4] See Debord's letter to Michel Prigent dated 29 August 1981.
[5] See letter to Pierre Besson dated 31 October 1989.
[6] Letter to Eduardo Rothe dated 21 February 1974.
[7] See letters to Floriana Lebovici dated 20 November 1984, January 1988 and 19 March 1988.
[8] "If Debord's strategies of resistance do not in fact jive with our version of the society of the spectacle, what is a budding anarchist to do?" McHugh asks with respect to Alex Galloway.
[9] See our review of Eyal Weizman's *Hollow Land*.
[10] Note well the following article, published on 19 December 2008 by *Haaretz* under the title "U.S. report: Hezbollah fought Israel better than any Arab army."

A new report from the U.S. Army War College warns that the American military must learn the lessons of the Second Lebanon War, in which Hezbollah operated more like a conventional army than a guerrilla organization.

The report, "The 2006 Lebanon Campaign and the Future of Warfare: Implications for Army and Defense Policy," warns against placing too heavy an emphasis on classic guerrilla warfare, and raises the possibility of further non-state actors following the Lebanese militant group's example.

"Hezbollah's 2006 campaign in southern Lebanon has been receiving increasing attention as a prominent recent example of a non-state actor fighting a Westernized state," the authors of the report state. "In particular, critics of irregular-warfare transformation often cite the 2006 case as evidence that non-state actors can nevertheless wage conventional warfare in state-like ways."

The authors of the report, Dr. Stephen D. Biddle and Jeffrey A. Friedman, state that changes made by the U.S. Army in conducting urban warfare against guerrilla fighters in Iraq could compromise the military's ability to deal with other enemies in the future.

The authors give a high grade to Hezbollah's performance in the 2006 war, describing it as more effective than that of any Arab army that confronted Israel in the Jewish state's history, and that Hezbollah militants wounded more Israelis per fighter than any previous Arab effort.

Unlike a traditional guerrilla force, however, Hezbollah emphasized holding territory and digging in to bunkers, instead of the usual tactic of hiding among civilian populations. Likewise, the militant organization's discipline and coordination highly resembled those of conventional armies.

This combination of conventional and guerrilla tactics, the report claims, places new challenges before the U.S. Army. It calls for preparing the military for asymmetrical urban warfare, while at the same time working closely with civilian populations. It also calls for reducing military activity likely to harm the image of the U.S.

The report indicates that no army can be ideally prepared to deal with both kinds of enemy, conventional and guerrilla, simultaneously, and that in light of the discrepancies between the lessons of the Second Lebanon War and the current U.S. experience in Iraq and Afghanistan, serious challenges confront military planners.

While fighting in Iraq and Afghanistan demands the ability to defeat guerrilla forces, the example of Lebanon may inspire enemies of the U.S. to adopt more conventional methods.

NOT BORED! #41, November 2009

Professor Galloway's Latest Stupidities

As if there weren't enough stupidities concerning Guy Debord emanating from a small group of academic "gamers" in New York City,[1] Associate Professor Alexander R. Galloway (NYU) has produced yet another collection of them. Entitled "Debord's Nostalgic Algorithm" and published in *Culture Machine* #10 ("Pirate Philosophy"), this article is mostly concerned with Debord's board game (sometimes called *Kriegspiel,* other times *The Game of War*), which Galloway digitized and exhibited with/under the name of The Radical Software Group.

Unlike Professor Galloway, we do not believe that "By March 8, 1978, Debord's former glory as a radical filmmaker and author had faded," because in 1978 Debord had yet to write his *Comments on the Society of the Spectacle* (1988) or *Panegyric* (1989), which are two of his finest and most celebrated books. Nor do we believe, as Galloway does, that Debord was quite serious when he claimed that *Kriegspiel* "might be the only thing in all my work – I'm afraid to admit – that one might dare say has some value"[2] (this claim is made, after all, from within the shifting sands of *Panegyric*). And so we are not interested in the few banalities that Galloway comes up with concerning *Kriegspiel* (his speculations as to whom played North and whom played South in the game recorded in Debord and Alice Becko-Ho's 1987 book *The Game of War*; his commentaries on the number and kinds of mistakes and/or instances of cheating in all three versions of the game's rule book, and – worst of all – his educated guesses about Debord's psychology and his possible motivations for being interested in what Galloway calls "first cinema and philosophy, and finally the bourgeois parlour game"). We are primarily interested in the bold new stupidities that Galloway's text contains. In particular, his remarks about the assassination of Aldo Moro.

But first, a brief sampling of the low quality of Professor Galloway's scholarship. "In 1991," he writes,

> Debord ordered all his published works destroyed, including this book [*The Game of War*]. But after Debord's death and under Becker-Ho's stewardship, the French publisher Gallimard reissued the book in 2006 as *Le Jeu de la Guerre: Releve des positions successives de toutes les forces au cours d'une partie.* After remaining untranslated for twenty years, an English edition of the work appeared a year later from Atlas Press, translated by Donald Nicholson-Smith, an ex-Situationist with whom Debord had kept in touch over the years. In 1986, as his publishing house was suffering hard times in the wake of the death of Gerard Lebovici, Debord suggested a scheme to Floriana Lebovici, the daughter, to relieve the publisher's debts by commercializing *The Game of War*.

There are no less than *five* serious omissions or errors of fact in these four sentences:

1) in 1991, Debord was able to get a court to order his former publisher, Editions Gerard Lebovici (EGL), to pulp all of the books that it had published under his name (Alice Becker-Ho asked for and was granted the same wish) because he/they wanted to make sure that EGL kept to its word, actually dissolved as a company, and didn't re-establish itself under a new name. Galloway makes

Debord's decision seem capricious or arbitrary, when it was in fact reluctantly taken in response to the unprofessional conduct of the inheritors of the Lebovici name.

2) it was in 1992, under the stewardship of Jean-Jacques Pauvert, that Debord started publishing his books with Gallimard. Unlike *Panegyric,* the *Comments,* and *The Society of the Spectacle*, Debord's *Game of War* book wasn't reissued by Gallimard during his lifetime because Debord himself did not in fact consider *Kriegspiel* to be as important as these other books/projects.

3) Debord didn't "keep in touch" with Donald Nicholson-Smith, whom he disliked and distrusted as early as 1979 and steadfastly all through the rest of his life. In fact, DNS kept pursuing Debord with the project of translating *Spectacle* into English, and Debord kept ignoring him.[3]

4) Editions Gerard Lebovici was not "his [Debord's] publishing house," which implies that he either owned part of it or was responsible for running it, neither of which was true. Indeed, Debord had been denying such foolishness as early as 1976.[4].

5) Floriana Lebovici was Gerard Lebovici's *wife,* not his daughter.

Of course, Professor Galloway also allows himself the liberty to *make shit up* (that is, project his own personality and preoccupations upon Guy Debord): the French occupations movement of May 1968 was merely "a student movement"; Debord *might not* have been at the barricades "in the flesh"[5] and he certainly wasn't a "frontline militant," unlike Gilles Deleuze(!); after 1974 Debord "stayed away from Paris for much of the rest of his downhill life, watching the passing parade from a safe distance" and he was "something of a fading violet when it came to actual conflict." Far from being a bad ass of *any* kind, Professor Galloway – a bland, politically cautious fellow – should know that *he* of all people would do well to refrain from publicly questioning Guy Debord's experiences with and taste for "actual conflict."

Galloway makes much of the following falsified juxtaposition: in March 1978, while Guy Debord was allegedly "dallying" with the idea that the cinema was over, "the world awoke to a dramatic turn of events":

> The long-time Prime Minister of Italy, Christian Democrat Aldo Moro, had been kidnapped during a brazen intervention by the far left communist militant group the Red Brigades. In Italy the progressive militancy of the sixties had metastasized during the following decade into an actually existing low-level guerrilla war. Moro was held for 54 days. During the hostage period, Moro appealed to the Christian Democrats to acquiesce and negotiate with what both the newspapers and government officials alike called terrorists, that newly evolved form of political actor so closely associated with the late-modern period. Held in secret and sentenced to death in a so-called people's trial on or about April 15, Moro received little solidarity from his

former government colleagues, and sensing the immanent culmination of events, the presumed future president of Italy stipulated that no Christian Democrat leaders should be present at his funeral. There were none.

In such a juxtaposition, Debord comes off very poorly.

> So as Moro lay in the trunk of the Renault R4, Guy Debord was at his rural home playing board games and toying with the idea of fashioning one of his own. The backdrop of European militancy in the seventies makes Debord's penchant for playtime all the more delicious.

But to make this cheap device work, Galloway must pretend that, prior to and during March 1978, Guy Debord said nothing about Moro, the Red Brigades, and the spectacle of artificial (state-sponsored) terrorism in Italy. Galloway claims:

> When he did finally address Moro and the Red Brigades, in his 1979 preface to the fourth Italian edition of *The Society of the Spectacle*, Debord spat on the guerrilla movement, claiming that the Red Brigades were in fact unknowing pawns of the state Stalinist forces. Writing to Sanguinetti *before the killing*, Debord predicted that Moro would be 'suicided' by his own government, thus allowing the state forces to consolidate power (known in Italy as the 'historic compromise') around the common fear of terror and anarchy. (Emphasis added.)

But the problem for Galloway is obvious: the 1979 preface *couldn't* have been the first time Debord addressed the subject, because he wrote to Gianfranco Sanguinetti *before the killing,* which took place on or just before 10 May 1978 (at least according to Galloway's source, which of course is the *New York Times*). Galloway makes no further reference to this letter to Sanguinetti, which was in fact dated 21 April 1978 and does quite a bit more than simply and correctly predict that Moro would in fact not be released, but killed by his captors. It also asserts that the Red Brigades (RBs) had long since been replaced or controlled by the Italian secret services; the "guerrilla war" was not being fought between the "far left" and the State, but by different forces active *within* the State that had differing ideas on what to do to quell Italy's workers movement; and that Aldo Moro wasn't "kidnapped" by the RBs, but by forces that *opposed* the "Historic Compromise" (these forces either controlled the RBs or didn't, but their hostility to Moro and others like him dates back to the 1960s).

Galloway's account gives the distinct impression that before, during and after March 1978, all Guy Debord was interested in was his toy soldiers, when in fact 1978 saw him write several other important letters (most to Paolo Salvadori, another former situationist) concerning the situation in Italy: their dates are 3 July 1978, 18 September 1978 and 12 November 1978. Significantly, all of Debord's assertions – proven true in the early 1990s – were completely foreign to the thinking of the people to whom Galloway praises for their lucidity and usefulness: Antonio Negri and Gilles Deleuze, both of whom quite foolishly believed that "the question of the Red Brigades" was that of over-zealous or under theorized politics, not state-sponsored artificial terrorism. Ironically, it is *not* Guy Debord who should be chided for avoiding the subject of Moro, but Sanguinetti, who had the power to the blow the lid off the Moro Affair – just as he did in 1975 on the subject of the bombing of the Piazza Fontana in his *Veritable Report on the Last Chances to Save Capitalism in Italy* – but who didn't, who waited until 1979, when he "finally" published *On Terrorism and the State*.

We'd be done now were if not for the fact that Professor Galloway felt the need to end his severely fact-challenged analysis with the following preposterous generalizations:

> Certainly the domain of simulation and modeling is always something of a bitter pill for progressive movements. This is the root anxiety lurking beneath the surface of Debord's game. The left will always be deceived in the domain of abstraction. This is not to say that Spirit or the logos are by necessity contrary to progressive political movements. Nevertheless the lofty realm of rational idealism has always been something of a hindrance to those suffering from the harsh vicissitudes of material fact. And here one must revisit a long history indeed, of traditionalism versus transformation, of philosophy versus sophistry, of essence versus process, of positivism versus dialectics, of social science versus 'theory', and so on.
>
> Progressive art movements are very good at beginnings, but terrible at endings. As Debord said in 1978 amidst his losses (the death of the SI, the 'end' of the cinema, his expanding waistline and vanishing sobriety): 'avant-gardes have but one time' (1999: 47). We might say something similar about leftist cultural production in general: (1) the left is forever true in the here and now, always in the grip of its own immediate suffering, but (2) it will forever be defeated in the end, even if it finds vindication there. This is why Debord can occupy himself with both 'struggle' and 'utopia'. It is also a window into why Debord became obsessed late in life, not with street revolt, but with the sublimation of antagonistic desire into an abstract rulebook. It is not that the past is always glorious and the future antiseptic. Quite the opposite, both past and future are internally variegated into alternately repressive and liberating moments. For the left, the 'historical present' is one of immediate justice won through

the raw facts of struggle and sacrifice. In short, the historical present is always true, but forever at the same time bloody. But the future, the utopian imagination, is a time of complete liberation forged from the mould of the most profound injustice. In short, utopia is always false, but forever at the same time free.

For Professor Galloway, obsessed as he is with binary oppositions (rational idealism vs. material fact, et al), *it's all the same*: "progressive [political] movements" and "progressive art movements," "the [political] left" and "leftist cultural production," what's the difference? None. And so, Guy Debord, the *enemy* of both political Leftism *and* "leftist cultural production," is easily conflated with partisans of "utopia" and "sacrifice," that is, with the wallflower dreamers and zealous self-abnegators. But Galloway has everything upside-down: the Situationist International didn't die, as if from exhaustion or recuperation, but because Guy Debord killed it. And that numbers among the best things he ever did.

[1] McKenzie Wark, Nathan Heller and Gene McHugh, among others.
[2] We would render the French slightly differently: "The surprises of the *Kriegspiel* seem inexhaustible; and it is perhaps the only one of my works, I fear, in which one will dare to recognize some value."
[3] See for example Debord's letter to Anita Blanc of EGL dated 20 November 1989.
[4] See Debord's letter to Jamie Semprun dated 26 December 1976 and printed in *Editions Champ Libre Correspondance, Volume I* (1981).
[5] Galloway says: "Much has been said about Debord being at those May barricades, certainly in spirit if not also in the flesh, with Situationist graffiti festooning the pediments of respectable French society." For the facts, see Debord's letter to Michel Prigent dated 29 August 1981.

NOT BORED! #41, November 2009

To Guy Debord in Hell
(Please forward if necessary)

"Although I have read a lot, I have drunk even more. I have written much less than the majority of people who write, but I have drunk more than the majority of people who drink." – Guy Debord, *Panegyric* (1989)

"Where's my mail? Who's messing with my mail?" – The Lone

Ranger, in Lenny Bruce's posthumous film short, *Thank You Mask Man* (1968)

In the 20 years since *Panegyric* was published, it has come out that the renowned French acrobat Guy Debord wrote *thousands* of letters during his lifetime (1931-1994). On average, he seems to have written a letter every day for more than 40 years! Avoiding telephones – not only because they could be bugged, but also because he found conversations on them to be intolerably impersonal – Debord used letters (and postcards and telegrams) to organize all kinds of conferences, exhibitions, and interventions; to receive and critique submissions to *Internationale Situationniste*; to write and distribute draft versions of declarations to be signed by the Situationist International; to distribute clandestine texts in foreign countries; to review books written by friends and offer proofreader's corrections to existing books or manuscripts that had been submitted to Editions Champ Libre; and to offer sketches of letters, statements or articles that would later be completed by other writers. He also relied upon letters to make arrangements to meet friends or newcomers for a casual drink or dinner; to gossip about friends or enemies; to renew old friendships; and to tell certain people to fuck off. In other words, he used the postal system the way today's writers and publishers use email: on a daily basis, and to do virtually everything.

An extraordinarily meticulous man, Debord made a carbon copy of each of his letters, which were typically hand-written and had to be typed up by someone else. Debord typed very poorly and disliked using a machine to write. (When computers "arrived" in the 1980s, Debord hated them and certainly wouldn't use one to write anything.) These carbon copies were collected and organized into files, which were stored and transported en bloc when necessary. Debord was quite certain of the historical character of his life, but he also wanted to be able to recall what had been said, when, to whom, despite his drinking. In sum, Guy Debord – heretofore known as a great writer of a modest number of books, essays and pamphlets, and a pioneering *cinematographer* (a "writer of films") – wrote more *letters* than the majority of the people who write letters. *Drink to it!*

Virtually none of these letters were published in his lifetime; only a few of them were reproduced, circulated to and discussed by people other than the original addressees.[1] Today, fifteen years after Debord's death (a suicide), most of his letters have been collected and published in well-designed, chronologically ordered volumes. Undertaken in 1999 by Librairie Artheme Fayard, the series entitled *Guy Debord Correspondance* has included seven volumes so far and claims to have covered the years 1957 to 1994. It is said one more volume in this series is to yet to come.[4] In addition to providing an index to the entire series, Volume 8 of *Guy Debord Correspondance* will apparently cover the years 1951 to 1957, which Fayard partially mined in 2004, when it published *Marquis de Sade a*

---

[4] It was published in October 2010.

des yeux de fille. A collection of facsimiles of some of the letters Debord wrote between 1949 and 1954, *Marquis de Sade* has apparently gone out of print. Perhaps it will be "reprinted" in Volume 8. If so, we will have Debord's letters from either 1949 or 1954 all the way to the end, 30 November 1994.

After five years of translating hundreds of the letters that Guy Debord wrote between 1957 and 1994, I have come to visualize a day in his life in the following manner: waking, drinking, reading, eating, going for a stroll, drinking some more, writing and *waiting for the mailman*. No matter where he was – in France or living in another country, in the city or in the countryside – Guy Debord was waiting for the day's mail, that is to say, to read the responses to *his* responses to other people's remarks. The usefulness, the regularity and even the novelty of the postal system never seemed to wear off. In several of his letters, but mostly strikingly in those written in 1994, the last year of his life, we encounter something like this: "Write to me at this address, because the mail follows me wherever I go." The temptation is irresistible: *Hey, Guy! Are you getting your mail down there in hell?*

Despite its grand appearance or our fondest hopes, *Guy Debord Correspondance* has *not* been "complete," and *will* not be "complete," even after the publication of Volume 8, which, according to Ken Knabb, will "also include various letters that were discovered too late to be included in the above volumes." There have been serious and systematic omissions, right from the start. *None* of the untold numbers of letters addressed *to* Guy Debord, by untold numbers of people, have been included. Furthermore, and for one reason or another, *none* of Debord's letters to the situationist Jacqueline de Jong, his one-time girlfriend Michele Mochot-Brehat, and his ex-wives (the situationist Michele Bernstein and Alice Becker-Ho) has been included. A cynical, but still unsatisfied buyer might ask: *Will there be a separate volume entitled "Guy Debord, Love Letters"?*[2]

While it is true that either "Alice Debord" (Alice Becker-Ho) or someone at Fayard (Patrick Mosconi?) has consistently provided summaries of the major events of each year, as well as explanatory footnotes, both have been kept very brief, and seem to have been added "only when necessary." In any case, they rarely quote from or even summarize the letters that have sent to Debord and to which he is always already responding. As a result, quite unnecessarily, and to the incalculable detriment of both contemporary understanding and the research of future historians, some passages in a few fairly crucial letters are difficult, if not impossible to understand, and some letters can't be properly or fully contextualized. At the global level, a complex and rich network of back-and-forth dialogues (true correspondences) has been turned into a simple set of monologues (letters primarily addressed to posterity and only secondarily to particular people at particular moments in time).

Only Jean-Pierre Baudet, Jean-Francois Martos, and Michel Bounan have publicly denounced the *Guy Debord Correspondance* series and Alice Debord's role in it, in particular.[3] Almost everyone else in the situ scene *hasn't* been outraged; at the very least, they have managed to stay ignorant or silent about the whole affair. Perhaps they feel that Alice can do anything she wants to do,[4] and/or that we are lucky to have the letters that we have been given. Most translators – Ken Knabb, Donald Nicholson-Smith, Stuart Kendall, John McKale, Keith Sanborn, et al – have continued to work with Alice, that is to say, to help her *capitalize* on her ex-husband's assets: not only his "correspondence," but his lesser known books, his films, his film scripts, and his cabinet game, known as *Kriegspiel* or *The Game of War*. But they should not be condemned too harshly: it is quite true that they do not get paid, or get paid very little, while Alice keeps the lion's share of the money for herself, even or especially if its ultimate source is the French Ministry of Culture in Los Angeles, New York or London. The sums involved here are probably substantial.

Harsh condemnation is best reserved for Semiotext(e), which recently published a perfectly good translation of Fayard's *already defective* version of Volume I (1957-1960), but did so without even mentioning the existence of the ongoing battle over the integrity of the *Guy Debord Correspondance* series as a whole. Of course Semiotext(e) didn't need to announce what position it was taking up on this particular battlefield. Its position spoke for itself: *The prestige of publishing Debord more than compensates for the inadequacy of the money we are paid.* And so Semiotext(e) must feign ignorance or keep quiet about the *prestige-killing* things Alice/Fayard have done to make the project happen in the first place: the ruthless suppression of Jean-Francois Martos' volume of *his* personal correspondence to and from Guy Debord, which allegedly compromised the "completeness" of then-nonexistent *Guy Debord Correspondance* series; the aforementioned omissions (the most important women in Guy Debord's life, no less!); and the satisfaction of a requirement that "X" replace a certain person's name wherever it appeared in Volume 6 (1979-1988). Semiotext(e) isn't simply helping Alice make even more money for herself; they are helping her to cover her tracks or, rather, helping her erase the tracks of others, without even being told why she is erasing these particular tracks and not others.[5] *See no evil, speak no evil.*

* * *

I have been reading Guy Debord's works since 1983. I *like* them. I learn a lot from them and enjoy them. I damn well know that he wasn't perfect, that he had his faults (in addition to the drinking), and that he was capable of saying stupid things, just like anyone else, especially in his "private" correspondence. I never met him nor thought to send him a letter while he was alive, even though I have long published an allegedly situationist fanzine in which Debord is often mentioned. I have never met or corresponded with Alice Becker-Ho; I do not have anything personal against her. But it has pleased me, especially since the man's death, to do my best to keep straight and/or complete the historical record about Guy Debord, to fill in the missing pieces, and to make sure the context is clearly understood.

Since the original volumes of the seven-volume-long series *Guy Debord Correspondance* are themselves selections, and not the complete correspondence, I have not felt compelled to translate every single letter in each volume. I just translated the interesting ones, the good ones. There were a lot of them; between 10 and 30 per year. In each case, I preserved the original footnotes. When desirable, I provided new footnotes, all of them clearly noted. More importantly, I did not drop out or soften the impact of any passages that might be seen or construed as unflattering to its author or that might be useful to Debord's many detractors (they tend to be the people who write biographies of him, for some reason). I always chose to include these letters, completely unabridged. This is *my* Guy Debord, yes; but it is my Guy Debord, *warts and all.*

I have placed these unauthorized translations on-line, at my own expense, and have made them available for free, without asserting any copyrights or rights reserved. When I have received emails pointing out mistakes, I have made the proper corrections immediately. Provided my translator's notes are included and attributed to "NOT BORED," I am always pleased whenever I discover that someone somewhere has copy-and-pasted one or several of my translations to the Internet. I have never received a cease-and-desist letter from either Alice Debord or Fayard, nor do I expect to. MIT Press? There'd be no point. Everyone knows that you *just can't trust* what you read on-line; you can only trust what's been *printed in a book.* Why? Books got a copyright symbol, an ISBN and a barcode, and what's on-line don't.

[1] Examples would include the Situationist International's orientation debate, which was largely conducted by mail between 1970 and 1971 (and collected and published by pirates in 1974); Guy Debord's letters to Alfonso Monteiro, concerning Portugal and dated March 1975 and 15 November 1975; and Debord's letter to Gianfranco Sanguinetti, concerning Aldo Moro and dated 21 April 1978.

[2] No doubt such a book would be veritably *Sadean.* "Sade was also recuperated to create the basis of the restricted section of the Bibliotheque nationale de France. Then why not Debord, yielded up in a bloc for the purposes of research?" Frederique Roussel wrote in the 17 June 2009 issue of *Liberation.*

[3] For more about Jean-Pierre Baudet, see "Signed X" (2007); for Jean-Francois Martos, see "On the Interdiction of My Correspondence with Guy Debord" (1999); and for Michel Bounan, see "Editorial Politics" (2000).

[4] So far, that has included 1) selling her ex-husband's letters through Fayard, which is owned by La Gardiere, one of the biggest arms-dealers and media-monopolists in the world; 2) selling his films through Gaumont, which one of the biggest corporate distributors in France; and 3) attempting to sell his *entire archives* – which have been estimated to be worth approximately $2,340,000 – to either Yale University or the Bibliotheque nationale de France (see news articles dated 14 June 2009, 17 June 2009 and 17 June 2009).

[5] For example: Jean-Pierre Baudet fell out of Debord's favor in 1988; and Jean-Francois Martos fell out of Debord's favor shortly thereafter because he questioned what happened to Baudet. They were thrown out of Debord's *social circle*. But this can't be taken as good reason to remove either of these men from the *historical record* of Debord's life. These were people who had known each other for years; while still close friends, they *collaborated* on texts together, properly "Debordian" texts – Baudet's book about Chernobyl and his translation of Clausewitz into French; Martos' pamphlet on Poland and his *History of the Situationist International*; and especially their collective work, as a trio, on the critique of the Encyclopedia of Nuisances – that, today, simply cannot be cut from the corpus without irreparably disfiguring it.

NOT BORED! #41, November 2009

Guy Debord in 2009: Spinning or Laughing?

Guy Debord wasn't buried. Following his wishes, his remains were cremated and scattered into the wind over a beloved Quay in Paris. The gesture couldn't be clearer: no place to come to worship his memory, to mark significant anniversaries or to leave tokens of appreciation. A refusal of eternity and posterity; an emphatic embrace of the ephemeral and disappearance(s). And so one can't say "Guy Debord is probably spinning in his grave" or "Guy Debord is probably laughing in his grave." But the question can still be raised. Fifteen years after he committed suicide at the age of 62: is Guy Debord, now in heaven or hell, spinning or laughing?

He's gotta be doing *something,* something other than resting peacefully. He has not been forgotten; he has not achieved oblivion. On the one hand, his works continue to inspire and motivate people: his 1950s-era notions and practices of psychogeography and urban drifting (*la derive*) continue to be popular, especially among urban theorists and contemporary performance artists; his chess-like cabinet game from 1977 (aka *Kriegspiel* or *The Game of War*) has become fairly popular among programmers and players of digital games in England and the USA; and his critique of the society of the spectacle (aka "the Spectacle") continues to be adopted as a starting point by young revolutionaries in France (cf. *Tiqqun* and *The Coming Insurrection*).

On the other hand, Debord's works have been repackaged and sold by his second wife, Alice Becker-Ho. Over the course of the last 15 years, "Ms Debord" has chosen to distribute her late husband's films in DVD form through Gaumont, a large and well-established producer and distributor of spectacular entertainment; to publish her late husband's "complete" correspondence in abridged form through

Fayard, a subsidiary of a large arms manufacturer; and to sell his complete archives to either the Bibliotheque Nationale de France (BNF) or the Beinecke Library at Yale University, whichever can come up with $2.34 million by 2011. "Ms Debord" has also used her commercial and legal clout to either change the presentation or completely suppress the "unauthorized" usage of her late husband's works by the Radical Software Group (re: *The Game of War*) and Jean-Francois Martos (re: *Correspondance avec Guy Debord*), neither of which came close to actually competing with the "official" copyrighted products. Were either of these heavy-handed actions really necessary? They certainly generated a ton of negative press for Alice.

I grant that her conduct could have been (even) worse. After all, she *could* have written books or appeared in the movies or the mass media to extol the virtues of her late husband. She *could* have licensed his image for use in an advertising campaign . . . "Spectacular eyeglasses," or some such. She hasn't, of course. Nevertheless, she *has* conducted herself like a classic recuperator. Would Guy agree? What would he think? Intriguing questions, *n'est pas*? I don't know what the answers would be, of course: I never met or corresponded with him; I am not in communication with either his ghost or his spirit; I have simply translated a bunch of his writings, especially his letters. And so, I can only make an educated guess.

I would say – all things considered, contrary to what others seem to think and despite what I personally might want or like – Guy Debord would have *approved of it all,* not just the "good" things (inspiring yet another generation of young people), but the "bad" (capitalist) things, as well. He would have found *no contradiction* between these two developments or, rather, he would have seen the contradiction between them *in a positive light.* His approval would of course be a matter of supporting everything that his wife and companion for the last 30 years of his life would do "in his name" – *only she knows* what his real wishes and intentions were – but also an affirmation that these would have been *the precise things that he himself would have done,* had he been alive. In short, Alice isn't to blame for the weird repackaging of Guy Debord's works; Guy himself is.

I say this despite the fact that "Ms Debord's" recent conduct – appearing in public and hobnobbing with high-level governments officials, wealthy patrons, and literary celebrities like Philippe Sollers so as to raise money for the BNF, or appearing alongside Jacqueline de Jong and allowing herself to be misidentified as a "member of the Situationist International" in the publicity for an art opening at Yale University – would have appalled her late husband, who detested celebrity and avoided celebrities, and had a mania for correcting "small" factual mistakes concerning membership in the Situationist International. She certainly would have done none of these things when he was alive. Though Guy had been litigious, he never sued a publisher of a "pirate" or copyright-infringing edition of his works. Though he allowed his works (both the new and the old ones) to be published by Gallimard, he did so provisionally, in response to a specific situation, and was ready to "jump ship" at any moment. And though he himself had created, organized and made plans for the eventual disposition of his archives, he would certainly have been mortified by the idea that the French government, in a fairly mysterious attempt to keep those archives in France, would declare them a "national treasure." Guy detested literary prizes and would certainly have hated the *explicitly anti-May 1968 politics* of the very French government (the Sarkozy gang) that has miraculously deemed his archives to be worthy of such great distinction.

Guy Debord was a very complicated person. While he was alive, he – he and Alice, as a matter of fact – were supporters, organizers and beneficiaries of various kinds of scams. According to his own *Panegyric,* he was a thief in his youth. In the 1950s and 1960s, Debord and his first wife, Michelle Bernstein, made some easy money by publishing cheap novelties (a horoscope for racehorses, a superficial novel about the depths of the "existentialist" scene, etc.). In a letter to Gianfranco Sanguinetti dated 26 October 1975, Debord referred to this kind of enterprise as "shit crushing": crushing shit and getting money as a result. For example: claiming to the Italian government that one's ships were destroyed during World War II and that one is therefore entitled to financial compensation. In August 1993, Debord justified the publication and sale of *Memoires* (originally produced as a gift to its recipients) in the following manner: "It was a gift, but now it must cease to be one [...] In sum, I prefer to sell my prestige and to recoup my losses with suitable liquid compensations."

The greatest emblem of this side of Guy Debord is the cover of his posthumous book, *Des Contrats* (1995), which was designed in accordance with Debord's own wishes. It shows "the Street Acrobat" (*Le Bateleur*), which is a card in the Marseille Tarot deck. In one of the last letters he ever wrote, Debord explains that this image is "the most mysterious and the most beautiful, in my sense of these words [...] It seems to me that this card will add, and without the duty to imply it too strongly, something that one could see as a certain mastery of manipulation, and will do so by opportunely recalling the extent of its mystery" (letter to Georges Monti). The "mystery" of truly masterful manipulation is that it achieves its intended effects without any apparent effort, without the manipulation ever being detectable, not to mention obvious. But then, if the manipulation is indeed undetectable, how do you know it is really there? In the Tarot card: note the deceptive simplicity of the Acrobat's movements.

Of course it isn't quite clear *who* was being manipulated in the pages of the *Contrats.* Was it Gerard Lebovici, Debord's patron in the 1970s and the co-signatory of his film contracts? Or was it Lebovici's heirs, with whom Debord had broken off both commercial and personal dealings in the early 1990s? I believe it was the latter. In 1992, Editions Lebovici had been forced to turn the rights to Debord's films over to Debord himself. Perhaps the *Contracts* book (and its Tarot-card-cover) were ways of signaling Editions Lebovici that they had been "manipulated" because they had failed to realize that, even though Debord's films had not been screened since 1984, the texts surrounding them (the film contracts, in this case) *could be* commercially exploited.

How could someone like Debord be devoted to "the objective truth" of the dialectic and History, and committed to the practice of transparency by and within revolutionary organizations, and yet still be a mysterious master of manipulation? Properly answered, it seems, this question is not a matter of ethics (the rhetorical demand/condemnation "How *could* you do that!"), but a question of practicality ("How did you *do* that?"). It is, of course, tempting to break Debord's life into parts, with – inevitably – the good parts coming early and the bad parts later on. With greater or lesser justification, people have said the "break" came in 1962, with "the expulsion" of "the artists" from the SI; in 1971, with the end of the SI; in 1975, with the appearance of the first-person "I" in his films; in 1984, with the murder of Gerard Lebovici; in 1988, with the publication of *Comments on the Society of the Spectacle*; or in 1990, with the on-set of chronic health problems. All were turning points, but "breaks"? I'm not sure.

And so let say this: during his lifetime, Guy Debord managed to juggle a lot of objects of different kinds; his genius was his ability to attempt to retrospectively demonstrate the consistency of his movements. *The Preface to the 4th Italian Edition of "The Society of the Spectacle* (1979), *Considerations on the Assassination of Gerard Lebovici* (1985), *Comments on the Society of the Spectacle* (1988), *Panegyric* (1989), and *Preface to the Third French Edition of "The Society of the Spectacle"* (1992) are all true feats of intellectual acrobatics. In each case, Debord shows that there had been no contradictions, no *real* contradictions, in the sense that he had never come to a halt or been stopped en route; at every turn, he'd found a way out. The line from 1952 to 1994 was surely irregular and meandering, but it was unbroken. But what happens *after* 1994, when the line must continue (the "legacy" must be protected, the Show must go on) despite and yet because of the death of The Acrobat himself? The answer is obvious: another acrobat must be found who can "step in" and keep the acrobatic feat going.

But why does the Show *have to* go on? What would it mean for the "Debord Show" to stop? Instead of being repackaged (sold piecemeal or en bloc), his archives could be *donated* to, say, the Institute for Social Research in Amsterdam, the Beinecke Rare Books Library at Yale University or the French National Library – someplace open to the public. The Debord estate could receive the appropriate tax deductions and write-offs, *plus* whatever it might make as sole copyright holder from the sales of individual components of the archives (Debord's films, film scripts, film contracts, essays, song lyrics, translations, books, letters, posters, audio recordings, paintings, etc.). That would be a lot of money, obviously; perhaps as much as $2.34 million. The estate would be free to make as much money as it wished, provided that the contents of the thing(s) being sold were complete and unabridged, and that the producers/distributors of the item(s) – the truly complete correspondence of Guy Debord, for example – were either independent or non-profit entities.

As things stand today, Alice Becker-Ho, doing as she pleases, will make a great deal of money in the coming years, perhaps much more than $2.34 million. I do not think it too much to ask, "Where is all that money going? To what purpose(s) is it being put, other than Alice's personal needs?" Unfortunately, unlike her late husband, "Ms Debord" doesn't explain herself. Except for a brief notice published shortly after Guy's suicide on 30 November 1994, she has remained silent and/or let her attorneys do her talking for her. Though the last 15 years have seen her publish several groundbreaking books about argot, she has published nothing that explains how her decisions, both individually and taken together, have been in line with those taken by Guy before 1994. Either she can't explain or she won't explain. Perhaps she feels no need to explain anything to anyone. Her silence might derive from the fact that she was *never* a member of the SI, even though she had known some of its members personally since 1964 and participated in the CMDO during May 1968 in France. Are the conceptual acrobatics necessary to explain, not to mention justify, Alice's conduct over the last 15 years even possible? Could Guy himself perform such a feat? Could *anyone*?

The answers to these questions are simple, just as the actions encouraged by them are unacceptable. If someone were to smash the glass vitrines that contained the manuscript of Debord's *The Society of the Spectacle,* steal the document, and hold it in exchange for ransom, then everything – everything "theoretical" – would become crystal clear. "Guy Debord" isn't property that can be owned. He is a weapon, and weapons are meant to be used.

On-line notice dated 7 December 2009

Re: Wayne Spencer
Let's Not and Say We Did

Wayne Spencer's call for the formation of a "new Situationist International" (5 March 2010) is an embarrassment. It embodies everything that is wrong with post-situationist thought, and I wouldn't blame anyone if they dismissed that thought on the basis of it.

"Towards a New Situationist International" is wrong about the proletariat: the "defining quality of proletarian life" is *not* "a craven acceptance of the separate commodity economy and the state as unchangeable givens" (Spencer's thesis #1), but a constant struggle to make a living in an unlivable world. Spencer's attention is on ideology, not socio-economic conditions, and – with respect to the proletariat – he places himself outside of it, as a naysayer to its "craven" acceptance, not inside, as an inmate in the same prison.

His text is wrong about the current state of the class struggle: the "discontent with the petty and idiotic lives" that we are obliged to lead is *not* "buried" (thesis #2), but front-page news: the student occupations movement in America; the on-going rioting and social strife in Greece; the popular demonstrations against the government in Iceland; the social movements in France against detention centers and expulsions; et al. Spencer speaks of a world that was destroyed more than 40 years ago.

His text is wrong about the current state of critical theory: "revolutionary theory" has *not* "almost completely failed to keep abreast of developments within advanced capitalism" (thesis #3); it is incorrect to say "revolutionary theory and practice stand at present in a state of *perfectly scandalous dereliction*" (thesis #6). In point of fact, since the dissolution of the SI, revolutionary theory has gone on to produce useful critiques of artificial terrorism, nuclear power, and political sovereignty, as well as such useful concepts as biopolitics, deterritorialization, and the integrated spectacle. Spencer speaks as if revolutionary theory stopped cold in 1972, which of course would come as a surprise (or insult) to Guy Debord, the ex-situationist who continued to develop situationist theory well after the SI dissolved and who personally associated with at least one other major critical theorist of the era (Giorgio Agamben). As for revolutionary practice, which Spencer hardly mentions, the revolutionary movement has produced tactics that were *unknown* before 1972: Black Blocs, flashmobs, and computer viruses, among many others.

His text is wrong about the situationists: one *cannot* speak of "the thought" of the SI, as Spencer does (thesis #4), because that "thought" changed several times between 1957 and 1972: after Debord's contact with Socialisme ou Barbarie in 1960 (the theme of workers councils); after the admission of Raoul Vaneigem in 1961 (the critique of everyday life); after the break with Henri Lefebvre in 1963 (the abandonment of unitary urbanism); after the admission of young revolutionaries and anarchists in 1966 and then again in 1968 (the emphasis on student life, occupations and general assemblies); and, of course, after the birth of the "pro-situ" phenomenon (the critique of the cadre). Spencer speaks as if everyone understands what "situationist theory" is, but he himself fails to outline its basic principles.

His text is wrong about post-situationists: "situationist thought" has not been "abandoned by individuals with revolutionary intent" (thesis #5). It certainly hasn't been "abandoned" by ex-situs such as Raoul Vaneigem, Jacqueline de Jong, Donald Nicholson-Smith, and T.J. Clark, or by first-generation pro-situs such as Michel Bounan, Ken Knabb and Michel Prigent (not to mention yours truly, who accounts himself a second-generation pro-situ). Spencer makes no mention of the French anarchist website Jura Libertaire: it consistently mixes together news items about current anti-capitalist and/or anti-state actions with situationist texts from long ago. The situationists are also dear to those (do not doubt their "revolutionary intent"!) who maintain the websites called Les Amis des Nemesis, Jules Bonnot de la Bande, and Debord-Encore. Spencer writes as if he doesn't read any other language than English. (Was his text translated into any other language? Not even French?! How "international" can this be?)

His text is *anti-situationist* when it comes to matters of organization: the SI *never* allowed its members the abilities to carry out "theoretical and other practical actions [...] in the *individual* names of those who produce them, and on their responsibility *alone*" and/or "carry out projects outside the framework of the international and to form other associations to do so" (thesis #7). Spencer writes as if he wants to found an organization that is "situationist" in name only, no matter how well he recites certain catechisms (thesis #8).

Last, but not least, his text is worse than a monologue: it is a sterile dialogue with himself ("it might be objected that such a proposal"; "it might also be objected"; "if I fail to heed these weighty objections") (thesis #9). This echoes Spencer's own situation: not a member of any organization, no matter how small, but an isolated individual. It is easy to foresee what would take place at a "conference between interested parties" that was based upon written answers to Spencer's five questions, so much so that a face-to-face meeting wouldn't be necessary (or so he claims): there would be a deluge of useless paper. Everyone would read what had been written and submitted, sure. But who would judge what was good and what was bad? Spencer himself? Note well his sudden recourse to the word "we" when the subject of whom to "exclud[e] from the outset" comes up. "We might save ourselves a little time by excluding from the outset anyone who . . ." (thesis #10). I have a better idea. Let's exclude from the outset anyone who would exclude anyone from the outset.

On-line notice dated 16 March 2010

On 23 March 2010, I received a lengthy reply from Wayne Spencer. Its conclusion is the following critique, which I reproduce without comment.

> No doubt Bill Bored can be assured that he is not speaking to himself. He presents his work at galleries. He lectures at subsidized cultural events. He speaks to the press and appears in documentary films. He leads walks. He stages plays and displays placards before passers-by and surveillance camera workers. He complains that his civil liberties are not upheld. He translates and comments. But after 25 or so years of presenting tepid social critique to spectators who have evinced no practical dissatisfaction and passively view his activities with no practical revolutionary purpose in view, nothing in the way of revolutionary contestation has been achieved. His efforts do not disrupt the processes by which his own life becomes foreign to him, however briefly. Nor do they attack the processes by which his audiences' lives become foreign to them. Yet he continues untroubled by the compatibility of what he does with the persistence of the

society of alienation and takes no steps to turn against his palpably inadequate praxis. Indeed, he seems quite content with the cultural and pseudo-oppositional niche he has found within that society. For him, it seems, revolution is a process that is satisfactorily unfolding at some distance from the everyday life around him and will one day deliver salvation to his door. All this is very different from the views that prompted my proposal for a new international association of situationist revolutionaries. It is no surprise that Not Bored views that proposal with contempt.

Cover, *NOT BORED!* #3, May 1984.

BOREDOM IS COUNTER-REVOLUTIONARY

—Situationist International

Back cover, *NOT BORED!* #4, July 1984.

Detail, *NOT BORED!* #6, November 1984.

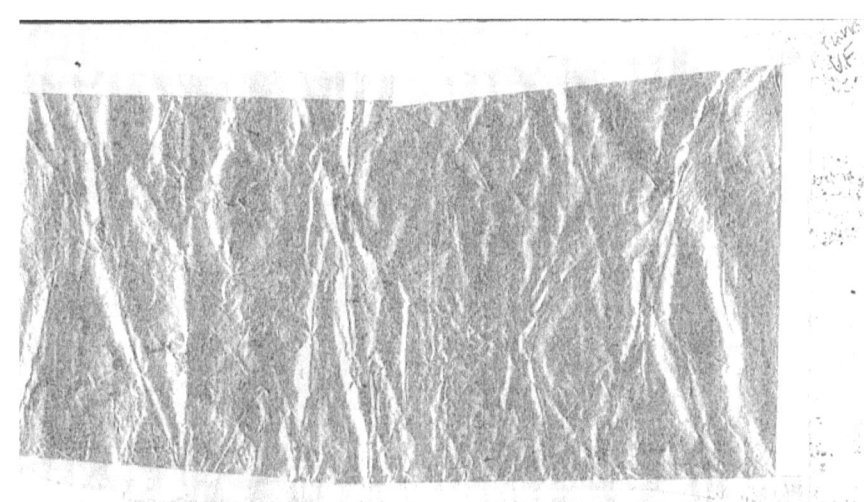

Cover, *NOT BORED!* #8, July 1985.

Text ("Expression is my enemy, the mistake I concentrate on avoiding at all costs, for to express myself would be to have my class be legible") taken from T.J. Clark
Cover, *NOT BORED!* #9, January 1986.

NOT BORED! #9, January 1986.

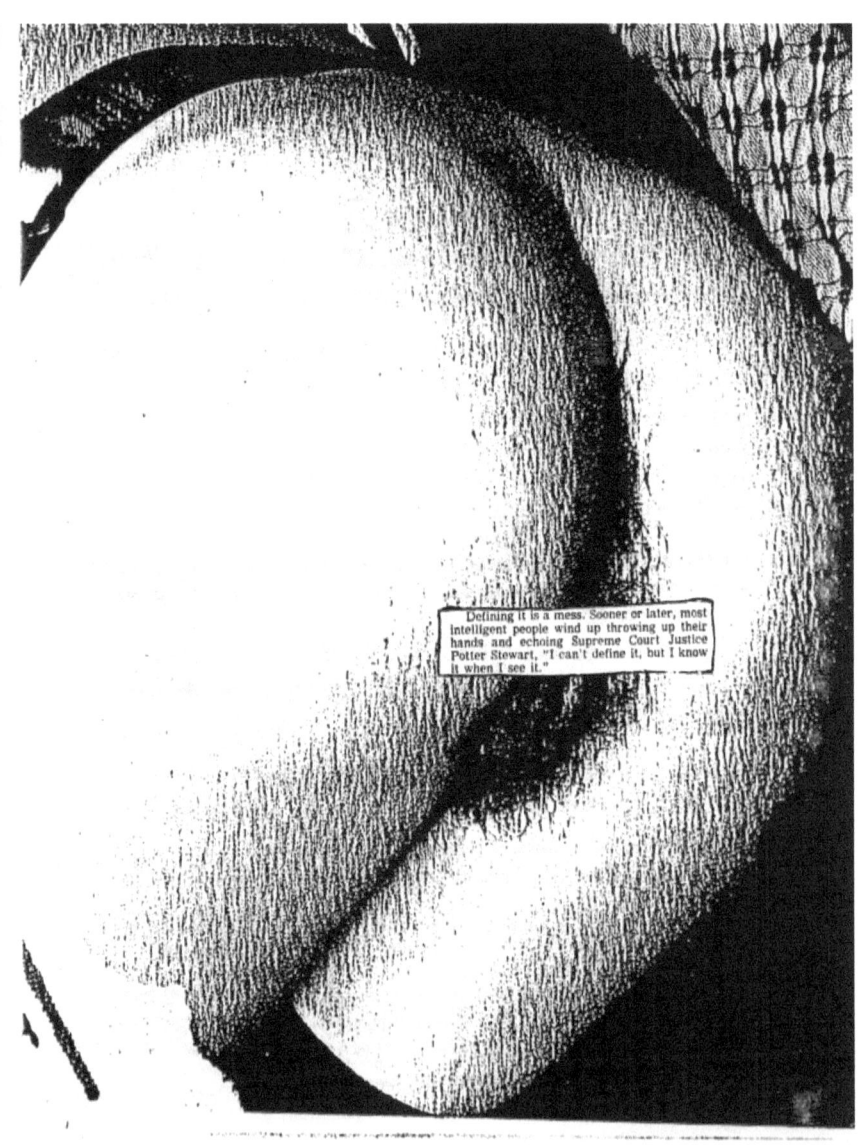

Text says, "Defining it is a mess. Sooner or later, most intelligent people wind up throwing up their hands and echoing Supreme Court Justice Potter Stewart, 'I can't define it, but I know it when I see it.'"
Back cover, *NOT BORED!* #13, May 1987.

Cover, *NOT BORED!* #15, April 1989.

Cover, *NOT BORED!* #16, December 1989.

In the dime-stores and bus stations, people talk of situations, read books, repeat quotations, write conclusions on the Wall.

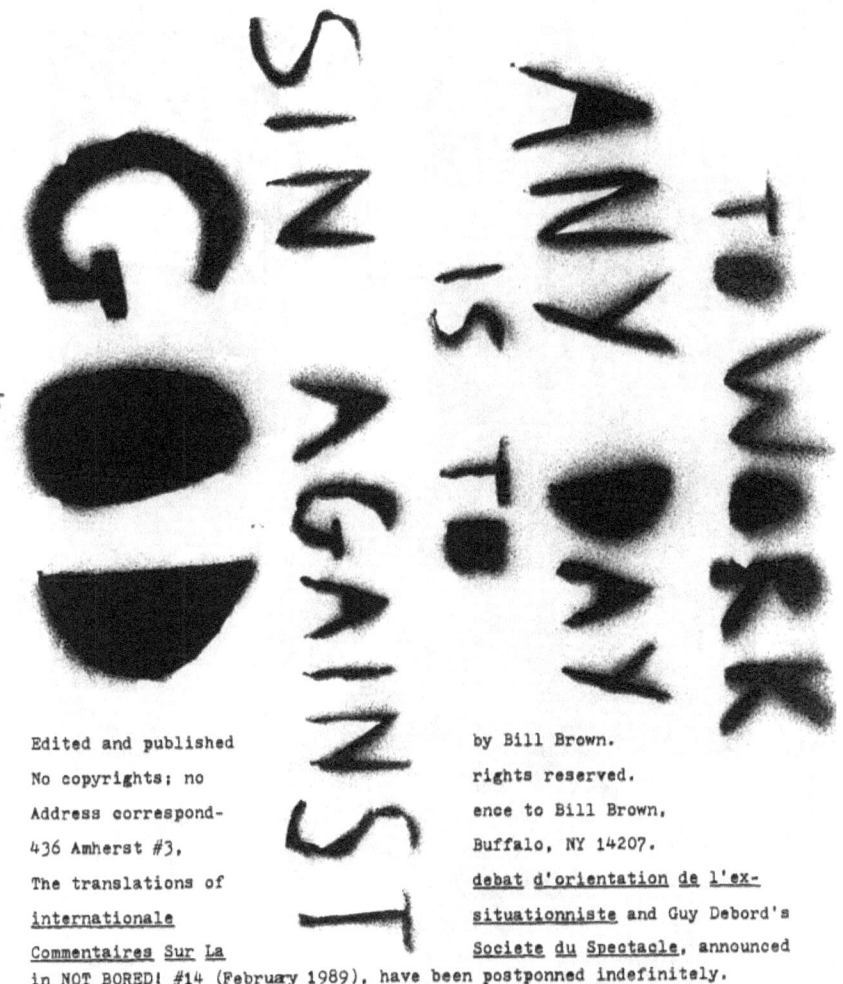

GOD IS SIN ANY DAY IS TO WORK TO AGAINST

Edited and published by Bill Brown.
No copyrights; no rights reserved.
Address correspond- ence to Bill Brown,
436 Amherst #3, Buffalo, NY 14207.
The translations of debat d'orientation de l'ex-
internationale situationniste and Guy Debord's
Commentaires Sur La Societe du Spectacle, announced
in NOT BORED! #14 (February 1989), have been postponned indefinitely.

WEISHAUPT WILL BE AVENGED

NOT BORED! #16, December 1989.

Text from Marc Shell
Cover, *NOT BORED!* #18, December 1990.

Cover, *NOT BORED!* #20, February 1992.

Text from Henri Lefebvre
NOT BORED! #21, July 1992.

Detail, *NOT BORED!* #22, August 1993.

Note: Very small print says "bloody repression" and "observation of the anniversary"
NOT BORED! #22, August 1993.

Back cover, *NOT BORED!* #22, August 1993.

Text from Machiavelli
Cover, *NOT BORED!* #23, January 1995.

Text from the Mekons, paraphrasing Guy Debord
NOT BORED! #23, January 1995.

Back cover, *NOT BORED!* #23, January 1995.

Cover, *NOT BORED!* #25, June 1996.

Cover, *NOT BORED!* #27, May 1997.

Cover, *NOT BORED!* #28, December 1997.

NOT BORED! #28, December 1997.

Back cover, *NOT BORED!* #29, July 1998.

NOT BORED! #31, June 1999.

NOT BORED! #32, January 2000.

NOT BORED! #34, July 2002.

Cover, *NOT BORED!* #38, October 2006.

Part IV:

Book Reviews

Book reviews
Manet in situ:
T.J. Clark's *The Painting of Modern Life*

According to the back flap of *The Painting of Modern Life: Paris in the Art of Manet and His Followers* (Knopf, 1985), the book's author

> was born in Bristol, England, and was educated at Cambridge University and the Courtauld Institute of London University. Before becoming professor of art history at Harvard University in 1980, he taught at Essex University, Camberwell School of Art, U.C.L.A. and Leeds University. He is the author of two previous books on nineteenth century French art, *The Absolute Bourgeois: Artists and Politics in France, 1848-51* and *Image of the People: Gustave Courbet and the 1848 Revolution.*

In his own "Narrative of Career," T.J. Clark writes,

> From fairly early on in my undergraduate career I was determined to do my graduate work in art history, and in particular to find a way to put the history of painting in contact with other histories, social, economic and political. From 1964 onwards I was enrolled for a Ph.D. at the Courtauld Institute of Art, London University, and in 1966-67 I was in Paris as a research fellow of the Centre Nationale de la Recherché Scientifique.

Perhaps most relevant to us is the fact that Clark was briefly a member of the Situationist International: in December 1967, Clark and the rest of the British section (Christopher Gray and Donald Nicholson-Smith) were excluded from the SI for reasons that are difficult, if not impossible to reconstruct.

But we should not prejudge Clark or his work because he was excluded from an organization we hold dear. Well after the exclusions of the British situationists, the SI considered all three of them to be (at the very least) quite talented and very likely to make excellent uses of their respective talents. Before their exclusion, the British situationists produced a collectively authored text and had translated several key situationist documents into English. In "The Latest Exclusions," an unsigned article that appeared in *Internationale Situationniste* #12 (September 1969), it was made clear the British situationists were not excluded for "their activity in England," which was otherwise exemplary; their exclusion was in response to mere "details regarding the SI's solidarity and general criteria for breaking." Thus, it makes sense that Donald Nicholson-Smith, in his translator's preface to Raoul Vaneigem's *The Revolution of Everyday Life* (Rebel Press/Left

Bank Books, 1983), says that the "parting of the ways seemed to me then – and still seems to me – thoroughly justified on both sides."

The Painting of Modern Life is a most unusual book: unlike the post-exclusion projects of Gray and Nicholson-Smith, which have been by and large limited to translations or translated anthologies of situationist writing, it is an attempt to write a properly situationist book about an important topic (impressionist painting and the birth of modernity), almost as if the SI itself had not disbanded in 1972 and was still in action. Furthermore, unlike Clark's two previous books on nineteenth century French art (both of which were published in 1973), *The Painting of Modern Life* is explicitly situationist in perspective. It is only nine pages into his introduction, which defines the terms that are used in the text (class, ideology, spectacle and modernism), before Clark tells his readers about the organization to which he once belonged. "About the concepts of 'spectacle' and 'spectacular society' it is not so easy to be cut and dried," Clark writes. "They were developed first in the mid-1960s as part of the theoretical work of a group called the Situationist International, and they represent an effort to theorize the implications for capitalist society of the progressive shift within production towards the provision of consumer goods and services, and the accompanying 'colonialization of everyday life.'"

And so here we have an excellent book on the nineteenth century by a professor of art history at Harvard University (of all places!) who is overtly attempting to keep alive the situationists' radical critique of the society of the spectacle and to update that critique in the light of the experiences of the last decade and a half. There are "problems" with such a book, and no one is more aware of them than Clark himself. In his introduction, he gives us a "standard proviso."

> The notion of spectacle, as I hope will be clear from even my dry summary, was designed first and foremost as a weapon of combat, and contains within itself a more or less bitter (more or less resigned) prediction of its own reappearance in some such form as this, between the covers of a book on art. Although I shall not wrestle in the toils of this contradiction too long, I wish to at least alert the reader to the absurdity involved in making 'spectacle' part of the canon of academic Marxism. If once or twice in the text my use of the word carries a faint whiff of Debord's chiliastic serenity I shall be satisfied.

But the critical concept of the spectacle doesn't make a "reappearance" between the covers of Clark's book: somehow it makes itself felt as an original appearance, as one of the first iterations of situationist socio-cultural critique.

Appropriately, Clark's critique of the spectacle of Impressionist painting involves a critique of the theory of the spectacle (itself). He writes in his introduction,

There are various problems here [in situationist theory]: for instance, deciding when exactly the spectacular society can be said to begin. One is obviously not describing some neat temporality but, rather, a shift – to some extent an oscillation – from one kind of capitalist production to another. But certainly the Paris [of the 1860s] that Meyer Shapiro was celebrating, in which commercialized forms of life and leisure were so insistently replacing those "privately improvised," does seem to fit the preceding description quite well. And it will be argued in chapter one that the replacement was not a matter of mere cultural and ideological refurbishing but of all-embracing economic change.

This isn't a trivial problem. If one can situate the beginnings of spectacular society, then one can also trace out the end of that society. Once traced out, the end of the spectacle can be set into motion, or accelerated in the movement of its own self-destruction, by revolutionaries such as the Situationists.

Guy Debord's remarks about the historical beginnings of the spectacle – he made at least two of them – are quite different than T.J. Clark's attempt. Significantly, Debord's datings are much closer to our own time. In *The Society of the Spectacle* (1967), Debord identifies the Russian Revolution of 1917 as the spectacle's beginnings; in *Comments on the Society of the Spectacle* (1988), he identifies the start of World War II. Taken together, Debord's and Clark's theories cover a very wide historical period, from the 1860s to the 1930s. Surely one can also detect (or would that be deduce?) the negative presence of the spectacle as far back as the 1840s, in the poetry and prose of Edgar Allan Poe and Charles Baudelaire.[1] Thus we must say there is a (meta)problem with the fundamental problem of deciding exactly when the spectacle came into being. But this is as it should be. The spectacle (even as it exists today) is not complete: indeed, what makes the spectacle the spectacle is that it is always under construction and never completed. The spectacle must never be fully realized, because it must always have a sphere from which to recuperate new forms of social practice, especially those that resist the spectacle's ceaseless turning of life into images of living. Thus the spectacle is very weak, its hold on power very tenuous.

Not surprisingly, *The Painting of Modern of Life* has been negatively reviewed by every major writer (except Greil Marcus) who has devoted more than a paragraph to it. The manner in which *The New York Times* responded to it may be paradigmatic: it chose to publish two reviews of Clark's book, one devoted to Clark's "politics" and one devoted to his "aesthetics," precisely because his book is an attempt to supersede the contradiction between politics and aesthetics. In its

---

[1] This idea is developed in William J. Brown, *American Colossus: the Grain Elevator 1843 to 1943* (Colossal Books, 2009).

review of the politics of *The Painting of Modern Life*, the *Times* claimed, "ultimately [Clark] remains weighed down by the chains of ideology." And in its review of the book's aesthetics, it claimed that Clark's book is "seriously flawed" in its lack of attention to the Impressionist painters' concern with "light and color." One isn't sure which is the more preposterous: the ridiculous content of the respective reviews, or their spectacular separation from each other.

Unfortunately, we do not have the space here to explore very much of Clark's book, which is quite rich and provocative: each of the book's four chapters could stand on its own, as separate statements on closely related issues. We have attempted to reduce the reader's sense of missing out by writing a separate article ("The Red Hot Chili Peppers: Rocks Off?") on the relevance of *The Painting of Modern Life* to rock music criticism. The rest of this article will be taken up with a relatively small, but hopefully very interesting point concerning Clark's treatment of Manet's famous 1863 painting, *Olympia*.

In his readings of Impressionist paintings (*Olympia* included), Clark is engaged in an analysis of the all-too-frequently ignored fact that "the perfect heroes and heroines of [the] myth of modernity were the petite-bourgeoisie" (the socio-economic group that, strange as this might seem, included prostitutes such as the one presumably depicted in *Olympia*). In Clark's words, the perfect heroes and heroines

> appeared in many ways to have no class to speak of, to be excluded from the bourgeoisie and the proletariat and yet to thrive on their lack of belonging. They were the shifters of class society, the connoisseurs of its edges and waste lands. And thus they became for a time the alter egos of the avant-garde – ironically treated, of course, laughed at and condescended to, but depended upon for a point of insertion into modern life. I believe that sometimes in depicting them the painters discovered the limits and insufficiencies of their own ideology, and in some sense described these people's belonging to the class system. That only happened occasionally. Clearly one such occasion was *Olympia*, which manages to describe both the prostitute's and the painter's own belonging to the (one and the same) class system, despite their respective and sometimes self-conscious detachment from or shifting within it. Properly speaking, the subject of *Olympia* is the class system.

In a footnote – the only one in the entire book – Clark states that "a text by Georges Bataille is sometimes enlisted in the argument that *Olympia* 'has no subject' (is purely pictorial, visual, or whatever)." It is strange that Clark should mention Bataille in a footnote, and not in the main body of the text: there is little question that Bataille's elaboration of the concept of the spectacle in his 1933 essay "The Notion of Expenditure" (not to mention his involvements with experimental micro-societies and radical politics) were crucial precedents for and influences upon the situationists' and thus Clark's own theory of the spectacle. And yet Clark stays within the footnote to relate that,

> in *Manet: Etude biographique et critique,* Bataille takes issue with Valery, who described *Olympia* as a "public power and presence of a miserable arcanum of Society," "the Impure *par excellence,* she whose position obliges a candid ignorance of any kind of shame. Bestial vestal, given over to absolute nudity, she makes one think of all the remnants of primitive barbarism and ritual animality which lurk beneath the routine of prostitution in great cities." Bataille comments: "It is possible (though questionable) that in a sense this was initially the *text* of *Olympia,* but this text is a separate matter from the woman . . . the text is *effaced* by the picture. *And what the picture signifies is not the text, but the effacement.* It is to the extent that Manet did not wish to say what Valery said – to the extent that, on the contrary, he has suppressed (pulverized) that meaning – that this woman is there; in her provoking exactitude, she is *nothing*; her nudity (in this, it is true, corresponding to that of the body itself) is the silence which issues from her as from a drowned and empty ship; what she is, is the 'sacred horror' of her own presence – of a presence as simple as absence. Her hard realism, which for the Salon visitors was the ugliness of a 'gorilla,' consists for us in the painter's determination to reduce *what he saw* to the mute simplicity, the open-mouthed simplicity, of *what he saw.*"

At this point, Clark's overly stuffed footnote should have come to an end. "O.K., Tim," we want to say to him, "we get the point: *Olympia* does indeed have a subject (the class system); if we want to argue otherwise – which we may not – we can call upon Bataille to help us do so."

But the footnote continues on, almost to the point of becoming a supplementary body of text and turning the book as a whole into a footnote to it. Clark writes of Bataille,

> This is a stranger argument than it seems. What Bataille objects to in Valery is the poet's attempt to situate *Olympia* in an older, established, pseudo-sacred text of prostitution – a text of ritual, mystery, pollution, animality. *Olympia* is the obliteration of that text, and the putting of another in its place – the text of literalness, the real silence of the body, the fact of *being nothing* – another sacred horror, that of presence so unmediated that it has no sign. Clearly Bataille sees this as reducing *Olympia to what a man sees,* but vision for Bataille is always wrapped up in some such complex act against

meaning ("it is the hard resolution with which Manet *destroyed* that was so scandalous": as before, Bataille's italics); seeing is making the world into nothing. These are themes which figure endlessly in Bataille's fiction and philosophical prose: presence as absence, the body as essentially inanimate, death as its purest and most desirable state, representation as colluding in this putting to death.

What is truly strange here is the fact that, in a footnote that has taken on a life of its own, Clark has not only put forward Bataille's argument, but he has also tried to elaborate on it, make it more comprehensible, even to contextualize it. If Bataille's argument is – in the final analysis – irrelevant or misleading (as Clark will argue that it is), then why pay so much attention to it? And if Clark is going to spend so much attention on Bataille's "strange" argument with Valery about Manet's painting, then why relegate it all to a footnote?

Perhaps the answer to this mystery is here, in the words with which Clark tries to conclude his footnote on Bataille.

> Bataille's untranslatable last words on *Olympia* – "Aux yeux memes de Manet la fabrication s'effacait. L'*Olympia* tout entiere se distingue mal d'un crime ou d'un spectacle de la morte . . . Tout en elle glisse a l'*indifference* de la beaute" – should therefore be read in at least two ways: as a reproduction of the cadaver fantasies of the critics in 1865, and as final, overt recuperation of *Olympia* into the terms of Bataille's own eroticism. Whatever else one might wish to say of this criticism, it has little to do with the simpler narratives of modernist art history.

Are there judgmental tones of snobbery, condescension and prudishness in Clark's last sentence? Yes, indeed, there are, and they give the reader the idea that, whatever those untranslated French words might mean – and they are the only untranslated words in the entire book – they must be pretty fucking sick, at least by the prim standards of "modernist art history" (which is presumably what Clark wants us to believe he is engaging in). This impression is perhaps unintentionally reinforced by the English translation of Bataille's 1955 book *Manet: Etude biographique et critique*, which acknowledges the difficulty of "Bataille's untranslatable last words on *Olympia*" only or precisely to the extent that it silently and completely omits them.

> "In the very eyes of Manet the fabrication effaces itself. In its entirety, *Olympia* distinguishes itself poorly from a crime or a spectacle of death . . . Everything in the painting [or everything about her] glides over the *indifference* of beauty."

According to Clark, these lines should be read "as a reproduction of the cadaver fantasies of the [Salon] critics in 1865, and as final, overt recuperation of Olympia into the terms of Bataille's own eroticism." That is to say, they should be read with the emphasis placed on the words "crime" and "a spectacle of death," not on the words "eyes" and "effaces itself." The nude woman (perhaps a prostitute) depicted in *Olympia* is dead; she is a corpse, a victim of the crime of murder. The *indifference* of beauty to death is "glided" over, not challenged nor negated. While this image or "fantasy" repelled the Salon critics of 1865, it attracted Georges Bataille. In either case, Clark's point seems to be, a fundamental perversion has taken place. The death of the spectacle (which was implied by Manet's discovery of the limits and insufficiency of his own ideology in the process that produced *Olympia*) is perverted into the spectacle of death (in which bourgeois alienation at its most gruesome is fetishized, "enjoyed," and reproduced). But surely the spectacle of death at some level contains within itself the death of the spectacle.

In addition to the theme of the eye's violence against meaning, "the spectacle of death" appears "endlessly in Bataille's fiction and philosophical prose." For Bataille (even for those others who are not hung up on images of necrophilia), the ultimate spectacle – the most "spectacular" spectacle, if you will – is the spectacle of death. More specifically, the ultimate spectacle is the spectacle of public execution (state-sanctioned murder). Indeed, in a very precise way, one can date the beginnings of the society of the spectacle in the decisions reached all across bourgeois Europe in the 1830s and '40s to ban "the spectacle of the scaffold" and public executions: they were stirring up the masses (the newly formed urban proletariat) in ways that seemed increasingly dangerous to the modern state. From then on, death was administered scientifically and secretly by a carceral society. Is *Olympia* in part a reaction to this specific situation? Did Clark ever explain from whence the Salon critics' cadaver fantasies came? Perhaps they did not come from the bowels of their immemorial collective unconscious, but from their repressed memories of recent history. Surely there is enough material to warrant a transplant of Clark's footnote on Bataille into a proper text of its own.

NOT BORED! #9, January 1986

Greil Marcus and
The Brethren of the Free Spirit

There is no more right to strike than there is to incest and adultery. – Proudhon

There's an interesting passage in "Alice in the Forbidden Zone," Howard Hampton's reading of the TV show *Twin Peaks* and *The Secret Diary of Laura*

Palmer; the latter is, in Hampton's words, "the wildly perverse popcult artifact" that appears to be "just another shiny cog in the *Twin Peaks* merchandising machine." Supposedly written by a girl who was later murdered, Laura Palmer's *Secret Diary* is "a product of pop images, and a strange apotheosis of them, but it mostly seems to come out of nowhere – a nowhere free spirits and rebellious daughters have disappeared into and reappeared from since civilization institutionalized the pagan universe in its own sanitarium." (*Artpaper* No. 3, November 1990, p. 17).

The key phrase here is "free spirits and rebellious daughters." It is in part a reference to – even a continuation of – Greil Marcus's seminal book *Lipstick Traces: A Secret History of the Twentieth Century* (Harvard, 1989), which is concerned in part with the Brethren of the Free Spirit, a nominally "heretical" group active in the 13th century in Europe. Certainly there are plenty of young writers currently deriving all kinds of inspiration from *Lipstick Traces*. But Howard Hampton is unique in that he seems to be tapping into something that can't be found in *Lipstick Traces*, but should be.

Hampton is obviously interested in the sexual politics of *Twin Peaks,* which unfolds as a narrative of investigation into the brutal rape and murder of Laura. "Orgies in the woods, secret ceremonies, drugged bliss," Hampton intones; "clear echoes of paganism that intensify throughout the course of *The Secret Diary of Laura Palmer,* until those echoes pass into a heresy that paganism is barely the dimmest shadow of." One of the "heretical" sexual practices clearly implied by the coupling together of "free spirits" with "rebellious daughters" – but not explicitly mentioned by Hampton – is incest. If we are all "sons" and "daughters" of the figure Hampton calls the "Father-Tyrant," then, structurally speaking, incest is inevitable and unpreventable, even when consciously avoided (as in the case of Oedipus). Phrased another way, all human sexual encounters are incestuous by definition. Thus, the taboo against incest is far from universal or unbreakable; indeed, it is hard to see how there could even be such an illogical taboo in the first place. "We're kissin' cousins," Elvis Presley once sang, with evident glee, "that's what makes it alright."

Certainly Greil Marcus is aware of the importance the deliberate breaking of the taboo against incest had to the Brethren of the Free Spirit. He writes in *Lipstick Traces,*

> If Original Sin was traced to lust, lust had to be pursued in all of its forms [by the Brethren]. One destroyed the lie of Original Sin by refuting it in acts. In Erfurt, Germany, in 1367, Robert E. Lerner says, free spirit Johann Hartman testified that "he could have intercourse with his sister or his mother in any place, even on the altar, and . . . it would be 'more natural' to have sex with one's sister than with any other woman. Nor would a young girl lose her virginity after sexual intercourse, but if she had already been robbed of it she would regain

it after having relations with one free in spirit. Even if a girl had successive intercourse with ten men, if the last of them was a free spirit, she would receive her virginity back."

But Greil doesn't place any special emphasis on incest as such. In *Lipstick Traces,* incest figures as a particularly vivid example of Free Spirit libertinism; but it is only an example; it isn't the distinctive feature of that libertinism itself, the thing that defines it. For Greil, the distinctive feature of the Brethren of the Free Spirit was their refusal of work. He writes,

> The house of the Free Spirit had many mansions. As the adepts believed that sin was a fraud, they believed that property – the result of work, humanity's punishment for Original Sin – was a falsehood. Thus all things were to be held in common, and work to be understood as hell, which was ignorance – only fools worked. Work was a sin against perfect nature.

"Like the Ranters, [the free spirits] stripped off their clothes and preached naked," Greil writes. "If they did not commit incest or murder it was because they wished not to." But what of those who *did* commit incest or murder? Did any free spirits commit these "unnatural" crimes? *Lipstick Traces* is silent on these points.

A recent book by Marc Shell, *The End of Kinship: "Measure for Measure," Incest and the Ideal of Universal Siblinghood* (Johns Hopkins, 1988), does take up these points. But we can't hold up Shell's book as an example of what Greil's book could have been if its author had taken up the free spirits' unique interest in incest. It would appear from some of the passages in *The End of Kinship* that Marc Shell would consider Greil Marcus's reticence on the subject of incest to be some kind of hysterical or near-hysterical repression of themes the author himself finds personally troubling. Shell would no doubt dwell on the fact that Marcus appears to be loath to refer to the *Brethren* of the Free Spirit, preferring instead to refer to "the heresy of the free spirit," "the house of the Free Spirit," and so forth. But this is not to say that *The End of Kinship* is without interest, or without relevance to *Lipstick Traces.*

In the light of Shell's book, we can return to Marcus's book and find an area or two in need of a certain amount of correction. "Though in some ways as old as Christianity, or even older than that," Marcus writes, "as an identifiable cult the heresy of the Free Spirit came to light not long after the founding of the orthodox orders." He writes, "The Free Spirit grew in strength and numbers when the Franciscans and the Dominicans began to slide into wealth and bureaucracy, leaving their roads [upon which they had wandered, preached and begged for sustenance] for monasteries." In other words, the popularity of free spirit ideas grew in proportion to the elitism of the Franciscans and Dominicans. But the "slide" into wealthy bureaucracy and the retreat from the roads to the monasteries did not necessarily entail the renunciation of experimenting with revolutionary forms of everyday behavior and social organization on the part of the orthodox orders. Like the Brethren, the orders continued to believe that private property was a falsehood, work was hell, and all things should be held in common. Furthermore, both the heretics and the orthodox orders believed that men and women are, literally speaking, the sons and daughters of a single father (God). The primary difference between the heretical Brethren and the orthodox orders seems to have been the fact that the former practiced and extolled physical incest with each other, the latter practiced and extolled spiritual incest with the Holy Trinity. But it is the secret connection between the two – the fact that both groups practiced and extolled incest of one sort or another – rather than their spectacular distance from each other, that seems the most startling to modern eyes. Had Greil taken this startling connection between heresy and orthodoxy into proper account, his book would have been less a heretical "secret history" than a history of how "secrets" (or "heresies," if you prefer) are produced, distributed and imposed.

NOT BORED! #18, December 1990

Henri Lefebvre and the First "Situationist Symphony"

Henri Lefebvre's *Introduction to Modernity: Twelve Preludes* has been translated into English by John Moore and published by Verso (London and New York, 1995). In his introduction to the book, Lefebvre writes:

> That this book is intended to have musical qualities should be obvious. It is constructed like a piece of music. Its wish is to be understood in the mind's ear, to be a cry, a song, a sigh, and not simply to be read as a theoretical and discursive statement. However, the subtitle *Twelve Preludes* in no way implies any kind of reference to music ancient or modern. It is not inspired by Bach's *Well-Tempered Clavier*, or by dodecaphony, although the presence of the number twelve is by no means fortuitous.

At the end of the book, it is quite clear to the reader that the apparently mystical number twelve is in fact a reference to the twelve-tone scale as it was developed by Arnold Schoenberg. In the early twentieth century, Lefebvre writes elsewhere in *Introduction to Modernity*, "Schoenberg was dismantling the monolithic structures of classical harmony; and regardless of whether we like the twelve-tone scale or not, we must admit that it was a revolutionary direction for music to take." The problem for Lefebrve – writing between September 1959 and May 1961, during the period of his "love affair" with Guy Debord and other members of the Situationist International – was that the "revolutionary direction" taken by music into the twelve-tone scale had turned out to be a dead-end. Not only was the music unlistenable, but the ideology surrounding it had become untenable.

Do we need to begin again? So soon? Perhaps the most memorable meta-musical theme developed by Lefebvre appears in "Towards a New Romanticism?" which is the last of his book's twelve preludes.

> We could take this analysis much further – but where is it leading? To a proposition and a theory. In the eighteenth century (particularly in the second half) and in the nineteenth century (but especially in the first half) there was one avant-garde art, [which was] the driving force behind the other arts: music. It was an art which was to undergo profound changes. The conditions and circumstances of this transformation were manifold: technical inventions (the harpsichord, the pianoforte, equal-tempered tuning), scientific discoveries (the study of resonances and harmonics), social developments (changes in the composition of the public and its taste), even movements in politics (the revolutionary crisis in France and in Europe). The debates this transformation provoked centered on philosophical concepts (the concept of nature, for example) and lasted for more than a century, often erupting in fierce quarrels, with significant repercussions. Music gives a far-reaching impetus to the other arts, to thought and to science, to life and manners and love and ways of living: harmony becomes the universal goal, everyone's desire, everyone's ideal way of life [...] We will go so far as to say that this creativity [of musical harmony] produced an upheaval which spread from music into poetry, painting, and finally – in France and thanks to Stendhal – into literature and ways of living. It was a tidal wave which became swollen with the ideological flotsam and jetsam it swept up in its path, and before finally dying away it had changed the way the world was perceived, and even ways of loving and satisfying the senses.

This is a catchy little tune about the revolution of everyday life, but Lefebvre doesn't want us humming it all day: "Instead we will concentrate on the following question: what impetus could create a comparable tidal wave capable of sweeping through aesthetics (leaving the social and political domains to one side) in the second half of what we conventionally call the twentieth century?" In other words, "What art, what form of thinking could assume the function of an avant-garde or a 'homing device'?"

Significantly, Lefebvre's book leaves music behind and begins to move on toward architecture and town planning: these could assume the leading roles of "pilot art," that is, "if they can be rescued from the prejudices of neoclassicists and functionalists." What happened to music? "Music?" Lefebvre echoes. "But what kind of music? Atonal? Concrete? Electronic? It would appear that modern music has still to find its direction; it can no longer claim to have the leading role of 'pilot art' it enjoyed in the old romantic era. Unless, one day soon, composers manage to pull something unexpected out of the hat . . . ." Needless to say, there is no point in sitting around, waiting for "composers" to do something really unexpected, for composers – as a privileged and specialized class of musical laborers – were only revolutionary within the "old romantic era" that had, by the early 1960s, been over for nearly a half-century.

Perhaps we should be astonished that – for a polymath such as Lefebvre, writing during the years that PFC Elvis Presley was stationed in Europe – "modern music," even the generic category "music," does not include rock'n'roll, or any other form of popular music. When Lefebvre asks himself about the kinds of music that are current, all his answers come from the field of "serious" music, from the world of High Art. Lefebvre presents himself as completely uninformed about (or completely uninterested in) the various forms of popular music. Why doesn't he think to mention the blues, or jazz, or soul? This question should be asked in unison with another question, one about Guy Debord's film *La Societe du Spectacle*: why is the only music in it a few short and unimpressive passages from a fucking violin and harpsichord sonata written in the 19th century by Michel Corrette? Why no contemporary music? Why no rock 'n' roll or jazz?

It seems that for both Lefebvre and Debord – as well as for the rest of the Situationist International, which systematically explored every "pop" art form available to it, except for music – most (if not all) of the "revolutionary" musical developments of the twentieth century are merely evidence of the larger process of spectacular cultural decomposition under capitalism. Furthermore, it seems that this lack of interest in musical forms marks a regression from the advances made by Isidore Isou's Lettrists in the early 1950s. As our *Lettrist Poetry* cassette (BSQR #1, 1995) makes clear, the Lettrists weren't simply interested in the concept of modern music: they were dedicated to and very good at making modern music.

Fortunately for all concerned, the progress of music isn't dependent upon and doesn't wait for the development of theory: the dialectical unfolding of the practice of music has its own autonomy. Each new musical instrument – even each new modification of an old instrument – facilitates the extension of musical technique; every time it is extended, technique offers new ideas of what kinds of music are now (and only now) "possible." In the words of Chris Cutler, drummer for such experimental "jazz-rock" groups as Henry Cow and the Art Bears, and author of *File Under Popular: Theoretical and Critical Writings on Music* (Autonomedia, 1993),

> Each discovery or 'solution' opens the door onto a new potentiality

and a new set of 'problems,' and in this way music organically develops and transforms: its techniques and vocabularies expand; its concerns change. None of these things can be called back or proscribed. If ignored they will not go away, undo themselves or cease to exert their transforming pressure on the whole.

Thus our purpose here is to update – if not actually produce – the situationist theory of music in the context of the developments in musical practice that have escaped the notice of our intellectual predecessors (in particular, Lefebvre and Debord). This updated theory will aspire to identify what is immanent in modern music and to hear the future as it exists in the music of the unliberated present. We are motivated in these efforts by *Situationist Symphony, No. 1: The First Situationist Symphony*, which we ourselves recorded on 4 May 1996.

To begin yet again: unlike Henri Lefebvre, we do not think that one fine day music was suddenly catapulted into the role of the central art of the times; we do not think that music, prior to that event, was not already the central art of the times; and we do not think that music is no longer the central art of our times. Music was, is and will always be *the* avant-garde art form. And that is because the human facility of memory is paradoxically the best at suggesting what the future might be like.

Like Chris Cutler, we see "a clear dialectic at work [in Western musical history], and that from quantitative changes within one form comes a qualitative change, a negation of that form, and this transformation accompanies, or rather is an aspect of, a revolutionary transformation in society in itself." Within this dialectic, we may discern three analytical and historical categories or levels of musical discourse: 1). the feudal; 2). the capitalist; and 3). the situationist.

In the feudal stage of music, the human body is the medium in which musical memories are stored, as well the primary instrument with which musical sounds are created. Musical practice is an "expressive attribute" of the whole community; the purpose of music is collective participation. As a result, no piece of music is ever "completed" and thus available to claims of personal ownership. In any case, in feudal music there is no productive distinction between musical composers and musical performers: specialization of roles has not yet occurred. Since no one is an "expert," improvisation plays an important role in the generation and perpetuation of this music.

In the capitalist stage of music, written notation is the medium in which musical memories are stored. Because of the precision of notation, new instruments are now in constant demand; indeed, under capitalism, the design and production of musical instruments becomes a central (even industrial) feature in the life of music. Musical practice becomes highly specialized: composers of music and performers of music begin to split into two groups, giving rise to tremendous advances in technique, but also to the loss of a common musical vocabulary and understanding. Notation also creates the necessity for "completed" works of music, "definitive" scores and copyrighted reproductions that can be circulated and consumed as commodities. Music becomes spectacularized by capitalism, for notation (or the phenomenon of "musical harmony") is a primarily a visual medium, while music is fundamentally aural. Improvisation, by definition, is impossible, as is participatory enjoyment on the part of the audience.

Finally, in the situationist stage, recording is the medium in which musical memories are stored. No "new" musical instruments are necessary for music to be played or to progress any further. Recording technologies themselves can be "played" as if they were instruments, rather than simply functional devices; they can be used to "memorize," analyze and manipulate their own sounds as well as any sound (created by a properly musical instrument or not) that has ever been recorded and made available. As a result, recording flattens out any distinctions that might have once been drawn between the "high" forms of Art Music and the "low" forms of Folk and popular music. Anyone with a machine capable of playing the recordings has access to (effective possession of) the memory of all music. Indeed, anyone with a combination tape player/recorder can now be a composer or a performer, as well as a mere consumer of musical commodities. The unity of player, instrument and community is reestablished. Improvisation again becomes something that everyone – even composers – can do; recording allows the extension of improvisation (back) into musical composition.

Where in this dialectical unfolding are we today, in 1996? It would appear from the longevity, creative vitality, cultural visibility, and resilient popularity of hip hop music – which is founded upon such recording-based techniques as sampling, scratching and looping – that we have reached the stage of situationist music. We have reached the stage at which relatively large numbers of groups of people – fans of alternative rock as well as hip hop – are carrying out revolutionary transformations of the relations of production, circulation and consumption of music. These groups satisfy the minimum requirements sketched out by Chris Cutler: they embrace and put to creative use the newest and the potentially most expressive media technologies; as egalitarian collectives, they unite within themselves the functions of composer and performer; they function as financially independent organizations, free from the dictates of controlled distribution; they bring to bear extra-musical skills and resources, such as theories of their own practice; and they are rooted in Afro-American musics, which somehow possess the ability to speak "to all the victims of the new economic order [of capitalism], whether they [are] conscious of their oppression or not" (Cutler).

But on the level of political economy, we are still at the capitalist stage. Let us remember that "classical" or Art music only came to command deep and universal cultural authority because it perfectly matched the ideological and aesthetic needs of the rising class, the revolutionary bourgeoisie. For situationist music to sweep aside the ideological flotsam and jetsam of what remains of the classical tradition of musical practice, and thereby have room to grow unimpeded, the proletariat – the class whose precise historical mission is the abolition of class society – must fight and win its own revolution. Truly situationist music can only exist when there is nothing to prevent it from developing, when society itself has become situationist (that is, truly classless). Needless to say, this has not yet happened, though it grows ever more necessary.

We sing in unison a theme – developed by Chris Cutler – that sounds as if it's a tune from Lefebvre's *Introduction to Modernity*.

> This is the critical point: ours is a culture saturated by commodities, a culture that is to say whose acts and products are characterized by the alienation intrinsic in the form of the Commodity. Any analysis that fails to take this into account will never be able to do more than grapple with outwards forms and appearances [...] This alienation permeates all cultural exchanges; it militates to atomise every aspect and element of them; it renders 'meanings' optional; and its ideological effect, though invisible, is devastating. For instance, commodities encourage, in place of active critical engagement, a passive absorption by their consumers of whole and undigested 'quanta' of information, opinion, values, – so long as they are acceptably wrapped – later to be regurgitated, still whole and undigested, but now as their own information, opinion or values – seemingly the product of evaluation and contemplation, actually a kind of involuntary [second-order] commodity-exchange. Of course, such an uncritical process can only work when it reinforces or elaborates what is already installed. 'Quanta' which 'don't fit' will be rejected or simply eliminated.

Thus we should be wary of premature celebrations of the first stirrings of situationist music. "The alienation inherent in the relations of commodity exchange will not be overcome until commodity exchange itself disappears," Cutler warns; "We shall [in the meantime] be able to do no more than struggle towards new relations of consumption, no more than strengthen liberating forces."

Situationist Symphony, No. 1: The First Situationist Symphony may be taken as (was designed to be) a good case in point, or, if you prefer, a point of departure. Technically speaking, the *Symphony* is a tape recording of a 30-minute-long performance that brought together in a single, flowing collage a very diverse assortment of commodified sounds. Inspired by the apparently trivial or alienated realization that our apartment is filled with a variety of modern sound-making devices, the *Symphony* was simultaneously composed and performed (that is to say, totally improvised) by playing at least two, but no more than three, of these meta-musical instruments at the same time. Thanks to the low cost of what the spectacle calls "consumer" electronics, we found ourselves in possession of no less than four very different and very versatile modern sound-making devices: an AM/FM radio; a stereo television set with remote control; a conventional radio/tape-player; and a new fangled combination radio/tape-player/CD-player. Each one of these situationist musical instruments is capable of transmitting or reproducing an immense – and ever-growing – variety of recorded sounds, voices, musics and noises. Indeed, the only factor that limited the range of the musical elements that we could call upon for our *Symphony* was the relatively small size of our collections of tapes and CDs. And yet – small as they might be – those collections were more than enough for one very rich symphony.

Precisely as if we were our own record-buying audience – even though no exchange of money for product took place – we listened to the play-back of the symphony we'd just performed with the surprise and delight that only a first listen to a piece of music can bring. Inevitably, we most enjoyed the parts that – despite their apparent internal logic and cohesion – were the results of fortuitous accidents, chance operations, and the aleatory. But who can believe now that these "inspired decisions" – to have John Coltrane take an alto sax solo right in the middle of an Indian war call, for example – were in fact pure accidents? Paradoxically, we ourselves can't believe it, even though we know better than anyone else that no one composed, wrote or intended any of those moments to take place in the way that they did. And so we are energized and excited by the very existence of the hidden possibilities of which we've caught just a glimpse. We yearn to perform yet another symphony – we yearn to perform the "same" symphony another time – without knowing or even caring if there is in fact a difference between the two. We yearn to make a whole symphony of situationist symphonies, to lose ourselves in a never-ending concert of the most beautiful music we can imagine. In a word, we yearn!

But until such time as our *Situationist Symphony* can be freely circulated and played on the radio and in concert halls, without fear of anyone being sued by the owners of all the copyrighted material we have appropriated, that is all we can do.

NOT BORED! #25, June 1996

The Movement of the Free Spirit: All the Things You Could Be Right Now if Raoul Vaneigem Were Your Father

Randall Cherry and Ian Patterson's translation of Raoul Vaneigem's 1986 book *Le Mouvement du libre-esprit* – published by Zone Books in 1994 as *The Movement of the Free Spirit: General Considerations and Firsthand Testimony Concerning Some Brief Flowerings of Life in the Middle Ages, the Renaissance and, Incidentally, Our Own Time* – is a crucial contribution to the development of the situationist movement in English-speaking countries such as our own. Predominantly Protestant, the United States needs a really good new book on the movement of the Free Spirit. "The first studies and publications of the supporters of the movement of the Free Spirit were the works of Protestants," Vaneigem writes in one of his many footnotes. Much like the now well-respected Freemasons, "[the supporters of the movement] were seen as antisacramental mystics, hostile to Rome and slandered by the [Catholic] Church."

As we reported in *NOT BORED!* #18 (December, 1990), there were at least two great books published in the late 1980s that indirectly concern the Brethren of the Free Spirit: Greil Marcus's *Lipstick Traces* and Marc Shell's *The End of Kinship*. But the last books written in English that directly concern this obscure Medieval "heresy" – Norman Cohn's *The Pursuit of the Millennium: Revolutionary Millenarians and Mystical Anarchists of the Middle Ages*, and Robert E. Lerner's *The Heresy of the Free Spirit in the later Middle Ages* – were written or revised between 1957 and 1972, at a time when America had global enemies and local anti-communist wars to fight. Great changes, of course, came in the late 1980s and early 1990s, wiping out the "international communist menace." Seeing the importance of the timing of an English translation of *The Movement of the Free Spirit,* Vaneigem wrote a special preface for the American edition in March 1993. In it, he delivers to his readers this simple, stunning and memorable remark: "The Middle Ages were no more Christian than the late Eastern bloc was communist."

In addition to commentary, Vaneigem's book contains new translations of a great many texts that today constitute "the principal manifestations of the movement of the Free Spirit from the thirteenth to the sixteenth century." These translations of documents originally published in Latin, Italian, Spanish, Flemish, Dutch, German and English were apparently done by Vaneigem himself. Written as a labor of love, "to do no more than satisfy a personal curiosity," *The Movement of the Free Spirit* nevertheless has an important function to fulfill. "I have tried here," Vaneigem writes toward the end of his book, "to pay homage to the alliance of pleasure and lucidity by rescuing from darkness and silence those who celebrated true life in a time when lies about its nature proliferated along with the violence of the repressed."

It is quite tempting to see *The Movement of the Free Spirit* as the book-length critique of religion that the Situationist International always needed and never produced. For Vaneigem's book doesn't simply concern the Middles Ages, the Renaissance and our own time, as its subtitle would suggest: it is in fact a kind of secret history of the world. Speaking about the first agricultural settlements in the Neolithic period, circa 7000 B.C.E., "when Paleolithic civilizations based on hunting, gathering and fishing were replaced by a communitarian organization founded on agriculture and trade," Vaneigem asserts the following:

It was at this point in human development that the fall from life into survival occurred. In place of a unitary mode of existence, slowly disengaging from nature without ever breaking with it, a society arose in which human beings, having become both their own enemy and the enemy of their fellow humans, saw the object of their actions turned against them. Instead of moving toward a human transcendence of the contradiction between a free life and the fight for survival that characterizes the animal kingdom, market civilization socialized both. The freedom of nature was sacrificed to a competitive struggle whose aim was no longer the brutal satisfaction of drives (which would now be satisfied in the form of a secret, shameful tribute to repressed animality), but rather the maintenance of a parasitic system [i.e., labor] offering the social collectivity an abstract guarantee of survival: the exploitation of nature through man's exploitation of man.

In sum, this most unfortunate development "imposed a global inversion on the evolution of human life, just as this life was slowly disengaging itself from nature, like a child developing in the womb." It is from this pre-natal traumatization of human life, commonly known as "economic necessity," that stem humanity's collective historical neurosis, "all those eternal truths and sacred causes that have governed master and slave alike, truths and causes to which generations, born simply to live, have been wantonly sacrificed." More precisely, "the attribution of earthly effects to heavenly causes [religious belief] depended on the inversion and separation caused by labor, which represses pleasure and sets up a division between the intellectual and the manual."

In Vaneigem's secret history of the world, the movement of the Free Spirit – which has its roots in a series of socio-economic developments that took place in the 11th and 12th centuries C.E. – does not represent or refer to an easily identifiable grouping of heretics who had a thoroughly systematized philosophy or doctrine. There are no *Brethren* of the Free Spirit here. There is only the movement of the Free Spirit; it is "among," "supported" or "propagated by" certain groups and individuals at certain times and places.

The very designation "Free Spirit" is vague, hard to pin down. Based on a line contained in one of Paul's epistles to the Corinthians – "Where the Spirit of the Lord is, there is freedom" – the words were, to quote Vaneigem, "seized by adherents of the movement of the Free Spirit, who would subvert [their] meaning and restore [them] to the clandestine life from which they came." Thus, the name "Free Spirit" – and such officially recognized Biblical phrases as "paradise," "innocence of pleasure," and "ecstasy" – are part of a kind of elaborate disguise: "The movement disguising itself under the clerical name of the Free Spirit traced, beneath the filaments of everyday life, a path more secret and less tolerable than the alchemical magistracy and its degeneration into the genesis of the work of art." The path traced by the movement of the Free Spirit was toward "a new world in which the goods necessary for survival [are] held in common, property [is] abolished, and marriage, which reduce[s] women to an object of ownership, [is] done away with." Heaven on earth.

The movement of the Free Spirit is thus an instance of anti-mercantilist class struggle, not an instance of anti-clerical heresy against the Church. "The freedom of nature" and a great many earthly pleasures were already available to rich members and supporters of the Church. According to Vaneigem, "it was on the basis of the right to these pleasures, which the rich claimed for themselves and which the poor constantly demanded, that the movement of the Free Spirit founded its project of transcendence." The contradiction to be transcended was between wealthy contemplative, orthodox hermits and the "simple people" of the working class. But the Church has no meaning or jurisdiction whatsoever if the "world" ceases to be identified with religious forms; thus it had little choice but to insist that the movement of the Free Spirit was, like Catharism before it, a religious heresy. In this effort, the Church was helped by the tricky designation "Free Spirit," which paradoxically "reflected a wish to reduce things to spiritual terms – which is of course the essence of all religion," as Vaneigem points out. "But the label, which placed the Free Spirit on the same shelf as heresies and pure ideas, was the despair of the ecclesiastical storekeepers: the mold did not fit, and because it bore the imprint of a reality that it could not contain, it broke."

What we are left with, then, is a uncanny and paradoxical situation in which "the Middles Ages seem closer to us, in their demand for immediacy, than the period that extended from the Renaissance to the 1960s, when every generation seemed to delude itself about its future history," Vaneigem concludes. "Well-being was the carrot that [modern society] dangled in front of itself, on the stick of future progress." The upheavals of 1968 have allowed the "forces of life" to "gradually become more distinguishable from what had once corrupted them." No doubt thinking of his first and best-known book, translated into English in 1983 as *The Revolution of Everyday Life,* Vaneigem notes soberly that "many observations that were considered ludicrous in 1967 have now become commonplace." Even so, we cannot find a "guide to the emancipation of all" in the simple reiteration of Free Spirit ideas, "because the dominant language has changed its vocabulary, and, with the collapse of religious power [in the nineteenth century], God has been eliminated, excreted through a cleansing purgative, only to be replaced by ideas that are even more constipating, and made of the same fecal matter." Indeed, all thinking bears the indelible shit-stain of survival. For Vaneigem, who perhaps has in mind here the orientation debates conducted within the Situationist International in 1970, "the idea that reliance on the lucidity of the few will lead to freedom of all is so ingrained in new forms of slavery that the leaders are worn away up to their knees or even higher, revealing their true nature as truncated men."

What then is to be done? At the very least, we should re-acquaint ourselves with "the appropriation of language," which for Vaneigem is "both the labyrinth and the Ariadne's thread that lead to the heart of life, to the latencies that wait to be born in each of us, and which economic necessity paralyzes and corrupts with its universal negativity and its fundamental inhumanity." Significantly, the language appropriated by Vaneigem for and in *The Movement of the Free Spirit* is not that of genealogy or critique. It is a language with no name, one in which a thoroughly, gleefully atheistic, fifty-two-year-old man – though an ex-international situationist, one of the "simple people" nevertheless – "prays to God" upon the birth of his first child, a daughter.[2]

"We are only just now realizing that bringing a child into the world is no longer simply a matter of reproducing intellectual and manual slaves," Vaneigem writes, somewhat vaguely, for he is talking about no one but himself. "A new consciousness is developing that sees every birth as the early stages of a creation that needs to be perfected, of a life to be saved before the closed universe of commodities stifles it in the polluted air of profitability." He looks at his child, and "prays" aloud that "I hope [survival] ceases to be a priority, as if surviving were necessary first in order to live." He sees that his child is nude, and realizes, perhaps for the first time, that "the nudity of Giles of Canter was a renewal of the innocence of childhood, so that the world could once again be ordered along the lines of satisfaction, not the parameters of duty." He looks at his daughter's naked vagina and is angered by the idea that – in the inverted perspective of the market – "Woman, except as mother or as pure object, is lascivious, useless and harmful, and arouses a horror of the feminine affecting even that part of femininity which male worshipers of the patriarchal and celestial menhir repress so thoroughly." He looks at the mother of his child, and realizes the most important lesson of all:

> The ultimate disgrace is aptly revealed in the title of 'Creator' applied to a God who has created [or fathered] from his own substance a universe in which his creatures, deprived of his resources, begin in a state of total deprivation and progress toward nothingness. A desert valley irrigated with tears is a rather pathetic creation. It is not difficult to understand how the men and women who tried to establish a paradise on earth, here and now, saw themselves as superior to God.

NOT BORED! #25, June 1996

The Unabomber's Manifesto

When we last saw the Unabomber, it was 19 September 1995, the day after we'd finished "The Spectacle of Information," a seven-part essay published in *NOT BORED!* #24 (September 1995). The sixth part of the essay is titled "Terrorism and the State" and is mostly concerned with the so-called Unabomber.

---

[2] This was a guess on my part.

So important was the discussion of the Unabomber to the essay as a whole that we felt compelled to add the following editor's note to the end of it.

> This text was completed and distributed on 18 Sept 1995. The following day, *The Washington Post* published the Unabomber's 35,000-word manifesto, 'Industrial Society and Its Future' – a text of central importance to it. Though the author of 'The Spectacle of Information' was fortunate enough to obtain copies of the 19 Sept 95 edition of *The Post*, he didn't feel that his text needed to be immediately recalled and rewritten to take account of the bomber's manifesto. In either the next issue of *NOT BORED!* or a pamphlet [exclusively] devoted to the Unabomber, the author will discuss the contents and significance of 'Industrial Society and Its Future' in its entirety, and in its relations to the general spectacle and to the spectacle of information, in particular.

The only thing in our essay's discussion of the bomber "risky" enough to possibly merit recall and rewrite turned out to be one of its most interesting features: our guarded speculation that "perhaps the recent publication in the mainstream press of excerpts from his texts indicates that, whether he knows it or not, his personal mission has been or will soon be completed." Theodore Kaczinski's personal mission – and here we are assuming that Theodore Kaczinski is in fact the Unabomber – was indeed soon to be completed: he was arrested by the FBI a little over six months later. And the publication of the manifesto was in fact the way in which a suspect in the Unabomber attacks was apprehended: a reading of manifesto led David Kaczinki to conclude that his brother Theodore might very well be the Unabomber.

In the half-year between the publication of "Industrial Society and Its Future" and the arrest of Theodore Kaczinski, the manifesto was published many times and in a variety of formats. It is now widely available, even for free. Ironically, the widespread availability of the manifesto comes at a time when its publication is, strictly speaking, no longer authorized. From the standpoint of the commodity-spectacle, the text of the manifesto is obsolete. Its publication was intended to do one thing and one thing only: catch a suspect. Now that the manifesto has in fact led to the capture of a suspect who seems to be the Unabomber, it can – indeed, must – no longer be "operative," as Nixon press secretary Ron Ziegler used to say. It should no longer be appreciated as a piece of writing published and distributed according to the express wishes and best interests of the People of the United States of America, as represented by the Department of Justice, the FBI and the combined resources of *The Washington Post* and *The New York Times*. The manifesto should no longer exist as anything detachable from the on-going criminal investigation into the identity of the bomber. It should now only be read by the lawyers, expert witnesses, judges and jury members directly involved in the case.

Even during the trial of Theodore Kaczinski himself, the manifesto will not be read as the peculiar state-distributed polemic against the state that it is, but as a simple reflection of its author's character and psychological state. The defense will surely want to introduce the manifesto into evidence, but only because it seems to lend credibility to the notion that Kaczinski – unlike Timothy McVeigh – is both an intelligent, reasonable man and a sympathetic figure, and not a sociopathic killer who has been using "politics" as his pretext, justification and excuse. The prosecution will surely claim that the manifesto and the circumstances of its writing are irrelevant to the question at hand: did or did not Theodore Kaczinski send bombs through the mail, bombs that killed 3 people and wounded more than twenty? But even if the judge rules for the defense, the manifesto can easily be used by the prosecution to make the defendant seem less sympathetic than he already is. An intelligent, reasonable guy – or, if you like, a poor fuck – like Kaczinki certainly should have realized that his tactics would only have been appropriate, if at all, in a totalitarian society in which dissent was impossible, and that America is in fact the world's leading democracy.

Before Kaczinski's arrest, there had, of course, been some general discussion of "Industrial Society and Its Future." In anarchist circles, the discussion mostly concerned the Unabomber's relationship to anarchism: was he or was he not an anarchist? But even these discussions didn't concern themselves with the specific contents of the manifesto, other than the fact that it announces itself to be opposed to technological industrialism.. These discussions were mostly concerned with the actions the Unabomber took on the basis of the ideas set forth in his manifesto. That is to say, the occasion of the official publication of the Unabomber's manifesto was turned into an opportunity to revive a very old and very uninteresting question, "Is there a role for violence in the anarchist movement?" But violence is only a tactic. What is anarchism's current strategy? The manifesto's official authorization was a unique opportunity for anarchist thought to revive itself, to bring itself out of the coma into which it lapsed amid the foul stench of Reaganism, and to glimpse the new conditions for its existence and ultimate success. This opportunity was lost, but we can take advantage of another.

We hold to our original assertions about the Unabomber:[3] that he didn't act alone or without the knowledge of others; that he was helped to one degree or another by the still unidentified members of the Freedom Club (FC); that this help largely consisted of fresh information about potential targets; and that the Unabomber himself might have been "selected and trained according to the progression signified by the words misguided, provoked, infiltrated, manipulated, taken over and subverted" (Debord). To date, nothing that has been reported or otherwise leaked about Theodore Kaczinski – and there has been a lot – has

---

[3] Most unfortunate, because none of these assertions were borne out by the facts that came out later.

concerned the crucial years between his arrival in Lincoln, Montana, in 1972 and the beginning of the Unabomber attacks in 1978. How did it come about that this guy – who'd not taken part in any of the ultraleftist or anarchist bombing campaigns of the late 1960s and early 1970s – suddenly got the bug to send and personally deliver explosive devices to establishment types in the late 1970s, when almost no one else was doing it any more? What accounts for Kaczinski's weird sense of timing? It certainly had nothing to do Teddy's being personally rejected, by girlfriends or academic magazine editors or both!

Let us listen to Theodore Kaczinski the manifesto-writer discuss his ideology at some length.

> It is necessary to develop and propagate an ideology that opposes technology and the industrial society if and when the system becomes sufficiently weakened. And such an ideology will help to assure that, if and when industrial society breaks down, its remnants will be smashed beyond repair, so that the system cannot be reconstituted [paragraph 166]. The pattern would be similar to that of the French and Russian Revolutions [para. 181]. But an ideology, in order to gain enthusiastic support, must have a positive ideal as well as a negative one; it must be FOR something as well as AGAINST something. The positive ideal that we propose is Nature. That is, WILD nature [para. 183]. The radical environmentalists ALREADY hold an ideology that exalts nature and opposes technology [para. 184]. A further advantage of nature as a counter-ideal to technology is that, in many people, nature inspires the kind of reverence that is associated with religion, so that nature could perhaps be idealized on a religious basis [footnote 30]. On the more sophisticated level the ideology should address itself to people who are intelligent, thoughtful and rational. The object should be to create a core of people who will be opposed to the industrial system on a rational, thought-out basis [para. 187]. On a second level, the ideology should be propagated in a simplified form that will enable the unthinking majority to see the conflict of technology vs. Nature in unambiguous terms [para. 188].

This isn't the voice of someone laying out a stable, logically consistent ideology that is "manifested" in a written document, not at all. This is the voice of someone repeating what has been told to him, and it is not anarchism or even libertarianism, but some sort of Leninism or fascism.

Thus this manifesto is offensive but harmless to the established order. It is rhetorically and emotionally empty, without personality, bereft of metaphor and imagery, utterly joyless and profoundly boring. It is as de-natured as its author's or authors' conception of "wild nature," which is illogically defined as "those aspects of the functioning of the Earth and its living things that are independent of human management and free of human interference and control" (para. 183). We note that the Unabomber has no animalistic or primal urges of his own. He seems to take pleasure in nothing, not even in the spectacular deaths, injuries and property damage he has caused. For him, killing people has been a simple, bloodless way "to get our message before the public with some chance of making a lasting impression" (para. 96). Even *fucking* is a duty to be performed in the service of the anti-industrial revolution: "Revolutionaries should have as many children as they can" (para. 204). What about having as many orgasms as you can, man?

Though the author(s) of "Industrial Society and Its Future" insist upon the desirability of religious fervor among the "revolutionaries," there is no religious fervor in the voice of the text itself, no confidence in the future, no joy taken nor dread felt in the knowledge that the future itself is possible. "True, there is no assurance that the industrial system can be destroyed at approximately the same time all over the world," FC writes woodenly; "and it is even conceivable that the attempt to overthrow the system could lead to the domination of the system of dictators: that is the risk that has to be taken" (para. 195). But why must it be taken? Why can't you make us *feel* something here? Perhaps it is because you don't let yourself feel anything yourself.

The personality or characterological structure projected by FC's manifesto is familiar, all-too-familiar. It is, at its most fundamental level, based on a lie: the attack laid out in the manifesto is not against "industrial society," as its title might indicate, but against leftists and leftism. Over and over again, FC's text rails against the "psychology of the leftism," which the author insists is dominated by "low self-esteem, feelings of powerlessness, depressive tendencies, defeatism, guilt, self-hatred, etc." While it is obvious to us that this is in fact the psychology of the author of the manifesto, FC is in haste to draw our attention to the "fact" that "the [psychological] problems of the leftist are indicative of the problems of our society as a whole" (para. 32). In FC's view of "society as a whole," there are simply no rightists or rightism to balance out with or complement the leftists and leftism. The only forces on the other side of the political spectrum are the mild-mannered "conservatives," who are "fools" (para. 50), even though they are very successful at "taking the average man for a sucker, exploiting his resentment of Big Government to promote the power of Big Business." The timing and circumstances of Kaczinski's arrest in Lincoln, Montana, pointed up at least one of the huge holes or blindspots in FC's manifesto: while Teddy was being carted off to jail, at the same time and on the other side of the state (in Jordan, Montana), the FBI was trying – indeed, as of this writing, still is trying – to negotiate the surrender of several members of the Freemen, a far-Right group.

Certainly many of the social and cultural positions taken in FC's manifesto could easily be construed as ultra-rightist. This is the Unabomber (though it could be the Nazi Minister of Culture, Joseph Goebbels) talking about modern art, or, rather, about the degenerates who like modern art: "Art forms that appeal to modern leftish intellectuals tend to focus on sordidness, defeat and despair, or else they take on an orgiastic tone, throwing out rational control as if there were no hope of accomplishing anything through rational calculation and all that was left was to immerse oneself in the sensations of the moment." What modern art needs is the very thing that leftists "tend to hate": that is, "an image of being strong, good and successful." Both leftists who like modern art and modern artists themselves "hate America, they hate Western civilization, they hate white males, they hate rationality" (para. 15).

It goes without saying that FC, like the National Socialist Workers' Party, hates gypsies: as the manifesto points out, everyone knows that "the gypsies commonly get away with theft and fraud because their loyalties are such that they can always get other gypsies to give testimony that 'proves' their innocence" (footnote 7). What about homosexuals, who can't of course have as many babies as possible? Surely they are "perverts" (footnote 6). And what about niggers? The Unabomber hates 'em, too, folks, but not as much as he hates leftist nigger-lovers.

> Many leftists push for affirmative action, for moving black people into high-prestige jobs, for improved education in black schools and more money for such schools. . . . In all ESSENTIAL respects most leftists of the oversocialized type want to make the black man conform to white, middle-class ideals. They want to make him study technical subjects, become an executive or a scientist, spend his life climbing the status ladder to prove that black people are as good as white. They want to make black fathers 'responsible,' they want to make black gangs nonviolent, etc. . . . In effect, however much he may deny it, the oversocialized leftist wants to integrate the black man into the system and make him adopt its values (para. 29).

All that's missing from these crypto-racist remarks is something along the lines of, "It's not like we're the racist segregationists – the blacks themselves *want* to be separate from us!"

Finally, like a great many modern fascists before him, the Unabomber is willfully ignorant about capitalism, a word that doesn't appear in the manifesto without ironic or distancing quotations marks around it. (In paragraph 229, "capitalism" is identified as a simple and "common catchphrase of the left," one which has as much objective reality as the phrases "social change," "social justice," or "social responsibility.") In paragraph 211, FC writes, "In the late Middle Ages there were four main civilizations that were about equally 'advanced': Europe, the Islamic world, India, and the Far East (China, Japan, Korea). Three of those civilizations remained more or less stable, and only Europe became dynamic. No one knows why Europe became dynamic at that time; historians have their theories but these are only speculation."

Correction: the "speculation" here is that people will forget that they already know that capitalism is the reason Europe became "dynamic" in the late Middle

Ages! This speculation will pay off if there is a systematic and profitable confusion surrounding the relationship between technology and capitalism. FC – as well as the society of the commodity-spectacle – profits when people believe that capitalism is just a stage through which "technology" or "technicity" is passing, rather than the truth, which is the reverse. Capitalism was "there" before technology, and it will continue to exist, even if technology is somehow abolished.

NOT BORED! #25, June 1996

Dennis Rodman: De-domesticated Man

It's the very first thing you notice about Dennis Rodman's remarkable autobiography *Bad As I Wanna Be*, published by Delacorte in June 1996 so as to coincide with the NBA Finals. The typography is "gimmicky." Over and over again, for the entire length of the text, the reader is confronted with whole sentences printed in different fonts, in **boldface** or *italics* (or ***boldface and italics***) and/or in FULL CAPITALS. Occasionally, single words or phrases are printed, shall we say, in ways different from the norm. **THAT'S JUST IT**, of course: Dennis Rodman is different from the norm. He's an "in-your-face" basketball player, and his autobiography is an "in-your-face" book. Get it?

But there's quite a bit more to "get" in *Bad As I Wanna Be* – to be precise, there's more being communicated by the "gimmicky" typography – than one might expect from a poorly-organized, all-too-short and irritatingly sketchy book that was clearly designed to cash in on Rodman's spectacular success as a member of the revitalized Chicago Bulls basketball team. Masquerading as a gimmick, the jumpy typography is a metaphor for Dennis's multi-colored hair, which is itself a metaphor for his sexual persona, which is itself a super-metaphor for the completeness of Dennis's refusal to be denied participation in the totality of what it means to be a human being. In a word, the typography is a metaphor for his total and therefore exemplary refusal to remain domesticated, despite all the pressures he is under to stay as he has been or to become what he "should" be.

An "animal" on the basketball court, Dennis Rodman is nevertheless the most human basketball star ever to play the game. This makes him a spectacle only to the extent that the other players, who generally pride themselves on being picture-perfect "role models," do not seem to be human beings at all. As has been noted elsewhere, it is Rodman's ceaselessly inventive performance of his "de-domestication" that makes him so, er, ah – sorry to use a word that even seems silly when it is uttered by revolutionaries – revolutionary. His much-vaunted "negativity" has created untold numbers of new radical possibilities and expectations for all kinds of people. Thanks to Rodman, some of America's most fixed and therefore oppressive images – of what it means to be a star professional athlete, a physically powerful male human, and a black male athlete – have been loosened and set adrift. If only critical theorists and professional revolutionaries could be as wild and distracting as Dennis Rodman is! But, alas, this is rarely the case.

Take for example the collection of essays written in the 1970s by the French communist Jacques Camatte and published in translation by Autonomedia in 1995 under the title *This World We Must Leave and Other Essays*. "Until now," Camatte announces in the title essay, "all sides have argued as if human beings [have] remained unchanged in different class societies and under the domination of capital." Supposedly striking out into completely new and unknown territory, Camatte claims that the widely observed "autonomization" and becoming-human of capital have been accompanied – indeed, made possible – by the capitalization or "domestication" of people living in advanced capitalist societies. This double movement of autonomization and domestication, Camatte writes, is ultimately responsible for "the return to 'barbarism,' as analyzed by R. Luxemburg and the entire left wing of the Frankfurt School; the destruction of the human species, as is evident to each and all today; finally, a state of stagnation in which the capitalist mode of production survives by adapting itself to a degenerated humanity which lacks the power to destroy it."

Let us leave aside the question of the becoming-human of capital – it has been adequately treated in our discussions of the situationists' critique of the society of the spectacle – and ask what, precisely, is domestication? In a 1980 text entitled "Echoes of the Past," Camatte explains that "the scientific presuppositions established in the neolithic era with the spread of animal husbandry went hand in hand with the development toward [human] domestication [...] And it shows up again in this vital contradiction: men always want to distinguish themselves from beasts [of burden], yet they constantly treat each other like animals." Forget about the way veal is produced: we are the veal.

"The result of . . . technological process has been that, not only animals, but also humans themselves have been domesticated and adapted to the needs of industrial society," says Chris Korda, founder of the Church of Euthanasia and member of the Unabomber for President Write-In Campaign 1996, perhaps unaware of Jacques Camatte's work in this area. When it comes to watching the spectacle of laboratory animals being used in so-called scientific research, Korda says, "we can see that's cruel, we can see that those animals are suffering, it's essentially 'inhumane.'" What a curious use of the word, because what we are not able to see is that our lives have been equally affected, and that humans have also suffered at the hands of industrial society."

Domesticated humans – people who have been successfully conditioned by the inhumane capitalist mode of production to "have a tendency to see themselves as a herd that they have to make prosper and grow" – have been dispossessed of the faculties of "action, language, rhythm, and imagination," Camatte says. In the society of the spectacle – Camatte's metaphor is "the community of capital" – "there are no longer classes, only generalized slavery, accompanied by massification and homogenization of human beings and products." There is now only one element relating the "reduced" or domesticated human being to the external world: sexuality, "which," Camatte awkwardly explains, "fills the void of the senses." Sexuality seems to make Jacques Camatte uncomfortable. For him, "pansexuality, or more exactly the pansexualization of being that Freud interpreted as an invariant characteristic of human beings" is in reality "the result of [human beings'] mutilation" at the hands of capital.

One look at Dennis Rodman tells us that Freud was right and Camatte was wrong. The fuel for Rodman's intense and continuously growing popularity clearly comes from the flamboyantly liberated and polymorphous perverse sexuality that he has – in the very process of healing his "mutilation" – discovered in himself. As Rodman says in his book, he'd be just another nigger without basketball, but he'd be just another black basketball player without sexuality.

It should come as absolutely no surprise that Dennis – like his ex-lover Madonna, who is perhaps the only American performance artist who is at his level of skill – is pansexual. Dennis Rodman – easily one of the strongest, most physically aggressive and intimidating players in the history of the NBA – sleeps with women, fantasizes about men, dresses in drag, and publicly supports gays and lesbians. De-domestication, which is, in Dennis's words, doing things that "make me feel like a total person and not just a one-dimensional man," is a profoundly sexual experience. De-domestication is allowing "your body to go and explore anything it wants." It is the revolution of bodily life, bro.

Where Dennis Rodman eclipses Madonna – indeed, where Dennis Rodman eclipses just about everyone these days, but especially the specialists in revolution – is in his awareness that his sexually charged efforts to become a fully de-domesticated man is an instance of class struggle. Nothing but a mere worker (a salaried slave) in the eyes of some of his coaches and all of the economic powers behind the NBA, Dennis Rodman refuses to be reduced to a thing, to a commodity, to a quantity of labor power to be bought and sold. And this refusal isn't so much a matter of money as it is a matter of working conditions at the point of production, so to speak. "The bottom line is, this league wants to control its players," Rodman writes. "They want to restrict players from doing things that are natural and human to do. They don't want anybody insulting the people who buy the tickets – the wealthy corporate types, because they're the only ones who can afford to go anymore." More than that, the NBA doesn't want players thinking and acting for themselves while they are on the court, even if it means that good teams lose important basketball games. In this regard, the NBA is just like every other capitalist enterprise, whether it is privately or bureaucratically owned.

Towards the end of his book – in a story that might easily be overlooked, for it concerns the mechanics of the game of basketball – Rodman recalls the playoffs in which the San Antonio Spurs (Rodman's putative owners and managers at the time) played the defending champion Houston Rockets. "We lost the first two games – at home, even – because the defense we were running was ridiculous," Rodman writes. "Do you want to know who changed the defense for the next two games, after we got to Houston? I did. I saw what we were doing wrong, and I set out to change it. I finally got [Spurs' coach] Bob Hill to see it my way, and it worked. David [Robinson] played Hakeem [Olajuwon] straight up. Hakeem got what he was going to get anyway, but we stopped everyone else. That's the whole key to stopping [the Rockets]: give Hakeem what he wants and clamp down on everybody else. It's not that hard to figure out." Shortly after this series, which the Spurs lost to the Rockets, the Spurs traded Rodman to the Chicago Bulls for next to nothing.

What pansexualist and typographical artist Dennis Rodman has got in his multi-colored head is socialist basketball, a basketball team that is collectively managed and coached by its own members. Who knows better how to do something than the people who can actually get it done? Bob Hill and the San Antonio Spurs' organization couldn't tolerate even the semblance of such a team, so they got rid of Rodman and have been a third-rate team ever since. But Chuck Daly and the Detroit Pistons and Phil Jackson and the Chicago Bulls know the value of socialist production (perhaps precisely because they themselves are employed by enterprises based in the industrial Midwest), and so have made a home for the greatest rebounder and all-around defensive player the NBA has ever seen.

After all, it is in the industrial Midwest that the working classes – the producers of automobile pistons and the crews at the slaughterhouses – have known for generations that there is a profound discontinuity between the way a productive enterprise is supposed to function and the way it actually functions, and that, if operated according to management's organizational plan and nothing else, the enterprise will not run at all. It is in the factories of the industrial Midwest that socialism is actually at work, for it is in these factories that collectivities of workers are allowed to band together and manage at least some of their own work, precisely because it is the only way their bosses can get the job done and make some money. The connection between Dennis Rodman's de-domestication and the on-going struggle in America to propagate and move closer towards socialism is so obvious it just jumps out at you. But can you catch the rebound, bro?

NOT BORED! #26, November 1996

Book reviews

Workers' Councils, Cornelius Castoriadis and the Situationist International

In our comments on the first and only issue of the review of the American section of the Situationist International, which was published in 1969, we began a discussion of the SI's championing of workers' councils as "the highest organizational form of direct democracy reached by the proletariat for the expression of its own power" and the place where "the renewed motion toward emancipation will begin" (to quote the American situationist Robert Chasse). We propose here to continue our discussion of this topic and its relevance to contemporary struggles.

1

The history of the SI's development of the theme of the councils is instructive. At least so far as one is able to judge by the contents of *The Situationist Anthology*, the first mention of workers' councils appears in *Internationale Situationniste* #6 (August 1961). "Of the tendencies toward regroupment that have appeared over the last few years among various minorities in the workers movement in Europe," an unsigned text pronounces, "only the most radical current is worth preserving: that centered on the program of workers councils." Unfortunately, this article – which is entitled "Instructions for Taking Up Arms" – does not specify which "tendency," "minority" or "current" in Europe is centered on the program of the councils. But, as we will see, the writer(s) certainly had the revolutionary group and journal Socialisme ou Barbarie in mind, for S. ou B. had been running articles on workers' councils all through the middle and late 1950s.

From 1961 to 1967, the situationists maintained their official adherence to the "program of the councils," and yet they never defined what that program might entail. The text "Minimum Definition of Revolutionary Organizations," adopted by the 7th Conference of the SI (held in Paris in July 1966), begins with the following bold sentence: "Since the only purpose of a revolutionary organization is the abolition of all existing classes in a way that does not bring about a new division of society, we consider any organization revolutionary which consistently and effectively works toward the international realization of the absolute power of the workers councils, as prefigured in the experience of the proletarian revolutions of this century." But nowhere does the SI define or describe the precise content of "the experience of the proletariat revolutions of this century." Without bothering to define what is meant by a "workers' council," the situationists' "On the Poverty of Student Life" (November 1966) confidently announces that "the democracy of workers councils is *the* solution to all the present separations" (emphasis added).

Only three theses in Guy Debord's *The Society of the Spectacle* (originally written between 1964 and 1965 and published in 1967) concern workers' councils.

The councils are defined in a single phrase: they vest "all decision-making and executive powers in themselves and [they] federat[e] with one another through the exchange of delegates answerable to the base and recallable at any time" (thesis 116). And yet Debord, quoting Karl Marx, feels entirely at ease with echoing the apparently unquestionable claim that the revolutionary workers' councils are that "long-sought political form whereby the economic emancipation of labor might finally be achieved." There can be no other form than that of the councils: though "the decision to set up workers' councils does not in itself provide solutions so much as it 'proposes problems,' " Debord writes, "the power of workers' councils is *the one context* in which the problems of the revolution of the proletariat can be truly solved" (thesis 116, emphasis added). Again: "the councils may be seen in their true light as *the only* undefeated aspect of a defeated movement," existing "not at the periphery of an ebbing tide but rather at the center of a rising one" (thesis 118, emphasis added).

And yet, during the whole 1961 to 1967 period – despite the apparent centrality of the councils to the situationist project – the development of what the situationists meant when they used the words "workers' councils" remained a peripheral concern. A story Raoul Vaneigem tells in his 1991 preface to *The Revolution of Everyday Life* (written between 1963 and 1965, published in 1967) is significant from this perspective. As a result of some insignificant events involving the changing whims of the editors at Gallimard, Vaneigem had to "cut short [i.e., leave unwritten] a closing discussion of workers' councils as a social model (the book's second postscript, added in 1972, shows signs of an attempt to redress this)." But the 1972 postscript, "A Toast to Revolutionary Workers," emphasizes the significance of wildcat actions and riots, not workers' councils.

When the much-anticipated revolution began in Paris in May 1968, the situationists stuck by their official but drastically underdeveloped theory of the power of the workers' councils. One of the "slogans to be spread now by every means," "POWER TO THE WORKERS COUNCILS," appeared on the situationists' banners, in their telegrams to world leaders, and in their leaflets. It was a slogan to be spread in "announcements over microphones, comic strips, songs, graffiti, balloons on paintings in the Sorbonne, announcements in theatres during films or while disrupting them, balloons on subway billboards, before making love, after making love, in elevators, each time you raise your glass in a bar."

But the workers of France did not organize themselves into workers' councils during the revolutionary crisis of May and June 1968. And so the situationists had to content themselves with such meager consolations as this idea, proposed by Raoul Vaneigem in the aftermath of May: "Without really manifesting itself, a movement toward councils was implicitly present in the resultant of two contradictory forces: the internal logic of the occupations and the repressive logic of the parties and unions." (How d'ya figure that, Raoul? But he doesn't say.) Other paltry consolations include this piece of speculation, offered up by the SI in

"The Beginning of an Era": "the occupations movement was objectively at several moments only an hour away from such a result" (the establishment of workers' councils). "If, in a single factory, between 16 May and 30 May," the SI continued, "a general assembly had constituted itself as a council holding all powers of decision and execution, expelling the bureaucrats, organizing its self-defense and calling on the strikers of all enterprises to link up with it, this last qualitative step could have immediately brought the movement to the final struggle, the struggle whose general outlines have all been historically traced by this movement." (Whoa, now: that's a pretty big "if," isn't it?)

The situationists spent much of their efforts after 1968 promulgating the "program of the councils," but this time in much greater depth than before. But at no point did they question the historical inevitability of workers' councils: "the power of the councils" remained a simple article of faith, a totally unexamined assumption. The last issue of *Internationale Situationniste* (#12, September 1969) contains two major pieces on the councils: Rene Riesel's "Preliminaries on the Councils and Councilist Organization," and Raoul Vaneigem's "Notice to the Civilized Concerning Generalized Self-Management."

Riesel's piece is politico-historical in nature: it offers a short introduction to workers' councils as they were established and briefly maintained in Russia (in 1905), Germany (1918), Italy (1920), Spain (1936) and Hungary (1956). Riesel sums up his critique of these events as follows: "Despite all the beautiful history of the councils, all the councilist organizations of the past that have played a significant role in class struggles have sanctioned separation into political, economic and social sectors." That is to say, all of the workers' councils to date have allowed themselves to be placed, as it were, alongside such fundamentally antiworker bureaucracies as the State or the Communist Party. And yet, as Riesel writes, the "coherence [of the councils] is guaranteed by the single fact that they are the power; that they eliminate all other power and decide everything."

Though a fully constituted workers' council has not yet come into existence in over a half century of struggles, Riesel is quite confident that the "new revolutionary proletarian movement" has no choice but to see the councils as "the sole form of antistate dictatorship of the proletariat, as the sole tribunal that will be able to pass judgment on the old world and carry out the sentence itself." Nothing other than workers' councils will ever do, even if Riesel finds that he cannot deny the fact that "it is quite likely that genuine councilist organizations will still take a long time to form and that other important revolutionary moments will occur before such organizations are in a position to intervene in them at a significant level." Why are workers' councils inevitable or unavoidable? Riesel answers: because "the workers continue to be the central force capable of halting the existing functioning of society and the indispensable force for reinventing all of its bases." Conclusion: we revolutionaries must have the workers with us if we want a total revolution; some of the workers in a handful of European nations have indicated – sporadically, over the course of the last 50 years – that they must have some kind of "council" for them to be involved in the revolution; therefore, we are all stuck with workers' councils, whether we like it or not.

Vaneigem's piece on "Generalized Self-Management" is purely speculative: it contains such helpful hints as "it will be a good idea for the councils to distinguish between priority sectors . . . reconversion sectors . . . and parasitical sectors [of the economy]," and "it will be a good idea for the assembly [of each council] to elect and control: an equipping section . . . ; an information section . . . ; a coordination section . . . ; and a self-defense section." All this flies right in the face of a very good point Riesel makes in his essay: "Only historical practice, through which the working class must discover and realize all its possibilities, will indicate the precise organizational forms of council power." In the meantime, it is nonproductive and even a little absurd to speculate in the manner Vaneigem does upon the nature of the workers' councils that the revolutionary proletariat should or will establish as it comes to power.

2

It has been our good fortune to locate and read copies of the two volumes of the *Political and Social Writings of Cornelius Castoriadis* (translated and edited by David Ames Curtis) that the University of Minnesota published in 1988. The first volume, subtitled "From the Critique of the Bureaucracy to the Positive Content of Socialism," covers the years 1946 to 1955, while the second, subtitled "From the Workers' Struggle Against Bureaucracy to Revolution in the Age of Modern Capitalism," covers the years 1955 to 1960. (A projected third volume will supposedly cover the 1960 to 1966 period, but it has not yet been published.) Castoriadis was a co-founder of the revolutionary group and journal Socialisme ou Barbarie, and the author of several important S. ou B. texts on workers' councils that clearly had a strong influence on the councilist theories and ideas of the members of the Situationist International. Though these two volumes arrived with the warning (issued by Castoriadis in 1972) that "We do not have any Good News to proselytize concerning the Promised Land glimmering on the horizon, any Book to recommend whose reading would exempt one from having to seek the truth for oneself," we can't help but look to them for a way through the impasse we have reached.

Since Castoriadis has used several pseudonyms – including Paul Cardan, Pierre Chaulieu and Jean-Marie Coudray – it might be helpful if we included a brief biography of him here. He was born in Greece in 1922; in Athens he studied law, economics and philosophy. A member of the Greek Communist Youth since the age of 15, Castoriadis became a Trotskyist in 1942, and thus spent World War II avoiding both Stalinist and Nazi agents. He moved to Paris in 1945, and has lived there ever since. (But because he didn't become a French national until 1970, Castoriadis conducted nearly all of his pre-1970 political activities in Paris under aliases.) He was a member of the French section of the (Trotskyist) Fourth International until 1949, at which time he (and several other members, including

Claude Lefort) left to form S. ou B. Over the course of the next 17 years, the group weathered and profited from two scissions between Castoriadis and Lefort, and included such other now well-known Parisian intellectuals as Jean-Francois Lyotard and Pierre Guillaume. According to David Ames Curtis, in 1966 "Castoriadis convinced the group to disband, complaining that readers of the journal had remained mere consumers rather than active participants." There was some consolation in the knowledge that the views of the group, in the words of Curtis, "already were gaining acceptance in left-wing and student circles."

The discussion about workers' councils within the S. ou B. group appears to have started with the publication of Castoriadis' essay "The Proletarian Revolution Against the Bureaucracy" in issue #20 (December 1956). Like many of the pieces Castoriadis wrote at the time, this essay attempts to evaluate and update the guiding principles of the S. ou B. group in the light of current events. Though the essay cites the revolutionary events that took place in East Germany in June 1953 and in Poland in June 1956, it is mostly a response to the Hungarian Revolution, which broke out in November 1956. There was nothing "academic," speculative or undialectic about Castoriadis' motivations to begin such a discussion at that particular moment in time. If he used his essay (in part) to launch a discussion of workers' councils, it is only because workers' councils were actually established in 1956 by the Budapest proletariat in its revolution against the Hungarian bureaucracy. (In theory, Castoriadis could have begun this discussion as early as 1950, when Anton Pannekoek published *The Workers' Councils*, an account of events that took place in the first third of the twentieth century.) Based upon what was actually happening at the time, Castoriadis presented what he thought was "the clearest and the highest expression of the tendencies and goals of the workers of our epoch": the formation of workers' councils, which are nonhierarchical and directly democratic groupings of people, organized at their place(s) of employment, that manage and direct their own productive activities without a separate class or strata of managers or supervisors of any kind "above" them; the federation of these councils with each other on the national level; and "the beginning of the whole set of tasks involved in directing the [entire] economy."

The unique strength of Castoriadis' work in this area consists in his awareness and careful documentation of the on-going existence of proto-councilist collectives – right in the very heart capitalism's most advanced sectors of production! Indeed, in part thanks to Castoriadis, we can clearly see that these proto-councilist collectives are not accidental occurrences, nor are they planned. Ironically, they are necessary and integral parts of the functioning of the capitalist mode of production, as well as the precursors of socialist society. Castoriadis writes:

> Modern social life has already created these [proto-councilist] collectivities and continues to create them. They are based in medium-sized or large enterprises and are to be found in industry,

transportation, commerce, banking, insurance, public administration, where people by the hundreds, thousands, or tens of thousands spend the main part of their life harnessed to a common task, where they encounter society in its most concrete form. A place of work is not only a unit of production: It has become the primary unit of social life for the vast majority of people.

"No modern factory could function for twenty-four hours," Castoriadis proclaims in "The Proletarian Revolution Against the Bureaucracy," "without this spontaneous organization of work that groups of workers, independent of the official business management, carry out by filling in the gaps of official production directives, by preparing for the unforeseen and for regular breakdowns of equipment, by compensating for management's mistakes, etc."

And yet these "elementary" or "primary" groups of workers – though they can be studied by bourgeois sociologists – cannot be officially recognized, sanctioned or empowered by the bureaucratic managers of these putatively capitalist enterprises. Such a recognition would be tantamount to admitting that the entire management strata is not only irrelevant and superfluous, but also wasteful, counterproductive and therefore (by its own logic!) irrational. "Those in authority in a large modern factory in fact spend less of their time organizing production than coping, directly or indirectly, with the resistance of the exploited," Castoriadis reminds us. "The net result is not only waste but perpetual conflict." And so the creation of workers' councils – based upon the existence and functioning of the "elementary groups" – would both dissolve the bases for perpetual conflict between directors and executants, and would put an end to capitalism's inhuman, irrational and wasteful "privatization" of the free, spontaneous creativity of the people it enslaves.

By the publication of "On the Content of Socialism, II," which appeared in *S. ou B.* #22 (July 1957), Castoriadis was ready to sum up what his investigations into the Hungarian revolution had produced. "There is no question for us here of trying to draw up 'statutes,' 'rules,' or an 'ideal constitution' for socialist society," he writes.

> From this point of view, we obviously should condemn any fetishism for the 'soviet' or 'council' type of organization. The 'constant eligibility and revocability of representatives' are of themselves quite insufficient to 'guarantee' that a council will remain the expression of working-class interests. The council will remain such an expression for as long as people are prepared to do whatever may be necessary for it to remain so. . . . [T]he council is an adequate form of organization: Its whole structure is set up to enable this will to self-expression [of the workers] to come to the fore, when it exists.

For Castoriadis, future revolutions would necessarily strive for the takeover of the management of all production by the workers, themselves organized into workers' councils; the federation of the councils into a central assembly; the expropriation of the capitalists; the dissolution of the police and the army, and the arming of the proletariat; and the issuance of what Castoriadis refers to as a "call on the workers of other countries . . . [that would] explain to them the content and meaning of these measures," which "contain all that is essential to the process of building socialism." Otherwise, these revolutions would be doomed to failure, precisely because they were partial or restricted in their fields of action.

3

In 1966, at least in so far as the extremists of the Situationist International were concerned, the views of the S. ou B. group were merely "impotent speculation." As early as 1961, the journal of the SI – which, like S. ou B.'s journal, got its name from the group that published it – made it clear that the SI, though it obviously valued the work of groups such as S. ou B. in France, Solidarity in England and Alternative in Belgium, did not wish to be associated with them. The SI's reasons for doing so were questionable, given the strong and explicit attachment both groups had to workers' councils. "Those who put all the stress on the necessity of changing work itself, of rationalizing it, of interesting people in it, and who neglect the idea of the free content of life (i.e., the development of a materially equipped creative power beyond the traditional categories of work time and rest and recreation time)," the SI wrote, "run the risk of providing an ideological cover for a harmonization of the present production system in the direction of greater efficiency and profitability without at all having called into question the experience of this production or the necessity of this kind of life" ("Instructions for Taking Up Arms," *I.S.* #6 August 1961). Despite this objection's lack of relevance to S. ou B.'s efforts, which appear to have been informed by a clear awareness of the "risk" cited by the situationists, the SI faithfully repeated it in the next two issues of their journal.

Starting in 1964, the SI attacked Castoriadis by name (or, rather, by alias) for the "specialization" of his efforts, which was one of the situationists' endearing ways of goading academics and militant intellectuals into forming their own autonomous revolutionary groups on the model of the SI. "Poor Heidegger! Poor Lukacs! Poor Sartre! Poor Barthes! Poor Lefebvre! Poor [Paul] Cardan!" mocks an unsigned article entitled "Now, the S.I." and published in *I.S.* #9 (August 1964). "Once the specialized thinkers step out of their domain, they can only be dumbfounded spectators of some neighboring and equally bankrupt specialization which they were ignorant of but which has become fashionable," the SI continues. "The former specialist of ultraleftist politics [Paul Cardan] is awestruck at discovering, along with structuralism and social psychology, an ethnological ideology completely new to him: the fact that Zuni Indians did not have any history to him appears as a luminous explanation for his own incapacity to act in our history. (Go laugh at the first twenty-five pages of *Socialisme ou Barbarie* #36)." In contrast to "specialists of thought" such as Paul Cardan, who can "no longer be anything but thinkers of specialization," the members of the SI lauded themselves for being thinkers of the totality in which specialization is negated. After that (that is, after 1964), the situationist line on Paul Cardan was set: "for a long time [we have] pointed out Cardan's unmistakable progression toward revolutionary nothingness, his swallowing of every kind of academic fashion and his ending up becoming indistinguishable from any ordinary sociologist" (*I.S.* #11, October 1967, p. 64).

Since we do not have access to volume 3 of Castoriadis's *Social and Political Writings* (as we have mentioned, it has not yet been published), we are not able to judge for ourselves if it indeed traces out an "unmistakable progression toward revolutionary nothingness" over the course of the 1961 to 1966 period. But the first two volumes make it clear that – over the course of a fairly long period, that is, from 1946 to 1960 – there is an unmistakable progression toward revolutionary significance in Castoriadis' writings. He begins as a Trotskyist and anti-Stalinist; he then breaks with Trotskyism over the question of the bureaucracy, and begins a sustained critique of what he was the first to refer to as "bureaucratic capitalism"; he finds that workers' councils are adequate means by which a revolution that is both anticapitalist and socialist can be fought and won; and he ends by formulating the centrality of the critique of everyday life to all revolutionary struggles. In a word, his progression takes him from the Trotskyists to the situationists.

On 20 July 1960, one Pierre Canjuers (the pseudonym of S. ou B. member and contributor David Blanchard) and Guy Debord signed their names to a text entitled "Preliminaries Toward Defining a Unitary Revolutionary Program." In his translator's footnotes to *The Situationist International Anthology,* which includes this text as one of several "Miscellaneous SI Publications (1960-1969)," Ken Knabb explains:

> Pierre Canjuers was at this time a member of the Socialisme ou Barbarie group. This text is described in *I.S.* #5 [December 1960] as 'a platform for discussion within the SI, and for its link-up with revolutionary militants of the workers movement.'

That is to say, the co-authored "Preliminaries" were intended as a platform for the Situationist International's link-up with Socialisme ou Barbarie in particular. The slogan of such a link-up is provided within the text: "Everywhere the vastness of the new possibilities poses the urgent alternative: revolutionary solution or science-fiction barbarism" (obviously another version of "socialism or barbarism," a phrase originally used by Rosa Luxemburg).

And so the co-authored "Preliminaries" offer a unique vision of the development of contemporary struggles: while Cornelius Castoriadis and the S. ou

B. circle steadily progressed from Trotskyist to situationists-in-all-but-the-name (much like ex-Communist Party theoretician Henri Lefebvre, who also collaborated with Debord around 1960), Guy Debord came out of nowhere (or revolutionary lettrism, if you prefer). For a brief moment in time, they were travelers along the same route. Thereafter – to hear the SI tell it – Castoriadis became a revolutionary nothing, while Debord went on to make all of Paris dance.

Though everything would suggest that it *should be* about workers' councils, "Preliminaries Toward Defining a Unitary Revolutionary Program" doesn't say a goddamned thing about them! Not one fucking word. "The revolutionary movement can be nothing less than the struggle of the proletariat for the actual domination and deliberate transformation of all aspects of social life," Blanchard and Debord write, "beginning with the management of production and work by the workers directly deciding everything."

> Such a change immediately implies a radical transformation of the nature of work and the development of a new technology tending to ensure the workers' domination over the machines. This radical transformation of the meaning of work will lead to a number of consequences, the main one of which is undoubtedly the shifting of the center of interest of life from passive leisure to the new type of productive activity. This does not mean that overnight all productive activities will become in themselves passionately interesting. But to work toward making them so, by a general and ongoing reconversion of the ends as well as the means of industrial work, will in any case be the minimum passion of a free society. All activities will tend to blend the life previously separated between leisure and work into a single but infinitely diversified flow. Production and consumption will merge and be superseded in the creative use of the goods of society.

It's as if the situationist project never knew about or (perhaps more to the point) never needed to know about workers' councils – or about any other revolutionary organizational form, for that matter, be it commune, soviet or factory committee – and yet, for all that, could still be given shape, launched and taken up by others acting for themselves and on their own. The situationist project suggested by Blanchard and Debord's text doesn't find it necessary to specify, lobby for or speculate upon which or what kind of mass organ or organizational form the proletariat will use to accomplish the shifting tasks of the revolution. It is enough for it to say that the revolution consists in the "radical transformation" or "reconversion" of work in general and (this is the important point) at every single workplace. The revolutionary proletariat will see to the rest on its own. Or it won't.

In the case of the French revolutionary crisis of May 1968, the proletariat rejected work in general but balked at radically transforming every single workplace. The Situationist International, as we have seen, took the position in the post-1968 period that workers' councils were just under the surface of the May "events," and that its members should continue to try to generate interest in them, so that workers' councils would, as it were, come to the surface of the next revolutionary crisis. What position did Castoriadis take on the councils in the post-1968 period? Did he continue to evolve (and so move beyond the situationists, who either remained stationary or regressed) or did he merely continue to devolve into revolutionary nothingness? The former: he evolved.

To be an advocate of "the councils" and their "power" presupposes that one believes that work in general and every single workplace (taken together) is at the very heart of human society, of what it means to be human. "To say that a workers' council will be an organ of popular self-administration (and not just an organ of workers' management of production)," Castoriadis wrote in July 1957, "is to recognize that a factory or office is not just a productive unit, but is also a social cell, and that it will become the primary locus of the individual 'socialization.'" It is precisely because councilists place the primary locus of socialization in work and in the workplace that they believe it is so important that the power of the workers' councils be complete and unchallenged by bureaucrats and capitalists on this terrain. If work *isn't* the center of social life, then workers' councils quite obviously cannot be truly revolutionary organizations, no matter how or why they are established.

According to Castoriadis, writing in a 1972 "General Introduction" to his S. ou B. essays, the "generalized contestation" or the generalization of "the revolutionary problem" to "all spheres of social life" signified and set in motion by the world-wide revolutionary events of 1968 marks the end of the historical centrality of the traditional proletariat (the factory workers) as the privileged, sovereign and exclusive bearer of the revolutionary project. If "the proletariat" exists (and it most assuredly does), it includes within itself such exploited groups as youth, chronically unemployed urban populations, women, gays and lesbians, the mentally ill, drug addicts and prostitutes – as well as factory workers and other wage slaves that fit the traditional Marxist paradigm. It makes no sense at all to try to get these exploited groups to organize their workplaces in the form of councils: they have no workplaces! Or, rather, if they *do* have workplaces, they are clearly not the centers of their respective lives. We would go so far as to say that, in the wake of the revolts of the late 1960s, very few "real" (that is, traditionally defined) workers place their jobs, careers or workplaces at the center of their lives, and those who do position work in this fashion will no doubt be the least likely to be revolutionaries, militant workers or socialists.

Though Castoriadis does not suggest what new form of organization might be adequate to antibureaucratic and anticapitalist struggles in post-1968 society, he does give us a valid jumping off point. Back in July 1957 he wrote,

> To achieve the widest, the most meaningful direct democracy will require that all the economic, political and other structures of society

be based on local groups that are concrete collectivities, organic social units. Direct democracy certainly requires the physical presence of citizens in a given place, when decisions have to be made. But this is not enough. It also requires that these citizens form an organic community, that they live if possible in the same milieu, that they be familiar through their daily experience with the subject to be discussed and with the problems to be tackled.

Anyone for a socialist society organized by, for and at the local level by neighbors' councils?

NOT BORED! #26, November 1996

Kryptonite: McDonough on the Situationists

It is alleged by Thomas F. McDonough (in "Rereading Debord, Rereading the Situationists," his introduction to *Guy Debord and the Internationale situationniste: A Special Issue of October* [#79, Winter 1997]) that Ken Knabb's *Situationist International Anthology* is a prejudiced selection of texts. "The material [Knabb] selects consistently obscures cultural analyses in favor of political ones – to the extent that these two can be separated in Situationist writings," McDonough claims. "This extends as far as a selective editing of articles to deemphasize the S.I.'s abiding interest in issues of visual and literary culture." For McDonough, "the cumulative effect of Knabb's choices is to enforce a misleading construction of the S.I.'s history: because cultural politics are placed in a decidedly secondary position, the reader is free to see the Situationists as one of many anarchist 'groupuscules' formed in the wake of the leftist critique of the Stalinist French Communist Party (1956-58)."[1]

In a footnote to this crucial sentence, McDonough advises his readers to seek a "more accurate political contextualization of the S.I." in – among other works – an essay unfortunately entitled "Situationism," despite the fact that the situationists themselves clearly stated from the outset and many times thereafter that "there is no 'situationism' as doctrine." (In a testament to the poor quality of McDonough's own understanding of the situationist project and the generally poor quality of the essays he selected for inclusion – a noteworthy exception is the interview with Henri Lefebvre – two of the "critical" essays in his volume refer to "situationism" as if this were quite simply the critical theory expounded by the situationists.)

Though McDonough's got Ken Knabb's number, he is dead wrong about the situationists. According to him, the reader who sees the SI "as one of many anarchist 'groupuscules' formed in the wake of the leftist critique of the Stalinist

French Communist Party" is only partly right, certainly misled, possibly even duped. *The Situationists can never simply be one of many groups, especially if these groups are anarchist.* And why the fuck not, Tom? *Because if they are only one among many, the situationists are not absolutely unique, and, if they're not absolutely unique, they cannot be "special."* It depends on what you mean by "special," doesn't it? *Something is "special" if I can act as if I personally discovered it, if I can claim that I have a unique relationship to it, and if, in claiming that no one else can possibly understand it like I do, it communicates to me something of its mystique, power and glamour.* I can see why anarchist groups are never "special" for you. *You got it: no one can act as if he or she discovered them, has a unique relationship to them, or understands them like no one else. The mystique, power and glamour just aren't transferable.*

So as to preserve his and his colleagues' vampiric access to the image of the Situationist International, McDonough – supposedly in the interests of the reader – must intervene in such a way as to prevent or discourage this reader from taking undue liberties or being too "free" in his or her vision of the SI. This anarchism stuff has got to be put in check. *The Situationists weren't merely or simply anarchists: they were primarily Artists, Avant-Gardists, Modernists, Cultural Revolutionaries, and Critical Theorists!* Consequently, only specialists in these fields – such as yourself and your academic colleagues – are their rightful legatees and proper heirs, right Tom? *Right! And the thing we as their rightful legatees and proper heirs should be doing right now is . . . historicize!* Not risking your professional reputations and futures by forming anarchist groupuscules appropriate to today, right? *Right! Now you got it.*

Restoring "cultural politics" ("issues of visual and literary culture") to its rightful place in the history of the SI – while making sure to keep anarchist politics in its proper place – does more than simply permit academics such as McDonough to further their careers by writing about and endlessly "rereading" Debord and all those other situationists. As Tim Clark and Donald Nicholson-Smith point out in "Why Art Can't Kill the Situationist International" (their fierce contribution to this otherwise meek and crappy little volume), those who would de-emphasize or even dismiss the importance of what the various members of the SI said in the 1962 to 1967 period about completely political subjects – such as the Algerian War, the Six Day War, the Chinese Cultural Revolution, and the riots in Watts – are trying to hide the fact that A). back in the 1960s they themselves were Stalinists of one stripe or another, and so were incapable of producing such "disabused and passionate" classics of Marxist analysis, and B). even today they are unable to produce good, coherent analytical work about current events or past events, for that matter.

The reason why art can't kill the Situationist International is that, in Clark and Nicholson-Smith's words, "it was the Left (as opposed to, say, the art world) that the Situationists most hated in the 1960s." To the SI, "the overwhelming reality was Stalinism: the damage and horror it had given rise to, and its capacity to reproduce itself, in ever newer and technically more plausible forms, within a Left that had never faced its own complicity or infection." If you take certain situationist concepts and "return" them to their presumed source in modern art, you won't kill the Situationist Superman – Clark's own book *The Painting of Modern Life* (1986) has already proved this to be true.

Are you tired of ineffective recuperations? Do you really want to know how to kill the SI? The kryptonite radiates out from the pictures that appear sprinkled throughout Clark and Nicholson-Smith's piece: "Toppled [statue of] Alexander III" (Moscow, 1917); "Dedication of statue of Heinrich Heine" (Petrograd, 1918); "Toppled Stalin" (Budapest, October 23, 1956); "Toppled Lenin" (Vilnius, August 30, 1991); "Toppled Dzerzhinsky" (Moscow, KGB headquarters, August 22, 1991); and, finally, "Anarcho-Situationist 'commandos' installing a replica of Charles Fourier's statue on a plinth left empty since the removal of the original by the Nazis" (Paris, Place Clichy, March 10, 1969). Bring all of humanity to life – that is the only way to kill the SI. Once wide-awake and truly alive, we will have no need for Great Men, no matter who they are. They do not make History. We do.

[1] McDonough is absolutely right about Ken Knabb. His *SI Anthology* is, in Knabb's own words, "admittedly weighted somewhat toward the situationists' later, more 'political' period," because, were it not for the existence of this later period, "no one but a few specialists in obscure avant-garde movements would have ever heard of them." Knabb the editor has no qualms about dropping out significant passages that do not suit his narrow, immediate needs – provided, of course, that proper ellipses mark the spots where text used to be.

For example, in *Public Secrets: Collected Skirmishes of Ken Knabb: 1970-1997*, Knabb reprints some of our text "Ken Knabb, R.I.P." (originally published in *NOT BORED!* #19, June 1991) in the section of his book devoted to "Selected Responses" to his work. In this text, we discussed Knabb's "The War and the Spectacle," which begins with the line, "The orchestration of the Gulf War was a glaring expression of what the situationists call the spectacle – the development of modern society to the point where images dominate life." In its entirety, our response to this opening salvo was as follows.

> Not only is the tone [here] appropriate to grade schoolers, and not only is the definition of what 'the spectacle' is simplistic, but the whole concept seems to be that recent events prove that the situationists were right. *It's always a drag when someone reverses things and has the practice prove the theory right (instead of having the theory prove the practice right), but especially where the situationists are concerned. Like they really need to have their theory proved right, again? and at this stage of things?* Rest in peace, Ken: the situationists were indeed right. And so, in a way, are you when you write, 'The point is to undermine [the spectacle-spectator relation]

– to challenge the conditioning that makes people susceptible to media manipulation in the first place.' But how?

In Knabb's version, the two sentences printed in italics are replaced by an ellipsis. The effect of this deletion is to remove all irony from the lines that conclude the text. Instead of ridiculing the importance attached to being right, our text seems to simply praise the situationists for being right, once again. Instead of expressing frustration with Knabb's refusal to focus on specific methods of contesting the spectacle as it exists today (he prefers to focus on the situationists and the theory that they "perfected" so many years ago), our final question seems to indicate that we are clueless and that we need specialists like Knabb to answer such questions for us.

It is significant that Knabb is unable to deal with the issues that we raised about the situationists being "right" without resorting to a complete suppression of them. (Read p. 150 of his new book and note well that Knabb is able to deal directly with points we raised in "Ken Knabb, R.I.P." provided that 1) they are minor points dealt with in parenthetical remarks, such as why it took him months to write, publish and distribute "The War and the Spectacle," which is both short and thin, and 2) he doesn't have to mention us by name and thereby give us the kind of publicity of which he no doubt considers us to be undeserving.) We dared to question Knabb's attachment to the always-right theories of Great Men such as Debord, Sanguinetti, Voyer, et al., and he responded by trying to deny us acknowledgment for what we have written and tried to do on our own.

NOT BORED! #27, May 1997

Len Bracken's *Guy Debord: Revolutionary*

Len Bracken's *Guy Debord: Revolutionary* (Feral House, 1997) is a competent, clearly written "critical biography" by a writer who is sympathetic to his subject and tells his story without prejudice, jargon, or rumor-mongering. Thanks to its strict reliance on a chronological narrative structure, which moves from "The Formative Years (1931-1957)" to "The Situationist Years (1958-1972)," and ends with "The Clandestine Years (1973-1994)," the development of the book is easy to follow. Two-hundred-and-sixty-six pages long, it is handsomely designed, well illustrated, and well-made. It contains a bibliography, an index, and relatively few typos. Most notably, the book includes as an appendix the entirety of a never-before-translated text by Debord, i.e., "The Game of War" (1987), which describes the rules of a 19th century-style board game (*kriegspiel*) that Debord invented. Scattered throughout the book are several previously untranslated texts, including letters, articles for *Potlatch*, taped lectures and tracts by Debord, parts of Debord's 1993 book *This Bad Reputation* and *Guy Debord: His Life and His Art* (Cornand's TV documentary), articles by Isidore Isou, letters by Gil Wolman, excerpts from Debord & Jorn's *Memoires*, flyers for LI exhibits, etc etc. There's even a picture of Raoul Vaneigem.

Though *Guy Debord: Revolutionary* includes material by Debord that has been translated into English for the first time, the book tells us nothing new about him – nothing, that is, that attentive readers of Debord's published works didn't already know. And that isn't very much: Debord said very little about himself, even in his putative autobiography, *Panegyrique*. And so the only "place" to go, if you want to compose a biography of Debord, would be to the people who knew him well. People like Alice Becker-Ho, his widow; Michelle Bernstein, his ex-wife; and Raoul Vaneigem, Rene Riesel, and Rene Vienet, the members of the Situationist International with whom he collaborated. Right? This is what Greil Marcus did before he wrote *Lipstick Traces* (1989); it is the interviews with people like Henri Lefebrve, Alexander Trocchi, Gil Wolman and Michele Bernstein that make Marcus's portraits of Guy Debord so vivid and compelling, and that makes Marcus's book such good reading and good research. (In the years since *Lipstick Traces* was published, Lefebvre, Trocchi, Wolman and Debord, of course, have died.)

Bracken evidently had access to people in Europe (principally Jean-Noel Clement, as well as the International Institute of Social History in Amsterdam and the Silkeborg Kunstmuseum in Denmark) who had and granted him access to never-before-translated texts. (Bracken says nothing about his methodology.) But no one of any consequence is interviewed in his book. Perhaps the surviving ex-members of the Lettrist and Situationist Internationals refused to be interviewed by Bracken; perhaps no one Bracken came in contact with knew Debord personally; or perhaps Bracken never saw the necessity of interviewing human beings, as well as reading and interpreting cultural artifacts, for *Guy Debord: Revolutionary*. It appears that no one was "looked up in the phone book" – both Greil Marcus and Tim Clark live in Berkeley, California; Bruce Elwell and Donald Nicholson-Smith live in New York City; Raoul Vaneigem lives in Brussels; etc. etc. – and interviewed "just for this book."

As a result, all of the first-person accounts of what Debord was really like as a person, that is, outside of the carefully constructed portraits of himself that he placed in his writings and films – the interviews with and quotes from Henri Lefebvre, Michelle Bernstein, and Alex Trocchi – were originally recorded and published by other writers, in particular Greil Marcus, from whose book Bracken also borrowed over half-a-dozen pictures of Debord and his closest associates. (And yet Bracken nevertheless directs confused criticism towards Marcus!) Because Bracken's portraits of Debord-the-person are composed of collages of pre-recorded material, they have a cheap, second-hand quality, and the book that contains them has a closed, claustrophobic feel. Debord never "lives" in the pages of Bracken's book. All Debord does here is create cultural artifacts that, when broken into pieces that are then arranged chronologically, *seem* to say something meaningful about the uniqueness of the personal life of their creator, but don't really.

Proudly advertised as "the first biography [of Debord] in any language," Bracken's book may quickly become obsolete. It doesn't include key material published before it came out, such as Kristen Ross's 1983 interview with Henri Lefebvre, which was finally published in *October*'s Winter 1997 special issue on Debord and the situationists, or Pierre Guillaume's recently translated 1995 article about Debord, which claims that Debord collaborated with the spectacle by remaining silent about the suppression of the writings of the historical revisionist Robert Faurisson. Indeed, Bracken's book contains *nothing at all* about the ongoing and alarming appropriation of Debord by the Far Right in France. (See for example Laurent Dandrieu's "Debord derriere le miroir," published in the May 1996 issue of *Le Spectacle du Monde* and Charles Champetier's "Debord est mort . . . vive Debord!" published in *elements* #82. At the conclusion of the latter essay, there appears a situationist-style detourned comic strip. A small man, apparently captured, says, "I come to learn the death of Debord. With him ends the history of the last avant-garde of the century!" He is answered by a man who appears to be in control of the situation. "End of the revolution! The place is finally free for a humanist and managerial Left, which allies liberal efficiency and social justice." The captured man raises his fist and says in reply, "Poor cunt! You have not realized that the New Right henceforth embodies the only way to have done with the market and the spectacle!")

Debord's *Panegyrique II* will be published in France soon, though it is unlikely that it will help any biographer's efforts. Perhaps someone who can interview the people who were close to Debord will write a real, personal biography of Guy Debord – if such a thing is actually needed in the first place. (A biography of Debord seems oxymoronic, an exercise in futility.) But until a real biography appears or is translated from whatever language it is written in (French, Italian or Spanish), Len Bracken's *Guy Debord: Revolutionary* is a novelty; it will be "in demand," talked about by all the right people, assigned a role to play in the spectacle. It will surely garner some positive reviews in the American bourgeois print media. It may even be assigned reading by professors who would teach *The Society of the Spectacle* in their classes. But it won't make anyone *feel* what Debord felt, namely, the necessity of social revolution.

NOT BORED! #28, December 1997

Book reviews
Exhibition of works by Jamie Reid

Peace is Tough – a touring exhibition of works by the graphic artist Jamie Reid, best known for his pioneering work for the punk band the Sex Pistols – came to Artificial, a gallery in New York City, for a few weeks in September and October 1997. (After leaving New York, the exhibit was bound for Tokyo and then Europe.) I found it necessary to see the exhibit twice, and to stay for a long time each visit, to fully appreciate its depth and diversity. The exhibit contained (in chronological order) the following:

1) about a dozen images from *The Suburban Press,* the clearly situationist-influenced zine Reid published between 1970 and 1974, and *Leaving The Twentieth Century,* the first anthology of writings by the situationists ever published in English (it was a 1974 collaboration between Reid and ex-situationist Christopher Gray). One of the best and yet rarely reproduced pieces from this period is entitled "Towards an Architecture of the Impossible"; it both reads and looks like a publication by the utopian radicals of the Lettrist International. Another superb and exuberantly situationist-influenced image from this period is a collage of bits of images depicting all the dreary things that concern us in our everyday lives (food, work, cars, money, and the city). This collage is very dense at the bottom, but lighter and made up of images of the sun, birds, airplanes in flight and other images of Utopia, even the word "hope," at the top;

2) a ton of Sex Pistols things, including a selection of huge, colorful, and exquisitely printed reproductions of several of the classic Pistols images from 1976 and 1977 (a steal at $350 each!); about a dozen original not-for-sale Sex Pistols graphics, most of which have been widely reproduced and were familiar to me, some of which were not (including an old record sleeve for Mexican pistolero music upon which Reid had put cutout block letters that spelled out "Los Pistoleros del Sexo"); and three huge wooden panels from the early 1980s upon which Reid made collages of all kinds of materials, both original and reproduced, concerning the band, their songs and their career (these materials included a Glitterbest cheque made out for 2,500 pounds and signed by Malcolm McLaren that bounced when Reid tried to cash it in 1979);

3) about two dozen posters, record sleeves and other images Reid made between 1980 and the present for radical political causes, punk bands such as the Dead Kennedys, or shows of his own work or of the work of others, including the Situationist International (Reid designed the poster advertising the 1989 Institute of Contemporary Art show in London, a gesture which seems to confirm others' claims that the situationists were a big influence on Reid and consequently the Sex Pistols). One of the most significant of the miscellaneous images – it was the one selected by Reid to go on the posters advertising *Peace is Tough* – was originally designed as the jacket art for Greil Marcus' book of writings on punk (originally

entitled *In the Fascist Bathroom* but changed to *Ranters, Ravers and Crowd Pleasers* by a cowardly publishing house). Reid's artwork – which includes a picture of John Wayne upon which Reid placed lipstick (a reference to Greil's book, *Lipstick Traces,* which is about the situationists' influence on the Sex Pistols) and a button saying "Peace is Tough" – was dumped along with the original title; and

4) about two dozen traditional-looking and very hippie-ish paintings, posters and printed tapestries that depict Celtic, mystical and other "shamanarchistic" visions (Reid is a spiritual-minded Welsh). I suppose it is terribly ironic that one of Reid's images (it was included in the show) proclaims "Never trust a hippie!" but I'd much prefer Reid's "backsliding" into hippie-ish mysticism to the Sex Pistols' head-long rush into cultural insignificance. The simple reason for this is that hippie-ish mysticism has enabled Reid to do something that neither John Lydon nor Malcolm McLaren has done since the 1980s, which is stay in meaningful touch with the politically engaged musical subcurrents that trace their inspiration (if not their sound, look or style) to punk. Reid is an avid fan of and has worked with several European electronic dance bands.

Not only did the *Peace is Tough* exhibit provide a lot to look at and a lot to think about – for example, can the ideas of the situationists be used again to produce effects as explosive as those produced by the "situationist punk band" called the Sex Pistols? is there really a relationship between shamanism and anarchy? – but the exhibit's curator arranged the items mentioned above within the existing space of the gallery in a very satisfying way. Perhaps a better way of saying this would be that the gallery space itself is rich with possibilities, and that the curator of the exhibit utilized the space well when the exhibit was installed. All the Sex Pistols stuff was exhibited on the ground floor, which is a typical gallery space with high-ceilings, white walls and white lights. While the shamanarchy stuff was evenly distributed between the ground floor and the basement, all of the pre-Sex Pistols stuff and all of the miscellaneous post-1980 political stuff was in the basement. Made out of brick, cozy, smaller and much less brightly lit than the main space, and filled with little pockets in which you could sit down and linger for a while, the basement would have been fun to hang out in even if it wasn't filled with great art work! The total effect of the arrangement was that you were hit with the Sex Pistols stuff as soon as you walked in the door, and so you got "it" – the Sex Pistols TWENTY YEARS LATER – over with right away. If you stayed long enough to realize that there was a whole second floor of stuff downstairs (not every visitor did, and so some got a literally superficial view of the exhibit), you could descend into and move around in the "underground" source and inspiration for Reid's work for the Sex Pistols. It sounds corny, but the psychogeographical effect was undeniable.

Underneath, say, a 1993 poster in which Reid pasted the phrase "DAMN THEM ALL" over pictures of British royalty from Henry VIII to Diana of Wales and Queen Elizabeth – the "damn them all" phrase refers to and extends the infamous Sex Pistols detournement of GOD SAVE THE QUEEN – you could sit in a comfortable and yet slightly disorienting space, and collect your thoughts and impressions, relatively undisturbed, for as long as wanted. Few visitors did. Most of them had wandered into the gallery because of its location in the trendy "SoHo" neighborhood, not because they knew Reid's work and had heard about the exhibit (it was pretty poorly advertised); most visitors moved through the wine cellar-like basement space quickly and efficiently, without sitting down. In all the hours I sat there on two different days, no one joined me. There were passersby, of course; but no one sat down and stayed on their own. The *absence* of a social scene within the gallery was telling, even appropriate to the exhibit itself.

In those hours in that space, I mostly pondered something that Jamie Reid himself said in an interview segment in a videotape that played on the ground floor of the exhibit. He said – or, if you will, he re-iterated the classic situationist theme – that the challenge to the modern artist is not to create, but to use what has already been created. This would seem to be a reduction or a narrowing of the scope of modern art, but it isn't. To find a way of using what has already been created – and there is a lot of all kinds of things that have been and continue to be created by this wasteful society – to say something that is really new, you have to widen your field of awareness to the point that you can see what is NOT being done, and what COULD BE done, with these creations. This clearly isn't easy. What makes Jamie Reid a great artist is that he sees what could be done, but isn't being done, with both the images and the productive forces that made these images possible. Lesser artists see the aesthetic usefulness of appropriating mass-produced images and the techniques of juxtaposition and collage, or they see that the proliferation of images in contemporary society says something about this society's fundamental possibilities and limits, but they don't bring these two visions together into a single coherent perspective in the way that Jamie Reid does. By consistently making emotionally compelling and socially relevant art out of such unlikely and potentially hackneyed things as collages of appropriated images, Jamie Reid dares his viewers to believe that constructing an architecture of the impossible is not only desirable, but possible as well.

NOT BORED! #28, December 1997

The Beginning of the End: France, May 1968

Enrages and Situationists in the Occupation Movement, France, May '68 – the Situationist International's official statement on the 1968 revolution – begins with the following quotation from Hegel's *Reason in History*.

> Concerning original history. . . . The content of these histories is necessarily limited; their essential material is that which is living in the experience of the historian himself and in the current interests of men; that which is living and contemporary in their milieu. The author describes that in which he has participated, or at least that which he has lived; relatively short periods, figures of individual men and their deeds. . . . It is not sufficient to have been the contemporary of the events described, or to be well-informed about them. The author *must* belong to the class and social milieu of the actors he is describing; their opinions, way of thought and culture *must* be the same as his own. In order to really know phenomena and see them in their real context, one *must* be placed at the summit – not seeing them from below, through the keyhole of morality or any other wisdom [emphasis added].

These formulations *must* be faulty, or, rather, they *must* have been overtaken and left behind by "reason in history," because *Enrages and Situationists in the Occupation Movement, France, May '68* is simply not at the level of Hegel's writings on history, despite the fact that it, like *Reason in History,* is a first-hand, insider's account, written by a participant and eyewitness.

Or so it appears now in 1998, after reading the new edition of Aneglo Quattrocchi and Tom Nairn's thrilling *The Beginning of the End*, which is certainly the best book on May 1968 that I have ever read. (Originally published by Panther Books, it has been reprinted by Verso.) Though both Quattrocchi and Nairn were well-informed contemporaries of the events described, only Quattrocchi was an active participant or an "actor" in the Hegelian sense. Nairn was not an eyewitness to the events: he was living in London at the time. Quattrocchi wrote his half of the book as a series of dispatches to his friend, Nairn, whom he had met years before. But Quattrocchi was Italian, not French, and this would seem to present a problem, if not concerning his ability to fully understand this very French revolution, then at least concerning the strict standards established by Hegel in *Reason in History*.

There is substantial irony in the fact that *The Beginning of the End* is a better book than *Enrages and Situationists in the Occupation Movement, France, May '68,* and this irony was most definitely not lost on "Uncle Bob," who designed the cover for the new Verso edition of the book. The cover photograph, which is attributed to AKG London/Paul Almasy, captures a moment in the life of the occupied Sorbonne. In the background, there are slogans spraypainted on the walls of a university building; in the middleground and towards the right, a handful of short-haired students (they are all male) sit on the steps and read newspapers; in the foreground and towards the left, a young man with long hair stands and reads a copy of (wait for it) *Internationale Situationniste.*

It is a truly arresting picture, almost too good to be true. For a moment you think the photograph must have been altered, in the way the situationists routinely "detourned" photographs to get them to express their real, hidden meanings. But the photo isn't altered: it is *reality* that has been altered; this photo simply captures a moment in the existence of that altered reality. The photo shows the degree of "penetration" of situationist texts into the radical student milieu, and more: it unintentionally captures a juxtaposition very similar to the one caught in the photograph reproduced on page 31 of the Rebel Press/Autonomedia edition of *Enrages and Situationists*. The caption to the latter photograph reads: "The Enrage Rene Riesel (left), and 'media spokesman' Daniel Cohn-Bendit (right)." Echoing the sitting students with their newspapers (headlines refer to a "Danny the Red"), Cohn-Bendit has short hair, and wears a blazer and a button-down shirt. Echoing the standing, longhaired student with his copy of the *I.S.*, Riesel has long hair, and wears sunglasses and a leather jacket (he looks like a Velvet Underground-era John Cale). "The difference in style, to which Vienet here refers," the editor of the Rebel Press/Autonomedia volume says in a clumsy note to the caption, "is here obvious."

And so "Uncle Bob" and the folks at Verso are having a little fun here. The photograph of the Parisian student with a copy of *I.S.* in his hands probably was not part of the book's original 1968 design, but *should have been*. This bit of fun was enough for me to buy this slender book, even though it retails for $15. But the fun doesn't last for long. For some reason, the photograph – though appropriate to the book's subject matter and content – just doesn't fit as the book's cover. It keeps peeling off, leaving a space, some kind of split, which won't close up.

The split is the fact that *The Beginning of the End* is divided into a poetic section (Quattrocchi's "What Happened," written in the form of a lyrical prose poem) and an analytical section (Nairn's "Why It Happened," written in the form of a scholarly essay). Though the content of Quattrocchi & Nairn's book concerns the explicit, practical supersession of the split between Art (poetic renderings of raw experience) and Politics (analyses of the causes of uprisings), its form re-enacts or reproduces that very split. There is nothing dialectical about this irony, this contradiction between the book's content and form. It is the simple result of the desire to get a book – any book – about May 1968 into print as fast as possible.

The split in the book – the difference between the photograph and its role as bookcover – is also the fact that neither Angelo Quattrocchi nor Tom Nairn seem to know very much about the Situationist International, the group that dedicated itself to the dialectical suppression and realization of Art and Politics, and that was quite active in the May revolution. For example, when Quattrocchi takes stock of "the extremists" active in Nanterre in March 1968, his list includes "a handful of Maoists, trotskyists, anarchists, situationists; yes, and even Cohn-Bendit," when in fact *no* situationists were active in Nanterre during this period. (It was only after May 1968 that the Nanterre Enrages joined the SI.)

Nairn fares little better. In referring to the circumstances of the publication of *On the Poverty of Student Life,* Nairn writes that in 1966 "a Situationist group got itself elected to the students' union of Strasbourg, and proceeded to dissolve the union," when in fact there was no situationist "group" at the University of

Strasbourg at the time. Elsewhere, Nairn mentions in passing "the Situationist theme of '*la societe du spectacle*' (modern society seen as already mainly devoted to the production of 'scenes,' appearances rather than things)":

> This concern [with "the whole subject-matter of communication and language"] extends from the spectacular manifestation of McLuhanism, on the one hand (a general theory of history as determined by modes of communication), and the Situationist theme of "*la societe du spectacle*" (modern society seen as already mainly devoted to the production of 'scenes,' appearances rather than things), to the abstruse theories of French structuralism, on the other.

As Nairn's tortured phrasing unintentionally makes clear, the apparently untranslatable "theme" of the society of the spectacle doesn't belong among such compromised and degraded company. Unlike both McLuhan and the structuralists, the situationists were active revolutionaries who weren't simply interested in the "subject-matter of communication and language." The concept of the society of the spectacle was for the SI a weapon of combat against modern society, not a way of acclimating oneself to it or a way of interpreting its history.

And so, it was for these reasons – one can only suppose – that Guy Debord referred to *The Beginning of the End* as "an unconsciously situationist text." (This "blurb" appears on the book's back cover, and is not included or referred to anywhere else in the 1998 edition.) Quattrocchi & Nairn's book doesn't know that it is in fact a situationist book; it thinks that it is something else (an anarchist book); it hasn't yet risen to the level of (self)-consciousness one calls "situationist" – it is difficult to know exactly what Debord meant by this phrase, which someone has turned into a blurb on a book jacket.

But this much is clear: *Enrages and Situationists in the Occupation Movement, France, May '68* was intended to be a consciously situationist book about May 1968. What does this mean? It means that the book was written by Situationists. (It has come out recently that Vienet didn't write the book on his own, but that he co-wrote it with Raoul Vaneigem, Mustapha Khayati and Rene Riesel.) It means that the book is primarily about the role(s) played by the Enrages and Situationists, and only secondarily about the occupation movement itself. It means that the book contains precisely what *The Beginning of the End* and so many other books on May 1968 does not contain: namely, accurate and plentiful information about the Situationists and their role(s) in the movement.

Unlike Quattrocchi & Nairn's book, *Enrages and Situationists in the Occupation Movement, France, May '68* – which was also assembled and published as quickly as possible (indeed, it was published a few months before *The Beginning of the End* came out) – is not internally divided into "Poetry" and "Politics." But this does not mean that this consciously situationist book manages to suppress and realize the separation between Art and Politics. Art is simply dispensed with: *Enrages and Situationists* is simply one long scholarly essay, enriched by the inclusion of an appendix of primary-source documents. That is to say, "Poetry" is not one of the strategies employed by the writers of this putatively situationist book: "poetry" appears inside of it, but the book itself is not poetic.

At the level of political analysis, Nairn's "Why it happened" is able to hold its own when compared to *Enrages and Situationists,* especially because the latter is so quick to dismiss the importance of the Fifth Republic in the origin of the agitation in France. "The Gaullist regime in itself had no particular importance in the origin of the crisis," the situationists state; "Gaullism is nothing but a bourgeois regime working at the modernization of capitalism, in much the same fashion as Wilson's Labor Party is" in England. As Nairn points out, such a perspective is unable to answer the crucial question, "Why did the May revolution occur in Paris, rather than anywhere else – rather than in Italy, for instance, where student revolt was more militant and on a larger scale?" To ask this question is also to ask, "Do the local circumstances of [the May revolution's] origin prevent one from considering it as a model for other times and places?" Something made de Gaulle's France – rather than Colombo's Italy or Wilson's England – "the most unlivable corner of the western world, when for so long it had been the most comfortable" (to quote Nairn again).

Nairn's answer to this riddle is that, "of all relevant and comparable nations, France was the one with the least 'control' of any kind from below."

> [France] was almost totally deprived of living democracy [...] Because the Fifth Republic was very much of a vacuum in this sense, clearly any resolute effort to grab some kind of 'participation' was more inherently explosive than elsewhere. After all, the vacuum was not mere absence or accident. It was the intended structure of the Fifth, without which the compensation for the void, the General [de Gaulle], would not have agreed to emerge from the clouds again and assume power. But this peculiar emptiness of the regime [...] was the logical counterpart of its success, on another level.

This is a far more insightful analysis than that of the situationists, who state that only "two specific features" of the French situation should be noted in passing: "the Gaullist accession to power by plots and a military putsch, which marks the regime with a certain contempt for legality, and de Gaulle's personal cultivation of archaic prestige." For Nairn, de Gaulle's accession to power is unique because of the "never-healed conflict between the political traditions of the revolution of 1789 and the predominantly anti-revolutionary reality of France." It was France, Nairn writes, "which produced the most perfect, the classical order of bourgeois political democracy, thanks to the revolutionary energy of the Jacobin leadership of 1791 to 1795. But she proved thereafter chronically incapable of making this order function properly."

This inability to ensure the political order with a relative stability, as Nairn points out elsewhere in his essay, has upset and marked the French State far more seriously than similar crises have affected England or the United States. "To the revolutionary and democratic tradition of 1789, 1830, 1848 and 1871," Nairn writes, "one must oppose the hideous *serie noire* of Napoleon, the Restoration, Napoleon III, Boulanger, Petain, and de Gaulle." The contrast to England and the United States is quite pronounced. "While the British Constitution, that unclassical rag-bag of oddments, survived industrial revolution and innumerable wars," Nairn writes, "the French Constitutions which succeeded one another after the great revolution habitually collapsed at the slightest crisis." To Nairn, the unique contradiction in French society is "a certain weakness of development [that] stemmed from the Revolution itself, which was essentially political in nature, not economic (like the English industrial revolution proceeding at the same time), and bought its political success by compromise with rural backwardness." Precisely because the Fifth Republic, in addition to everything else, "was also a model of enlightened, technocratic neo-capitalism – not at all a sick man in the capitalist world," the fundamental contradictions in French society became so acute that an explosive, far-ranging and unprecedented crisis was inevitable. All that was necessary for the whole thing to burst into flames was the proper spark.

Everyone familiar with these discussions will know that the Situationist International – unlike all the other revolutionary groups and theorists active in the 1950s and the early 1960s – was so confident in the inevitability of political revolution in France that it based its entire programme and position in capitalist society on this certainty. But the uniqueness of the SI – indeed, the very reason we continue to give a shit about this obscure group, 30 years after its "heyday" – lay in the fact that it was committed to "losing" or realizing itself when the insurrection broke out. *"We will only organize the detonation,"* the SI wrote in 1963; "the free explosion must escape us and any other control forever." These are anarchist positions, at least in the sense that Tom Nairn uses this word in his essay; and the remarkable thing about the situationists was that – despite their explicit denunciation of anarchism – they acted like anarchists and let the free explosion of May 1968 "escape" them. That is to say, the Enrages and Situationists were active in the occupation movement, but they refused to lead it or speak for it at any time. They acted in their own name, as the Committee of the Enrages and the Situationist International, and – when the proverbial dust settled – they wrote, in their own name, about what they had done in their own name.

And yet *The Beginning of the End* is still a better book than *Enrages and Situationists in the Occupation Movement,* precisely because the former (Quattrocchi's prose poem, in particular) is strongest where the latter is weakest: on the events before the Sorbonne was occupied on 13 May 1968; that is to say, on the events that led up to the detonation. The situationists only devote two chapters – a mere 26 pages out of a total of 110 – to these salient events, while Quattrocchi devotes half of his prose poem to them. But it is, of course, not only the quantity but also the quality of what Quattrocchi has to say about the two weeks immediately prior to the free explosion that makes his writing on 1968 superior to that of the situationists.

I am not arguing that Quattrocchi is a better writer or prose poet than the writers of *Enrages and Situationists in the Occupation Movement*. This is not be a matter of style, or, rather, it is not primarily be a matter of style or poetic expression. This is in fact a matter of content, of the quality and quantity of useful information contained in these two works about May 1968. This is not a matter of the relative superiority of first-hand accounts to second-hand accounts. It is a matter of the "details" that eyewitnesses and even participants choose to focus on in their writings.

To the situationists, the police were not a factor in the detonation, or, rather, they were part of it only insofar as they were a reaction to it.

[On 3 May 1998, the situationists write] the police and the *gendarmerie mobile* invaded the courtyard of the Sorbonne without meeting resistance. The students were encircled. The police then offered them free passage out of the courtyard. The students accepted and the first to leave were in fact allowed to pass. The operation took time and other students began to gather outside in the [Latin] quarter. The remaining two hundred demonstrators inside the Sorbonne, including all the organizers, were arrested. As the police vans carried them away, the Latin Quarter erupted. One of the two vans never reached its destination. Only three policemen guarded the second van. They were beaten up, and several dozen demonstrators escaped. It was the first time in many years that several thousand students in Paris had fought the police for so long and with such energy. Endless charges, greeted with hails of paving stones, failed to clear the Boulevard Saint-Michel and the adjoining streets until several hours later. Some six hundred people were arrested [...] The whole of May 6th was marked by demonstrations which turned into riots early in the afternoon. The first barricades were thrown up at the Place Maubert and defended for three hours. At the same time, fights with the police were breaking out at the bottom of the Boulevard Saint-Michel, at the Place du Chatelet, and in Les Halles [...] Insofar as the rioters were able to strengthen the barricades, and thus their own capacity for counterattack, the police were forced to abandon direct charges for a position strategy which relied mainly on offensive grenades and tear gas [...] The battle was very rough [on the night of 10 May]. The CRS, the police, and the *gendarmerie mobile* succeeded in making the barricades untenable by an intense bombardment of incendiary, offensive and chloride gas grenades, before they would risk taking them by assault. The rioters responded with paving stones and

Molotov cocktails [...] The police swept the quarter until noon, beating up and taking off anyone who looked suspicious.

The impression created by these remarks is strong: though numerous, the police are outnumbered; in general, the police seem weak; they generally restrict themselves to tear gas grenades, and don't kill anyone; indeed, it seems like the police are beaten up more often than the demonstrators are! If there is violence here, it is the revolutionary "energy" of the demonstrators; if there is frenzy here, it is the frenzy of demonstrators spontaneously turning into rioters.

The impression created by Angelo Quattrocchi's account is quite different:

Unwritten rules, the ones which can be unearthed in cryptograms of balance sheets and profit margins, silently and categorically state that rebellious workers must be faced by the army, and shot at. Agitating students are best dealt with by clubs and tear-gas. A threat is a threat, a nuisance is a nuisance. And the ruling society mustn't be caught in the act of murdering its own children. The consequent outcry would be more disruptive than the actual disturbance [...] And dawn [on the morning of 7 May] brings more fighting and the two water cannon trucks ready into position but vulnerable to the bravest *paves* which shatter the windscreen and make them retreat. It slowly gets quieter, exhaustion takes over, the *flics* [cops] are masters of a dark Latin Quarter, watching the corners, fearful of shadows, but ready to maim and hurt the isolated and beat the unaware and scare the 'civilians' who are just passing there [...] Two cafes are besieged [by the police] and filled with gas. Unmentionable acts of savagery are committed late at night on isolated people and small groups [...] The government doesn't know if it's better to open the Sorbonne and take away the *flics* or to continue the beating which is sharpening the consciences of those listing on their radios [...] The masters [of society] think the government and its police are stupid and dangerous. They have been instrumental in bringing about this revolution, this escalation. Here the police are armed with water cannons and clubs; they are stupid, dangerous, vicious, indiscriminate in who they beat up, in control of the situation and yet totally out-of-control, unmentionably savage, and instrumental in bringing about the detonation.

Police brutality – now *this* is an explanation that makes sense. "The local inhabitants [of Paris]," writes the anonymous author of *Paris: May 1968* (Solidarity pamphlet, June 1968), "saw what happened [on the night of 10 May 1968], the viciousness of the CRS charges, the assaults on the wounded, the attacks on innocent bystanders, the unleashed fury of the state machine against those who had challenged it." When the police beat up, arrest or kill your sons and daughters;

when the police beat up or arrest you ("A man in a bow tie is hit [by the water cannon] and rolls over the pavement" – Quattrocchi); when there appears in the sudden explosion "a taste of revenge for a struggling people who count their pennies" – *that* is when the detonation occurs, when the revolution begins. The detonation does not occur when "our ideas are in everyone's heads," as the situationists were fond of saying; the detonation occurs when the police's batons are on everyone's heads.

NOT BORED! #29, July 1998

Gianfranco Sanguinetti's *Veritable Report on the Last Chance to Save Capitalism in Italy*

Gianfranco Sanguinetti, an active member of the Italian section of the Situationist International from January 1969 to the SI's auto-dissolution in April 1972, is someone about whom we English-speakers know relatively little. We know that he was a close friend of and collaborator with Guy Debord, with whom he authored "Theses on the Situationist International and Its Time," the document that formally dissolved the SI, and that Sanguinetti helped produce Debord's important 1973 film *The Society of the Spectacle*. As English translations of *Section Italienne de L'Internationale Situationniste: Ecrits complets 1969-1972* (published in 1988 by Contre-Moule, Paris) become available, we will begin to know even more about Sanguinetti's contributions to the international situationist movement.

In August 1975, under the pseudonym Censor, Sanguinetti (with help from Debord) wrote, produced and distributed to 520 members of the ruling class a little-known pamphlet entitled *Rapporto verdico sulle opportunita di salvare il capitalismo in Italia*. Putatively written from the perspective of an educated, well-connected and ruthless member of Italy's economic elite, Censor's pamphlet announced its intention to be the saving of capitalism, not only in Italy but also all over the world. By October 1975, the printing of three more editions were necessary to satisfy the public's interest in this pamphlet. After it was hypocritically praised by the bourgeois press, Sanguinetti published *Prove dell 'inesistenza di Censor, enunciate dal suo autore* (December 1975), which revealed that *a situationist* was in fact its author. A major public scandal ensued.

As Sanguinetti reported in a preface to *On Terrorism and the State*, published in 1982 by Chronos Publications, the owners of the world and their salaried critics were exasperated and vexed at having to note that only their most indomitable enemies have the ability to really understand [the world]; and the ruling classes [saw], with justifiable anxiety, its veritable problems exposed only by these enemies, who work towards its subversion. Our ministers and all politicians [were] disturbed, not without reason, at having to read our writings in order to contemplate themselves with realism at last, but in the perspective of the destruction of their powers. The heads of the secret services of the bourgeoisie, appointed in the last ten years or so for the purpose of provocation, assassinations, and State terrorism, will understandably be infuriated at seeing their maneuvers constantly unmasked by those very people against whom they were always conceived.

In 1976, Debord translated both Censor's *Report* and Sanguinetti's January 1976 exposure of it as a fake into French, got them published as *Verdique rapport sur les dernieres chances de sauver le capitalisme en Italie* and defended Sanguinetti when he was refused entry to France. Censor's pamphlet remained a powerful influence on Debord's writing, including his 1979 "Preface to the 4th Italian edition of *The Society of the Spectacle*," and especially his *Comments on the Society of the Spectacle* (1988), despite the fact that he broke with Sanguinetti around 1980.

With the exception of an excerpt that was published in *Italy: Autonomedia: Post-political Politics* (Semiotext[e], 1980), Sanguinetti's pamphlet has never been translated into English. And so Flatlands Books is right to say that Len Bracken's new translation of the pamphlet under the title *The Real Report on the Last Chance to Save Capitalism in Italy* (1997) is the first ever in English. According to Bracken's August 1996 translator's forward, this new translation "is based on the original Italian (in consultation with M.C. Quilter, the translator of *Renzo Novatore*), and, primarily, the French translation by Guy Debord." In a remark that should alarm any intelligent reader, but especially readers of Bracken's *Guy Debord: Revolutionary*, he goes to say of Debord's translation, "Like many books, this one appears to have been bolstered through translation." One shudders at the idea that Bracken, who evidently does not speak Italian, tried to mimic Debord-the-translator and somehow "bolstered" Debord's translation of Sanguinetti's pamphlet.

It seems to us quite plainly inaccurate to translate either *verdico* or *verdique* as "real" (as opposed to "veritable"). (In their translation of the SI's book *La Veritable Scission dans L'Internationale* – which includes Debord & Sanguinetti's "Theses on the SI and Its Time" – Forsyth and Prigent translate *veritable* as "veritable.") Bracken's unconvincing explanation for deliberately botching part of the pamphlet's title: "It was decided that fewer syllables would make the title a little less daunting to the U.S. reading public." *Who* exactly decided to dumb down the title? Was it Bracken or not? With this senseless alteration, the title is 19 syllables long instead of 22. Wotta difference those three syllables make to the easily daunted American members of the English-speaking world!

Unfortunately, it appears that Bracken's approach to the pamphlet's title is also operative in his translation of the body of the text. Elsewhere in his foreword, he notes that "[Sanguinetti's] prose is not in the telegraphic style now favored in North America," and that "the words erupt and flow like molten rock, burning everything in their path and burying the lies of his times with the blazing truth." Here we are (again) in danger of being buried under a pile of Brackenish bullshit, for it is Bracken himself who prefers to use the "telegraphic style." You tell me which "flows" like molten rock and which is choppy and irregular – the Semiotexte[e] translation (done by Richard Gardner) or the Bracken translation?

Gardner, p. 93:

> And who better than the communists can today institute a period of convalescence in the country, during which the workers will have to stop fighting and resume working? Who, better than a Minister of the Interior like Giorgio Amendola, could weed out the delinquency which has spread to every level, and make the agitators shut up, by good methods, or not so good ones? We must undertake long-term governmental action, and to do so we must have a solid and resolute government: not accepting a 'compromise' like that in question today in reality signifies fatally compromising, for ourselves, the very existence of tomorrows. Let us remember that neutrality, in such an affair, is the daughter of irresolution, and that 'Irresolute princes, in order to flee present perils, most often follow this neutral path, and most often collapse.' (Machiavelli) In order not to see the real peril, we pretend to see an accord with the P.C.I. as a peril, and we flee them both.

Bracken, p. 75:

> And who better than the communists can now impose a period of convalescence on the country when the workers stop fighting and begin to work again? Who better than a Minister of the Interior like Giorgio Amendola could extirpate the spreading delinquency and silence the agitators by good, or less good, methods? What is necessary is government action for a long duration, and for this a solid and highly resolved government is required. Not to now accept the compromise in question actually signifies, for us, accepting to fatally compromise the existence of our tomorrows. We always remember that neutrality in such affairs is the daughter of irresolution, and that 'To banish a present danger, irresolute princes most often follow the

neutral path, and most often they lose themselves.' In order not to see the real peril, one pretends to view the accord with the PCI as a peril, and one banishes the peril before both of them.

Maybe this is quibbling. Maybe Bracken's translation – six choppy sentences instead of five flowing ones, in this instance – is "less good" than it could have been, but is good enough. . . . Until someone else, Gardner perhaps, publishes a better translation,[4] we are stuck with the one made by Len Bracken.

Too bad, because the *Report* itself, quite obviously, is a most unusual document: global in scope and yet subtle and nuanced. One is never quite sure how to contextualize what one is reading. Are we to concentrate on what we know to be the hypothetical existence of Censor and his desire to save capitalism, or on the real existence and revolutionary perspective of Sanguinetti, "standing behind" Censor and occasionally winking at us?

The *Report* works on at least four levels: as a situationist prank; as a critique of capitalism and its communist "adversary"; as a call to revolutionary action; and, most importantly, as an expose of terrorism conducted by the Italian State against its own people from 1969 to 1975.

We work in the absence of translations of reviews of Censor's pamphlet and responses to the announcement that Sanguinetti was in fact its author. (The Flatlands edition of Bracken's translation includes none of the latter and about a half-dozen of the former, but these are two-sentence-long excerpts from reviews of Censor's pamphlet, and are too short, arbitrarily chosen and arranged, and unrelated to each other to base any well-considered opinions upon them.) And so we are unable to say much about the pamphlet-as-prank, other than to observe that the text contains several barely concealed, in-joke references to the Situationist International, something about which someone like Censor might or might not have known. Appropriately enough, there is a sly reference to Debord's *Society of the Spectacle* – "over the last ten years in all the democratic countries, it seems intelligent censorship would only have had to been applied to three or four books," books that "should have disappeared completely using all possible means," but did not, books that "are susceptible to creating adepts over a long period, and, finally, disturbing our power." There is also a reference to Sanguinetti's own "Advice to the Proletariat on the Present Occasions for Social Revolution" (not yet translated into English), of which Censor claims to have seen a copy in the very midst of the worker riots in Milan on 19 November 1969.

Sanguinetti's *Report* contains a short exposition on "the characteristics and permanent effects" of the "development and expansion of economic power" that has "changed the face of the world much more than any revolution in the past." There are five distinctive traits of contemporary capitalism with which Censor

---

[4] In 2005, I personally translated the Censor pamphlet, as well as Sanguinetti's subsequent statement that he was its author and all related newspaper accounts published in French.

wishes his readers to become familiar:

1). the "quantitative and qualitative *progress of political lies* to a level of power that has never been seen in history." (Though political lies only serve the interests of the ruling class, Censor perceives a danger in relying upon them overmuch: "too often [the] results are not in accord with the higher interests of the whole of the economic order.")

2). "*a grandiose reinforcement of State power* as an increasingly sophisticated organism of surveillance."

3). "*the isolation, or better said, the separation of people has been highly perfected.*"

4) "an unprecedented growth in the power of the economy and of industry" to the point that "nothing exists that cannot be industrially produced, that is to say, that does not conform to the exigencies of profit."

5) "the vertiginous growth in the complication of the everyday intervention of human society on all aspects of the production of life, and its replacement of every natural element with a new factor that one could call artificial," which justifies and requires "the unmitigated power of every expert who erects and corrects the new economic and ecological equilibriums outside of which people can no longer live."

Readers of Guy Debord's *Comments on the Society of the Spectacle* (published in 1988) will find strong similarities between the five features of contemporary capitalism listed by Censor and the "five principal features" of what Debord calls "the society whose modernization has reached the stage of the integrated spectacle." For Debord, those features are 1) incessant technological renewal (which corresponds with #4 in Censor's list); 2) integration of state and economy (#2 in Censor's list); 3) generalized secrecy (#5 in Censor's list); 4) unanswerable lies (#1 in Censor's list); and 5) an eternal present (#3 in Censor's list).

Though an analysis of the influence of Sanguinetti's *Report* on Debord's *Comments* is too broad a topic to be adequately addressed here, we should note that this influence may account for the notoriously guarded tone and paranoid outlook of the latter book: Debord knew from the moment Censor revealed his true identity that the secret services in Italy (and perhaps France as well) would be paying *very* close attention to both of their activities and writings, if they were not doing so already. When Gerard Lebovici was murdered in 1984, the factual basis for Debord's paranoia in particular was brutally confirmed.

Censor's critique of the Italian Communist Party (the PCI) is practical, not theoretical: that is to say, he bases his remarks on what the PCI had actually done and not done, rather than on the PCI's "theories" or propaganda. "In France and Czechoslovakia, where the revolutionary movement was on the best footing," Censor asks, "who favored or imposed the return to normal in the factories and streets?" The "first lesson to be learned from these events" was that "in both cases it was the communists: in Paris thanks to the unions, and in Prague thanks to the

Red Army." According to Censor, "it was in the middle of 1969 that the Italian Communist Party was explicitly asked what guarantees it would offer the government to work with it to stop the [workers'] movement before autumn, and what they wanted in return." But because both the Christian Democrats (the politicians in power) and the PCI were mistaken in their respective calculations, a formal deal between them wasn't made at that time. However, as Censor reports, "the force of the Communist Party and unions has already been useful to us, and it has been our principle support since the autumn of 1969." (When Sanguinetti wrote and published his pamphlet, the possibility of a formal "historic compromise" between the Christian Democrats and the PCI was again in the offing, because the government still could not contain the continuing labor unrest in Italy.)

As a call to revolutionary action, the *Report* is very powerful, precisely because Sanguinetti has Censor speak more honestly about class society than any member of the elite ever has (at least in public). "From the point of view of the defense of our society, there only exists one danger: that workers succeed in speaking to each other about their condition and their aspirations *without intermediaries*," Censor writes. "All other dangers are secondary, or proceed directly from the precarious situation in which we place, in multiple respects, this unavowable problem." This sort of honest appraisal of both the "unavowable" problem and its solution – especially when the appraisal is celebrated by newspaper reviewers and other political commentators ignorant of the real identity of Censor – calls for equal honesty on the part of the workers. With the same ruthlessness shown by Censor, the workers must collectively and totally "deny the right to property" and "contest the necessity of work."

Precisely because the *Report* was a situationist prank, it no doubt made the undertaking of these projects in earnest seem like *fun*. "The *principal* irrationality of contemporary capitalism," Sanguinetti has Censor say, "is that it does not do all that it can do to defend itself from the dangerous attacks against it." All too true, especially when *the one who is ostensibly proposing that this irrationality be corrected, is actually taking the greatest advantage of it!* (It is perhaps fitting that we share a little laugh before approaching the most serious level upon which the *Report* works.)

In the deadly game of social poker known as class struggle, the *Report* called the Italian state's bluff. When the Italian state pretended that 1) starting in 1969 it did *not* perpetrate acts of terrorism against its own people, and 2) somebody else, perhaps an ultra-leftist or an ultra-rightest group (it need not matter which one), had in fact been the perpetrator of acts of terrorism such as the bombing of the Piazza Fontana in Milan on 12 December 1969, Sanguinetti knew that *the state was bluffing.* He knew as early as the end of 1969 – when he and the other members of the Italian section of the SI wrote and distributed "Il Reichstag Bruccia?" ("Is the Reichstag Burning?") – that the state's secret services were the real culprits, and he knew *why* they had been called into service in this fashion.

"It was necessary," Censor reports, "to launch a diversionary tactic during the summer [of 1969]: artificial tension, the principal goal of which was to *momentarily* distract public opinion from real tensions that are destroying the country." Elsewhere in the *Report,* Censor relates that,

> disoriented and shaken to a stupor by the number of innocent victims, the workers remained hypnotized by this unforeseen event, and were distracted by the rumors that followed [...] As if by magic, a strike movement that was so widespread and so prolonged forgot itself and stopped.

Thus, the initial bombings immediately achieved their desired effects. But precisely because after 1969 the Italian state *continued* to use the "strategy of tension," as it became known, its bluff could be called at any time. The genius of the card played in the *Report* is not so much the fact that it called the state's bluff, but the *confident manner* in which it did it.

Sanguinetti called the State's bluff by having Censor think, write and act as if it was *an established fact,* not a matter for speculation (among the members of the elite), that the secret services were responsible for the Milan bombing, and that this bombing was *desirable.* "We can see the undeniable, long term advantages of such a tactic," Sanguinetti has ruthless Censor say, "and [also] the harm it entails in transforming itself into strategy." And so – as far as Censor and the interests for which he speak are concerned – the problem with artificial tension was not its use as a tactic in 1969, but its continuing use as strategy in all of Italy since then. "We argue that the *theatrical killing* (the scenic protagonists of decadence and of its political chronicle in Italy) demonstrated the weakness of those who govern as much as it displayed the general desire to *change the scene,* intrigue and actors," Censor writes. "We will say it for once and for all, and clearly: the time has come to put an end to the uncontrollable use of this parallel action that is brutal, useless and dangerous for order itself."

The brilliance of Sanguinetti's use of tactics (his manner of calling the bluff) was that the State could neither answer it nor ignore it. To answer the call – either by folding (admitting that the State's secret services were indeed the perpetrators of the Milan bombing) or by showing its cards (admitting that the people that the State had prosecuted for the crime could not and did not commit it) – would be too risky in either case. Instead, the State chose to try to prosecute Sanguinetti for crimes he did not commit, thus forcing him into exile.

NOT BORED! #29, July 1998

Book reviews
Simon Sadler's *The Situationist City*

"[In the June Insurrection, Paris, 1848] they broke through walls so as to be able to pass from one house to another." – Sigmund Englander, 1864, *History of the French Workers' Association*.

Like Moliere's Monsieur Jourdain, who spoke prose without knowing it, Mr. Cohn Bendit and the other student radicals were situationists without quite realizing it. According to Guy Debord, around whom the fragile movement circled, "a situationist" is "one who engages in the construction of situations." When students turned the Boulevard St Michel into a lecture hall, or invited workers into the Sorbonne to set up workers' councils, they were being situationists. – *The Economist*, June 1998.

It's *not* a difficult image to visualize. But Simon Sadler, author of *The Situationist City* (The MIT Press, 1998; 232 pages; no color illustrations; $35 hardcover only), just can't bring this image into focus, despite the fact that he is a Postgraduate Researcher and Tutor in the Department of Art History at the Open University in Great Britain who pledges (in his own words) "allegiance to academic rigor and objectivity." He makes only two references to the May 1968 revolution in his entire book, and both of those references are glancing. In an academic book that pretends to concentrate on the Situationist International and its close attention to modern architecture and urban planning, this oversight – if that is what it is – is more than just glaring: it is *blinding*.

The first reference to the event around which the entire history of the SI (1957 to 1972) revolves appears buried in a paragraph about the mainstream and very uninteresting architectural group Team 10.

By 1967 [Shadrach] Woods was writing in a vein so radical that it might have been acceptable even to situationists. "Our weapons become sophisticated; our houses more and more brutish. Is that the balance sheet for the richest civilization since time began?" In 1968, the year of the political chaos that the situationists claimed to have sparked, Woods assisted students in the removal of his own work from the Milan Triennale.

If the situationists claimed to have "sparked" anything in particular – which they didn't – it would *not* have been the "political chaos" of that one year, 1968. The situationists were interested in neither politics nor chaos; their concerns, rather, were with general social revolution and the new organization of life to come. The

281

situationists had been engaged in anti-capitalist subversion ever since 1957, well before there was a student movement in France; and they continued to be active after 1968. More to the point: in 1968, while people like Shadrach Woods were *evacuating* their art work from places like the Milan Triennale, the situationists were *occupying* buildings such as the Sorbonne and the National Pedagogic Institute, and filling them with their art work (graffiti, posters, banners, et al).

Sadler's second and last reference to the events of 30 years ago appears at the beginning of his last chapter, entitled "Conclusions."

> The sort of doubts about planning and [architectural] modernism expressed by situationists have since met with spectacular consensus [...] Many city centers became dominated by leisure use. It was of course a commercial rather than an anarchic leisure, since larger situationist demands remained marginalized by capitalism – which always seemed likely to be the case, except perhaps for a few heady days in May 1968.

Sadler assumes that his readers know all about those "few heady days," and that he therefore doesn't need to say a thing about them, other than to observe that May 1968 might perhaps have been a striking exception to the normal functioning of advanced capitalism. Of course "larger situationist demands remained marginalized by capitalism": those larger demands concerned nothing other than the immediate *destruction* of international capitalism and its replacement by a superior form of social organization! Quite obviously, if May 1968 produced even a few heady days in which "larger" situationist demands were no longer marginalized, but were freely heard in the very center of society, *any* competent academic who pledges allegiance to the flag of rigorous and objective research would focus on May 1968, at least for one solid paragraph, if not for an entire chapter.

But Assistant Professor Simon Sadler will have none of it, and this marks him as an unapologetic defender of the capitalist system. His basic attitude towards capitalist society seems to be an echo of the argument made by "some members of Britain's Independent Group," namely, that "mass consumption and the capitalist spectacle were things that intellectuals would simply have to come to terms with if they were to appreciate the revolution taking place in the electric city." By "to come to terms with" Sadler obviously means "to accept without any further questioning."

Sadler's unstated but obvious assumption is that the 1990s are very much like the 1950s, which he characteristically describes as a "time when it was fashionable for avant-gardes to disengage from notions of social revolution." Sadler would have us believe that, by some swing or turnaround that he doesn't trouble himself with defining, exploring, or explaining, it became "fashionable" in the 1960s to be politically engaged, but that this new political engagement was fundamentally false, because it was just an empty echo of the 1920s,

> when artists, architects, and designers had pursued disparate, open-ended experiments; for a time when the conditions of modern life – above all, the relationship between "man and machine" – had been addressed head-on; [...] when fundamental shifts in thought, like those engineered by Marx, Freud and Nietzsche, still felt fresh and vital; and for a time when general revolution was regarded as necessary, even inevitable.

Sadler wants his readers to believe that the days of genuine revolution were already long-gone in 1968, when even the "peculiarly risque" and "seductive" Situationist International – which stood out in such marked contrast to all the Maoists, Stalinists, Leninists, and Trotskyists of the time – "seemed rather old-fashioned" because of its "preoccupation with class," its "belligerent class-consciousness." For Sadler, there is no point in talking about *any* of it in the 1990s – when all of Marxism itself is completely outdated; when international capitalism is triumphant; when general revolution is neither possible nor even desirable. "Though history denied us" – once and for all, Sadler makes it seem – "the opportunity to spend our leisure time wandering around situationist space," he writes, "we have been offered the chance to while away our free time in cyberspace, with its potential to produce a version of social space with even greater finesse than [the situationist Constant's] New Babylon."

The central paradox of *The Situationist City* is this: if class-conscious, general revolutionary movements were old-fashioned in the 1960s and are as dead as a door-nail in the 1990s, then why bother with the situationists at all? Why not throw the SI out along with the rest? Quite clearly, Sadler would love to do just that, for, in his eyes, the situationists were *idiots*. "It was almost by default, creditable to the eccentricity, complicity, and tenacity of psychogeographical technique" – and not to the situationist inventors of psychogeography, apparently – "that situationism yielded any worthwhile social geography," he writes. As for Debord:

> When [he] drew our attention to the wonders of the Metro map of Paris, and when he collaged into *Memoires* an old map of London's railway network, he might have been construed as offering some insight into the capital and social growth of cities. But he more likely enjoyed the way the drifting nets of track reminded him of psycho-emotional meanderings generally.

It is as if Debord were a precocious child or a monkey that can paint abstract images; a being incapable of even understanding such big words as "capital" and "social growth," which must only be used by fully qualified adult humans, who, of course, know what these words and images *really* mean.

To Sadler, the situationists were dangerous idiots, "anarchic" people to be neither trusted nor under-estimated, despite their child-like obsessions with games and play. "Like revolutionaries before them" – like *all* revolutionaries, it would appear – "situationists had no compunction about using the same tactics as the authorities that they rebelled against," Sadler writes. "Early situationism did indeed threaten to replace the totalitarian ideologies of capitalism and communism with a new totalitarian ideology of situationist play, enforced by peer pressure and the situationist appropriation of space." In a revealing phrase, Sadler writes metaphorically of "card-carrying members of the SI," but it is clear that he is trying to get his readers to believe that his metaphor is to be taken literally and seriously: the situationists, no matter what they said or even did to the contrary, were no different from the Communists.

And so Sadler – good defender of the capitalist order that he is – seizes upon every opportunity available to him to slander, insult, ridicule or dismiss the situationists. According to Sadler, who loves to dispense his "objective" value-judgments while playing the role of psychologist, the situationists "seem to have had difficulties getting on with 'everyday' citizens"; they were "among the most megalomaniac heirs of *urbanism*"; their "encounters with the ghetto could be immature or deliberately provocative"; Debord was "overambitious"; the SI's ambitions were "preposterous"; some of their texts (especially the ones written in collaboration with other situationists) are "schizophrenic," rather than self-contradictory....

Perhaps the most telling series of objections to situationist theory and practice that Sadler makes is the one in which his personal discomfort with the situationists as people is made clear.

> In relating their visions the situationists relied, of course, on a sympathetic relationship with one another and with their audience [...] Anyone who has really lived understands psychogeography, it was assumed, and anyone will understand it once they have experienced *real life*. This simply assumed that we all want the same things from the city, and that our experience and knowledge are homogenous; in short, that we are the sort of person who was attracted to the SI or, more to the point, that we *should* be that sort of person [...] More than anything this high-mindedness revealed the social descent of the situationists – from the avant-garde, the *flaneur*, and the connoisseur – which they combined with the tiresome cockiness of youth.

Here Sadler – a person who has become visible precisely and only because of his putative interest in "situationism" – is telling us that he is, in short, *not* the sort of person who is attracted to the SI, that is to say, someone who wants to destroy capitalism and replace it with a superior form of social organization. He's telling us – no, he's whining – that he bitterly resents the fact that – when it comes to the "field of study" that he's marked off as his own, the hot little bit of intellectual property called "situationism" – it is expected that *he* should have to be such a person. To make sure we know how bloody unfair the whole thing is, Sadler lets it be known that the situationists themselves had "no class"; that they were stupid and arrogant enough to give up their class privileges and "descend" down the socio-economic ladder; and that they were no better than the "students" (cocky louts and layabouts, one and all) that, every semester, poor university professors such as Simon Sadler are forced to instruct in classes on the elementals of art history and architecture. *Why do people have to be so bally principled when it comes to this situationist stuff?* Sadler wants to know. *Why can't I have my cake and eat it, too?*

But poor, tortured Simon Sadler just can't throw the Situationist International into the trashcan of history along with the Stalinists, Trotskyists, Maoists and all the rest; it appears it would be really fucking stupid to do so. The SI is just too valuable to Sadler *personally* as just another upwardly-mobile young professional who needs to distinguish himself from the others; as a proletarianized intellectual who dreams of becoming one of the elite. *The Situationist City* – which is obviously an illustrated version of his recently completed Ph.D. dissertation – is not the only thing he has written about the SI: far from it. Indeed, in 1993 Sadler wrote his (still unpublished, alas) M.A. dissertation on the subject of "'Situationism' and Architecture" for his professors at the University of Central England. Sadler also wrote a paper entitled "The Situationist City" for the Association of Art Historians, which met in Birmingham, England, in 1994. In other words, dangerous idiots though these situationists might have been, they are helping one Simple Simon Sadler make an academic career for himself as The Young Architectural Historian Who Specializes in "Situationism."

Not surprisingly, Sadler – judging from his work in *The Situationist City* – hasn't troubled himself to learn very much about the SI over the course of the last few years. The pages of his book, like the streets of any major city, are littered with garbage. Rather than try to present in an organized fashion the various pieces of garbage we have retrieved from Sadler's book ("trashcan in book form" would be a more accurate description), we will just dump out a few of the pieces that are the most revealing of its general ambience and odor.

— Sadler is willing to make conclusions based on the following suppositions – "if situationist testimony is to be believed," "if the claims for three-month drifts were true," and "if situationists spent as much time drifting as they claimed" – without bothering to test them, that is, without bothering to conduct an interview or two with a living situationist such as Constant or Michele Bernstein, and, no doubt, without really believing that the situationists actually did any of the incredible stuff that they claimed to have done.

— In one part of his book, Sadler writes that world-renowned *painter* Asger Jorn "apparently concentrated upon the production of situationist theory rather than of genuine situationist works, and hopelessly ambitious projects rarely went much further than the written idea." In a footnote to this staggeringly ignorant remark, Sadler adds, "the only 'situationist' productions of Jorn were some exercises in 'detourned' painting." But, in yet another part of his badly-edited book, Sadler informs his readers that Jorn "modified his own house in Albisola, Italy, between the late 1950s and the early 1970s" – thereby creating the situationist Garden of Albisola, which inspired Guy Debord to write "On Wild Architecture" in 1974.

— Debord's unforgiving "attitude" about bad books and poisoned food, according to Sadler, has "its roots in the Marshall Plan era, when the French left chose to drink wine instead of Coke as an act of defiance against 'Coca-Colonisation.'"

— The "moments of euphoria and *fete* actually present in the memories of Lefebvre and of many situationists" comparable to the Paris Commune of 1871 were "the 1936 election victory of the French Popular Front, and the liberations of 1945." (For Debord's fiercely critical comments on the French Popular Front – the election of which he believed to have been a *disaster* for the French working class – see *Refutation of all judgments brought to bear on the film 'Society of the Spectacle,'* the extraordinary film he made in 1975.)

Despite the fact that he is boring, lazy, ill-informed and willfully ignorant (even for an academic), Sadler has been published, and – happy coincidence! – by a publisher that since 1994 has also published or agreed to distribute two important situationist-related books: Donald Nicholson-Smith's translation of Debord's 1967 book *The Society of the Spectacle* and a translation of Raoul Vaneigem's 1986 book *The Movement of the Free Spirit.* Quite obviously, the utility of someone like Sadler – the reason that you would publish a bad book by him and not a good book by someone else – is not who he is, nor even what he has written or done, but the simple and arbitrary fact that the *timing* of his manuscript was fortuitous. Turned into a book, it could be made to serve as advertising for other titles in Zone Books' catalog.

As far as academic career moves go, Sadler's specialization in architectural "situationism" has been very well timed, and very successful. Thirty years ago, *no one* in the academic fields of "postmodern" architecture knew or cared about the situationists. As Sadler himself notes, "situationism was conspicuous by its absence from *Experimental Architecture,* the key retrospective account published in 1970 by Archigram's Peter Cook." It has only been in the last ten years – since the exhibits of situationist artifacts at the Institute of Contemporary Arts in London and at the Georges Pompidou Center in Paris – that "situationism" has really begun to catch on as something new among architectural historians. Sadler's bibliography lists four articles on the subject of "situationism" that have been published in highly respected urban planning or architectural journals over the course of the last four years.

(The most recent article listed by Sadler, Thomas F. McDonough's "Rereading Debord, Rereading the Situationists" – which is, in Sadler's words, one of "the important additions to the literature" – was lambasted in *NOT BORED!* #27 May 1997. The two other "important additions to the literature" mentioned by Sadler are both books published in Barcelona in 1996 and edited by Libero Andreotti and Xavier Costa: *Situationists: Art, Politics, Urbanism* and *Theory of the Derive and other situationist writings on the city*. Both books clearly demonstrate that the situationists' interest in architecture and urbanism remained a central feature of their program before 1957, from 1957 through 1972, and beyond. "It may be argued," Andreotti writes, "that the core animating principles of the movement, which were so clearly spelled out at the start, remained essentially unchanged; among them, a passionate rejection of all forms of utilitarian economism, an understanding of the city as a space of play and human self-actualization, and a faith in the possibilities of urban space to generate moments of genuine democratic participation." Later and overtly political situationist writings – such as "The Decline and Fall of the Spectacle-Commodity Economy" [1965], which Sadler relegates to a mention in a caption to an illustration – are included by Andreotti because they "locate urban issues in the wider perspective of radical change advocated by the SI.")

And so – to make his on-going personal exploitation of the situationists work, despite his strong dislike of the situationists and much of what they stood for – Simon Sadler must carefully watch his step and walk a very thin line in *The Situationist City*. He has to take his readers on a tour that is both rewarding and thorough-going (not to mention "rigorous and objective," and "fastidiously academic"), but he also has to make sure that the readers' footsteps never deviate from the intended path, that the readers' eyes never stray from what is being presented and accidentally glimpse something that they should not see, and that the readers' minds should not wander and find themselves in a place that is not supposed to exist.

To keep his readers "on the straight and narrow," Sadler has got two kinds of rewards. Every so often, he will claim that – despite the fact that they were dangerous idiots, worthy of being constantly insulted and ridiculed – the situationists were occasionally *right*. "Despite the initial popularity of *grands ensembles* and *villes nouvelles* like Sarcelles and Mourenx," a caption to an illustration taken from the SI's journal declares, "situationists correctly predicted their long-term social and architectural failure." Nowhere in his book does Sadler elaborate or follow-up on this provocative statement. Elsewhere, Sadler notes in passing that, "exactly as the situationists seemed to be warning us, the social is implicated in the aesthetic: Jussieu's nightmarish corridors, vertiginous stairwells, and campus deserts, fashioned from *beton brut* to meet the demand for popular higher education, barely conceal an indifference for their users."

The situationists, Sadler occasionally points out, were also right when they judged reformist architectural groups and movements to be without real value. The architectural proposals of Constant Nieuwenhuis, Sadler says, echoing Debord's critique of the Dutch situationist, do indeed have "a whiff of reformism about them." Even "later situationism" is credited with being right on occasion. In the course of a discussion of Constant, Sadler quotes Reyner Banham: "In one sense they [the later SI] were right [about Constant, who was forced to resign from the SI in 1961]; once you begin to clothe the naked concept of homo ludens in usable equipment, and to connect the constructed situations to the power mains, the result is liable to look remarkably like a swinging affluent society and its mobile, leisure-seeking citizens." (Sadler wishes to make it appear that situationists both "early" and "late" were themselves merely "swinging" "leisured nomads," instead of the fiercest critics of empty capitalist "happiness.")

The other means by which Sadler tries to keep his readers from drifting away from him is to throw into his tour guide's patter a few "interesting" tidbits garnered second-hand from other academic sources: in 1956, the situationist Giuseppe Pinot-Gallizio arranged for Constant to design an encampment for a group of Gypsies who lived in Alba, Italy; during the Paris Commune, the "lateral piercing" of buildings was used by the insurgents as a way of creating routes of travel that could not be cut off by the army; and, in the minds of the situationists active in the 1957 to 1961 period, "psychogeography was merely a preparation, a reconnaissance for the day when the city would be seized for real." Any one of these tidbits could have been – but was not – used to launch a very interesting and relevant discussion of situationist architectural theory – especially the last one, which concerns the use of psychogeography in the placement and defense of barricades in the Latin Quarter on the night of 10 May 1968.

It must be said – though we hated reading this bad book on the situationists more than reading any of the others – there is no small degree of drama in Sadler's dilemma and the peculiar ways in which he tries to resolve it.

> The constructed situation [Sadler writes] would plunge its participants into an examination of individual and collective consciousness: redeeming Shakespeare's famous dictum that "All the world's a stage, And all the men and women merely players," the Lettrist International envisaged the construction of situations as a twenty-four-hour tragedy played out for real.

As it played out in reality, the story of the Lettrist International was in fact a romance, a love story that came true, not a tragedy. About Debord in 1957, Sadler writes this:

> He was desperately casting around for a way out of the impasse of five years of lettrist activity. And about five years after *that* he was instrumental in escaping another impasse, redefining situationism as a "non-art" movement [emphasis in original].

But even Simple Simon knows that Debord got himself *out* of the labyrinth in

1957, when the Situationist International superseded the Lettrist International, just as he got himself out of the labyrinth *again,* in 1962, when the Situationist International transformed itself into the type of organization that both expected and could act effectively during the revolution (which, as we all know, did indeed break out in France in May 1968).

And so, dear readers of mine, let us see how Simon Sadler, the protagonist in a tragedy of his own making, is the cause of his own undoing. . . .

Right from the start, the situationists were very clear on these points: that a "situationist" is someone who "engages in the construction of situations," someone who is "a member of the Situationist International"; and there is no such thing as "situationism," which would be – in the words of the first issue of *Internationale Situationniste* – "a meaningless term improperly derived" from the word situationist, as well as "a doctrine of interpretation of existing facts." According to the situationists, "the notion of situationism is obviously devised by anti-situationists."

In his apology to his fellow academics for his "the reductionist tactics," Sadler writes:

> I have suppressed the considerable differences among avant-garde groups that contributed to situationism, instead drawing out their common ground. And I have claimed this common ground for situationism because the nexus of ideas that I want to explore in this book was almost completely formulated in the decade before the Situationist International finally inaugurated it as a program. Subsequently [sic] I have chosen to identify the people who formulated these ideas as "situationists."

Throughout his book, Sadler refers to "situationists," and not to *the* situationists, thereby destroying the carefully established and diligently maintained boundary constructed by the SI between its members and people who had ideas or methods that might be construed as similar to those that they held or used. Consequently, all kinds of people ignored or even explicitly repudiated by the SI are referred to as "situationists." Alain Touraine – described by the SI as "foaming at the mouth and howling," in the midst of the agitation at Nanterre in March 1968, "I've had enough of these anarchists and more than enough of these situationists! Right now I am in command here, and if one day you are, I will go somewhere else where people know what it means to work!" – has a nice, comfortable place in *The Situationist City,* among other "situationists." So does Henri Lefebvre – dismissed by the SI in the same breath as Touraine – whose work Sadler describes as "so seamlessly assimilated by situationism, and vice versa, that for the purposes of this discussion it is hardly possible or useful to distinguish the two."

(In a telling footnote to this strikingly ignorant and lazy remark, which clearly suggests the *uselessness* of his own book, Sadler reports that Eleonore

Kofman and Elizabeth Lebas – the translators and editors of Lefebvre's *Writings on Cities,* published posthumously in 1996 – are "correct in their opinion that 'the relationship between Lefebvrian and Situationist concepts awaits a serious study' and it will doubtless be forthcoming." In the meantime, Sadler seems to think he can say whatever he likes about the relationship between Lefebvre and the situationists, without fear of being contradicted by a "serious" authority on the subject. He is wrong.)

With the exceptions of Simon Sadler, the other architectural historians who are, like him, only now discovering the situationists, and Stewart Home (author of *What is Situationism?*), all of the writers who have approached the subject in recent years have respected the SI's wishes that the distinction between "situationist theory" and "situationism" be observed. Insensitive or simple readers may find no difference between the two phrases, because it is thought that the difference would, no doubt, directly concern the situationists: i.e., either they were ideologues (builders of an "ism"), or they were thoroughly anti-ideological (nomads of free thought). But the real difference between the two phrases has more to do with the consciousness of the SI's readers than with the situationists themselves: i.e., either the readers – like the situationists themselves – are enemies of all "isms," but especially such "isms" as Leninism and Stalinism, and are therefore quite willing to give the SI the benefit of the doubt on this score, or the readers are people who believe that it is impossible for *anyone* to be thoroughly anti-ideological (nomads of free thought), and who therefore think, without any further investigation, that the situationists *had* to have been ideologues.

Simon Sadler, who falls into the second category of readers, has one and only justification for referring to "situationism" throughout his book:

> The situationists' caution about a 'situationism' was a clever way of reminding themselves of the dangers of becoming 'academic' in their procedures, a fate that had befallen their avant-garde predecessors, the surrealists, 'policed' as they were by their spokesman Andre Breton. But as a way of throwing academics off the scent forty years later – well, no tactic could be more misguided than denying the existence of situationism. Academics are precisely the people with the time and inclination to unravel such riddles.

Only a seriously ill-informed, guilt-ridden, and totally self-absorbed academic could think that the situationists were obsessed with being recuperated by academia and by academia only. "Situationism" in fact represented the dangers of the recuperation of situationist theory by such diverse institutions as the art world (the galleries and the art magazines far more than the professors of architecture and art history), the world of newspapers and journalism, and, most importantly, the world of the Communist and Socialist political parties and their theorists – all of which responded to the SI while it was still in existence, and not "forty years later," as have the riddle-unraveling academics with plenty of free time on their hands. (Note that Breton and surrealism had flirted with and were recuperated by the French Communist Party in the 1930s, well before they were recuperated by academic art historians and Madison Avenue.)

Quite obviously, if the SI disbanded in 1972, its members can't still be using the term "situationism" forty years after its original refusal or anti-coinage to throw academics "off the scent." (Off the scent – of *what* exactly?) The only people who are properly using the term "situationism" in the 1990s are "the radicals who have carried the candle for situationist ideas since the demise of the Situationist International" (Sadler's words); they typically use the term to condemn enterprises such as Sadler's. In a sweeping and preemptive counter-dismissal, Sadler refers to these candle-holders as "Pro-situs," whom – Sadler boldly predicts – will not like his book at all.

> Many Pro-situs [Sadler writes] seem uncomfortable that they and their discourse are largely products of academia, even when they are its anti-products [...] They apparently wish to direct the full force of the class war against academics.

More obsessive self-absorption on Sadler's part: "Pro-situs are uncomfortable with academic books on the situationists because these books reveal the source of 'situationism' in academic discourse." If this were true – and it isn't, because the sources for such crucial situationist concepts and practices as the derive and psychogeography lie in *modern art,* not in academic histories or interpretations of it – then there would be no reason for Sadler's book to exist in the first place. In other words, if the premise of Sadler's pop sociology were true, then *The Situationist City* would have been a book called *The Postmodern City* and it would have been about how so very interesting and relevant the architectural theories and writings of Reyner Banham and the Independent Group, Archigram, Team 10, and the Smithsons (the theorists and movements with whom Sadler is most comfortable) are. There would have been no need at all to refer to the situationists, except perhaps in a snide footnote or two.

No: if pro-situs such as myself hate *The Situationist City,* it is because Sadler wants to have it both ways, at all times. He wants to write a "fastidiously academic book" (though this will offend the uncomfortable Pro-situs), and yet, at the end of his introductory chapter, he wants to settle in comfortably with the highly principled Pro-situs so that his readers won't, you know, get the wrong idea.

> I hope that this [Sadler writes of the three-part organization of his book] makes the book fairly easy to follow. But in case it settles readers' ideas about situationism too much –

and consequently ends the demand for bad books about the situationists

> – I end this introduction by siding with my imaginary Pro-situ detractors. Early situationism was *never* quite as containable as this book might make it seem [emphasis added].

To insulate himself against the obviously valid claim that – because he nevertheless decided to refer to situationist theory as "situationism" throughout his book – he wrote it in *bad faith*, Sadler wants his readers to know that the fault with "situationism" lies squarely and completely with the situationists, and not with him.

> But for all the propagandist brilliance of situationist critique, virtual incomprehensibility was an inherent feature of the situationist architectural project. Situationists were nearer the mark than they realized when they said that "situationism" did not exist. At the center of the project was a methodological vacuum, a groping for the nonspectacular, some kind of everyday "other." [...] The situationist process envisaged can barely be claimed to have occurred. There wasn't even any evidence that a situation was ever constructed as prescribed. The program that situationists set themselves was so ambitious and uncompromising that it condemned itself to failure [...] And if the Situationist International couldn't even decide how to construct a situation, it seemed unlikely that they would agree upon how to transform the city itself [...] The best that *Internationale situationniste* could suggest for those wishing to carry on envisaging the situationist city was that they return to the principles of *detournement*.

But the situationist architectural project is easily comprehensible by anyone willing and able to see where it leads, which is straight to such revolutionary insurrections as the one in France in May 1968. "We have invented the architecture and the urbanism that cannot be realized without the revolution of everyday life – without the appropriation of conditioning by everyone, its endless enrichment, its fulfillment," Raoul Vaneigem and Attila Kotanyi wrote in "Elementary program of the Bureau of Unitary Urbanism," a text from 1961 paid little attention by Sadler. When the precondition was met or when it began to be met – when the revolution of everyday life broke out in Paris and then in other French urban areas (especially Nantes) – the situationist city began to be constructed, or, rather, situationist cities began to be constructed as detournements of existing cities. To make it plain: a street barricaded against intrusions by the police is a detourned street.

In order to prevent his readers from taking an unauthorized stroll down the Street of Modern Urban Insurrection, Sadler tries to cut the situationist city into pieces, to create "off-limits" zones, in short, to separate the situationist city from itself. For those who don't know or need reminding: the 15-year-long history of the Situationist International is commonly divided into three periods: 1957 to 1961, during which the SI was primarily focused on modern art and its revolutionary legacy; 1962 to 1967, during which the organization developed its critical theory of contemporary capitalist society; and 1968 to 1972, during which the members of the group participated in the May 68 insurrection and attempted to deepen, broaden and spread it to other countries. Sadler's announced intentions in *The Situationist City* are to cleanly separate the first period ("early situationism") from everything else that follows it (he doesn't distinguish between the middle and late periods, and prefers to call them both "later situationism"), to cherish a simulacrum of "early situationism," and to belittle and mock "later situationism" for its abandonment of its own architectural theory.

> I reserve for academics my apology for the reductionist tactics of this book [Sadler writes]. I have concentrated on the earlier phase of situationism, when art, architecture, design, and urbanism were still primary concerns for the movement [...] This book takes perverse care in extracting situationist architectural theory from a revolutionary program that attempted to confront the ideological totality of the Western world

and *failed* (that is, if you stubbornly refuse to acknowledge that May 1968 actually happened). According to Sadler:

> Over time [the SI], sidelined the art theory that had been the springboard of the entire endeavor [...] The intensely critical turn situationist theory took after the first few issues of *Internationale situationniste* effectively terminated the direct situationist interest in art and urbanism [...] It seemed that the Situationist International quickly lost control of its architectural theory [...] In this book I concentrate on the early situationist program and so try to save it from the obscurity to which it was later banished by the Situationist International.

There *is* a point to be made here. In fact, Henri Lefebvre had already raised it in an interesting and forceful way in an interview conducted with him in 1983 by Kristin Ross, who, for some reason, waited until 1997 before she got it published in *October* 79 (special issue on Debord and the SI).

> After 1960 . . . [the situationists, Lefebvre reported] abandoned the theory of Unitary Urbanism, Unitary Urbanism only had a precise meaning for historic cities like Amsterdam that had to be renewed, transformed. But from the moment that the historic city exploded into

peripheries, suburbs [...], the theory of Unitary Urbanism lost any meaning. I remember very sharp, pointed discussions with Guy Debord, when he said that urbanism was becoming an ideology. He was absolutely right, from the moment when there was an official doctrine on urbanism [...] That doesn't mean that the problem of the city was resolved – far from it. But at that point [the situationists] abandoned the theory of Unitary Urbanism. And then I think that even the derive, the derive experiments, were little by little abandoned around then, too.

Unlike Sadler, Lefebvre clearly appreciates the fact that the SI's apparent abandonment of Unitary Urbanism and their other architectural theories (the derive and psychogeography) in the early 1960s was based on a carefully reasoned and highly principled argument, not a whim. This argument, spelled out in detail in "Critique of Urbanism" – a crucial text published in *Internationale situationniste* #6 (August 1961), not included in Ken Knabb's *Situationist International Anthology,* but available in both *October* 79 and *Theory of the Derive and other situationist writings on the city* – holds that:

> Confrontation with the whole of present-day society is the sole criterion for a genuine liberation in the field of urban architecture, and the same goes for any other aspect of human activity. Otherwise, "improvement" or "progress" will always be designed to lubricate the system and perfect the conditioning that we must overturn, in urbanism and everywhere else.

Sadler gives his readers the impression that the SI's rejection of urbanism was executed in isolation, that it wasn't part of a long-term, systematic and largely successful attempt to protect the revolutionary core of situationist theory from immediate recuperation by reformist and neo-liberal forces in the capitalist system. Sadler doesn't believe that recuperation is a real concern, of course. Both times that he uses the word, it appears enclosed within doubtful quotation marks; the second time he uses it, "recuperation" is quickly dismissed as a "highfallutin" word. (I'm serious: "The situationists found highfallutin reasons for their failure to meet this requirement," Sadler writes in the voice of a country hick about a complex installation the SI wanted to put in Amsterdam's Stedelijk Museum. "They would withdraw from 'recuperative' space, their journal said.") Furthermore, Sadler refuses to admit that the "supposedly historic split between pro-art and non-art factions" in the SI around 1962 was in fact a real split: it was "in fact rather a crude representation of the difficulties that had been inherent in situationism." After 1962, Sadler insists, "Debord and the Debordists," who had "an increasing stranglehold on the movement," did not "question directly the universalizing assumptions of the situationist project," but struck out "the most visible reminder of its fracture: the continued production of it."

For his part, Henri Lefebvre – even though the SI consigned him to the trashcan of history in 1962 – couldn't disagree more with Sadler. The split and regrouping of the SI in 1962 was "more than a transition, it was the abandonment of one position in order to adopt the exact opposite one," Lefebvre is quoted as saying. "Between the idea of elaborating an urbanism and the thesis that all urbanism is an ideology is a profound modification." Debord might say that between the two ideas, within the profound modification of one by the other, is the adventure of the dialectic.

But neither Simon Sadler nor Henri Lefebvre are willing to admit that the SI made tremendous strides as a revolutionary organization committed to the overthrow of global capitalism in the 1962 to 1967 period, that is to say, when they stopped considering the "problem of the city" in the context of individual behavior and started considering it in the context of global conditions. Though Lefebvre, unlike Sadler, doesn't refuse to acknowledge the facts that (a) the May 1968 revolution took place and (b) it was clearly "situationist" in its use of public space, Lefebvre still speaks of the SI's "abandonment of the problem of the city," and refuses to acknowledge that it was precisely their insistence on the importance of life in the capitalist city that allowed to the situationists to play such an important role in May 1968 (the urban revolution in which "situationist architectural theory" was directly tested by being put into practice).

So Sadler is simply doing capitalism's ideological dirty work when he claims that, dentist-like, he is "extracting situationist architectural theory" so as to *save* it from the rotten Situationist International, which was so stupid as to deform and abandon it. Sadler is trying to turn one of the SI's greatest successes – its evolution within and beyond the limited "artistic" framework in which it was originally conceptualized – into one of its failures. He is suppressing the later SI's attempts to go beyond architecture – to go beyond their own architectural theory – so as to remain in control of "his" privileged subject matter and consequently his personal niche as the architectural historian who specializes in "Situationism."

To do this, Sadler needs to create the impression that, in the years leading up to 1968, the situationists wasted their time with talk of revolution. In a pointed comparison between the SI and Team 10's Aldo van Eyck, Sadler states that van Eyck – despite the presumably situationist-like "revolutionary threat" contained in a statement he had issued in 1947 – "had preferred to reshape space in the here-and-now, under the respectable patronage of De 8 (a Dutch CIAM group), rather than await the revolution." Sadler's unstated but obvious point seems to be that, were it not for the historical accident or aberration commonly referred as the May 1968 revolution, the situationists would have been exposed as frauds, and people like Aldo van Eyck – *not* the situationists – would have achieved the fame that they deserved but were deprived of. "Ironically," Sadler writes, "Debord, virtually the inventor of the constructed situation, obstructed maneuvers to construct one, as if he suspected that it was of little revolutionary value: that its realization would, indeed, be faintly ridiculous." In Sadler's view, Debord and the SI didn't actively make history: their passive hands were forced by it.

Were it not for the *deus ex machina* of the May 1968 revolution, Sadler wants us to know, the situationists would have been exposed as (gasp!) architectural conservatives. Sadler, confusing the activities of the Lettrist International with those of the SI, writes:

> Most of the architecture and spaces that were endorsed by situationists existed by chance rather than by design: back streets, urban fabric layered over time, ghettos. Perhaps situationist exemplars could not adequately be synthesized, abstracted, or even "detourned" – only preserved, the passing of time itself being an architectural agent, the fourth-dimensional attribute of use, weathering, and legend that psychogeographers keenly noted. Probably most situationists realized the near-impossibility of constructing truly situationist architecture.

But we are *not* embarrassed by the facts that the situationists were not builders, that their architectural theory was "nothing more" than the direct application of detournement to already existing buildings and streets, and that – in pre-revolutionary periods – their architectural practice was "nothing more" than the protection of certain areas of the city from destruction. The situationists were not architectural specialists, and their "programme" didn't require experts for its execution. Anybody can detourn a building or a street; anybody can drift through the city and find a place in it that should be protected from the ravages of capitalism.

"If we wish to know more, we must descend to the streets ourselves," Sadler writes, as if he's actually been there. But he hasn't; and it is quite plain that the very idea of "descending" to the streets terrifies him more than any haunted house has ever disturbed the dreams of little children.

NOT BORED! #29, July 1998

Jacques Attali's *Noise*

When Jacques Attali's spectacular book *Noise: The Political Economy of Music* was first published in translation by the University of Minnesota in 1985 (as volume 16 in its "Theory and History of Literature" series) – and every time the book was reprinted, which happened five times between 1985 and 1996 – it came carefully wrapped. In front of it was Frederic Jameson's seven-page-long "Foreword," and after it was Susan McClary's nine-page-long "Afterword." Such thick wrapping for a book so thin (only 148 pages and four chapters long)! And such *heavy* people to put the wrapping on it, too: Jameson, identified simply by the book jacket as the William A. Lane Jr., Professor of Comparative Literature at Duke University, was at the time America's best-known Marxist academic; and McClary, identified as professor of musicology at the University of California at Los Angeles, was a rising star in academic feminist music theory (today her star has risen).

Why was such protective (explanatory) wrapping deemed to be necessary? Was it thought that Attali's book would not be understood, accepted or even read seriously by English-speaking academics if it did not come wrapped in long explanations by well-known experts? Was the text, originally published in French in 1977, really that difficult to comprehend? Or did it have to do with the book's ostensible subject matter (the history of Western classical music), widely known to be one of the most boring topics in the world?

In his "Foreword," Jameson locates the significance and originality of Attali's book in its contribution to "a general revival of history, and of a renewed appetite for historiography," and in its specific insistence on "the possibility of a superstructure to *anticipate* historical developments, to foreshadow new social formations in a prophetic and annunciatory way." In her "Afterword," Susan McClary – throwing caution to the wind and allowing herself to "take Attali at his most daring and permit ourselves to assume that music truly heralds changes that are only later apparent in other aspects of culture" – wants only to have Attali help her "find explanations for several problems in seventeenth-century music scholarship."

OK: so we know that *Noise* was not wrapped carefully because of its *content*. Then why? Because of who wrote it, and why it was written.

On the book jacket, Jacques Attali is identified simply as "the author of numerous books, including *Millennium: Winners and Losers in the Coming World Order.*" But ol' Fred Jameson knows better: he is, Jameson notes in passing, "a practicing economist and a close adviser to President Mitterand," and "a central figure in France's current socialist experiment," as well as a "distinguished scholar, the author of a dozen books whose subjects range from political economy to euthanasia." In other words, Jacques Attali is a prominent financial capitalist, a "socialist," a technocrat, and a close personal friend of the President of one of the G-7 nations. He seems, shall we say, a little out of place in the company of other authors published in the "Theory and History of Literature" series, who include Georges Bataille and Mikhail Bakhtin.

In the two decades since he wrote *Noise,* Jacques Attali has authored books about Francois Mitterand; was the first person to head the European Bank for Reconstruction and Development (created in 1990 to assist the former Soviet Union); was the president of A & A, an international consulting firm based in Paris; and has been one of *Foreign Policy* magazine's contributing editors. As his recent writings indicate, he is a leading advocate of neo-liberal capitalism. In "The

Crash of Western Civilization: The Limits of the Market and Democracy," published in *Foreign Policy,* Number 107, Summer 1997, pp. 54-64, Attali writes that, in order to avert the destruction of western democratic societies by the unfettered rule of the capitalist market,

> the West should improve and strengthen democracy in order to achieve a balance with the power of the market. To accomplish that, we must foster a new government role in enforcing the rule of law, supporting the principles of education, ensuring social justice and the participation of workers in corporate decision making, and leading the fight against corruption and the drug economy.

This perspective has *nothing* to do with Marxist "political economy," and Jameson was able to spot it way back in 1985: "The positioning of Marxism as an older world paradigm clearly marks Attali's affinities with certain poststructuralisms and post-Marxisms, at the same time that it expresses the French Socialist party's complicated relationship to its Marxian tradition." *Complicated* ain't the word, Freddy: "severed" or "inverted" would be much more like it.

Though it appears to be a work on music by a committed revolutionary – indeed, by a situationist-inspired revolutionary – *Noise* is one long justification for the formation and continued existence of France's "socialist" government. "Without music, no State could survive," Attali quotes a character in Moliere as saying; Attali, of course, believes that his own French state is no exception to this rule. But Attali is not a musician, nor does he use *Noise* to advise the members of his government to don sunglasses and play Elvis Presley songs on their saxophones. In his discussion of the music of the 18th century, Attali brings up the rhetorical question, "How could an order that brought such wonderful music into the world not be the one desired by God and required by science?" It is clear that Attali would like the voters of contemporary France to say, "How could a government that brought such a wonderful *book* about music into the world not be the one desired by the majority of the people and required by the global economy?" (It is also clear that Wlad Godzich, Jochen Schulte-Sasse, and the other "socialists" at the University of Minnesota Press – not to mention academic Marxists such as Frederic Jameson and Susan McClary – have a vested interest in seeing to it that the American perception of the results of the socialist "experiment" in France is favorable.)

To make *Noise* a convincing and effective work of political propaganda, it must silence or, rather, expose as "mere noise" certain discourses that insist on the immediate destruction of both the capitalist economy and the technocratic State. Of these discourses, the situationist critique of the society of the spectacle appears to be the most dangerous to the socialist "experiment," and so must be silenced first. Why is this? For the same reason that Mitterand presented himself as the leader of the Party that would "Change life" once it was voted into office: "Situationism" –

the enemy of situationist theory – was the French government's unofficial ideology in the 1980s.

It is staggering that the only situationist author Attali quotes in *Noise* is "Gian Franco Sanguinetti Censor" [sic], the author of *Veridique rapport sur les dernieres chances du capitalisme en Italie*, which was translated from Italian into French by Guy Debord (whom Attali does not mention) and published in Paris by Champ Libre in 1976, just one year before Attali published his "political economy of music." Censor's pamphlet, unlike every other situationist text, was addressed directly to the ruling class, of which – as we have pointed out – Attali is a member. Though the pamphlet was part of a deliberately constructed scandal, which was designed to embarrass, if not topple, the ruling class – for Censor was not, as he claimed, a member of the ruling class to which he addressed himself, but the situationist revolutionary Gianfranco Sanguinetti writing under a pseudonym – incredibly, Jacques Attali uses it as a relatively straight-forward source of good practical advice on the running of a modern State such as France!

Both of the direct references Attali makes to Sanguinetti's pamphlet lay bare Attali's foul ulterior motives for writing *Noise*. Seeking to avoid social "errors" – or, rather, lamenting the fact that "many errors would have been avoided in social science over the past two centuries," that is, had his insights been available back then – Attali writes the following:

> The [classical] concert is then seen to be the place used by the elite to convince itself that it is not as cold, inhuman, and conservative as it is accused of being. For the rest, the [popular] concert is mediocrity camouflaged in an artificial festival, for 'whatever is distributed to the poor can never be anything more than poverty.'

In a footnote, Attali correctly attributes this quote to Censor, who got it from Marx. But when he evokes this "law," Censor is not advocating its overturning: he is advocating that certain illusions must be given up by the elite, for capitalism is impoverishing and poisoning the entire world, even or *especially* for the elite that control it.

> For a long time [Censor writes] one pretended to believe that the abundance of industrial production slowly elevated everyone to the conditions of an elite. This argument has so completely lost its very slight appearance of seriousness that it has been degraded to being nothing more than the ephemeral incitations of publicity [...] The mechanically egalitarian tendency of modern industry to want to make everything for everyone, and to break and maim everything just to distribute its most recent merchandise is what has poisoned almost all space, and most of our time, with its piles of cheap goods: cars and "second homes" are everywhere. If words remain rich, the same is not

true of things, and the countryside is deteriorating everywhere. The law that dominates all this is, of course, that the only thing one distributes to the poor is poverty: cars that do not circulate because there are too many of them, wages paid in inflated currency, meat from animals fattened up in a few weeks by chemicals means, etc.

For Censor – and for Jacques Attali, as well – the trick is (once again) *extricating the elite from the ranks of the poor,* but without incriminating the "justice" that is meted out to the poor under this fundamental law, which must remained unchallenged.

As for the nature of the elite, the simple truth is that it is indeed "cold, inhuman, and conservative," and Attali doesn't deny it: in fact, he is trying to protect modern capitalism by getting the elite to do a lot more than attend musical concerts, that is, if its members want not to be perceived accurately and, as a result, fought more effectively.

"Capitalism," Attali writes a couple pages later, "has become 'a terrorism tempered by well-being, the well-being of each in his place' (Censor)." But when Censor uses these words, he is *not* referring to modern day capitalism, *but to the Republic of Venice,* which Censors cites as "the model of a qualitative society, a model that was sufficient in its time, even perfect." The *contrast* with modern day capitalism couldn't be starker.

> This [Censor writes, referring to the Republic of Venice] was the most beautiful dominant class in history: no one resisted it, or even pretended to reckon with it. For centuries, no demagogic lies, hardly any troubles and very little bloodshed. It was *terrorism tempered by happiness,* the happiness of each in his place.

By conflating modern day capitalism with what the ruthless capitalist Censor defines as the society most desirable in history for *his* social strata (the ruling class), Attali has taken Sanguinetti's bait – and this is, of course, what Censor's pamphlet was all about: getting the ruling class to take the bait. In the conflation, Attali has indicated clearly what is for him and his "socialists" buddies the *desirability of the current state of affairs,* terrorism and all.

Looking back on the 19th century, Attali correctly points out that:

> The commodity quickly became an object of spectacle. Already in the eighteenth century, music-turned-commodity was announcing the future role of all commodities under representation: a spectacle in front of silent people. In representation, commodities speak on behalf of those who purchase the spectacle of their order, their glory. Usage, as soon as it is represented, is destroyed by exchange. The spectacle emerged in the eighteenth century. . . .

But as soon as he has said this, Attali wants it to be known that he has grave doubts – no more than that, but grave doubts are enough for him – about the continued relevance of the theory of the spectacle to modern society.

> The spectacle emerged in the eighteenth century, and, as music will show us later on, it is now perhaps an obsolete form of capitalism: the economy of representation has been replaced by that of repetition [...] *Music announces that we are verging on no longer being a society of the spectacle.* The political spectacle is merely the last vestige of representation, preserved and put forward by repetition in order to avoid disturbing or dispiriting us unduly. In reality, power is no longer incarnated in men. It is. Period. [...] Even the spectacle is now only one form of repetition among others, and perhaps an obsolete one [...] The spectacle [has been replaced by] recordings of it [...] In the end, the political spectacle itself, already now limited to the highest echelons, may disappear – without, however, a dissolution of power – just as it disappeared in the large corporation, in which legitimacy is now founded upon efficiency and the competence of anonymous, interchangeable cadres, and hardly at all in the personality of the president.

The source of this hardly disinterested speculation, though not made explicit by Attali, is obvious: the "post-situationist" writings of Jean Baudrillard, former teaching assistant to Henri Lefebvre and member of the pro-situ group Utopie in the 1960s. Drawing upon Baudrillard's *Political Economy of the Sign* and *The Mirror of Production,* Attali puts forth the following "succession of *orders* (in other words, differences) done violence by *noises* (in other words, the calling into question of differences) that are *prophetic* because they create new orders, unstable and changing."

> The simultaneity of multiple codes, the variable overlappings between periods, styles and forms [Attali writes], prohibits any attempt at a genealogy of music, a hierarchical archeology, or a precise ideological underpinning of particular musicians. But it is possible to discern who among them are innovators and heralds of worlds in the making [...] Briefly, we will see that it is possible to distinguish on our map three zones, three stages, three strategic usages of music by power. In one of these zones, it seems that music is used and produced in the ritual in an attempt to make people *forget* the general violence; in another, it is employed to make people *believe* in the harmony of the world, that there is order in exchange and legitimacy in commercial power; and finally, there is one in which it serves to *silence,* by mass-producing a

deafening, syncretic kind of music, and censoring all other human voices.

This last usage of music – repetition that silences – is the zone of the spectacle, or rather, it corresponds to the "bureaucratic power" of the society of the spectacle.

Attali's anecdotal descriptions of the third "zone" are accurate and compelling. In this stage, *"people buy more records than they can listen to. They stockpile what they want to find the time to hear."* While the second stage "stockpiled exchange-time in the form of money," the third stage "stockpiles use-time." In effect, Attali writes, "transforming use-time into a stockpileable object makes it possible to sell and stockpile rights to usage without actually using anything, to exchange ad infinitum without extracting pleasure from the object, without experiencing its function." In the final analysis, *"the stockpiling of use-time in the commodity object is fundamentally a herald of death."*

One couldn't agree more: the death heralded by the appearance and on-going development of repetitive or spectacular society (and its forms of music, especially Muzak) is the death of music as a separate sphere of human cultural activity, the death of human pre-history, and the death of the entire capitalist socio-economic system in and through which this three-stage process unfolds. This death is quite literal, unfortunately: it is the death of the human species due to lethal accumulations (stockpiles) of toxins, pollutants, and radioactive wastes. The only alternative to this death is revolution, the global destruction of capitalism and its replacement with a higher form of social organization.

But Attali does not want to see people all over the world rise up in open revolution against both private and bureaucratic capitalism: as a member of the "socialist" government of a leading Western nation – especially one that as recently as 1968 was nearly toppled by a popular revolution – his job depends on the infinite delaying and deferring of this necessary revolution; indeed, his job *is* the infinite delaying and deferring of it.

And so, out of nowhere – illogically, arbitrarily, but "poetically" – Attali posits the "embryonic" existence of a fourth zone or stage, which he calls "composition," that "heralds the arrival of new social relations" in which "freedom" is an essential and irreducible feature. Signs of its eventual birth are everywhere, in both "avant-garde" and "pop" music. Attali writes:

> Both [John] Cage and the Rolling Stones, *Silence* and "Satisfaction," announce a rupture in the process of musical creation, the end of music as an autonomous activity, due to an intensification of lack in the spectacle. They are not the new mode of musical production, but the liquidation of the old.

As we have seen, Attali claimed that "a precise ideological underpinning of particular musicians" is not possible (yet this is precisely what he has just done with John Cage and the Stones); furthermore, Attali claimed that "it is possible to discern who among them are innovators and heralds of worlds in the making." But, when "push comes to shove," he locates the beginnings of the fourth stage in technological innovations, not in the efforts of particular musicians such as Cage or the Stones (better references would have been La Monte Young and the Velvet Underground). Notice the total absence of *human agents* in Attali's description of "radical" anti-capitalist subversion:

> Already, from within repetition, certain deviations announce a radical challenge to it: the proliferating circulation of pirated recordings, the multiplication of illegal radio stations, the diverted usage of monetary signs as a mode of communication forbidden political messages – all of these things herald the invention of a radical subversion, a new mode of structuring, communication that is not restricted to the elite of discourse.

Without the presence of self-conscious human agents, this description clearly suggests that the passage from the deadly third stage to the "free" fourth stage is an inevitable and technological one, not a determined choice, made for dire social reasons, by organized but anti-hierarchical groups of people. For Attali and other "socialist" technocrats, no human intervention is needed: technological progress itself, if allowed to develop unimpeded, is what will overthrow the society of the spectacle and save us from death.

With the arbitrary addition of this fourth stage, Attali's three-part cycle suddenly becomes a linear progression, an evolutionary and inevitable course of development, a happy story ("Fear, Clarity, Power, and [then] Freedom") rather than a terrifying paradox. And yet Attali is canny enough to want to make clear that this fourth stage will directly answer and satisfy the human needs – totally ignored by capitalism – that situationist theory and practice so successfully exposed.

> Hear me well [Attali writes]: composition is not the same as material abundance, that petit-bourgeois vision of atrophied communism having no other goal than the extension of the bourgeois spectacle to all of the proletariat. It is the individual's conquest of his own body and potentials. It is impossible without material abundance and a certain technological level, but is not reducible to that.

This is double-talk: technological "progress," if allowed to continue to develop unimpeded, will poison us all, even the members of the elites. For the society of the spectacle to be overthrown, both capitalism and the bureaucratic state must be overthrown as well. No happy "free zone" is possible within the society created and managed by these institutions, except perhaps for members of their elites. Hear *me* well, Mr. Eurobank who likes Eric Clapton: these are established facts for every person part of the international current of radical subversion channeled in certain ways by the situationists. We won't be satisfied with simple "conquest" of our own "bodies" and "potentials": we want the liberation of all of human society from the shackles of private property, work and the state, and the permanent, unending realization of *society's* potentials. Only then can we realize our own potentials as individuals.

NOT BORED! #29, July 1998

Cornelius Castoriadis, 1922 to 1997

In "Workers' Councils, Castoriadis and the Situationist International" (*NOT BORED!* #26, November 1996), we demonstrated that – subsequent to Guy Debord's membership in both the SI and Cornelius Castoriadis's Socialisme ou Barbarie group in the 1960-1961 period – the situationists adopted and claimed as their own the basic programmatic points that had been outlined and explored in great detail by Castoriadis in *Socialisme ou Barbarie* in the 1950s. Those basic points were workers' self-management and workers' councils. We noted that the situationists, especially after the May 1968 revolution, never really elaborated or expanded upon these basic points, and yet continued to make them the center of their position on modern revolution. The fact that the situationists' readership grew in both size and activity during the 1961 to 1967 period suggested to us the validity and richness of these basic points, even when they are left undeveloped. Finally, we noted that, despite the SI's indebtedness to S. ou B. and to Castoriadis in particular, the situationists refused to acknowledge it and were openly hostile to Castoriadis, whom they insulted relentlessly.

In this essay – which we intend, along with "Workers' Councils, Castoriadis and the Situationist International," to be a contribution to an appreciation of the work of Castoriadis, who died in late 1997 at the age of 75 – we will briefly explore the development of the S. ou B. group after 1961, that is, after Debord's departure. Our assumption will be this: just as the situationists needed the ideas and work of S. ou B. to transform the SI from an informal to a formal revolutionary organization, Castoriadis needed the ideas and work of the SI to give S. ou B. a genuinely "new orientation." The paradoxes here are that, though the situationists simplified (even reduced) the ideas of S. ou B., their organization flourished in the early and mid-1960s, while the S. ou B. group, despite the rigor, complexity and originality of its theoretical work, did not.

The crisis within Socialisme ou Barbarie began in October 1962, when Castoriadis – acting on behalf of "a certain number of us comrades from the Paris area" – wrote and distributed to the entire S. ou B. group a series of texts that are assembled in the essay entitled "For a New Orientation," which appears in *Political and Social Writings, 1961-1979* (University of Minnesota Press 1993, translated and edited by David Ames Curtis).

> The group has arrived at a decisive turning point in its history [Castoriadis wrote]. This turning point has been imposed upon it by both external events and by its own internal situation. External events: with the end of the Algerian War, we can no longer continue to avoid answering the following question: In a modern capitalist country, in what does revolutionary activity consist? Internal situation: the great majority of the comrades, in fact nearly all of them, clearly feel that the extreme empiricism and the refusal to respond, as far as we are capable, to basic questions that have characterized for the past two years the conduct and the existence of the group cannot go on any longer without leading to a certain split.

For Castoriadis, the single most important problem facing the S. ou B. group in 1962 was this: "What can revolutionaries say and what can they do in a capitalist country where the regime has achieved stability and does not encounter any difficulties in the short term, where the population is not politically active, where (as is the case in France in particular) even industrial actions occur very rarely and remain very limited in scope?" Castoriadis's provisional answers to this question were simple and direct. "We propose," he wrote, "that the organization adopt, either in a national conference or in a general assembly of the Paris-area comrades broadened to include comrades from the provinces, a platform for the group's ideological and political orientation; a text on the orientation of the group's propaganda; a text on the orientation of the group's activity; [and] statutes and rules for the provisional functioning of the group."

Though Castoriadis did indeed go on to write the platform for the group's ideological and political orientation in March 1963 – see "Recommencing the Revolution" in *Political and Social Writings, 1961-1979* – neither the national conference nor the general assembly ever took place. But Castoriadis's texts nevertheless had a strong effect on the members of the group. In "Recommencing the Revolution," he writes that "our reconstruction effort" has encountered "at each of its crucial stages, bitter opposition from conservative elements [within the S. ou B. group] representing the type of militant who retains nostalgia for the golden age of the workers' movement (a golden age that, like all golden ages, is, moreover, perfectly imaginary) and who moves forward in history only by preceding backwards, constantly wishing to return to the era in which, as he believes, theory and program were indisputable, established once and for all, and constantly corroborated by the activity of the masses."

The ultimate result was indeed a split within the group. Castoriadis writes that, "The comrades who separated themselves from us [in 1963], among whom are P. Brune, J-F Lyotard, and R. Maille, propose to continue publication of the monthly journal *Pouvoir Ouvrier*." But the scission – no matter how acrimonious it was (in a long translator's footnote, David Ames Curtis explains that Jean-Francois Lyotard was still complaining about it as late as 1974) – did nothing to clarify the underlying issues. Castoriadis writes that,

> The customary and logical thing would have been to discuss publicly the reasons for this scission, and the opposing theses. Unfortunately, that is not possible for us to do. This opposition has remained without any definable content, positive or even negative; to this day we know nothing about those who reject our ideas want to put in their place, and just as little about what precisely they are opposed to. We therefore can only explain ourselves concerning our own positions and, for the rest, we can merely note once again the ideological and political sterility of conservatism.

As a result, the S. ou B. group – unlike the Situationist International, which experienced a very public scission in the 1961-1962 period, during which a *Second Situationist International* was constituted by a group of members who had either resigned or been excluded – came out of the experience an organization whose days, as one says, were numbered. In June 1965, what would turn out to be the last issue of *Socialisme ou Barbarie* was published. Two years later, Castoriadis wrote and distributed "The Suspension of Publication of *Socialisme ou Barbarie*" as a circular addressed to the journal's subscribers and readers.

"The Suspension" is a *very* strange document. In retrospect, we may find it nearly impossible to believe that it was written just *one year* before the May 1968 revolution in France. But then again – at the time "The Suspension" was circulated – some people probably found it difficult to believe that this deeply skeptical text was written during the "long hot summer" of 1967, during which riots broke out in dozens of major American cities. More than guardedly pessimistic about the possibility of people forming a truly revolutionary organization in the midst of these putatively non-revolutionary conditions, "The Suspension" seems closed to this very possibility. If S. ou B. couldn't do it, well then *no one* can: "the construction of a such a [new] political organization under the conditions in which we live – and in which, no doubt, we take part – was and remains *impossible* due to a series of factors that are in no way accidental in character and that are in fact closely interconnected" (emphasis added). Castoriadis's tone seems to suggest that, not only hasn't S. ou B. lived up to its announced intentions since its founding in 1949, but it was on a fundamental level doomed to failure, doomed *despite* the scission of 1962-1963, doomed in fact from the very first.

> We have had a negative experience, regarding both a working-class

membership and an intellectual membership [he writes]. As to the former, even when they view a political group sympathetically and recognize in its idea the expression of their own existence, it is not their habit to maintain permanent contact with it, still less active association, for its political views, insofar as these go beyond their own immediate preoccupations, seem to them obscure, gratuitous, and excessive. For the others – the intellectuals – what in particular they seem capable of satisfying when they come into contact with a political group is their curiosity and their 'need for information.' We should state here clearly that we have *never* had, on the part of the public readership of the review, the kind of response we had hoped for, which could have aided us in our work. The attitude of this public has remained, save for the rarest of exceptions, that of passive consumers of ideas. Such an attitude coming from the public, which is perfectly compatible with the role and aims of a review presented in a traditional style, in the long run renders the existence of a review such as *Socialisme ou Barbarie* impossible [emphasis added].

It is very significant that in "The Suspension" Castoriadis complains that forming and maintaining a revolutionary organization in the mid-1960s was impossible because *young people* were the only people who, "under these circumstances," wanted to join it.

> Our experience has been [Castoriadis writes] that those who came to us – basically young people – often did so based, if not on a misunderstanding, at least on motivations that derived much more from an emotional [trans: *affective*] revolt and from a need to break with the isolation to which society today condemns individuals than from a lucid and firm adherence to a revolutionary project. This initial motivation perhaps is as good as any other; what really matters is that the same conditions for the absence of properly political activity also prevent this motivation from being transformed into something more solid.

The significance of this complaint should be obvious: it was among the young people of France (the deplorable *students*) that the May 1968 revolution originated. It appears that – unlike the situationists, who intervened quite smoothly and successfully in the student milieu at the University of Strasbourg in 1966 – the members of S. ou B. just didn't know what to tell or what to do with all the young people who were, after reading their review, approaching them personally. Since no one else was approaching them personally – since the "real" working-class either was not reading the review or had decided to remain "passive consumers" of it – Castoriadis and the rest decided to call it quits.

Someone named Alain Guillerm was among the four members of the S. ou B. group who opposed the suspension of publication of the review and tried to continue the S. ou B. project under another name. It was Guillerm who, in the wake of Guy Debord's departure in 1961, wanted to form a "situationist tendency" within S. ou B., but was unsuccessful. In 1967, David Ames Curtis reports,

> the group formed by the dissenting S. ou B. members called itself Communisme ou Barbarie [a.k.a. Groupe Bororo]. It met frequently in the Marais section of Paris, managed to be denounced by the Situationist International during its brief existence, and picked up a few members, including Dominique Frager, who had wanted to join S. ou B. soon before its dissolution. Contacts also were established with people from Noir et Rouge, the Situationists, and radical students from Germany, among others. Right before Christmas, 1967, Frager introduced the group to the soon-to-be student leader of May '68, Daniel Cohn-Bendit. Cohn-Bendit [...] thus was in direct contact with the group that made itself the continuator of Socialisme ou Barbarie in the months leading to the March 22 takeover of the Nanterre University Administration building and to May '68. To my knowledge, this quite slender, but significant, thread of historical continuity has never before been revealed in print. Also of significance, Guillerm participated in the Nanterre occupation on March 22 and in the formation of the March 22d Movement. He was on the barricades the first evening in Paris.

Despite the admirable attempts of Castoriadis's translator to locate and call attention to the "slender, but significant, thread of historical continuity" between what we are calling the larger S. ou B. project and the May 1968 revolution, the reader of Castoriadis's "The Anticipated Revolution" (written between 20 and 25 May 1968) is struck by the fact that its author was far more critical than he was excited about the May 1968 revolution.

> The students and workers were not even united on a negative objective [Castoriadis writes about May 1968]. Among the students, at least among their revolutionary and active elements, the negative objective of opposition to the government was understood in a different sense than it was by the workers. For the former, the aim is to eliminate the government, whereas the great majority of workers, even though they do not favor the government, are absolutely unprepared to work toward its overthrow. A worker/student alliance cannot materialize under these conditions; it remains a mere wish, based on a misunderstanding.

Indeed, Castoriadis seems no partisan of revolution itself!

> Historically [Castoriadis writes], it is revolution that permits the world of reaction to survive as it transforms and adapts itself – and today we risk experiencing a fresh demonstration of this truth. These explosions shatter the imaginary or unreal setting in which alienated society, by its very nature, tends to enclose itself – and they oblige alienated society to seek out new forms of oppression better adapted to today's conditions, even if it finds them through the elimination of yesterday's oppressors.

Quite obviously, neither Castoriadis nor the rest of the S. ou B. group did what the situationists did: namely, foresee or "anticipate" the advent of the May 1968 revolution. David Ames Curtis mentions that "this text ['The Anticipated Revolution'] could just as well bear the title 'The Revolution Anticipated.'" That is to say, for Castoriadis, May 1968 was only an anticipation of the real revolution to come, and was not, as the Situationist International called it, the much anticipated "beginning of an era."

And yet Curtis, in his "Foreword" to *Political and Social Writings, 1961-1979,* claims that "the May 1968 French student-worker rebellion came as a striking confirmation – both in its negative and its positive aspects – of the new orientation Castoriadis was developing in the 1960s." Let us offer a corrected version of this sentence: the May 1968 French student-worker rebellion came as a striking confirmation – both in its negative and its positive aspects – of the new orientation Castoriadis called for but failed to develop, especially in his October 1962 text "For a New Orientation." (If the "new orientation" was developed by *anyone* in the early 1960s, it was the situationists.)

The striking thing about Castoriadis's "For a New Orientation" is that it is completely preoccupied with *content,* and totally unconcerned with *form.* Though Castoriadis claims that "today" S. ou B. is at a momentous turning point, he is unable to embody his sense of urgency in his *writing.* "For a New Orientation" is thoughtful and very clearly expressed – it patiently lays out fairly detailed suggestions concerning the group's propaganda, its main themes, and the group's means of expressing it – but it is also affectless, boring and uninspiring to read. "For a New Orientation" lacks the very same emotional qualities – passion, anger, love, rage – that Castoriadis found so plentiful in the revolt of the young people who approached the S. ou B. group. Quite obviously, if you can't feel what other people are feeling, there is no way that you can really communicate with them, no way that you can "know how to welcome and accept the collaboration and the contributions of people outside the group, and to do so within the framework of a very broad ideological sense of agreement."

Though Castoriadis is clearly aware of this serious problem –

> To break with the conceptions and practice of bureaucratic organizations [he writes] is also to break with traditional jargon, which has lost all meaning for people, and even has become an object of derision [...] We must transform our way of speaking and writing, pitilessly eliminating from our speech and from our texts insider terms and a didactic expository style.

– there seems to be nothing he can do to solve it.

> Obviously on this point no one can provide recipes or resolve the problem by fiat in one day [he writes]; only by multiplication of examples and of trial efforts will it be able to yield results (some of the texts written by our English and American comrades show the way in this regard). But this need to change our language must become a preoccupation, a permanent obsession for everyone [...] To break with the bureaucratic ideology is, first of all, to break with the *themes* of this ideology and its corresponding propaganda. It is to broaden the subjects we are talking about so as to embrace all aspects of people's lives in society. It is, moreover, the most profound content of our ideas that makes this incumbent upon us.

But messing around with *quantities* – "eliminating" this and "multiplying" that; "broadening" this and narrowing that – will never produce or guarantee superior *quality*. Revolutionary style is not just a matter of adding good things and subtracting bad things from your texts; it is not a matter of changing what you talk about, but changing *how* and *why* you talk about it.

Not surprisingly, Castoriadis's total lack of attention to form (and to quality) is apparent in his discussions of the revolution itself.

> People will not make a revolution over their wages – not today, in any case; they will not even make one for workers' management as such, and rightly so, since workers' management as such is only a tool, not an end in itself. People will make a revolution in order to make a radical change in the way they live, and this concerns the *content* of the revolution, its *ends,* and its *values.*

What Castoriadis fails to realize is that the desire to change life itself is dialectical: it concerns the *form* of the revolution, its *means* and its *pleasures,* as well as its content, ends and values. If the revolution remains obsessively concerned with its *content,* and ignores its form, it will be a partial revolution: it surely will not be the "total revolution" that Castoriadis insists elsewhere in "The New Orientation" is necessary ("The crisis of society and of culture is total, and the revolution will be total or it will not be at all"). Quite obviously, revolutionary theory and action must be concerned with both the content *and* the form of the revolution for that revolution to be total.

Unlike the situationists of 1962, who were obsessed with recuperation by the dominant society, Castoriadis has nothing to say about partial revolutions and the dangers they pose once they have been defeated. Precisely because he unaccountably sees around him *no* revolutionary activity, *no* struggles by workers that, "on certain points at least, tend to break with the established order," Castoriadis is not concerned with capitalism's capacity or efforts to recuperate such struggles. His thinking seems to be this: "By definition, there is no such thing as a partial revolution; the revolution will either be total or it simply and literally will not be; when the revolution breaks out, there will of course be no need to be concerned with recuperation, because it won't exist; until such time as the revolution breaks out, there is no need to worry about the recuperation of partial revolutions, because they aren't really revolutionary and therefore can't be co-opted."

It is almost *funny* that Castoriadis – when he finally addresses himself to the concept of recuperation – does so in "The Anticipated Revolution," of all texts, and does so to categorically dismiss its importance to revolutionary organizations.

> Someone who is afraid of cooptation has already been co-opted. His attitude has been co-opted – since it has been blocked up. The deepest reaches of his mind have been co-opted, for there he seeks guarantees against being co-opted, and thus he has already been caught in the trap of reactionary ideology: the search for an anticooptation talisman or fetishistic magic charm. There is *no* guarantee against cooptation; in a sense, everything can be co-opted, and everything is one day or another.

This is *psychobabble,* and I'm sure it convinced no one in the aftermath of May 1968, precisely because this revolution was dominated by concerted and consistent efforts to *defeat* cooptation. What other way is there to understand the workers' "brutal" rejection of the "incredible swindle" (Castoriadis's words) of the Grenelle Accords? If this rejection *wasn't* a counter-attack against cooptation, why was it necessary – just two days later – for the police to start removing workers from the factories they had been occupying?

Our conclusions are this: though the Situationist International did not have a particularly nuanced and deep understanding of workers' self-management and workers' councils, its members knew well *how to communicate these basic programmatic points in a style suitable for the time and for a young and enraged audience,* and thus prospered in the 1962 to 1967 period; while the radical elements in the Socialisme ou Barbarie group knew that their positions were scandalous by bourgeois and bureaucratic standards, they did not know *how to create scandals in the bourgeois world that would disseminate and attract people to their positions,* and thus steadily declined in relevance in the 1962 to 1967 period.

Quite obviously, these conclusions suggest a new starting-off point: namely, the image of the Situationist International and the Socialisme ou Barbarie group working together, rather than insulting or ignoring each other. We will look into this image in a third and final essay on Cornelius Castoriadis, which will be published in a future issue of *NOT BORED!*

NOT BORED! #29, July 1998

Norman Cohn's
The Pursuit of the Millennium

Norman Cohn's purpose in writing *The Pursuit of the Millennium: Revolutionary messianism in medieval and Reformation Europe and its bearing on modern totalitarian movements,* which was originally published in 1957 and then re-printed in 1961 in an expanded edition, was two-fold. First, Cohn intended to add to the existing literature on the "heresy" of the Free Spirit. "There exist only two comprehensive studies of the heresy of the Free Spirit," Cohn writes in a footnote. Neither of these studies – Mosheim's *De Beghardis et Beguinabus commentarius,* which was published in 1790, and Jundt's *Histoire du pantheisme populaire au Moyen Age et au 16e siecle,* published in 1875 – have been translated into English. And so Cohn's book was intended to be the very first comprehensive study of the Free Spirit in English.

One of the reasons for this dearth of historical research, Cohn notes, is that, "unlike the Cathars and the Waldensians," about whom a great deal has been published, "the adepts of the Free Spirit did not form a single church but rather a number of likeminded groups, each with its own messiah and each with its own particular practices, rites and articles of belief." Cohn's very ambitious book – he reports in the first edition that it took him 10 years to write it – attempts to gather together and present in chronological order translations of rare or previously unknown texts by and about many of these likeminded groups. A measure of the success of *The Pursuit of the Millennium* is the fact that it is cited as a reliable authority by people who otherwise disagree strongly with the conclusions its author makes on the basis of his research.

Let's take as our example a member of the Situationist International, a modern Marxist – and anti-Nazi and anti-Communist – revolutionary organization that was, not without some irony, strongly inspired by some of the groups described in Cohn's book. As Greil Marcus notes in *Lipstick Traces: A Secret History of the Twentieth Century,* the 11th (October 1967) issue of *Internationale*

Situationniste includes a page in which a photograph that has been intentionally miscaptioned "ALLEGED MEETING PLACE OF THE INTERNATIONAL SITUATIONISTS IN PARIS" has been juxtaposed with the following unattributed quote from Cohn's book:

> It is characteristic of this kind of movement that its aims and premises are boundless . . . Whatever their individual histories, collectively these people formed a recognizable social stratum – a frustrated and rather low-grade intelligentsia . . . And what followed then was the formation of a group of a peculiar kind,

– as Marcus notes, the situationists here dropped out the phrase "a true prototype of a modern totalitarian party" –

> a restlessly dynamic and utterly ruthless group which, obsessed by the apocalyptic phantasy and filled with the conviction of its own infallibility, set itself above the rest of humanity and recognized no claims save that of its own supposed mission . . . A boundless, millennial promise made with boundless, prophet-like conviction to a number of rootless and desperate men in the midst of a society where traditional norms and relationships are disintegrating – here, it would seem, lay the source of that peculiar subterranean fanaticism.

The situationist Raoul Vaneigem, who knew the book in its French translation (which was published in the early 1960s under the title *Fanatiques du l'apocalypse*), cites Cohn as an indisputable authority in his free-spirited book *The Revolution of Everyday Life*.

> The facts themselves will soon come to the aid of the mass of men in their struggle to enter at long last that state of freedom aspired to – though they lacked the means of attaining it – by those Swabian heretics of 1270 mentioned by Norman Cohn in his *Pursuit of the Millennium,* who "said that they had mounted up above God and, reaching the very pinnacle of Divinity, abandoned God. Often the adept would affirm that he or she had no longer 'any need of God.'"

This reference to Cohn's book was made in 1967. Some twenty years later, in his *Movement of the Free Spirit*, Vaneigem again cites Cohn as a reliable authority. "It is necessary to mention here a legend, substantiated by Norman Cohn and Romana Guarnieri, which originates not in any historical fact but in a novel by Georges Eekhoud. . . ." Such glancing references to *The Pursuit of the Millennium* may strike one as peculiar, because it is not a neutral book: it is in fact a relentless and spirited polemic. Cohn wrote it in part to expose and neutralize Marxist interpretations of the significance and nature of the movement of the Free Spirit.

Cohn notes that "the extent to which medieval heresy as such was a social protest by the unprivileged has been much debated." According to him, "the Marxist view maintained by Kautsky [in the book translated in 1897 as *Communism in Central Europe in the Time of the Reformation*] and Beer [in the 1924 translation of *Social Struggles in the Middle Ages*] and, with more scholarship, by de Stefano [in *Riformatori ed eretici del medioevo*] and Volpe [in *Movimenti religiosi e sette ereticali nella societa medioevale italiana, secoli XI-XIV*], is certainly an over-simplification." Elsewhere Cohn claims that, "in interpreting voluntary poverty as specifically a movement of the oppressed, Marxists such as Beer and Volpe certainly distorted the facts." And so *The Pursuit of the Millennium* was written to correct the over-simplifications and distortions made by Marxist historians.

But there is more to Cohn's relationship to Marxists and Communism than just this. For Cohn, "more curious" than the fact that the memory of the medieval free spirit Thomas Munzter "should have been venerated" by the Anabaptists, "even though he had never called himself an Anabaptist," "is the resurrection and apotheosis which he [Muntzer] has undergone during the past hundred years." Cohn continues:

> From Engels down to the Communist historians of today – Russian as well as German – Marxists have inflated Munzter into a giant symbol, a prodigious hero in the history of the 'class war.' This is a naive view, and one which non-Marxist historians have countered easily enough by pointing to the essentially mystical nature of Muntzer's preoccupations, his general indifference to the material welfare of the poor. Yet it may be suggested that this point of view too can be over-emphasized. Munzter was a *propheta* obsessed by eschatological phantasies which he attempted to translate into reality by exploiting social discontent. Perhaps after all it is a sound instinct that has led Marxists to claim him for their own.

To Cohn, contemporary Marxists – just like medieval *prophetae* such as Thomas Muntzer – do nothing but exploit social discontent, and are totally unconcerned – despite their grand-sounding pronouncements – with eradicating its underlying causes. Indeed, Marxists actually need social discontent to continue uninterrupted, for, without it, there is nothing to recommend their "Communism," their "heaven on Earth." And so *The Pursuit of the Millennium* has a certain sort of built-in reversibility: it is as much about contemporary Marxism – and German Nazism, which Cohn often mentions in the same breath as Communism – as it is about medieval heresies.

In a key passage, Cohn writes:

As for the Communists, they continue to elaborate, in volume after volume, that cult of Thomas Muntzer which was inaugurated already by Engels. But whereas in these works the *prophetae* of a vanished world are shown as men born centuries before their time, it is perfectly possible to draw the opposite moral – that, for all their exploitation of the most modern technology, Communism and Nazism have been inspired by phantasies which are downright archaic. And such is in fact the case. It can be shown (though to do so in detail would require another volume) that the ideologies of Communism and Nazism, dissimilar though they are in many respects, are both heavily indebted to that very ancient body of beliefs which constituted the popular apocalyptic lore of Europe.

Either people such as Thomas Muntzer anticipated and set the stage for the totalitarian leaders of the twentieth century, or people such as Lenin and Hitler were throwbacks to the leaders of heretical medieval sects. Take your choice: the results are the same. For Cohn, there is only massacre and terror to be expected from the realization of Munzter's or Hitler's or Lenin's respective "phantasies" of the "mystery and majesty of the final, eschatological drama"; there is only death and despair to be expected from these leaders' "restlessly dynamic and utterly ruthless group[s] which, obsessed by the apocalyptic phantasy and filled with the conviction of its own infallibility, set itself above the rest of humanity and recognized no claims save that of its own supposed mission." For Cohn, all three of them – Muntzer, Hitler, Lenin – are, in plain English, *mentally ill*. The theories of each sound like "a paranoiac expounding his private systematised delusion." All three were obsessed with purifying the world by destroying the agents of corruption, who are consistently identified as the Jewish people. As for the followers of these mass-murdering, anti-Semitic madmen, they are simply "the great mass of the disoriented, the perplexed and the frightened."

And so this is Cohn's ultimate message, despite the reversibility at the heart of his book: nothing has really changed in Northern Europe since the medieval period; for the last eight hundred years, Northern Europe has been a barbaric place.

Unlike Raoul Vaneigem, who merely uses Cohn's book as a reliable source of information (and does not call attention to the irony of his doing so), the situationist Guy Debord is explicitly interested in the strange reversibility contained within it. In his 1967 book *The Society of the Spectacle,* Debord writes:

> The social revolt of the millenarian peasantry defines itself naturally first of all as a will to destroy the Church. But millenarianism spreads in the historical world and not on the terrain of myth. Modern revolutionary expectations are not irrational continuations of the religious passion of millenarianism, as Norman Cohn thought he had demonstrated in *The Pursuit of the Millennium*. On the contrary, it is

millenarianism – revolutionary class struggle speaking the language of religion for the last time – which is already a modern revolutionary tendency that as yet lacks *the consciousness that it is only historical.*

And so Debord re-establishes the Marxist position (reversed by Cohn) that medieval free spirits such as Thomas Muntzer were really forerunners of today's social revolutionaries – but he does so while making a crucial alteration in its fundamental assumptions.

> The millenarians [Debord goes on to say] had to lose because they could not recognize the revolution as their own operation. The fact that they waited to act on the basis of an external sign of God's decision is the translation into thought of the practice of insurgent peasants following chiefs taken from outside their ranks. The peasant class could not attain an adequate consciousness of the functioning of society or of the way to lead its own struggle; because it lacked these conditions of unity in its action and consciousness, it expressed its project and led its wars with the imagery of an earthly paradise.

Unlike both Marxist and Nazi historians, Debord insists that the millenarians of the twentieth century must not make the same mistake made by their medieval predecessors. That is to say, Debord insists that modern millenarians will lose if they allow a "socialist" political party to conduct the revolution for them or on their behalf. Leaders must never be drawn from outside the ranks of the insurgents, and moments for insurrection must never be chosen on the basis of external signs or concerns. The revolution must be recognized and conducted as the operation of the millenarians themselves if it is to be successful.

Let us note that there is some irony in the fact that Debord's reversal of Cohn is not located in the chapter of *The Society of the Spectacle* entitled "The Proletariat as Subject and Representation," in which it clearly belongs – precisely because Cohn himself uses the word "proletariat" to designate the mass of urban workers who consistently participated in "heretical" movements and microsocieties throughout the Middle Ages. Instead, Debord places his reversal of Cohn in the chapter entitled "Time and History," which seems to indicate that Debord is uncomfortable with the fact that he himself is (still) a Marxist; it indicates that Debord is uncomfortable with the validity of Cohn's attacks on Marxism. Or, rather, it indicates that Debord knows that his situationist Marxism must be clearly *set apart* from "Marxist" Communism, from the Marxism of Lenin and Stalin. This setting apart is in fact accomplished in "The Proletariat as Subject and Representation," which evaluates and strongly criticizes both the Marxists and the Bakunists, who, in their own time, clashed with the Marxists over their support for authoritarian use of state power to abolish class society.

Unfortunately, no one has undertaken a sustained discussion of *The Pursuit of the Millennium* – that is to say, of how its author demonstrates *the opposite* of what he sets out to do, of how the book in fact shows:

1) that the medieval "heresy" of the Free Spirit is not doomed to be reborn in fascist or otherwise authoritarian milieus, and that it can in fact be reborn in anarchist or otherwise *anti-authoritarian* formations; and

2) that "heaven on earth" is in some sense historically possible, that is to say, realizable, in the modern era.

Not surprisingly – given the fact that "Never work" is a central, if not *the* central situationist slogan – the theme of refusing to work for one's living is a consistent one in *The Pursuit of the Millennium,* or, rather, it is a consistent theme in the various pronouncements of the adepts of the Free Spirit over the course of some six centuries. Cohn notes that Irenaeus interpreted the remark, attributed to Jesus of Nazareth, "And I appoint unto you a kingdom . . . that ye may eat and drink at my table in my kingdom," as meaning that "during the Millennium the Saints would do no work but would sup of a banquet prepared for them by God with all sorts of fine dishes." Cohn notes that for Joachim of Fiore,

> The Age of the Spirit was to be the sabbath or resting-time of mankind. In it there would be no wealth or even property, for everyone would live in voluntary poverty; there would be no work, for human beings would possess only spiritual bodies and would need no food; there would be no institutional authority of any kind.

Cohn notes that John of Leyden (aka Jan Bockelson) wrote that, come the New Jerusalem, "all things were to be in common, there was to be no private property and nobody was to do any more work, but simply trust in God." Cohn notes that the "phantasy" of never working was part of the Roman Stoics' legend of the Golden Age, in which (in the words of Seneca) "no labourers ploughed up the soil, nobody was allowed to mark out or divide the ground; when men put everything into a common store, and the earth bore all things more freely because none demanded it."

In addition to all this, Cohn notes that, throughout the six centuries under consideration, millenarians actually did refuse to work for relatively long periods of time. The flagellants of Thuringia in the 1360s; the Beghards of Cologne in the 14th century; the radical Taborites in 1419-1420 – all of them refused to work, even if or precisely because it meant becoming destitute and having to beg for bread "for God's sake." But for Cohn, these attempts at "heaven on earth" were "wildly impractical," and consequently led to the abandonment of these "anarcho-communistic experiments." He contrasts them with the German Peasants' War, in which

> the peasants showed themselves not at all chiliastically minded but, on the contrary, politically minded in the sense that they thought in terms

of real situations and realizable possibilities. The most that a peasant community ever sought under the leadership of its own peasant aristocracy was local self-government; and the first stage of the movement, from March 1525 to the beginning of May, consisted simply of a series of local struggles in which a great number of communities really did extract from their immediate lords, ecclesiastical or lay, concessions giving them greater autonomy. And this was achieved not by bloodshed but by an intensification of the tough, hardheaded bargaining which the peasantry had been conducting for generations.

The intended polemical parallel with conditions in the twentieth century couldn't be clearer: *if only the working-classes would abandon their wildly impractical "chiliastic" hopes for revolutionary change, and just stick to working for reforms within the trade union ("bargaining") format!* In case his readers have any doubts about this, Cohn insists that the question has at any rate become academic, closed. "In the seventeenth century," he states simply, "voluntary poverty was no longer practicable as a consistent way of life." Incredible as it seems, this is what Cohn would have his readers believe: that with the advent of the Industrial Revolution, never working became not *more* possible, but *impossible*. Quite obviously, he's wrong. As a matter of fact, the Industrial Revolution was truly or was only "revolutionary" in that, for the first time in human history, it made the "phantasy" of never working a real, actualizable possibility. But Cohn isn't the only one who refuses to admit that something profound changed in Northern Europe since the Medieval period: our whole society is based upon the stubborn refusal to admit that work is no longer necessary, that "heaven on earth" is realizable now, for everyone, and without the need for either bargaining or bloodshed.

If the slogan "Never work" doesn't strike you as *heresy,* it can only be because – after centuries of becoming historical – the dream of not working is no longer an illusion or a matter of speculative doctrine. Never working has become something for the eye to see and desire, and for the hand to reach out for, hold and enjoy.

NOT BORED! #30, February 1999

Henri Lefebvre's *The Production of Space*

And do you know what "the world" is to me? Shall I show it to you in my mirror? This world: a monster of energy, without beginning, without end; a firm, iron magnitude of force that does not grow bigger or smaller, that does not expend itself but only transforms itself; as a whole, of unalterable size, a household without expenses or losses, but likewise without increase or income; enclosed by "nothingness" as by a boundary; not something blurry or wasted, not something endlessly extended, but set in a definite space as a definite force, and not a space that might be "empty" here or there, but rather a force throughout, as a play of forces and waves of forces, at the same time one and many, increasing here and at the same time decreasing there [...]. Frederick Nietzsche, *The Will to Power.*

Henri Lefebvre is a name that will be familiar to our readers. One of the most important French thinkers of the twentieth century, Lefebvre – in particular, his 1947 book *The Critique of Everyday Life* – exerted a profound influence on, among others, the members of the Situationist International; Lefebvre even became associated with the situationists personally in the years immediately following 1958, when he was excluded from the French Communist Party. Lefebvre's close association with the situationists lasted until 1962, when there was a nasty falling-out; their respective paths did not cross again after that. Though the situationists never regretted the bitterness and permanence of their separation from Lefebvre, he clearly did. *The Production of Space* was originally published in French in 1974, and translated into English by the ex-situationist Donald Nicholson-Smith in 1991. In it, the situationists are located in a certain space; their existence and contributions to the revolutionary movement are neither ignored nor over-emphasized. The very fact that *The Production of Space* is able to handle the situationists in such an even-handed way is a sure measure of the intellectual honesty and integrity of both the book and its author.

Unlike most English translations of situationist books, *The Production of Space* is a popular title with book buyers: it has been reprinted every year since 1991, and twice in 1994 (the year its nearly 90-year-old author died). No doubt comparatively few of the book's buyers are deeply interested in Lefebvre's relationship with the situationists and how it underpins or informs *The Production of Space*. Most buyers are probably drawn to the book by one of the many diverse topics that it covers in depth (spatial practices, architecture, urban planning, the history of the city, "the environment," representation and language, art, ideology, knowledge, epistemology, capitalism, Marxism, and the writings of Nietzsche). No doubt Lefebvre's brief and scattered comments about and references to the situationists will not inspire many of his readers to find out more about them. But the reader who knows well the writings of the situationists – in particular Guy Debord's *The Society of the Spectacle* (1967) – will get much more out of certain passages in *The Production of Space* than someone who doesn't; and the fan of the situationists who has read *The Production of Space* will be struck by the degree to which Lefebvre's book is an explicit attempt to continue the situationist project by means other than the International itself.

In his discussion of appropriation, which he (following Marx's discussions of human nature) defines as a spatial practice in which nature has been modified in order to satisfy and expand human needs and possibilities, Lefebvre writes: "Appropriation should not be confused with a practice which is closely related to it but still distinct, namely 'diversion' (detournement)." Knowing full well that detournement is a central concept in both situationist theory and practice, Lefebvre goes on to say the following:

> An existing space may outlive its original purpose and the *raison d'etre* which determines its forms, functions, and structures; it may thus in a sense become vacant, and susceptible of being diverted, reappropriated and put to a use quite different from its initial one. A recent and well-known case of this was the reappropriation of the Halles Centrales, Paris's former wholesale produce market, in 1969-71. For a brief period, the urban centre, designed to facilitate the distribution of food, was transformed into a gathering-place and a scene of permanent festival – in short, into a centre of play rather than of work – for the youth of Paris.

This is an extraordinary passage. As every pro-situ and situphile knows, the situationists were great fans and "reappropriators" of Les Halles as early as 1960; members of the French section no doubt spent a good deal of time there during the period in question (between the occupations movement of 1968 and the disbanding of the SI in 1972); Guy Debord includes several scenes of the market at dawn in his 1973 film *The Society of the Spectacle*. But this passage from Lefebvre is more than a tip-of-the-hat to the situationists, to one of their most important concepts, and to one of their favorite hangouts in Paris.

When the situationists defined the concept of detournement in the first (1958) issue of their journal *Internationale Situationniste* – actually, the concept of detournement dates back to Debord's days in the Lettrist International, circa 1956 – the references were to "pre-existing aesthetic elements," to "present or past artistic production," to "propaganda." In other words, the references were very broad: they took in all forms of cultural production, and were not limited to a single one. "In this sense," the SI wrote in 1958, "there can be no situationist painting or music, but only a situationist use of these means." In the definition provided by Lefebvre, however, the reference is very narrow: to "an existing space." Detournement is best understood as something done with pre-existing buildings, streets, fields, neighborhoods or cities. In this view, Lefebvre's definition is part of a larger effort to return the situationist project to its origins in architecture and "unitary urbanism." As has been pointed out before in the pages of this journal, Lefebvre felt that, after the reorganization of the SI in 1962, the group abandoned both "diversion" and "psychogeographical" experimentation as it perfected and disseminated its critical theories.

But this isn't the only way to read Lefebvre's "diversion" of the situationist concept of detournement. It may be misleading or inaccurate to say that the situationist definition of detournement is broad (all forms of art) and that Lefebvre's is narrow (only architecture and urbanism) – that is, to imply that the former includes the latter within its much-larger space. It may very well be the reverse: namely, that Lefebvre's insistence that "diversion" is essentially a spatial practice (and not an artistic one) is the broader of the two conceptions; and that revolutionary artistic practices are enclosed and only possible within revolutionary spatial practices. In this view, Lefebvre's re-definition of detournement might be part of a larger effort to critique, re-invigorate and extend the situationist project, even if this means demonstrating the limitations of and detonating several key situationist concepts and practices in the process.

Since Lefebvre's book is an explicit attempt to demonstrate the limitations of a great many concepts and practices (situationist and otherwise), it seems best to focus upon Lefebvre's specific references to and discussions of the limitations of situationist concepts before we turn our attention to the book as a whole. Otherwise, we risk losing sight of the fact that *The Production of Space* – though it is "a situationist book" – is not a book about the situationists or the situationist project. (We give away no secret when we say that Lefebvre's book is about "a space," a society, "which is determined economically by capital, dominated socially by the bourgeoisie, and ruled politically by the state.") The situationists and the situationist project are relevant to *The Production of Space* only insofar as this project is an effort to divert the totality of capitalist space.

Not surprisingly, Lefebvre focuses on the critical theory of the spectacle, especially as it is elaborated in Guy Debord's *The Society of the Spectacle*. Lefebvre's personal contact in the 1958 to 1962 period was primarily with Debord. After the 1962 reorganization, it was Debord's theory of the spectacle that replaced the theories of psychogeography, diversion and *la derive* at the center of the situationist project. Finally, and most importantly, *The Society of the Spectacle* – despite the impression that situationist definitions of detournement tend to under-emphasize or even ignore spatial practice – devotes several chapters to two closely inter-related topics (time and space) that are central to Lefebvre's concerns in *The Production of Space*.

In a passage that could very well have come from *The Society of the Spectacle* – and drawing upon the very same sources as Debord did (Georg Lukacs' *History and Class Consciousness* and Jean Gabel's *False Consciousness*) – Lefebvre writes:

> With the advent of modernity time has vanished from social space. It is recorded solely on measuring-instruments, on clocks, that are isolated and functionally specialized as this time itself. Lived time loses its form and its social interest – with the exception, that is, of time spent working. Economic space subordinates time to itself;

political space expels it as threatening and dangerous (to power). The primacy of the economic and above all of the political implies the supremacy of space over time.

Compare this passage with two comments taken from the chapter of *The Society of the Spectacle* entitled "The Organization of Territory" in the standard Black & Red edition. (Note that this chapter is titled "Environmental Planning" in Donald Nicholson-Smith's 1994 translation of *The Society of the Spectacle*, which is the translation we have used for these and all other quotations.)

> The same modernization that has deprived travel of its temporal aspect has likewise deprived it of the reality of space [...] The requirement of capitalism that is met by urbanism in the form of a freezing of life might be described, in Hegelian terms, as an absolute predominance of "tranquil side-by-sideness" in space over "restless becoming in the progression of time."

Though Lefebvre and Debord agree that historical or human time has been dominated by capitalist space, they disagree strongly as to what to do about it. Is the rediscovery of time the key to the liberation of space? Or is the reappropriation of space the key to the liberation of time? *Are these questions mirror images of each other?*

Debord insists on the primacy of time and its rediscovery: "The spectacle," he writes, "as the present social organization of the paralysis of history and memory, of the abandonment of history built on the foundation of historical time, is the false consciousness of time." Elsewhere in the "Spectacular Time" chapter of *The Society of the Spectacle*, he writes,

> As Hegel showed, time is a necessary alienation, being the medium [the Black & Red edition uses the word "environment" here] in which the subject realizes himself while losing himself, becomes other in order to become truly himself. The opposite obtains in the case of the alienation that now holds sway – the alienation suffered by the producers of an estranged present. This is a spatial alienation, whereby a society that radically severs the subject from the activity that it steals from him [also] separates him in the first place from his own time. Social alienation, though in principle insurmountable, is nevertheless the alienation that has forbidden and petrified the possibilities and risks of a living alienation within time.

For Debord, "spatial alienation" comes into existence as a result of the capitalist production of frozen time, not the reverse. To destroy the spectacle, then, fluid historical time must be rediscovered. "The revolutionary project of a classless society, of a generalized historical life, is also the project of a withering away of the social measure of time in favor of an individual and collective irreversible time which is playful in character and which encompasses, simultaneously present within it, a variety of autonomous yet effectively federated times," Debord concludes. "[The revolutionary project is] the complete realization, in short, within the medium [the Black & Red edition uses the word "context" here] of time, of that communism which 'abolishes everything that exists independently of individuals.'" For Debord, social space ("human geography") is only subjected to radical critique after frozen, spectacular time has been shattered and historical time has begun to flow again. If "the entire [social] environment" is to be reconstructed, it will be "in accordance with the needs of the power of established workers' councils – the needs, in other words, of the anti-State dictatorship of the proletariat."

Typical anti-Hegelian Hegelianism is what Lefebvre would – and does – say about this ideological fetishization of time, which involves a reduction of the multi-dimensional complexities of space. "Rediscovered time," he notes dryly, "under the direction of a class consciousness elevated to the sublime level at which it can survey history's twists and turns at a glance, breaks the primacy of the spatial." To Lefebvre, such "restorations" or "rediscoveries" of time are understandable but regrettable and increasingly useless counter-balances to what Lefebvre calls Hegel's "fetishization of space in the service of the state."

According to Lefebvre, "only Nietzsche, since Hegel, has maintained the primordiality of space and concerned himself with the spatial problematic." Significantly, "Nietzschean space preserves not a single feature of the Hegelian view of space as product and residue of historical time," Lefebvre asserts. "Cosmic space contains energy, contains forces, and proceeds from them [...] An energy or force can only be identified by means of its effects in space, even if forces 'in themselves' are distinct from their effects." For Lefebvre, "just as Nietzschean space has nothing in common with Hegelian space, so Nietzschean time, as theatre of universal tragedy, as the cyclical, repetitious space-time of death and life, has nothing in common with Marxist time – that is, [with] historicity driven forward by the forces of production and adequately (to be optimistic) by industrial, proletarian and revolutionary rationality."

Building upon Nietzsche – and to an extent alongside the work of Deleuze and Guattari, despite his strong criticisms of their work – Lefebvre insists on the primacy of space and its reappropriation. For him, capitalist false consciousness is not the false consciousness of time, but the false consciousness of space. To abolish the capitalist state, space must be reappropriated on the planetary scale; historical time will be indeed be rediscovered, but "in and through [reappropriated] space." And this is because everything (all the "concrete abstractions") that revolutionaries seek to abolish – ideology, the state, the commodity, money, value, and class struggle – do not and cannot exist independently of space.

"What is an ideology without a space to which it refers, a space which it describes, whose vocabulary and links it makes use of, and whose code it embodies?" Lefebvre demands. "What would remain of the Church if there were no churches?" The answer is nothing, for the Church does and can not guarantee its endurance otherwise. "The state and each of its constituent institutions call for [pre-existing] spaces – but spaces which they can then organize according to their specific requirements; so there is no sense in which space can be treated solely as an *a priori* condition of these institutions and the state which presides over them," Lefebvre writes. "The world of commodities would have no 'reality' without such [spatial] moorings or points of insertion, or without their existing as an ensemble," he reminds us. "The same may be said of banks and banking-networks vis-à-vis the capital market and money transfers." It is only in space that each idea of presumed value "acquires or loses its distinctiveness through confrontation with the other values and ideas that it encounters there"; it is only in space that competing sociopolitical interests and forces come effectively into play.

As for the spectacle, it is an ideological force – another "concrete abstraction" – that is taken quite seriously by Lefebvre. He writes:

> People look, and take sight, take seeing, for life itself. We build on the basis of papers and plans. We buy on the basis of images. Sight and seeing, which in the Western tradition once epitomized intelligibility, have turned into a trap: the means whereby, in social space, diversity may be simulated and a travesty of enlightenment and intelligibility ensconced under the sign of transparency.

But the process of spectacularization is, for Lefebvre, less "important" than and "in any case subsumed by" the "predominance of visualization." According to Lefebvre, the process of spectacularization is merely one of the functions of the "logic of visualization"; the "spectacle" is one of the "moments or aspects" of visualization.

Despite what was said at the beginning of this piece about Lefebvre's intellectual honesty and integrity, his distinction between the processes of spectacularization and visualization – which, it should be noted, entails the assignment of Debord to the intellectual ranks of such second-class theorists as Erwin Panofsky and Marshall McLuhan – seems arbitrary and specious. While it is obvious that a spectacle (an attractive, uncanny or repulsive visual phenomenon) presupposes the ability to perceive visually, it is not self-evident that spectacles only exist, that things are only attractive, uncanny or repulsive (that is, worth looking at) after vision has been established as the most important of the five senses. It is more likely that "the spectacle" (as opposed to a spectacle, or this or that spectacle) and "the predominance of the visual" are simply different names for the same phenomenon.

But this doesn't mean that Lefebvre has nothing new or interesting to add to what Debord says about the society of the spectacle (Lefebvre might have referred to "the society of abstract space," had he been interested in such terminology). Indeed, precisely because he approaches the spectacle from the "perspective" of space rather than time, Lefebvre is able to re-illuminate and enlarge the terrain on which the battle to abolish the spectacle is being fought. The freshness of Lefebvre's take on the spectacle can be detected in both the form and the content of his book.

Unlike Debord's *The Society of the Spectacle*, which is short, direct, and clearly intended to be definitive, Lefebvre's *The Production of Space* is long, meandering, and clearly intended to be preliminary. While Debord's book accumulates invulnerable sentences into numbered theses, and numbered theses into numbered and subtitled chapters – in imitation of the spectacle, which is "capital *accumulated* to the point that it becomes an image" (emphasis added) – Lefebvre's book imitates space by being written in such a way that it "is actually experienced, in its depths, as duplications, echoes and reverberations, redundancies and doublings-up which engender – and are engendered by – the strangest of contrasts." While the internal divisions (the nine sharply-defined chapters) of *The Society of the Spectacle* – reminiscent somehow of wide boulevards that ensure the smooth circulation of traffic – make sure that the book's major themes do not interfere with each other, *The Production of Space* (to once again quote its author out of context) is "penetrated by, and shot through with, the weaker tendencies characteristic of networks and pathways." Unlike Debord, who uses the same paths to arrive at different points, Lefebvre arrives at the same points by using different paths.

As for the content of Lefebvre's analysis: the society of abstract space has three essential aspects, two of them unmentioned by Debord in his book(s) on the spectacle: the visual-spectacular; the geometric; and the phallic. For Lefebvre, these three aspects "imply one another and conceal one another," in part because they arose as part of the same historical process. Speaking about supposedly pre-spectacular thirteenth century Gothic architecture, Lefebvre says that "the trend towards visualization, underpinned by a strategy, now came into its own – and this in collusion on the one hand with abstraction, with geometry and logic, and on the other with [phallic] authority." And so, rather than speak of "the predominance of the visual" in abstract space, Lefebvre speaks (rather awkwardly) of "the predominance of the geometric-visual-phallic."

Let us focus, then, on the two aspects of spectacular or abstract space apparently overlooked by Debord: the geometric and the phallic. Though he knows well that –

> A society that molds its entire surroundings has necessarily evolved its own technique for working on the material basis of this set of tasks. That material basis is the society's actual territory. Urbanism is the mode of appropriation of the natural and human environment by capitalism, which, true to its logical development toward absolute

domination, can (and now must) refashion the totality of space into its own peculiar decor. ("The Organization of Territory," *The Society of the Spectacle*.)

– Debord stops short of describing that "peculiar" decor, of analyzing its distinctive features and shapes, of tracing out its geometry. A curious impression is created by the absence of references to the increasingly obvious use and overuse of straight lines, right angles, symmetrical shapes, and strict rectilinear perspectives in spectacular space. There seems to be a kind of blindspot in Debord's analysis. Paradoxically, it is only in some of the images included in the film version of *The Society of the Spectacle* (1973) that Debord is seen to take direct note of the specific geometrical characteristics of capitalism's "own peculiar decor." The same may be said for the phallic aspect of the spectacle: it is suggested – but not made explicit – by the obsessive quality of the film's repetitious use of images of half-nude women. But the book itself never refers to gender, sex, or sexuality. Curious.

As for the "geometric formant," Lefebvre writes, it "is that Euclidean space which philosophical thought has treated as 'absolute,' and hence a space (or representation of space) long used as a space of reference."

> Euclidean space [he continues] is defined by its "isotopy" (or homogeneity), a property which guarantees its social and political utility. The reduction of this homogenous Euclidean space, first of nature's space, then of all social space, has conferred a redoubtable power upon it. All the more so since that initial reduction leads easily to another – namely, the reduction of three-dimensional realities to two dimensions (for example, a "plan," a blank sheet of paper, something drawn on paper, a map, or any kind of graphic representation or projection).

In its geometric aspect, the "abstract spectacle" is a double reduction: first the heterogeneous spaces of nature and social space are reduced to the homogenous space of Euclid; and next homogenous Euclidean space is reduced to the illusory space of two-dimensional representations. Space is no longer something concrete and opaque, that is, something to be experienced and lived (as well as perceived and conceived); it is now something abstract and transparent, something to be looked at passively and from a distance, without being lived directly. What is seen is not space, but an image of space. Space becomes "intelligible" to the eye (but only to the eye); space appears to be a text to be read, a message that bears no traces of either state power or human bodies and their non-verbal flows. Certain basic geometrical forms – the rectangular, the square, the circle, the triangle – are elevated to the level of the exemplary (microcosms of the universe) and are reproduced everywhere as images of rationality, harmony and order.

Because abstract space "cannot be completely evacuated, nor entirely filled with mere images or transitional objects," and still exist, its geometry is a phallic one. A "truly full object – an objectal 'absolute'" is required by abstract space. A monumental, vertically oriented, steel-and-glass *architectural erection* "fulfills the extra function of ensuring that 'something' occupies this space, namely a signifier which, rather than signifying a void, signifies a plenitude of destructive force." This plenitude is the violence of state power, of the state's monopoly on "legal" violence. Thus there is a tension within the phallic aspect of the spectacle, or, rather, between its phallic and geometric aspects. "Abstract space is not homogenous," though it wishes to appear and be perceived as homogenous, Lefebvre writes; "it simply has homogeneity as its goal, its orientation, its 'lens'." Abstract space appears to be transparent and readable-intelligible, but "this transparency is deceptive, and everything is [actually] concealed," he points out. "Space is illusory and the secret of the illusion lies in the transparency itself."

The three aspects of abstract space – the spectacular-visual, the geometric, and the phallic – combine in such a way that, Lefebvre concludes, "the visual realm is confused with the geometrical one, and the optical transparency (or legibility) of the visual is mistaken for logico-mathematical intelligibility. And vice versa." What, then, are we to make of the fact that Debord either folds the geometric and the phallic aspects into the visual aspect (so that the visual aspect is the only one worth mentioning), or completely overlooks the geometric and the phallic, and so only mentions the visual?

From Lefebvre's perspective, Debord is too much of a Marxist, and too little of a Nietzschean. That is to say, Debord is far too concerned with the commodity and its monopolization of time, and too little concerned with state power and its production of space. He is too confident that the economy has indeed completely established itself at the heart of society, and that the state is simply a tool of economic interests, without any autonomous existence, powers or effects. And so, if Debord focuses exclusively on the visual aspect of abstract space, it is because this aspect is the closest to the spectacular appeal of the commodity (its social appearance); and if he turns away from the geometric and the phallic, it is because they are to be associated with the state and its "logical" monopoly on "rational violence."

But let us give Debord the benefit of the doubt. In 1967, the role of the state in the imposition and maintenance of social homogeneity wasn't as clear as it became after 1969, that is, after the state began to defend itself in earnest against the social revolutions of 1968. The books Lefebvre himself wrote before 1970 – *Introduction to Modernity,* for example, or *Everyday Life in the Modern World* – are also preoccupied with the commodity, and relatively unconcerned with the state. And so one can't blame the Debord of 1967 for not asserting (in the words of Lefebvre) "with reasonable confidence" – and in direct contradiction with one of the central situationist hypotheses about the banalizing effects of the global commodity-spectacle – "that the process of producing things in space (the range of so-called consumer goods) tends to annul rather than reinforce homogenization."

One can't blame the Debord of 1967 for not seeing what Lefebvre saw in 1974, namely that:

> A number of differentiating traits are thus permitted to emerge which are not completely bound to a specific location or situation, to a geographically determinate space. The so-called economic process tends to generate diversity – a fact which supports the hypothesis that homogenization today is a function of political rather than economic factors as such; abstract space is a tool of power.

Judging from the dramatic shift in his emphasis from the commodity to the state in his 1988 book *Comments on The Society of the Spectacle*, Debord realized his miscalculation and attempted to correct it (without, for all that, admitting that his 1967 book wasn't perfect). Furthermore, Debord recognized his mistake early. More so than any other European revolutionary, with the notable exception of his situationist comrade Gianfranco Sanguinetti, Debord quickly and fully recognized the international significance of the bombings of civilian targets executed in covert fashion by the Italian secret services in December 1969. On this score, one might very well ask Lefebvre: why doesn't *your* book – if it indeed it is concerned with the opaque machinations of state power – contain a single reference to terrorism?

Today, in 1999, it seems very clear that the hypothesis about the role of the state in social homogenization – which Lefebvre indicates was originally inspired by the Czech writer Radovan Richta – is absolutely correct. Thanks to an ever-expanding commodity economy, young people today look more rebellious, less socialized, and less like each other in matters of personal appearance than ever before. Piercings and tattoos are a clear sign that certain forms of social conformity and homogenization are at an end. And yet, Lefebvre (following Wilhelm Reich) wants to know, "Why do they allow themselves to be manipulated in ways so damaging to their spaces and their daily life without embarking on massive revolts?" An even better question: "Why is protest left to 'enlightened,' and hence elite, groups who are in any case largely exempt from these manipulations?"

Lefebvre's own answer to these questions is: the nature and effects of abstract space. It is abstract space (the space of bureaucratic politics) that produces, imposes and reinforces social homogeneity. In order to destroy the society of abstract space, Lefebvre prepared *The Production of Space*, which attempts to define and develop some of the necessary concepts ("the production of space," "the political economy of space," and "the science of space" among them).

The space produced by Lefebvre is big, almost too big, for it is easy to get lost in it or confused by the return to the same points. Voices echo off the walls. Lefebvre himself hears them, and answers back. "Change life!" and "Change society!" the voices call out; they are the voices of situationists. "These precepts mean nothing without the production of an appropriate space," he answers back. "Seize the time!" and "History's not made by great men!" other voices call out.

And we enter the conversation to say that these precepts should be detourned so that they say "Seize the space!" and "Space is not made by great men!"

NOT BORED! #30, February 1999

T.J. Clark's *The End of An Idea*: Beginning Well and Ending Badly

"If I can't have the proletariat as my chosen people any longer, at least capitalism remains my Satan." – T.J. Clark.

T.J. Clark's *Farewell To An Idea: Episodes from a History of Modernism* (Yale University Press, 1999) is announced to be a book about art and politics – about modernist art and socialist politics, and their relationship to each other – by someone who is sympathetic to both, er, "parties."

The book was written after the Fall of the Wall [Professor Clark writes in his "Introduction"]. That is, at a moment when there was general agreement, on the part of the masses and elites in most of the world, that the project called socialism had come to an end – at roughly the same time, it seems, as the project called modernism. Whether those predictions turn out to be true, only time will tell. But clearly something of socialism and modernism has died, in both cases deservedly; and my book is partly written to answer the question: If they died together, does that mean that in some sense they lived together, in century-long co-dependency? Socialism, to remind you, was the idea of "the political, economic and social emancipation of the whole people, men and women, by the establishment of a democratic commonwealth in which the community shall own the land and capital collectively and use them for the good of all" [here Professor Clark – without a trace of irony – is quoting quotes from the 1906 "Platform of the Church Socialist League"]. Co-dependency, we know to our cost, does not necessarily mean mutual aid or agreement on much. Modernism was regularly outspoken about the barrenness of the working-class movement – its politics of pity, its dreary materialism, its taste of the masses, the Idea of Progress, etc. But this may have been because it sensed socialism was its shadow – that it too was engaged in a desperate, and probably futile, struggle to imagine modernity otherwise. And maybe it is true that there could be and can be no modernism without the practical possibility of an end to capitalism existing, in whatever monstrous or pitiful form.

Let me put aside any immediate objection I might have to the implied metaphor of a co-dependent "marriage" between modernist art (husband) and socialist politics (wife) – Professor Clark is evidently married to and raises three children with Anne Wagner, the author of the recently published book *Three Artists (Three Women): Modernism and the Art of Hesse, Krasner and O'Keeffe*, which looks to be the "better half" of Professor Clark's *Farewell To An Idea* (a book that only deals with dead, white males) – and note that Professor Clark's book should not and cannot be politically neutral. It must take sides, for the stakes are indeed very high. As Clark writes in his "Introduction":

> Since the "Fall of the Wall" – an expression which is, as the situationist Guy Debord has pointed out, an all-too-facile shorthand for the rather complicated and deceptive events in Central and Eastern Europe beginning in 1989 – advanced capitalism appears to be, shall we say, the only "super-power" in the world of economics. Like the United States of America, advanced capitalism seems to be able to do what it wants to do on the stage of universal history; it is the only actor of consequence. Our post-1989 world is horrible; it is a horrible intensification of the conditions that have prevailed all century long.

Since I have already made and put aside one small but pertinent objection, let me not avoid adding another: that 1989 is a very late date to start a chronology of post-modernism. As early as 1969, Leslie A. Fiedler was referring to the novels written by William S. Burroughs and others in the 1960s as "Post-Modern"; in the early 1970s Jean-Francois Lyotard was already referring to "the postmodern condition." Professor Clark's dating of the birth of post-modernism – or, shall we say, his dating of the sudden death of modernism – at the end of the 1980s is at one, as we shall see, with his book's failure to deal with either the art or the politics of the post-1950 years.

Professor Clark's book must take sides, and by this I mean that it must take sides in the on-going battle between capitalism and its enemies, which include modernism and socialism. The implication throughout *Farewell To An Idea* is that the "death" of the husband-and-wife team of modernist art and socialist politics was prematurely announced: in writing about the coincident "births" of modernism and socialism during the French Revolution, for example, Professor Clark writes that "modernism also ended with the revolution, and began again when the revolution began again, and so on. (The cycle continues.)" Surely "the cycle" continues beyond 1989. What would authorize us to say that it doesn't, that the "age of revolutions" came to an end 10 years ago and that we are now living in a permanently post-revolutionary age? Not Professor Clark's book, which ends with these hopeful lines: "The myth will survive its historic defeat. The present is purgatory, not a permanent travesty of heaven." (What's up with all these straight-faced references to "the Chosen People," "Satan," "heaven," and the Church Socialist League? I don't know, but they stink of the rotten-egg smell of God.)

Clark voices modernism's critique of "the barrenness of the working-class movement," that is to say, "its politics of pity, its dreary materialism, its taste of the masses, the Idea of Progress, etc." but he voices no corresponding or reciprocal critique of modernism. This makes it appear that he is more apt to take sides in the lively battle of the sexes (modernist art versus socialist politics) than he is to take sides in the battle to the death between capitalism and its enemies. He writes in his "Introduction":

> Socialism occupied the real ground on which modernity could be described and opposed; but its occupation was already seen at the time (on the whole, rightly) to be compromised – complicit with what it claimed to hate. This is not meant to be an excuse for the thinness and shrillness of most of modernism's occupation of the *un*real ground. There could have been (there ought to have been) an imagining otherwise which had more of the stuff of the world to it. But I am saying that modernism's weightlessness and extremism had causes, and that among the main ones was revulsion from the working-class movement's moderacy, from the way it perfected a rhetoric of extremism that grew the more fire-breathing and standardized the deeper the movement bogged down on the parliamentary road.

Without getting too far ahead of myself, I'd like to note the way in which Professor Clark – who does not double-up his terms when it comes to modernism – conflates the terms "socialism" with "the working-class movement": the two appear to be the same for him. "You will see in what follows that I interpret the terms 'socialism' and 'working-class movement' broadly," he writes in his "Introduction," but then immediately goes on to say, without further explanation, "Two of my main cases are Jacobinism and the *sans-culottes* in 1793, and anarchism in the early 1890s." Quite obviously, using two terms broadly is not the same thing as using two terms interchangeably. It makes no sense to refer to Jacobinism as a "working-class movement," and Professor Clark knows this well (indeed, it is one of the main points of his chapter on David's *Marat* and the French Revolution). But he fails to apply this basic insight to the conceptual structure of the book as a whole, which ultimately comes crashing down in the chapter on his "third test case, War Communism in Russia in 1919 and 1920" – that is, during the ultimate and complete betrayal of "the working-class movement" in the name of "socialism." Indeed, helping to rescue the working-class movement from the poisoned legacy of so-called socialism – which, as Cornelius Castoriadis has clearly shown in "The History of the Working Class Movement," necessarily involves completely abandoning Marxism, something that Professor Clark clearly refuses to do – is precisely one of the things that *Farewell To An Idea* should be doing, but alas is not.

The first chapter of *Farewell To An Idea*, which is the one devoted to David's *Marat*, keeps to the plan of the book announced in the introduction: that is to say, the chapter keeps both modernist art and socialist politics in its sights. But, by the end of the book, the theme of socialism has completely disappeared, and so has any consideration of the inter-relatedness of socialist politics and modernist art. All that is left of Professor Clark's project is a fragment of what could and should have been a complete and coherent analysis of contemporary class society.

Despite the fact that it can only come full circle if it concludes with the period immediately before, during or after the "Fall of the Wall," Professor Clark's book ends with two chapters about Abstract Expressionism. There is one chapter about Jackson Pollock (previously published, it has its roots in work Clark began back in 1986, that is, the year after the publication of *The Painting of Modern Life*), and one chapter that offers a new "Defense of Abstract Expressionism," fifty years after its appearance in New York. *And why should we give a shit about Abstract Expressionism?* Because it appeals to America's petite bourgeoisie; because the petite bourgeois is the class that buys Pollocks and other Abstract Expressionist paintings. *Didn't Tom Wolfe already write about this years ago?* Yes, but, in his chapters on petite bourgeois Abstract Expressionism, Professor Clark introduces a new wrinkle in the well-worn fabric: the theory of "the vulgar." America's petite bourgeois like and buy Abstract Expressionist paintings because they (the paintings) are vulgar in the very narrow sense of having to do with a "well-to-do or rich person" who "betrays" his or her socio-economic position by behaving in a manner "having a common and offensively mean character; coarsely commonplace; lacking in refinement or good taste; uncultured, ill-bred." The vulgar is the ideological meeting point for the slumming big bourgeois and the upwardly-mobile petite bourgeois.

This fragment – whatever its relative value as a scheme in which to read certain Abstract Expressionist paintings – *has nothing to do with what the book set out to do.* The working-class movement doesn't come up even once in these last two chapters. Rather than opening up or living up to its noisily announced aspirations, *Farewell To An Idea* closes down and gives up on them. It stops short, way back in 1950, and – despite Professor Clark's altogether-strange references to the paintings Asger Jorn did in the 1950s and early 1960s – doesn't even come close to discussing the (post)modernist art of the years since the "Fall of the Wall." The failure here is monumental: complete and indisputable. The edifice of Professor Clark's Marxism isn't in disrepair, nor is it abandoned: it is collapsed, it is a ruin, a pile of broken bricks.

"It is the case that many, maybe most, of my chapters come to a bad end,"

Professor Clark writes at the end of his introduction. "Trust the beginnings, then; trust the epigraphs." *No, Tim, I cannot let you off that easily: others may, but not me.*

* * *

The quiet but complete ruination or evaporation of the theme of socialist politics from *Farewell To An Idea* has a striking parallel in the complete but quiet disappearance of the theme of situationist politics from Professor Clark's discourse as a whole.

Briefly a member of the British section of the Situationist International in 1966-1967 (when he was a 25-year-old grad student), Tim Clark has since then both publicly defended the situationist legacy, and has indicated the strength of his involvement with it, back in the day, in a preface for a recent translation of Anselm Jappe's biography of Guy Debord. *Farewell To An Idea* is this ex-situationist's fourth book. His first two books, *The Absolute Bourgeois* and *Courbet and the Image of the People,* derived from his work as a grad student and were published, by an academic press, as small volumes in 1973. In 1985, Clark published *The Painting of Modern Life: Paris in the Art of Manet and His Followers,* both his first major book (it was published by a well-known commercial house) and, perhaps not accidentally, his first explicitly situationist one. I have always thought the world of *The Painting of Modern Life*: it is both an excellent book on Impressionist painting and an excellent exposition and application of the situationist theory of the urban spectacle. And yet *The Painting of Modern Life* plays no role at all in *Farewell To An Idea,* despite the fact that the latter book, in Clark's words, "tries to pull together the work and teaching of three decades."

The shocking thing is that, for Professor Clark, the consignment of *The Painting of Modern Life* to the trashcan of history (or, at the very least, to the status of a supplement or footnote) is simply a matter of not talking about Manet a second time. "Above all," the Professor writes in his introduction to the new book, "there is an ominous leap in what follows from 1793 to 1891 [that is, from the chapter on David's *Marat* and the French Revolution to the chapter on Pissarro and anarchism]."

> Partly this is accident: I have had my say in previous writings on aspects of nineteenth-century art that would connect most vividly to the story I am telling (Courbet's attempt to seize the opportunity of politics in 1850, for example, or the pattern of risk and predictability occurring in paintings of Hausmann's new Paris), and I saw no way to return to them properly here. In any case, I want Pissarro and anarchism to stand for the nineteenth century's best thoughts on such topics. I believe they do stand for them. The true representativeness of 1891 and Pissarro is one of my book's main claims. But I know full

well the claim is disputable, and that some readers will see my leap over the nineteenth century as the clue to what my argument as a whole has left out. I cannot bear to face, they will say, the true quiet – the true orderliness and confidence – of bourgeois society in its heyday, and the easy nesting of the avantgarde in that positivity. I will not look again at Manet because I do not want to recognize in him the enormous distance of modern art from its circumstances, and the avant garde's willingness to seize on the side of secularization – the cult of expertise and technicality – that seemed to offer it a consoling myth of its own self-absorption. Of course I bring on this skeptical voice because one side of me recognizes that it points to something real – how could anyone looking at Manet fail to? But equally, I am sure this view of Manet and the nineteenth century is wrong.

"the true quiet" indeed: Professor Clark says not a fucking word about the situationists' critical theory of the spectacle, that is to say, about the theory that he so brilliantly and productively used to talk about Manet and the nineteenth century in *The Painting of Modern Life*. There isn't a single word from the famously thoroughgoing and detail-oriented Professor Clark about there not being a word about the situationists in this three-decades-in-one book! (Note that, when it comes to his decision to distance himself from the explicitly situationist project begun by Henri Lefebvre in *The Production of Space* – a most unfortunate decision, as we shall see – Professor Clark feels himself compelled to say to his readers, "I want to avoid thinking of modernism in spatial terms, even in terms of conceptual space. I want modernism to emerge as a distinctive patterning of mental and technical possibilities.") The contrast between Professor Clark's current silence on the situationists and all the noise he made in his "Introduction" to his book on Manet – about his own membership in the SI, about his personal role in the art world's just-beginning recuperation of one of the SI's primary "weapons of combat" and about Debord's "chiliastic serenity" that something like this would eventually happen to the critical theory of the spectacle – couldn't be more pronounced.

I do not know if the following passage from *Farewell To An Idea* (Clark is writing about Pissarro) fits the professor himself as well as it seems to.

> Such a painter makes problems for himself, of course. He will most likely be a fearsome mixture of hedonist and Puritan, and puritanical above all about the possibility of repeating himself, and leaning on his skills. He will have an infuriating habit of not understanding how good he has been at certain moments; he will not understand that trying to reproduce one's own classic style is no sin [sic], because the attempt will always fail and give rise to further variations.

But I do know this: there is no mystery as to why Professor Clark no longer mentions the situationists in his writing about painting. It doesn't have to do with pressure from editors at Yale University Press or commercial considerations, though *Farewell To An Idea* is sure to be better reviewed and better received than was *The Painting of Modern Life*, which got slammed for both its politics and its take on Impressionism.

Speaking about El Lissitzky and UNOVIS – people he describes a couple dozen pages earlier as "a wild-looking bunch" (they are) – Professor Clark says, "Anyone who has spent time teaching in art schools will recognize early on that UNOVIS' pamphlets and bad behavior have the flavor of any art school putsch." Our response: *anyone who has spent too much time teaching in art schools will eventually come to say condescending things like this*. Phrased another way: Professor Clark no longer mentions the situationists because he no longer has contact with revolutionaries: the only intellectuals he has contact with are other academics. *Academics*. . . . In France they proclaimed "the end of the age of revolutions" right up until the May 1968 rebellion broke out! And today, at the University of California at Berkeley, they are proclaiming the age ended again. (Will they *ever* learn?)

Rather than call upon Debord and the situationists, Professor Clark brings on such unfashionable but solid academic stalwarts – nice words for *boring old farts* – as Sigmund Freud, Paul de Man and Noam Chomsky. (I know you are saying, in disbelief: "No Stephen Greenblatt?!") Come to think of it, brothers and sisters, *it's a bloody miracle* that Goodman Clark managed to resist the *ungodly temptation* to analyze state propaganda in Bolshevik Russia during the late 1910s, or Trotsky's references in the 1920s to "public spectacles" and "show trials," or Freud's pronouncements in the 1930s that "Everything past is preserved" in terms of the critical theory of the spectacle! For surely the temptation to give in to Debord's devilishly seductive book *The Society of the Spectacle* was powerful indeed as Professor Clark read over these wooden lines from his horrible chapter on El Lissitzky and UNOVIS:

> Noam Chomsky, for instance, has argued over the past several years that the representation of American interests and actions in the media – both those directly financed and managed by the government and those independently owned – has a degree of coherence and partiality to it that deserves the description "propaganda system." I think the evidence of flattening and exclusion he presents is overwhelming. But I know this will remain a minority view. Why? Surely because of something in the nature of propaganda itself. One of the main jobs of a propaganda machine is to define the enemy's system of representations as propaganda. That is, it poses the question of propaganda in terms of style. The style of the Other is uniform and monistic. (The Other totalizes all the time.) Our system is different. A good propaganda machine is able to promote and sustain a degree of

difference within itself (within limits, of course), a plurality of voices, styles, and "viewpoints." For present purposes, the feature of Chomsky's model I want to emphasize is simply the idea that the effective unit of propaganda is what he calls the propaganda system.

But, no, the Puritan Professor successfully resisted temptation – at the cost of completely impoverishing his analysis of modern capitalist society. All through *Farewell To An Idea*, Professor Clark attempts to do without the situationist concept of the spectacle, even when it is obviously called for, and put something else (bad political writing of one kind or another) in its place, and the results are, not surprisingly, uniformly disastrous. He might well have tried to re-invent the bloody wheel!

To list some of the book's really serious theoretical deficiencies: 1) it is very confused about anarchism, which it tries to position as the "nineteenth century's best thoughts on such topics" as art, politics and the modern city; 2) it doesn't say a single thing about bureaucratization (which, along with the spectacle, clearly distinguishes modern society from its predecessors), nor does it comment on the bitter historical irony that it was so-called War Communism that invented the modern bureaucracy (cf. Cornelius Castoriadis); 3) it contains not a single reference to either Dada or surrealism, that is to say, to the moments at which the marriage of modernist art and socialist politics was in its hey-day; 4) the book appears to be completely unaware or completely uninterested in any of the strong "post-structuralist" critiques of Freud, especially those made by Deleuze & Guattari, and various feminists; 5) the book points to but fails to express the significance of the widespread use of paper money in modern times; and 6) as I've already noted, the book ignores everything (and it is a great deal) that points to the originality and relevance of Lefebvre's *The Production of Space*.

It doesn't seem much of a coincidence that, by and large, Professor Clark's writing is flat and uninteresting in his new book, at least, that is, by the standards of *The Painting of Modern Life*. One of the most striking features of Clark's situationist writing about Manet is that it is dramatic: though there are exceptions, by and large the narrative moves from an informative background sketch of the circumstances surrounding the creation of an individual painting, to a detailed and highly evocative description of the painting itself, and then to the characteristic ways in which the critics of the time responded to the painting (i.e., the scandal caused). As a result, *The Painting of Modern Life* – especially the chapter on Manet's *Olympia* – is both satisfying and compelling. It is in fact great writing, great political writing on painting. Debord and the other situationists – their unfettered ambitions and their beautiful language – clearly inspire Tim Clark to write at his very best. It appears that at this stage of his career, without them, he is lost.

It is striking that Clark himself should call attention to the fact that "many, maybe most" of the chapters in his new book begin well but "come to a bad end," precisely because the pattern is set early, indeed, by the book's very first chapter (the one on David's *Marat*). In the "classic style" of *The Painting of Modern Life*, Clark first describes the circumstances of the painting's first public showing; then he addresses the painting's subject matter, that is, the cult of the martyred Jacobin revolutionary Marat and the various and conflicting claims made upon it immediately after the murder; and then he *concludes* with a detailed and highly evocative description of the painting itself. Something is missing, *n'est pas*? There are no reactions from the critics, nor are there any from the People, the masses whom Marat idolized and who idolized him in return; there is no scandal. There is just the next chapter – the one that skips 100 years to take up Pissarro and anarchism. Whatever tension or mood Clark managed to create in the opening pages of the chapter – and thus of the book itself – is destroyed. Not surprisingly, none of the remaining chapters takes up the "classic [narrative] style" of *The Painting of Modern Life*.

This leaves the chapter on Jackson Pollock – which, at least in its original version, was primarily concerned with Pollock's conscious effort, based on what he knew of the history of the avant-garde since the time of Picasso, to defeat in advance the recuperation that a scandalous painting often is subjected to, after the original scandal has died down – high and dry. Professor Clark was clearly aware of this problem, for he clumsily tried to hide the facts that the both the theoretical underpinnings (the necessity of scandal) as well as the dramatic set-up (the expectation of scandal) for this chapter have been flushed down the pipes, by changing the last phrase in this crucial passage –

> It is hard to tell at present whether ideas of resistance and refusal have any sustaining force left in them, or have been hopelessly incorporated into *the* general spectacle.

– so that it reads "incorporated into *a* general spectacle." The difference between the two versions is small, but consistent with what I've already pointed to: there are spectacles, sure; but there is no such thing as *the spectacle,* and, consequently, no such thing as *the general spectacle* or *the society of the spectacle.* Or, at least, none worth mentioning in a book of modernist art criticism.

I mentioned that Professor Clark refers to the paintings of Asger Jorn. Jorn is not simply any old modernist (dead white male) painter: he was a founder and, for several years, a central member of the Situationist International, as well as a close personal friend of and collaborator with Guy Debord. In his "Defense of Abstract Expressionism," Professor Clark suddenly blurts out that Jorn was "the greatest painter of the 1950s."

> European painting after the [Second World] war, alas, comes out of a very different set of class formations. [Unlike in America], vulgarity is not its problem. In Asger Jorn, for example – to turn for a moment

to the greatest painter of the 1950s – what painting confronts as its limit condition is always refinement.

A very strange passage, to be sure. *To turn suddenly and only for a moment to the greatest painter of the 1950s.* Knowing that "eyebrows will be raised" in response to this sudden and startling assertion – which, because it is contained in an aside, seems nothing short of ridiculous – Professor Clark writes the following a few lines later, in a tone that sounds defensive:

> In calling Jorn the greatest painter of the 1950s I mean to imply nothing about the general health of painting in Europe at the time (nor to deny that Jorn's practice was hit and miss, and the number of his works that might qualify as good, let alone great, is very small). On the contrary. The clichés in the books are true. Jorn's really was an end game. Vulgarity, on the other hand, back on the other side of the Atlantic, turned out to be a way of keeping the corpse of painting hideously alive – while all the time coquetting with Death. An Asger Jorn can be garish, florid, tasteless, forced, cute, flatulent, overemphatic: it can never be vulgar. It just cannot prevent itself from a tampering and framing of its desperate effects which pulls them back into the realm of painting, ironizes them, declares them done in full knowledge of their emptiness. American painting by contrast – and precisely that American painting which is closest to the European, done by Germans and Dutchmen steeped in the tradition they are exiting from – does not ironize, and will never make the (false) declaration that the game is up. Hofmann and de Kooning, precisely because they are so similar to Jorn in their sense of "touch" and composition, register as Jorn's direct opposites.

In a footnote, Professor Clark goes on to say:

> You could apply the same rule of thumb to Jorn as Greenberg was fond of doing to abstract painting in general: most Jorn paintings from the 1950s and early 1960s are considerably worse than most from the same period by Gottlieb, Still, Hofmann, de Kooning, Kline, even Tomlin; but a very few Jorns are better than anything by any of the above – in my view, decisively better. (I leave Pollock out of it, mainly because he painted so little, and, by his standards, so badly, after 1951.) A short, though certainly not exhaustive, list of the Jorns I have in mind would include, besides the ones I illustrate [*Paris by Night*, 1959, and *To Become, That is the Question. To Have Been, That is the Answer*, 1961]: *La Grande Victoire: Kujaski, Lodz* (1956), *Shameful Project* (1957), *Alcools* (1957), *Le Canard Inquietant*

(1959), *The Abominable Snowman* (1959), *Dead Drunk Danes* (1960), *L'Homme Poussiere* (1960), *Faustrold* (1962), *Les Pommes d'Adam* (1962), *Triplerie* (1962), *Deux Pingouins, Avant et d'apres David* (1962), *The Living Souls* (1963), *Something Remains* (1963), probably several other *Modifications* and *Defigurations,* if I could get to see them, and one or two late works, like the great *Between Us* (1972). This list is skewed and limited by accidents of availability, but I have a feeling that even if my knowledge of Jorn was more comprehensive it would not swell enormously.

And that's all Professor Clark has to say about "the greatest painter of the 1950s," who happens to be, like Professor Clark, a former member of the SI.

Quite obviously, if anyone, but especially a situationist, really were the greatest painter of any decade – but especially the 1950s (the decade beyond which Professor Clark's book cannot seem to go) – there should be an entire chapter in *Farewell To An Idea* devoted to him or her. Had Professor Clark done this, he could have saved his entire book from ruin: not only was Asger Jorn an explicitly Marxist modern artist, but he was also active before, during and after the period that presents such an obstacle to Professor Clark's chronology. A chapter on Jorn at the end of the book would have allowed it to come to some real kind of completion, would have given it an opportunity to reach pertinent conclusions about the inter-relationship between modernism and socialism. A chapter on Jorn would also have linked up with and made sense of Professor Clark's interesting but scattered references to such situationist or lettrist chestnuts as "painting machines," "the unity of architecture," and the fact that certain "[a]rtists have invented a new alphabet." But no: all we get from Professor Clark on Asger Jorn are the two passages quoted above. That is to say, a fragment, *another* fragment.

This is most unfortunate. The English-speaking world needs a really good chapter on Asger Jorn, as well as chapters on the other great situationist painters, Hans Peter Zimmer and Giuseppe Pinot-Gallizio, among them. (Just what the fuck does Tim mean when he says, in his first paragraph on Asger Jorn, "The clichés in the books are true"? *Which* clichés about Jorn? Are they situationist clichés? Which *books* about Jorn? Are they situationist books? Professor Clark does not anticipate these questions, unlike so many others, and so doesn't answer them, not even in a footnote.) The situationist painters, precisely because they were revolutionary socialists, and not academic or petite-bourgeois socialists, have never been written about by someone of T.J. Clark's caliber. It's a very exciting prospect – the T.J. Clark of *The Painting of Modern Life* writing about situationist painting – but one very unlikely to be realized.

* * *

In his discussion of Jackson Pollock, Professor Clark hedonistically tosses out the idea that "Modernism is full of novels and poems rescued from the wastepaper basket by their author's best friends." We are not prepared to rescue Asger Jorn and the other situationist painters from Professor Clark's trashcan and launch a situationist evaluation of situationist painting of our own. We plan to do something similar, but perhaps much less ambitious: using the research and other raw materials contained in *Farewell To An Idea*, we will offer alternative readings of some of the paintings on which Professor Clark focuses. In particular, we will detourn Professor Clark's chapters on Pissarro's *Two Young Peasant Women* (1892), Cezanne's three paintings entitled *The Large Bathers* (1895-1906), and Picasso's *The Architect's Table* (1912). As the reader will see, we will not deal directly in what follows with the chapters on David's *Marat* (1793) and El Lissitzky's propaganda board (1920). Though stunted, the former is quite adequate; the latter is simply beyond repair. Nevertheless, to the extent that these two chapters touch upon modern paper money, we will deal with them in an extended digression that immediately follows. As for Professor Clark's chapters on Abstract Expressionism, we plan to leave them right where they are: perched high and dry. Perhaps our detournements of his readings of Pissarro, Cezanne and Picasso will raise the metaphorical water level sufficiently high, so that Pollock and the others (including Jorn) can get back in their boats and be on their respective ways.

On Money

Professor Clark states in his "Introduction":

A book about nineteenth- and twentieth-century culture will inevitably turn on the question of money and the market, and their effect on artmaking. This book does so three times: in its dealings with the Terror and War Communism, and with Pissarro in 1891. Again, two of the three cases are extreme. In 1793 in France and 1920 in Russia the very relation between markets and money seemed, for a while, to be coming to an end. We shall see that certain Bolsheviks looked back to Year 2 explicitly, and exulted in the notion of the socialist state's being able now to drown its enemies in a flood of paper. It was a fantasy, but not an entirely empty one. Money is the root form of representation in bourgeois society. Threats to monetary value are threats to signification in general. "Confidence in the sign" was at stake, to quote one historian of Jacobinism, talking of inflation in 1793 and the role of the new booknotes. In their different ways David and Malevich confronted the crisis of confidence, I think, and tried to give form to its enormity. In coming to terms with money, or with money seemingly about to evaporate as a (central) form of life, modernism at moments attained to true lucidity about the sign in general.

What I will be focusing on here is the failure to clearly distinguish between coined money and paper money, and the effect this failure has on Professor Clark's analysis of the crises of "confidence in the sign" in revolutionary France and Bolshevik Russia.

Money is an important, even central theme in Jacques-Louis David's famous painting *Marat* (1793). Upon the orange crate that the martyred revolutionary was using as a writing-desk moments before his assassination, the painter has placed an inkwell, an extra quill, a partially legible letter, and, directly upon the letter, an *assignat* (a printed banknote). The text of the letter (or that part of it which is visible) is, "You will give this banknote to this mother of five children whose husband is off defending the fatherland." As is the case with the letter that was written to accompany it, the printing on the *assignat* is difficult to make out, almost impossible to read. Both therefore stand in stark contrast to the letter held in the dead man's hand, that is, the letter to him from his assassin, Charlotte Corday, which can be seen clearly and is quite legible: "On the 13th of July, 1793: Marie Annie Charlotte Corday to citizen Marat: It suffices that I am truly Unfortunate for me to have a Right to your benevolence." With this ruse, she gained access to Marat. She might even be the "mother of five children" for whom the *assignat* was intended. But, if she (pretended that she) was, she left the paper money behind after she stabbed him. The blurriness of the *assignat* suggests that both Corday and Jacques-Louis David didn't think much of its value.

For reasons that are far from clear, Professor Clark presents himself as positively embarrassed by having to talk about the *assignat* (he will present himself in much the same way when it comes to having to talk about at the naughty bits in Cezanne's *The Large Bathers*).

> There is, I think, one further small piece of the picture which might have the power to reconcile the warring parties. Up to now I have brushed it aside. I mean the scrap of paper whose tiny weight keeps Marat's letter eternally balanced on the edge of the orange box. It is an *assignat*, a piece of revolutionary paper money – writing which stands for property. I have to say something, in consequence, about what the *assignat* was. Many of the issues concerning it are for experts, and leave me as far behind as they left most revolutionaries. Marat was notably bone-headed on the subject. But one or two things are clear. The *assignat* was a form of paper currency first issued in January 1790, partly in response to the flight of gold and coin which had followed the storming of the Bastille. It only gradually became a mainstay of government finance. There was considerable skepticism about the whole idea of paper money, which was thought to be an

English sort of thing. In theory the notes were guaranteed by land. Inscribed on each was the legend: "Mortgaged on the National Estates." That is to say, on the wealth generated from the sale of crown and church properties, and later from the lands and belongings of *emigres, emigres'* properties, and foreigners. From a Jacobin point of view, this rootedness of the paper in the earth was an important ideological consolation. [...] No one calls the economic policy of Robespierre and co. a success, but it did have one paradoxical result for a while: it managed to stabilize the value of its multiplying paper. [...] And how had they done it? By Terror, of course. By forcing the pace of expropriations, by seeking out and melting down gold and metal coinage, by a general and ruthless *cours force*. [...] In the end, in 1794 and 1795, the new form of money collapsed. The government was forced to conspire against its own currency – buying up the paper in secret and burning it, as a desperate hedge against inflation.

Professor Clark's embarrassed disclaimers about his lack of expertise in the presumably specialized field of monetary studies should not make us feel that *we* should be accepting or tolerant of *his* "bone-headed" mistakes. Nor should we be swayed by the fact that his short discussion of the *assignat* is only designed to show that "Marat's *assignat* is densely coded, then." Money is in fact not that difficult to understand, and elementary mistakes of the type Professor Clarks makes should be avoidable.

To begin with, "coin" and "metal coinage" (despite the implication in Professor Clark's gloss that they are raw material resources in the way that land and unminted gold are) are forms of money. Indeed, stamped gold coins were the first form of money. But money is not "writing that stands for property." *Money is a combination of writing (a unique inscription) and a special substance into which this writing is inscribed.* It therefore both "stands for" something else (the authority, trustworthiness and reliability of the power that both selected the special substance and inscribed the message) and is something in its own right (the special substance). Paradoxically, money – unlike all other commodities –- is both a useful or otherwise desirable thing *and* the standard by which one measures all other useful or otherwise desirable things, including itself.

When coins were the only form of money, and when coins were stamped out of gold (which is quite costly to unearth and quite useful on its own), there was a clear, logical and reassuring connection between inscription and inscribed thing. The apparent arbitrariness of the inscription, which pretended to indicate the value of the coin as a whole, was limited by the actual value of the inscribed metal itself. A coin could only be worth so much: it depended on the amount of gold it was made out of. And there needed to be such a strong connection between inscription and inscribed thing, because, in an age accustomed to barter, there was perceived to be a radical split between the sign (the inscription or the stamped coin as a whole) and the reality it was supposed to represent (the inscribed thing or the useful things for which the coin could be traded). Two thousand years before the French Revolution, a severe "crisis of confidence" occurred as a result of the invention and widespread use of coined money. A measure of its severity can be found in the split that coined money created between Socrates and Plato.

Paper money has been used, in one form or another, ever since the Middle Ages, when checks were first introduced to Europe by soldiers who had been to North Africa and the Middle East. As indicated by the context of Professor Clark's remarks, paper money was most frequently or only used as an emergency measure when neither unminted gold nor coined money was readily available. Banknotes could be used to pay soldiers, for example. But paper money was always used on a limited basis, for a limited time or in a limited geographical area. It was never used as a government's primary form of currency, at least until the French Revolution. The Jacobin introduction of the *assignat* set into motion yet another, or, rather, a second-order "crisis of confidence in the sign." Unlike coins, banknotes were not made out of a substance that was useful or otherwise desirable; or at least paper was not as useful or otherwise desirable a commodity in its own right as gold was. Gold was still scarce and difficult to extract from the earth; stamping coins took time and skill. But paper was plentiful and cheap, and the printing press made this new form of "coinage" quick and easy. The chains upon the arbitrariness of the sign (the inscription and its pretense to ascribe value on its own) seemed to have been suddenly broken; now the inscription seemed to float above and completely detached from the world of objects, material goods and the human needs they satisfy. *The spectacle* was born, and Plato's worst fears were realized.

And yet strange new possibilities opened up as well. Gold was natural, but human beings manufactured paper. If governments (mere human beings!) could say that a scrap of paper with "special" writing on it was money, why couldn't other writers say that *their* papers with "special writing" on it (poetry, for example) was also money? Who or what gave governments the exclusive right to write the form of poetry known as money? No one, if not the people themselves.

Professor Clark completely misses this last point. In his chapter on El Lissitzky and the concentrated spectacle of "War Communism," Clark only grasps the negative aspect, and not the positive aspect, of the spectacularization of the money-form. He states:

> Most people capable of reading the papers in 1920 thought they were living through the end of capitalism. They were in the *Economics of the Transition Period.* And maybe the clearest symptom of that passing from one system to another was the crisis in capitalism's most precious means of representation, money. Mahkno as usual saw the point. The money he issued in his anarchist republic had printed on it the message that no one would be prosecuted for forging it. But Mahkno was only carrying to its logical conclusion the general

collapse of "confidence in the sign," which not only anarchists thought would be terminal.

If there was such a message on the anarchists' paper money (I do not know for sure), this may have been simply or quite logically because, as anarchists, the citizens of the republic did not believe in maintaining a centralized and repressive judicial system, which would have been necessary to prosecute counterfeiting and other such "crimes against the state." (There was probably a moratorium on the prosecution of thefts of bread, as well, but this doesn't mean that the anarchists were participating in the general collapse of confidence in the nutritional value of grain!) The logic of the anarchist message is clear: if money (or bread) be needed, let money (or bread) be had. And if there is indeed a collapse of "confidence in the sign" at work here, there is also at work a growing confidence among the people in their ability to write and print their own banknotes.

Pissarro's Two Young Peasant Women

All told, Professor Clark has a relatively easy time showing that Camille Pissarro was an anarchist. Not only did the painter subscribe to Brousse's newspaper and then to *La Revolte,* the newspaper founded by Kropotkin, but he wrote forcefully about anarchism in his letters: "I firmly believe that our ideas, impregnated with anarchist philosophy, give a color to the works we do, and hence make them antipathetic to the ideas of the moment." The problem for Professor Clark is that, like any good anarchist, Pissarro was vehemently anti-socialist. The painter wrote:

> Well yes, things passed off peacefully [during the May Day observations of 1890] in Paris. But the strikes are continuing, *the socialist chiefs have done everything in their power to put a stop to the demonstrations,* but the [working-class] movement is under way, and you will see in due course that this eight-hour day, which is absolutely useless and will not give the working class a thing, will be the spark that will lead to one demand after another. The bourgeois will not have stolen it all!!! [Emphasis added.]

Not surprisingly, our Marxist Professor of Art History can't let socialist-bashing such as this go on for too long. After a few such excerpts, he says, "Pissarro was no great political thinker. He knew his limits, and ducked the occasional invitation to put his anarchism in publishable form," and stops quoting from the painter's letters altogether. But by then it has been clearly established that Camille Pissarro was the type of man who, when he heard news that a fellow anarchist named Ravachol had been arrested for bombing the houses of princesses, magistrates, and prosecutors, wrote to his friend Mirbeau: "Ravachol must have really put the wind up those good magistrates. They only got away by the skin of their teeth! Devil take it! It is not a good thing to pass judgment on others! If you get a taste for it, you're damned! They are going to have to surround them [the magistrates] with soldiers from now on." (Ravachol is, of course, also presented as something of a hero in the situationist Raoul Vaneigem's book *The Revolution of Everyday Life*.)

Professor Clark has a difficult time defining anarchism itself. Because anarchism emerges between the French Revolution and the 1890s, that is, in the 100-year-long gap between the book's first two chapters – and because anarchism doesn't figure at all in his books on Courbet and Manet – Professor Clark's definitions of it cannot help but be typically fragmentary and off-balance. For Professor Clark, anarchism "crystallized out of the struggles within the working-class movement in the 1870s and early 1880s, in response to the freezing and splitting that followed the [crushing of the Paris] Commune," and Brousse and Kropotkin are the first great anarchist theorists, writers and activists. The Professor is wrong, of course: the roots of anarchism go back to the 1840s, and any list of the first great anarchists must include Godwin, Stirner, Proudhon, and Bakunin, none of whom are even mentioned in *Farewell To An Idea*.

If anarchism arose in response to anything, it arose in response to the authoritarianism of the Marxists and the negative effects this authoritarianism had on the International Working-Men's Association in the late 1860s and early 1870s, that is, immediately prior to the Commune. (Professor Clark himself refers to "Marx's insistence on new forms of centralization and authority within the International," an insistence that unfortunately comes in the aftermath of the Paris Commune, which surely taught the working-class movement that the masses can be mobilized and organized *without* recourse to centralized authority.) And yet, for our Marxist Professor of Art History, "a side of anarchism figures, and wants to figure, as the Other to socialism." The only way this can be the case is if Marxism and socialism are interchangeable words for the same thing. But they are not: Marxism is just one version of socialism, one idea of how to conceive and move toward a socialist society.

Professor Clark himself keeps pretty accurate tabs on the major differences between Marxism and anarchism in the 1890s: while the Marxists were militarists (and often nationalists, as well), the "[a]narchists were anti-militarists, working to subvert the loyalty of soldiers .... They believed in confronting the police and the courts – in pushing new forms of working-class resistance and demonstration toward the breaking-point of class demand and state reply." While the Marxists ignored the revolutionary potential of the peasantry, "[a]narchists had long been preaching the folly of socialism's exclusive preoccupation with the city proletariat." Unlike the Marxists, who plodded along believing that the laws of historical development were pre-determined and unalterable, the anarchists "knew that that the question of whether the proletariat would choose, or be obliged, to accommodate with capitalism rather than try to defeat it was very much an open one." Unlike the Marxists, who dismissed moral indignation as a bourgeois conceit, the anarchists, in their very "bombast" and "naïveté," "had the measure of the bourgeois beast in the late nineteenth century: [anarchism's] rhetoric of horror and denunciation was the only one adequate to the new color of events. To Fourmies, Tonkin, Panama, Dreyfus. To the whole escalating vileness of patriotism and Empire that ended (but did not end) in 1914." Finally, unlike the Marxists and the so-called socialists, "the anarchists," Professor Clark writes, "were the only ones capable of turning revulsion at this turn of events into resistance."

For Professor Clark, anarchism – despite the lip service it might pay to collectives and federations – knows no other kind of resistance than "the lone bomber."

> "Propaganda by the deed" was a proposal for socialist tactics which, like its main rivals, first came to self-consciousness in the 1870s [Professor Clark writes]. [...] There were plenty of arguments among anarchists about the particular occasions, forms and combinations such a tactic should take. No doubt violence would be useless unless it connected with other kinds of agitation and political work. But the tactic itself (the examples of Ireland and Russia kept recurring) was mostly accepted. "As for me," said Kropotkin, "I approve entirely of this way of acting . . . it will be propaganda by cudgel blows, or revolvers if necessary." You will notice that the model is trouble at the edge of a demonstration, or a quick strike at tax records in an isolated Town Hall. Not (yet) the lone bomber.

You will notice that "the model," which is Professor Clark's creation, and not the creation of Kropotkin or any other anarchist, involves nothing but acts of cowardice. Both "a quick strike at tax records in an isolated Town Hall" and the work of a "lone bomber" are cowardly acts; there is no real "movement" (descent, devolution or turning) possible between the two; it is only a matter of degrees of cowardice. And so it is somewhat disingenuous of Professor Clark to play the role of judge and say that, with Ravachol, "a new (and ultimately disastrous) turn in the history of anarchism had begun," even if "anarchists did not immediately realize" it. No such decisive turn took place, or, rather, this turn, as well as several other decisive turns, some of them in the precisely the opposite "direction," took place in the history of anarchism in the twentieth century. You would never know from reading *Farewell To An Idea* that the twentieth century held such people and events in store for anarchism as Emma Goldman, Jules Bonnot, Bueneventuri Durutti, the Spanish Revolution of 1936-37, the Hungarian Revolution of 1956, and the May 1968 revolt in France, among others.

Because of the limits of his understanding of anarchism, Professor Clark fails to connect all this to the particular painting by Pissarro that he has chosen for careful examination. (The painting, *Two Peasant Women,* was never put up for sale by Pissarro and is not part of the modernist canon of great works.) The closest Clark gets to offering a reading of the painting in terms of anarchism is this:

> The moment of anarchist politics in late 1891 was specific, I think, and had effects on Pissarro's *Two Peasant Women.* Not dramatically. Not in terms of particular imagery or even firmly identifiable tone. . . . I see no outright socialist [sic] politics in it.

This is a rather pathetic admission. *Sorry, folks, all this stuff about anarchism has nothing to do with the subject at hand; I've been wasting your time this whole chapter.*

So let us try to forget about Pissarro and turn our attention to what Professor Clark says about Georges Seurat. "Somewhere here, I think, in the continuing encounter with Seurat, is the key to the question of art and anarchism in Pissarro," Professor Clark writes. "I believe that if we can identify what Pissarro thought Seurat had to offer, we may understand what he thought, or hoped, anarchism in painting would be like." And again: "Seurat was profoundly anarchism's painter: cruel and elusive and infinitely fond of the city's foibles and moments of freedom." (If this is true, there seems no justification on Professor Clark's part for writing his chapter on Pissarro and anarchism instead of on Seurat and anarchism.) Provided that we accept the proposition that "the lone bomber" is representative of anarchism, which is a highly debatable notion (and, unfortunately, still very much with us a hundred years after Ravachol), we can say that the discrete points or dots of color out of which Seurat composes his paintings are symbols for the piece-by-piece reconstruction of the image of society after the anarchists' bombs have gone off. Or they are symbols for the moment immediately after the detonation but before the explosion of the shattered pieces. Or they are symbols of the fact that the image of society is already exploded, and needs only a bomb to make this fact plain. Professor Clark writes:

> What the dot [in Seurat] seemed to promise, at least for a while, was a truly naive visualization of the singular and uniform as the same thing. The dot exploded the opposition. And this was wonderful. It planted a bomb in the middle of the bourgeois idea of freedom – and order, and individuality, and Art-ness, and taste, and "touch," intuition, variety expressiveness. [...] [Seurat] worked quietly at perfecting his explosive device.

(Interesting parallels might be drawn here between Seurat and the "shot-gun" paintings made by William S. Burroughs in the last decade of his life. These abstract paintings were produced by lining up spray-paint cans in front of a blank canvas and exploding the cans with a blast from a shot-gun.)

The Seurat that Professor Clark chooses to illustrate these ideas (*Channel at Gravelines*, 1890) is apt for our purposes, as it turns out, precisely because it is a landscape. "Never had it been so clear," Professor Clark writes about the late 1880s and early 1890s, "that the built form of the state was now very much more than a set of prisons, *palais de justice, fortifs, zones,* and customs posts. The state was a landscape." Expressed in terms familiar to readers of Henri Lefebvre's *The Production of Space*, the state – always the master of space – was in the process of totally re-ordering it, of creating a new, *abstract* space. "[The state] was [now] a pattern of agriculture and subsidy and monopoly and communication, whose forms had less and less to do each year with the facts of climate, geology, or regional specialization," Professor Clark writes, as if he knows exactly what Lefebvre was talking about. "These things were still in their infancy" around 1890; "not even the gloomiest dystopian had an inkling of what was to come." Except for the anarchists, of course: "But at least anarchists knew already in the 1890s that fighting the state meant thinking geographically and biologically."

Cezanne's *The Large Bathers*

The circumstances of the creation of three closely related paintings by Paul Cezanne, all of them entitled *The Large Bathers*, are quite provocative. Though they were begun at different times (one in 1895, another in 1900 and the last in 1904), all three paintings were finished in 1906. They were among the very last paintings Cezanne completed in his life. Apparently worked on side-by-side and comprising a kind of trilogy, the three *Large Bathers* are an obsessive working-over of a set of themes that were clearly dear to Cezanne himself, for he allowed Emile Bernard to photograph him sitting in front of one of the *Bathers* (still unfinished) in 1904. In these photographs, Cezanne is a small, pleasant-looking, slightly impish old man.

Though two of these three paintings have entered the canon of great modernist paintings, "there are no eulogies of Cezanne's last *Bathers* – or no descriptions (no extended, nonobvious interpretations) to go with the eulogistic noises." The questions that arise for Professor Clark, the person who made this observation, are, "Why, even if these works did eventually enter some kind of modernist canon in the twentieth century, could they not be described by those who did the canonizing? What was it that stood (and stands) in the way of description?" Good questions. He has a few answers, of course: referring to the *Bathers* that was started in 1895 and is now housed by the Barnes Foundation in Pennsylvania, Professor Clark writes, "I take the Barnes painting to be a staging of some ultimate sexual material – ultimate for Cezanne, that is – which could only gradually be dragged into the light of day, and even more gradually (if at all) brought into order. It took ten years." The same interpretation is extended to the so-called Philadelphia, started in 1904 and now housed by the Philadelphia Museum of Art, but not to the *Bathers* owned by the National Gallery in London, which, begun in 1900, is the most conventional (less scandalous) of the three paintings. Professor Clark's thesis is that, in the Barnes and the Philadelphia paintings, the repressed attempts to return. To bring these paintings to completion, Cezanne had to possess a courageous determination to face directly what had been repressed (and then feared), a determination that must have been lacking in those who canonized these very paintings.

"Some ultimate sexual material": the subject matter of all three *Bathers* is the following scene: a group of eight to thirteen nude women are seen lounging around by the side of a river or some other body of water. Some of the women are standing; others sit on or squat above the ground; still others are lying on their stomachs, their naked buttocks facing us. Unlike the tone and "tactics of representation" in *Bathers At Rest,* which Cezanne painted between 1875 and 1877, the scene obsessively re-created in the three late *Bathers* is not clearly dream-like, and yet neither is it presented as if it were a somewhat unusual scene from waking life. There is something uncanny about the emotionally charged atmosphere evoked, especially by the Barnes and the Philadelphia. To Professor Clark, the best (only) word for it is "phantasy," which Clark struggles to think through in a language borrowed from the unfashionable but solid academic stalwarts Laplanche and Pontalis, who in 1973 defined "phantasy" as an "imaginary scene in which the subject is a protagonist, representing the fulfillment of a wish (in the last analysis, an unconscious wish) in a manner that is distorted to a greater or lesser extent by defensive processes." For Professor Clark, there is no question about the fact that the three *Bathers* obsessively recreate a phantasy in which Cezanne's unconscious wishes concerning the sexual difference(s) between men and women are staged.

> In the Barnes, the nude form leaning against a tree at the far right of the painting appears to be both male and female: he or she has what appear to be small breasts and an erect penis (though the painted marks that are here taken to signify "erect penis" could also be interpreted as a long vaginal fold that travels up the stomach from the crotch). The nude form standing at the far left of the Barnes appears to be a woman, but her head looks like the head of a (circumcised) penis. In the Philadelphia, further to the right of the form (here she is clearly a woman) leaning against the tree, the figures of two women are combined in such an optically illusionistic way that the buttocks of one are easily confused with the shoulders of the other. The woman with the penis-head (in the Barnes) has been replaced (in the Philadelphia) by a standing woman whose right hand reaches out to touch a set of painted marks that could either be the back of one of the sitting women or the back of the head of one of the women squatting on the ground, or both at the same time.

In part because of the (sexual? certainly biological) subject matter of the paintings, and in part because of the serendipity of the dates of composition, Professor Clark juxtaposes Cezanne's three *Bathers* with the work done in this same decade by Sigmund Freud. Though psychoanalysis has occasionally been put in the service of revolutionary theory by such Freudo-Marxists as Andre Breton and Wilhelm Reich, Freud himself was neither a Marxist, a socialist nor an anarchist. Psychoanalysis itself, to the precise degree that it abandoned its original discoveries and re-fashioned itself in the image of the dominant society, long ago became a powerful institutional force for the repression of human desiring, and little else. At this stage in the game, no one expects psychoanalysis to be anything but a prop for the established order. And so Freud's presence in this book about modernism and socialism is irrelevant, totally gratuitous, even insulting to the intelligence. This is a chapter in *Farewell To An Idea* that both begins and ends badly.

"I have never understood why writers about Cezanne shy away from the strict coincidence of the ten years spent on the three large *Bathers* with those of the founding of psychoanalysis – the years of Freud's self-analysis and the publication of *The Interpretation of Dreams* (1900), the letters to Fliess, the treatment of Dora, [and] the writing of *Three Essays on the Theory of Sexuality*," Professor Clark writes. "I like to think of the Barnes picture as roughly the equivalent of *The Interpretation of Dreams*, and the cooler atmosphere of the painting in the Philadelphia Museum as corresponding to that of the *Three Essays*." As we will see, this juxtaposition does not become active; it never becomes an interruption and intermingling of the separate(d) canonical discourses on Cezanne and Freud.

Not surprisingly, the epigraph for Clark's chapter on Cezanne is taken from Freud, but not, as one might expect, from one of the well-known psychoanalytic works referred to above. It is taken from an earlier and largely unknown text, an essay from 1895 entitled "Project for a Scientific Psychology."

> The intention of this project is to furnish us with a psychology which shall be a natural science: its aim, that is, is to represent psychical processes as quantitatively determined states of specifiable material particles and so to make them plain and void of contradictions.

This is not the Freud we know as "Freud." As Professor Clark says, "the Freud I quote is the Freud before Freud, still struggling to think the unconscious in a language borrowed from Heimholtz and Fechner." After quoting a passage in which Freud evokes the "picture" of a living organism as an "undifferentiated vesicle of a substance that is susceptible to stimulation," Clark writes, "present-day readers of Freud tend to skim such passages, which crop up all through the later work – the one quoted here is from *Beyond the Pleasure Principle* – or denounce their 'scientism.'" Professor Clark goes on to say that "I imagine Cezanne's reading them all agog." I can imagine Cezanne reading them all agog, too. But

Cezanne's reading of Freud is not the point: Clark's is.

Referring to the Freud of scientific psychology, Professor Clark says that "this is the Freud, ultimately, whom I take to be closest to the *Bathers'* mental world." *Which is it, Tim? Freud or 'Freud'? For it certainly can't be both.* While it is true that elements of the abandoned project for a "scientific psychology" keep cropping up in the later Freud, it is not the case that all or even certain crucial aspects of the later Freud appear in the early Freud. Though psychoanalysis can at times be informed by the natural science of "scientific psychology" – though psychoanalysis can even "struggle" to free itself from the vulgarity of the language and conceptual apparatus borrowed from Heimholtz and Fechner – the science of "quantitatively determined states of specifiable material particles" *knows nothing* and *needs to know nothing* of such "mature" Freudian concepts as the phallus, castration, and the Oedipal complex, in order to function. These concepts are little more than "contradictions" to be "voided" by the Project. Unfortunately, Professor Clark doesn't recognize this difficulty in his self-avowedly vulgar appropriation of Freud, and mixes the two Freuds together as if they were the same. (Only Freud himself could get away with doing this, and he had a rough time of it.) By having his Freud and eating him, too, Clark produces scenes far more terrifying and oppressive than poor little Paul Cezanne ever did, even in the most "phantastic" parts of the putatively scandalous Barnes and Philadelphia paintings.

Despite or perhaps precisely because Professor Clark says that his reference to (the) Freud(s) "is not meant as preliminary to a Freudian reading of the three late *Bathers*," he goes straight off to offer what – if there were a competition for such achievements in the field of academic specialization – would surely be the big winner in the no doubt bitterly contested and very close contest for The Most Pat, Pre-Packaged, Reductive, Boring and Unconvincing Freudian Reading Ever Written. Even if it were written back in the 1930s or 1940s, when such monsters of the academic imagination were novel, Clark's non-Freudian Freudian reading of Cezanne would win the award. Hands down. Yes, it's *that* bad.

Based on these deceptively simple, clearly fragmentary, inconclusive and not very germane bits of psycho-biographical evidence –

> Here, to begin, is a fragment [note: it is all we will get] of Cezanne's self-description. It occurs in Bernard's 1905 memoir. Cezanne is trying to explain to Bernard his horror of human contact, after a pathetic scene in the street the day before. He reaches back to an ancient memory: "I was going quietly down a staircase, when a *gamin* who was sliding down the banister, going full speed, gave me such a kick up the arse as he [sic] went by that I almost fell down; the shock being so unexpected and unlooked for, it hit me so hard that for years I have been obsessed by its happening again, to the point that I cannot abide being touched or even brushed by anyone." One can almost hear the analyst breathing a discreet sigh of relief. The patient's phantasies

are close to the surface. [...] The script . . . is easy to write. This patient's phantasies are close to the surface.

– Doctor Clark reaches the following unappealable verdicts about the "patient's" sad case.

> The Barnes picture, then, is a staging of that moment in the dissolution of the Oedipus complex at which the threat of castration is so intense and overwhelming that the male child is unable to take the exit into repression; and instead remains frozen in a world where, in spite of everything, the Father is absent and the phallic mother's return is awaited. She will possess the phallus and restore it to her son. And everyone will have the same sexuality. [The Barnes picture] shows us the moment of inconsolable clinging to infantile sexuality, the stage of psychic development which "knows only one kind of genital: the male one." Freud called it the phallic stage. [...] You will gather that if I saw it necessary or possible to psychoanalyze Cezanne, I would hazard the guess that in his case the moment never did dissolve, and that the late *Bathers* were his attempt to reconstitute a world of sexuality which, at some level, he had never left. Maybe the Barnes picture does reconstitute it – but of course it also summons up its doom-laden atmosphere. There has never been a subject so constituted under the sign of loss and despondency as the figure leaning on the tree. Maybe he does not even see the phallic mother arriving. Maybe in a sense he does not want to. [...] It was not until the Philadelphia picture that a narrative of sexual difference (sexual difference actually happening, as if it had never happened before) gave way to a kind of tragic positing of sexuality as fate.

Yuck. There is nothing "new" or even particularly modern about this kind of poisonous shit. Nietzsche or Bataille would have easily recognized in it nothing but the age-old religion-based hatred of the human body gussied up as a "theory" of its materiality: castration, loss, lack, tragedy, doom, despondency, fate, and the final "exit into repression" (rather than the exit *from* repression). Professor Clark should have wondered why its "script . . . is easy to write," indeed so easy to write that it practically writes itself. But he didn't, and so ended up repeating and thereby helping to legitimatize the worse justifications for the on-going repression of real human desiring and its replacement with its spectacular representation.

Can one use Freud to look at Cezanne's *Bathers* and not reach the same dreadful results as Professor Clark did? Without trying to re-invent the wheel – that is, without repeating what has already been laid in great detail, and quite brilliantly so, by Gilles Deleuze and Felix Guattari in *Anti-Oedipus* (1973) – I think it is indeed possible to do so, but provided that one insist on and carefully observe an important distinction, which is not between Freud and "Freud," but between Freud's basic discoveries about the unconscious and those aspects of psychoanalysis that do not take account of, ignore or even obscure (by "defensive processes") these basic discoveries.

What Freud discovered and reported upon in *The Interpretation of Dreams* is the fact that the unconscious doesn't "wish" for anything, because it lacks nothing. The unconscious is actively productive, not passively representational; it is a kind of factory that produces "dream-works," not a theater for re-presentations of already-accumulated (already exploited) "work." It makes no sense to speak of the unconscious as "the machine of representation," as Professor Clark does. *The machinic unconscious is fundamentally anti-spectacular.* It doesn't signify; it works and produces. What is striking about spectacle-dreams is not the way they passively "re-present" past psychological states, events and truths. It is precisely the way in which spectacle-dreams work upon and thereby produce their images (the way they produce totally new states, events and truths) that is truly noteworthy. I think Professor Clark knows this well, for he writes at one point that the method of the *Bathers* (like the method of the unconscious itself) is "more like interruption than juxtaposition, more like the grating and locking of the parts of a great psychic machine than the patient disclosure of a world." But Clark still relies upon the wooden Freudian concept of "wish-fulfillment," in which the wishes that the dream or phantasy fulfills are pre-packaged (virtually eternal and indestructible), and come directly from the theater of spectacular representation (Oedipal triangulation). The "meaning" of dreams lies in the way they work, in the work that they perform on their "raw materials," and in the effects they produce, not in some codebook or system of interpretation, which is bound to repeat and reinforce the most oppressive prejudices and hatreds of the dominant system.

The language Freud uses in "The Project for a Scientific Psychology" shouldn't simply and only be understood as "borrowed from Heimholtz and Fechner." Otherwise, the untenable presumption is that Freud evolved out of and at least partially beyond the simplistic, steam-engine mechanics of his era and thereby inaugurated something new, something "modern," namely psychoanalysis. But are not some forms of borrowing also forms of detournement? It is quite true that Freud's discourse is more advanced than that of Heimholtz and Fechner, but this is precisely because Freud did not conceive of the detourned phrase "specifiable material particles" as a designation for stable, singular and equivalent units (as Professor Clark thinks he does). Freud conceived of these "particles" as both discreet units *and* indivisible flows. (Cf. contemporary theories of the nature and behavior of particles of light.) The language of "quantitatively determined states of specifiable material particles" – the language of flows, cuts or breaks in flows, couplings and uncouplings – is directly and quite productively connected to the discovery of the fundamentally productive machinic nature of the unconscious. Despite being vulgar or "uncritically" borrowed, the detourned language of Heimholtz and Fechner *worked* for Freud. Perhaps this is the reason why he "struggled" with it all through his career: it worked too well for bourgeois Vienna.

Enough about fucking Freud already: let's talk about Cezanne's *The Large Bathers*. Quite obviously I believe one can look at them and not see the rather typical and altogether not very frightening nightmares that Professor Clark sees. There are several reasons for this. First and foremost, when it comes to human sexuality and sexual "wish fulfillments," very little is generalizable (so be forewarned all those who would pass judgment on others!). Human beings are far too diverse and their situations are far too different to do so with anything approaching confidence. We are not all white heterosexual men. For some of us, the visual content of even the most fantastic parts of the *Bathers* is not a phantasy, but the physical reality we live every day. There are in fact sexual freaks of all kinds, and they are both natural (involuntary) and man-made (voluntary). Fear or even avoidance of all physical contact does not mean that sexuality is impossible and desire is blocked. Desire flows freely in the (onanist) sexuality of the voyeur, the exhibitionist and the fetishist – all of whom, need I tell you, can experience sexual pleasure and orgasm without touching or being touched by someone else.

One's take on Cezanne's *The Large Bathers* may also be a simple matter of personal temperament or sense of humor: the "double figures" (Clark's drab phrase) of the women joined at the buttocks and shoulders, the woman with the penis-head, and the man/woman with the erect penis/very long vaginal fold may strike you or me as funny instead of dreadful, liberatory instead of oppressive, and a mockery of bourgeois neurosis instead of an instance of it. After all, these "double figures" are all *visual puns*. Though puns are considered the lowest form of humor, their crudity or vulgarity need not make them terrifying, oppressive or evocative of inconsolable despair.

Can you feel the way Georges Bataille's "The Solar Anus" rises and falls with the movements of Cezanne's paintings? First Cezanne, then Bataille.

> *What do women talk about privately – what are they really like – when they are by themselves? What's it like to touch a nude woman? And several nude women, all at once?*

> A man who finds himself among others is irritated because he does not know why he is not one of the others. In bed next to a girl he loves, he forgets that he does not know why he is himself instead of the body he touches. Without knowing it, he suffers from the obscurity of intelligence that keeps him from screaming that he himself is the girl who forgets his presence while shuddering in his arms.

> *Why does it please me so to see women's buttocks becoming shoulders and shoulders becoming buttocks? Why do I want to stick my penis's head atop one of their heads?*

Ever since sentences started to circulate in brains devoted to reflection, an effort at total identification has been made, because with the aid of a copula each sentence ties one thing to another; all things would be visibly connected if one could discover at a single glance and in its totality the tracings of an Ariadne's thread leading thought into its own labyrinth. But the copula of terms is no less irritating than the copulation of bodies.

What then is the relationship between these three paintings?

It is clear that the world is purely parodic, in other words, that each thing seen is the parody of another, or is the same thing in a deceptive form.

Why are they always bathers? Why water?

Animal life comes entirely from the movement of the seas and, inside bodies, life continues to come from salt water. The sea, then, has played the role of the female organ that liquefies under the excitation of the penis.

This is modernist as fuck, yo, but what has it to do with socialism?

This eruptive force accumulates in those who are necessarily situated below. Communist workers appear to the bourgeois to be as ugly and dirty as hairy sexual organs, or lower parts; sooner or later there will be a scandalous eruption in the course of which the asexual noble heads of the bourgeois will be chopped off.

Picasso's The Architect's Table

Though Pablo Picasso is often associated with strong anti-war sentiments (cf. *Guernica*), one doesn't associate him with Marxism, socialism or anarchism. And so his presence in *An End to An Idea* is questionable, though not nearly as much as that of Freud. For, after all, Picasso was a modernist painter, and this is supposed to be (and really is) a book in part about modernist art. According to Professor Clark, "Cubism . . . is the moment when modernism focused on its means and purposes with a special vengeance. The idiom that resulted became *the* idiom of visual art in the twentieth century: Picasso's and [Georges] Braque's way of organizing a picture was borrowed, adapted, or fought against by almost all subsequent art, and very often taken as the still point of modernism – the set of works in which modernity found itself a style." I would claim pride of place here for Dada, and not Cubism, but I've probably spent too much time reading the situationists and Greil Marcus to make an unbiased judgment.

Professor Clark is most interested in the paintings Picasso (and, to a lesser extent, Braque) completed between 1907 or 1908 and 1912 – that is, in the period after "the aftershock of *Demoiselles d'Avignon* (which is another story) had subsided" and before 1914, which is when Clark dates the birth of abstract art. For Clark, "clearly there is something eye-catchingly sequential to the work Picasso and Braque did between 1908 and 1912."

> It looks to have a kind of logic and consistency, to be looping back and back to the same or much the same set of problems, edging forward to new ways of doing things, plotting a syntax and testing it out across the usual range of subjects – still life, landscape, nudes, figure paintings, portraits of dealers and friends. This look is not misleading. There is a quality of insistence and repetitiveness to Cubism that sets it apart from all other modernisms, even the most dogged [...].

And yet, Clark writes, "everyone agrees" that "the moment of summer 1910 and the pictures done on vacation in Cadaques" are "odd." Picasso's art dealer Kahnweiler recalls that, "dissatisfied, [Picasso] returned to Paris in the fall [of 1910], after weeks of painful struggle, bringing back works that were unfinished." And so Professor Clark believes that, "we can best understand the painting Picasso did in 1911 and 1912 if we see it as *not* issuing from the process of inquiry of the previous three years." Thus, within the larger 1907 or 1908 to 1912 period, there is an internal division between the work Picasso did before and after 1910, the year that found Cubism "near freezing point" (Clark's phrase). It was in 1910 that Picasso's paintings demonstrated "their inability to conclude the remaking of representation that was their goal." And it was in the following two years that Picasso decided to try something radically different – and succeeded. "Everyone agrees," Clark writes, "that the painting Picasso did in 1911 and 1912 represents some ultimate test-case and triumph of modernism."

Despite its precise focus, Professor Clark's entire chapter on Picasso doesn't offer any explanations as to why the painter made the art-historical decisions he made between 1908 and 1912, or between 1910 and 1912, for that matter. What motivated Picasso to undertake the project to "remake representation"? Was he, like Cezanne, motivated by an unresolved Oedipal complex? Was he, like David during the French Revolution or Pissarro in the year of Ravachol, motivated by the possibility of a revolutionary uprising? No, neither.

According to Professor Clark (he's writing about Picasso's *The Architect's Table*), "what is being done to the world in the oval [of the painting] is done not by 'painting' alone but painting-in-the-service-of-epistemology; and that pretense is necessary precisely in order to keep 'painting' alive, since painting in Picasso's view is a set of means generated out of imitation, and unthinkable – empty, inconsistent, unconstrained – without it." *Painting is threatened with death.* Why? How? By what? *Painting must be kept alive.* Why? *Being placed in the service of epistemology will keep painting alive.* Why? No answer. No answers at all, other than this: "So a formal task presents itself, which Picasso carries out to perfection." A strictly formal task, one without any political or social content?! Not bloody likely. And so: here we go, back into the Good Professor's wastepaper basket!

Though it doesn't serve as the centerpiece for the chapter – a photograph by Picasso himself of several of his paintings displayed at Sorgues in 1912 has the honor – *The Architect's Table* (1912) is discussed at length by Professor Clark. Of all the paintings by Picasso that Clark reproduces and discusses, this one is both the most interesting and the one that brings him to (even over) the brink of thinking of modernism in explicitly spatial terms.

Let us recall that Clark announced in his "Introduction" that he didn't want to think of modernism in terms of space, but in terms of a "distinctive patterning of mental and technical possibilities." Clark doesn't explain or develop what he means by this last phrase, so it isn't possible to determine why such "patterns of possibilities" should be opposed to or precluded from spatial conceptualization. But it appears that Clark understands these patterns to have something to do with time, and not space. At the conclusion of his chapter on the French Revolution, he writes, "If I wanted to argue more fully for the 1790s and early 1800s being the decades that usher in a decisive new structuring of time, I think my best evidence would be music. Naturally, since this is the art that feeds most deeply on a culture's imagining of temporality – its sense of sequence and repetition, or of discontinuity and inauguration." How very similar to Debord and Jacques Attali, as well! The passage of time, not the usage of space, is primary in modernity. It really is a history, and not a psychogeography of modernism that Clark wants to be write.

And yet, when he comes face-to-face with Cubist paintings, Clark does not talk about a new structuring of time, but about a new structuring of space: In Cubist paintings, "the surface [is] chock-full, almost overwhelmed by spatiality," he says. Summing up his remarks on the 1912-1913 painting *Man with a Guitar*, Clark writes, "This is the kind of spatiality that Picasso was struggling to retrieve." Elsewhere, Clark says that:

> If one were feeling for a means, that is, to cancel the equation of presence with salience, then maybe there would prove no other way of doing it than reducing the body to a set of contingent positions and directions in space – possible not actual, mapped not materialized. In which case [...] the organizing structure of representation would no longer be edges and surfaces – solids folding out into spaces abutting them – but a tissue of virtual locations, relations, kinds of orientation or topology. That all locations are now virtual is expressed, in *The*

Guitarist [1910], by the fact that more and more surfaces seem to be transparent or nearly so, opening onto other possible positions, declaring themselves not to be solids, or even forms of transparent material, but rather configurations of space.

In other words, Picasso's paintings from the early 1910s demonstrate that space isn't "empty" when there are no discernible objects in it, that space is *never* "empty," and that the supposedly sharp distinction between space and solid objects (between absence and presence) is illusory. "There is no [such thing as] empty space," Professor Clark quotes Kasimir Malevich as saying, "because everything is already filled, occupied."

Clark's rather complete turnaround concerning space, or, if you will, the sudden and violent "return" of what he has "repressed," is provocative, for it in part suggests that, to the extent Cubism is in fact central to twentieth century modernism, Clark's discussions of the art that followed Picasso's (El Lissitzky's, Jackson Pollock's, and Abstract Expressionism in general) should be in spatial terms as well. Not surprisingly, the theme of space is present in Clark's discussions of El Lissitzky's interest in architecture, and in his discussions of Jackson Pollock's works from 1947 to 1950. (In the latter, Clark quotes Michael Fried, who speaks about the "new kind of space" opened up in Pollock's *Number 1*, 1948.) But these are not sustained discussions of spatiality in modernist art. Professor Clark only takes up the theme of space in his chapter on Picasso (just as anarchism is only discussed in his chapter on Pissarro and Freud only comes up in his chapter on Cezanne).

The theme of space is certainly unavoidable when one turns to *The Architect's Table* – in part because of its evocative title, which was not given to the painting by Picasso. At some point, it was just a "still life."

> For instance [Professor Clark writes], the one that includes Gertrude Stein's calling card, which Picasso identified in a letter to her as "*votre nature mort (ma jolie)*": the phrase from the pop song appears again, with what look to be lines of music (or maybe guitar strings) in the vicinity. The sexual humor hoped for in the counterpoint between *"Ma Jolie"* and *Mis (sic) Gertrude Stein* is about up to Picasso's usual standard. Kahnweiler preferred to take his cue from the carpenter's T-square visible upper left, and christened the painting *The Architect's Table*.

Evidently Picasso accepted this unusual title, which evokes magic, alchemy, and the philosopher's stone. Despite the title's richness – despite all the puns that are possible – Professor Clark does very little with it, which is noteworthy, given how much attention he pays to the titles given to paintings by Jackson Pollock.

"Run your hand over *The Architect's Table*," Clark writes in a rare instance;

"pick up the unlovely Miss Stein's calling card, hang on to the knife by its handle." These suggestions fit the painting, which has a fascinating visual texture, a spatiality that you want to enter into and experience directly, personally. But Clark ignores the fact that he himself is writing "on" *The Architect's Table*, that he is trying to make his mark on the critical reception of it. He ignores the fact that *The Architect's Table* is not a square or rectangle, but an oval. (Most architect's tables are square or rectangular, and not oval-shaped, right? Architects don't move around their tables; they sit for long periods of time at a particular end or side of it.) But, most notably, Clark ignores the fact that *The Architect's Table* – despite our modern expectation that such a table must be as clean and orderly as both the plans for buildings that are drafted upon it and the buildings themselves – is incredibly cluttered. (I mean that though Clark understands and speaks at length about the visual clutter of the painting itself, he does not point out the irony of the fact that it is an *architect's* table – of all things! – that is overwhelmed with decorative architectural elements, objects of all types, and words both floating about "in thin air" and fixed upon calling cards.)

The spatial-visual clutter of *The Architect's Table* is obviously the key element in understanding it. This is Gertrude Stein writing in 1912 about Picasso's most recent paintings:

> Something had been coming out of him, certainly it had been coming out of him, certainly it was something, certainly it had been coming out of him and it had meaning, a charming meaning, a solid meaning, a struggling meaning, a clear meaning . . . . This one [Picasso] was always having something that was coming out of this one that was a solid thing, a charming thing, a lovely thing, a perplexing thing, a disconcerting thing, a simple thing, a clear thing, a complicated thing, an interesting thing, a disturbing thing, a repellent thing, a very pretty thing.

Note: not one thing with a great many diverse aspects or sides, but simply a great many diverse things. This is Picasso himself writing about the paintings he's doing in 1911 and 1912:

> For certain I am sending you [Kahnweiler] the pictures I told you about yesterday in my letter . . . there are three of them the biggest a violin on its side and then a still life done at Druetrx the hotel-keeper's place with the letters Mazagran armagnac cafe on a round table a fruit bowl with pears a knife a glass. The other still life Pernod on a round wooden table a glass with strainer and sugar and bottle written Pernod Fils with in the background posters mazagran cafe armagnac 50.

Again: a great many things, not so much cleanly juxtaposed as all jumbled together, each thing unrelated to the others.

Clark's interest in these passages is rather narrow. They are simply "evidence for these [Cubist] paintings' being best construed as descriptions of an object-world," a world in which there are "objects, or aspects of objects, accumulated, intersecting, fighting for room in the oval." That need be all. "If we do agree on that much," Professor Clark writes, "we have already come far in the interpretation of Cubism, for this opening onto an object-world has always been disputed or downplayed in the case of the paintings from 1911 and 1912, often by those with most to say about them." The point? Apparently that Cubism is not yet abstract art, for in abstract art there are no objects – no "real" object-world to which the painting might refer – just shapes, colors and textures.

In Clark's fumbling hands, the objects in Picasso's paintings – "Miss Stein's dog-eared calling card, a pipe and liqueur glass, Victorian furniture, fringes with little tassels, curtains with heavy silk cords" – are simply "bits and pieces of a bourgeois world." Clark notes that "viewers of Cubism have always relished the sheer banality of the things it does denote," but is unable to rise above this banality himself. He asks, half-rhetorically, "What could we find to say about them?" If this were the T.J. Clark of the chapter on Pissarro and anarchism, the answer would be: "These bits and pieces are fragments of the world hated and bombed to pieces by Seurat and Ravachol." But it isn't; this chapter is written by T.J. Clark the Academic Semiotician, and so the answer, "provisionally" (of course), is this: "The claim or pretense in *The Architect's Table* to articulate an order made out of perception . . . is a mighty one, but a pretense." The purpose of creating a painting such as *The Architect's Table* in 1912 was to (yet again!) show "the arbitrariness of the sign." Not the arbitrariness of the "object-world" of architecture and architects, but that of the sign. *Forget about the oppressive day-to-day reality of overcrowded modern cities! O, save me from the arbitrariness of the sign!* "Here I think I cross the path of the semioticians," Professor Clark says. You are incorrect, sir: here is where you *tripped over* the path of the semioticians and fell flat on your face.

A few basic banalities, then: *The Architect's Table* is cluttered by objects that had traditionally been either hand-made or produced by relatively simple, if not pre-industrial techniques. That is to say, the "object-world" evoked or depicted by this and other such Cubist paintings is the precisely object-world that was – at that very time – being rapidly destroyed, and replaced with a new one, by mass industrial production. Every conceivable object – no matter how "aristocratic" or "banal" in past times – was then beginning to be mass-produced and widely distributed by huge industrial combines. The reign of the spectacle-commodity had begun. Tables and carafes and posters and pieces of furniture and glasses and calling cards and knives were now mass-produced by complex electrically powered machines. The skilled artisans of the past were now unneeded, obsolete; the relatively scarce objects formerly reserved for the bourgeois alone could be increasingly be purchased by anyone, anywhere. Clark mistakenly claims that the "particular representational repertoire" of *The Architect's Table* attempts to "contradict experience, [and] set up impossible orders, and imagine otherwise." On the contrary: *The Architect's Table* attempts to reaffirm everyday experience, and to resist the setting up of the impossible cluttered new "order" of mass-produced objects. The representational space of the painting is overwhelmed by handmade objects precisely because they were starting to disappear, not one by one, but *en masse* and rapidly.

It is surprising that Professor Clark says so little about Gertrude Stein's calling card, which would seem to offer a unique opportunity to make an interesting comparison with the half-legible letters and the *assignat* in David's *Marat*. Is the misspelling of the word "Miss" solely an instance of "vulgar" sexual humor? ("Duh, I get the joke: the Miss is missing an S.") But perhaps Picasso dropped the last "s" because he knew that Stein was interested in misprints. Perhaps Picasso was signaling that he knew that certain forms of money – but especially modern paper banknotes and postal stamps – increase rather than decrease in value if they contain a misprint. Perhaps Picasso meant to indicate that misprints on official papers said a great deal about the creation of artistic value in his own paintings. (Note well that, despite what Picasso wrote to Stein about "Ma Jolie," it is in fact the phrase "*La* Jolie" that floats "in thin air" in *The Architect's Table*.)

It so happens that Gertrude Stein was fascinated by money, not so much by what it could buy, but by the literal object itself, all through her literary career, but especially when she lived in Paris. In particular, she was fascinated by paper money, which had been introduced to the United States as early as the 1840s (cf. Edgar Allan Poe's "The Gold Bug") and which became fully institutionalized in 1913 when the Federal Reserve Bank was established. Stein used to sign autographs on paper money and frequently commented upon the practice. She knew well that wartime hyper-inflation wasn't a "crisis of confidence" that arrived *later*, when too much paper money had been printed up. She knew well that, from the perspective of the gold coin, paper money has (or is) inflation at its very heart; that paper money itself is inflationary and floats "in thin air," above the ground. She knew well that, with the total separation of the money-form from gold and other precious metals, the value of money itself had become inflated. And so Miss Gertrude Stein based her entire mature work on a simple but very productive device: the systematic "hyper-inflation" (over-production) of literary value. When she wrote obsessively repetitive passages such as the one quoted above – "Something had been coming out of him, certainly it had been coming out of him, certainly it was something, certainly it had been coming out of him" – she was imitating the way printed money unceasingly and quite miraculously makes something meaningful (indeed, the measure of all meaningful value) come from nothing or almost nothing (a few magic words on a mere scrap of paper).

What has architecture or oval architect's tables to do with all this? In the very years under consideration here, European architecture was undergoing something of a "crisis of confidence" of its own. According to Walter Gropius, the German modernist who wrote a groundbreaking and widely distributed essay about the subject in 1913, European architecture was mired in its past and morbidly obsessed with ornamentation, which was deemed to be a "crime" by the Austrian architect Adolph Loos. The old historical city, over-crowded with people and objects, was being overwhelmed by industrial mass production. Circulation was becoming impossible. The only way out, according to Gropius, was for European architecture to wholeheartedly embrace the monumental and apparently completely undecorated industrial and commercial buildings being put up by engineers (not architects) in the United States, Canada and South America. That is to say, Gropius was arguing that *the techniques that were then proving so successful in the mass-production of commodity-objects (money included) should be applied to the design and production of buildings and cities.*

European architecture did in fact embrace the quick and cheap building materials and methods, as well as the sleek "functional" look, of industrial buildings. Under the guidance of Le Corbusier, Frank Johnson and Mies Van der Rohe, among others, this form of architectural modernism became known as the International Style. Monumental or superhuman in scale, obsessed with simple geometric shapes, always clad in spectacular mirrored surfaces, and strangely in need of "empty spaces" surrounding its rigid steel-and-glass monoliths – abstract architecture now orders (dominates) the social space of the entire planet. That is to say, abstraction now dominates everything, from money to commodities and art to social space itself, precisely because abstract social space is the space needed for the production and maintenance of modern bureaucracies and total (uncontested) state power.

Perhaps Walter Gropius would have interpreted Picasso's *The Architect's Table* as either a parody of the old and overwhelmed European city, or as an open call to modern architects to create the New Abstract City. Space needed to be changed to accommodate the proliferating new object-world. ("Either that, or industrial mass production needed to be changed to accommodate people, not profits," a Marxist, a socialist or an anarchist would say.) *The Architect's Table* certainly disorients and enriches our perception of what space is and could be. But does it in fact change space? Certainly the impulse or the desire to change space was very strong. Clark aptly summarizes it in a remark he imagines Picasso might have made: "I will get the world in order – just watch me! I will have the picture be more than the sum of its parts!"

Nevertheless, the answer to our question must be "No." This painting cannot – indeed, no painting can – change space on its own. "It may even be that Pollock never thought the project of abstract painting had a chance of succeeding without its becoming part of some such general reordering of space," Clark writes. (A "general reordering of space" does nicely as shorthand for *social revolution.*) As for Picasso, his painting was not "a devising of a new description of the world –

one in which, to take the most widely touted example, the terms of space and time were recast in a way that responded to changes out there in physics or philosophy," Clark writes; "it was a *counterfeit* of such a description – an imagining of what kinds of things might happen to the means of Western painting if such a new description arose" (emphasis added). Though it may circulate in the meantime, Picasso's counterfeit could only be cashed in "after the revolution."

There is something ominous about Jacques Riviere's 1912 statement that, in the paintings of Picasso, shadows become incarnated as space. (As quoted by Clark: "By becoming incarnate as shadows, space will preserve the discrete existence of objects in the picture itself.") What *ideology* is in fact materializing before our eyes? "I will get the world in order – just watch me! I will have the picture be more than the sum of its parts!" It is in fact the ideology of totalitarian state power.

I can't help but wonder what Adolph Hitler – surely the twentieth century's greatest hater of both modernism and socialism (and yet unmentioned by Clark) – would have made of Picasso's *The Architect's Table*. An architect and a painter in his own right, Hitler would have had strong opinions on the subject. Certainly he would have hated the painting, hated its "decadence," "ugliness," and "deformation" of the human body. But Hitler would have been unable to forget it, even if he had it destroyed or locked up in a museum of decadent (and obsolete) culture. For did not Hitler, too, feel overwhelmed by life in the over-crowded city? Did not he, too, dream of a New City in which space and the object-world were reconciled?

NOT BORED! #31, June 1999

Cornelius Castoriadis and Guy Debord: "Strangers in the Night"

Let us review the story so far. For the last three years, we have been working our way through all three long and dense volumes of Cornelius Castoriadis's *Political and Social Writings* (translated and edited by David Ames Curtis, and published by the University of Minnesota Press between 1988 and 1993). A former Trotskyist born in Greece, Castoriadis founded the ultraleftist group Socialisme ou Barbarie in Paris in 1949, and published a great many essays in the eponymous journal published by that group until its dissolution in 1967. Curtis's superb three-volume anthology includes essays written as early as 1946 and as late as 1979. Previously unknown to us, these essays have been and continue to be extremely useful (in part because they are both informative and insightful, and in part because they clearly had a strong and enduring influence on the Situationist International, the revolutionary group that has had a strong and enduring influence on us). Even if we were to complete our anticipated trilogy of articles on *Political and Social Writings* as planned, we would barely scratch the surface of the ground covered by these three books.

In "Workers' Councils, Cornelius Castoriadis and the Situationist International" (*NOT BORED!* #26, December 1996), we reported the little known fact – at least among American situationists of our generation – that the situationist Guy Debord had briefly been a member of and, one might say, received his education in the history of the workers' movement thanks to Socialisme ou Barbarie, to which he belonged in 1960. Our essay traced the post-1960 influence of the writings of the S. ou B. group and Castoriadis upon Debord and the other situationists, as well as noted that this influence primarily consisted in the situationists' sudden adoption of and repeated insistence upon the theme of workers' councils (long one of Castoriadis's central concerns). Our essay also criticized the situationists, both for hiding their significant indebtedness to the excellent work done by Castoriadis and the S. ou B. group all through the late 1940s and 1950s, and for heaping indiscriminate and undeserved abuse on them, Castoriadis in particular. (One of the enduring effects of this abuse – whatever its purpose back in the day – is that people who are today turned on to politics, sometimes for the very first time, by the situationists know absolutely nothing about the people the SI insulted, people such as Henri Lefebvre, Daniel Guerin, and Castoriadis.)

Because "Workers' Councils, Cornelius Castoriadis and the Situationist International" was intended to follow-up on commentary we'd previously made upon the manner in which the American section of the Situationist International adopted the "situationist" theme of the councils ("Highway 69 Revisited," *NOT BORED!* #25, May 1996), our essay did not mention or discuss all of the other "classic" situationist themes that, it turns out, have their roots in the work and writings by Castoriadis and S. ou B. One might do a detailed study of the date and manner of appearance in situationist writing of such original Castoriadian concepts as "bureaucratic capitalism" (adopted wholesale and without attribution by Debord in *The Society of the Spectacle*) and the fundamental split in capitalist society between "directors" and "executants" (adopted wholesale and without attribution by Raoul Vaneigem in *The Revolution of Everyday Life*).

What would be accomplished by such a study? On the one hand, it would add to the on-going posthumous evaluation of the extent and nature of S. ou B.'s and Castoriadis's influence on the young radicals who rose up en masse in May 1968. While the influence of the situationists on these young radicals has been well-documented (in part because some of the situationists were themselves among the young radicals who rose up), the direct and indirect influence of the S. ou B. group upon them has not. This is unfortunate, because Castoriadis's after-the-fact evaluation of the May 1968 revolt was quite different from that of the situationists. Somewhere between the situationists' triumphant proclamations and Castoriadis's sober reservations about what "really" happened lies an accurate, comprehensive and tempered version of May '68 that will help rather than hurt our current efforts to incite and participate in similar revolts.

On the other hand, a detailed study of S. ou B.'s influence on the Situationist International would aid in the constructive de-mythification of the situationists, who were able to recontextualize a variety of ideas in such a way that, although some or even most of these ideas were originally given form by other people, they came across as though they could only be situationist ideas. The presence and role of Raoul Vaneigem would be central here, for, according to Pierre Guillaume (a member of S. ou B. in the early 1960s), it was through S. ou B. that Vaneigem originally entered the SI, and it was as a result of the Belgian wildcat strikes of 1961 – documented and praised in S. ou B.'s journal, but not in the pages of *Internationale Situationniste* – that Vaneigem became interested in joining a revolutionary organization. (To the extent that situationist writing – especially Vaneigem's *The Revolution of Everyday Life* – remains exciting to read, while some or even most of the writing published in S. ou B.'s journal is not [and perhaps never was] exciting to read, an evaluation of the manner in which the situationists plagiarized or detourned such Castoriadian concepts as "self-management," "bureaucratic capitalism" and "directors/executants" would be quite useful to contemporary polemicists, propagandists and agitators.)

In "Cornelius Castoriadis, 1922-1997" (*NOT BORED!* #29, July 1998) – the second installment of our anticipated trilogy of articles about *Political and Social Writings* – we contrasted the respective attempts of the SI and S. ou B. to "re-orient" themselves in the early 1960s, that is to say, at a time when revolutionary struggles, after a long hiatus, began to break out, not only in the "socialist" bureaucratic countries, but in the capitalist "democracies" as well. (One might say that what the SI and S. ou B. were really doing in the 1961 to 1962 period was re-orienting themselves in the light of their contact with each other.) Our second essay noted that, unlike the SI (which flourished in the mid-1960s and thus was able to play a direct role in the May 1968 uprisings), S. ou B. was unable to re-orient itself adequately, and was forced to disband itself in 1967 – a fact we tried to explain by highlighting Castoriadis's lack of attention to the form of revolutionary exposition and action, and to his over-emphasis upon content. We associated this imbalance with an inability to communicate effectively with rebellious student youth, precisely the people who rose up with so much style in May 1968.

Had "Cornelius Castoriadis, 1922-1997" not been narrowly focused on May '68 (the revolution that Castoriadis neither anticipated nor totally approved of), it would have included a discussion of all of the formal, youth-oriented things that S. ou B. and Castoriadis – unlike the situationists – didn't have a feel for: late 19th century French poetry; modern art (especially Dada and surrealism); popular culture in all its forms (including street posters and graffiti); architecture, urbanism, and social space; and intoxication, passion, desire and love. Indeed, though Castoriadis continued writing (and continued writing well) long after the dissolution of S. ou B., so far as we can tell he never took up these situationist themes. (Note that "Social Transformation and Cultural Creation," the only essay on music in volume three of *Political and Social Writings* is totally untroubled by the sudden appearance of punk, despite being written in December 1978.) As for Debord and Vaneigem, they continued to dwell upon "romantic" themes – poetry, modern art, and so forth – in their various works, long after the dissolution of the SI and long after they stopped talking about workers' councils and directors and executants. (Note that Debord says nothing about workers' councils in the film version of *The Society of the Spectacle*, despite the importance given to them in the book version.)

In a certain sense, what is truly remarkable about the relationship between the SI and S. ou B. is not the fact that, after brief contact in 1960, the former adopted and popularized certain key themes of the latter – it's the fact that the two organizations, despite the agreement they came to have for a brief moment in time, were so different from each other in the pre-1960 period. Unlike the very cool and "ultra-modern" Situationist International, S. ou B. was a very traditional revolutionary organization (despite breaks with "paleo-Marxists" in 1959 and again in 1962) whose roots lay in the dissident factions of the French Communist Party and the Fourth International. The roots of the SI, in sharp contrast, lay in revolutionary surrealism. Which is the stranger of the two, a group of ex-Trotskyists embracing workers' councils a good 30 years after Trotsky's suppression of the Kronstadt uprising or a group of ex-surrealists discovering workers' councils a good 5 years after the Hungarian Revolution (in which the councils played a prominent role)?

Castoriadis himself "came a long way." In the late 1940s, he was a Marxist, a member of the French Communist Party, and a dissident Trotskyist. By the early 1960s, Castoriadis was no longer a member of the Communist Party nor was he a dissident Trotskyist. Indeed, though he remained a proponent of radical autonomy, generalized self-management and workers' councils, Castoriadis wasn't even a Marxist anymore, a point to which we will return. Compare Castoriadis's trajectory to that of Debord, who, in the early 1950s, was a surrealist-inspired poet, filmmaker, and flaneur. By the early 1960s, Debord was a Marxist theoretician and a founding member of an increasingly formal revolutionary organization. Who is the stranger of the two, the former Communist Party member who renounces Marx but remains a partisan of workers' radical self-management, or the former surrealist who becomes a Marxist and a partisan of workers' councils?

The obvious answer is that both trajectories are *passing strange*. The temptation to stage a speculation (or series of speculations) about the two of them meeting in the night is strong. Castoriadis writes in "The Diversionists," a stiff essay from 1977 included in volume three of *Political and Social Writings*: "You can search with a magnifying glass *for one single sentence* in Sartre, Levi-Strauss, Lacan, Althusser, Foucault, Barthes, etc., that is even remotely relevant either for the preparation of May '68 or for its subsequent comprehension" (emphasis in original). But what about Debord and Vaneigem? What about Rene Vienet, author of a book on the subject? But, all told, it would be just too strange to try to position the very different trajectories of Castoriadis and Debord along a common axis, or to imagine what S. ou B. would have been like if Debord had remained a member, or what the SI would have been like if Castoriadis had become a member.

It is, therefore, with some embarrassment that we recall that the conclusion of "Cornelius Castoriadis, 1922-1997" calls for a third article from us that would bring together into one "image" the best aspects of the SI and S. ou B. When we made this call, we imagined that we'd take from the situationists their style (their love of scandal; their youthfulness; their passion and reckless creativity) and from Castoriadis and the other members of S. ou B. their smarts (their thoroughness and patience; their knowledge of relevant facts; their insistence on informed judgments based on accurate information). We imagined that we'd be able to envision a group that was 1). organized like the SI (unstable, intentionally small, and nonhierarchical); 2). composed of people such as were attracted to the SI (painters, writers, and architects, on the one hand, and profligates, hedonists and criminals, on the other), as well as those who were attracted to S. ou B. (professors, union militants, and dissident Party members); and 3). capable of speaking intelligently about both complex economic and political issues, and complex aesthetic and social issues.

But it just won't work. The whole project is too mechanical, too much of an abstract or speculative enterprise. *Fuck!* Combining the best of one long-defunct revolutionary organization with that of another long-defunct revolutionary organization – *why bother?* It isn't the early-1960s anymore! It's more than 35 years later, and it is quite possible (even likely) that neither the SI nor S. ou B. are particularly relevant to today's conditions. But, even if it were, metaphorically speaking, "still 1962" – even if it still made sense to speculate upon the possibility that the radical elements in the SI and S. ou B. might have joined together in 1962 and formed a new revolutionary organization that would still be relevant today – there is a problem that will not be ignored or easily resolved. And that problem can be indicated by the words "Marx and Marxism." *Rather than being the grounds upon which the meeting between the SI and S. ou B. could or might take place, Marx and Marxism are the chasms that separate the two groups from each other.*

From very early on, Castoriadis realized that the rejection of Stalinism – that is, the rejection of what "socialism" had become in "Soviet" Russia – necessitated or entailed the rejection of central, even fundamental, aspects of Marxism itself. In "The Problem of the USSR and the Possibility of a Third Historical Solution" (originally written in 1947, first published in 1949 and reprinted in the first volume of *Political and Social Writings*), Castoriadis insisted that the very fact that neither true "socialism" nor "barbarism" (another word for capitalism) was instaurated by the October 1917 Revolution meant that Marx – as well as Lenin, Stalin and Trotsky – had been wrong about the historical process (the very thing that Marx and the Marxists claimed that they and they alone had mastered). For Marx as well as for Lenin, Stalin and Trotsky – that is, for what Castoriadis called "the classical schema for the end of capitalism from Marx to Trotsky" – it was inevitable that, faced with the choice between socialism and barbarity, the international working class movement would eventually choose the former. But what was instaurated in Soviet Russia was in fact "a third historical solution," one not foreseen by any of the great Marxists, including Marx himself: the instauration of the modern bureaucratic state.

Though Trotsky granted that the unprecedented growth of the bureaucracy under both Lenin and Stalin was regrettable, he continued to remain faithful to Marxism's unwavering belief in the scientific inevitability of socialism. Consequently, Castoriadis and his comrades (Claude Lefort, among them) broke with the Trotskyists, who obstinately refused to draw and act upon the following obvious conclusions, which Castoriadis draws in "The Problem of the USSR and the Possibility of a Third Historical Solution": 1). "The historical process is neither fated nor necessarily determined in advance," and 2). "The historical process does not follow a straight and narrow line of ascent."

But Castoriadis's real disagreement was with Marx. "But we must go back even further," Castoriadis writes in "On the Content of Socialism, II," originally published in 1957 and reprinted in the second volume of *Political and Social Writings*; "we must go back to Marx himself." For it was Marx himself who insisted on – *who attacked Bakunin and the anarchists because they refused to recognize and act in accordance with* – the "scientifically" verifiable "facts" that capitalism would be overthrown in a Western European industrialized nation (not in a backward Eastern European nation such as Russia), that capitalism would be overthrown by a mass uprising of the revolutionary proletariat (not by a palace coup), and that "the dictatorship of the proletariat" would instaurate socialism (not the modern bureaucratic state) in place of capitalism. To Castoriadis, these mistakes were not small, incidental or limited, but indicative of the essential uselessness of Marxism as an effective revolutionary theory in the second half of the twentieth century.

All through the 1950s – that is, long after dispensing with the Trotskyists – Castoriadis continued to criticize the writings of Marx. Indeed, Castoriadis's break with the classical Marx-Trotsky scheme grounded all of his later work in the S. ou B. period, and beyond. In his "General Introduction" (1972), reprinted as the preface to volume one of *Political and Social Writings*, he states, "There is not, as Marxism implied, borrowing a three-thousand-year-old belief, an irresistible advance toward truth in history, neither under its liberal-naive-scientistic form nor under some form of dialectical accumulation." Within this general critique of the historical process as it is theorized and practiced by Marx and the Marxists, Castoriadis offers a number of very valuable examples of Marx(ism)'s blindness to various forms of contingency, which, as T.J. Clark shows in both *The Painting of Modern Life* and *Farewell to an Idea*, is the very essence and expression of modern society. We have already seen that "the classical schema for the end of capitalism from Marx to Trotsky" is blind to the historical contingency of socialism. But Marx and the Marxists were also blind to the organizational contingency of capitalist production.

In "On the Content of Socialism, II," one of his most important essays, Castoriadis writes,

> Marx shed a great deal of light on the alienation the producer experiences in the course of the capitalist production process and on the enslavement of man by the mechanical universe he has created. But Marx's analysis is at times incomplete in that he sees only alienation in all this. In *Capital* – as opposed to Marx's early writings – it is hardly brought out at all that the worker is (and can only *be*) the *positive* vehicle of capitalist production, which is obliged to base itself on him *as such*, and to *develop* him *as such*, while simultaneously seeking to reduce him to an automaton and, at the limit, to drive him out of production altogether. Because of this, the analysis fails to perceive that the primary crisis of capitalism is the crisis at the point of production, due to the simultaneous existence of two contradictory tendencies, neither of which could disappear without the whole system collapsing. Marx shows in capitalism "despotism in the workshop and anarchy in society" – instead of seeing it as *both* despotism *and* anarchy in *both* workshop *and* society. This leads him to look for the crisis of capitalism not in production itself (except insofar as capitalist production develops "oppression, misery, degradation, but also revolt," and the numerical strength and discipline of the proletariat), but in such factors as overproduction and the falling rate of profit. Marx therefore fails to see that as long as *this type of work* persists, this crisis will persist with all it entails, and this not only whatever system of property but also whatever the nature of the State, and finally whatever even the system of *management* of production.

Even back in Marx's time, workers experienced more in the capitalist production process than simply alienation and enslavement, though alienation and enslavement were undeniably and unfortunately part of that experience. Producers (factory workers) also experienced participation in what industrial sociologists term "elementary groups," that is, the informal bands that must be created and unofficially allowed to function if the production enterprise is to work at all. For capitalist enterprises – especially large-scale enterprises – do not actually function simply or only according to the way they were designed or according to the way managers want them to function. They function only because the workers at the point of production have discovered and collectively implemented all of the various but absolutely necessary shortcuts and modifications without which the production process would not in fact function properly. By the very requirements (complexity and scale) of capitalist production – by virtue of the "collective reality of production" – the worker can never be simply or only the negative vehicle of capitalist production, the only-temporarily-necessary element in the process that eventually will be totally replaced by machines. The worker must also be the "positive vehicle" of capitalist production; the worker must always be involved in the day-to-day practical aspects and applications of the very process that is nevertheless designed to exclude him or her. This *organizational contingency* was the fundamental contradiction of capitalism in Marx's time and – long after capitalism solved its strictly economic problems with the falling rate of profit and over-production – it remains capitalism's fundamental contradiction.

Not surprisingly, there is no contingency when it comes to *commodified labor*, according to Marx and the Marxists. In "The Question of the Workers' Movement" (an important essay written in 1973 and published in volume three of *Political and Social Writings*), Castoriadis starts with the classic Marxist notion (now a commonplace of bureaucratic thought) that, in the employer-employee relationship, "a quantity of 'commodity' labor power" is sold or exchanged for "a quantity of money, that is, wages."

> But are these definite quantities? [Castoriadis asks]. Apparently so: so many hours of work, so much in wages. In reality, however, *absolutely not*: labor power is not a commodity like any other, not only because it "produces more than it costs its buyer," but because it is indefinite in advance in its concrete content – which makes it a commodity only in a formal and empty sense – and ultimately because it *is not a commodity at all*. When the capitalist buys a ton of coal, he knows [exactly] how much heat he can extract from it; for him, the business is settled. When he buys a day of work, the matter has only begun. What he will be able to extract from it in terms of actual output will be the stakes in a struggle that does not stop for a second during the entire workday.

Quite obviously one cannot codify and enforce an unchanging "law of value" or even a provisional "labor theory of value" if the amount of value extracted from labor or the cost of labor per workday is always contingent upon the outcome of myriad daily struggles. One can't adequately define and contest capitalist alienation at the political or "world-historical" level if one pretends it that it isn't being effectively contested every single day at the point of production. One can't base a theory of alienation or a theory of commodity fetishism on the fiction that, because labor power has become "completely" commodified, the commodity-form now dominates all of society. And yet these are precisely the things that both Marx and Marxism set about doing – forming an army of worthless concepts.

As serious as these wounds are (*on their own* they could prove fatal),

Castoriadis's analysis reveals other and far more serious casualties among the upper echelons of central Marxist concepts and revolutionary practices. "When workers launched wildcat strikes to win a fifteen-minute coffee break," Castoriadis writes in "The Question of the Workers' Movement," "trade unionists and Marxists tended to consider such a demand as trivial or indicative of the workers' backwardness." But, "by lodging such a demand, the workers were challenging the very foundation of the capitalist organization of the business enterprise and of society – namely, that man exists for production – and they opposed to this the principle of organizing production around the needs and life of man the producer." (The reason for the Marxists' long-standing and unbroken tradition of denigrating and even helping to suppress these revolutionary struggles is clear to Castoriadis: "autonomous and anonymous collective activity, implicit and informal struggle on the part of workers has no place in the traditional conceptualization." We might add that Marxism is also hostile to autonomous and anonymous leaderless collective activity because there is no place for it in Marxism's hierarchical and authoritarian organizational practice.)

What Castoriadis has revealed is that *both revolution and capitalism are themselves contingent.* Capitalism it does not develop according to pre-determined economic laws or its own "logic"; it develops as a result of the daily struggles at the point of production. "Through its activity, the proletariat, going on two centuries, has profoundly modified its situation in capitalist society, as well as this society itself," Castoriadis observes. Conversely, in these daily struggles, the working class movement does not confront an enemy that remains unchangeably the same. The boundaries, if you will, between capitalism and socialism – and between reformism and revolutionary action – are always shifting and thus difficult to precisely determine, but especially "scientifically" and once-and-for-all.

Therefore, if we notice that capitalism has the uncanny ability to adapt and to survive all kinds of crises – or that capitalism changed its strategy in the 1940s and has since then "endo-colonialized" the inhabitants of the First World – we must conclude that one of the prime causes of these changes and adaptations has been the conscious, collective and revolutionary actions of the international working class movement. Contrary to Marx, it turns out that, in Castoriadis's words, "the objective assigned to the working class, the historical role inscribed in its position within the capitalist relations of production, was to maintain capitalism against everything that capitalists represented and immediately aimed for; for those who think the cunning of reason is at work in history should have the courage to say that it has made of the proletariat not the gravedigger, but the savior of capitalism."

But this last point does not mean that for Castoriadis revolution – the overthrow of capitalism and its replacement with genuine socialism – is impossible. (Both the situationists and our previous essay on Castoriadis have made this erroneous claim.) Only a Marxist would believe that the proletariat and (the) revolution are inseparable, that giving up on one is giving up on the other.

One of the challenges made by Castoriadis's "The Question of the Workers' Movement" is to re-examine this movement before the appearance of Marx (especially the English struggles in the 1820s) – that is to say, before Marx introduced into this movement his only original contribution, which was the always already poisonous and ultimately fatal idea of "the dictatorship of the proletariat" – and conceptualize it without recourse to any Marxist concepts. (Though Castoriadis doesn't say so, it seems clear that anarchists are best suited to this on-going theoretical enterprise.) A related challenge to the international revolutionary movement is not to find the one social class that "really" is the vanguard or embodiment of anti-capitalist and anti-bureaucratic revolution – and that would be "put in the place" of the proletariat – but to promote generalized autonomy and self-management among all people. "What was intended by the term 'socialism' we henceforth call autonomous society," Castoriadis writes in "Socialism and Autonomous Society," the last essay in volume three of *Political and Social Writings*. "An autonomous society implies autonomous individuals – and vice versa. Autonomous society, autonomous individuals: free society, free individuals."

Unlike Castoriadis, Debord and the other situationists never realized or allowed themselves to admit that the rejection of Stalinism necessitated or entailed the rejection of fundamental aspects, if not the whole theoretical apparatus, of Marxism. Despite all of their "detournements" of Marx, the situationists remained Marxists all through the 1950s and 1960s. (Indeed, as we can see in the case of Professor T.J. Clark, some situationists remain Marxists long after they've stopped being situationists! One imagines the same thing is true for such other English-speaking ex-situationists as Donald Nicholson-Smith and Bruce Elwell.) Significantly, the Marxism of Debord and the SI is not seen in some quarters as the central weakness of situationist theory, but as its strength, as the very quality that sets it apart from (on a higher level than) other contemporary critical theories.

This is in fact the argument of young Anselm Jappe's recent biography *Guy Debord*, which is shortly to be published in an English edition that will have a preface by T.J. Clark. Jappe's very traditional (boring) book, which is actually about the critical theory of the spectacle, and not about Guy Debord, places Debord's theory squarely in line with Marx's theory of commodity fetishism and Lukacs' theory of reification. Hardly a new idea! But the problem – more intense here because Jappe presses the point so hard – is the fact that it is all-too-fitting to position the critical theory of the spectacle along this axis. Marx and the great Western Marxists: *this* is the company Debord wanted to keep. Bakunin and the other anarchists and Pannekoek and the other council communists were just so many big sticks with which to thrash the Stalinists.

If we review what we have just seen of the blindness of Marx(ism) to various forms of contingency – the historical contingency of socialism, the organizational contingency of capitalist production, the contingency of "commodified labor," and the contingency of capitalism and revolution – we quickly find that the only blindness not evinced by Debord and the other situationists concerns the historical contingency of socialism. The situationists do not expect "miracles" from the working class, Debord writes somewhere in *The Society of the Spectacle*. Hardly "adventurists," the situationists certainly knew how to wait, and didn't become impatient, suspicious, or bitter during the very years (1964 and 1965) in which Castoriadis and the other S. ou B. radicals found no reason to stay together. Unfortunately, all the other forms of contingency pass in the night without being visible to Debord the Marxist.

Against the background of Castoriadis's critique of Marx, certain passages of Debord's *The Society of the Spectacle* read like a caricature and not a detournement of Marxism. This is from Thesis 31:

> Workers do not produce themselves: they produce a force independent of themselves. The success of this production, that is, the abundance it generates, is experienced by its producers only as an *abundance of dispossession*.

Who is Debord to make such a sweeping generalization about all producers all over the world (or even just Western Europe), who are employed in a staggering variety of productive enterprises? Nothing backs this statement up – what possibly could? For surely there are producers who, despite the degradations they are forced to endure at work day after day after day, actually enjoy those things that they have created with their fellow workers; surely there are producers who are not "fragmentary individuals completely cut off" from the production process. Otherwise, what could explain the obviously genuine feelings of brother- and sisterhood among unionized workers? Absolutely nothing. Elsewhere in *The Society of the Spectacle* (Thesis 42), Debord writes:

> With the advent of the so-called second industrial revolution, alienated consumption is added to alienated production as an inescapable duty of the masses. The *entirety of labor sold* is transformed overall into the *total commodity*. A cycle is thus set in train that must be maintained at all costs: the total commodity must be returned in fragmentary form to a fragmentary individual completely cut off from the concerted action of the forces of production. [Emphasis in original.]

"The entirety of labor sold" – how much is that, exactly? Over what period of time is that value calculated: a fiscal year? a fiscal quarter? a business day? an honest hour? It is clear that one can at best or must speak of *an average* here: "The time in question is always that which is needed *on average* to manufacture a particular product in a given society under working conditions," Anselm Jappe writes in *Guy Debord*. But an average won't do here; it is too imprecise, too contingent. Despite

Jappe's belief that "more complicated jobs have a value that is simply a multiple of that of simpler ones (i.e. a greater quantity of simpler labor)," things aren't that simple, don't "add up" so neatly. Doesn't the value of the labor that has been purchased vary according to the effectiveness of the labor-extraction process? Are there not some set-backs experienced along the way that are so serious that they completely wipe out the successes of the past? What sense is there in averaging those setbacks in with a series of successes that turned out to be temporary? None. And so there is no fucking way "the entirety of labor sold" is going to be "transformed overall" into anything, not even "the total commodity," because the entirety of labor sold can only be approximated, that is, rendered on a contingent basis.

And so we are forced to conclude that, in order to get rid of Stalin, you must get rid of Marx, too; and, if you *do* get rid of Marx, you must get rid of Debord, as well. Not that Debord is to be likened to Stalin – Debord wasn't an authoritarian, mass murdering dictator, and wasn't likely "to become one" if he ever came to power. But Debord based his entire theory of the spectacle-commodity upon Marx's theory of commodified labor: the former, putatively the most radical theory of the alienation experienced in consumption, was designed to be the complement of the latter, putatively the most radical theory of the alienation experienced in production. They fit all too well. If one goes down, the other goes down with it.

We can still hold on to Castoriadis, it seems, but this is a decidedly mixed blessing. As we showed in "Cornelius Castoriadis, 1922 to 1997," his writing is short on precisely the rhetorical and emotional satisfactions contained in the best writing by Debord and the other great situationists. There are other problems as well: Castoriadis appears to have spent far too much time writing about getting rid of Marx: indeed, a good deal (far too much) of Castoriadis's *The Imaginary Institution of Society* (translated by Kathleen Blamey and published in 1987 by MIT Press) is taken up with this subject. Thus it seems premature on Castoriadis's part to replace "socialism" with "autonomous society," when there has been absolutely no discussion of anarchism, and its various relationships to Marxism, socialism, and autonomy. All of this has been left up to us to do. *Enough preparation then: let's get to it.*

NOT BORED! #31, June 1999

Mass Murder and Slavery: The Invention of Capitalism

> "For globalization to work, America must not demur from acting like the omnipotent super-power that it is. The invisible hand of the market

never functions without the hidden fist. McDonalds cannot prosper without McDonnel Douglas, the builder of the F-15 fighter. And the hidden fist that guarantees a secure world for the technologies of the Silicon Valley is called the US Army, Air Force, Navy and Marines."
– Thomas Friedman, *New York Times,* 28 March 1999

Between the 1750s and the 1840s, a series of disparate economists and philosophers tried to understand, encourage and, when necessary, apologize for the development of capitalism, which became the dominant form of socio-economic organization during this crucial period, especially in England, the birthplace of the Industrial Revolution. These writers, most of whom were English, Scottish or French, later became known as "the classical political economists." In *The Invention of Capitalism: Classical Political Economy and the Secret History of Primitive Accumulation,* published in 2000 by Duke University Press, Michael Perelman argues that the pantheon of the classical political economists – a group usually dominated by Adam Smith and, to a lesser extent, by David Ricardo – should be expanded so that it includes writers traditionally thought to be too obscure, insignificant or unorthodox to be worthy of inclusion.

A Professor of Economics at California State University at Chico and a Marxist scholar of capitalist agriculture, Perelman argues that his proposed expansion has important consequences for both historians of the period and contemporary economists. "The center [of classical political economy itself] is [now] nearer to Sir James Steuart and Edward Gibbon Wakefield than to Smith and Ricardo," Perelman writes. Of the two "stars," Adam Smith gets the worst of it. In Perelman's "new cosmology" of classical political economy, the author of *An Inquiry into the Nature and Causes of The Wealth of Nations* (published in 1776) "appears less like the sun than a moon, a lesser body whose light is largely reflected from other sources." Though not all of us will want to enter into the fray, these are fighting words, and they're certain to elicit scorn, hostility or stony silence from those who think of the Scottish economist (1723-1790) as the founder of modern economics as well as the first theorist of the "free market."

Unlike David Ricardo, who isn't much discussed these days, Adam Smith still fascinates people. As pointed out by a recent reviewer of Emma Rothschild's *Economic Sentiments: Adam Smith, Condorcet, and the Enlightenment* (Harvard University Press, 2001), "it's hardly an accident that a contemporary investment guru took 'Adam Smith' as his nom de tube." The name "Adam Smith" still has meaning and authority for contemporary political economists – whose job, it should be clear, is justifying the unjustifiable – because Smith was, as Perelman says, a "great master of capitalist apologetics" and uniquely committed to "obfuscating all information that might cast doubt on his ideology." In particular, Smith made sure his readers had no relevant information about the relentless campaign in Great Britain to 1) destroy subsistence farming and "self-provisioning" or self-sufficient households in the rural areas; 2) de-populate these areas and use them for animal husbandry and livestock production, not farming; and 3) put the former inhabitants of these areas to work in commodity-producing factories located in the major city centers. (Taken together, these merciless reorganizations of what Marx called "the social division of labor" constitute the conditions necessary for the invention of capitalism.) As a result of his deliberate omissions, Smith's "charming obfuscations" – unlike the more realistic, intellectually honest and insightful works by Steuart, Wakefield and others – have long been extremely useful to those who must promulgate the myth that capitalism is the happy product of a "natural" evolution, and not the ghastly, man-made monstrosity that it really is. Today, in the era of the General Agreement on Tariffs and Trade (GATT), the North American Free Trade Agreement (NAFTA) and other neo-liberal "free trade" agreements, the need to promulgate this myth is stronger than ever.

With Smith and Ricardo in their proper places, Perelman says, it's no longer possible to see "an uncompromising advocacy of *laissez-faire*" in classical political economy, nor is it possible any longer to cite the precedent of classical political economy as a justification for the adoption of a *laissez-faire* (a "hands-off" or non-interventionist) approach to stimulating economic growth and development. Perelman writes that, "For more than two centuries, successive generations of economists have been grinding out texts to demonstrate how these early theorists discovered that markets provide the most efficient method of organizing production." But what the classical political economists actually discovered were the facts that "the invisible hand" of the market wasn't sufficient and that concerted interventions by the state – i.e., the creation of new legal frameworks and the apparatuses to enforce the changes in society mandated by these frameworks – were absolutely necessary, that is, if the new invention (capitalism) was going to work.

It was obvious to the classical political economists that, if left to itself, the free market would require centuries to produce the conditions necessary for the invention of capitalism. A great many things stood in the way of a quick and "orderly" transition from feudalism to capitalism, but especially the remarkable tenacity with which the rural peasants adhered to traditional agricultural practices and subsistence farming. Even when wages in the city were high, the peasants refused to accept factory jobs and stayed on their farms. They preferred a life full of holidays, not manufactured goods. And, when times got rough, the peasants would agree to make salable commodities, but only if they could make the commodities in their homes, out of which they could not be enticed, even when the wages for the exact same work was twice as high in the factories! To the political economists and "moral philosophers" of the 18th century, the peasants weren't within their rights; they revolted because they were rude and uncivilized, morally defective or psychologically impaired. In any case, the peasants were standing in the way of "progress" and "civilization." What capitalist had time to wait around until the peasants evolved on their own? None. Only the state – that is, only the state's monopoly on and ability to use legalized violence – could force these people to do what the "economic rationality" of others dictated that they do. And what if the peasants resisted, which they did in fact do? "*Send troops into the blazing districts,*" screamed Edward Gibbon Wakefield in 1831; "*proclaim martial law; shoot, cut down, and hang the peasants wholesale, and without discrimination.*"

Following Marx, who originally found a variation of the term in *The Wealth of Nations,* Perelman calls these concerted interventions by the state instances of "primitive accumulation."

> The very sound of the expression, primitive accumulation, drips with poignant echoes of human consequences [Perelman writes]. The word "primitive," first of all, suggests a brutality lacking in the subtleties of more modern forms of exploitation. It also implies that primitive accumulation was prior to the form of accumulation that people generally associate with capitalism. Finally, it hints at something that we might associate with "primitive" parts of the world, where capital accumulation has not advanced as far as elsewhere.
>
> The second term, accumulation, reminds us that the primary focus of the process was the accumulation of capital and wealth by a small sector of society, or as Marx described it, "the conquest of the world of social wealth. It is the extension of the area of exploited human material and, at the same time, the extension of the indirect and direct sway of the capitalist." Certainly, at least in the early stages of capitalism, primitive accumulation was a central element in the accumulation process.

Both Marx and Perelman need a little help here. It might be clearer if they referred to "state-sponsored organized crime" instead of primitive accumulation. Acting on behalf of a gang or a group of gangs, the state steals valuable resources from its traditional owners. (These resources need not always be land, and can also include self-representations, art, methods of using plants, intellectual property rights, genetic material, "airspace" and sources of water.) The new owners of the stolen property use it to finance or equip their enterprises, which not coincidentally encourage the dispossessed to accumulate valuable little scraps, so that they too can one day become rich.

Before moving on, let us note well that state-sponsored organized crime need not be limited to 18th century Great Britain or contemporary Third World countries. But Michael Perelman isn't sure about primitive accumulation. He asks, "Why does this process, or at least most accounts of Marx's treatment of it, seem to stop so abruptly with the establishment of a capitalist society [in England and then elsewhere in Europe in the 19th century]? Marx himself offered few examples of primitive accumulation that occurred in the nineteenth century outside of colonial lands." Striking out on his own, Perelman notes that "the process of primitive accumulation [...] lasted well into more modern times," and says it can be seen at work in the destruction of small-scale farming by the U.S. government in the 1940s. But he notes in an awkward sentence that, "like Marx, most contemporary references relegate the concept to a distant past, except perhaps in the case of the proletarianization that the less-developed countries of Africa, Asia and Latin America are experiencing." To both introduce and conclude his book, Perelman limits himself to saying that "primitive accumulation *played* a continuing role in capitalist development" (my emphasis). But this careful wording begs several important questions. Can primitive accumulation or "proletarianization" continue to play a role in capitalist development? Can it re-occur in a nation in which it has already taken place, centuries ago? Can it occur and re-occur at the international level, as well as on the national level? Etc.

Drawing upon personal diaries, letters written to colleagues and newspapers, and lectures delivered to college classes, i.e., texts that are usually ignored by contemporary political economists, Perelman shows that all of the classical political economists – yes, even Adam Smith – believed in, lobbied for and directly benefited from English or French primitive accumulation. Drawing upon these same texts, Perelman is also able to suggest why Adam Smith worked so hard to avoid the subject in *The Wealth of Nations*. The history of primitive accumulation, especially in Ireland and Scotland in the 17th and 18th centuries, proved that Smith was right when he told his students: "Laws and government may be considered *in every case* as a combination of the rich to oppress the poor, and preserve to themselves the inequality of the goods which would otherwise be soon destroyed by the attacks of the poor, who if not hindered by the government would soon reduce the others to an equality with themselves by open violence" (emphasis added). It just wouldn't do to discuss or even openly acknowledge the reality of primitive accumulation and the oppression of the poor by the rich, especially in a book such as *The Wealth of Nations,* which was written as much to curry favor amongst politicians, potential benefactors and Smith's peers, as it was to set forth a theory or methodology of modern economics. And so, Smith carefully followed the advice he himself had given his students ten years before *The Wealth of Nations* was published: if we desire to sway the opinion of sensitive or unsympathetic readers, "we are not to shock them by affirming what we are satisfied is [in fact] disagreeable, but are to conceal our design and beginning at a distance, bring them on to the main point and having gained the more remote ones we get the nearer ones of consequence."

Smith thus managed to avoid the fate of his fellow Scot, Sir James Steuart, who was imprudent enough to be completely honest. Ten years before Smith's book came out, Steuart published *An Inquiry into the Principles of Political Economy,* which was not, as Perelman says, based "on the airy fiction of a [voluntary] social contract." It was instead based upon the frank recognition that ancient slave societies such as Sparta offered, in Steuart's own words, "the perfect plan of political economy." Because they forced people (the poor and the conquered) to produce for others as well as for themselves, slave societies suppressed what Steuart called "idleness" and "the laziness of the people," and thereby allowed the masters and rulers to eat and live luxuriously without doing any work of their own. Thus, Steuart argued, slave societies were able to become much wealthier, stronger and longer-lasting than free societies, in which the poor and the conquered are allowed to produce only as much food as they themselves need. But Steuart thought Sparta to be a "violent" and barbaric republic because it wasn't Christian: e.g., it allowed people to enslave other people. And so Steuart championed capitalism, a putatively enlightened form of slavery in which "men are [instead] forced to labor because they are slaves to their own wants," in particular, to their need for food. But Steuart wasn't willing to wait for plagues, famines or wars to make the British masses hungry enough to submit to capitalist slavery. It was in fact possible that these catastrophes wouldn't come or wouldn't be severe enough to do the job and in precisely the way desired. And so Sir James advocated that the state should forcibly evict the masses of rural peasants from the land, turn their farms into pastures, and thereby create the hunger, poverty and misery necessary to provide capitalism with sufficient numbers of people willing to submit themselves to wage labor. Though he wasn't the only writer of the time to be completely honest about the brutality of the invention of capitalism, Steuart's book was objected to, taken to task and then completely forgotten about. It struck a nerve, the very one Adam Smith tried to soothe.

This is a great story, this "secret history," but Perelman doesn't tell it very well, or, rather, he doesn't tell it nearly as well as it could have been told. It takes him six chapters (almost 140 pages) to set it up. When he finally gets around to telling the story, he puts Steuart first and Smith second. While this ordering is chronologically accurate, it's weak dramatically, especially since Perelman devotes a single chapter to Steuart and spends three chapters on Smith. If Smith is such a willful idiot, why dwell on him? Why not spend three chapters on Sir James, the one who is unjustly obscure and underappreciated? Furthermore, going from Steuart to Smith points the reader in the wrong direction, i.e., away from reality and towards propaganda. But going from Smith to Steuart points the reader in the right direction, i.e., away from the contemplation of the past and towards activism in the present.

Unfortunately, there are other problems with the book's organization. The last of the three chapters on Smith should also have been the last chapter in the book. But it isn't: it's followed by four more chapters (another 110 pages), which introduce the reader to a large number of classical political economists (Benjamin Franklin, Robert Owen, David Ricardo, Thomas Robert Malthus, Robert Torrens, Robert Gourlay, Edward Gibbon Wakefield and John Rae), but without adding anything new to the discussion. If there is to be a second edition of this book, the entire last third of it should be deleted, no harm done. Indeed, the book would be greatly improved by being shortened in this way. The last third is poisoned by turds of lazy writing, something the reader doesn't find elsewhere in the book. "Yes, I know that sections 3 through 5 of Ricardo's first chapter of his *Principles* are filled with considerations about the durability of capital," Perelman writes irritably at one point, "but by the time we get to the chapter on machinery, all concerns with durability have fallen by the wayside." Who the fuck is he talking to? Himself? An imaginary critic? The reader certainly doesn't know what he's talking about, unless he or she happens to have a copy of Ricardo's *Principles* on hand and has opened it to the correct pages. Not bloody likely! "Ricardo was, after all, a master of making his models analytically intractable," Perelman writes elsewhere. "Just consider how cleverly he [Ricardo] eliminated any consideration of rent from his value theory." It's as if the reader couldn't possibly be unfamiliar with the nuances of Ricardo's theory of value! But, alas, I was, and so I didn't get Professor Perelman's reference to how clever Ricardo was. Another great example of lazy writing is this sentence, also taken from the last third of the book: "The mere mention of this period, however, seems to suggest an important policy dimension to the model." Our thoughts exactly, dude!

But these defects are small when compared to the atrocious manner in which the book ends. In the last chapter, Perelman turns his attention away from the political economists and moral philosophers of the 18th century, and directs it towards some of the 20th century's worst political criminals: V.I. Lenin, Joseph Stalin and Mao Tse Tung. It is clear that the only reason that Perelman didn't include Benito Mussolini and Adolph Hitler in his discussion of "unlikely" supporters of the "Smithian interpretation of history," is the fact that these last two mass murderers were not Marxists, and the others were. The writings and personal authority of Karl Marx are very dear to the author of *The Invention of Capitalism.* According to Perelman, Marx "intended this [his] historical analysis to refute the contention of classical political economy that markets supposedly work fairly because invisible hands somehow guide the world toward inevitable prosperity and even a higher level of culture," and was successful. *Das Capital* refutes classical political economy, once and for all, and that's what's important. "In the end," Perelman writes, "Smith's confusion about the origins of capital seems to have served a good purpose, since it put Marx on the track of his own theory of the so-called primitive accumulation." Hooray!

Where does this leave us today, at the beginning of the 21st century? With the most famous Marxists of the 20th century, of course! Lenin?

> Lenin [Perelman writes] understood the essence of the classical theory of primitive accumulation. He knew that once the traditional sector becomes sufficiently impoverished, poor peasants will have no choice but to accept wage labor. Lenin praised Karl Kautsky, whose work on agriculture [...] demonstrated how political acts, such as cutting off the peasant's freedom to gather firewood or hunt game, increased the number of hours that a family would have to work to produce the

same amount of use value.

Stalin?

> After Joseph Stalin took over the reigns of power, the imagery of Steuart continued to echo in the Party deliberations. Stalin called for a shift in policy relative to "the bond between town and country, between the working class and the main mass of the peasantry." He emphasized the role of producers' goods delivered to the peasantry rather than the consumer goods, as Steuart had done [...] Stalin's bond, unlike Steuart's, was intended "not to preserve classes but to abolish them." [...] Ultimately, the Russian countryside was also cleared of many "superfluous mouths."

Mao?

> Unlike Stalin, Mao believed that the proper arrangements could not be created by fiat. [...] Mao [...] stood for the substitution of the visible bond of politics for the invisible bond of Smith. In this sense, Mao's vision may nonetheless properly be called Smithian. In spite of the best precautions, he recognized that "the spontaneous forces of capitalism have been steadily growing in the countryside."

"Such sentiments accurately echoed Marx's vision," writes Perelman, summing up his little tour of those who overthrew capitalist slavery, only to replace it with communist slavery. "Indeed, Marx's socialism may be said to be the proper heir to the best of classical political economy in this regard."

I'll be honest with you, dear reader. I don't give a shit if Marx inherited the best or the worst of what classical political economy had to offer, or if Lenin, Stalin and Mao positioned themselves or can be positioned on one side or the other of the Steuart/Smith debate. All I care about at this point is the fact that Perelman thinks he can get away with referring to "blind spots" in the vision of contemporary political economy and "the mistakes of the Stalin era," and leave it at that. These kind of lies might have been believed by a few gullible idiots back in the 1930s or 1940s, when American communists could plausibly claim that they didn't know much about what was happening in the Soviet Union. But no one is going to believe them today. When Stalin murdered tens of millions of peasants in the 1930s, he didn't make a "grave error" in understanding the theory of primitive accumulation; he committed a crime against humanity. And if Stalin was a good Marxist or an "echo" of Marx's vision, then Marxism – like Adam Smith's *The Wealth of Nations* and Sir James Steuart's *Inquiry in the Principles of Political Economy* – is nothing but a justification for mass murder and slavery.

Raptor, Rapist, Rapture: the Dark Joys of Social Control in Thomas Pynchon's *Vineland*

"With his own private horrors further unfolded into an ideology of the mortal and uncontinued self, Brock came to visit, and strangely to comfort, in the half-lit hallways of the night, leaning in darkly in above her like any of the sleek raptors that decorate fascist architecture." Thomas Pynchon, *Vineland.*

Between 1963 and 1973, the American author Thomas Pynchon (born in 1937) published three novels: *V.* (1963); *The Crying of Lot 49* (1966); and *Gravity's Rainbow* (1973). Taken together, these dense, critically acclaimed books form a kind of loosely intertwined trilogy in which certain characters and themes occasionally reappear. The very length of *Gravity's Rainbow* (over 700 pages long) seemed to suggest that, with its publication, a cycle – perhaps *the* cycle – had been completed. Maybe Pynchon would never publish another novel. How could he? What more could he have left to say? As the years (the 1980s) went by and a fourth Pynchon novel didn't come out, it seemed that the author – well-known for keeping his "private life" truly private, for not even allowing his photograph to be taken – had indeed quit when he was ahead, and stopped writing novels.

And so, it was something of a surprise when, in 1990, Pynchon finally published *Vineland,* his fourth novel. Inevitably, perhaps, it was perceived to be a disappointment. Take for example these fairly typical comments, made at the time the novel was published by Brad Leithauser, writing for *The New York Review of Books.* For Leithauser, *Vineland* "fails in any significant degree to extend or improve upon what the author has done before"; it "marks a return to what was weakest in his patchy novella," i.e. *The Crying of Lot 49*; it contains "no pleasure [...] to compare with the one great delight of *Lot 49* – its madman-in-a-library's hunger for arcana"; the humor in *Vineland* "has no bite"; and the characters "are strictly one-dimensional." After a couple of months on *The New York Times'* bestseller list, *Vineland* dropped from sight. It wasn't made into a movie, not even a "Made for TV" movie, despite all the hints dropped in the novel about how appropriate that would be.

Vineland is weak, there's no doubt about it. The text is too long and padded out with filler. Future editions should delete the superfluous characters (DL, Takeshi, and Blood & Vato) and cut everything after page 293 in the first edition, that is, the last 100 pages. "Used to think I was climbing, step by step, right? toward a resolution," says one of the novel's characters (Weed Altman, killed by Roscoe, now floating around as a "Thanatoid") about his murder. "First Roscoe, above him your mother, then Brock Vond, then – but that's when it begins to go dark, and that door at the top I thought I saw isn't there anymore, because the light behind it just went off too." Unfortunately, many of Pynchon's readers may feel the exact same way about *Vineland* about two-thirds of the way though the book, well before they've reached this ironic passage.

To be fair, both *V.* (450 pages long) and, of course, *Gravity's Rainbow* could also use some serious editing. . . . But I don't want to defend *Vineland* or try to convince others of its high quality. All I want to do is provide the right setting for a single stunning sentence that it contains. If future editions of *Vineland* are edited as I've suggested, this sentence will become the novel's centerpiece, its otherwise missing resolution, the steadily illuminated door at the top of the stairway.

* * *

"Carking care is my feudal castle. It is built like an eagle's nest upon the peak of a mountain lost in the clouds. No one can take it by storm. From this abode I dart down into the world of reality to seize my prey; but I do not remain down there, I bear my quarry aloft to my stronghold. What I capture are images." – Soren Kierkegaard, *Entweder-Oder* (1911)

Since terms taken from architecture seem especially useful in this project, let's say that both *V.* and *Gravity's Rainbow* are constructed like gigantic labyrinths, through which the Reader must, very slowly at times, make his or her way through narrow passages, totally alone, except for the narrator's voice(s) and those of the characters. Narratively speaking, *The Crying of Lot 49* is a more straight-forward affair, but the Reader still travels, alone, in a labyrinth, this time somewhat wider but still narrowly passaged, that matches the twists and turns of a mysterious, centuries-long conspiracy against the Post Office. To quote *Vineland's* narrator somewhat out of context, Pynchon's first three novels describe "a Kasbah topography," created by "the arrangements of hillside levels, alleyways, corners, and rooftops," which is "easy to get lost in quickly, terrain where the skills of the bushwhacker became worth more than any resoluteness of character."

Vineland, by contrast, is constructed like a large public square. It is intended to be open, easy to get through, and big and wide enough so that masses of people can see the "attractions," all at the same time. In *Vineland,* the Reader isn't alone, but can hear, in addition to the narrator's tour-guide voice, the sounds made by other Readers, lots of them locals, most of them tourists snapping pictures and chattering away like birds. It is certain that Pynchon has failed to build, removed or blocked off a great many of the sidestreets, cul-de-sacs and alleys that Readers would normally find in one of his novels. But if the Reader knows how to drift or wander "aimlessly," he or she can still come upon several passages in or through which it is possible to get completely and intoxicatingly lost, like a madman in a library.

Here's one of them. On this tour, we'll only take a few steps into it.

> Fortunately [for musician Billy Barf, playing at an Italian Mafia wedding without knowing any Italian songs] Ralph Wayvone's library happened to include a copy of the indispensible *Italian Wedding Fake Book,* by Deleuze & Guattari.

While they weren't authors of books that help chart-reading musicians fake their way through songs that they don't know – though the idea is pretty amusing, given their occasional attempts to imitate or "fake" schizophrenic writing – Gilles Deleuze and Felix Guattari were the authors of a series of books about capitalism and schizophrenia, most notably *Anti-Oedipus,* published in 1972 with a preface by Michel Foucault about the book's relevance to fighting contemporary fascism. In a passage that applies to them as well as it applies to Wilhelm Reich, author of *The Mass Psychology of Fascism,* Deleuze & Guattari write, "Reich is at his profoundest as a thinker when he refuses to accept ignorance or illusion on the part of the masses as an explanation of fascism, and demands an explanation that will take their desires into account: no, the masses were not innocent dupes; at a certain point under a certain set of conditions, they *wanted* fascism, and it is this perversion of the desire of the masses that needs to be accounted for."

Like *Anti-Oedipus* and *The Mass Psychology of Fascism, Vineland* is an attempt to account for the fascist "perversion of the desire of the masses." There have been fascists in America for decades. Take for example someone like Brock Vond, the U.S. Attorney, COINTELPRO specialist and anti-drug zealot who is the novel's anti-hero. He's called a "fascist" several times. Though the word is often used casually and inaccurately, Brock Vond is a real old-time fascist. Like the Nazis,

> he was a devotee of the thinking of pioneer criminologist Cesare Lombroso (1836-1909), who'd believed that the brains of criminals were short on lobes that controlled civilized values like morality and respect for the law, tending instead to resemble animal more than human brains, and thus caused the crania that housed them to develop differently, which included the way their faces would turn out looking [...] By Brock's time the theory had lapsed into a quaint, undeniably racist spinoff from nineteenth-century phrenology, crude in method and long superseded, although it seemed reasonable to Brock.

In the aftermath of what the narrator calls "the Nixon Reaction" or "the Nixon Repression," which began in 1969, overt fascists such as Brock Vond were able to find both a home and plenty of financial support in Washington, D.C. Despite changes in personnel and presidents during the 1970s, "the Repression went on, growing wider, deeper, and less visible," culminating in Ronald Reagan's "war on drugs," in which – in Pynchon's version – Brock Vond features prominently.

Vineland is set in 1984, the year that Reagan was re-elected President. Of course, it was also the year that George Orwell set his famous anti-Stalinist and anti-fascist novel, *1984*. Orwell – or, rather, the betrayed relationship between Winston and Julia – is clearly the reference when Brock Vond tells Zoyd, just after Vond has gotten him to snitch on his ex-wife for the FBI, "Believe me, she'd have done the same to you." But Orwell wasn't really given his due back in 1984, perhaps because nothing exactly like the following scene from *Vineland* ever took place.

> Was Reagan about to invade Nicaragua at last, getting the home front all nailed down, ready to process folks by the tens of thousands into detention camps, arm local 'Defense Forces,' fire everybody in the Army and then deputize them in order to get around the Posse Comitatus Act? Copies of these contingency plans had been circulating all summer, it wasn't much of a secret [...] Could it be that some silly-ass national emergency exercise was finally coming true? As if the Tube [television set] were suddenly to stop showing pictures and instead announce, 'From now on, I'm watching you.'

Pynchon clearly believed that, just because the year 1984 didn't bring actual "telescreens" into every home in the country, this didn't mean that Reaganism *wasn't* an American form of fascism. The year 1984 was in fact the perfect occasion to ask what Pynchon calls "the perennial question of whether the United States still lingered in a prefascist twilight, or whether that darkness had fallen long stupefied years ago, and the light they thought they saw was coming only from millions of Tubes all showing the same bright-colored shadows," that is, *the old question* that brings forth "the names – some shouted, some accompanied by spit, the old reliable names good for hours of contention, stomach distress, and insomnia – Hitler, Roosevelt, Kennedy, Nixon, Hoover, Mafia, CIA, Reagan, Kissinger, that collection of names and their tragic interweaving that stood not constelled above in any nightwide remoteness of light, but below, diminished to the last unfaceable American secret, to be pressed, each time deeper, again and again beneath the meanest of random soles, one blackly fermenting leaf on the forest floor that nobody wanted to turn over, because of all that lived, virulent, waiting, just beneath."

In hindsight it seems clear that 1984 did indeed mark the end of the Twilight and the beginning of the Dark Night of Fascism in the United States. But to see down on the forest floor that rotting tramped-down leaf, to pluck out that hideous worm-like truth and to digest it – why, you'd have to have a bird's eye, a bird's beak and a bird's stomach to do it.

Look, birds are everywhere in *Vineland,* from the message-laden carrier pigeons "taking off one by one" on the novel's very first page to the "redtail hawk in an updraft soaring above the ridgeline" on its very last. In between, there are pigeons, mockingbirds, sparrows and, of course, chickens-coming-home-to-roost and parrots that tell bedtime stories to troubled children. Even when you can't see them, the birds are out there, in the trees, making loud, strange, even "delirious" sounds. The effect, Pynchon's narrator notes, is especially striking at twilight.

There's a passing reference to the "shelter" snitches can find in "the shadow of the federal wing," that is, under the protection of the federal wing of the United States Government, here visualized as something similar to the fatherly, even Godlike giant bird in Prince von Bulow's *Memoirs: The World War and Collapse of Germany, 1909-1919.*

> An eagle spreads his wings
> Over his young
> So, ever and anon,
> His might has covered me.

But most of the birds in *Vineland* are predatory, not protective. On the second page, there are blue jays "who came screaming down out of the redwoods and carried off the food in it piece by piece" and, right in the middle of the novel, there are "city falcons who hunted pigeons in the booming prisms of sun and shadow below." Raptorial birds such as these – others include eagles, hawks and owls – use their sharp claws and pointed beaks to seize and carry off their living prey. There's a strong etymological link between *raptor* and older definitions of *rapist,* someone who seizes human beings and carries them off by force. In the Greek myth of the rape of Ganymede by Zeus, who takes the form of an eagle to perpetrate the crime, the two meanings co-exist.

The aforementioned fascist, Brock Vond, is *a human raptor.* In the words of the novel's narrator, "the narc's natural prey," that is, "an average doper of the sixties," would expect that a cop like Vond would have "the reflexes of a predator." Vond doesn't disappoint: he almost literally preys upon stool pigeons, a "classical pigeon" like Roscoe, who kills his mentor because of a rumor that he was really an FBI agent, and any of "the birds" that Vond puts in cages in his prison-like Political Re-Education Program. A professional sadist, Vond is also fond of fantasizing about rape. "Smart mouth," the narrator says. "One day he would order her [Frenesi Gates, the woman Vond is obsessed with] down on her knees in front of all these cryptically staring children [hippies], put a pistol to her head, and give her something to do with her smart mouth. Each time he daydreamed about this, the pistol would reappear, as an essential term."

Vond also has a weird predilection for using helicopters to spot, fly above, descend upon, seize and carry off individual people. "Death From Slightly Above" is the nickname Vond's colleagues give him. In his raptorial use of helicopters, Brock Vond was a pioneer. "No hour day or night was exempt from helicopter visits," the narrator says about the late sixties, "though this was still back in the infancy of overhead surveillance." By 1984, as a result of Reagan's "war on drugs," aerial surveillance – especially the helicopter surveillance of marijuana-growing areas of the United States such as Vineland, California – had become fully developed.

Significantly, "Death From Slightly Above" is terrified of being raped. "In nightmares he [Brock Vond] was forced to procreate with women who approached never from floor or ground level but from steep overhead angles, as if from someplace not on the surface of Earth, feeling nothing erotic but only, each time it was done, a terrible sadness, violation . . . something taken away. He understood, in some way impossible to face, that each child he thus produced, each birth, would only be another death for him." Perhaps these nightmares of being raped by bird-like women replay a trauma Vond experienced as a child; perhaps they express his guilt and remorse for the crimes he's committed as an adult. Either way, Vond's way of coping with these nightmares is to *reverse the positions,* so that *he* is the rapist from above and not the one below being raped. But the structure of oppression remains intact.

An average novelist, perhaps even a good one, would have been content with these twin images of anti-hero Brock Vond: raptor/rapist. But sometimes-a-great novelist Thomas Pynchon went ahead (reached above?) and added a third term, namely, *rapture,* which is commonly taken to mean the state of being joyous or deeply engrossed. Following this meaning, the narrator describes Frenesi's (mostly sexual) feelings while being transported on the back of DL's motorcycle as "biker rapture, for sure." But other, less innocent meanings of the word are also at play in the novel. Etymologically linked to both "raptor" and "rapist," rapture can also mean to have one's imagination, feelings or sense of self transported, seized or carried off. And so Pynchon is careful to highlight the aspects of passivity, acceptance and surrender.

In a memorable description of an on-coming storm (more "death from above"), his narrator says that "Weather commentators tried to maintain the tradition of wackiness the job is known for, but could not keep out of the proceedings an element of surrender, as if before some first hard intelligence of the advent of an agent of rapture." One might have expected those words to have been *an angel* – "the advent of *an angel* of rapture" – and not *an agent.* "Agent" sounds too instrumental, too human, too mortal, especially for the advent of "the Rapture," otherwise known as the first resurrection of the Elect, which is supposedly prophesied in the Bible.

> I saw the souls of those executed with the ax for the witness they bore to Jesus and for speaking about God, and those who worshipped neither the wild beast nor its image and who had not received the mark upon their forehead and upon their hand. And they came to life and ruled as kings with the Christ for a thousand years. The rest of the dead did not come to life until the thousand years were ended. This was the first resurrection. Happy and holy is anyone having part in the first resurrection; over these the second death has no authority, but they will be priests of God and of the Christ, and will rule as kings with him for the thousand years. (*The Book of Revelations*, Chapter 20, Verses 4-6.)

There's an obvious reference to the Rapture in the scene in *Vineland* in which a band wakes up Thanatoid Village by playing J.S. Bach's *Wachet Auf*: "To one of the best tunes ever to come out of Europe, even with the timing adapted to the rigors of a disco percussion track able to make the bluest Thanatoid believe, however briefly, in resurrection, they awoke, the Thanatoids woke." But it is *the agent*, Brock Vond, who is morbidly obsessed with death, resurrection and rapture.

At a press conference held in the aftermath of a brutal and possibly murderous police attack on a "subversive" university campus, Vond is asked about the whereabouts of the large numbers of students who have turned up missing. "Why underground, of course," Vond says. "That's our assumption in this, from all we know about them – that they've gone underground." He's pressed by someone who asks, "You mean they're on the run?" This doesn't seem at all likely. The questioner persists, "Are there warrants out? How come none are listed as federal fugitives?" Before having the questioner removed from the room, Vond answers, "Underground, hm? Rapture below." In other words, the missing students aren't on the run and disguising their identities to avoid capture. Brock had them "axed" and buried "below," in the (under)ground. And if they were good Christians while they lived, ha ha ha, they will live as kings with Christ. On another occasion, Vond cries out to one of his colleagues as they try to use a helicopter to kidnap Frenesi's daughter, Prairie, "The key is rapture. Into the sky, and the world knows her no more."

And so "rapture" is a powerful, highly ambivalent, even troubling word here. Brock Vond the rapist fancies himself to be a raptor in the service of Jesus Christ. But does this mean that his prey are enrapt or experience rapture? that his victims don't merely "surrender" to him, but willingly give themselves over, in other words, that they actually enjoy being raped?

To answer these questions, Pynchon gives his readers Frenesi Gates, whose perverse relationship with Brock Vond began back in the sixties, when he "convened his roving grand jury in Oregon to look into subversion on the campus of a small community college, and 24fps" – a radical filmmaking collective of which Frenesi was a member – "had gone there to film the proceedings, or as much as they could find with Brock always changing venues and times on them at the last minute." Like hunters, the members of 24fps stayed on Vond's trail, and, thanks to luck and Frenesi's eagle-eyes, were able to capture him on film.

> They chased him from the courthouse, *through the rain,* to a motel, then to the fairground exhibition hall, the college and the high school auditoriums, the drive-in-movie lot, finally back to the courthouse again, where Frenesi, by then not expecting him, just trying to shoot some old WPA murals about Justice and Progress [...], in the middle of a slow pan across the rotunda, happened to pick up in her viewfinder this compact figure in a beige double-knit, *striding toward* the staircase. Another camera *eye* on the same crew might've dismissed him as one more pompous little functionary. Zooming in a little on his face, she began to track him. She didn't know who he was. Or maybe she did. (Emphasis added.)

This scene has a kind of twin. About 70 pages later, the narrator explains that the proto-fascist criminologist Cesare Lombroso "had divided all revolutionists into five groups, geniuses, enthusiasts, fools, rogues, and followers, which in Brock's experience about covered it, except for the unforeseen sixth, the one without a label Brock was waiting for, who at last came *striding toward* him now *through the drizzle,* a few pounds thinner, her hair full of snarls, barelegged, her camera taken away, no weapon of witness but her *eyes."* The parallelism or symmetry between these two scenes suggests that Brock Vond and Frenesi Gates are a "natural" pair, destined to be lovers, despite their political differences.

But do these lovers have political differences worth speaking of? According to the narrator,

> Brock Vond's genius was to have seen in the activities of the sixties left not threats to order but unacknowledged desires for it. While the Tube was proclaiming youth revolution against parents of all kinds and most viewers were accepting this story, Brock saw the deep – if he'd allowed himself to feel it, the sometimes touching – need only to stay children forever, safe inside some extended national Family. The hunch he was betting on was that these kid rebels, being halfway there already, would be easy to turn and cheap to develop. They'd only been listening to the wrong music, breathing the wrong smoke, admiring the wrong personalities. They needed some reconditioning.

When it came to Frenesi, Brock's "hunch" was right on. Though Frenesi and her mother, Sasha, were long-time Leftists surveilled and persecuted for their political beliefs and activities, both women have a half-childish, fully fascist fetish for uniformed authority.

> Sasha believed her daughter had "gotten" this uniform fetish from her. It was a strange idea even coming from Sasha, but since her very first Rose Parade up till the present she'd felt in herself a fatality, a helpless turn toward images of authority, especially uniformed men, whether they were athletes live or on the Tube, actors in movies of war through the ages, or *maitre d*'s in restaurants, not to mention waiters and busboys, and she further believed that it could be passed on, as if some Cosmic Fascist had spliced in a DNA sequence requiring this form of seduction and initiation into the dark joys of social control.

What's disturbing about this irrational and perverse "turn" toward fascism – also described by Sylvia Plath's poem "Every Woman Loves a Fascist" – is the unexpected fact that awareness of it doesn't trigger terrible realizations about the "bad" things one has done, but terrible realizations about the "good" things. "Long before any friend or enemy had needed to point it out to her," Pynchon's narrator says, "Sasha on her own had arrived at, and been obliged to face, the dismal possibility that all her oppositions, however just and good, to forms of power were really acts of denying that dangerous swoon that came creeping at the edges of her optic lobes every time the troops came marching by, that wetness of attention and perhaps ancestral curse." And so it seems that only evil is possible; good intentions are constantly betrayed by one's eyes, lobes and desires.

Then why not stop "denying that dangerous swoon," that rapture, and give oneself over to it completely? This is in fact what Frenesi does, only she chooses to call it *love,* not self-betrayal.

> She came and lay next to him, but not touching. The storm held the city down like prey, trying repeatedly to sting it into paralysis. She lay on her elbow, unable to stop gazing at Brock [...] [She thought that] someplace, lost, stupefied, needing her intercession, was the 'real' Brock, the endearing adolescent who would allow her to lead him stumbling out into light [...], returning him to the man he should have grown into . . . it could've been about the only way she knew to use the word *love* anymore, its trivializing in those days already well begun, its magic fading [...] Yet if there was anything left to believe, she must have [believed] in the power even of that weightless, daylit commodity of the sixties to redeem even Brock, amiably, stupidly brutal fascist Brock.

And so Frenesi became this fascist's lover and, what's worse, a COINTELPRO agent in his employ. She told a fool named Roscoe that political leader Weed Altman was really an FBI agent and then gave Roscoe the gun that he eventually used to kill Weed. And, worst of all, she did it – all of it – because she wanted to, *not* because she was ignorant, stupid, drugged or duped. Note well the conclusion of the scene that takes place during the storm: Frenesi and Brock entered into their tangled relationship with both of their respective pairs of eyes wide open to the truth.

> At some point he must have gone drifting to sleep, and she hadn't noticed. She watched over him, hers for a while, allowing herself to shudder with, even to *surrender* to, her need for his bodily presence, his beauty, the fear at the base of her spine, the prurient ache in her hands . . . at last, so swept and helpless, she *leaned in to whisper* to him her heart's overflow, and saw in the *half-light* that what she'd thought were closed eyelids had been open all the time. He'd been watching her. She let out a short jolted scream. Brock started laughing. (Emphasis added.)

Like the twin scenes in which Brock and Frenesi meet each other, this "eyes wide open" scene is doubled. It so happens that this second doubling or twin contains the single stunning sentence for which I've been preparing the arrival. Here it comes: in the aftermath of Prairie's birth, Frenesi was deeply depressed. She felt an irrational hatred for her newborn, "the tiny life, raw, parasitic, using her body through the wearying months and now still looking to control her." Fearing that she might kill Prairie, Frenesi sent her to Sasha for safekeeping. According to the narrator, "It was in those hours of hallucinating and defeat that Frenesi had felt Brock closer to her, more necessary, than ever." Was Frenesi active? Did she "fly" to Brock, wherever he was? No, she was passive; he flew to her.

> With his own private horrors further unfolded into an ideology of the mortal and uncontinued self, Brock came to visit, and strangely to comfort, in the *half-lit* hallways of the night, *leaning in* darkly in above her like any of the sleek raptors that decorate fascist architecture. *Whispering*: "This is just how they want you, an animal, a bitch with swollen udders lying in the dirt, blank-faced, *surrendered,* reduced to this meat, these smells. . . . " Taken down, she understood, from all the silver and light she'd known and been, brought back to the world [...] (Emphasis added.)

Brock Vond once again reversed the positions while leaving the oppressive structure intact. Like the TV set that declared, "From now on, I'm watching you," Brock switched from *watched-over* to *watcher*. He was then seen as and for what he really was: a gargoyle on a fascist building. Confronted by this uncanny vision, Frenesi didn't experience "rapture" of any kind. But the fascist perversion of her desire didn't depend on her enrapture. She was in fact strangely comforted by what had at first made her scream, and *that* was enough for Brock to "take her down."

* * *

Note the loose ends. Why does Pynchon refer to "any" of the sleek raptors that decorate fascist architecture? Are all raptors the same? Are all raptors sleek? And what about his vague reference to "fascist architecture"? Does Pynchon intend to evoke architecture that is designed and built by fascists? If so, *which* fascists? The reactionaries who, during World War II, referred to their own governments as fascist (Mussolini in Italy, Hitler in Germany and Franco in Spain), or the reactionaries who, since WWII, have referred to their own governments as democratic, though they are actually fascist (Reagan/Bush in America, Thatcher in England and Sharon in Israel)? Perhaps Pynchon intended "fascist architecture" to signify a generalizable *style* of architecture that can appear anywhere, in either "democratic" (implicitly anti-fascist) countries or those countries that are explicitly fascist.

It's tempting to reduce Pynchon's allusion to "any of the sleek raptors that decorate fascist architecture" to a very specific reference: the gigantic eagles that appear on buildings that were designed or constructed in Nazi Germany between 1932 and 1945. Pynchon refers to these very raptors – "Eagles cast in concrete stand[ing] ten meters high at the corners of stadiums where the people, a corrupted idea of 'the People,' are gathering" – in *Gravity's Rainbow*. Ancient symbols of tele-vision, independence, speed, and power, these sleek raptors are easy to visualize. Not only did the Nazis perch them at the entrances to highways and at the tops of stadiums, government buildings, train stations, and buildings that overlooked public squares, but they also used them in their songs, banners, sketches, models, paintings, photographs and propaganda films. (Though the Italian fascists didn't share the Nazis' obsession with eagles, the German fascists were hardly the first conquerors to use them as symbols or emblems of their military power. Eagles have been used in this way at least since the time of the ancient Egyptians.)

Sleek is an interesting word to use in this context. Not only does it describe the smoothness or glossy look of a bird's feathers, but it also suggests that the bird is well-fed and thus not necessarily preoccupied with its next meal. It is not immediately dangerous. There is time to escape while the raptor – like Brock Vond before one of his televised press conferences – takes time to groom himself properly, to make himself look "slick," that is, suave, sly, shrewd, seductive. The raptor will kill when he's good and ready. He will not depend upon that which accident or good fortune has placed within his grasp. He will select and kill what he wants, when he wants.

Significantly, other than being sleek, the raptors decorating fascist architecture in Germany had little in common. There was no model or prototype, no standardization of presentation. (Same thing for the *hackenkreuz,* or "swastika," which, for example, could either spin clockwise or counter-clockwise.) And so the German raptors differed, sometimes quite substantially, as to their respective stances, postures, attitudes, and head positions. As a result, they communicated a very powerful but very confusing message. Why couldn't the symbol of power get control over of its own representations? Why was it always the same (an eagle) but always different (a different eagle)?

In Nazi Germany, this paradox was also played out at the level of architecture itself. Unlike the Italian fascists, who favored a certain definable style (stripped-down, unadorned neo-classical forms built on a truly monumental scale), the Germans made do with whatever worked: neo-classicism, *volkische* or vernacular forms, American engineering designs, even Bauhaus-style modernism. For the German fascists, form *didn't* follow function. As long as the building or the symbol functioned as intended (facilitated total control), it didn't matter what form the building or the symbol took. Significantly, the Nazis weren't worried that the inconsistency of their forms or symbols would eventually undermine their meanings and thus their usefulness. Indeed, the Nazis *wanted* their symbols to "inflate" to the point that they became emptied of all meanings. With meaning exploded, without anything to know, there are no longer two groups of people that the State has to control (those "in the know" and those who don't know anything). There's only one big group, which makes total control so much easier.

First published *Art Paper* (May 1990)
Substantially revised September 2002
NOT BORED! #35, July 2003

Wanted: More Books Like These

One really wants the two books under consideration here – Jean-Michel Mension's *The Tribe* and Ralph Rumney's *The Consul* – to be part of a series, in part because that's exactly what they appear to be. Both books were published by City Lights Books (in 2001 and 2002, respectively). Both books were designed by Stefan Gutermuth/doubleu-gee. Each book is filled with illustrations designed to provide a context: translations, reminiscences by friends and acquaintances, captioned photographs, and black-and-white reproductions of art works, posters and manuscripts. These illustrations sometimes appear as full-page reproductions but most often as marginalia in the style of the Situationist International's journal, *l'internationale Situationniste*.

Both books are oral histories, long autobiographical interviews with men who were either members of the Situationist International (SI) or close associates of Guy Debord, who was the SI's central figure. (Jean-Michel Mension was a member of the Lettrist International, a pre-SI group that also included Debord, while Ralph Rumney helped found the SI in 1957 with Debord, Michele Bernstein, Asger Jorn, and four other radical artists.) In both books, the interviewer is Gerard Berreby, who has published several books on the SI. And, finally, both books are subtitled "Contributions to the History of the Situationist International and Its Time." *The Tribe,* which was translated from the French by Donald Nicholson-Smith (a former member of the SI), is called "Volume I" and *The Consul,* which was translated from the French by Malcolm Imrie (who has also translated Debord's *Comments on the Society of the Spectacle*), is called "Volume II."

Unfortunately, one hears from City Lights that no more titles are planned for this series. This is really a shame, because there is a pressing need to record and publish interviews with those Situationists who are still alive, especially Constant Nieuwenhuys, who is in his 80s,[5] and Michele Bernstein and Raoul Vaneigem, both of whom are in their 60s. There is also a pressing need to publish whatever interviews were conducted with Asger Jorn (who died in 1974). And though Gil J Wolman (1994), Francois Dufrene (1980), Eliane Brau (?) and Isidore Isou (?)[6] were Lettrists but not Situationists, there is also a pressing need to conduct new interviews with them or publish whatever old ones are in existence.

Without such a series of candid interviews, historians of the SI will have no choice but continue to base their accounts of the group's history on *what Guy Debord said* and little else. Of course, Debord had every right to monopolize the discussion of the SI's development. After all, he was the only founding member to remain in the group all through its existence, all the way until its end in 1971. But his writings on the subject – "Theses on the SI and Its Time," written in 1972 with Gianfranco Sanguinetti, and parts of his autobiography, *Panegyrique* (1989) – are full of self-congratulation, intentional obscurity and polemic against his enemies. Though such things make Debord's writings interesting to read, they also make them unreliable as objective historical records.

Originally published in 1998 by Editions Allia, *The Tribe* is by far the better of the two books. The illustrations are excellent, especially the pictures of the youth scene at the Parisian bar Moineau's circa 1952 taken by the Dutch photographer Ed Van Der Elsken. There are also several items that have never been published in English before, including a newspaper article from 1953 about "Wayward Youth" (Jean-Michel Mension and his friend Auguste Hommel, arrested for theft), translations of passages from books by Maurice Rajsfus and Eliane Brau, and several posters designed by Debord.

One might expect that, compared to the superb illustrations, the interview(s) with Jean-Michel Mension might be a major disappointment. During the early 1950s, Mension didn't produce any paintings or posters. Though he wrote an article or two for *Internationale Lettriste* – one of them, the provocative "General Strike," is both reproduced and translated into English in *The Tribe* – Mension

---

[5] Constant died on 1 August 2005.
[6] Isou died on 28 July 2007.

wasn't much of a writer either. Indeed, in Lettrist circles, he was best known for *writing slogans on his pants,* which was why he was described as "merely decorative" when Debord and the other Lettrists voted to exclude him from the group in 1954.

One might also expect to be disappointed by *The Tribe* because, after his expulsion, Mension joined the French Communist Party, become a Trotskyist militant, and helped found a university group called Revolutionary Communist Youth, which was dismissed in 1966 as a bunch of *petit con* (little cunts) by the pro-Situationist comic strip, "The Return of the Durutti Column." In other words, Mension moved in a direction that was *the exact opposite* of the direction(s) pursued by such other associates of Debord as Cornelius Castoriadis and Henri Lefebvre, both of whom left the Communist Party in disgust in the 1950s. (One imagines that when he was informed of Mension's political regression, Guy Debord said that it simply and amply confirmed the prescience and appropriateness of his exclusion from the Lettrist International.)

But *The Tribe* isn't a disappointment, not at all. Mension isn't bitter about his expulsion from the Lettrists or the way his group was insulted by the Situationists; and though he admits that he didn't read Debord's 1967 book *The Society of the Spectacle* until the late 1980s, Mension isn't made uncomfortable or defensive by Berreby's presence or even by some of his questions. No matter what the subject, Mension answers Berreby's questions fully, honestly and clearly. Despite his claim that "I have always been a drunk," Mension is still able to think sober thoughts.

Not surprisingly, Mension has a lot of interesting things to say about Guy Debord. This remark was especially impressive, given the fact that Mension never learned the real reason for his exclusion from the Lettrists: "There was another side to Guy, too, a certain courage: he was always prepared to break off relations even though he didn't always know what he would find next. He took the risk of finding himself alone." And yet, Debord never did find himself alone. He always had a tribe with and around him. "I was very surprised in May 1968," Mension recalls, "[because] I couldn't imagine Guy surrounded by three thousand people; that wasn't his style at all."

Originally published in 1999 by Editions Allia, *The Consul* is weak where *The Tribe* is strong. Though Ralph Rumney was a painter, very few of his pictures are reproduced in the book. The paintings that *are* reproduced are reproduced in black-and-white, and so look like crap. Too many of the texts and images reproduced as marginalia have little or nothing at all to do with Rumney and thus seem included because nothing better could be found. To make matters worse, a good deal of this superfluous marginalia is either illegible or not translated into English.

Most unfortunately, the interview(s) with Rumney are just as bad as the book's illustrations. Like Mension, Rumney did a number of interesting things in the 1950s: he created and exhibited a number of paintings; he helped organize a screening of Debord's film *Hurlements en favor de Sade* at the Institute for Contemporary Arts in London; and he founded and edited an art journal called *Other Voices*. He participated in the July 1957 conference at which the Situationist International was founded and took the photographs of the gathering that later went on to become famous. According to him, he was the one who proposed that the journal *Internationale Situationniste* come wrapped in metallic covers and that it include anthropometric photographs or "mug shots" of the group's members.

But unlike Mension, who continued to lead an interesting, politically engaged life after his expulsion, Ralph Rumney did very little of interest after he was expelled from the SI in 1958. "After my expulsion from the SI," Rumney says, "my life became quite ordinary, or normal, I should say. I was too busy finding the money to enable my family to survive." If it weren't for the facts that his first wife, Pegeen Guggenheim, was the daughter of the wealthy art-maven Peggy Guggenheim, that Pegeen killed herself in 1967, that Peggy blamed him for her daughter's death, and that his second wife was Michele Bernstein, Ralph Rumney and what he did after 1957 wouldn't be of much interest to anyone except gossips and scandal-mongers.

Though Rumney says that he was expelled from the SI "politely, even amiably," he admits that it "hit me very hard." He goes on to say, "It was very demoralizing. I really believed in the SI, and I still do. You don't have to become a turncoat because you've been excommunicated." But Rumney *was* treated like a turncoat, especially after 1962, when the SI "excommunicated" *all* of the artists and all of the group's founders, except for Debord, his wife Michele Bernstein, and Asger Jorn. "Art once played a real role in society, and I thought it might be possible to reproduce that situation," Rumney says, obviously still bitter. "In 1962, Debord didn't believe that at all. He was wrong, I think."

Not surprisingly, the ex-situationist is very uncomfortable with Berreby. At least a half-dozen times, Rumney completely ignores or doesn't acknowledge the question Berreby has posed to him. It's quite possible that these very noticeable problems are the result of the fact that Rumney was born an Englishman and that Berreby is interviewing him in French, not English. "Ralph spoke French just as well as English," says Malcolm Imrie, the book's translator, in his epilogue. "Still, it always seemed a bizarre enterprise to be translating the edited transcripts of French interviews with him [Rumney] into his native language. He could have rewritten it in English himself, I suppose, but even if he hadn't been ill, he had better things to do with his time."

Perhaps Rumney's illness(es) – he had emphysema, suffered from years of alcohol abuse, and eventually died of cancer at the age of 68 – caused these interviews to be so awkward. "Where was I?" he asks at one point, which happens to be the end of a rambling and pointless story. "And the pioneers are as lost as Hansel and Gretel in the forest," he says at another point and, though his reference is to the situationists of 1962, the remark is better applied to Rumney himself. *He's* the one who's lost.

Book reviews

Unfortunately, Berreby doesn't do much to help Rumney find his way back. In the course of their not-very-enlightening discussion of Asger Jorn, Berreby says, "There was an exhibition later at the Eugene Boucher Gallery with a text by Jorn entitled 'Peintures Detournees' and an introduction by Jacques Prevert." Perhaps because this is a statement of fact, and not a question, Rumney can only say in response to it, "Exactly." In an instance of really atrocious interviewing, the very next thing Berreby says is, "To change the subject slightly, it seems that you beat Duchamp at chess?" But of course Berreby has in fact changed the subject completely.

Berreby is clearly bored with Rumney and his ideas. "So let's talk about artism," Berreby says wearily at one point, as if he'd rather not and is only doing so because he knows it is expected of him. Same thing for what Berreby describes as "your argument" that "the American secret services played a role in French art, even in European art in general." Though Rumney immediately warms to the subject – his response is, "You're trespassing on a project I've been researching for the past two years! Frances Stoner Saunder's book *Who Paid the Piper?* which published not long ago in London, reveals what Gremoin and others could only suspect" – Berreby doesn't ask a follow-up question about Saunder's book, what Gremoin suspected or even what Ralph Rumney thinks about these things. Instead, he moves on to another subject.

One final thought: both Mension and Rumney have high praise for Francois Dufrene, an obscure Lettrist poet, filmmaker and writer. To Mension, Dufrene was one of the "two real Lettrists" (the other was Gil J Wolman). To Rumney, Dufrene was – like Wolman – "too brilliant" and so had to be expelled because Debord couldn't tolerate any competition. "Was Dufrene hurt?" Berreby asks Rumney. "Terribly," Rumney replies. "Guy told me of the incident with pride. Francois was mortally wounded. I learned this when I started meeting him [...] I quickly understood two things: the first was that he had been grievously hurt by this split, and the second was that he didn't deserve it. He considered Guy Debord to be his best friend. I think being unable to understand why it happened that was the worst part." And so, if there are going to be more volumes in this series of situationist books, let one of them be devoted to Francois Dufrene. He deserves it.

NOT BORED! #35, July 2003

Trashing Georges Bataille, "Accursed" Stalinist

Born in France in 1897, Georges Bataille was a very creative, controversial and *strange* person. A librarian by profession, he wrote a great many poems, essays and books during his life (he died in 1962). Some of these writings were novels; most were works of critical theory (non-fiction writings on society and politics). Bataille's name is often closely associated with Freudian psychoanalysis, Surrealism, Marxism and the occult.

Because of the very strong and mostly acknowledged influence of Bataille's various concepts and methodological approaches on the writings of such younger and sometimes better known critical theorists as Guy Debord ("potlatch"), Jean Baudrillard ("gift exchange"), Michel Foucault ("the order of things"), and Jacques Derrida ("nonlogical difference"), almost all of Bataille's many books have been published in English translations by university presses in America. No doubt many of these books are required reading in courses in literary theory, the history of modern art, sociology, political economy, psychology, and ethnology.

Originally written in French and privately published in 1949, the first part of Bataille's massive trilogy *La Part Maudite* was re-printed by Les Editions de Minuit in 1967. It was re-printed again in the 1970s, when Gallimard began publishing Bataille's *Oeuvres Completes* (nine volumes so far). In 1989, Zone Books in New York City published a hardcover translation under the title *The Accursed Share, Volume I: Consumption* (the trilogy as a whole is subtitled "An Essay on General Economy"). In 1998, Zone published a paperback edition of the book, as well as both hardcover and paperback editions of translations of Volumes II and III.

Though we have only commented upon them once before, Bataille's books, especially the ones on art and politics, have long been of interest to us here at *NOT BORED!* We were excited by the prospect of reading Volume I (hereafter referred to as *The Accursed Share*) because it clearly marked a return to the subject matter – unproductive ("wasteful") expenditures, human sacrifices, potlatch, and the critique of classical utility – Bataille first explored in one of our favorite essays, "The Notion of Expenditure" (written in 1933 and published in English translation in *Visions of Excess*, a collection of essays Bataille wrote between 1927 and 1939).

It's pretty damn strange that Bataille's "Theoretical Introduction" to *The Accursed Share* mentions neither "The Notion of Expenditure" nor *any* of his previous writings. It's as if Bataille wants us to believe that this is the very first time that he is pointing out that 1) classical political economy is built on the unquestioned and yet demonstrably false premises that *scarcity* is the defining aspect of the economy, that individuals will always act according to their self-interest, and that self-interest always involves growth, the accumulation of wealth, and a reduction of waste; but that 2) a study of non-European, non-Christian cultures shows that *surplus* is actually the defining aspect of the economy, that growth can never be an end in itself, that wealth can indeed be accumulated but precisely for the purposes of *deliberately* wasting it in spectacular displays of power (human sacrifices, wars, religious monuments, festivals and mass entertainments); and that, in any case, 3) waste is unavoidable. And Bataille almost gets away with it, too: he introduces so much new material, material not covered in

"The Notion of Expenditure" – Islam, Buddhism, the 13th Dalai Lama, and the connections between Calvinism and Marxism – that his 1933 essay is apparently outmoded, superseded, *discarded* and forgotten. Bataille has discretely tried to place "The Notion of Expenditure" into the proverbial "Trashcan of History," hoping that no one would notice or care.

Bataille also wants to pretend (wants us to believe) that the entire book, all of *The Accursed Share,* might also have ended up in the trash. In his preface, he writes:

> Writing this book in which I was saying that energy finally can only be wasted, I myself was using my energy, my time, working; my research answered in a fundamental way the desire to add to the amount of wealth acquired for mankind. Should I say that under these conditions I sometimes could only respond to the truth of my book and could not go on writing it? A book that no one awaits, that answers no formulated question, that the author would not have written if he had followed its lesson to the letter – such is the oddity that today I offer the reader. This invites distrust at the outset [...]

It's a fitting conceit, a pretty good joke, and it's irony certainly brings a smile; but it does indeed invite distrust at the outset. Note the (intentional?) ambiguity of "Should I say that under these conditions I sometimes could only respond to the truth of my book and could not go on writing it?" The only response to this evasively rhetorical question is: "Look, Georges: You should say that you stopped writing it, but only if it's true. If it *isn't* true, then you shouldn't say it."

Bataille doesn't say why he decided to put aside his reservations and complete all three volumes of *The Accursed Share.* He certainly didn't finish Volume I because of the uniqueness of the Marshall Plan, which is the subject of its very last chapter, or because of the unprecedented scale and extent of the devastation during the Second World War. Bataille finished the book because, like Breton, Aragon, Eluard and others in the Surrealist movement, *he'd become a Stalinist* (15 years after the others!), and because Stalin – the whole Soviet Union, even – really needed people like Georges to come to its defense.

Though many radical artists and intellectuals in France and elsewhere in Europe were Trotskyists in 1949 (Cornelius Castoriadis, for example), very few were open supporters of Stalinism. Andre Breton and most of the others had distanced themselves from or openly denounced Stalinism (if not the Communist Party, as well) because of the Soviet Union's murderous campaign to "collectivize" the kulaks in 1937 (an infamous example of what Karl Marx called primitive accumulation) and because of the Hitler-Stalin Pact of 1939. The same may be said for 1967, when *The Accursed Share* was first re-printed: though there (still) were Trotskyists in France, there were very few Stalinists. Those who were Stalinists – Jean Paul Sartre, among them – were denounced by the Situationist

International. But there is no denunciation of Bataille in *Internationale Situationniste,* Guy Debord's *La Societe du Spectacle* or one of the books by his one-time colleague, Henri Lefebvre. The only thing Allan Stoekl – the editor and translator of the *Visions of Excess* collection – can say on the subject of Batatille's post-War writings is: "In his later writings (of the 1940s and 50s) Bataille is no longer overtly Marxist." While this remark might be taken as indirect evidence that Stalin himself wasn't much of a Marxist, it doesn't even admit that Bataille was a Stalinist.

In the chapter called "Soviet Industrialization," Bataille writes:

> The collectivization of lands is in theory the most questionable part of the changes in economic structure. There is no doubt that it cost dearly; indeed, it is regarded as the cruelest moment of an endeavour that was never mild. But if one judges this development of Russian resources in a general way, one risks forgetting the conditions in which it was begun and the necessity that compelled it [...] These considerations had all the more force since industrialization always demands a large displacement of the population to the cities [...] But a sudden [industrial] development creates a call for manpower to which the response cannot long be delayed. Only agrarian "collectivism," coupled with mechanization, could ensure the maintenance and growth of agricultural production; without them, the proliferation of factories would have only led to disequilibrium [...] Situations arise in which, wrongly or rightly, acts of cruelty, harming individuals, seem negligible in view of the misfortunes they are meant to avoid [...] Today it is easy to see that the Soviets organizing production were replying in advance to a question of life and death. I do not mean to justify, but to understand; given that purpose, it seems superficial to me to dwell on horror [...] Apparently the Soviet Union, and, even, speaking more generally, Russia – owing to the czarist legacy – would not have been able to survive without a massive allocation of its resources to industrial equipment. Apparently, if this allocation had been even a little less rigorous, even a little less hard to bear than Stalin made it, Russia could have foundered [...] And we would rather die than establish a reign of terror; but a single man can die, and an immense population is faced with no other possibility than life. The Russian world had to make up for the backwardness of czarist society and this was necessarily so painful, it demanded an effort so great, that the hard way – in every sense the most costly way – became its only solution.

What's most striking about this chilling passage – aside from its monstrous cynicism – is the fact that, despite the passing reference to costliness in the last sentence, it has *nothing* to do with the discussions that introduced them. Forced social displacement on a massive scale, systematic theft of land by the State and mass murder ("terror") *aren't* "understood" here in scientific or empirical terms, that is, in terms of the structural unavoidability of waste and the stark contrast between primitive practices such as potlatch and the puritanical maintenance of accounts in modern capitalist society. Ironically, these terms only come (back) into play when Bataille turns to the Marshal Plan, which he asserts was a potlatch-like response – not to the poverty created by the defeat of the Nazi regime – but to the glorious success of the Russian Army at Stalingrad.

No, Bataille justifies Stalinist terror in the calculating, moralizing, ideological terms of political expediency. Despite the radicality of some of Bataille's ideas, here he doesn't question *anything* of real importance: neither the historical inevitability of Bolshevism, the political legitimacy of the so-called Soviet Union itself (the soviets themselves were forcibly suppressed in the early 1920s), the necessity of industrialization (both in general and in the specific case of the Russian economy), nor the desirability of Russia's survival. As Bataille himself showed in a preceding chapter, the Aztecs were conquered; Islam declined; Tibet was undermined. The United States, Bataille says, is also doomed. Why shouldn't Russia meet the same unavoidable fate?

It's also striking that Bataille's argument includes the following remark: "But if one judges this development of Russian resources in *a general way,* one risks forgetting the conditions in which it was begun and the necessity that compelled it" (emphasis added). In other words, one must concentrate on specific circumstances, not the general situation. This plainly contradicts two other remarks made by Bataille – "Situations arise in which, wrongly or rightly, acts of cruelty, harming individuals, seem negligible in view of the misfortunes they are meant to avoid," and "[B]ut a single man can die, and an immense population is faced with no other possibility than life" – as well as *the central premise of general economy.* "Are there not causes and effects that will appear only provided that *the general data of the economy* are studied?" Bataille had asked, *rhetorically,* in his introductory remarks concerning "the meaning" of general economy. "Will we be able to make ourselves the masters of such dangerous activity (and one that we could not abandon in any case) without having grasped its *general* consequences? Should we not, given the constant development of economic forces, pose the *general* problems that are linked to the movement of energy on the globe?" Yes, Georges, we should, even when looking at a "special case" such as Stalinist Russia.

And so, it's regrettable that Bataille decided to persevere and complete Volume I of *The Accursed Share.* Even though this Stalinist's analyses of eroticism and sovereignty are no doubt fascinating, we will nevertheless refrain from reading Volumes II and III of his trilogy. And we will also be quick to question those who say they are avid readers of Bataille's books to see if they know about his apologies for Stalinism.

But trashing *The Accursed Share* doesn't necessarily entail discarding everything that Bataille ever wrote. We still value the essays contained in *Visions of Excess,* especially "The Notion of Expenditure," which speaks of class struggle and revolution against bourgeois society as a whole in precisely those places that *The Accursed Share* speaks of the evolution of socialism in the Soviet Union and a "dynamic peace" between the USSR and America.

> One notes [Bataille wrote in 1933] that in primitive societies, where the exploitation of man by man is still fairly weak, the products of human activity not only flow in great quantities to rich men because of the protection or social leadership services these men supposedly provide, but also because of the spectacular collective expenditures for which they must pay. In so-called civilized societies, the fundamental *obligation* of wealth disappeared only in a fairly recent period [...] Everything that was generous, orgiastic, and excessive has disappeared; the themes of rivalry upon which individual activity still depends develop in obscurity, and are as shameful as belching. The representatives of the bourgeoisie have adopted an effaced manner; wealth is now displayed behind closed doors, in accordance with depressing and boring conventions [...] Such trickery has become the principle reason for living, working, and suffering for those who lack the courage to condemn this moldy society to revolutionary destruction [...] As the class that possesses the wealth – having received with wealth the obligation of functional expenditure – the modern bourgeoisie is characterized by the refusal in principle of this obligation. It has distinguished itself from the aristocracy through the fact that it has consented only to *spend for itself,* and within itself – in other words, by hiding its expenditures as much as possible from the other classes [...] In opposition, the people's consciousness is reduced to maintaining profoundly the principle of expenditure by representing bourgeois existence as the shame of man and as a sinister cancellation [...] As for the masters and exploiters, whose function is to create the contemptuous forms that exclude human nature – causing this nature to exist at the limits of the earth, in other words in mud – a simple law of reciprocity requires that they be condemned to fear, to the *great night* when their beautiful phrases will be drowned out by death screams in riots.

NOT BORED! #35, July 2003

Book reviews
Anarchism: Left for Dead

Alan Antliff is an Assistant Professor of Art History at the University of Alberta, Canada. He's making a name, indeed, *a career* for himself as a specialist in modern art and anarchism. His dissertation, accepted by the University of Delaware in 1998, was entitled *The Culture of Revolt: Art and Anarchism in America, 1908-1920.* In 2001, he published both *"Only a Beginning": An Anthology of Anarchist Culture* and *Anarchist Modernism: Art, Politics, and the First American Avant-Garde.* There will be another book out soon, concerning Anarchist Dadaism in New York. Anarchism, anarchism, anarchism: one might think that the State was actually in danger of being smashed sometime soon!

It's surprising that Antliff, who's right on (tenure) track, would stop the train to respond, and at length, to a negative review of one of his books, especially to a negative review published in a marginal, non-academic journal. What does a negative review in some rag mean to a professor with a hot specialty? N-o-t-h-i-n-g. Professors do not earn their living from book sales; it is the simple fact that they've published a(nother) book that helps them get promotions, tenured positions, administrative posts, etc etc. And yet issue #54 (Winter 2002-2003) of *Anarchy: A Journal of Desire Armed* carried Antliff's long response to a review of *Anarchist Modernism* that was written by Patrick Frank and published in *Anarchy* #53 (Spring-Summer 2002).

Though critical, the original review wasn't completely negative or dismissive of Antliff's accomplishments. Patrick Frank merely asserted that the main argument of *Anarchist Modernism* – that "anarchism was *the* formative force lending coherence and direction to modernism in the United States between 1908 and 1920" (emphasis in original) – is "inflated." Not incorrect, but inflated or overstated. And of course Patrick Frank is right: Antliff *could have* made the more modest claim that anarchism was *one* of the forces lending coherence and direction to early American modernism and not provoked any objections. But Antliff pressed on, not because (as an anarchist) he felt anarchism didn't have to share the glory with other "formative forces," but because (as an academic) the more modest claim made his own specialization look less relevant, less important. And so Antliff made anarchism the single decisive factor, made himself indispensible, someone who has, in his own words, made "new discoveries" that require everyone to "reset the boundaries of debate." He shifted the center of attention away from anarchism to his "bold" claims about it.

After dispatching with poor Patrick Frank, Antliff's response doesn't end (as it should). Instead, it goes on to provide blurb-like quotes from four positive reviews of *Anarchist Modernism* and to encourage the readers of *Anarchy* to read the book for themselves. These gestures make Antliff seem overly impressed with his own accomplishments, overly sensitive to criticism, and – perhaps most importantly – desperate for a single good review in an anarchist publication. Antliff describes himself as an anarchist. And yet none of the positive reviews from which Antliff quotes were written by anarchists. Most of them were published in art magazines; only one of these positive reviews was published in a political publication and it was the decidedly non-anarchist *Left History.*

But it is unlikely that *Anarchist Modernism* will ever get the type of review that its author wants, that is, a positive review from an anarchist. Why? Antliff's anarchism is both too inclusive and too narrowly defined. In the introduction, he writes,

> In the course of discussion I refer to a number of tendencies in the American anarchist and socialist movements, all of which contributed to the makeup of the diverse milieus I am examining. These are anarchist mutualism, anarchist collectivism, anarchist communism, anarchist syndicalism, anarchist individualism, parliamentary socialism, and Bolshevism.

For Antliff, anarchism isn't incompatible with such explicitly *anti*-anarchist movements as socialism, communism, and Bolshevism. As we read his book, we find out that, for Antliff – and perhaps *only for Antliff* – anarchism is also compatible with mysticism (theosophy) and reactionary nationalism (the writings of Coomarasamy). Antliff's anarchism is actually a misnomer for individualism. In the body of his book, despite what he says in his introduction, Antliff *never* finds or discusses any artists influenced by anarchist mutualism, anarchist collectivism, anarchist communism or anarchist syndicalism. Instead, all he finds are artists who are "anarchist individualists," "philosophical anarchists," people who define themselves as rebels against "mass society" or "the masses," people who don't form collectives, forge collective (anonymous) styles, or work in collaboration with each other, but instead form schools that preserve and reinforce uniqueness and individuality.

Ironically, Antliff's book gives voice to a couple ringing critiques of individualism. Paraphrasing Irwin Granich (only to say that he was wrong), Antliff says "Individualism in the arts was the epitome of bourgeois social and psychological decay." Quoting Carl Zigrosser (only to say that he, too, was wrong), Antliff says "Under capitalism the artist had become 'a curious being, an anarchist, a product of spontaneous generation, a being apart from the crowd' who spoke 'a strange language, unintelligible to those who lived in the world.'"

It is shocking, but not surprising, that Antliff believes that around 1920 both anarchism and anarchist art were dead and buried, murdered by two hands: the US government, which, ever since the 1902 assassination of President McKinley, had been tracking, arresting and deporting foreign-born anarchists; and the young Soviet Union, which first attracted anarchists (back) to Russia and then imprisoned or slaughtered them as counter-revolutionaries. For Antliff, there was simply *no* anarchist culture in the 1920s or 1930s; not even ghosts.

> [B]y the early 1920s [Antliff writes] Bolshevism had vanquished anarchism, and with it the political relevance of artistic innovation [...] Once this link [between creativity and anti-capitalist rebellion] was severed, "anarchist" modernism withered on the vine [...] Anarchist modernism's demise was setting the stage for what Richard Fitzgerald calls the "great failure" of the communist-dominated thirties.

For Antliff, Bolshevism also "vanquished" Anton Pannekoek and the other council communists, for whom "Lenin dealt the death blow" in 1920, after which they, a mere "scattering of isolated individuals," were headed for "oblivion."

Ummm. . . . *Someone* should tell Professor Antliff that *left for dead* isn't the same thing as *actually dead*. The Kronstadt rebellion of 1921; the creation of the "Organizational Platform of the General Union of Anarchists" by Nestor Makhno, Peter Arsimov, and other exiled Russian and Ukrainian anarchists in 1926; the anarchist uprising in Spain in 1936; the formation of workers' councils in Hungary in 1956; and mass rebellion in France in 1968, Portugal in 1975 and Poland in 1980 – none of this would have taken place if anarchism had indeed been "vanquished" in 1920! But Antliff doesn't seem to know a-n-y-t-h-i-n-g about these clearly anarchist events or how they might follow from or retrospectively illuminate those that took place in America between 1908 and 1920.

One would expect that a book such as *Anarchist Modernism* – an expensive, hardcover-only volume published by the University of Chicago Press – would be full of pretty pictures and that they would make the book worth looking at, despite its ah political shortcomings. But, no, not even that. Sure, the book has plenty of illustrations, 84 in total. But only 4 of them are color; 6 of the black-and-white images are very badly reproduced, and so make "close reading" impossible.

Not a problem for Alan Antliff, who doesn't offer a close reading of any of the images in his book. Most often, these images simply "stream by" as one turns the pages, without Antliff saying anything about them, as if they "speak for themselves," which of course they don't. Sometimes Antliff will stop the image-stream to offer a brief description of one of them: "In the *Figure* Benn depicts a woman standing against a forested background that looks more like a decorative screen," he writes in one of his better moments. "The face and arms of the woman are rendered in outline and she wears a brightly patterned smock that is equally hard-edged, with no modeling to distract from the work's formal qualities." Occasionally there are mistakes in labeling (Walter Pach's paintings described as "cubist" or "muted cubism") and some really atrocious sentences ("Man Ray's Dadaism, therefore, was the end game in a Stirnerist passage from materialism in painting to antiontological conceptualism").

It's telling that Antliff gives a pessimistic reading of the image that appears as both a color plate and the book's cover: Man Ray's 1914 painting *War (AD*

MCMXIV).

The coldly mechanized soldiers and blasted landscape of *War,* therefore, reflect Man Ray's conviction that World War I was the dehumanizing progeny of the modern state and the capitalist economic system it sustained [Antliff writes]. Pressing the point home, the invading soldiers attack a mother whose fallen child lies in the right foreground, left for dead amid the carnage. Here, the expressive power of abstraction melded with an equally powerful politics of protest: intent on destruction, these soldiers trample on all humanity.

But we see a different painting, one that depicts an army of faceless red people who are riding horses and attacking an army of faceless blue people on foot; the latter appear to be out-numbered and on the verge of defeat. Completed at the beginning of World War I, this painting seems to be a prediction or perhaps an allegory. But what do "red" and "blue" stand for here? Whose colors are they? Like a dream, this painting cries out for interpretation. At the bottom right, underneath the block that bears the portentous date AD MCMXIV, a small child-sized figure is curled up on its side. The child isn't dead: it's sleeping! And what is being dreamed? Perhaps that one day we will wake up from the nightmare of war.

NOT BORED! #35, July 2003

Lester Bangs: Great American Moralist

Religious truth is always of a categorical and dogmatic nature: "I am *the* way and *the* light." Use of the definite article conveys the concept of one and one only. *The* way. *The* universe. *The* truth. No proof or argument is admissible. Religious truth is *absolute* [...] Religious truth [...] is lifeless repetition of dogmatic formulations. – William Burroughs, *The Adding Machine.*

The dictionary's definitions (emphasis added) are not at all flattering.

moralism: 1. the habit of moralizing. 2. the practice of morality, as distinct from religion.
moralist: 1. a person who teaches or inculcates morality, 2. a person who practices morality, 3. a person who believes in *regulating the morals of others, as by imposing censorship.*

morality: 1. conformity to the rules of right conduct, 2. virtue in sexual matters, 3. a doctrine or system of morals.

morals: 1. principles or habits with respect to right or wrong conduct, 2. generally accepted customs of conduct and right living in a society, and to the individual's practice in relation to these.

But when people condemn "moralizing," they are making a mistake: they mean to condemn the dogmatism and inflexibility of *religious truth,* not the provisionality and flexibility of *moral truth.*

And so Greil Marcus (editor of Lester Bangs' first posthumous collection, *Psychotic Reactions and Carburetor Dung,* published in 1987) was absolutely right to say that, "Moralism in the very best sense – the attempt to understand what is important, and to communicate that understanding to others in a form that somehow obligates the reader as much as it entertains – surfaced at the end of [Bangs'] tenure at *Creem,* and found a field in New York at the *Village Voice.*" Free sprit and self-proclaimed "Drug Punk" Lester Bangs was indeed a moralist, one of the finest this country (America, "the Great Satan") has ever produced.

Praise for other great moralists runs through *Mainlines, Blood Feasts and Bad Taste,* the second posthumous collection of Bangs' writings, which was edited by John Morthland and published in 2003. "Black Sabbath," Bangs wrote in 1972, "are moralists – like Bob Dylan, like William Burroughs, like most artists trying to deal with a serious situation in an honest way." Burroughs' work, Bangs wrote, "amounts to a demonology for our times, portraying the forces currently threatening our planet's survival as evil gods operating from without." And Bangs clearly saw himself as a moralist, too: "Me," he wrote in 1979, "I have this problem separating people's music from the stance or value system behind it."

But what was it that kept Lester Bangs from being a moralizer in the worst sense of the word (that is, a regulator or censor)? Once again, Greil Marcus gets it right, when he quotes a remark Bangs made to interviewer and biographer Jim DeRogatis: "I double back all over myself." Unlike the so-called Moral Majority, who were neither moral nor the majority, Lester Bangs wasn't dogmatic; he didn't judge music or the people who made it in accordance with an eternal, unchanging code of right-and-wrong. *His* morality constantly changed, constantly doubled back upon and questioned itself.

Though one might pick other instances, for example, his writings about the Sex Pistols (especially "Bye Bye Sidney, Be Good"), Lester Bangs' writhing, constantly changing moralism was at its best when he wrote about the music Miles Davis recorded and released in the early 1970s. *Mainlines* contains two such essays: "Kind of Grim: Unraveling the Miles Perplex," published in 1976, and "Miles Davis: Music for the Living Dead," published in 1981.

As someone who was greatly influenced by Bangs' great (and still not reprinted) essay "Free Jazz / Punk Rock," I was shocked by "Kind of Grim," which dismisses Miles' 1972 recording *On the Corner* as "garbage," "the absolute worst album this man ever put out." "On this experiment in percussion and electronics," Bangs wrote in 1976, "what little actual trumpet you could pick out of the buzz-whiz and chockablocka was so distorted as to be almost beyond recognition." But because *On the Corner* wasn't simply "an off-note unaccountably put on record," but the beginning of a series of releases that included such other depressing "horseshit" as *Big Fun* and *Get Up with It*, Bangs claimed that "this music indicat[ed] that something was wrong with the progenitor, that he was not [merely] indulging himself or tapped out or merely confused," but that Miles was "sick of soul."

Five years later or, if you count "Free Jazz / Punk Rock," three years later, Bangs was claiming that *On the Corner* was "something genuinely new," "the first jazz of the Eighties." Instead of being dead, of "having no discernible emotion in it," *On the Corner* is "almost obscenely, frighteningly alive." And this change of mind doesn't fail to implicate Bangs himself. He makes sure his readers know that, back in 1976, he "couldn't even *hear* it, much less feel its cold flame and realize its intentions," and "we could only grow into it [...] as time caught up with us and we caught up with Miles."

But this new-found appreciation is *not* an occasion for self-congratulation. No, far from it: back in 1976, Bangs writes, "*there was something wrong with me* [...] I was sweeping some deep latent anguish under the emotional carpet, or not confronting myself on some primal level." He'd dismissed *On the Corner* because "it exposed me to myself, to my own falsity, to my own cowardice in the face of dread or staved-off pain." And this, precisely, is the value of reading Lester Bangs so long (22 years!) after his death: like Miles' music, his writhing "will pry [pain] out of your soul's very core when he hits his supreme note and you happen, coincidentally, to be a bit of an open emotional wound at the moment yourself. It is this gift for open-heart surgery that makes him the supreme artist" – or, if you will, the great moralist – "that he is."

NOT BORED! #36, July 2004

Kurt Cobain: Looking at the Corpse, 10 Years Later

Negation is not nihilism. Nihilism is the belief in nothing and the wish to become nothing [...] Negation is the act that would make it self-evident to everyone that the world is not as it seems – but only when the act is so implicitly complete that it leaves open the possibility that the world may be nothing, that nihilism as well as creation may occupy the suddenly cleared terrain [...] Along the way to the realization of the wish for negation, though, the tools one seems forced to use – real or symbolic violence, blasphemy, dissipation, ridiculousness – change hands with those of the nihilist [...] Often the same rooms are rented, and sometimes the same bills are paid. Usually the coroner – be he or she critic, historian, epigone, or even loved one – cannot tell the difference by looking at the corpse. – Greil Marcus, "Gulliver Speaks," *Artforum,* November 1983.

People just left me alone. They were afraid. I always felt they would vote me Most Likely to Kill Everyone at a High School Dance. – Kurt Cobain, 1993.

Death is on every stained page of Kurt Cobain's notebooks, excerpts of which were published as *Journals* in November 2002. But it's *not* the death you think it is, the obvious one: Kurt's own death, a suicide by gunshot, on 5 April 1994. No, it's something else.

On page 140 (the entries are not dated), he says that he's in "absolute and total support" of many things, including "full scale violently organized terrorist-fueled revolution." Killing is necessary because "you cannot de-program the glutton," and because "it would be nice to see the gluttons become so commonly hunted down that eventually they will either submit to the opposite of their ways or be scared shitless to ever leave their homes." And so Kurt's advice is "arm yourself, find a representative of Gluttony or oppression and blow the motherfuckers head off."

This isn't an isolated outburst of anger and pain, but a theme, perhaps an obsession. Five pages later, above a figure ("Fig. A") that shows an assassin standing above a line of Ku Klux Klan members, Cobain writes "And hairy, sweaty, macho-sexist and racist dickheads who will soon drown in a pool of razor blades and sperm from the uprising of your children, the armed and de-programmed crusade." And on page 162, "Fig. A" returns, only this time more vehemently: one of the KKK guys carries a sign with a Nazi swastika on it and the assassin's gun is filled in, better drawn.

But of course Kurt wasn't an assassin, a lone gunman standing on the roof. He might have composed, sang and played several *killer songs* ("School," "Negative Creep," "Paper Cuts" and "Teen Spirit," among them) but he never wielded a gun against anyone but himself. No, not negation but nihilism: the death in the pages of *Journals* isn't Cobain's suicide, but the killings and suicides that took place almost exactly five years later at Columbine High School.

NOT BORED! #36, July 2004

Book reviews

The Deception of Strategy

"We want them [the Iraqis] to quit, not to fight, so that you have this simultaneous effect, rather like the nuclear weapons at Hiroshima, not taking days or weeks but minutes." – Harlan Ullman, creator of the "Shock and Awe" tactic, January 2003.

"As we move toward a new Middle East, over the years and, I think, over the decades to come . . . we will make a lot of people very nervous. We want you [Egyptian President Hosni Mubarak and the leaders of Saudi Arabia] nervous. We want you to realize now, for the fourth time in a hundred years, this country and its allies are on the march and that we are on the side of those whom you – the Mubaraks, the Saudi Royal family – most fear: We're on the side of your own people." – ex-CIA Director James Woolsey, 3 April 2003.

Today, 25 June 2004, just five days before the US military is scheduled to "hand over" political control of Iraq to a provisional governing body, it became official: the Bush Administration has lost the support of the American people for its allegedly humanitarian war against Saddam Hussein. A public opinion poll conducted by CNN-*USA Today*-Gallup has found that a majority (54 percent) of the 1,005 Americans who responded think that going to war in the first place (no matter what the justification) was a mistake; they are increasingly *disappointed* with the results, which are appalling and grow worse every day. They are also increasingly *disillusioned* with George W. Bush, whose disapproval ratings are higher than they have ever been.

This is the Bush Administration's *second* major military campaign that has produced mixed results, that is, a rapid and deceptively easy military victory followed by a humiliating political defeat. The first one, of course, was the phony victory over the Taliban, which, though swift, failed to capture or kill Osama Bin Laden, didn't so much weaken Al Qaeda as force it to become more decentralized, mobile and willing to work with other, more "localized" jihadist groups, destabilized Afghanistan, and put new pressure on Pakistan. The *entire* post-September 11th global war on terrorism (GWOT) has been a disaster, at least from the political or strategic standpoint. The total number of Al Qaeda-like terrorist attacks since "911" has *risen* and spread to previously unaffected countries, most notably Spain and Saudi Arabia. The GWOT has also, of course, been a resounding success from a certain, rather limited economic standpoint, i.e., billion-dollar, no-bid, "cost-plus" contracts with Halliburton, Kellogg Brown & Root, and other politically well-connected companies.

George W. Bush and the "chickenhawks" in his Administration have no monopoly on mixed (ultimately disastrous) military campaigns. The Clinton Administration conducted at least two of them: the 1998 Cruise missile attacks on Osama Bin Laden's positions in Afghanistan and the Sudan; and the phony 1999 victory over Slobodan Milosevic in Kosovo. And George Bush Senior conducted at least two of them, as well: the Gulf War of 1991, which left Saddam Hussein in power and thus created the precondition/justification for the *second* war against Iraq; and the 1992 "humanitarian" intervention in Somalia, for which Bill Clinton ended up taking the blame. The last time America conducted a truly successful military offensive, or at least one that didn't leave the defeated country in the midst or on the verge of a bloody civil war, was in 1988, when Reagan ordered the US military to invade Panama and arrest Manuel Noriega. But, like Reagan's invasion of Grenada, this victory held no strategic significance whatsoever.

Two themes emerge here: a long history of increasingly humiliating political defeats, which may be said to have started when the US military, despite its nuclear arsenal and superior air force, lost the war against Vietnam; and an increasing *infantilization* of the American presidency. The step from Reagan to Bush Senior was a step down, from Grandfather to Father; and the step from Bush Senior to Bush Junior was literally a step from Father to Son. But this change isn't merely a decrease in age. Unlike Reagan, each one of these clowns (Bush Senior, Clinton and Bush Junior) experienced some sort of memorable public humiliation during their terms as President (throwing up while at a official dinner in Japan, denying an affair with Monica Lewinsky, and failing to win the popular vote count in 2000, respectively). Ever since 1988, there's been the increasing suspicion that these guys just aren't the real people in control of the US military. Instead, the US military seems to be in control of *them*.

Over these same 16 years, there has been a self-avowed "revolution in military affairs," that is, a rapid, technology-fueled but incomplete movement away from ground wars, troop-heavy deployments, mechanized divisions and an essentially defensive posture (*a la* NATO), and towards aero-space or "star" wars, precision-guided munitions, "special" and covert operations, and an offensive or pre-emptive posture (the so-called Rumsfeld Doctrine). The idea is that one no longer defeats an enemy by attacking it on the ground, but by attacking it from the air with increasingly lethal weapons. Because there will be far more deaths among the civilian population than among the armed forces, one must also be skilled at "relating" to the mass media, controlling "spin," deploying decoys, creating distractions, and circulating disinformation.

Paul Virilio's *Strategie de la Deception* is one of the few books that addresses itself to these developments. Originally published in 1999, it is made up of four newspaper articles Virilio wrote during and immediately after the Kosovo War. In 2000, Verso published a translation by Chris Turner under the title *Strategy of Deception*. Despite September 11th, which is the "gulf" that supposedly separates us from the world as it was back in 1999, *Strategy of Deception* retains its relevance. Indeed, it may even be much more relevant today than it was five years ago.

In a "Translator's Note," the entirety of which is quoted below, Chris Turner explains why *Strategy of Deception* is a "disappointing" rendering of the book's title into English.

> It is always disappointing to report something lost in translation. In this case, the element lost is that of disappointment itself, for this is, of course, the everyday meaning of the French word *'la deception.'* The term does, however, also have a more recondite military sense, the *deception* of missiles being the overall process of the deflection of such weapons from their course (this part is, technically, their *seduction*) and their redirection to some other – preferably harmless – target. Virilio uses the term to refer to the bundle of techniques of decoying, distraction and disinformation which make up a classically 'deceptive' strategy in the English sense. However, in his title he is alluding also, and more directly, to the (possibly intended) disappointment and disillusionment which remains after the massive Allied military efforts in the former Yugoslavia, where, were we nineteenth-century speakers of English, we might contend (*pace* Jamie Shea [cf. James Mills, *The History of British India,* 1817]) that 'never was expectation more completely deceived.'

And so, there are three meanings of "deception": 1) disappointment and disillusionment; 2) the deflection of missiles; and 3) disinformation, decoys and distractions ("classic deception"). By choosing to employ *deception,* instead of *tromperie* or *duperie,* both of which denote classic deception, Virilio has insisted on the importance of disappointment and deflection. Not only are disappointment and deflection weapons that can be used against an external enemy, but they can also (Turner says "possibly") be used against internal enemies, rival factions and the like.

These meanings make Virilio's book different from others on the subject. Note well that all of the authors cited in the massive bibliography entitled *Deception in Warfare,* which was compiled in 1996 by the Air University Library at Maxwell Air Force Base, Alabama, concentrate exclusively on decoys and distractions, and do not touch upon the other two meanings of deception at all. Same thing with authors on the subject of the deflection or interception of incoming missiles. There is an extensive literature on such relevant subjects as the re-programmable "Tomahawk" Cruise Missile, "Patriot" Anti-Missile Launchers, and the National Missile Defense System, aka "Star Wars," but the various authors define the deflection/interception of missiles as a tactic, not a strategy, and their works have little or nothing to do with either disappointment or classic deception.

Virilio's basic point is that, despite or perhaps *because* of the spectacular success of Hiroshima, "when *a single B 29 bomber and a single atom bomb put an end to the war in the Pacific,*" it is impossible to conduct a politically successful or "humanitarian" war if its ideology and strategy are based upon on the false premise that wars can be won using nothing but air power. Virilio points out that, "during the Cold War years, the development of 'intercontinental missiles' and control of satellite space for the guidance of high-precision missiles sadly caused us to forget that aero-spatial war goes hand in hand with extremes of destruction and *the imperative need for an absolute weapon,* whether it be an atomic or neutron device, or chemical/bacteriological agents." Because this fact was forgotten, Virilio says, "or rather obscured by the illusion of Allied victory in Iraq [in 1991]," a "fatal error was [able] to arise during the Clinton presidency of an all-out multiplication of these 'automatic strikes,' aimed at punishing so-called 'rogue states,' from which the USA aspires to protect the world by way of its telematic technologies." That "fatal error" continues to be made under Bush Junior: for both him and Bill Clinton, Iraq and Afghanistan were "rogue states" that richly deserved and *would benefit from* punitive bombings from the sky.[7] Both presidents were quite wrong, and in both cases.

Thus a question arises: *In whose interest works the strategy of deceiving infantilized American Presidents so that they once again make the fatal error of relying exclusively upon air power?* The answer seems relatively straight-forward: the faction of the military-industrial complex that concentrates on nuclear weaponry and delivery systems, the "nuclear priesthood," the true believers in "mini-nukes."[8] But, like many of his other books, Virilio's *Strategy of Deception* isn't a long, systematic or comprehensive effort. Instead, it is short, fast and full of lightning flashes, puns and coinages. As a result, even though *he's* the one who has managed to pose the question "Who profits from the strategy of deception?" Virilio doesn't give his answer the attention that it obviously deserves.

NOT BORED! #36, July 2004

On-line notice dated 17 June 2007: In a famous passage in *The Art of War,* Sun Tzu remarks, "The Way of War is a Way of Deception." That is to say, the general "changes his ways and alters his plans to keep the enemy in ignorance. He shifts camp. He shifts camp and takes roundabout routes to keep the enemy in the dark." But Sun Tzu also remarks that the general "must be able to keep *his own troops* in ignorance, to deceive their eyes and their ears" (emphasis added).

---

[7] Under President Obama, who ran as an anti-war candidate in 2008, remote-controled drones are being widely used to bomb targets in Pakistan as well as in Afghanistan and Iraq.
[8] See for example, William J. Broad, "New Advice on the Unthinkable: How to Survive a Nuclear Bomb," *New York Times,* 16 December 2010, p. 1.

Book reviews

1968: the Year that Never Ended

What follows are the primary ingredients of the "political-cultural stew" in which the Mexican historian and essayist Paco Ignacio Taibo says that he and many other militant students involved in the 1968 Movement "came of age": Che Guevara, Che's face, Guevarism, the Cuban Revolution, the Vietnamese resistance, the Spartacists, Lenin, Mao, Maoists, neo-Maoists, Trotsky, *four different species* of Trotskyism, no sex, no drugs, "rock" musicians such as Leonard Cohen, Joan Baez, Bob Dylan, Pete Seeger, Peter Paul & Mary, Donovan, the Beatles, Donovan ... shall I go on? I didn't think so.

What a bizarre combination of the repulsive and the utterly bland! On the one hand: where are Emilio Zapata, the young Karl Marx, *forty different species of anarchism,* Blanqui, Durruti, Nestor Mahkno, Kropotkin, the Paris Communards, the Kronstadt sailors, Rosa Luxemburg, the Spanish anarchists of 1936 and Wilhelm Reich? And, on the other hand: Elvis Presley, Little Richard, Frank Zappa, Jimi Hendrix, the Rolling Stones, the Who, the Kinks and the Velvet Underground? All missing.

But Taibo's brand-new book, *'68* (Seven Stories Press, 2004), doesn't deserve the scorn and insults that are heaped upon repulsive/bland student radicals in the Situationist International's 1966 pamphlet *On the Poverty of Student Life.* Originally published under the title *Fantasmas nuestros de cada dia* (Our Everyday Ghosts) in 1991, supplemented by two epilogues, and translated from the Spanish by ex-situationist Donald Nicholson-Smith, *'68* is an exemplary exercise in constructive self-criticism:

> Our militancy was old-style even as we aspired to the new. We were sectarian. The enemy was powerful, alien, and far away. The State was a bookish abstraction, so it made more sense to devote ourselves to interminable disputes with our pseudo-allies – the militants of the neighboring party, the next sect along, the devotees of some parallel cult. We were absorbed by ideological warfare, and we produced unreadable newspapers laden with quotations from Lenin or Mao, Trotsky or Bakunin – depending on which particular club we belonged to [...] In the working-class neighborhoods we visited on occasion (after all, the manuals we had been reading and quoting until we bored ourselves stiff decreed that it was up to the working class to make the revolution), we were strange birds who showed up, then took off after showering the factory with unreadable pamphlets that the employees of the Azcapotzalco refinery or the workers at the Vallejo or Xalostoc plants would later use for ass wipes [...] We were barely aware of the railroad-workers' movement and its jailed leader

Demetrio Vallejo [...] We felt absolutely no connection to Morelos, Zapata, [and] Villa.

Over the course of Taibo's recollection of the three months of strikes, rallies and marches that preceded the massacre of 2 October 1968, "we" begin to develop a new "style" of militancy, remember "a lost language in which we could converse with the rest of the people," and have real conversations. During a massive demonstration in late July 1968,

> one brigade of left-wing militants from the Department of Sciences found itself surrounded [and protected] by a group of vocational students who had learned to belt the riot police with stones using slingshots, then take refuge in the courtyards of their school. The militants taught the vocational students how to produce fliers and organize propaganda brigades. And the militants in turn learned that bricks need to be aimed high and that Molotov cocktails should have very short fuses [...]

And then, in late August 1968: "Groups of workers started showing up at the schools, and workers' committees for solidarity for the students started to form." By September, "we had taken over the street, a street that led to other places, to points of no return, to the end of the world." Taibo asks,

> Could the government see further than us? Did they anticipate the emergence of a vast student movement, and were they out to strangle it in its infancy? Was one faction of the government using this as a stick with which to beat another in the presidential race? [...] The May [1968] events in France had made headlines in all the papers, as had the Prague Spring, the student mobilization in Brazil, the occupation of Columbia University in New York, and the Cordoba uprising in Argentina. Did these idiots [in Mexico] really think that some sort of international contagion was at work?

Yes, that's *exactly* what those idiots thought. And they also believed that, with the Olympic Games scheduled to be held in Mexico City on 12 October 1968, they had to act quickly and effectively. "We expected the blow," Taibo writes, "but we did not know how brutal it would be."

On 2 October, the Mexican Army, under the command of General Crisoforo Monzon, confronted the hundreds of thousands of striking students and workers who'd assembled in the Plaza de las Tres Culturas in Tlatelolco. Though the truth was denied for a very long time, "today," Taibo writes, "everybody knows that the provocateurs were soldiers disguised as civilians, each wearing a single identifying glove, soldiers from the Olimpia Battalion. Today everyone knows that flares thrown from a military helicopter were the signal to open fire, the signal for the army to begin to shoot into the unarmed crowd." Over a 1,000 people were seriously injured; hundreds more were killed.

As if it were trying to demonstrate the ruthlessness of its special forces, showcase the modernity of its spectacle, and/or destroy all of the evidence of the terrible crime (mass murder) that it had just committed, the Mexican Army collected the dead bodies, took them to a hangar in the military part of a near-by airport, and loaded them into planes that eventually dumped the bodies into the Gulf of Mexico. Judicial-police officers visited near-by hospitals, looking for survivors of the massacre who'd sought treatment for their injuries, and either arrested, tortured or "disappeared" the survivors that they found. (The next day, President Diaz Ordaz could plausibly deny that the massacre even took place.) And so a terrible question gets asked at the beginning of Taibo's book, never gets answered, and so continues to echo and resound throughout what follows: "Where did they throw our dead? Where did they toss our dead? Where, for fuck's sake, did they throw our dead?" This echo is the sound of 1968, the year that never ended.

"In memory," Taibo says, "the second of October has replaced the hundred days of the strike [that preceded it]. The black magic of the cult of defeat and of the dead has reduced '68 to Tlatelolco alone." But Taibo knows that the 1968 movement was much more than just 2 October, that it was also about "real democracy practiced for 123 days [...] of university occupations and assemblies at all levels." And so he reconstructs '68, both with and against his memories of it. "Memory tends to simplify," Taibo says, "whether by retaining absurdly trivial anecdotes or by seeing the big picture strictly in black and white terms." The key to the reconstruction of '68 is combining the anecdotal with the analytical, "the poetry of everyday life" with the critique of the State. In regards "[c]ollective memory, but also even the tiniest, most insignificant memory of a personal kind," Taibo says, "I suspect, in fact, that the one can barely survive without the other, that *legend* cannot be constructed without anecdote" (emphasis added).

The reconstructed '68 must be more than just history: it must also be a legend, a *living legend* of freedom. Otherwise, it will disappear. In his 1993 epilogue, Taibo explains that, in response to the first edition of his book and the political activism that accompanied the commemoration of the 25th anniversary of the massacre, there was a concerted attempt to produce an "objective" or "digestible version of the facts that would in no way upset the present of the yuppies of Ali Baba and his forty (PRI-ist) thieves," a version of the atrocity that could be "aired in public in all its certitude, then duly vanish from the popular middle-class imagination." To keep '68 true to itself and safe from these "objectivity hounds," Taibo declares, "I am thus in favor of the fantasy, the antiauthoritarian myth of the Movement [...] As for objectivity, I don't give a royal shit about objectivity. Because, when you get down to it, this is a myth that gives them [the government] a major pain in the ass."

A great writer, Taibo gets the balance between the anecdotal and the analytical right every time. Of particular delight are his chapter titles. Some are one or two words long, and function like index entries or file names, such as "Confetti" and "Nabbed"; others are longer and descriptive, such as "Wherein We Learn That the Tanks Have Arrived" and "When Maricarmen Fernandez Grabbed My Ass"; still others – the best ones – don't name or describe the action about to unfold, but float above or around it, like titles for or lines from poems ("It is Made Clear that Barricades, Once Built, Lodge Immediately in Memory" and "Memo to Amnesiacs on How to Dent the Armor of a Tank with a Metal Pipe").

Some of Taibo's chapters are devoted to the "big picture" of the Movement's development; others are devoted to details or stories along the way. In one remarkable chapter, "Menu" (quoted below in its entirety), these two orders of memory are presented on the same dish:

> Menu for the Nguyen Van Troi Cafeteria, Department of Political Sciences, in early August 1968. Cooks: a Maoist, a leftist Christian Democrat, a Trotskyist, two miniskirted Guevarists. To drink: *agua de Jamaica* (hibiscus flower tea). To eat: chicken soup, boiled potatoes with salt, and bananas for dessert. Menu remains unchanged for four days, until food donated by Mixcoac Market vendors is finished. No siesta. Brigade activity in Ciudad Nezahualcoyotl: newspaper distribution, factory visit, assembly. At night: massive graffiti-painting campaign. There are one hundred painting brigades in this school. Thousands of painting brigades to paint the entire humanities wing. The city as rainbow. A quick slogan: HOCICON! (Big mouth – in reference to the supremo of the Republic). A not-so-quick slogan (because it has one letter more): LIBERTAD!

But the greatest thing about Taibo is that, despite all the twists and turns, he *never* gets distracted from what's important. In the 1993 epilogue, he wants a "Truth Commission" and he wants it to deal with the following six issues:

1. Clarification of the charge against the Movement that it was the outcome of a plot or conspiracy.
2. Origins and motives of the repressive action of July 1968.
3. Genesis and unfolding of the events of 2 October 1968 and the identification of those responsible.
4. Clarification of the contradictory information released concerning those killed and wounded during the '68 movement.
5. Legitimacy of the penal judgments passed as part of the repression of the Movement.
6. Definitive assignment of responsibility for those events.

Ten years later, in his epilogue dated November 2003, Taibo is still saying, "However, as long as the murderers are not brought to justice, the wounds will fester [...] As for us, obdurate as ever, thirty-five years down the line, we are back in the street yet again."

NOT BORED! #36, July 2004

Greil Marcus' *Like a Rolling Stone*

The development of capitalist concentration, and the diversification of its function at the global level, have produced the forced consumption of the abundance of commodities, as well as the control of the economy and all of life by bureaucrats, through their possession of the State; or direct or indirect colonialism. Quite far from being the definitive response to the incessant revolutionary crises of the historical era begun two centuries ago, this system has now entered into a new crisis: from Berkeley to Varsovie, from the Asturians to Kivu, it is refuted and combated.
– Guy Debord, "Summary of 1965"[1]

In the dime stores and bus stations
People talk of situations
Read books, repeat quotations
Write conclusions on the wall.
– Bob Dylan, "Love Minus Zero/No Limit," *Bringing it all back home*[2]

Greil Marcus must know that he leaves himself open to a predictable objection when he refers to Guy Debord in most recent book of music criticism, *Like A Rolling Stone: Bob Dylan At the Crossroads. An explosion of vision and humor that forever changed pop music* (Public Affairs Books, 2005). In the middle of a quotation from a detective novel that uses comfortable, pre-riot Watts as its psychogeographical backdrop, Greil tells us, "as the critic Guy Debord wrote of Watts from Paris, 'comfort will never be comfortable enough for those who seek what is not on the market.'"

The quote is from Debord's strategic analysis of the Watts riots, "The Decline and Fall of the Spectacular-Commodity Society," which – as Greil notes in his list of works cited – was first published clandestinely in America, in an English translation, in December 1965 by the Situationist International and later published in French in *Internationale Situationniste* #10 (March 1966).

In *Like A Rolling Stone,* Greil is only interested in the Watts riots to the extent that they chronologically preceded the release of Dylan's "Like a Rolling Stone" as a single on 20 July 1965. Unlike, say, Frank Zappa's 1966 song "Trouble Everyday," Dylan doesn't refer to or try to comment upon those riots. In the same way that Greil doesn't really need the riots to tell the story of "Like a Rolling Stone," he doesn't really need Guy Debord ("from Paris") to tell the story of the riots. Thus, Greil can afford to call Debord "a critic" and leave it at that; to neglect to tell his readers that, in *Lipstick Traces on a Cigarette: A Secret History of the Twentieth Century* (Harvard University Press, 1989), Greil himself had written extensively (and very productively) about Debord's writings, theories and relevance to rock 'n' roll music.[3] Some readers might have benefited from this knowledge: just like *Like a Rolling Stone, Lipstick Traces* is a risky, rarely undertaken adventure: an entire book – footnotes, an index, a discography with its own internal digressions and asides – about a single great rock 'n' roll song (the Sex Pistols' "Anarchy in the UK" in the case of *Lipstick Traces*).[4]

The objection that Greil leaves himself open to here isn't really factual, though Debord *wasn't* a "critic," but a filmmaker, writer and political revolutionary. Though he wrote about art, he refused to write "art criticism," which he denounced as "a second-degree spectacle" in a 1961 text entitled "For a Revolutionary Judgment of Art." Nor is the objection ideological: Greil isn't a "recuperator," to use the phrase that Debord and the situationists used to describe those who use revolutionary ideas or practices to maintain, rather than destroy, the existing order. No: the objection is aesthetic in nature. It is *boring* to bring Debord onstage (just this one time), only to describe him as a critic. If he is *just* a critic, why mention him at all? This boredom is far from dissipated or relieved when, in his "Works Cited" entry, Greil writes that "this shocking analysis of the Watts riots ('Looting is the *natural* response to the society of abundance . . . The flames of Watts *consummated* the system of consumption') was written in Paris in French." Shocking?! Not for readers of *Lipstick Traces* or the reprinted editions of Debord's "Decline and Fall of the Spectacular-Commodity Society" that were circulated in both French and English in response to the 1991 Rodney King riots.

Greil Marcus' *Like a Rolling Stone* is not a boring book and it includes very few boring passages or references. As a matter of fact, it is a truly excellent book: well-researched, well-illustrated (photos of the recording sessions) and – as always – very well-written. I feel confident in saying that one can't really go any further in or with music criticism than Greil has gone. He is simply the best.

To adopt the terminology Greil used in the years leading up to the publication of *Lipstick Traces,* Dylan's "Like a Rolling Stone" is a negation: an "act that would make it self-evident to everyone that the world is not what it seems – but only when the act is so implicitly complete that it leaves open the possibility that the world may be nothing, that nihilism as well as creation may occupy the suddenly cleared terrain" ("Gulliver Speaks," *Artforum,* November 1983). "The world is not what it seems": in so many words, this is exactly what the young woman to whom the whole song is addressed has just realized; in any event, it's what the narrator of the song keeps telling her (and us). His harsh truths are indeed implicitly complete (she'd been warned; what else could there be left to say after *four* detailed and merciless verses?). But the song's chorus – the music and the way Dylan sings, as well as the question posed ("how does it *feel*?")[5] – open up many possibilities, among them the possibility that the young woman may now feel *absolutely nothing*. Her experience? It might also mean *absolutely nothing*.

But there is nevertheless something missing, not so much from within *Like a Rolling Stone,* but *around* it. Greil's half-hearted reference to Guy Debord – very French, but unmistakably an internationalist – emphasizes what's missing. Greil's book does a lot of things – it educates, it amuses, it satisfies – but it doesn't *impassion.* Unlike *Lipstick Traces,* which, according to one of its blurbs, inspired a woman to dye her hair the colors of the rainbow, *Like a Rolling Stone* will simply inspire readers to listen to Dylan's incontestably excellent song one more time or seek out a copy of one of those many bootlegged recordings the book refers to. Greil is right when he says that "Like a Rolling Stone" hasn't aged since 1965 and is always new, always different to our ears, but *we* are not. We've aged; we've grown tired of ourselves, of our perpetual sameness; we lack the passion of our youth.

Greil writes that the release of Dylan's "Like a Rolling Stone"

> was an event. It defined the summer, but like the Watts riots the performance also interrupted it – as, ever since, the song has interrupted whatever might be taking place around it as it plays. It was an incident that took place in a recording studio and was then sent out into the world with the intention of leaving the world not quite the same. This is not the same as changing the world, which implies a way in which one might want the world to be changed. This is more like drawing a line, to see what would happen: to see who the song revealed to be on which side of the line, and who might cross it, from either side.

Unlike *Lipstick Traces,* which was divisive, if not negationist, because it broke through the separation between "the pop world" (music and cultural criticism) and "the greater world" (contemporary events and political struggles),[6] *Like a Rolling Stone* doesn't aspire to make its readers choose sides or make immediate and important decisions about everyday life. It stays within "the pop world," and uses "the greater world" (the Watts riots, for example) as backdrop.

Who could say that "Like a Rolling Stone" *isn't* the greatest rock 'n' roll song of all time? It's a great song and Greil argues for it very persuasively. Even if one *did* disagree – preferring instead Elvis Presley's "Hound Dog," the Rolling Stones' "Gimme Shelter" or the Sex Pistols' "Anarchy in the UK" – what would be the point? It's only a popularity contest: it doesn't really matter who wins. Or, rather, it's like a democratic election, in which everyone who votes is supposedly a winner. Paraphrasing what Frank Zappa said about Dylan's song, Greil's book will sell ("win") but nobody will respond to it the way they should: that is, by commencing the social revolution.

Greil seems unsure about *the intention* behind or within "Like a Rolling Stone."[7] To the extent that he *is* unsure, or confused, his book stays away from drawing a line that would force his readers to choose sides. Has he mellowed over the course of the last 16 years?[8] I seem to remember him (in *Dead Elvis: A Chronicle of a Cultural Obsession,* from 1991) insisting on the deliberateness, the willfulness, of Elvis Presley's' songs and onstage appearances in the 1950s: this wasn't some simpleton who stumbled out from behind his plow one day to sing some songs he thought his Momma would like; this was a self-conscious actor who clearly intended to change the race relations of his era, if not "the world." In the years leading up to "Like a Rolling Stone," Bob Dylan obviously had some very clear ideas about the precise ways in which *he* wanted to change the world: an end to war and nuclear weapons, an end to racism and segregation. "Like a Rolling Stone" demands several very precise changes: an end to condescension and snobbery, vanity and phoniness, trendiness and vicarious pleasures.

Paradoxically, it is Greil himself who reminds his readers that, thirty years after he wrote and recorded "Master of War," Dylan was *still* against war, against a *particular* war (as always). He played the old song on the 1991 telecast of the Grammy Awards, which happened to take place during the first American war on the people of Iraq, and again at Madison Square Garden on 11 November 2002, that is, while the second American war on the people of Iraq was being prepared and publically announced. Taking their cue but also sharing the vision, American anti-war protesters performed the song or quoted it in the flyers, posters and speeches they made in 2003 and 2004.[9]

And so *there's* where the potentially explosive line could have been drawn: not between Dylan's fans and everyone else, but between Dylan fans who are pro-war ("anti-terrorism") and Dylan fans who are not. Greil could have attacked, insulted or mocked pro-war people who love Dylan's music and think "Like a Rolling Stone" (or even "Masters of War"!) is the greatest rock 'n' roll song ever. But he didn't, perhaps because he didn't want to appear mean-spirited, perhaps because he feared the possible repercussions, which might include pro-Bush, right-wing lunatics accusing him of being unpatriotic or even *anti-American.*

It is, precisely, America that Greil Marcus loves and writes about so well in his many books, especially *Mystery Train: Images of America in Rock 'n' Roll Music* (1975) and *Invisible Republic: Bob Dylan's Basement Tapes* (1997). Dylan's "Like a Rolling Stone" isn't simply American, as American as Coca Cola and Mickey Mouse. It is *about* America and it is literally and figuratively addressed *to* America. But what is "America"? It is two – no – three things: 1) a "promise," a Promised Land, a Heaven-on-Earth; 2) a whore, a betrayal, a Hell-on-

Earth; and 3) an invisible republic or an unknown or unmapped country (both a geographical location and a society) in which nothing is settled and everything is up for grabs.

It's an ingenious schema, and very useful in the fields of musicology, cultural history and American Studies, but it begs important questions: is this geo-theological drama unique to America? or is it performed in/by other countries, as well? Does each country have its own unique geo-theo drama? or do the countries of the world share a few basic geo-theo dramas? How does religion – Dylan as a Jew, as a born-again Christian, as a Muslim (?) – figure in here?

None of this is resolved, and it kinda spoils the ending of *Like a Rolling Stone*:

> The unmapped country prophesied in 'Like a Rolling Stone' is still there too, hanging in the air as a territory of danger and flight, abandonment and discovery, truth and lie, but as [Dylan's song] 'Highlands' plays, there is the sense that no one has been there for years. The singer has long since traversed the country; he knows his way around. He wouldn't mind company, but he can do without it. Every once in a while he hears his old song on the radio, and the country is new again, that will have to do.

But this isn't enough, not in 2005,[10] when both #1 and #3 in the schema above (America as Paradise and America as unsettled territory) are vanishing and #2 (America as Hell) is becoming a worldwide reality – Abu Graib, Guantanamo Bay, officially sanctioned "extraordinary renditions" and torture, secret CIA prisons, etc ad nauseum.

One of the primary merits of *Like a Rolling Stone* is that it demonstrates so well that "Like a Rolling Stone" was a collaborative effort (not just between Dylan and his muse, but between these two and *all* of the other musicians on the track *and* the people who recorded, produced and mixed what the musicians played). But the book's ending is a vision of a solitary individual who can "do without" company. That is to say, it is a vision of America as it is today – a loner, a dusty cowboy, haunted by his own echoes, completely isolated from the rest of the world, and not particularly worried about it.

But what if America is no longer #1 with a bullet in the Top 40 of all-time great countries? What if America is, to quote "Anarchy in the UK," "just another country"? What if America, like God, Elvis, and rock 'n' roll itself, is dead? Could Dylan and "Like a Rolling Stone" be salvaged from the wreckage of America and embraced as citizens of the world, at home everywhere? Could Greil have written *Like a Rolling Stone* from the perspective of an internationalist, and not that of a specialist in American Studies?

[1] Appended to the Situationist International's English translation of "Decline and

Fall of the Spectacular-Commodity Society," December 1965. The full text of this "Summary" was recently translated into English for the first time.

[2] The graffiti in question here is "NEVER WORK," inscribed by Guy Debord on a street-wall in Paris in 1953 and cited ten years later as a "preliminary program of the [entire] situationist movement." One need not marvel at the "earliness" (March 1965) of Dylan's awareness of the existence of the Situationist International, which one might have expected to come after December 1966, that is, after the publication of "On the Poverty of Student Life" and the Strasbourg scandal. Note Allen Ginsberg's poem, "How to Make a March a Spectacle," also written and published in 1965: when asked about it in 1987, Ginsberg confirmed that at the time it was written, he'd certainly been aware of the situationists and their theory of the spectacle. No doubt both Dylan and Ginsberg learned of the SI through William S. Burroughs' friend, the ex-situationist Alexander Trocchi, who launched his "Project Sigma" in 1964. It doesn't really matter. The point is this: if Dylan knew about the situationists, why shouldn't one use situationist ideas and approaches to appreciate his music?

[3] In contrast, in the "Works Cited" section, Greil makes sure to let his readers know that some of the content in *Like A Rolling Stone* (Dylan's performances with the Hawks in 1965 and 1966) overlaps with that of *Invisible Republic: Bob Dylan's Basement Tapes* (1997).

[4] Unless I'm mistaken, the only other such book is Dave Marsh's book about "Louie Louie," but it (the book) is both thin and filled with padding. Both of Greil's books are thick and all-business. [I am in fact mistaken: there are entire books about such songs as "White Christmas," "Rock Around the Clock," "Strange Fruit," "Stack-O-Lee," and more. Thanks to Greil Marcus for the correction.]

[5] Greil astutely notes that the narrator himself surely knows how it feels, but he might not know what it *means*. His repeated refrain "How does it feel?" might actually ask, "What does it mean?" If so, the woman in the song, despite her fall, has learned something the narrator doesn't know, and so is "still" above him. (In *L'Anti-Oedpide*, Gilles Deleuze and Felix Guattari are not interested in "How does it feel?" or "How does it mean?" but "What does it do?" What does "Like a Rolling Stone" do? It stops and starts time; it recalls time and takes time; *it negates time*.)

[6] "[In 1965] the race was not only between the Beatles, Bob Dylan, the Rolling Stones, and everyone else. The pop world was in a race with the greater world, the world of wars and elections, work and leisure, poverty and riches, white people and black people, women and men – and in 1965 you could feel that the pop world was winning" (*Like a Rolling Stone*). One might say that, in *Lipstick Traces,* you can feel both worlds collapsing.

[7] Elsewhere in *Like a Rolling Stone,* he writes that, "If society did not raise itself as a single brave, terrified soul and leave itself behind, sometimes, listening to Dylan's voice as everything around him dropped away, as the demonic, despairing figure in the song threw off everything around itself, you could imagine that

society had done just that. If people did not leave their homes to travel the roads making speeches and barbeque – though many did, and many already had – you could hear intimations of that, too. Or you could hear that event in its absence, as if, in its failure to instantly *change the world*, unlike any recording before it 'Like a Rolling Stone' had proved that that was precisely what a work of art was supposed to do, and the standard by which a work of art should be judged" (emphasis added).

[8] In the "Works Cited" section of *Like a Rolling Stone,* Greil describes an essay he wrote in May 1985 ("Number One with a Bullet") as "mean-spirited." You can't tell if he's joking or not.

[9] In *The Invisible Republic,* Greil quotes a question that Dylan once asked an interviewer in 1968: "How do you know that I'm not, as you say, for the war?" This is how we know.

[10] Relevant here is the myth of the American frontier, which was both a place and a weird socio-theological process in which so-called savages (native Americans) were supposedly transformed or converted into civilized beings, and ex-Europeans were supposedly transformed into Americans, *real* Americans. The question today would be what it had been back in 1890: Is the American frontier still open, or has it finally closed? Looking back to 1965, to Dylan's "Like a Rolling Stone," it seems that the American frontier was still open. But in mid-2003, when he was writing *Like A Rolling Stone,* Greil Marcus obviously found that something was bothering him, something was preventing him from peopling "the unmapped country," from imagining that "the unmapped country" was full of people. Did he sense that, in the forty years since Dylan's song, the American frontier had indeed finally closed? Did the myth of the Frontier finally expire when Bush, the Warrior Cowboy, attacked Afghanistan in October 2001?

NOT BORED! #38, October 2006

Pitying Paul Virilio

It isn't particularly easy to read Paul Virilio's books. He writes in French, and it is difficult to translate his idiosyncratic puns, metaphors and neologisms into English. He doesn't really write books, though he has certainly published a great many texts. Virilio mainly writes articles and essays; he reads aloud papers he's written at conferences; and he gives in-depth interviews. Various collections of these furtive texts have been assembled and published as books that are often very short and, in the English translations, not illustrated. Finally, Virilio tends to develop his themes slowly, across the span of several books, which makes it especially difficult for the newcomer to enter into his discourse, which dates back to the late 1970s (he was born in 1932). But Virilio needs to be read. He is the only post-World War II radical French theorist to write extensively on the inter-related subjects of war, the military, speed, and the acceleration of time, and his writings are uniquely useful in describing and theorizing terrorism, militarism, and September 11th.

Most recently, there's this weird little book called *Art and Fear* (Continuum, London/New York, 2003). Composed of two short texts, "A Pitiless Art" and "Silence on Trial," and only 61 pages long, it was originally published in 2000 by Editions Galilee under the title *La Procedure Silence* ("The Silence Procedure"). In 2002, the book was translated into English by Julie Rose, who had previously translated Virilio's *The Art of the Motor* (University of Minnesota Press, 1995). Slender as it is – no price listed, but my copy cost an unmerciful $15 – this volume is also absurdly padded out. Not only does it contain a two-page-long translator's preface, a bibliography of works cited and an index, but also a completely unnecessary thirteen-page-long "introduction" by John Armitage, who is clearly uncomfortable with the book itself or this particular line of thought in Virilio's books. And so Armitage feels compelled to offer various defensive responses to what commentators on the book might claim about it. When all is said and done, *Art and Fear* contains a mere 35 pages of worthwhile material. But this material is so strong and provocative that it is more than worth the difficulty of obtaining it.

In "A Pitiless Art," Virilio reports that, "as [the] sole explanation" for staging *The World of Bodies* exhibition at the Mannheim Museum of Technology and Work in 1998 – it is in fact on display here in New York City as I write these very words – the German anatomist-turned-contemporary-artist Gunther von Hagens "resorted to the modern buzzword: 'It's about breaking the last remaining taboos,' he says." It is precisely the overlap of modern science (in this case, necrology) and modern art that Virilio finds so distressing. Modern art is no longer the only field in which the deliberate breaking of taboos is the central motivation. It now appears in fields as disparate and socially important as commercial advertising; sports, pornography, music and other activities that privilege "performance" and increasingly rely upon specialized pharmaceuticals (Viagra, Human Growth Hormones, steroids, amphetamines and so forth); scientific research, but especially in the fields of bio-technology, genetic modifications, mutations, and cloning; and the strategic planning and execution of military campaigns. Each one of these fields is, in its way, an extreme art that seeks to "shock and awe." Taken together, these various fields constitute a kind of *official art*, indeed, the official, State-sponsored art of the twenty-first century.

Precisely because modern art has been so successful in convincing nearly everyone that there should be no limits to freedom of expression – up to and including *the call to murder and torture* – this official art is terrorist, lethal and inhuman. It is best likened to the experiments performed by the Nazis' artist/doctors at Auschwitz-Birkenau. Over the course of a few dense pages, Virilio writes:

Having *broken the taboos* of suffocating bourgeois culture, we are now supposed to *break the being,* the unicity of mankind, through the impending explosion of a genetic bomb that will be to biology what the atomic bomb was to physics [...] *Ethics or aesthetics*? That is indeed the question at the dawn of the millennium. If freedom of SCIENTIFIC expression now actually has no more limits than freedom of ARTISTIC expression, where will *inhumanity* end in [the] future? [...] Ethical boundary, aesthetic boundary of sport as of art. Without limits, there is no value; without value, there is no esteem, no respect and especially no pity: *death to the referee!* You know how it goes.

Citing Charles Baudelaire – whose poem "The Man Who Tortures Himself" (*Les Fleurs du Mal,* as translated by William Aggeler) proclaims "I am the wound and the dagger! / I am the blow and the cheek! / I am the members and the wheel, Victim and executioner!" – Virilio asks, "How can we fail to see that, in the wake of the hecatomb of the Great War [...] modern art for its part forgot about the wound and concentrated on the knife – the bayonet." That is to say, after WWI, modern art become absolutely pitiless: it inflicted suffering, and had no empathy for its victims. Punning – perhaps somewhat clumsily or in a way that can't easily be translated into English – Virilio claims that one of modern art's pieties is to be without pity. As a result, modern art – especially that which calls itself "contemporary art" – is complicit in the terrorism of everyday life and should be denounced. Either it "indirectly promot[ed] the rise of TOTALITARIANISM" or, after the rise and *apparent defeat* of totalitarianism, it started openly mimicking and adopting its aesthetics, especially the aesthetics of the concentration camp. For Virilio, it hardly matters which. Either way, so-called contemporary art is only *contemporary with* the multi-media arts experimented with at the concentration camps: "Whether Adorno likes it or not," – Virilio says, in response to Theodor Adorno's famous insistence that writing poetry after Auschwitz would be barbaric – "the spectacle of abjection remains the same, after as before Auschwitz. But it has become politically incorrect to say so."

This is as much a moral judgment as it is an intellectual analysis. Its politics? They would seem, at first glance, to be right-wing. Virilio marshals a great many allusions and examples, most of which are well-chosen and end up confirming his point, a few of which are badly chosen and end up contradicting him or even making him seem like a bit of a crackpot. He is right on target when he attacks body-oriented performance artists and the videos that document their self-imposed tortures; multi-media presentations or installations of live TV images of calamities and terrible suffering; and the "sonorization" of perception (see below). But his remarks about Guy Debord are ludicrous.

Book reviews

> Avant-garde artists, like so many political agitators, propagandists and demagogues, have long understood what TERRORISM would soon popularize: if you want a place in 'revolutionary history' there is nothing easier than provoking a riot, an assault on propriety, in the guise of art. Short of committing a real crime by killing innocent passers-by with a bomb, the pitiless contemporary author of the twentieth century attacks symbols, the very meaning of a 'pitiful' art he assimilates to 'academicism.' Take Guy Debord, the French Situationist, as an example. In 1952, speaking about his *Film Without Images,* which is a defense of the Marquis de Sade, Debord claimed he wanted to kill the cinema *'because it was easier than killing a passer-by.'*
>
> A year later, in 1953, the SITUATIONISTS would not hesitate to extend this attack by trashing Charlie Chaplin, *pitiful actor par excellence,* vilifying him as a sentimental fraud, a mastermind of misery, even a proto-fascist!
>
> All this verbal delirium seems so oblivious of its own century and yet condescends to preach to the rest of the world in the name of freedom of artistic expression, even during a historical period that oversaw the setting up of the *balance of terror* along with the opening of the laboratories of a science that was gearing up to programme the end of the world – notably with the invention, in 1951, of thermonuclear weapons. It corresponds equally to *the auto-dissolution of the avant-gardes,* the end of the grand illusion of a *modernite savante.*

Obviously Virilio doesn't know what the fuck he's talking about. Debord's film without images was in fact entitled *Hurlements en Faveur de Sade* and was hardly a "defense" of the Marquis. In 1953, the Situationist International had not yet been founded, and Debord was in fact a "left-wing" lettrist, that is, a member of the Lettrist International. Debord was in fact hyper-aware of his century, detested "artistic expression," etc etc. It would obviously be easy to be pitiless in one's (counter) attack on Virilio: Debord himself certainly would have been.[1]

Despite these problems, Virilio has certainly convinced us of this much – to quote George Bernanos, writing in 1939:

> The world is sick, a lot sicker than people realize. That's what we must first acknowledge so that we can take pity on it. We shouldn't condemn this world so much as feel sorry for it. The world needs pity. Only pity has a chance of cobbling its pride.

"Sixty years on," Virilio says, "the world is sicker still," and "pride has gotten completely out of hand, thanks to globalization." To which we can only say, *Amen,*

Brother.

In the second text, "Silence on Trial," Virilio examines the extent to which sound, music and noise are involved in or implicated by the emergence of the official art of the Twenty-First century. He reminds us that the photograph was always silent; that the cinematograph was, at first, silent, and then started "sounding" (the birth of the "talkies"); and that the videograph (the "televised" image) was, from the start, a live synchronization of image-track and sound-track. What's been ignored in these well-known developments, Virilio notes, is the fact that silence has disappeared and can't readily be found in contemporary society. "From the end of the 1920s onwards," he asserts, "the idea of accepting the absence of words or phrases, of some kind of dialogue, became unthinkable." Today, Virilio contends, "silence no longer has a voice [...] The voices of silence have been silenced; what is now regarded as obscene is not so much the image as the sound – or, rather, the lack of sound [...] Warhol does not so much document the end of art as the end of the man of art: *he who speaks even as he remains silent*."

In this hundred-year-long procedure, which seems to have culminated in the condemnation of silence, Edvard Munch's painting, *The Scream* (1883) stands out. In this famous canvas, Virilio says, "Munch tried to puff up the [silent] painted image with a sort of SOUND RELIEF, which was until that moment the sole province of music and its attendant notations." In other words, influenced by the power of then-contemporary music, Munch tried to make the viewer want to *hear* the scream and not just "see" it, or see it represented. (Virilio also cites Kandinsky's interest in Wagner's music and Kandinsky's statement that "the clearer the abstract element of form, the purer, the more elementary, the sound.") But in neither example did the viewer of the painting ever feel him- or herself deficient in some way, *deaf*, as if he or she couldn't hear the actual, the real scream. Things changed with the advent of the talkies in 1927. Virilio asserts that "When Al Jolson [...] launched his celebrated 'Hello mammy' in the first talking film, he was answering the unarticulated scream of Edvard Munch." Yes, he was metaphorically answering *The Scream* (giving voice to it and answering it back), but he was also *putting on trial* all those who had not been able to hear that scream, who must have been deaf *not* to have heard it.

As if to shame or punish those who were or still are deaf, or to reassure one and all that at least *it* can hear perfectly well, contemporary art makes as much noise as it possibly can. Today, everything is either accompanied by soundscapes/music (art exhibitions and installations of all kinds, Muzak-polluted elevator rides, even screenings of "silent" films) or expressed as sound/music (a voice that announces, "You've got mail"). Everyone – or at least every contemporary artist since Andy Warhol collaborated with the Velvet Underground – wants to be rock star, a *singer,* especially. Virilio or, rather, his translator, refers to this incredibly widespread phenomenon – it's more than mere noise pollution, and appears to be a kind of socio-technological obsession – as "sonorization." As one knows, this word doesn't really exist in English; the words that are close to it (such as "sonorous") suggest sounds that are harmonious, but this works against Virilio's point, which is not only how much "sound" there is these days, but how noisy it is, too. In French, *sonorisation* denotes either a public-address system or a movie soundtrack, both of which are relevant here: everything has a sound-track, and it is always played loud, so as to drown out everything else.

Today, silence – if or when it exists – signifies nothing, nothing, that is, but consent. "No silence can express disapproval or resistance, only consent," Virilio notes; "whoever says nothing is deemed to consent." The significance of this turn will not be lost on readers of Virilio's *Speed and Politics, The Strategy of Deception*[2] or any of his other texts that focus on the political repercussions of near instantaneous military response-times, which amount to this: *there isn't enough time* to ask every member of the Joint Chiefs of Staff, or every member-state of NATO, if they each approve of a particular rapid-strike (based, as always, upon "timely" intelligence); there's only enough time for them to disapprove. He who speaks up always speaks to say "No," and everyone else is assumed to say "Yes." But neither Virilio, his translator, nor John Armitage make this connection, and so it will likely escape most readers of *Art and Fear*: militarist and artistic sonorization go hand-in-hand.[3]

It is interesting that Virilio mentions music ("you can bet that soon, thanks to digital technology, *electro-acoustic* music will generate new forms of visual art") but he doesn't seem to realize that music is important enough to discuss at some length. If the presentation of reality is indeed being sonorized, then the role of music properly speaking would appear to be central. The music of composers who have tried to create or at least appreciate the musical qualities of silence (chiefly John Cage, but also Erik Satie),[4] or composers who tried to make music that was so deliberately noisy or anarchic that it was practically or actually unlistenable (John Cage's "Variations II" or Lou Reed's *Metal Machine Music*), would appear to be of particular interest. But Virilio lets it all go.

In a circumstance that might be familiar to readers of Virilio's other books, it is "A Pitiless Art" – and not "Silence on Trial" – that contains a really stunning (but brief, too brief!) discussion of music. In the context of a discussion of the disappearance of ephemerality due to the 20th century's socio-technological mania to record, digitize and make everything permanent, Virilio brings on a famous musician to discuss the related disappearance of analog recordings.

> *All the music you hear these days is just electricity!* [emphasis in original]. You can't hear the singer breathing anymore behind this electronic wall. You can't hear a heart beating anymore. Go to any bar and listen to a blues group and you'll be touched, moved. Then listen to the same group on a CD and you'll wonder where the sound you heard in the bar *disappeared* to [emphasis added].

It's a very good point, one worthy of extended discussion, perhaps an entire piece devoted to contemporary music. But Virilio misplays this point when he introduces it with, "Things have reached such a pitch that a *pitiful* musician par excellence like Bob Dylan can bemoan the fact that [...]" Yes, Bob Dylan has pity on a great many down-trodden peoples, which means he is full of pity ("pitiful") and thus open to the complaint or brush-off that he personally is pitiful – *but is this really the time to bring all this up?* No, it is not, and so some confusion is caused and a few interesting questions get ignored. Are pitiful musicians the only ones upset about the disappearance of the analog? What has Dylan, a practicing musician, done to combat the digitalization or, if you will, 'sonorization' of his own music? etc.

There is, of course, a single and fairly thick thread that not only connects "A Pitiless Art" with "Silence on Trial," but also connects these essays with those Virilio has been writing since the early 1990s: the theme of the disappearance of representation (cf. *The Aesthetics of Disappearance,* published in French in 1991). Both pitiless, taboo-breaking art and silence-killing sonorization seek to present reality unmediated, not to re-present it or mediate its appearance; both seek to negate deferrals and delays, and to be instantaneously, perpetually present. In "A Pitiless Art," Virilio warns that this is "a situation that reinforces the dreadful decline of *representative democracy* in favor of a democracy based on the rule of opinion, in anticipation of the imminent arrival of *virtual democracy,* some kind of 'direct democracy' or, more precisely, a *presentative* multimedia democracy based on automatic polling." And, in "Silence on Trial," he fears that "the way that pressure from the media audience ensures that crime and pornography never cease dominating AUDIO-VISUAL programmes [...] the bleak dawn of the twentieth century was not only to inaugurate the crisis in figurative representation, but along with it, the crisis in *social stability* without which representative democracy in turn disappears."

Now, while we *might* agree that the disappearance of figurative representation implicates or threatens all representation, all political representation, including representative democracy – which supposedly governs the hyper-industrialized capitalist nations in North America, Europe, Australia, Japan, Israel, et al. – we might *not* agree that this is a bad drift of events. Same thing with "social instability." If we are anarchists, council communists or even situationists, we might find this drift quite encouraging![5] And that would be because, unlike Virilio, we do not associate or confuse direct democracy with a slide into "virtual democracy" or "multi-media democracy based on automatic polling." For us, direct democracy is something practiced *in-person,* in large, on-going public assemblies, at which everyone gets to speak as well as to listen, and everyone gets to vote and decide. Democracy can exist and function perfectly well without representation! But it would take a revolution and that's the rub: Virilio doesn't believe in revolution. "Those days are long gone," he says. "No one is waiting any more for the REVOLUTION, only for the ACCIDENT, the breakdown, that will reduce this unbearable chatter to silence." But does Virilio know of any contemporary revolutionaries? Forget Guy Debord, obviously. Virilio – who only gives himself one crack at it – goes with a "former revolutionary," someone named Ieng-Sary, "who today declares, apparently by way of excuse, 'The world has changed. I no longer believe in the class struggle. The period from 1975 to 1979 was a failure. We went from utopia to barbarity.'" And who is this disillusioned person? Someone in some way relevant to representative democracies, one presumes. Virilio doesn't tell us, but Ieng-Sary was the infamous head of the Khmer Rouge's "Foreign Ministry," that is, a murderer and torturer, and so not a fair choice, by any stretch. So, let's begin again. . . .

[1] Note well that Vincent Kaufmann's recent biography – *Guy Debord: Revolution in the Service of Poetry,* translated from the French by Robert Bononno, University of Minnesota Press, 2006 – praises Debord for precisely the thing that Virilio would condemn, namely, his aesthetics of disappearance.
[2] See my review of *The Strategy of Deception,* dated 25-26 June 2004.
[3] Recent installations by the Cincinnati-based contemporary arts group SimpArch incorporate recordings of sonic 'booms' made by high-speed military aircraft as a kind of accompaniment, background music or soundscape.
[4] William S. Burroughs strove to de-sonorize the spoken word and thereby produce (more) silence. See, especially, *The Ticket That Exploded* (Grove, NY: 1967).
[5] For example: I do not equate *noise* with the end of civilization. See my essay "Unanswered questions about 'rough music'."

NOT BORED! #38, October 2006

Paul Virilio: Another Dupe of the 'War against Terrorism'

Paul Virilio makes a few good points about "the doctrine of security" in *Popular Defense & Ecological Struggles,* a short book that was originally published in French in 1978, translated into English by Mark Polizzotti, and published by Semiotext(e) in 1990. Noting that France was already "considering merging police information with military intelligence," and that "turnstile-hopping is now likened to much more serious crimes, such as assault and vandalism," Virilio predicts that the nations of Europe "will try to initiate a new unanimity of need, a permanent feeling of insecurity which will lead to a new kind of consumption: *the consumption of protection.*" In such a situation, he concludes, "we find [...], completely normalized, the conditions of the state of siege of military security."

Virilio based these predictions – which have obviously been borne out by the post-September 11th waging of the "Global War on Terrorism" – upon the way in which the nations of Europe responded to the emergence in the early 1970s of so-called Euro-terrorism, that is, terrorist attacks allegedly carried out by domestic groups, such as the Red Brigades (Italy) and the Red Army Faction (Germany). "Since there is Euro-terrorism," Virilio quotes the French Minister of Justice, Alain Peyrefitte, as saying; "then let the struggle against terrorism know no borders!" Virilio is very clear on the fact that such a struggle is deeply cynical and a convenient cover for other, even more cynical strategies:

> They are stretching the repression of Euroterrorism to include the industrial as well as the criminal. During the French electric company strikes of December 1977, the term "union terrorism" was frequently heard. But, in 1975, in Germany, they had already set up a crisis headquarters to deal with the strike in the Ford auto plants.

In other words, the economy of security – the deliberate production of "insecurity" and the consumption of "protection" – is simply a way for capitalism to protect itself when it is threatened by proletarian subversion.

But the problem with Virilio's analysis is the simple fact that "Euro-terrorism" was *not* the product of ultra-leftist revolutionaries, but the product of the capitalist State itself. In other words, unlike Gianfranco Sanguinetti,[1] Virilio believes everything that he's been told about the Red Brigades. First and foremost, he believes that the Red Brigades continued to exist after 1970, and were not quickly infiltrated and then completely taken over by the Italian secret services. Virilio finds nothing weird about the fact that, as he says, "Renato Curcio, 'historic leader of the Red Brigades,'" was "also a former neo-Fascist in the *Ordre Nouveau* group." Virilio seems to know absolutely nothing about NATO's anti-Communist "Operation Stay-Behind," its Italian branch ("Gladio"), or the role of the P2 Lodge. He seems to think that it was by accident or mere coincidence that Euro-terrorism was used to launch and maintain a state of permanent insecurity. "In 1977," he writes, "the terrorism which *providentially* sustained the international repression and systems of mass incrimination praised by the various media already afforded a glimpse of this kind of asocial organization" (emphasis in original). But, perhaps worst of all, Virilio believes the exact same lie that was used by Italian prosecutors to arrest, convict and imprison such theorists as Tony Negri:[2] "the Autonomists," he says, "destroy the transmitters of State television networks, obstruct roads and railways, blow up tax offices and airports in Corsica, in Brittany. . . ."

As a result, *Popular Defense & Ecological Struggles* does nothing to help us in these days of Al-Qaeda-style terrorism, which is also – and obviously so – the creation of the very State that claims that it is under sustained attack. But this shitty little book *does* help us explain why Virilio has never taken the revolutionary movement seriously. (Note for example the weaknesses of the recent collection entitled *Art and Fear*.)[3] To him, technology is the only agent of change: "When the European revolutionaries in the nineteenth century claimed that *to control the streets is to control the State*, they had no idea of the technological way in which they would in fact lose both the streets and the State at the same time!" Virilio takes this idea to ridiculous extremes: "And, in 1868, Gambetta was already denouncing Louis-Napoleon's *coup d'etat* as having depended on 'the new means of communication that science has placed in the hands of men: the telegraph and the steam engine.'" And so, far from being a technophobe,[4] Paul Virilio is a technological determinist.

[1] See especially the pamphlet he wrote with Guy Debord in 1975: *On the Last Chances to Save Capitalism in Italy.*
[2] See our comments entitled "The relevance of Antonio Negri to the Anti-globalization Movement."
[3] See our review of this text, especially its concluding paragraph.
[4] Joseph Nechvatal, review of Virilio's "Unknown Quantities," in *Film-Philosophy*, vol. 6, no. 47, November 2002.

NOT BORED! #38, October 2006

McDonough and *October* on Guy Debord, Again

In 1997, someone named Thomas F. McDonough edited a special issue of *October* that focused upon "Guy Debord and the *Internationale situationniste*."[1] This collection had an announced agenda: to provide a counter-weight to Ken Knabb's *Situationist International Anthology* (1981), which, as Knabb himself says, is "admittedly weighted somewhat toward the situationists' later, more 'political' period." But McDonough's special issue of *October*, though it focused on the situationists' earlier, more "artistic" period, wasn't really weighty enough to offer an effective counter-balance to Knabb's massive *Anthology*. And so, in 2002, *October* expanded the collection and published it as a 500-page-long, illustrated tome entitled *Guy Debord and the Situationist International: Texts and Documents*. Its editor: Tom McDonough.

Centered around 1958, the year the first issue of *Internationale Situationniste* came out, this book certainly reveals a few glaring omissions from Knabb's collection: the complete text of Debord's 1957 "Report on the Construction of Situations," (Knabb only offered excerpts);[2] Debord's "Theses on the Cultural Revolution" (1958); the unattributed "Critique of Urbanism"

(1961); and Raoul Vaneigem's "Comments Against Urbanism" (1961). But Knabb is not just "countered" as an editor, but as a translator, as well. McDonough ignores Knabb's translations of such early, cultural texts as the "Report on the Construction of Situations," "All the King's Men" (1963) and "The Situationists and the New Forms of Action in Art and Politics" (1963), and either brings in other translators (John Shepley or Thomas Y. Levin) or translates the texts himself.[3]

But Knabb's *Anthology* holds its own against this onslaught. Though it *is* in fact more heavily weighted towards the SI's second period (1962-1971) than its first (1957-1961), Knabb's book still provides a good selection of early documents, some of them produced well before 1957. But McDonough's book only offers *four* texts written after 1963: Theo Frey's "Perspectives for a Generation" (1966), Mustapha Khayati's "Captive Words" (1966), Rene Vienet's "The Situationists and the New Forms of Action against Politics and Art" (1967), and the unattributed "Cinema and Revolution" (1969). With the exception of the unremarkable essay by Theo Frey, which was only included, perhaps, because Frey was excluded from the SI,[4] all of these texts were already available in Knabb's *Anthology*. None of them are major contributions to the situationist project.

Here's the kicker: although Tom McDonough provides an introduction to the big and weak volume that he's put together, he's no longer interested in Ken Knabb's *Situationist International Anthology* nor in rectifying its over-emphasis of the SI's later, political period at the expense of its earlier, artistic period. Tom McDonough has *moved on*. "This introduction is meant polemically," he writes,

> as an initial foray into new interpretive territory, as a suggestion for moving beyond the stale categories into which we have compartmentalized our thought on the Situationist International. Those categories – of avant-garde purity, or of chronological and ideological division ('artistic' versus 'political' phases or wings) – now simply hinder any understanding of this group; it is time to move beyond them.

Tom McDonough is not Thomas F. McDonough and *harrumph!* Tom McDonough is not interested in what Thomas F. McDonough was interested in way back in 1997. Tom McDonough is interested in what he calls "a 'Tafurian' critique of situationist positions" – 'Tafuri' being Manfredo Tafuri, an Italian architect (1935-1994) and the author of *Architecture and Utopia* (MIT Press, 1976). And so the reader is confronted with a *double* deflection. First, there's a deflection away from Knabb's political preoccupations and (back) towards the SI's early, artistic period; and then a deflection away from the SI *as a whole* and towards Manfredo Tafuri's critique of artistic avant-gardes. But fast-moving Tom McDonough didn't update the body of his book to keep pace with the bold initiatives of his "Introduction: Ideology and the Situationist Utopia." Not one of the ten critical essays that he includes in his book mentions Tafuri or the relevance of his "critique" to the situationists. Tom McDonough moved on, but he forgot to take his book with him. And so it just sits there, thick as a brick.

An introductory essay should make us want to read what follows it; but McDonough's introduction doesn't. More like a negative essay that *might* be included in a volume (as a counter-weight to more positive evaluations) than a neutral or objective essay that introduces the volume as a whole, McDonough's introduction is a hatchet job masquerading as a "critique." It openly accuses the situationists of *unintentionally* working on the side of "the police," socioeconomic rationalization, and the Stalinist "planification" of the future. So poisonous are these outright lies that McDonough feels compelled to reassure his readers that "This 'Tafurian' critique of situationist positions is not intended as a blanket dismissal, needless to say." The situationists didn't intend to work for the police, and Tafuri didn't intend to blow their cover, *but* . . . . Should we be surprised that the arbitrary and clearly political drift of McDonough's stewardship of these "Texts and Documents" didn't raise any red flags at *October* or the MIT Press? Maybe not. After all, McDonough is certainly not the first academic scholar we've encountered who is openly torn between his resentment of (and ignorance about) Debord and the SI, and his need to make a living by continuously discovering *new* things to "historicize" and "interpret."[5]

Not surprisingly, the justification for McDonough's "Tafurian" critique of the situationists lies in an obvious, perhaps even intentional misunderstanding of their ideas.[6] According to McDonough, *everyone* – Tafuri, even Marx himself – agrees that "Constant revolutionizing of production, uninterrupted disturbance of all social conditions, everlasting uncertainty and agitation distinguish the bourgeois epoch from all earlier ones." But Guy Debord, says McDonough, identified "the salient characteristic of bourgeois society" with "what he called in a telling phrase 'a freezing of life.'" Later McDonough will refer to something of his own invention, i.e., the situationists' "belief in capitalism's fundamentally static, affirmative quality," which allows him to proclaim that, "What is at issue here is the potential misrecognition on the part of the Situationist International of the role of the avant-garde in advanced capitalist society; rather than being the latter's absolute contestation, Tafuri raised the possibility that it was this society's necessary adjunct."

But here McDonough is moving (away) too fast and speaking too generally. As always, Debord was historically specific when he spoke about "a freezing of life." The phrase didn't pertain to *all* of bourgeois society, at all stages of its development, but to bourgeois society since the 1930s. And Debord carefully distinguished between a freezing of history, a freezing of "life" as lived experience, and the continuing and continuous flow of "revolutionary" new commodities, fads and ideologies. It was precisely this split that made real revolution necessary and desirable, and that suggested ways of bringing that revolution about. Furthermore, the situationists didn't "misrecognize" the "role of the avant-garde in advanced capitalist society." From the beginning, they were extremely critical of Dadaism and Surrealism[7] – in all his talk of Tafuri's critique of artistic avant-gardes, McDonough gives the erroneous impression that the Situationists uncritically followed or repeated Dada's gestures – and this is precisely why they eventually started conceiving of themselves as a properly revolutionary organization, *not* as an avant-garde group. But of course one won't find a reprint of Debord's "Minimum Definitions of a Revolutionary Organization" (1966) in Tom McDonough's book – it's got nuthin' to do with art, dontcha know.

[1] *October* #79, Winter 1997. See *NOT BORED!* #27, May 1997.
[2] Knabb's worse offense as an editor is certainly his replacement of sometimes lengthy passages with ellipses [...] Note my recent translations of "How Situationist Books Are Not Understood" and "Remarks on the SI Today," both of which Knabb did not translate in full.
[3] Knabb may be not be a good editor, but he's a pretty good translator: that is to say, he doesn't make really egregious mistakes. For example, McDonough titles his translation of Debord's *Le Grand Sommeil et Ses Clients* (from 1955) "The Great [sic] Sleep and Its Clients," as if he's never heard of the Howard Hawkes classic 1946 film, *The Big Sleep* (Debord assuredly had).
[4] See "The Alsatian Ideology," in *Internationale Situationniste* #11, October 1967.
[5] See our review of Simon Sadler's pathetic book *The Situationist City* (1998).
[6] Note the obvious manner in which McDonough carefully maintains his own confusion about what only he insists is "that murky differentiation" between the SI and the police, which, he says, "was described as follows . . . in 'Now, the SI': 'The path of complete police control over all human activities and the path of infinite free creation of all human activities is one: it is the same path of modern discoveries.' The confusion that this might engender was little dispelled by adding that 'we are inevitably on the same path as our enemies – most often preceding them – but we must be there, without any confusion, *as enemies*.' The same path, a shared race, a mutual goal: how could one not be confused?" But only McDonough insists on maintaining that these *enemies* have "a mutual goal" (when clearly they don't) and so he is the only one who is confused.
[7] See, for example, Guy Debord's comments about the avant-garde in his letter to Robert Estivals dated 15 March 1963.

NOT BORED! #38, October 2006

Book reviews

Elizabeth Byrne Ferm's
Freedom in Education

In fact, the truths set forth or the facts recorded must be endorsed and supported by man's own experience before man can appreciate or understand them. Words become living agencies as soon as they express the thing we know to be true. The words of the writer may be used to convey a live thought, a spiritual message, but if we are unprepared mentally and spiritually, there is no thought exchange or spiritual message transferred to us. Look, observe, think and assimilate and thus create your own book. – Elizabeth Byrne Ferm

Over the course of the last year or so, Factory School has published many interesting books, two of which are closely related: *Freedom in Education,* by Elizabeth Byrne Ferm (2005), and *The Modern School of Stelton: A Sketch,* by several different authors (2006). The latter was originally published in 1925 by the Modern School Association of North America, which intended to celebrate the tenth anniversary of its founding of the first libertarian school for children in the United States. Reprinted by Factory School in its entirety, complete with the original photographic illustrations, *The Modern School of Stelton* was mostly written by Joseph J. Cohen, who had been instrumental in re-locating the Modern School from New York City, where it had been founded in 1911 as an outgrowth of the anarchist-inspired Francisco Ferrer Center, to Stelton, New Jersey. (The Ferrer Center stayed in New York City, where it was dissolved in 1918.) Another contributor to *The Modern School of Stelton* was Alexis C. Ferm, who had been – along with his wife, Elizabeth Byrne Ferm – brought in to be the school's principals between 1920 and 1925, and then again in 1933. The book also includes short essays by Harry Kelly and Leonard D. Abbott, who had been the Ferrer Center's first Chairman and President, respectively.

It is interesting that Elizabeth Ferm, or Elizabeth Bryne, as she is sometimes called, isn't given very much attention in these histories of the Modern School. Harry Kelly doesn't mention her at all; Joseph Cohen and Leonard Abbott only mention her in passing. She is, of course, mentioned several times by Alex Ferm, but once again only in passing; he offers no sustained portrait or appreciation of her efforts. One might get the impression from all this that Elizabeth was a relatively minor figure, and perhaps only mentioned because of her husband. But that impression would be quite incorrect: *Freedom in Education* shows her to be a groundbreaking theorist and an excellent writer. Thanks to Factory School, she is no longer an unread or forgotten author.

Apparently a series of essays written for *The Modern School* magazine in the 1920s, *Freedom of Education* was originally prepared for publication by Alex and first printed by Lear Publishers (New York) in 1949, five years after Elizabeth's death. The Factory School edition of the book reprints the original text, which included a biographical note on the author by Alex, plus "The Spirit of Freedom," a short text that Elizabeth published in *The Modern School* magazine three years before she joined the endeavor at Stelton. It is an excellent collection: without announcing itself as such – there is no preface or introduction of any kind – *Freedom in Education* is a major contribution to the fields of infant development, children's education, and libertarian social theory.[1]

One of the striking things about "The Spirit of Freedom" is that, despite its date of publication (October, 1917), it does not refer to the Bolsheviks. Nor does it refer to Lenin, Marx, Bakunin, Nietzsche, Goodwin, Stirner, Proudhon or any other anarcho-communist writer. Perhaps Elizabeth Bryne sees all of these men as mere reformers: "If reformers could inaugurate or legislate into existence a perfect social and economic state of Society," she writes, "we should nevertheless fail to realize any real benefit or permanent change." The problem with reformism is the fact that "a free state – to be permanent – must evolve from a free people. We cannot bestow free conditions," which "must be worked for and established consciously." Compounding the problem is the fact that "A simple natural state could not be enjoyed by Society today." So-called adults, "who have not expressed themselves self-actively since babyhood, would feel awkward and perplexed in a natural condition." In short, "A free Society, a free condition, would naturally result [only] from a spontaneously self-active, self-employed, self-directing body of humans." To create this new "body of humans," one must start – not with the adults, the teens, nor even the children – but with *the infants,* the only ones in whom "the instinct and impulse for freedom" is completely un-self-conscious and unrestrained. "If we succeed in fostering the instinct and impulse of freedom which the infant reveals, we may reasonably count on building a free Society," Bryne says, to conclude her revolutionary manifesto.

For her, the only source of inspiration seems to lie in the work and example of the man she refers to simply as "Froebel," never giving his first name. A "successor" to "the educator, Pestalozzi," this Froebel is the only one to have "based his whole educational work upon a close study of the simple mother with her first born" (so says "The Spirit of Freedom"). Froebel is also mentioned several times in the pages of *Freedom in Education,* but once again without saying who is he, what he's written, whether he's alive or not, etc. It's as if we are supposed to know who he is. Ahhhh, yes: Froebel!

Friedrich Froebel (1782-1852) was in fact the inventor of the kindergarten, for which he laid the theoretical groundwork in 1826, when he published *Die Menschenerziehung*. The first German kindergartens were established between 1837 and 1840. It appears that, as far as American educators go, Froebel and the German kindergarten system were discovered by Susan Blow, a member of the St. Louis Philosophical Society, while she was on holiday in Germany in 1870. Like Blow and the other St. Louis philosophers, Froebel was strongly influenced by the work of GWF Hegel (1770-1831), particularly his writings on education and history. Susan Blow was so impressed that, upon her return to the United States, she began to campaign for an American kindergarten system, which was begun – under her auspices – in 1873, with the creation of the Des Peres School in Carondelet, Missouri. The idea caught on, thanks in part to a timely translation of Froebel's book into English, under the title *The Education of Man* (1877). In 1889, Susan Blow moved to New York City, where, among other activities, she translated the prose sections of Froebel's *Mutter- und Koselieder* (originally published in 1844) into English as *Mother Play* (1895) and wrote *Letters to a Mother on the Philosophy of Froebel* (1899).

The year that Susan Blow arrived in New York (1889) was also a significant one for Elizabeth Bryne. Born Mary Elizabeth Bryne in Illinois in 1857, she moved to New York to open a bookstore with her first husband, Martin Battle, in 1877. After they separated, Elizabeth got a degree in piano from the New York Conservatory of Music (1885), and became active in the struggles against poverty and in favor of women's rights.

In the late 1880s, her sister died after a long illness and Elizabeth decided to adopt and take care of her two infant children. "To do the job properly," Alex Ferm says in his biographical note on his wife, whom he married in 1898, "she resolved to take a course in child education." Elizabeth's studies were greatly enriched and deepened by the facts that, technically speaking, she had no children of her own and thus no "ulterior motive" nor "self-interest" in their education and development. She writes in *Freedom of Education* that,

> It is said of Darwin that he watched and studied frogs for twenty years. When shall we be able to tell of having studied children for so long, not only in the study room or on paper, but in the open of the child's own life? And studied without any ulterior motive, without self-interest, except the one great interest that should ever unite adulthood and childhood – the unity of life. The test for earnest seekers after truth – no matter what field – is, keep your hands off! Wait and observe the life in its freedom, and the truth will be revealed to you.

In 1899, Elizabeth Byrne graduated from the Training School for Kindergartners, which was sponsored by Dr. Newton's All Souls' Church in New York. Alex Ferm reports that "the theories" Elizabeth learned at school were "based on Froebel's ideas of child education." Indeed. During the precise period in which Froebel's texts were becoming widely available in English, Elizabeth Byrne was the head of the Brooklyn Guild Kindergarten (1890); the co-founder (with Alex Ferm) of The Children's Playhouse (1901), located in Dyker Heights, Brooklyn; and the co-founder (again with Alex) of a free kindergarten on Madison Street in New York City (1906-1913). And so, when she was finally invited to the Modern School at

Stelton in 1920, Elizabeth Byrne – then 63 years old – had been studying, thinking about and using Froebel's ideas for more than 30 years.

To this remarkable woman, the importance and usefulness of Froebel's ideas were located in his insistence on the primacy of creativity in all human endeavors. In *Freedom of Education* she explains, "Froebel held that through *self-expression* man would objectify his desires and impulses and thus develop and become aware of his own nature, his own individuality; and through this consciousness of self, he would eventually comprehend the unity of all endeavor, of all life." But without true self-expression, or with expression that simply reproduces what has been internalized, "we have a thing that is not self-revealing," that "has no message for anyone," and that "clutters the road which should be left open and free." Because young children do nothing but express themselves – every infant "has a self-centered, self-conscious, self-determining and self-directing instinct which shuts out the useless and unnecessary things which would serve only to distract and confuse him" – they are both the role models for adults who would like to free themselves from capitalist oppression and the ones most likely to benefit from a new pedagogy, organized around self-expression.

Elizabeth Byrne doesn't say so, but this Froebel – several decades before Marx – seems to have taken what Hegel said about mankind's objectification of impersonal nature ("the outside world") through labor, and applied it to mankind's objectification of human nature ("the inside world") through creativity. And so, by becoming a devout Froebelian, Elizabeth Byrne also became a kind of *left-wing Hegelian* (even if she didn't know it).[2] This might explain why she seems far more modern to us today than do her allegedly anarchist contemporaries, most of whom had little or no interest in critical theory. I say this with full awareness that, despite or alongside her fierce libertarianism, Ms. Bryne was also a deeply spiritual person. She occasionally refers to creepy shit like *The Ascension of the Virgin,* a painting "which depicts how insensitive the churchmen were to the spiritual truths they were supposed to protect." But Elizabeth Bryne was no "Church lady." In a truly remarkable passage, she proclaims,

> No design, no example for life can be given to man. Froebel passionately declares that 'no life, not even the life of Jesus, can serve as an example.' Each life is particular and unique in itself. Each life must create its own form.

Here she sounds like a religious heretic: not only is she an anti-clerical, but she's against all representation, even that of Jesus! As a result of this unusual mix of socio-political libertarianism and religious heresy, some of Elizabeth's declarations sound a lot like those made decades later by the members of the Situationist International, especially Raoul Vaneigem, who has written many books about the heresies suppressed and/or absorbed by the Catholic Church.[3]

To go back to what Elizabeth says about the primacy of self-expression: the distinction between the outside and the inside is central to her practical philosophy. At the beginning of her book's first chapter, which, following Froebel, is devoted to the role of "Creative Development in Education," she proclaims,

> Unless an act is the outcome of an inner necessity it is not creative. If it is not creative it cannot educate. In the degree that a human expresses himself creatively, in that degree he lives. In the degree that man does not reveal himself in his daily life, in that measure he exists as a material thing and he in no way fulfills his destiny as a self-conscious being, self-determining, self-directing and self-revealing.

It is precisely here – at the beginning – that Byrne finds that she must distinguish between Froebel's ideas and the way that Froebel's ideas were put into practice in kindergartens in the New York City area. Elsewhere in "Creative Development in Education," she states,

> One of the gravest objections to our present school system is the initiation of the young into forms which have not been called out by any need or desire of the child [...] In the school the child soon finds or senses that his acts are caused by an outer influence or permitted by an outer authority. The flow of his former life is diverted and consequently its course no longer normal. His inner voice is stifled and though he may still feel the impulse to act independently, there are too many voices in that child center for him to distinguish his own. From the standpoint of human growth, the outer voice is always false and totally unrelated to man's inner life. When the school succeeds in deadening the sound of the inner voice, it becomes an enemy to human development and a hindrance to life.

Later in *Freedom of Education,* Byrne goes so far as mention and criticize the great Froebel by name.

> After many years of practical kindergarten work, we realized that the kindergarten system did not serve to help the child to develop as an individual. Froebel's educational principles we fully agreed with, because they were verified in the life of the child; but we found that his system, *like all systems,* hindered the very thing that Froebel most desired to help the child to realize, i.e., self-consciousness through 'spontaneous self-activity' [emphasis added].

Unlike Froebel and other reformist system-builders, Byrne is an improvising or spontaneous revolutionary theorist.

> Education cannot be reduced to a system [she writes]. It cannot be standardized. There is no method for demonstrating its efficiency. Every *locality* must reveal its educational need in a particular manner. Education is a spiritual union of unconscious youth and conscious age. No degree can make an educator. The spiritual development of adult life is the magnet which attracts and holds the developing child. The bond is an inner one [emphasis added].

We might call her a localist: it is *the local situation* – that is, the particular children to be educated – that determines what the educator should do, not the reverse.[4] The educator can't be a specialist or dogmatist of any kind.

There's no phony liberalism here: educators must learn not to manage, criticize, judge or intervene (chapter 3), even if a lot of toys get smashed to pieces (chapter 12). Such toys – all of them – *deserve* to be smashed.

> Commercial toys may be taken as symbols of the present stage of human consciousness [Byrne writes]. How many realize today that their outer lives should be necessitated by an inner need? The intense diversion which surrounds us all tends to distract the individual from any realization. Tabloids, movies, phonographs, radios and the automobile serve to exaggerate the importance of external life. The reaction of man to all this is a sense of emptiness, loneliness and discontent.

Play is central to the child's inner life. It is, Byrne says, "what religion is to the adult": "an earnest and serious inquiry into the nature of life through and by means of an external form." Play is a "continuous, permanent expression of all forms of life; […] the law of development demands that every living thing must express and reveal itself in play." And so child's play must be encouraged (chapters 13 and 14), even if it turns "rough and tumble" (chapter 15). How rough? "I am inclined to think," she says "that, deplorable as a criminal start may be, there is more hope in it than in a submissive condition."

It is positively thrilling to read Byrne as she – decades before the great theorists of play[5] – imagines the place that the New Kindergarten will occupy in the New City and the New Society:

> But what have I to offer in place of all the things that I would abolish? Well, I too would establish play centers, but in every neighborhood. Mine would include the whole block, for I would go back of the city houses, tear down the fences and utilize the wood for a playhouse which I would build in the center. If the wood were not fit for building purposes, I would pile it in the center and make one great bonfire to celebrate the event. With the barriers removed, the work-a-day life of

the neighborhood would be seen.

But let's not get carried away. Every theorist has his or her blind spots, and childhood sexuality, unfortunately, is Elizabeth Bryne's. She does not give it its own chapter and the subject is raised, somewhat awkwardly, in the chapter ostensibly devoted to "Rough and Tumble Play" (chapter 15). She wants children to engage in sexual activity only when they have achieved a proper age, but does not specify what that age should be. If children are "pre-maturely" engaging in sex, it is simply because "artificial conditions help to breed artificial states of being," because "hothouse treatment tends to foster a general exotic state favorable to delicacy, cowardice, morbidity, sex curiosity and sex precocity." Of course, Byrne is also opposed to masturbation ("self-abuse") and I wouldn't doubt that she means homosexuality when she speaks of "delicacy" and "morbidity." But such a drawback should not prevent us from reading and praising *Freedom in Education.* It simply means that when it comes to books, we need to create our own.

[1] Is Elizabeth Byrne really best described as "a libertarian"? As an "anarchist"? These questions should also be asked of both the Modern School and the Francisco Ferrer Center, both of which were staffed by spiritualists, socialists and rugged American individualists, as well as by libertarians and anarchists. In this regard, see my review of Alan Antliff, *Anarchist Modernism: Art, Politics, and the First American Avant-Garde* (2001).
[2] For example: in *Freedom of Education,* the image – which is either truly or falsely reflected back to its creator – can be used to describe capitalist society as a whole. Elizabeth Bryne writes, "When we review the arbitrary discipline of the home, school and society, we find [...] that their discipline is not designed to foster the spirit of life. It is intended to reproduce *images of life,* to perpetuate old forms of life, and to guard against the creation of new forms. Nature abhors an imitation, but not so with these self-appointed guardians. They value the imitative uniform thing far more than the genuine natural thing" [emphasis added]. Note the striking similarity to Feuerbach's *The Essence of Christianity* (1841): "But certainly for the present age, which prefers the sign to the thing signified, the copy to the original, representation to reality, the appearance to the essence, *illusion* only is sacred, *truth* profane." Here one might also be reminded of the visual metaphors used by the Marxist critical theorist Georg Lukacs to discuss modern alienation (*History and Class Consciousness,* 1926), as well as those used decades later by the situationist theorist Guy Debord (*The Society of the Spectacle,* 1967).
[3] Raoul Vaneigem's books include *The Movement of the Free Spirit* (1986) and *The Resistance to Christianity: The Heresies at the Origins of the 18th Century* (1993).
[4] "Pedagogy implies localized practices, not socialized centrality." Henri Lefebvre, *The Right to the City,* contained in *Writings on Cities* (Blackwell, 1996).
[5] For example, Johan Huizinga, *Homo Ludens* (1938). See also the work of

Constant.

NOT BORED! #38, October 2006

The Secret of George W. Bush's Power: The State of Exception

In 2005, Factory School published a book by Francis Shor, a professor in the Department of Interdisciplinary Studies at Wayne State University. Entitled *Bush-League Spectacles: Empire, Politics, and Culture in Bushwhacked America*, it brings together some of the entries that Shor wrote between 2001 and 2005 for such liberal news/commentary blogs as *Common Dreams, CounterPunch, The History News Network* and *Bad Subjects*. The book is divided into four parts, all of which refer to the spectacle: "The Spectacles of Empire" (essays about international events); "The Spectacles of Politics" (domestic events); "The Spectacles of Culture" (domestic pop culture); and "Countering Bush-League Spectacles" (domestic political action). Shor begins his collection with a preface that, in its turn, begins with a quotation from Guy Debord's *The Society of the Spectacle*: "The spectacle cannot be understood as a mere visual deception produced by mass-media technologies. It is a worldview that has actually been materialized." But what Shor says right after this epigraph proves that he doesn't really understand Debord. To him,

> Spectacles have played a significant part of empires and public life throughout history. From the circuses of Rome to the Nuremberg rallies of Nazi Germany, the staging of public events for mass mobilization has served the interests of the ruling elite. However, in this era of the society of the spectacle where images dominate beyond just the media environment, the spectacle is even more integral to the functioning of society.

But for Debord, the society of the spectacle is *not* a trans-historical phenomenon: it can be dated fairly precisely (capitalist society since the 1920s/1930s). As a matter of fact, Debord's society of the "integrated spectacle"[1] has only existed since the 1960s! And the integrated spectacle – dominated, as it is, by atomization, separation and privatization – is obviously quite different from the "concentrated" spectacle of Nazi Germany (public events for mass mobilizations, etc). As we will see, Shor realizes this, too. But he's not concerned with appearing incoherent, and he need not be. His book is not a serious work about the society of the spectacle, but a collection of topical and thus highly perishable essays about the spectacle of the Bush Administration. It needs nice "fresh" packaging a lot more than it needs theoretical coherence, and it gets it: the book's cover depicts a pair of spectacles (eyeglasses) in which George W. Bush appears in one oculus and an Abu Ghraib detainee appears in the other.

Underneath the packaging is a very well-intentioned but ultimately inconsequential writer, who takes positions – to be fair, they are indeed the "right" positions, morally responsible positions – on the controversial issues of the day, but who has no strategic overview and no real plan of action. Note, in this regard, his sensitive but rather naive and superficial remarks about Abu Ghraib:

> Only our callousness and denial, characteristics built into the political culture of empire, prevent us from effectively countering the gruesome spectacle of Abu Ghraib and what it represents. One does not need a radical imagination to break free from such horror; just a sense of common humanity. But to recognize that common humanity requires overcoming ethnic, religious, and national prejudices that also inform the political culture of empire.

In a certain way, Shor represents everything that is wrong with the left-wing of the Democratic Party (his list of additional resources includes Air America Radio, Code Pink, Move On, United for Peace and Justice, etc). Ironically, though Shor is quite clear about his belief that "George W. Bush and his right-wing cabal" stole both the 2000 and the 2004 presidential elections, he is not the type of person you would want next to you at the barricades, which have in fact been built and defended in recent years in countries in which similar electoral frauds have been perpetrated (Mexico, the Ukraine, Argentina et al). Note Shor's pathetic reluctance, his total inability to *name his enemy*, even when it is standing right in front of him:

> Perhaps it may be time to raise the whole matter of the "F" word. It certainly seems reasonable to call this erosion of liberties and rights creeping fascism, albeit a postmodern fascism that does not need to rely on mass mobilization [hic] for realizing a proto-fascist agenda. In one of the most brilliant analyses of everyday life in Nazi Germany, Detlev Peukert devoted a whole chapter to 'The Atomization of Everyday Life' in his *Inside Nazi Germany* (236-242). Combining a form of psychic numbing with political numbing, many Germans just retreated from any public political life and took refuge in their own isolation. Since there is much evidence to support the tendency towards atomization and privatization of everyday life in the United

States, it may not require utilizing any reference to fascism, whether postmodern or not. On the other hand, when an administrative authority relies on the militarization of everyday life to pursue a repressive and aggressive agenda, it may be necessary to raise the specter of fascism.

Such hemming and hawing! *Come right out and say it, man*: Fascism is the precise worldview that is materializing in America today. Earlier in his book (in less of a mood to beat around the bush?), Shor had said,

> Of course, the racism that led the U.S. military to see every 'gook' as VC in Vietnam has also re-appeared in Iraq. According to one British commander in Iraq, American troops often saw Iraqis as '*undermensche*n – the Nazi expression for sub-humans.' Although embedded U.S. reporters rarely provided an insight into the racist mindset, Mark Franchetti of the *London Times* quoted one U.S. soldier as asserting that 'Iraqis are sick people and we are the chemotherapy.' And with chemotherapy if the sick person dies it was only to help cure the person.

This certainly sounds like fascism, and classic 1930s-era fascism, too. But Fran Shor simply doesn't want to face it, much in the same way that – even though he believes that "certain players acted out of their own personal interests at the expense of the safety and security of the nation" – he stands by the ridiculous idea that "to suggest that the Bush Administration arranged the 9/11 tragedy is to resort to wildly speculative conspiracy theories." Shor wants to restrict himself to discussing the Republicans' tactics (how they *capitalize* on terrorism) and does not want to talk about their strategies (how they *instigate* or even *perpetrate* terrorism). Significantly, he also does not want to think about anything that took place prior to 1960:

> To view the Bush regime as an aberration in U.S. politics, notwithstanding the electoral shenanigans of the presidential elections of 2000 and 2004, is to neglect the right-wing trends in American life during the last 30 years. These trends have been part of a reaction to the democratization fostered by the movements of the 1960's and the crisis of U.S. hegemony in the 1970's in the aftermath of the conflict in Southeast Asia. Starting with the Reagan Administration of the 1980's, attempts have been mounted at the national, state, and local levels to turn back the clock by repealing or undermining legislative advances made by minorities and women and to reverse environmental protections.

(Don't you just hate hippies? They think everything that's being done today is in response to what *they* did forty years ago!) But it is plain that the roots of the contemporary situation go back a lot further than the 1960s. It is also plain that the Bush Administration is employing something a lot more complex than a "strict father model of government." According to Shor:

> To prove they have compassion, albeit constricted and exclusionary, Republicans mount high-profile campaigns such as their intervention in the Terry Schiavo case. Congressional Republicans obviously believe that they can play on the sentiments of a media-manipulated public, too busy or numbed to realize the details of their awful budgetary cuts. Furthermore, and most tragic of all, hewing to a strict father model of government, Congressional Republicans have arrogated to themselves the desire to play god, dispensing life and death according to their own narrow-minded whims and truly heartless politics.

This is a nice, easy and all-too-obvious set of analogies: strict father in the home (the Republican social agenda); "a strict father model of government"; above it all a strict God (presumably God the Father). The ideology of the strict father's authority is often called "authoritarianism."[2] But authoritarianism does not explain the full extent of Bush's fascism.[3] It does not account for Bush's weird two-step: an inclusive and warm embrace of people who are inside of his literal and metaphorical family (the international family of Judeo-Christian nations), and an exclusive and murderous rejection of those who are outside this family (in particular, fundamentalist Muslims). *Quicunque finem iuris intendit cim iure graditur* ("Whoever intends to achieve the end of law, must proceed with law").[4] Strict fathers do not capture outsiders and deport them for torture or preemptively murder them in foreign lands to prevent attacks at home. Strict fathers *enforce* the law; they do not act outside of it or suspend it due to an emergency.

No, to really understand the spectacle of the Bush Administration, it seems we must go beyond Francis Shor, America and blogs, and read the truly difficult but rewarding work of Giorgio Agamben.[5] An Italian philosopher and professor of aesthetics, Agamben might be described as a political Jacques Derrida. He intends his audience to be much wider than university-affiliated intellectuals and postmodern artist-types; he also intends to appeal to anti-authoritarian and anarchist activists.

"The weakness of anarchist and Marxian critiques of the State," Agamben says in his introduction to *Homo Sacer: Sovereign Power and Bare Life,* "was precisely to have not caught sight of this structure" – the "originary structure" of the "state of exception" – "and thus to have quickly left the *arcanum imperii*[6] aside, as if it had no substance outside of the simulacra and the ideologies used to justify it. But one ends up identifying with an enemy whose structure one does not understand, and the theory of the State (and in particular of the state of exception, which is to say, of the dictatorship of the proletariat as the transitional phase leading to the stateless society) is the reef on which the revolutions of our century have been shipwrecked." It is clear that Agamben wrote *Homo Sacer* so that the next revolution, the revolutions of the next century, would have much smoother sailing.

In archaic Roman law, the "state of exception" describes the juridical situation of *homo sacer* (sacred man), a human being who – for one reason or another – "may be killed but not sacrificed," that is, someone who is no longer included in human society nor even covered by its most basic protections. Condemned to exist in a state of exception, the *homo sacer* can be killed by anyone, without a murder being committed. To Agamben, the striking thing is that this situation (which concerns the extra-juridical order) was inscribed within Rome's juridical order. The rule and the exception to it became confused, indistinct: the exception now becomes the rule. The *homo sacer* is not simply excluded from society; he or she is also included into its "constitution," its legal code. But he or she is included only as "bare life," only as a body, a mere creature without political or human rights of any kind. This was a major historical development, which constituted "the first paradigm of the political realm of the West." Prior to that, bare life (*zoë* in Greek) had not been "included in/excluded from" the politico-juridical realm, which merely concerned itself with *bios* (living in the *polis* as a citizen).

As Agamben notes, Michel Foucault's *History of Sexuality, Volume I* had already recognized the birth of modern politics ("biopolitics") in this change. But Agamben asserts that the key development was "not so much the inclusion of *zoë* in the *polis* – which is, in itself, absolutely ancient – nor simply the fact that life as such becomes a principal object of the projections and calculations of State power," but, "together with the process by which the exception everywhere becomes the rule, the realm of bare life [...] gradually begins to coincide with the political realm, and exclusion and inclusion, outside and inside, *bios* and *zoë,* right and fact, enter into a zone of irreducible indistinction." Thus, the key question becomes, "Who decides who is a citizen and who is a *homo sacer*?" Following Carl Schmitt, who early in the Twentieth Century defined "the Sovereign" as "He who decides on the state of exception," Agamben concentrates his efforts on *sovereign power,* which isn't simply "the question of who within the political order was invested with certain powers," but also the constitution (the "threshold") of the political order itself.

It seems clear that Agamben would not have written a second book about the state of exception – *Stato di eccezione* (2003, translated into English as *State of Exception* by Kevin Attell and published by Stanford University Press in 2005) – had it not been for the "global civil war" (the global war on terrorism) that George W. Bush started in response to the September 11th attacks on the Pentagon and the World Trade Center. As Agamben notes, things have changed since the Nazis' concentration camps: "the state of exception tends increasingly to appear as the dominant paradigm of government in contemporary politics"; "the voluntary creation of a permanent state of emergency (though perhaps not declared in the technical sense) has become one of the essential practices of contemporary states, even so-called democratic states"; "the state of exception has today reached it maximum worldwide deployment."

Rather than citing a great many examples and dealing with them in a verbose but ultimately superficial manner, *a la* Fran Shor, Agamben gets to the heart of the matter.

> The immediately biopolitical significance of the state of exception as the originary structure in which law encompasses living beings by means of its own suspension emerges clearly in the 'military order' issued by the President of the United States on November 13, 2001, which authorized the 'indefinite detention' and trial by 'military commissions' (not to be confused with the military tribunals provided for by the law of war) of noncitizens suspected of involvement in terrorist activities [...] What is new about President Bush's order is that it radically erases any legal status of the individual, thus producing a legally unnamable and unclassifiable being. Not only do the Taliban captured in Afghanistan not enjoy the status of POWs as defined by the Geneva Convention, they do not even have the status of persons charged with a crime according to Americans laws. Neither prisoners not persons accused, but simply 'detainees,' they are the object of a pure *de facto* rule, of a detention that is indefinite not only in the temporal sense but in its very nature as well, since it is entirely removed from the law and from judicial oversight. The only thing to which it could possibly be compared is the legal situation of the Jews in the Nazi *Lager* (camps), who, along with their citizenship, had lost every legal identity, but at least retained their identity as Jews. As Judith Bulter has effectively shown, in the detainee at Guantanamo, bare life reaches its maximum indeterminacy.

The noncitizen "enemy combatant" detained by the US military at Guantanamo Bay, Cuba – itself an indeterminate place, beyond the reach of national and international law – is the modern-day *homo sacer*. And George W. Bush is much more than an "imperial president": he is a modern-day Sovereign. "President Bush's decision to refer to himself constantly as the 'Commander in Chief of the Army' after September 11th 2001, must be considered in the context of this presidential claim to sovereign powers in emergency situations," Agamben writes in *State of Exception*. "If, as we have seen, the assumption of this title entails a direct reference to the state of exception, then Bush is attempting to produce a situation in which the emergency becomes the rule, and the very distinction between peace and war (and between foreign and civil war) becomes impossible." But a protected democracy is not a democracy at all and, as Agamben notes with respect to the history of the Weimar Republic, "the paradigm of constitutional dictatorship functions instead as a transitional phase that leads inevitably to the establishment of a totalitarian regime."

The great value and difficulty of Agamben's books is that they show that Bush's post-September 11th drift towards totalitarianism has actualized or made use of a potential that has existed in the politico-juridical structure of the West since the ancient Romans. Though one must "ceaselessly [...] try to interrupt the working of the machine that is leading the West toward global civil war," one must also realize the superficiality of focusing on "driving out the Bush regime" and the immensity of the real task at hand, which, as Agamben states, "is not to bring the state of exception back within its spatially and temporally defined boundaries in order to then reaffirm the primacy of a norm and of rights that are themselves ultimately grounded to it. From the real state of exception in which we live, it is not possible to return to the state of law, for at issue now are the very concepts of 'state' and 'law.'" And if we can't return, where do we go from here? Not towards totalitarianism, but towards insurrection and revolution. There is no other option.

[1] See Debord's *Comments on The Society of the Spectacle* (1988).
[2] A critique of "authoritarianism" is easily made these days by liberal Democratic opponents of President Bush. Note in this regard John Dean's recent thesis (*Conservatives without Conscience,* Viking 2006) about "the authoritarian personality" and the frequency with which he is called upon to apply it to Bush, Rumsfeld, Cheney, et al on MSNBC's liberal news/comedy show, *Countdown with Keith Obermann.* See also Theodor Adorno and Else Frenkel-Brunswick, *The Authoritarian Personality,* Harpers, 1950.
[3] For a denunciation of "the liberal identification of totalitarianism with [mere] authoritarianism," see Hannah Arendt, "What is Authority?" in *Between Past and Future* (1961).
[4] Dante, *De monarchia,* cited in Giorgio Agamben, *State of Exception* (2005).
[5] Note well that Guy Debord's theory of the spectacle will come with us. Agamben is a serious student of the Situationist International: he is the author of "Difference and Repetition: On Guy Debord's Films" (1995, included in Thomas McDonough, *Guy Debord and the Situationist International: Texts and Documents*). In his introduction to *Homo Sacer: Sovereign Power and Bare Life* (1995), setting up one of his major themes, Agamben writes that, "Modern democracy's decadence and gradual convergence with totalitarian states in post-democratic societies (which begins to become evident with Alexis de Tocqueville and finds its final sanction in the analyses of Guy Debord) may well be rooted in this aporia, which marks the beginning of modern democracy and forces it into complicity with its most implacable enemy."
[6] Latin: the secret of power.

NOT BORED! #38, October 2006

Henri Lefebvre's *Writings on Cities* and *The Right to the City*

OK. Before we can say anything about the contents of the book called *Writings on Cities,* published under the name of Henri Lefebvre, and translated and edited by Eleonore Kofman and Elizabeth Lebas (Blackwell Publishing, 1996), we must say the following about the book itself, as a product. Ahem. This *piece of shit* is only 250 pages long, uses large type, has a soft cover, includes no illustrations, and yet costs a whopping $45. From cover to cover, it is riddled with unchecked facts, missing punctuation marks, dropped words, words that appear unaccountably and should be dropped, misspelled words, etc. For example, the publisher's page is dated 1996 and yet fails to record that Henri Lefebvre *died* in 1991 (the bio line still reads "1905 – "). It's obvious that this book was never properly proofread. All of this can be blamed on Blackwell, which seems to have published *Writings on Cities* as a way of capitalizing on the success of its edition of *The Production of Space* (1991)[1].

But the editor/translators must take their share of the blame. A fifth of "their" book (50 pages) is devoted to their ultra-self-conscious and unnecessarily long introduction, which, if deleted, would necessitate the deletion of a large number of entries in the book's 10-page-long index that refer to subjects raised *not* by Henri Lefebvre, but by Kofman and Lebas. The selection of texts they made is very unsatisfactory: the reader gets a full translation of Lefebvre's *Le droit a la ville,* first published in 1968; but instead of getting a full translation of *Espace et Politique* – published in 1973 as the sequel to *Le droit a la ville* – the reader only gets a translation of the book's introduction and a single and very short chapter. These regrettable decisions weren't based on "space limitations": there appears to have been *plenty* of room for such obvious filler as the two interviews with Lefebvre and the two texts snatched from the book called *Elements de rythmanalyse,* published in 1992. The reason why the majority, if not all of *Espace et Politique* was not included in the *Writings on Cities* anthology is explained as follows: "Some of it has already been translated (Antipode, 1976) and much of it announces the subsequent and more elaborate *Production of Space.*" But Kofman and Lebas's own list of references shows that Lefebvre didn't publish any *books* in 1976 and that none of the books he did publish were published by "Antipode," which is in fact a *journal* in the field of radical geography. Quite obviously, the existence of overlap between *Espace et Politique* and *The Production of Space* does not require that the former should not be published in its entirety.

Last but not least, Kofman and Lebas's translation tends to be a literal word-for-word affair (did they dash it off in a hurry? did they never get a chance to polish it properly?), which means that their English renderings are often awkward, even confusing. But rather than provide examples, let us simply proceed with our discussion, which will of course involve extensive quotation of Lefebvre and will thus provide a number of opportunities for the reader of this text to decide for him- or herself if Kofman and Lebas's translations/typographical renderings are good or bad.

* * *

Le droit a la ville (*The Right to the City*) was written in 1967 to mark the centenary of the publication of Karl Marx's *Das Kapital* (1867) but it wasn't published until the following year. Lefebvre had been thinking about cities since 1947, when he published the first volume of his pioneering study, *Critique of Everyday Life*. But he remained lodged in and attached to the countryside in which he'd been born and raised until the mid-1950s, when he moved to Paris. In the city, Lefebvre eventually met several young, very attentive readers of his book, including such future members of the Situationist International as Constant Nieuwenhuis, Guy Debord, Michelle Bernstein and Raoul Vaneigem. As a result, Lefebvre decided to take up the issue of the city once more. His decision came at an interesting time. As he says in *The Right to the City,*

> Over the last few years and rather strangely, the *right to nature* entered into social practice thanks to *leisure,* having made its way through protestations becoming commonplace against noise, fatigue, the concentrationary universe of cities (as cities are rotting or exploding). A strange journey indeed! Nature enters into exchange-value and commodities, to be bought and sold. This 'naturality' which is counterfeited and traded in, is [in fact] destroyed by commercialized, industrialized and institutionally organized leisure pursuits. 'Nature,' or what passes for it, and survives of it, becomes the ghetto of leisure pursuits, the separate place of pleasure and the retreat of 'creativity' [...] In the face of this pseudo-right [to nature], the *right to the city* is like a cry and a demand [...] The claim to nature, and the desire to enjoy it, displace the right to the city. This latest claim [the right to nature] expresses itself indirectly as a tendency to flee the deteriorated and unrenovated city, alienated urban life before at last, 'really' living [...] The *right to the city* cannot be conceived of as a simple visiting right or as a return to traditional cities. It can only be formulated as a transformed and renewed *right to urban life.*

Between 1958 and 1962, Lefebvre and the Situationists worked together closely.

As has been pointed many times, the Situationist concept of the "situation" was closely related to the Lefebvrian concept of the "moment."[2] In 1963, there was a dreadful falling-out between them concerning excerpts from Lefebvre's book on the Paris Commune, *La Proclamation de la Commune,* which was eventually published in 1965. In *Aux Poubelles de l'Histoire* ("Into the Trashcan of History"), dated 21 February 1963, the situationists alleged that these excerpts were clearly plagiarized from a situationist text entitled "Theses on the Commune" and dated 18 March 1962. There were of course several other bones of contention: the Situationists' boycott of *Arguments* magazine, in which the allegedly plagiarized excerpts were published; ex-girlfriends; etc etc.[3] Whatever: the point here is that the split was far worse for Lefebvre than it was for the Situationists, whose work deepened and thrived in the aftermath. But the split clearly troubles *The Right to the City,* and the two other books Lefebvre published in 1968: his *Cliff Notes*-style summary of his own ideas, translated as *Everyday Life in the Modern World,* and his May 1968 cash-in gambit *L'Irruption a Nanterre au sommet.* Indeed, it wasn't until 1973 or 1974 – the very years in which he published *Espace et Politics* and *The Production of Space* – that Lefebvre fully recovered his balance, and started producing good work again.

The problem for Lefebvre in *The Right to the City* is that there is little in Karl Marx's works – even in the later, "mature" writings – from which to offer a properly Marxist critique of the city. Lefebvre himself is very clear on this.

> Until now, in theory as in practice, the double process of industrialization and urbanization has not been mastered. The incomplete teachings of Marx and Marxist thought have been misunderstood. For Marx himself, industrialization contained its finality and meaning, later giving rise to the dissociation of Marxist thought into economism and philosophism. Marx did not show (and in his time he could not) that urbanization and the *urban* contain the *meaning* of industrialization. He did not see that industrial production implied the urbanization of society, and that the mastery of industrial potentials required specific knowledge concerning urbanization. Industrial production, after a certain *growth,* produces urbanization, providing it with conditions, and possibilities. The problematic is displaced and becomes that of urban *development.* The works of Marx (notably *Capital*) contained precious few indications on the city and particularly on the historical relations between town and country. They do not pose the urban problem. In Marx's time, only the housing problem was raised and studied by Engels. Now, the problem of the city is immensely greater than that of housing.

And so, in the absence of Marx, Lefebvre needs the situationist critique of the city to successfully bring Marx's *Capital* into the world of 1967. Unfortunately, due to his strained personal relations with Debord and the other situationists, Lefebvre feels he can't mention them, their theories nor their publications. For example, when it comes time for him to note that "the problem is to put an end to the separations of 'daily life/leisure' or 'daily life/festivity'. It is to restitute the *fete* by changing daily life," Lefebvre restrains himself from mentioning either the Paris Commune – an importance instance in which the "right to the city" was forcefully asserted – or his book about the subject, only two years old at the time. And yet, inevitably, it would seem, Lefebvre's critique of the city is unmistakably situationist or, rather, strongly reminiscent of the Situationists of 1962.[4]

In this critique, the city has been thoroughly commodified: it is a privileged space for the consumption of commodities and it is consumed as if it were one big commodity. "They city is no longer lived and it is no longer understood practically," Lefebvre writes. "It is only an object of cultural consumption for tourists, for estheticism, avid for spectacles and the picturesque." And yet, "the *urban* remains in a state of dispersed and alienated actuality, as kernel and virtuality." In short, "urban life has yet to begin." For urban inhabitants to start really living, they must *make use* of their cities. But the word "use" must be considered as broadly as possible; it must include *appropriation,* which inevitably involves re-creating ("inventing" or "sculpting") existing space(s), that is to say, the production of new space(s).

To end the chapter called "The Right to the City," Lefebvre gives us a fascinating portrait of class relations in today's commodified city.

> Who can ignore that the Olympians of the new bourgeois aristocracy no longer inhabit? They go from grand hotel to grand hotel, or from castle to castle, commanding a fleet or a country from a yacht. They are everywhere and nowhere. That is how they fascinate people immersed into everyday life. They transcend everyday life, possess nature and leave it up to the cops to contrive culture. Is it essential to describe at length, besides the condition of youth, students and intellectuals, armies of workers with or without white collars, people from the provinces, the colonized and semi-colonized of all sorts, all those who endure a well-organized daily life? Is it here necessary to exhibit the derisory and untragic misery of the inhabitant, of the suburban dweller and of the people who stay in residential ghettoes, in the moldering centers of old cities and in the proliferations lost beyond them? One only has to open one's eyes to understand the daily life of the one who runs from his dwelling to the station, near or far away, to the packed underground train, the office or the factory, to return the same way in the evening and come home to recuperate enough to start again the next day. The picture of this generalized misery would not go without a picture of 'satisfactions' which hides it and becomes the means to elude it and break free from it.

Great stuff, solidly within the orbit of the Situationists' *On the Poverty of Student life* – except for the description of "the Olympians of the new bourgeois aristocracy," who use high-speed technologies (airplanes chiefly, but also wireless telephones and/or radio transmitters) to get to and from, and also up and *out of* the cities of the world. In short, they use time (accelerated speeds) to both control and transcend the slow space(s) of everyday life. But these are not really situationist themes. One thinks instead of the writings of Paul Virilio, who is certainly neither Marxist nor situationist.[5]

Significantly, there are many passages in which Lefebvre does not even mention such basic Marxist concepts as the proletariat and the revolution. Both themes emerge rather late in *The Right to the City* and, when they *do* appear, they do not dazzle the world with their brilliance. No: unlike the passages on everyday life, they are dull and boring, and they are certainly not helped in this regard by Kofman & Lebas's stilted translation. The entirety of thesis #9 in "Theses on the City, the Urban and Planning" (the final chapter of *The Right to the City*) states:

> The revolutionary transformation of society has industrial production as ground and lever. This is why it had to be shown that the urban centre of decision-making can no longer consider itself in the present society (of neo-capitalism or of monopoly capitalism associated to the State) outside the means of production, their property and their management. Only the taking in charge by the working class of planning and its political agenda can profoundly modify social life and open another era: that of socialism in neo-capitalist countries. Until then transformations remain superficial, at the level of signs and the consumption of signs, language and metalanguage, a secondary discourse, a discourse on previous discourses. Therefore, it is not without reservations that one can speak of urban revolution. Nevertheless, the orientation of industrial production on social needs is not a secondary fact. The finality thus brought to plans transforms them. In this way urban reform has a revolutionary bearing. As the twentieth century agrarian reform gradually disappears from the horizon, urban reform becomes a revolutionary reform. It gives rise to a strategy which opposes itself to the class strategy dominant today.

A revolutionary reform?! Sheesh: there's no such thing for a Marxist! Perhaps this book didn't find a publisher in 1967 because it just wasn't very good. Perhaps it only found a publisher because of the revolt of May 1968, which aroused interest in *all* of the contemporary French Marxist theorists, no matter what the caliber of their latest works or their actual connection to the May movement.

* * *

Lefebvre's *The Right to the City* certainly looks rather weak in comparison to Giorgio Agamben's writings on the city, or, rather, Agamben's writings expose several serious weaknesses in Lefebvre's book. In *Homo Sacer: Sovereign Power and Bare Life* (1995, translated from the Italian by Daniel Heller-Roazen, 1998, Stanford University Press), Agamben calls attention to the fact that the French philosopher Michel Foucault – despite introducing the concept of biopolitics in the late 1970s (see his *The History of Sexuality, Volume I*) – "never dwelt on the exemplary places of modern biopolitics: the concentration camp and the structure of the great totalitarian states of the twentieth century." Instead Foucault dwelt on disciplinary institutions, in particular, the prison. But, to Agamben, "the camp – and not the prison – is the space that corresponds to this originary structure of the *nomos*."

> This is shown [Agamben continues], among other things, by the fact that while prison law only constitutes a particular sphere of penal law and is not outside the normal order, the juridical constellation that guides the camp is (as we shall see) martial law and the state of siege. This is why is not possible to inscribe the analysis of the camp in the trail opened by the works of Foucault, from *Madness and Civilization* to *Discipline and Punish*. As the absolute space of exception, the camp is topologically different from a simple space of confinement.

The implication is obvious: if the concentration camp is the most important *topological* (structural or spatial) phenomenon of the Twentieth Century,[6] and if Foucault does not discuss nor even mention the camp, then Foucault's works can't be very important, insightful or useful. (Almost all of the great post-World War II French theorists have an original theory that also functions as a kind of litmus-test for the interest of the works of their contemporaries: for Debord, it is the spectacle; for Foucault, it is the carceral or "disciplined" society; for Lefebvre, it is everyday life in the city; for Paul Virilio, it is the acceleration of time; for Jean Baudrillard, it is the hyper-real, etc etc. Note in this regard Virilio's ideological break with Baudrillard and his embrace of Deleuze & Guattari's war machine, as well as Baudrillard's dismissal of Foucault, etc etc *ad nauseum*.)

It is indeed quite curious that neither Lefebvre's *The Right to City* nor anything else contained in *Writings on Cities* discusses or mentions the concentration camp. (*The Production of Space* is also silent on the subject.) This omission is especially felt during Lefebvre's discussions of the dialectic of urbanization and industrialization: is it not interesting that the Nazis constructed their highly industrialized concentration camps as if they were self-contained little cities and yet never situated these "mini-cities" *within* any German cities (like factories, they were built in the outskirts or in conquered nations such as Poland)? To Agamben, the answer is "yes." It is this precise topology – the *doubled structure* of inclusion (modeled on the city) and exclusion (outskirts) – that makes the camp the exemplary (urban) space of modern biopolitics. Lefebvre's omission is especially glaring in light of how much attention both Guy Debord and Raoul Vaneigem gave to the similarities between concentration camps and contemporary architecture and urbanism.[7]

The second weakness highlighted by Agamben's work concerns Lefebvre's decision to cast his putatively Marxist critique of the modern city as the declaration of a "right," which as a matter of fact is the only original thing about *The Right to the City.* In *Homo Sacer,* Agamben, introducing a chapter on the "Rights of Man," declares:

> Yet it is time to stop regarding declarations of rights as proclamations of eternal, metajuridical values binding the legislator (in fact, without much success) to respect eternal ethical principles, and to begin to consider them according to their real historical function in the modern nation-state. Declarations of rights represent the originary figure of the inscription of natural life in the juridico-political order of the nation-state. The same bare life that in the *ancien regime* was politically neutral and belonged to God as creaturely life and in the classical world was (at least apparently) clearly distinguished as *zoë* from political life (*bios*) now fully enters into the structure of the state and even becomes the earthly foundation of the state's legitimacy and sovereignty.[8]

For Agamben, it's a simple matter of re-reading the documents that founded modern democracy: the 1679 writ of *habeas corpus* and the 1789 "Declaration of the Rights of Man and Citizen," among others. What one finds is this:

> It is not the free man and his statutes and prerogatives, nor even simply *homo,* but rather *corpus* that is the new subject of politics. And democracy is born precisely as the assertion and presentation of this 'body': *habeas corpus ad subjiciendum,* 'you will have to have a body to show' [..] *Corpus is a two-faced being, the bearer both of subjection to sovereign power and of individual liberties.*

Another (hopefully not contradictory) way of saying this is that, when rights are codified in or as law, they become *suspendable* under certain extraordinary but lawful conditions, such as martial law, a state of siege, etc etc. And when "human" or "democratic" rights *are* suspended, there is a split between the old laws, which supposedly protected everyone, and the new provisional laws, which protect "the majority," but not everyone. (Note, in this regard, the beauty of the "silence" of the Ninth Amendment to the U.S. Constitution: "The enumeration in the constitution of certain rights shall not be construed to deny or disparage others retained by the people." Here rights are protected from suspension to the precise extent that they escape enumeration!)

And so, we are not surprised when we find that these precise problems appear in – and fatally compromise – the documents that, over the course of the last five years, have been drafted by international human rights groups on the subject of "the right to the city." The first of these documents is entitled *World Charter for the Human Right to the City* (January 2003) and was collectively authored by the various groups that first came together 1-4 February 2002 at a "World Seminar for the Human Right to the City" sponsored by the World Social Forum. The second document is the *World Charter on the Right to the City,* which was first presented in July 2004 at the Social Forum of the Americas and then in September 2004 at the World Urban Forum. It is not clear to what extent the various organizations involved – which include UNESCO – have been aware of Lefebvre's *The Right to the City*. But they must be aware of the connection now, that is, since 2003, when Don Mitchell published his study entitled *The Right to the City: Social Justice and the Right to the City* (New York: Guilford). Mitchell writes:

> It is peculiar that these documents should ever have wanted to be have been defined as "charters." A charter is not only a document that sets forth the principles, functions and organization of a corporate body, but it is also a grant of rights and privileges from the sovereign power of a particular nation. Nothing in a charter is guaranteed. The rights and privileges, *even the very existence* of a corporation ("corpus") can be suspended by the sovereign in certain "emergency" situations.

Significantly, neither charter offers a good definition of "the city." *World Charter for the Human Right to the City* notes that cities "represent much more than physical space distinguished by a higher density of living space" (paragraph 2), but says no more than that. Much more formal and precise, the *World Charter on the Right to the City* says that, "For the purpose of this Charter, the denomination of City is given to any town, village, city, capital, locality, suburb, settlement or similar which is institutionally organised as a local unit of Municipal or Metropolitan Government independently of whether it is urban, rural, or semi-rural." And so "the City" is everywhere: it exists everywhere there's a local government. But isn't "the City" much more than just local politics? Hasn't the City's essence, particularity and specificity been lost in this definition?

As for the right to the city itself, it is apparently nothing new. In the words of the *World Charter for the Human Right to the City,* it "actually amalgamates a bundle of already-existing human rights and relate State obligations, to which, by extension, local authorities are also party" (paragraph 7); it "encompasses the internationally recognized human rights to housing, social security, work, an adequate standard of living, leisure, information, organization and free association, food and water, freedom from dispossession, participation and self-expression, health, education, culture, privacy and security, a safe and healthy environment" (paragraph 11); and it "embodies claims to the human rights to land, sanitation, public transportation, basic infrastructure, capacity and capacity-building, and access to public goods and services – including natural resources and finance" (paragraph 12). In other words, "the right to the city" is just an empty slogan, a catch-all phrase.

Both charters have a remarkably narrow idea of what the city's inhabitants are allowed to *do* with and to the city, which, as we will see, is not really their city. The *World Charter for the Human Right to the City* says "these standing rights and obligations are supported by the concepts of equal usufruct of the city" (paragraph 7), and the *World Charter on the Right to the City* says that "the cities attend its function if to guarantee to all persons the full usufruct of its economy, culture and resources" (Article II, paragraph 2: all mistakes are in the original). In the law, "usufruct" means the utilization and enjoyment of *someone else's property* so long as that property is not altered or damaged. It is a right usually reserved for those who lease or rent property. Such agreements can lawfully be terminated and the inhabitants can lawfully be evicted if they appropriate ("misappropriate") the property. Only those who *own* the property have the right to properly appropriate it.

But the real weakness of these documents lies in the confused and confusing way that they each define, address and refer to the bearers of the enumerated rights. The *World Charter for the Human Right to the City* declares, "the Human Right to the City is both an individual and a collective right of the city's inhabitants, especially protecting and serving members of vulnerable and disadvantaged groups" (paragraph 8). It is clear that this "collective right" would *never* be democratically exercised if *some* individuals (it wouldn't matter if they are members of dominated or dominating groups) could receive greater, increased, or better protection and service. It would violate the principle of equal protection under the law.

The *World Charter on the Right to the City* says that "everyone has a right to the city without discrimination of gender, age, race, ethnicity, political and religious orientation" (Article I, paragraph 1) and yet also says that, "for the purpose of the Charter, *citizens* are all persons who live in the city either permanently or in transit" (Article I, paragraph 5), thereby creating a potentially confusing distinction between "everyone" (which even includes people who do not dwell in the city) and the city-dwelling "citizens." Further distinctions within city-dwelling "citizens" are drawn by Article II, which states, "For the purposes of this Charter vulnerable people are the following: persons and groups in situation of poverty, in health and environmental risk, victims of violence, the disabled people, migrants, refugees and all other groups which, in the reality of each city, are in a situation of disadvantage with respect to *the rest of the inhabitants*" (paragraph 6, emphasis added); and Article XIV, which states that "This present Article" – which is titled "The Right to Housing" – "shall be applicable to all persons, including but not limited to, families, tenants without ownership titles, the homeless, and those whose living conditions vary, such as nomads, travelers and the Roma" (paragraph 10).

But what rights do people possess – what good are their "rights to the city" – if their *citizenship* has been suspended by the sovereign? This is the crucial question when it comes to "nomads, travelers and the Roma," that is to say, people who don't have a "proper" nationality or a "homeland" they wish to return to someday. Under these two charters, the City can do absolutely nothing to prevent sovereign power – remember, the city is merely a "locality" – from arresting, detaining and eventually deporting these "illegal immigrants" from the Nation-State.[9] Worse still, by rendering indistinct the notion of citizenship – it applies to non-city dwellers, permanent city dwellers and temporary city-dwellers – these Charters have created a conceptual framework in which the state of exception[10] can "logically" be extended to include not only "nomads, travelers and the Roma," but also the native-born or legally naturalized "persons and groups [who are] in a situation of disadvantage with respect to the rest of the inhabitants," *and even* "the rest of the inhabitants" themselves: absolutely everyone. For that's what totalitarianism is: the state of exception applied to everyone.

[1] See our essay on Levebvre's *The Production of Space*.
[2] See Guy Debord's letter to Andre Frankin, dated 22 February 1960. See also Debord's letter to Lefebvre concerning "revolutionary romanticism," dated 5 May 1960.
[3] See Guy Debord's letters to Bechir Tlili dated 14 May 1963 and 15 April 1964.
[4] After which the SI supposedly abandoned urbanism, derives and psychogeography, in favor of extolling wildcat strikes, Workers' Councils and the theory of the spectacle. See Kristin Ross's interview with Lefebvre.
[5] See for example my essay on Virilio's *Art and Fear*.
[6] For Asger Jorn's interest in topology, see "Open Creation and Its Enemies," *Internationale Situationniste* #5, 1960.
[7] Debord: see "Critique of Urbanism" (*Internationale Situationniste* #6, August 1961) and the montages in the film version of *The Society of the Spectacle* (1973). Vaneigem: "Comments against Urbanism" (*Internationale Situationniste* #6, August 1961), which contains the great line: "If the Nazis had known contemporary urbanists, they would have transformed their concentration camps into low-income housing."
[8] Here Agamben is following Michel Foucault, who writes in *The History of Sexuality, Volume I*: "We have entered a phase of juridical repression in comparison with the pre-seventeenth-century societies we are acquainted with; we should not be deceived by all the Constitutions framed throughout the world since the French Revolution, the Codes written and revised, a whole continual and clamorous legislative activity: these were the forms that made an essentially

normalizing power acceptable."
[9] See Guy Debord, "Notes on the 'Immigration Question'."
[10] In archaic Roman law, the legal-juridical status of the *homo sacer,* the person who could be killed but not sacrificed. For more, see our reviews of the books by Giorgio Agamben.

NOT BORED! #38, October 2006

One Step Forward, One Step Back: Ken Knabb's *Pas de deux*

In December 2006, Ken Knabb took the occasion of the twenty-fifth anniversary of the first edition of his *Situationist International Anthology* (Bureau of Public Secrets: Berkeley, 1981) to publish a "revised and expanded edition." A major development in Anglo-American radical politics, Knabb's *Situationist International Anthology* was the first such collection of translated texts[1] since 1974, when the ex-situationist Christopher Gray published *Leaving the Twentieth Century.* Though Gray's selections were far from complete and his translations and commentaries were weak, *Leaving the Twentieth Century* was also an important work. Illustrated by Jamie Reid,[2] it exerted a strong influence on English punk. But unlike *Leaving the Twentieth Century,* which was not reprinted in its original format, well distributed or widely read, Knabb's *Situationist International Anthology* became a kind of "Bible" for that part of the English-speaking world that loved and learned from the situationists. It was reprinted once in 1989, and then again in 1995.

The new version of the *Situationist International Anthology* is both longer (532 pages, up from 406) and smaller (the size of the type has been decreased and there are more lines per page). It includes six "new" texts: one from the pre-1957 period ("Proposal for Rationally Improving the City of Paris"); three from the 1958 to 1962 period ("Theses on the Cultural Revolution," "Another City for Another Life" and "The Use of Free Time"); and two from the 1966 to 1969 period ("Contribution to a Councilist Program in Spain" and a selection of graffitied slogans from May 1968). Ten texts that had only been partially translated in the first edition have now been translated in full. They include such important documents as Guy Debord's "Report on the Construction of Situations" and "The Situationists and the New Forms of Action in Politics and Art"; Raoul Vaneigem's "Ideologies, Classes, and the Domination of Nature"; and the unsigned "How Not to Understand Situationist Books."[3] Knabb has also greatly expanded his "Translator's Notes" (annotated references to historical events) and his "Bibliography" (Pre-SI Texts, Guy Debord's Films, French SI books, SI Publications in Other Languages, Post-SI Works, and Books About the SI).

And yet the *Situationist International Anthology* remains a deeply flawed book. It continues to under-represent the SI's early period: only a few texts are included from the following issues of the group's French-language journal, *Internationale Situationniste*: #2 (1958), #3 (1959), #4 (1960), #5 (1960) and #9 (1964). And so Knabb seems rather silly when he criticizes Tom McDonough, the editor of *Guy Debord and the Situationist International,* for presenting "a misleadingly one-sided selection of 150 pages of SI articles (mostly early ones on art and urbanism, with virtually nothing from the last two-thirds of the group's existence)," precisely because Knabb's book is such a good symmetrical match for it (mostly later articles on politics, with virtually nothing from the first third of the group's existence). Unfortunately, *neither book* documents such important moments as the formation and subsequent collapse of the Dutch and German sections of the SI.

Knabb's *Anthology* also under-represents is the SI's final period. Absolutely nothing from *The Veritable Split in the International* (published in 1972) – not even Vaneigem's letter of resignation[4] or Debord's famous response to it[5] – is included because, as Knabb says, "anyone who is serious" will want to read them in their entirety. And though *forty* texts were contributed to the group's "orientation debate" (also called the "debate on organization"), which took place between August 1969 and February 1971, Knabb only includes *five* of them. Worse still, nothing changed between the 1981 and 2006 editions: Knabb offers us *the same five texts* and *three* of them are still not offered in their full versions. It is misleading, perhaps even mendacious, to say that Knabb's translations of two of these five texts – "Remarks on the SI Today" (27 July 1970) and "Document Beyond Debate" (28 January 1971), both by Debord – are "excerpted." They are *flat-out butcheries,*[6] just as Knabb's previously "excerpted" (and now restored) version of Attila Kotanyi's "Gangland and Philosophy" (at one time the *only* text from issue #4 of the SI's journal) was a bloody murder. Note well that one of Knabb's other crime scenes – his "excerpted" version of "Maitron the Historian" (from 1969) – has been dropped from the 2006 version of the *Anthology,* and *without any acknowledgement or explanation whatsoever.*

And so, Ken Knabb has a lot of goddamned nerve to haughtily ignore or look down his nose at other translators and readers of the situationists' texts. His "Bibliography" contains such *pompous idiocies* as these:

> The online translations tend to be less reliable than the published ones, but many of the latter are also inadequate. The three main faults are excessive literalness, excessive liberty, and pure and simple carelessness [...] I have not attempted to mention, let alone review, the

thousands of printed articles or online texts about the SI. Suffice it to say that the vast majority are riddled with lies or misconceptions, and that even the few that are relatively accurate rarely offer much that cannot be found better expressed in the SI's own writings.

And, as a kind of postscript to "The Blind Men and the Elephant (Selected Opinions on the Situationists)," which he has not updated since 1981,[7] Knabb claims that "most of the recent reactions are as laughably clueless as the earlier ones."

This isn't merely a matter of Ken Knabb's great opinion of himself. It also exposes a basic contradiction in his presentation of the situationists and their writings. On the one hand: "Despite the situationists' reputation for difficulty," he says, "they are not really all that hard to understand." On the other: *only Knabb himself* is smart, educated, patient and attentive enough to understand the situationists; everyone else is a fucking idiot. Well, not *everyone*: "In certain regards, however, the general level of comprehension has improved (particularly among those engaged in radical practices), because the [sic] society's increasingly evident spectacularization has made some of the situationists' insights more clear and undeniable." And *there* it is folks, the root of the problem: despite everything that the situationists said and did, Knabb does not seem to realize (or remember) that what's important is *not* "comprehension," especially not its "general level," as if comprehension can be quantified or averaged out. No: what's important is "radical practice." And Ken Knabb hasn't engaged in *any* "practice," radical or otherwise, since the early 1970s, when he did precisely those types of things that he thought that the situationists would approve of. But the situationists were not prophets of some eternal truth, nor were they scientists who discovered undeniable facts. They worked in and for their own time.[8] And the times have certainly changed since 1972.[9] The situationists' texts or theories can't be used today "as is": they can only be useful when they are used, that is, when they are detourned.

[1] Though most of the surviving documents were written in French, there were also situationist publications in German, Italian, Spanish, Danish and English.
[2] See our comments about Jamie Reid's exhibition for more about the link between the situationists and the Sex Pistols.
[3] See our translation of this text, which we have preferred to title "How situationist books are not understood."
[4] See our website.
[5] See our website.
[6] Knabb's translation of "Remarks on the SI Today" hacks out more than *a third* of the original.
[7] Knabb sent a copy to Debord, who didn't seem very impressed with it or its compiler. In his letter to Gianfranco Sanguinetti dated 31 January 1975, he merely stated: "An American has sent me a poster on which he has assembled many very

droll citations about the SI (generally unfavorable)."
[8] In a letter to Jean-Francois Martos dated 14 September 1985, Debord wrote: "It is necessary to make it understood how the adventure of the SI was narrowly circumscribed *in time*; and contrary to many other 'avant-gardes' with pretensions to lead several [subsequent] generations. Literally, it existed from 1957 to 1972. And counting the period of the 'origins,' it existed from 1952 to '57. And here was the profound meaning of the operation of 'dissolution,' which one can say took place between the autumn of 1970 and the first months of 1972."
[9] In a letter to Eduardo Rothe dated 21 February 1974, Debord wrote: "The epoch no longer simply demands a *vague* response to the question 'What is to be done?' [...] It is now a question, if one wants *to remain in the present*, of responding to this question almost every week: '*What is happening?*'"

NOT BORED! #39, September 2007

Vaneigem's *Declaration*: The Worst Book Ever Written by a Situationist

Nothing strengthens foolishness better than to honor it with a polemic.
– Raoul Vaneigem, 2000.

Raoul Vaneigem's *A Declaration of the Rights of Human Beings: On the Sovereignty of Life as Surpassing the Rights of Man*[1] is easily one of the *worst* books we have ever read, and it is certainly *the worst book* ever written by a former member of the Situationist International (SI). Indeed, it is so bad that, were it not for the fact that we recently passed six months translating Vaneigem's superb book *La Resistance de le Christianisme*,[2] we would not have felt the need to write this review. We would simply have said "Avoid Vaneigem's book about human rights" and left it at that. But this would not have been intellectually honest nor particularly helpful to our readers: there is something *wrong* with Raoul Vaneigem. It isn't simply the case that some of his books are "good" and that others are "bad." It is almost as if there is Vaneigem, the author of a handful of great books, and then there is *someone else* who calls himself "Vaneigem" and writes books that would be unthinkable and even offensive to "the other Vaneigem."

The central thesis of *A Declaration of the Rights of Human Beings* is that human rights are a mere by-product of the rights that the State has accorded to the so-called free market. "The rights of man are no more than specific amplifications of a single right, which is the right to survive merely for the sake of working towards the survival of a totalitarian economy which was imposed untruthfully as the sole means of sustaining the human race," Vaneigem writes. As a result, "the rights of man sanction in a positive form the negation of the rights of the human being": that is, political freedom is a simple compensation for economic unfreedom. As a historical matter,

> the upsurge of the rights of man stems from the expansion of free trade [...] The earliest charters of freedoms appear during the ferment of uprisings in the communes, from the eleventh to the thirteenth centuries, which opposed the entrenched agrarian situation and its parasitical aristocracy with the redoubt of the towns then in full commercial expansion. The air of city freedoms inspired the pre-industrial bourgeoisie to establish a right of recourse against the arbitrariness of the feudal regime, whose predatory parasitism widely hindered the free circulation of merchandise.

The watershed of this period was the Magna Carta (15 June 1215), which, Vaneigem claims, "confirmed an economic revolution which reckoned on a greater energy and profit from the free man selling his labor to the corporations than from the serf bound to the glebe and forced into wearisome corvees."

This is a very simplistic argument, and its weaknesses are clearly exposed when Vaneigem moves on to discuss the declarations of rights that were issued after the Magna Carta. In each case, there is an obvious split or lack of complete overlap between natural rights and those rights that are protected by the law of the land (sometimes this split/difference even appears in the very title of the declaration of rights): "All men are by nature equally free and independent, and have certain inherent rights, of which, when they enter into a state of society, they cannot, by any compact, deprive or divest their posterity" ("The Virginia Declaration of Rights," proclaimed on 12 June 1776); "The Declaration of the Rights of Man *and* the Citizen" (emphasis added), adopted by the French National Assembly on 26 August 1789; and "The Declaration of the Rights of Woman *and* of the Citizen" (emphasis added), written by Olympe de Gouges in 1791. As Giorgio Agamben has pointed out,[3] this split – which appears in many more documents than Vaneigem mentions – becomes a crisis when the laws of the land are suspended due to national emergency. Do "natural rights" still exist during such emergencies? Have these rights been completely absorbed into the now-suspended "political rights"? If they have, does this mean that people who are no longer (or have never been) "citizens" are now completely outside all protections and can be imprisoned, tortured or murdered with impunity?

These are not economic problems nor are they problems caused by the economy's domination of society as a whole. They are properly, even exclusively *socio-political* problems, and – though Vaneigem is too ill-informed or hasty to take note of the fact – they were explicitly addressed by the "Founding Fathers" of the United States. In *The Federalist* (No. 84), Alexander Hamilton pointed out that,

> bills of rights, in the sense and to the extent that they are contended for, are not only unnecessary, but would even be dangerous. They would contain various exceptions to powers not granted; and on this very account, would afford a colorful pretext to claim more than were granted. For why declare that things shall not be done, which there is no power to do? Why, for instance, should it be said, that the liberty of the press shall not be restrained, when no power is given by which restrictions may be imposed? I will not contend that such a provision would confer a regulating power; but it is evident that it would furnish, to men disposed to usurp, a plausible pretence for claiming that power. They might urge with a semblance of reason, that the constitution ought not to be charged with the absurdity of providing against the abuse of an authority, which was not given, and that the provision against restraining the liberty of the press afforded a clear implication, that a right to prescribe proper regulations concerning it, was intended to be vested in the national government. This may serve as a specimen of the numerous handles which would be given to the doctrine of constructive powers, by the indulgence of an injudicious zeal for bills of rights.[4]

Of course, the split between natural rights and political rights reappears in (and tears apart) Vaneigem's *A Declaration of the Rights of Human Beings*. There are certain issues – contraception, suicide, euthanasia and abortion, what to do with dangerous lunatics, violent rapists and murderers – that cannot be merely or simply left up to the billions of "free" individuals in the world or, rather, to what Vaneigem calls "a bundle of individual decisions," because these are properly *social* questions. Who or what holds "the bundle" together? There are no easy answers here, and Vaneigem himself inadvertently proves this to be the case when he refers to certain actions – "bringing children into the world when they are not assured of the benefits of loving care and sensitive intelligence" – as "crimes against humanity." Who should or could punish such a crime: the law of natural selection or the law of the land?

To return to Vaneigem's simplistic sketch of modern history: at the end of the 20th century, economic expansion – after reaching and conquering the entire planet – came to an end. As a result, human rights are now in a period of "decline within democracies" and are subject to "prohibition by despotic regimes." In an attempt to sound "cynical" (that is, uncompromised by illusions), he writes, "there are no grounds for anyone to be surprised, upset or made indignant because the freedoms bestowed on men should have been taken away from them, and, having been emptied of their meaning or negated through the use that is made of them, [that they] should everywhere become inaccessible and illusory, even in the very principle of hope that nourishes them."

And so, *what is to be done,* today, at this moment of crisis, which neatly coincides with the beginning of a new millennium? Well, "we cannot limit ourselves to demanding liberties which have come out of free trade," nor can we "be satisfied with abstract rights in a society where economic ascendancy abstracts human beings from themselves." What *should* we demand, what *would be* satisfactory? Because he is thought to be a revolutionary, Vaneigem feels obliged to offer his readers a revolutionary formulation, fourteen pages into this 133-page-long book:

> We recognize no power other than the pre-eminence of life. Wherever the will to live and its awareness claim an undivided sovereignty, the very notion of rights cancels itself out. All we need is to be human in order to attain an awareness of never being human enough.

But the revolution, though it is apparently already underway, hasn't yet destroyed "the will to power" and replaced it with "the will to pleasure." First, Vaneigem says, there needs to be a period of a *gradual transition*: "The transitional phase which marks the passage from an archaic society to a new society [...] Gradual emancipation from compulsory work authorizes everyone to allocate their time as they see fit [...]." And what should we be doing during this "transition"? Waiting! "While we wait for a guaranteed basic income for everyone [...] As a transitory measure, while waiting for the inauguration of a social system based on free prevision [...]." And how long will we have to wait for this transition to be completed, and – other than waiting – what should we be doing in the meantime? Vaneigem has given his answer by way of personal example: *he* filled up 119 pages of a book with 58 declarations of human rights!

Our readers will probably not be surprised that *every single one* of these articles either comes from or belongs in what Vaneigem himself (in the book's last paragraph) calls the "land of make-believe in which children pretend to die, kill, to flatten mountains and make mountains out of plains." Let us take "Article 10b3" as our example, although any of the other 57 articles (and/or any of their respective subsections) would have sufficed:[5] "Every human being has the right to replace state governments with a world federation of small local collectivities in which the quality of the individual guarantees the humanity of societies." Only those who are completely incapable of logic will need it explained to them that "Article 10b3" is *impossible,* even after any or all "revolutionary" transformations of society have been completed. It could only be through coercive force that "every human being" – the key word here being "every" – could instaurate "small local collectivities" *and* create a worldwide federation of them, but then such a situation have *nothing* to do with "humanity"!

But our readers – especially those who believe that Vaneigem is or was a genuine revolutionary – will be *shocked, if not nauseated* when they learn what

Vaneigem thinks is powering the "gradual [...] transition" to a fully and truly human society. It is *not* the proletariat, the working class, nor even human beings; it is *capitalism itself* or, rather, what Vaneigem calls "neo-capitalism."[6]

> We are engaged in a process of economic transformation where the exploitation of nature and of human beings by other human beings has reached its stage of stagnation, and is gradually giving way under the impact of a new economy [...] The economic transformation under way opens on to a transformation of culture. The former is already at work on producing renewable sources of energy, organic farming and technologies destined to rebalance the environment. The latter is in our hands, exposed to the confusion that always accompanies the conjunction of an old era's ending and the coming of the new, forcing a path through the rubble [...] The economy experienced a reaction of self-preservation at the end of the second millennium. The will to recover some fresh dynamism set its hopes on a regeneration of use-value and quality. The rise of organic farming, the development of natural sources of energy, the emergence of a civil, humanitarian ethics and the return to use-value, all laid down the objective conditions for a time which, liberated from measurement in terms of productivity and consumption, is in the process of becoming the time of market humanism, from which we still have to set it free in order to make it the time of pleasure [...] The decline of the old economy ushers in a new form of harvesting. By drawing on the arsenal of technical progress which is in continuous anarchic development, the new economy has the capacity to add to the profusion of good things which the earth richly offers for the benefit of humankind as a whole [...] The reconversion of the huge market of technologies by a neo-capitalism which takes advantage of a planetary reconstruction that is human and environmentally sound will bring about the application to peaceful ends of a great many discoveries inspired by the art of war and destruction. It is up to us to ensure that the passage from the archaic economy to the setting up of natural sources of energy, organic agriculture, an ethic of human respect and 'clean' merchandise goes hand in hand with that ending of the conditions of survival which will be brought about by the creative making of life.

There is a word for this ideology: it is *neo-liberalism,* and it is espoused by any number of progressive politicians and green capitalists. There is a *very* good reason that, in its review of this book, *Le Monde* said that "all opponents of globalization should carry it in their luggage": this book will help make sure than the "anti-globalization" movement never becomes an *anti-capitalist* movement.

But this critique of *A Declaration of the Rights of Human Beings* – valid though it may be – assumes that the real subject of this book is indeed "human rights" and that Vaneigem wrote it to be read by "opponents of globalization." These assumptions might be false; there are certainly insufficient when it comes to how many of the "rights" enumerated by this book concern (attempt to justify) such things as "the freedom to shun deliberately those subjects for which they feel no curiosity or attraction," "the right to ugliness, to flaws, to what is unaccomplished, to what falls short, the self-same pleasure of the sketch, the botched draft, the skew-whiff line, the false note," "regression, crudeness or silliness," "baby talk, deliberate errors, childish puns and private languages," "the right to rest, to be lazy, to gorge oneself, the right to regression or to nonconformity, the right to oppose, to contradict, to act the clown or the fool," "the wildest speculations, the most lunatic assertions," "the most far-fetched fiction, the most ephemeral lie," and "the most abstruse speculations, crazy systems, immense stretches of the imagination, geometries of the impossible." Precisely because these various kinds of self-betrayal so well describe the very book in which they are justified, one gets the impression – no, one is convinced – that the real subject of *A Declaration of the Rights of Human Beings* is Vaneigem's resignation from the Situationist International (SI), and that he only wrote it for himself, to make himself feel better about what happened back in 1970.

Vaneigem says nothing about the SI in particular,[7] but he says a great deal about groupings of revolutionaries, and *none* of it is favorable.

> The factitious antinomy between individualism and collectivism, normal and abnormal, conformist and anti-conformist, banal and extravagant has always functioned as a trap for rebels, insurgents and outlaws. How could singularity avoid self-betrayal when it takes up a stance of insubordination which derives its meaning from the subordination against which it fights? [...] The ties of solidarity are a hindrance unless they are willingly bound by the affinities which animate a common desire for pleasure, independence and individual creativity. Wherever the will to live abolishes the will to power, those who come together save themselves most surely from the ways of thinking that have turned groupings, associations, collectivities and other fellowships into hotbeds of resentment, hatred and bogus attachment [...] The spirit of subversion has made its claims even through vandalism, by assuming the right to destroy, to soil and degrade a world which, appropriated by those who decreed themselves the masters, did not belong to us [...]

But these are not the worst practices of groupings like the unmentioned SI. No, their worst practice is that they make *judgments*. According to Vaneigem, *no one* should ever make judgments of anyone else: "the right to make mistakes implies a refusal to judge or to be judged," "the propensity to judge derives from the trade in things being applied to the trade in people." As so, where does this leave someone like Raoul Vaneigem, who was judged to be *all talk and no action,* and who consequently was forced to resign from the SI? Alone, completely alone. He pretends that he is happy with being all alone: "Being alone is not the same thing as being forsaken," he writes; "there is no solitude *we* inhabit that does not ultimately live in the world" (emphasis added). "We"?! Who is this "we"? Who is the "we," in the following bold statement, "We are resolved no longer to follow any of the ways that lead to the concentration-camp universe of master and slaves." Elsewhere Vaneigem quotes Heinrich von Kleist – "I can be happy only in my own company, because it is where I am allowed to be completely true" – either forgetting or hoping that his readers do not know that *Kleist killed himself at the age of 34.*

[1] Written in French, dated 11 December 2000 and published by le cherche midi editeur in 2001, this book was translated into English by Liz Heron and published by Pluto Books in 2003.
[2] Written in French in 1992 and published by Librairie Artheme Fayard in 1993, we translated it into English as *The Resistance to Christianity.* In our translator's introduction to this book, we noted the intensity of the antagonism between Vaneigem and Guy Debord, another member of the Situationist International, but tried to maintain a neutral position: "we do not wish to choose sides."
[3] See *Homo Sacer: Sovereign Power and Bare Life* (1995) or *State of Exception* (2002).
[4] Another passage in this text offers an excellent retort to Vaneigem's entire project: "It has been several times truly remarked, that bills of rights are, in their origin, stipulations between kings and their subjects, abridgments of prerogative in favor of privilege, reservations of rights not surrendered to the prince [...] It is evident, therefore, that according to their primitive signification, they have no application to constitutions professedly founded upon the power of the people, and executed by their immediate representatives and servants. Here, in strictness, the people surrender nothing; and as they retain every thing, they have no need of particular reservations [...] This is a better recognition of popular rights, than volumes of those aphorisms, which make the principal figure in several of our state bills of rights, and which would sound much better in a treatise of ethics, than in a constitution of government."
[5] Another good choice here would have been section 2 of "Article 27," which is made up of *questions,* not declarations. "How are we to bring about the elimination of the institutions of police and criminality, by which they are simultaneously incited and repressed, if we continue to maintain within ourselves the way of thinking of a cop, giving it license to subjugate us in the ordering of our everyday affairs and even in our movements of protest and subversion? How are we to guard against an increase in epidemics, epizootics and disasters which are allegedly natural, if we put them down to bad luck, instead of sabotaging the tyranny of

profit which provokes them, more and more frequently, through chaotic disorganization, negligence and contempt for humanity?" Vaneigem obviously has *no answers to these questions,* and so has *no business* pretending that he is capable of writing "a declaration of the rights of human beings."

[6] There is a strong similarity between Vaneigem's serene confidence in the ability of capitalism, through its own development, to produce the "new society" and the confidence displayed in *Facing Reality,* a book that was written in 1958 by C.L.R. James, Grace C. Lee and "Pierre Chaulieu" (a pseudonym for Cornelius Castoriadis) and reprinted in 2006 by Factory School. In the latter volume, the "socialist society" *already exists* on the factory floor, in the ways in which the workers have banded together to make things run smoothly. The task of "the Marxist organization" in such miraculous circumstances is rather simple and passive: "Our task then is to recognize the new society, align ourselves with it, and record the facts of its existence."

[7] But the SI – Guy Debord, in particular – had a great deal to say about Raoul Vaneigem, and all of it is worth citing here.

According to Debord, writing in the "Communiqué from the SI concerning Vaneigem," which was offered in response to Vaneigem's letter of resignation from the SI, his former friend and collaborator wrote his superb book *Treatise on Living for the Younger Generations* (1967) precisely so that he would not have to actually live it out or live up to its demands. Why? Because Vaneigem is fundamentally a "timid" man, Debord says.

> Apart from his opposition, affirmed once and for all, to the commodity, the State, hierarchy, alienation and survival, Vaneigem is quite obviously someone who is never opposed to *anything* in the specific life that is made for him [...] Vaneigem seems to have never wanted to face the simple fact that he who speaks so well commits himself to *being there a little* in a number of analyses and practical struggles, under pain of being radically deceptive.

In other words, Vaneigem's life was "disastrously" divided between bold theory and timid practice. "Nevertheless," the "Communiqué" goes on to say, "the importance of this book [the *Treatise on Living*] does not escape anyone, because (over time) no one, not even Vaneigem, can escape its conclusions." And so, painfully aware of his failure to truly *become Vaneigem,* Vaneigem "disappeared" over the course of the years 1965-1970; he contented himself with the way things were in 1961, when he first joined the SI. He continued to rely upon "a certain generality, a certain abstraction, sometimes even the usage of the tone of the lyrical utterance." For him, "the goal [revolution] being total, it was only envisioned in a pure present: it was *already here* as a whole insofar as one could try to make it believed, or it remained quite inaccessible; one never succeeded in defining it or approaching it [...] The vulgar problems of real society and real revolution could be instantaneously abolished *even before one had the displeasure of considering them.*"

After his resignation from the SI, Vaneigem "disappeared" again: except for an introduction to a volume by Ernest Coeurderoy, he published *nothing* under his own name. In 1974, when he published *From Wildcat Strike to Total Self-Management*, he took the pseudonym "Ratgeb." Once again, Debord's analysis was harsh but very insightful. In a letter to Eduardo Rothe dated 21 February 1974, he wrote:

> What today prevents the Vaneigems from writing – even in the *quantity* of their fuckery, they have been very sober – is the fact that the epoch no longer simply demands a *vague* response to the question "What is to be done?" [...] It is now a question, if one wants *to remain in the present,* of responding to this question almost every week: "*What is happening?*" It is this richness of the return of modern history that puts their poverty into the light of final judgment, and condemns them to silence.

Vaneigem, still believing himself to be in 1961, had not yet caught up to 1968, when revolution returned to modern life, not to mention 1974, when the Portuguese Revolution went further than any before it, even the Hungarian Revolution of 1956.

Nine years later, when Vaneigem finally published a book – *The Book of Pleasures* (Encre, 1979) – under his own name, Debord noted that little had changed. "Vaneigem can only follow the road that was traced for him" in the "Communiqué of the SI concerning Vaneigem." "Fundamentally," Vaneigem's *Book of Pleasures* is "the repetition of a unique stupidity," which was the following:

> The French or Russian worker, the black miner from South Africa or the peasant in the Andes – without considering anything else – goes from pleasure to pleasure, and thus the revolution will quickly be made. Long live strategy, death to the realities of refusal! *What has always defined the parish priests is the promise of paradise.* (Guy Debord, letter to Paolo Salvadori dated 30 November 1979)

The only difference that Debord could detect in Vaneigem was that, "after ten years of reflection, he dares to spout a great stream of resentment, finding himself so alone. He *returns* to childhood; he denies time; he hates all judgments (not without motivations); he no longer refuses anything, *except refusal.*"

NOT BORED! #39, September 2007

Book reviews

Eyal Weizman's *Hollow Land*

We believe we know the basics of the central conflict in the Middle East: the conflict between the Israelis and the Palestinians, that is to say, the conflict over the partition of Palestine. Even before the Israeli "War of Independence," or the Palestinian "Catastrophe," depending upon your viewpoint (either way it took place between 15 May 1948 to 20 July 1949), no one could propose a partition that would be satisfactory to both sides. Jewish and Arab areas were either intermixed and far too close to separate out, or they virtually overlapped. In 1947, for example, the United Nations Special Committee on Palestine (UNSCOP) was unable to carve out a contiguous Israeli state out of Palestine, and so had to content itself with proposing the creation of two politically separate but geographically overlapping and interconnected states, one Israeli, the other Palestinian. Over the course of the creation of the "Green Line," which marked the separation between the new State of Israel and its neighbors at the moment of the 1949 Armistice, more than 700,000 Palestinians were either displaced from or forced out of their homes in Israel "proper."

A great many of the refugees took up "temporary" residence in camps in the Gaza Strip and the West Bank, which were, unfortunately but not unexpectedly, among the precise territories that Israel would seize and begin occupying in the aftermath of the June 1967 war. Starting in late 1967, and in clear violation of both international law and its own laws – battles have been fought in the Israeli High Court of Justice ever since – Israel began to systematically "settle," that is to say, colonize the West Bank (especially "Greater Jerusalem") and the Gaza Strip. Though the Sinai Peninsula was returned to Egypt by 1982, illegal settlements continued to proliferate throughout the Occupied Territories. There have been two *Intifadas* (rebellions) against Israel's on-going occupation and colonization: the first was fought between 1987 and 1993, when the first Oslo Peace Accords were signed; and the second began in September 2000 and ended in 2005. In 2003, supposedly as a result of the second *Intifada,* Israel began the construction of a massive "West Bank Wall," which – though still incomplete – now winds a complicated, highly controversial (totally illegal) path, separating illegal settlements from a patchwork made up of hundreds of parcels of land under the partial sovereignty of the Palestinian people, but actually remote-controlled, if not directly occupied, by Israel.

Yes, we know all this, and yet – despite the fact that this conflict is 60 years old – we have very few widely available maps of the Occupied Territories. I mean good maps; accurate, informative and useful maps; ones that actually show what's happening "on the ground." This makes one wonder: Is it even possible to make a map of the West Bank? Is the West Bank a political geography that is so intensely complicated that it cannot be mapped?

In *Chicago* (Stiedl, 2006), their book about a mock-Palestinian town in the middle of the Negev Desert created for war games by the Israeli military, the photographers and authors Adam Broomberg and Oliver Chanarin note that "maps, land deeds, names, and documentary evidence [of Palestinian life before 1948] have been systematically erased." The only maps that have been available are Israeli maps, that is, maps created and/or approved by the Israeli Defense Forces (the IDF), and not everyone has had access to – or even realized the importance of – these maps. As Edward Said reported in "Palestinians under Siege" (*London Review of Books,* 24 December 2000), the Palestinian negotiators "had no detailed maps of their own at Oslo; nor, unbelievably, were there any individuals on the negotiating team familiar enough with the geography of the Occupied Territories to contest decisions or to provide alternative plans [...] In none of the many dozens of news reports published or broadcast since the present crisis began has a map been provided to help explain why the conflict has reached such a pitch." One must remember that, across the table from the mapless Palestinians at Oslo weren't civilian Israeli negotiators, but military men who certainly knew "the lay of the land" very, very well: they were precisely the ones who had shaped it.

Remarkably, virtually anyone can confirm this maplessness. Go online, call up the much-celebrated Google Maps, and search for either "Israel" or "the Occupied Territories." In either case – the blurring between the two is highly significant – you will find that, in the "Map" setting, absolutely *none* of the major highways, cities and towns are indicated, nor are any of these basic facts presented by the "Satellite" and "Terrain" settings. (As per normal, such basic information *is* indicated in the corresponding displays for Lebanon, Syria or Egypt). And so, strictly speaking, *Google Maps does not have a map of either Israel or the Occupied Territories.* Yes, it is true that there are satellite pictures of the highways, cities, towns, streets and houses in these areas, but pictures do not make a map, which must be read as well as simply looked at, questioned as well as simply appreciated for existing. It is also true that the "Terrain" setting works perfectly well, but such topographical information is completely useless if it can't be combined with a map of the areas under consideration, especially in Israel and the West Bank, where the terrain changes, as one moves from west to east, from beaches to mountains within the space of just a few miles, and where, especially in the West Bank, the illegal Israeli settlements (and other "security" installations) are built on the hilltops and the Palestinian towns and refugee camps are consigned to the valleys. It is for these precise reasons that a picture of an Israeli settlement taken from above is likely to be pleasing, while a picture taken from ground level, where the disparity between hill and valley, Israeli and Palestinian, rich and poor, is likely to be disturbing. Only the latter could reveal the presence of houses permanently divided between floors, houses with roads constructed upon their roofs, or true highways that connect hilltop enclaves together via lengthy elevated platforms. Finally, in all three of Google Maps' settings, one is prevented from zooming in close to the ground or, rather, as vertiginously close as one can when viewing, say, Beirut, Damascus or Cairo. Especially in East Jerusalem, "clouds" (intentional distortions of the images?) prevent one from seeing certain buildings and streets clearly.

Odd things, certainly. But mysteries? No: the answer is simple. Google Maps, which gets all of its satellite imagery as declassified feeds from the American Department of Defense (which of course has close ties with the Israeli military), has agreed to make the deletions mentioned above in the name of protecting the security of Israel against its many enemies: "we do not use our satellites against our allies."[1] Like any other enemy, whether they are state-conscripted armies, volunteer armies, mercenaries, or groups of alleged terrorists, Israel's enemies require maps, which furnish crucial information about Israel ("The company [Google Earth] estimates that 80 percent of the world's information can be plotted on a map in some way," The Associated Press, 8 April 2008). Because these enemies might be anywhere in the world, the IDF has decreed that the whole world cannot have a map of Israel or the territories that it is occupying. In a way, these limits set upon the world's perception and knowledge of itself (these limits to "globalization," if you like) also help Israel to assert *absolute sovereignty* over both its own territory and the territories it occupies: a sovereignty that exists over both airspace and outer space. (And *this* at a time when both the national sovereignty and the sovereign airspace of such nations as Afghanistan and Iraq has been violated, captured and occupied by the United States and its allies.) Furthermore, to the extent that some military planes and satellites have ground-piercing radar, the worldwide blackout on maps of Israeli space extends downwards into the ground as well as upwards into outer space.

And so it was a major event when the Israeli architect Eyal Weizman published the world's first comprehensive map of the Occupied Territories in May 2002. In the postscript to his remarkable book *Hollow Land: Israel's Architecture of Occupation* (Verso, 2007), Weizman notes:

> Establishing its perspective with the triangulations of high points of the terrain, later with aerial photography and satellite imagery, mapping has until recently been almost exclusively associated with the mechanisms of colonial power. However, since the start of the [second] Intifada, it has increasingly become more commonly associated with attempts to oppose and disrupt it [...] In 2001 Yehezkel Lein, a researcher from B'Tselem, invited me to collaborate on the production of a comprehensive report, *Land Grab,* which aimed to demonstrate violations of Palestinian rights through the built environment, especially in the planning of Israeli settlements. Analyzing [many] series of drawings, regulations, policies and plans, undertaking a number of on-site measurements and oversite flights,

we identified human rights violations and breaches of international law in the most mundane expressions of architecture and planning [...] The crime was undertaken by architects and planners in the way they drafted their lines in development plans. The proof was in the drawings. Collecting evidence for this claim against the complicity of architecture in the occupation, we synthesized all drawings and collated all the master plans onto a single map. (pages 261 and 262)

Entitled "Map of Jewish settlements in the West Bank," Weizman's work is still available on-line and was reprinted in *Hollow Land,* which also includes Weizman's map of Gaza, which he completed in 2005. Both maps are professionally designed, very detailed and color-coded. They are "difficult." But the thing that makes them "difficult" is in fact not their method of presentation, but the super-complexity of the spatial arrangements and practices that they depict. For example, Weizman's map of the West Bank carefully and legibly reveals the presence of ten different types of areas (three kinds of Israeli settlements, areas occupied by the IDF, and six kinds of Palestinian lands, including two classifications for Hebron). It turns out that to map the Occupied Territories, Weizman did not need to develop a new method of mapping: he needed to work in and through new conceptions of space, spatial practice and the built environment.

In Weizman's words, his map quickly "became one of the geographical tools for advocacy actions against the Israeli government"; it caused "a 'spatial turn' in the discourse surrounding the occupation," which "has helped extend our political understanding of the conflict to a physical, geographical reality, and led to the production of a wide range of maps, drawn and distributed by a multiplicity of political and human rights groups" (page 262). In a footnote to these lines, Weizman proudly reports that his map (plus the accompanying research) was "produced as evidence by the Palestinian legal team at the International Court of Justice in the Hague in its rulings on the Wall in the winter of 2003" (page 309). He also frankly declares that "Lein and I were later alarmed to learn that the Israeli Ministry of Defense planners had themselves made use of it for their own purposes."

Though he makes no claims to be a revolutionary, Weizman's map was a revolutionary accomplishment, a revolutionary endeavor that was specifically intended to end the Israeli occupation of the West Bank and Gaza, not "reform" or humanize it. He rather modestly likens his work to the efforts of such independent Palestinian organizations as the Applied Research Institute of Jerusalem (ARIJ) and Bimkom (Planners for Planning Rights), and the Israeli Committee Against House Demolition (ICAHD), all of which, he says, engage in "acts of advocacy aiming to put pressure on the Israeli government to end the occupation" (pages 259-260). Weizman opposes the work of these groups to the efforts of "other architects, [who] operating especially through humanitarian organizations and different UN agencies, help in the designing and improvement of Palestinian refugee camps, in the reconstruction of destroyed homes and public institutions, and with the relocation of clinics and schools cut apart from their communities by the West Bank Wall" (page 260). These efforts do not intend to end the occupation, but to "make somewhat more bearable the lives of Palestinians under Israel's regime of occupation" (page 260). As a result, they are open to the following critique:

> Poorly considered direct intervention, however well intentioned, may become complicit with the very aims of power itself. Interventions of this kind often undertake tasks that are the legal – though neglected – responsibility of the military in control, thus relieving it of its responsibilities, and allowing it to divert resources elsewhere. Furthermore, by moderating the actions of the IDF they may even make the occupation appear more tolerable and efficient, and thus may even help, by some accounts, to extend it. This problem is at the heart of what came to be known as the 'humanitarian paradox.' (page 260)

In a footnote to this passage, Weizman refers his readers to Giorgio Agamben's *Homo Sacer: Sovereign Power and Bare Life* (1995; translated from the Italian 1998): "This is one of the reasons [...] Agamben observed that humanitarians 'maintain a secret solidarity with the powers they ought to fight.' For him, both concentrate on the 'human' rather than on the 'political' aspect of being. Agamben further warned that 'there are no humanitarian solutions to humanitarian problems.'" (page 308). Elsewhere in his book, Weizman gives a concrete example of the "process by which the military incorporates into its operations the logic of, and even seeks to cooperate directly with, the very humanitarian and human rights organizations that oppose it" (page 152): the IDF's cynical "Another Life" program (summer 2003), which was supposedly intended to "minimize the damage to the Palestinian life fabric in order to avoid the humanitarian crisis that will necessitate the IDF to completely take over the provision of food and services to the Palestinian people" (quoted by Weizman, page 149).

It is important to note that Weizman's reference to Giorgio Agamben is uncharacteristic of his book as a whole. With the exception of the works of Michel Foucault – in particular, the 2003 collection entitled *Society Must Be Defended: Lectures at the College de France, 1975-1976,* to which Agamben himself often refers – Weizman doesn't mention, re-present or borrow from any critical theorist other than himself. (One might especially question the complete absence from *Hollow Land* of Gaston Bachelard and Henri Lefebvre, two pioneering theorists of space and spatial practices.) Generally speaking, Weizman discusses well-known contemporary critical theorists – Gilles Deleuze & Felix Guattari mostly, but also Guy Debord and Georges Bataille – because parts of the IDF have taken such a strong interest in the military applications of their work. Though Weizman's self-sufficiency hurts him a bit when he comes up with boxy phrases and sentences such as "optical-political camouflage" and "like a theatrical set, the panorama [of the Israeli settlement at Shiloh] is seen as an edited landscape put together by invisible stagehands who must get off the set as the lights come on" (pages 91 and 137, respectively) – why not just refer to Debord's theory of the society of the spectacle? – it helps him in the overall effect of his book, which is very impressive indeed.

Hollow Land concentrates on the post-1967 period: "It looks at the ways in which the different forms of Israeli rule inscribe themselves in space, analyzing the geographical, territorial, urban and architectural conceptions and the interrelated practices that form and sustain them" (page 5). To organize his material, Weizman has neatly superimposed topography and chronology:

> Starting in the deep aquifers of the West Bank, it progresses through its buried archaeology and then across its folded topographical surface to the militarized airspace above. Each chapter, describing different spatial practices and technologies of control and separation, focuses on a particular period in the history of the occupation. (page 15)

But this method is not an academic or self-interested exercise, i.e, not the use of the example of Israel to demonstrate a certain theoretical approach to spatial practice. This is a reckoning. If the occupation has indeed been a "laboratory of the extreme," a laboratory that has acted "as an accelerator and an acceleration of other global political processes, a worst-case scenario of capitalist globalization and its spatial fall-out" (Weizman, pages 9-10), then its experiments have produced definitive results. "In this way, the succession of episodes following the development of Israel's technologies of domination and Palestinian resistance to them also charts a tragic process of cumulatively radicalizing violence," Weizman writes. "However, with the technology and infrastructure deemed necessary for the physical separation of Israelis from Palestinians, it appears that the vertical politics of separation and the logic of partition have been fully exhausted" (page 15). The "human/humanitarian solution" (the demographic separation of populations) has failed; it must be abandoned and replaced by a "political solution" (the unification of all of Palestine into a single nation that brings the various populations together as equals).

Though Weizman refers to "the traditional perception of political space" (page 178), which "is no longer relevant" (178) because "a new way of imagining space has emerged" (182), he does not adequately define or illustrate what the new way is, which deprives his readers of a full understanding of its nature and significance. He only gives us the following (quite useful, but not sufficient) distinction between borders and frontiers.

Against the geography of stable, static places, and the balance across linear and fixed sovereign borders, frontiers are deep, shifting, fragmented and elastic territories. Temporary lines of engagement, marked by makeshift boundaries, are not limited to the edges of political space but exist throughout its depth. Distinctions between the 'inside' and the 'outside' cannot be clearly marked. In fact, the straighter, more geometrical and more abstract official colonial borders across the 'New Worlds' tended to be, the more the territories of effective control were fragmented and dynamic and thus unchartable by any conventional mapping technique. The Occupied Palestinian Territories [can] be seen as such a frontier zone [...] The frontiers of the Occupied Territories are not rigid and fixed at all; rather they are elastic, and in constant formation. The linear border, a cartographic imaginary inherited from the military and political spatiality of the nation-state has splintered into a multitude of temporary, transportable, deployable and removable border-synonyms – 'separation walls', 'barriers', 'blockades', 'closures', 'road blocks', 'checkpoints', 'sterile areas', 'special security zones', 'closed military areas' and 'killing zones' – that shrink and expand the territory at will [...] Elastic territories could thus not be understood as benign environments: highly elastic political space is often more dangerous and deadly than a static, rigid one." (pages 4 and 6-7)

And so, we offer the following sketch, not to make any definitive statements, but to help fill in the background that Weizman has left blank.

In the traditional perception of political space, such as it has been defined by Henri Lefebvre's *The Production of Space* (or at least our understanding of it):[2]

> 1) Space is a pre-existing given; it is available, naturally, like a raw material; it is not socially "produced" or "refined" in any way before it is claimed and put to use.
> 2) Space itself is either empty or partially or completely filled: it is likened to a container of some kind (a sphere or a cube).
> 3) Empty space is "neutral" space; space is only "political" or "political space" when it is partially or completely filled, that is, put to use.
> 4) In this apparently pre-political geometrical space, the key feature is the boundaries or borders that clearly separate inside from outside, and outside from inside. They are fixed and rigid, and cannot be bent, compressed, stretched or broken (even temporarily).
> 5) Internal space (within the sphere or cube) is homogenous; it is external space that is varied, diverse or fragmented. Thus, power originates in internal space and is exerted upon the external.
> 6) Internal space can thus be divided or multiplied "cleanly"

(concentric spheres or smaller cubes fitting snugly within larger cubes to follow the examples in #2 above).

7) In part due to #3 and in part due to other factors, social or political space is understood to be a simple three-dimensional embodiment, transference or materialization of two-dimensional, geometrical space.

This perception/conception of space cannot see or understand such "conceptual" or "theoretical" phenomena as frontiers; temporary interruptions or suspensions of the law (states of exception); trans-boundary flows; interstitial space(s); "elastic" or "pliant" lines, or even optical-political camouflage. But when it is confronted with the built environment in the Occupied Territories – that is to say, with such apparently arcane, extraneous, irrelevant or insignificant phenomena as "cladding and roofing details, stone quarries, street and highway illumination schemes, the ambiguous architecture of housing, the form of settlements, the construction of fortifications and means of enclosure, the spatial mechanisms of circulation control and flow management, mapping techniques and methods of observations, legal tactics for land annexation, the physical organization of crisis and disaster zones, highly developed weapons technologies and complex theories of military maneuvers" (Weizman, page 6) – the traditional perception of space becomes a hindrance to seeing what is actually happening, and why. It keeps looking in the wrong direction. As the IDF showed in its March 2002 raid into the Balata refugee camp near Nablus – during which its commando units completely avoided the major intersections, streets, building exteriors and entrances (all of which were barricaded and booby-trapped), and burrowed into and through the walls of civilian homes, instead, thus completely surprising their adversaries, despite the high degrees of their vigilance and preparation – such oversights can be fatal.

When one compares the map ("Starting in the deep aquifers of the West Bank, it progresses through its buried archaeology and then across its folded topographical surface to the militarized airspace above") to the territory, one finds that Weizman's book primarily concerns the region's "folded topographical surface." The aquifers and sewage disposal systems are discussed in a single chapter ("Interlude – 1967," which a kind of second introduction to the book as a whole). Archeology and the government-mandated use of stone as a building material and/or cladding are also discussed in a single chapter (Chap. 1: "Jerusalem: Petrifying the Holy City"). Also discussed in single chapters are the central role played by Ariel Sharon, who served in a variety of key government and military positions over the course of his 40-year-long career (Chap. 2: "Fortifications: The Architecture of Ariel Sharon"), and "militarized airspace" (Chap. 9: "Targeted Assassinations: The Airborne Occupation," which is the last chapter). The remaining six chapters, Chapters 3-8, are devoted to the Occupation's "folded topographical surface." This arrangement gives the book as a whole the topography of a plateau: a quick rise, a long leveling out, followed by a steep incline.

"One of the most crucial battlegrounds of the Israeli-Palestinian conflict is below the surface," Weizman writes in "Interlude – 1967."

> About 80 percent of the mountain aquifer is located under the West Bank [...] The erosion of the principles of Palestinian sovereignty in its subsoil is carried out by a process so bureaucratically complex that it is almost invisible. Although the aquifer is the sole water source for residents of the West Bank, Israel uses 83 per cent of its annually available water for the benefit of Israeli cities and its settlements, while West Bank Palestinians use the remaining 17 percent. Hundreds of thousands of Palestinians in the West Bank and virtually all Palestinians in Gaza thus receive water irregularly and in limited amounts. Israel's 'politics of verticality' is also manifested in the depth to which water pumps are allowed to reach. Israeli pumps may reach down to the waters of the common aquifers, whilst Palestinian pumps are usually restricted to a considerably shorter reach, only as far down as seasonal wells trapped within shallow rock formations, which, from a hydrological perspective, are detached from the fundamental lower layers of 'ancient waters'. (page 19)

And yet both lower and upper water tables are being contaminated by raw sewage.

> The Israeli authorities failed to provide the minimum necessary sewage infrastructure for Palestinians throughout the period of direct opposition although this is the legal duty of an occupying force [under international law]. The sanitary conditions of West Bank Palestinians were aggravated by Israel's segregation politics that isolated Palestinian towns and villages behind barriers of all kinds. This policy generated more than 300 pirate dumping sites where truckloads of waste were poured into the valleys beside towns and villages. Paradoxically, the restrictions on the flow of people [in the West Bank and between the West Bank and Israel "proper"] accelerated the transboundary flow of their refuse. Furthermore, Israeli companies have themselves used sites in the West Bank for their own waste disposal. [...] In the wild frontier of the West Bank, Israel's *planning chaos* means Jewish neighborhoods and settlements are often [hastily] constructed without permits, and populated before and regardless of sewerage systems being installed and connected. This sewage runs from the hills to the valleys, simply following the force of gravity and topography, through and across any of the boundaries that may be put in front of it. [...] Mixing with Palestinian sewage, traveling along the same open valleys, [Israeli sewage] will eventually end up in Israeli territory. Instead of fresh water flowing [from underground aquifers]

in the specially conceived water pipes installed under the Wall, Israel absorbs large quantities of raw sewage from all across the West Bank. The enclosures and barriers of the recent [counter-measures against the] Intifada thus created the very condition against which they sought to fortify. (pages 19-20, emphasis added)

"Planning chaos" should not be simply taken to mean that Israeli planning is chaotically organized, but also that the chaos that results from it is not completely accidental and has to some extent been planned. "The spatial organization of the Occupied Territories is a reflection not only of an ordered process of planning and implementation, but, and increasingly so, of 'structured chaos', in which the – often deliberate – selective absence of government intervention promotes an unregulated process of violent dispossession" (Weizman, 5). And so, the very thing that is feared (contamination by "dirty" Palestinians) is brought about by the measures taken against it. But instead of seeing the stupidity of its intelligence, the Israeli government asserted that this breakdown in fact confirmed its hygienic xenophobia. "By inducing dirt and raw sewage, Israel could go on demanding the further application of its hygienic practices of separation and segregation," Weizman writes. "The result is an ever-radicalizing feedback loop" (page 20).

Archeology has also been a crucial battleground in the Israeli-Palestinian conflict. Weizman reminds his readers that,

On 27 June 1967, twenty days after the Israeli Army completed the occupation of the [formerly Jordanian] eastern part of Jerusalem, the unity government of Levi Eshkol annexed almost 70 square kilometers of land and incorporated almost 70,000 Palestinians within the newly expanded boundaries of the previously western Israeli municipality of Jerusalem. [...] The new boundaries sought to 'unite' within a single metropolitan area the western Israeli city, the Old City, the rest of the previously administered city, 28 Palestinian villages, their fields, orchards, and tracts of desert, into a single 'holy', 'eternal' and 'indivisible' Jewish capital (page 25).

The problem, of course, was the unwanted presence of those 70,000 Palestinians. And so, "following [the] [urban] masterplan [of 1968] and a series of subsequent master plans, amendments and updates during the forty years of Israeli occupation, twelve remote and homogenous Jewish 'neighborhoods' were established in the occupied areas incorporated into the city," Weizman reports. "They were laid out to complete a belt of built fabric that enveloped and bisected the Palestinian neighborhoods and villages annexed to the city" (pages 25-26). "An outer, second circle of settlements – termed by Israeli planners the 'organic' or 'second wall,' composed of a string of dormitory suburbs – was established beyond the municipal boundaries, extending the city's metropolitan reach even further," he says. "An ever-expanding network of roads and infrastructure was constructed to weave together the disparate shards of this dispersed urban geography" (page 26). In 2007, when *Hollow Land* was published, Greater Jerusalem included 200,000 Israeli settlers, which was approximately the same number as all of the other settlers in the West Bank combined.

To ensure that this "land grab"[3] remained permanent, that is, capable of surviving any future attempts to partition the City in a different way, the very *soil* underneath, adjacent to and surrounding these settlements had to be secured, and done so "legitimately." And so: "On 27 June 1967, the same day that Arab Jerusalem and the area around it was annexed to Israel, the Israeli government declared the archaeological and historical sites in the West bank, primarily those of Jewish or Israeli cultural relevance, to be the state's 'national and cultural property,' amounting to a *de facto* annexation of the ground beneath the Occupied Territories, making it the first zone to be colonized" (page 40).

In an attempt to naturalize and standardize the unification and on-going expansion of Greater Jerusalem, Mayor Kollek Teddy inaugurated the biennial Jerusalem Committee, the Advisory Committee of which included prominent urban planners, architects, architectural critics, historians, theologians and biblical scholars. As Weizman bitterly notes, these people "never challenged the political dimension of the municipal plan and Israel's right or wisdom in colonizing and 'uniting' the city under its rule, nor did it discuss the dispossession of Palestinians that it brought about" (page 37). In addition to calling for the systematic excavation and exact reconstruction of archaeological finds, and their incorporation into the overall urban design scheme – as the American architect Louis Kahn did for the 18th Century (A.D.) Hurva Synagogue – these advisors insisted upon tightening a bylaw from the British Mandate circa 1918 that required the use of certain kinds of limestone as the only material allowed on the exteriors of the city's buildings and streets, and extending the bylaw's reach to the entire area annexed to the city. "Stone cladding was used to *authenticate* new construction on sites remote from the historical centre, giving the disparate new urban shards a unified character, helping them appear as organic parts of the city" (Weizman, 27-28, emphasis added). We can say that, because these new buildings strove to reject modernism and to look old (biblical era), rooted in archaeological sites (which in fact were *not* beneath them), and yet genuinely "authentic," they can be identified as *simulacra* (copies of things that never existed). And because the "unified character" of Greater Jerusalem was in fact produced according to plan rather than restored according to discovery, we can call stone-clad Jerusalem a *spectacular* city, that is, unified by and in appearance only.

For Weizman, the "folded, topographic space" of the Occupation is dominated by four spatial practices (all of them spectacular):

1) the Israeli settlements in the hills, which are "intensely illuminated [...] visible as brilliant white streaks of light that contrast with the yellowish tint of the light in the Arab villages and towns [in the valleys]" (page 133). Weizman calls

this spatial practice "optical urbanism" (page 111).

2) the West Bank Wall, which, "although none of the maps released by the media or independent [human] right[s] organization[s] actually show it, and all photographs of it depict a linear object resembling a border (and which all foreigners from territorially defined nation states will immediately understand as such), [...] has in fact become a discontinuous and fragmented series of self-enclosed barriers that can be better understood as a prevalent 'condition' of segregation – a shifting frontier – rather than one continuous line neatly cutting the territory in two" (page 177).

3) the spectacle of surveillance, which not only is staged at the hilltop settlements ("During the [second] Intifada, the military finally ruled that settlements be surrounded by several layers of fencing systems, cameras equipped with night-vision capability and even motion detectors placed on the perimeter fence, further extending the function of the naked eye" [page 133]), but also at terminal checkpoints ("the architecture of the Allenby Bridge terminal incorporated within the scale of a building the [same] principle of surveillance that [had] dictated the distribution of settlements and military bases [on the hilltops] across the Occupied Territories" [page 141]) and along the aforementioned West Bank Wall ("The main component of the barrier is a touch-sensitive, 'smart', three-metre-high electronic fence [...] It also has day/night vision video cameras and small radars" (page 292). Note well that surveillance is also the central element in the "militarized airspace" above the Occupied Territories: since 2004, "with the development and proliferation of drone technology," Weizman explains (page 242), most targeted assassinations of Palestinian "militants" and "terrorists" are carried out by remote-controlled Unmanned Aerial Vehicles ("drones") that were originally designed to engage in video surveillance and have been freshly equipped with laser-guided, anti-tank "Spike" missiles.

4) the IDF's methods of conducting urban warfare. Because this particular spatial practice is so closely associated with "complex theories of military maneuvers," including the theories of space elaborated by several bellicose critics of what Weizman calls "the capitalist city" (Deleuze & Guattari, Debord, Bataille, et. Al), it warrants being treated at some length.

Weizman reports that, "following global trends, in recent years the IDF has established several institutes and think-tanks at different levels of its command and has asked them to reconceptualize strategic, tactical and organizational responses to the brutal policing [...] in the Occupied Territories known as 'dirty' or 'low intensity' wars" (page 187). One of these institutions was the Operational Theory Research Institute (OTRI), which instructed all high-ranking Israeli officers – as well as some members of the US Marine Corps – between early 1996 to May 2006, under the co-directorship of Shimon Naveh and Dov Tamari, both retired brigadier generals.

One avid disciple of the OTRI was Brigadier General Aviv Kochavi, who was the commander of the IDF's March-April 2002 attacks on the Balata refuge camp in Nablus and several Palestinian cities in the West Bank. In an interview with Weizman, Kochavi explained that "the enemy interprets space in a traditional, classical manner," that is to say, "the alley [is] a place forbidden to walk through and the door [is] a place forbidden to pass through, and the window [is] a place forbidden to look through, because a weapon awaits us in the alley, and a booby trap awaits us behind the doors" (page 198). It is precisely this potentially deadly situation that has prevented urban warfare from being widely or frequently conducted by traditional, state-conscripted armies.[4] In the situation sketched out by Kochavi, the Palestinians' defensive position is far too strong for any attacking force to be successful, that is to say, any attacking force that feels itself bound by the constraints of international law and therefore would not, for example, simply drop a bomb on the entire neighborhood and kill everyone. But the IDF under the command of Kochavi did not feel itself bound by *any* law.

> I do not want to obey this interpretation [of space, but also international law] and fall into his [the enemy's] traps. Not only do I not want to fall into his traps, I want to surprise him. This is the essence of war. I need to win. I need to emerge from an unexpected place. And this is what we tried to do (Kochavi, quoted in Weizman, page 198).

And so, the IDF "won" in Balata and elsewhere by committing war crimes: it penetrated into, occupied, fought from within and eventually destroyed the domiciles of the civilian population in a zone "temporarily" occupied after a war.

> This is why opted for the method of walking through walls . . . We took this micro-tactical practice and turned it into a method, and thanks to this method, we were able to interpret the whole space differently (Kochavi, quoted in Weizman, page 199).

As Weizman notes, "the reference to the need to interpret space, and even to re-interpret it, as the condition of success in urban war, makes apparent the influence of post-modern, post-structuralist theoretical language" (page 199). Kochavi was indeed introduced to "theory" while at the OTRI, which taught it to help the IDF understand "urban fighting as a spatial problem" (Shimon Naveh, quoted in Weizman, page 200). According to Weizman, Naveh gave a presentation on military and guerrilla operations in 2004 that "employed the language of French philosophers Gilles Deleuze and Felix Guattari," whose books, Weizman says, "draw a distinction between two kinds of territoriality: a hierarchical, Cartesian, geometric, solid, hegemonic and spatially rigid state system; and the other, flexible, shifting, smooth, matrix-like 'nomadic spaces'" (page 200). Weizman goes on to explain that, "within these nomadic spaces," Deleuze and Guattari "foresaw social organizations in a variety of polymorphous and diffuse operational networks," and "organizations composed of a multiplicity of small groups that can split up or merge with one another depending on contingency and circumstances and are characterized by their capacity for adaptation and metamorphosis" (page 200). Naveh concurs:

> Several of the concepts in [Deleuze & Guattari's] *A Thousand Plateau* became instrumental for us . . . *allowing us to explain* contemporary situations in a way that we could not have otherwise explained [...] Most important was the distinction Deleuze & Guattari have pointed out between the concepts of 'smooth' and 'striated' space . . . [which accordingly reflected] the organizational concepts of the 'war machine' and the 'state apparatus'. In the IDF we now often use the term 'to smooth out space' when we want to refer to operations in a space in such a manner that borders do not affect us. Palestinian areas could indeed be thought of as 'striated', in the sense that they are enclosed by fences, walls, ditches, road blocks and so on. . . . We want to confront the 'striated' space of traditional, old-fashioned military practice with smoothness that allows for movement through space that crosses any borders and barriers. Rather than contain and organize our forces according to existing borders, we want to move through them (quoted in Weizman, 200-201, emphasis added).

As Weizman points out, "the Israeli military hardly needed Deleuze to attack Nablus" (page 214). Indeed. Naveh clearly doesn't know what Deleuze & Guattari talking about. It is nonsensical to pair "striated space" with the "state apparatus" on the Palestinian side, and "smooth space" with the "war machine" on the Israeli side. First and foremost, the Palestinians haven't created or chosen their "striated space": all of the "fences, walls, ditches, road blocks and so on" were built and imposed upon them by the Israelis. Second, Israeli space (that is to say, space in Israel "proper") is in fact not "smooth," but striated (like the typical capitalist city), and its architecture and urban design is, as we have seen, closely controlled by the "state apparatus" and *not* the nomadic tendencies of the "war machine." Third and last, the precise thing that the Palestinians lack is a "state apparatus": they have no homeland of their own and only partial autonomy in the Occupied Territories.

Indeed, if you are going to systematically commit crimes against humanity, you need nothing other than a reckless disregard for human life. Shimon Naveh reports that, during the March-April 2002 raids, "the [Israeli] military started thinking like criminals. . . like serial killers [...] like professional killers" (quoted in Weizman, 197). So why refer to Deleuze at all? Recall that Naveh said theory allowed the IDF *to explain* contemporary situations. Theory didn't allow the IDF to fight, or to fight better, but to explain, to talk about fighting. Explain it *to whom*? To the IDF's Palestinian victims? "The IDF didn't destroy your village; it smoothed it out." Perhaps to future war-crimes tribunals? "The IDF wasn't breaking the law, but merely borders and barriers."

In any event, Eyal Weizman wasn't fooled. On the one hand, he knows that theory is "an instrument in the power struggles within the military itself," "a new language with which it can challenge existing military doctrines, break apart ossified *doxas* and invert institutional hierarchies," and a means for "the critique of the existing system, to argue for transformations and to call for further reorganizations" (page 215). This "language" need not be expressed properly nor even understood by those who claim to speak it; this "language" need only be wholeheartedly embraced so as to exclude those who cannot or will not (allow themselves to) understand even little bits of it. "Theory" – even if a great deal of it is enunciated from a Marxist perspective – can be used to sell the Occupation as the work of a "smart" military (smart bombs, smart theories), that is to say, a surgically precise and thus "more humane" killing machine.

On the other hand, Weizman knows that "claims for the 'non-linearity' and the 'breakdown of vertical hierarchies' in contemporary warfare are [...] largely exaggerated [...] Military networks are still largely nested within traditional institutional hierarchies, units are still given orders [from a central command], and follow plans and timelines" (page 212). The "theory" cadre in the IDF was dealt a fatal set-back in spring 2006, when OTRI graduate Brigadier General Gal Hirsh was unable to defeat Hizbollah in Lebanon, which quickly led to the de-commissioning of the OTRI itself. The only measure of success in military operations is victory, and neither "theory," "intelligence" reports, nor magic spells can guarantee it.[5]

[1] Quoted in Weizman, page 270.
[2] See Henri Lefebvre's *The Production of Space*.
[3] See Eyal Weizman, *Land Grab* (May 2002).
[4] Weizman points out that "the technique of moving through walls was first recorded in writing by Marshal Thomas Bugeaud's 1849 military manual *La Guerre des Rues et des Maisons,* in the context of anti-insurgency tactics used in the class-based urban battles of nineteenth century Paris. 'Are the barricades too strong to be broken down by the *tirailleurs*? Then one enters into the first houses that line either side of the street, and it is here that the detonator is a great advantage because he quickly achieves the goal. One climbs to the top floor and systematically blasts through the walls, finally managing to pass the barricade'" (page 212). A striking parallel with the spatial practices of the IDF! But Weizman makes a mistake when he imagines that, "on the other side of the barricades and a decade later, Louis-Auguste Blanqui wrote this micro-tactical maneuver into his *Instructions pour une prise d'armes*" (212), as if the there were some kind of a symmetry, likeness, symbiosis or "co-evolution" (page 189) between the tactics of insurgents and those of anti- or counter-insurgents. But there isn't. The materials used by the Blanquists and others – "elements of circulation," "paving stones and carriages" that "became elements of blockage (blockades)" (Weizman, 212) – were

retrieved from the streets, from public space, and *not* from the insides of people's homes, from private space. Likewise, as Weizman himself says, "the Israeli and Palestinian methods of fighting are fundamentally different" (page 198).
[5] It seems that Weizman has only recently reached these conclusions. In an early version of Chapter 7 of *Hollow Land* ("Urban Warfare: Walking Through Walls"), he wrote:

> The practical or tactical function, the extent to which Deleuzian theory influences military tactics and maneuvers, raises questions about the relation between theory and practice. Theory obviously has the power to stimulate new sensibilities, but it may also help to explain, develop or even justify ideas that emerged independently within disparate fields of knowledge and with quite different ethical bases [...] Deleuze and Guattari were aware that the state can willingly transform itself into a war machine. Similarly, in their discussion of 'smooth space' it is implied that this conception may lead to domination ("The Art of War," published in issue #99 of *Frieze Magazine* [May 2006], emphasis added).

Perhaps Weizman was suggesting or implying that theory or, rather, particular theorists, were partly to blame for the IDF's war crimes. Perhaps he believed that Deleuze and Guattari, like the "humanitarian" organizations active in the Occupied Territories, "maintain a secret solidarity with the powers they ought to fight." It is certainly true that the language of the version in *Hollow Lands* is much softer: "This is not to place blame for Israel's recent aggression in the hands of radical theorists or artists, or to question the purity of their intentions" (page 211); "Deleuze and Guattari were aware that states or their agents may transform themselves into war machines, and that, similarly, the concepts of 'smooth space' may help form *tools* of domination" (page 298, emphasis added). Unfortunately for his readers, Weizman maintains that "it is not my aim here to try to correct imprecisions and exaggerations in the military 'reading', use and interpretation of specific theories," because "I am primarily concerned with understanding the various ways in which theory, taken out of its ethical/political context, may perform within the military domain" (page 211). But this explanation begs several important questions: Is theory still "theory" (that is, an apprehension of the totality) if it is taken out of context? Isn't theory more than mere *jargon*? What roles other than *generator of and apologist for criminal stupidity* can out-of-context theory play within the military domain?

NOT BORED! #40, May 2008

Book reviews
Steal this book

Now that Semiotext(e) – after thirty years of ignoring Guy Debord and the other members of the Situationist International in favor of such ex-Maoist "post-structuralists" and "post-modernists" as Jean Baudrillard and Michel Foucault – has published its translation of volume I (June 1957-August 1960) of Guy Debord's letters, I know you fuckers are expecting me – the guy who has been translating and uploading these letters to the Internet for free for the last four years – to write one of my patented, very detailed and thoroughly devastating 5,000 word critiques. But frankly I can't be bothered. And so y'all are going to have to content yourselves with the following list, presented *en vrac*.

1) The entire volume is presented exactly as it was in the original French, which means this volume says that it is the first of six such volumes, when in fact *seven* habe been published to date.

2) The translators have reproduced all of Alice/Fayard's footnotes, but have added none of their own; untranslated texts that are referred to by Debord have been left untranslated; the book also does not include an index or a list of "Who's Who"; as a result, the people, publications and events described can be unnecessarily difficult to follow.

3) The back cover claims that these letters are "published here for the first time in English," as if what appears on the Internet is not actually published and therefore isn't real and/or doesn't exist.

4) The back cover insists that the Situationist International was a "cultural" avant-garde, a "cultural movement" with a "cultural mission," and *completely* ignores and thereby falsifies its political character – and this at a time when Guy Debord *continues* to inspire and be cited by political revolutionaries in France and Greece, who would not recognize themselves in, nor would they settle for, what Semiotext(e) calls "a complete transformation of personal life *within* the Society of the Spectacle" (emphasis added).

5) After waiting to see how well this book sells – McKenzie Wark's preface suggests that it will be marketed to "today's individualist sensibility," "to an ear trained by the Cold War to protect its precious individualism," "the individualist sensibility of what Debord will call 'bourgeois civilization,'" and (worst of all) "the contemporary reader" – Semiotext(e) is going to try to convince Alice/Fayard that publishing translations of all seven volumes in their entirety isn't commercially viable, and that, after 1969, "superfluous" letters will need to be edited out,[1] thus placing the full weight of the series on the first two or three volumes, which of course will be complete.

6) The overall effect of this operation will be just like Tom McDonough's *Guy Debord and the Situationist International: Texts and Documents*, which emphasized the early "artistic" SI at the expense of the later "political" SI, but

much worse because Debord's *entire life* will be reduced to what he did between 1957 and 1967, and the English-speaking world will once be deprived of the opportunity to learn about the explicitly political work Debord did in Portugal in 1974 and 1975, Italy in 1975 and 1976, Spain in 1980 and France in 1986 and 1987.

7) Of course, Guy Debord himself would have *hated* such a weighting, which not only concerns the SI, but his whole life. He would have been familiar with it from Greil Marcus' *Lipstick Traces* (1989) and the various exhibitions of situationist art works held at the Pompidou Center and the Institute for Contemporary Arts that same year. And, even worse for Semiotext(e), Debord diagnosed the motivations behind such weightings in his letter to Pascal Dumontier dated 24 October 1989:

> This exhibition wanted to evoke the origins of the SI by refusing and hiding its destiny. 'Becoming is the truth of being.' This phrase by Hegel can be applied, even better than elsewhere, to revolutionary efforts (and often to their detriment, of course). The museographs have thus assembled the 'artistic victims' sacrificed by the SI, who – except for [Asger] Jorn, who was not a victim, but one of the lucid protagonists – wouldn't ever be gathered together in a museum if they had not once upon a time had such important and bad associations. Which are only important and bad thanks precisely to May 68.

I believe that this is why McKenzie Wark's preface is preoccupied with the theme of exclusion, which is mentioned and discussed a total of eight times in the course of a 22-page-long text. He knows full well that, had Debord been alive, he would have tried to prevent and, failing that, would have publicly denounced, such blatantly reactionary moves as those made by Fayard and Semiotext(e).

8) Just like the yellow journalism of Stewart Home, Andy Merrifield, Andrew Hussey, and Nathan Heller, McKenzie Wark's preface to this volume is hostile and suspicious, presenting Debord as if he were a career-minded, manipulative Communist-Party-style apparatchik. Does Semiotext(e) seriously think "the contemporary reader" is going to be interested in and want to buy a book by such a caricature?

9) Wark's preface (which we suspect was actually written by Sylvere Lotringer)[2] mentions *none* of the considerable controversy that, from start to finish (1999 to 2008) surrounds the publication of this series of volumes: a) the fact that in 1999 Alice/Fayard suppressed a book by Debord's former historian and friend, Jean-Francois Martos, who actually produced a real volume of correspondence in which two people exchange letters; b) the fact that Michele Bernstein refused to allow any of Guy's letters to her to be printed, which completely undermined the integrity and legitimacy of the entire project, given the unique importance of this woman to Debord's life, politics and thought; c) the fact

that none of the letters addressed to Alice herself, Jacqueline de Jong or Michele Mochot-Brehat are included, either; d) the fact that Debord's former friend and physician Michel Bounan condemned Alice in 2000 because Fayard is the publishing arm of a huge corporation that makes and distributes military weapons; and e) the fact that, in 2006 and 2007, Debord's former friend and collaborator Jean-Pierre Baudet – as a protest against all of the above, but especially the fact that Alice/Fayard's "Correspondence" is *not* a correspondence precisely because none of the letters addressed to Debord are included – insisted that none of the letters Guy addressed to him be included in Volumes 6 and 7, and that his name be replaced by an "X" in those instances when he is referred to.

10) The entire book is thus both an Orwellian suppression of these relevant and important historical events, and an implicit validation and approval of the similar suppressions that preceded it and made it possible.

[1] Email correspondence with Semiotext(e)'s Hedi El Kholti, 20 January 2009.
[2] In an email sent 22 January 2009, Wark maintained that he is the one who wrote it. *Tant pis.*

NOT BORED! #41, November 2009

Reading Greil Marcus Listening to Van Morrison

When I was a teenager, living on Long Island in the 1970s, I wasn't a fan of Van Morrison's music, which I only knew because several of his songs were always on the radio: "Moondance," "Domino," and "Brown-Eyed Girl." I didn't *dislike* these songs; they were pleasant enough; I just didn't find anything in them for me. They were too "mellow," too smooth, too goddamned happy. I liked loud guitars and songs about strife. In 1979, when a good friend of mine told me, with great passion, that he *loved* Van Morrison's music, I couldn't understand why. Of course, we were going in very different directions that year, which was the year we both turned 20. While he and the rest of our friends celebrated New Year's Eve by staying home and listening to their favorite records, I – inspired by what I'd read in Lester Bangs' essay "Free Jazz/Punk Rock" – went into New York City by myself and saw a performance by a new band called the Lounge Lizards, who didn't even have a record out yet.

Over the next few months, and always by myself, I would return to "the City" (there was only one) again and again, and, in addition to learning a few essentials – how to order a drink, how to chat up a stranger, and how to dance – I saw several other new bands (Eight-Eyed Spy, the Raybeats, the Contortions, DNA, and Pere Ubu, among others) that my high school friends didn't know about and didn't like when I played their records for them. To them it all sounded like noise, not like "real music," not like ... say ... Van Morrison.

Personally, I only started to like Van Morrison's music when, thanks to Lester Bangs' essay about *Astral Weeks,* I knew what to listen for and what songs to listen for it. (They were not the songs that were, even then, still being played on the radio, nor were they the songs that Morrison had just recently recorded.) Ever since then, I have been a fan, not a fanatical one, it is true, but a fan, nonetheless. My favorites: the albums Van recorded under the name Them in 1965 and 1966; the live concert from 1971; and *St. Dominic's Preview,* released in 1972. But do I like Van Morrison's music as much as I like Lou Reed's or Bob Dylan's? No.

Greil Marcus' newest book is about Van Morrison's music. As my readers will know, I have long been a fan – indeed, a fairly fanatical fan – of Greil's articles and books. For the last 30 years, I have been seeking them out, reading them carefully, and then seeking out the songs that he's mentioned, listening to them, and seeing if what he has said is in fact "true" and "really there." More often than not, he's been right on the money, and I have been thrilled. Greil isn't just a great storyteller; he knows what stories to tell. Of course, sometimes he's been wrong or, rather, sometimes I have found that I'm not convinced that he's "right" and, of course, I have felt disappointed. My favorite books are the early ones, *Mystery Train: Images of America in Rock 'n' Roll Music* (1975), *Lipstick Traces: A Secret History of the Twentieth Century* (1989), *Dead Elvis: A Chronicle of a Cultural Obsession* (1991), and *Invisible Republic: Bob Dylan's Basement Tapes* (1998). I don't particularly like some of the later ones, for example *Double Trouble: Bill Clinton and Elvis Presley in a Land of No Alternatives* (2001), *Like A Rolling Stone: Bob Dylan at the Crossroads* (2005), and *The Shape of Things to Come: Prophecy in the American Voice* (2006). Though I am a political animal and feel that Greil's politics have become rather mild over time – he's more a Social Democrat than an anarchist or a situationist[9] – I always look forward to reading his next book, whatever it might be about.

Entitled *When That Rough God Goes Riding: Listening to Van Morrison,* Greil's latest book was published in March 2010 by Public Affairs. It is excellent, and I thoroughly recommend it to anyone interested in Van Morrison's music and/or anyone who is interested in writing about music in general. (If writing about music is like dancing about architecture, as is sometimes said by people who don't believe that good writing about music is possible, then Greil Marcus is a bell-

---

[9] The book that Greil published later in 2010, *Bob Dylan By Greil Marcus: Writings 1968-2010* (Public Affairs), concludes with two essays from 2008 that have nothing to do with Dylan. Celebrations of the election of Barack Obama, these essays were published without any footnotes that might suggest any disappointment or dissatisfaction with the new president, despite his failures to close the illegal prison at Guantanamo, to pull the troops from Iraq, to end the war in Afghanistan, to prosecute Bush-era war crimes, etc.

ringing ballerina.) His book's narrative structure is both unusual and typical of his approach to historical writing. It both begins and ends in the present or, rather, the very recent past (2009 and 2008, respectively), and thus mimics or echoes the "continual present" in which Greil says that "the most valuable instances" of Van Morrison's music "exist," not a part of history, which is the field of the predictable and repeatable, but outside it, in a virtual geography (an unmapped territory) of unrepeatable events.

Like its subject matter, Greil's book turns on a slightly crooked axis. The author's introduction, which is an overview and summation –

> To those who were listening, it was clear that Van Morrison was as intense and imaginative a performer as any to have emerged in the wake of the Beatles and the Rolling Stones [...] Yet it was equally clear [...] that Morrison lacked the flair for pop stardom possessed by clearly inferior singers [...] What he lacked in glamour he made up in strangeness – or rather his strangeness made glamour impossible, and at the same time captivated some who felt strange themselves [...] [He sought] the deepening of a style, the continuing task of constructing musical situations in which his voice can rise to its own form [...] Van Morrison, then, is a bad-tempered, self-contradictory individual whose work is about freedom.

– appears *after* the brief discussion of the singer's appearance at the Greek Theater in Berkeley, CA, on 3 May 2009, and not before it, as one might expect. Or, if you prefer, the brief discussion of the Greek Theater show is placed *before* the "Introduction," and thus somehow outside of the historical framework it sketches out. As we will see, this sort of displacement or disruption of established conventions and/or expectations will be given an appropriately ugly name: the yarragh.

Like what used to be called a double album, Greil's book is divided into four sections, each of which bears its own title. These sections are of roughly equal length, and all of the essays within them are short. Each section presents the historical material in a zigzag. For example, the first section, "A Grimy Cinderella in a Purple Suit" (a description of what Morrison looked like at "The Last Waltz" performance, which was filmed by Martin Scorsese), starts out in 1965, jumps to 1971, returns to 1965, jumps to 1975, moves on to 1976, and then ends up in 1966. Quite obviously, such a book can be read and then re-read in any order the reader likes. In fact, the reader can even read the book's ending "out of order." Speaking of a particular moment in "Behind the Ritual," a song from 2008, Greil writes: "You never get back to the rest of the album, or for that matter to the rest of Morrison's career. It could stop right here. But over the course of that career one might have said the same thing a dozen times." Especially because the first "end" in Morrison's career came so early: in 1964 or 1965, when the original incarnation of the band Them broke up, and Morrison had to start all over again.

Expressed as a traditional, linear chronology, Van Morrison's best music according to Greil was produced in 1965 ("Mystic Eyes" and "Baby Please Don't Go"), 1966 ("It's All Over Now, Baby Blue"), 1968 (all of *Astral Weeks,* but especially "Madame George" and "Sweet Thing"), 1970 ("Caledonia Soul Music"), 1971 (two songs recorded in the studio, "Tupelo Honey" and "Moonshine Whiskey," and two songs performed live, "Just Like a Woman" and "Friday's Child"), 1972 ("Almost Independence Day" and "Listen to the Lion"), 1974 ("Linden Arlen Stole the Highlights"), 1975 ("John Brown's Body"), 1976 ("Caravan" performed live at "The Last Waltz") and 1979 (the *Into the Music* album). After more than a decade's worth of "colorless" albums, he returned to produce more great music in 1991 ("Take Me Back"), 1996 (a live performance of "Saint Dominic's Preview"), 1997 ("The Healing Game"), 2000 ("The Last Laugh"), and 2008 ("Behind the Ritual").

Greil's zigzag mimics or echoes Van Morrison's music, or at least "Mystic Eyes." The last line of his essay about this song ends this way: "You're caught up in an irresolvable adventure that is taking place as you listen, in the notion that you can drop someone into the middle of a story and then jerk him or her out of it as if it were nothing more than a few minutes on the radio, now a bad dream you're certain is yours alone." The zigzag also makes it clear that Greil is setting his own pace, preceding as slowly as he needs to, to get the story right. Throughout the book, there are references to musicians who have done the same thing: Bob Dylan on his album *John Wesley Harding,* Van Morrison on *Astral Weeks,* and Mattie May Thomas in her song "Workhouse Blues." The ending of Greil's essay on "The Healing Game" hits the nail on the head: "For both [Van Morrison and Mattie May Thomas], it's all in the refusal to be rushed. Ordinary life, after all, guarantees only death and oblivion [...] In their tone they both say the same thing. Death has waited all these years; it can wait another day."

And yet, within the essays themselves, Greil doesn't mimic or echo Van's singing, which is characterized by "unusual repetitions" of certain words or phrases. To Greil, such repetitions "in Morrison's music always signify freedom, a love of words, and a lack of fear for what they might say." Significantly, I think, it is these very qualities – a preoccupation with freedom, a love of words, intensity and imagination, and no fear of getting carried away – are what make him such a compelling writer. No: in his essays about Van Morrison, Greil moves fast and doesn't repeat himself. His essay about "Moonshine Whiskey" is only two sentences long! ("It's the way he affirms 'I'm gonna put on my hot pants' as if he's trying to twist himself into them. But were they pink?") Several of the other essays end too soon. In the essay about "Baby Please Don't Go," Greil writes (to begin the last paragraph): "Quickly, there's nothing between the singer and the song: no reverence, no respect, no hesitation in taking the fruits of someone else's culture." I know "quickly" refers to the pace of the music's development, but it also applies to Greil's discussion, which ends a sentence or two later with the following terse summary: "In 1965, Them's 'Baby Please Don't Go' was loud, on the radio, and its yarragh was its heedlessness." In his essay about Morrison's version of Bob Dylan's "It's All Over Now, Baby Blue" – Greil's own heedlessness brings him to ignore (or at least end the essay without mentioning) everything that happens in the song after the line "Drawing crazy patterns on your sheets," that is to say, the entire second half of the song! In particular, he misses Van's strangely mournful singing as the song fades out.

Of course, there are other missed opportunities, a few missed connections. The Velvet Underground's song "I Heard Her Call My Name" is clearly inspired by Them's "Mystic Eyes." Though he is quoted on the book's sleeve – "This is someone who can abandon himself. For a Protestant from East Belfast, Van Morrison has a lot of the Holy Ghost in him." – and though he performed a strong version of Morrison's "Full Force Gale" for the 1994 album *No Prima Donna: The Songs of Van Morrison,* Elvis Costello isn't mentioned once by Greil. In an essay often published alongside *Naked Lunch,* William S. Burroughs quotes from Gene Austin's "The Lonesome Road" – "Look down LOOK DOWN along that junk road before you travel there" – a song that Greil says fascinates everyone who is "over eighty or under twenty." Oh! and it was *Jimi Hendrix,* not Neil Young, who came up with "the harsher, louder, wilder, even triumphant treatment" of Dylan's "All Along the Watchtower" that "the song needed" and that "Dylan himself immediately adopted."

Though regrettable, these missed connections (or lamentations for them) are in some way beside the point. Greil writes at the end of his entry on *Astral Weeks*: "I no longer altogether trust the sort of explanations that along with other people I used to pursue so passionately – not, of course, philistine, literal explanations, of course not, but imaginative, contextualizing explanations that made both a work [of art] and its setting richer for the introduction of one to the other." Why the change or, rather, why the newfound distrust? Great art is fundamentally or essentially "inexplicable" – it is "something that could not have been predicted and could never be repeated," Greil says – and it so always remains beyond even the most imaginative and contextualizing explanations. Though I have no doubt about the truthfulness of these assertions, I'm not sure how far I'd want to take them. Certainly Greil would not write essays that simply say, "This is a great work of art, it is inexplicable, and so there is nothing more to say about it," because the greatness of great art is not self-evident. It requires some explanation at the very least.

As you read through Greil's short-and-to-the point entries, as he takes you here, then there and then over there, the book gathers momentum. It is only at the very end of Side Two (which is entitled, "I'm Going to My Grave With This Record," a reference to Greil's love of *Astral Weeks*) that we get the first reference to something recent, i.e., Morrison's guest appearance on Mark Knopfler's song "The Last Laugh." Until then, we've been reveling in the past, in Van's very best music. At the beginning of Side Three ("A Belief in the Blues as a Kind of Curse

One Puts on Oneself"), Greil stops the band and tells us, not only that Morrison produced 15 uninspired and uninspiring albums between 1980 and 1995, but also why. He was overcome by what we might call the anti-yarragh: a defensive, self-satisfied commitment to "music of affection, sensuality, and acceptance," with "everything [...] pitched to a middle range: desire and pleasure, never joy or rage." And then Greil lets his readers float for the rest of the section. First they look back to 1974, then forward to 2005, before settling in, in 1997.

It is on Side Four (entitled "There Was No False Face the Song Could Not Erase") that the heavy essays appear, the ones tasked with facing "Madame George" head on (she'd already been approached once in the essay on Side Two about *Astral Weeks,* and then again in the essay on Side Three about her song's appearance in the film *Breakfast on Pluto*). By the third-to-last essay, written about Van's song "Take Me Back" and how it appears in a bad film from 1995 starring Jennifer Jason Leigh, the reader can feel that Greil has put on the brakes, and has begun to end his rough ride. And when he finally does, in the essay on "Behind the Ritual," he leaves you with his most important insight (there have been others, including the idea that fiction is often dismissed or distrusted because many people lack imagination and even fear it). What in the end is it all about? Not just Van Morrison's music, but Greil Marcus' book as well? It's about "life," Greil says, "and what you want from it between the time you wake and the time you sleep." In the words Greil uses to summarize the many achievements of *Astral Weeks*: "there's more to life than you thought. Life can be lived more deeply – with a greater sense of fear and horror and desire than you ever imagined." Van Morrison's music doesn't make you love life and want to live it as deeply as possible? Well, there's no accounting for taste. Greil Marcus' books don't do it for you either? Well, that's OK, too, provided that *something* does it. If not, then the problem doesn't lie with Van Morrison or Greil Marcus, but with *you.*

A review for *The Washington Post* (reprinted as a blurb for *When That Rough God*) has claimed that Greil "achieves a primary goal of important music criticism: to turn readers back into listeners." But this is an impoverished goal, and one that Greil only passes by on his way towards a much richer one: turning both listeners and readers back into people.

P.S. What about the yarragh? OK: let's talk about the yarragh. According to Greil, this bit of onomatopoeia comes from a cinematic biography of the Irish tenor, John McCormack. According to Ralph J. Gleason – it appears Greil himself hasn't seen the film; otherwise why complicate things by bringing Gleason into it? – there's a moment in the film in which McCormack says that, to be a truly great singer, "you have to have the yarragh in your voice." I think it is clear that McCormack is referring a certain roughness, a kind of roaring, in the timbre of a singer's voice. But Greil defines it as an "event" that takes place during a song: "the moment when the magic word, riff, note, or chord is found and everything is transformed"; "a note so exalted you can't believe a mere human being is responsible for it, a note so unfinished and unsatisfied you understand why the eternal seems to be riding on its back"; "moments of disruption, when effects can seem to have no cause, when the sense of an unrepeatable event is present, when what is taking place in a song seems to go beyond the limits of respectable speech"; "the moments of upheaval, reversal, revelation, and mirror-breaking." In Van Morrison's case, the "quest for the yarragh" is pursued through "the twist of a phrase or the dissolution of words into syllables and syllables into preverbal grunts and moans," and "perhaps most of all in repetition, railing or sailing the same sound ten, twenty, thirty times until it has taken his song where he wants it to go or failed to crack the wall around it."

Greil obviously realizes there's a difference between a rough timbre and the "event" that the use of a rough timbre may or may not cause in a particular song when a particular person sings it. He is not trying to produce a "theory of the yarragh," that is, a concept that might be picked up and applied to other singers. The yarragh isn't "detournement" under another name. The "yarragh" is simply a way of labeling a phenomenon that is unique to Van Morrison and Van Morrison alone. And this is fitting, because no other singer has a style that includes – no other singer has based his or her style on – verbal tics, stutters, and repetitions. Lou Reed or Bob Dylan may sing in ways that include or produce disruptions, and Roger Daltry may have imitated a stutter to sing "My Generation," but none of them are wrestling with the yarragh. That lion has only one tamer.

For Van Morrison, the yarragh is both blessing and curse. It is a blessing to be such a talented singer, but talented singers are not always comfortable with audiences, especially those who have heard recordings of the singer's songs and demand to hear them reproduced live in concert, just as they are on record. Perceptive as always, Greil sees that in Van Morrison's case "the quest for the yarragh […] is also a performer's quest to evade and escape the expectations of his audience. It's a struggle to avoid being made irrelevant and redundant, a creature tied as if by chains to his hits of forty, thirty, twenty years earlier, even to the song that hit last month – forbidden, by the laws of the pop mind and the pop market, from ever saying anything he hasn't said before." Lou Reed and Bob Dylan have struggled with this, too, and the result for them, as well as for Van Morrison, "is a distrust of the audience, coming out, on any given night, in anger, insult, drunkenness, disdain directed at the singer's own songs as much toward whatever crowd might be present." But unlike Lou Reed and Bob Dylan, who have always needed, sought out and thrived on audiences, and have even pandered to them, "from the time of his first hits Morrison has, in a way, set himself against *any* possible audience: he does his work in public, but with his back turned, sometimes literally so" (emphasis added). He is an exile who will never return to Main Street.

It a different way, the yarragh is both a blessing and curse for Greil. It is certainly an apt term for Van Morrison and the way he uses his full, expressive, and sometimes rough voice. But it is also an unnecessary term, unworthy of repetition ("the yarragh in this song is," "Here the yarragh is in the," etc.) For example, Lester Bangs writes about Van Morrison's "whole set of verbal tics," but he doesn't give a special name to the affect(s) these tics produce on certain occasions; he simply identifies and describes them as needed. Furthermore, Bangs recognizes the events or moments in Van Morrison's music, but he doesn't register them as disruptions. For him, "Van Morrison is interested, obsessed with how much musical or verbal information he can compress into a small space, and, almost conversely, how far he can spread one note, word, sound, or picture." For Bangs, Morrison may compress or expand the sung word, but he never breaks it or breaks with it. But for Greil – and I suspect it is the temptation of having a concept at his disposal, rather than just an idea, that leads him in this direction – the yarragh has a relationship with and thus affects upon language itself. He writes about "Listen to the Lion": "Morrison cries, moans, pleads, shouts, hollers, whispers, until he finally breaks with language and speaks in tongues, growling and rumbling. The feeling is that whoever it is that is singing has not simply abandoned language, but has returned himself to a time before language, and is now groping toward it." I'm going to have to call bullshit on this. Speaking in tongues is not "breaking with language" but speaking an unknown language. There is no way to "abandon language," because language is the means by which we think *and* the means by which we communicate. There literally never was "a time before language," because time, a creation of language, didn't exist before language was invented. Finally, I believe that Shakespeare's *A Midsummer's Night's Dream* has already shown the bottomless comic perils that await those who mistake an actor pretending to be a lion for a real one.

The concept/non-concept of the yarragh really becomes a problem when the subject of Belfast comes up or, rather, when the subject of *avoiding the subject* of Belfast comes up. Greil writes:

> If, as more than one person has written, the title of Seamus Heany's 1975 poem "Whatever You Say, Say Nothing" summed up both the aesthetic and the everyday life of avoidance in Northern Ireland in that time, when the cause writing your name on a bullet could as well be that of your presumed fellows as of your fated enemies, if not chance itself, could Morrison's work up to this moment have been a version of the poem itself, with "Whatever You Say, Say Nothing" boiled down, in the manner of a song to nothing more than its phrase, sung over and over in endless variation? "Is there a link between that attitude, which Morrison seems to embody," a friend wrote, "and the yarragh? Can't we understand aspects of the yarragh as being at once a safe place beyond language" – when the wrong words could get you killed, or, with you safe at home in Marin County or New York or England, get someone who sang your song in the wrong place at the wrong time killed – "and an attempt to stretch for the sublime when the world, and Belfast is a world whether you're there in the flesh or

not, is crowding you very tightly, and even a gut cry, a howl beyond words, is an embrace of the failure of language, a celebration of the faith that some things not only should not but can't be spoken of or even named?"

This paragraph is entirely made up of questions; Greil doesn't answer a single one. I think he implies that the answer to all three is "yes," but I'm afraid the real answer is "no" in each case. *No*, Morrison's work up to that moment (or at any point) couldn't have been a version of the poem, with the phrase "Whatever You Say, Say Nothing" sung over and over in endless variation, precisely because Greil has argued so convincingly (especially in his remarks about *Astral Weeks*) that Van Morrison never writes or performs his songs in response to "current events." To associate Morrison's reductions and repetitions to the political situation in Northern Ireland is to attempt to do the impossible. As Greil himself notes, "*Astral Weeks* refused to speak the language of the time" and consequently it cannot "be translated back into that language," even if what Greil calls the "single rotting cliché of VIETNAM STUDENT POWER RIOTS LBJ LSD SEXUAL REVOLUTION BLACK POWER NIXON" has "IRA" and "UDA" added to it, which is what I think the first question that he's asked is proposing to do. *No*, there is no link between "that attitude, which Morrison seems to embody," and the yarragh. Or, rather, if there *is* a link between them, then that link places Van Morrison squarely on the side of the spectators and other cowards who believe it is possible to be "neutral" on a moving train. *No*, the yarragh is not "a safe place beyond language" because it is meaningless for human beings to speak, talk or write about what is "beyond language." For human beings, there is *nothing beyond language.* Lastly, it seems that what is being discussed here as "the failure of language" is actually a failure of courage, and that "the faith that some things not only should not but can't be spoken of or even named" is a religious cop-out worthy of the Vatican.

On-line review dated 1 August 2010

Part V:

Musicians

Musicians
David Bowie: Friend or Foe?

There you go. Less than a year ago MTV jocks, the rock press, the radio stations and the music trade journals were rife with predictions that David Bowie, after a three-year-hiatus from both recording and performing, would be back strong in 1983. Sure enough, in 1983 Bowie was back, and back in a big way. He now has a $17 million contract with EMI-America; a Top 10 LP in *Let's Dance,* and a number 1 single in the album's title track; a string of superb new video clips on MTV; a triumphant major-arena tour of the United States (Detroit dates are July 30-31 at Joe Louis arena); and now, NOW, to top it all off, he's got the cover story in the July 18 issue of *Time* magazine.

Yup. The current issue of *Time* is really thin, but I'm sure David Bowie's face (actually, an artist's rendering of same) will attract plenty of newsstand sales. Immediately following the Bowie article, which was written by the dubious Jay Cocks, the magazine's editors have placed an article on music entitled "New Rock on a Red-Hot Roll: Sizzling sales have record execs dancin' in the suites." I think the boosterish title is sufficient indication of what the content of the article is like.

There are many ways to react to the appearance of this *Time* magazine piece, the most common of which will likely be, "Wow, man, David Bowie has really sold out." But we think it would be more productive to look at the image of Bowie that is being presented, and then to decide if we like or agree with that image. Is David Bowie a mercurial superstar or a potentially dangerous egomaniac? Is he our friend or our foe? Neither?

We all approach the *Time* cover story with different feelings for Bowie and the history of his musical development. By and large, most people see David Bowie quite positively. Though there have been some lapses, he's been one of the most successful artists in a troubled decade (the 1970s). Very, very few English musicians who've come up after him have avoided his influence.

Yet there are those who don't like David Bowie at all. Take Steve Wynn, the singer/songwriter/rhythm guitarist for the L.A. band The Dream Syndicate, for example. In the March 1983 issue of *Sweet Potato,* Wynn says, "Bowie's made some good records. He had some good costumes. He has good cheekbones. But man," Wynn continues, "if there'd never been such a thing as David Bowie, we'd have been spared from all the worst music alive. If the Beatles made all of 1970s rock unbearable, then Bowie has made 1980s rock even more unbearable. The worst. Everything that's horrible in music is David Bowie's fault. Oh, he didn't mean any harm. Goebbels didn't mean any harm, either, but there he goes."

Pretty hot stuff, huh? Sounds like a personal problem, right? Maybe even a slight case of sour grapes? You betcha. But the thing is, the guy's got a point. The heirs to mid-period Beatles – groups like Fleetwood Mac, REO Speedwagon and the rest – are indeed "unbearable." The heirs to Bowie, which include nearly everyone from Duran Duran to Prince to Missing Persons, have also produced some terrible stuff, worse than REO et. al. because of their pretensions of being something new and different. In short, Wynn – though he's a bit too extreme for our tastes (Bowie is the rock equivalent of Joseph Goebbels?!) – has convinced us that good intentions on Bowie's part have paradoxically have had very bad effects.

Take a look at the photo we've reprinted. It was taken in 1980 by Kevin Cummins and published in *Cool Cats: 25 Years of Rock 'n' Roll Style*. The photo depicts "Bowiephile" Paul McVey in his bedroom. The caption in the book reads, "His wife's name is Angie, his daughter is Zoe. Rock style influences at its strangest and most obsessive." Though it is true that McVey is strange and obsessed with David Bowie, we don't think the caption goes far enough. It implies that people like Paul McVey are the exceptions to the rule that says that there is a time to wash off your party makeup and go back to your own life.

This guy is what Bowie himself would call a "vampire drug creature of the night." And Paul's quite obviously got his Bowie impersonation down to a T. He's got Ziggy Stardust hair; a Thin White Duke suit; a pair of *The Man Who Fell To Earth* bracelets – he's got it all. It may be true that this man's obsessions with the fantasies of another person would have eventually found expression, even if David Bowie had never existed. But it's equally true that the image of David Bowie gives purpose and meaning to this guy's life. And that means that, on some level, David Bowie is indeed responsible for Paul McVey's obsessions.

Being a vampiric drug and sex creature of the night is a dangerous hobby. Even Bowie himself says so. In the *Time* magazine piece, he's quoted as saying, "that same attitude, that same image, has been coming from one particular area of rock for the last 15 years, but it hasn't done anything except produce casualties." Bowie should know: he predicted in "Rock 'n' Roll Suicide" what the likely result of his post-Ziggy Stardust superstardom would be. Yet Bowie pressed on anyway. In Jay Cocks's words, "Bowie became a zombie [in the 1970s], sending back musical dispatches from the dead zone. He was a casualty, but he endured." And now, five years after Bowie hit the depths of *Low,* the rock 'n' roll survivor is back, "resplendently straight and sincere," as Jay Cocks puts it.

But what we wanna know is, What about Paul McVey? Bowie's helped get him addicted to glitter, dancing, technology, sex and desperation. What will McVey do, how will he be able to structure his life, now that Bowie's reportedly forsworn all roleplaying that isn't for a movie or a stage production? Unlike his role model, Paul McVey doesn't possess or have access to a nearly unlimited amount of cash. He can't, like Bowie has done, just move to the Swiss Alps for "a much needed vacation."

Nope. Paul McVey is stuck. He can't reinvent a new Bowie persona, and he can't very well go back to being plain old Paul McVey. What if (and we know that this is a big *what if*) Paul's decision is to try to murder Bowie, as David Mark Chapman did with his idol, John Lennon? Who's fault would that tragic event be? This isn't asked for the sake of outrage or sensationalism. It's asked because it could conceivably happen: "When the kids had killed the man, I had to break up the band" ("Ziggy Stardust"). When Chapman killed Lennon in 1980, few people bothered to discuss how such murders could be prevented from happening to other celebrities.

Dig. Hinckley saw *Taxi Driver,* identified with the character played by Robert DeNiro, and went on to shoot Ronald Reagan in 1981. Several months later, the film's director, Martin Scorsese, was interviewed in *Rolling Stone.* When asked for his reactions to the outcome of the Hinckley trial (the shooter was acquitted), Scorsese said (words to the effect) that he makes films for personal reasons, that it was unfortunate that *Taxi Driver* had been misconstrued by a sick person, and that he couldn't be bothered with figuring out what it all meant morally. Much more so than Scorsese, David Bowie isn't concerned with dodgy moral issues. Let's hope that someone like Paul McVey doesn't force him to become so.

NOT BORED! #1, July 1983

Gang of Four Surrender!

If the Sex Pistols were the aestheticians of late-70s punk – here defined as something greater than the sum of its precedents (the Velvets, Stooges and NY Dolls) – and the Clash were its most committed proponents, then Gang of Four were its most radical theoreticians. According to Van Gosse, writing in the *Village Voice* in 1981, Go4 came up with a "deeper aesthetic for pop," once which made it possible, for the first time ever, for pop to have some genuine content, "other than the unconscious, accidental and purely reflective content it has always had." Unlike the Pistols, who were primarily concerned with questions of content, and the Clash, who were primarily concerned with the forms punk could take, Go4 seemed to be after the supersession of the content/form contradiction, and were thus able to present a "concrete and dynamic totality, one that can be conscious of itself on many different levels, and organize them" (Van Gosse).

The nature of the totality was neatly summed up by the band's name, which was of course borrowed from the post-Mao Chinese government led by Hua Kua Feng, which originally used the phrase "gang of four" to designate the widow of Mao and three other Chinese officials accused of "counter-revolutionary" activities in the 1970s. Everything Gang of Four (the band) did – whether it was on stage or in the recording studio – was animated by a perpetual battle between revolution and counter-revolution, between class consciousness and false consciousness, between desire and need. It is commonly thought that the Go4's best expression of these battles was their 1980 debut LP *Entertainment!* With the possible exception of their second LP, *Solid Gold*, the band has since then proved increasingly unable to produce work on a par with their best. Unfortunately, this decline has paralleled, if not inspired, the band's desperate attempts to record a hit single, which finally culminated in the band's awful last LP, the (in)appropriately titled *Hard*. As things stand now, no one is particularly upset that the band has evidently decided to break up. The most common reaction seems to be relief.

A possible reason for the decline and fall of the Gang of Four could be the facts that they were always more of a conceptual or "political" aggregation than a musical one, and that their musical limitations – lead singer Jon King's lack of range, guitarist Andy Gill's underdeveloped melodic sense – eventually caught up with them. In 1982, Gill told *Musician Magazine* that "ours was a quite thought-out approach, thought-out almost before we picked up the instruments. We weren't really interested in melody, but with making different drum patterns." (As we will see, one of the primary inspirations for the Go4's "thought-out approach" was the Situationist International.) Another possible reason for the entropic end of the Go4 could be the fact that the band's conceptual and personal dynamisms couldn't survive the 1981 departure of original bassist Dave Allen. Unlike the rest of the band (King, Gill and drummer Hugo Burnham), Allen had been a working-class youth before he joined, and not a film, drama or art student at the University of Leeds. With his departure, which was apparently precipitated by the pressures and problems the band encountered during their tour of North America, the Go4 lost its rhetorical (if not practical or social) connection to the class to which and for which the band aspired to be an inspiration: the modern proletariat.

Though these are perfectly reasonable explanations, we think it might be more productive to examine that which has been assumed to be beyond reproach or beneath consideration: their "neo-Marxist" politics. When considered from this perspective, it seems clear that it wasn't the Go4's melodies or instrumental abilities that failed their lyrics and cultural stance, but the reverse. Or, rather, both failed each other. As a result, the Gang of Four ended up tracing out a trajectory than ran counter to their original purpose, which we take to have been the destruction of false consciousness and passivity.

When Go4 first emerged with the knock-'em-dead energy of their 1978 EP, which included "Damaged Goods," "Anthrax" and "Armalite Rifle," the band's musical style was nearly impossible to designate or describe. The band's own pre-Dave Allen description ("fast R&B") didn't even apply any more. Eventually, the rock press – seizing on the lyrics rather than the totality constituted by the words and the music properly speaking – came to pigeonhole the Go4 as a "neo-Marxist rock 'n' roll band." Apparently a gigantic oxymoron, this ugly sounding description was not without a certain accuracy. Many of the band's early compositions, especially "Damaged Goods" and "At Home He Feels Like A Tourist," drew heavily upon Marx's notion of commodity fetishism (advanced in the first volume of *Das Kapital*). The genius of the Go4 might very well have been their ability to compress and express such unwieldy concepts as commodity fetishism and alienation in a well-chosen phrase or two.

But the Go4 were taking their inspiration and ideas from a source a lot more contemporary than 19th century Marxism: namely, the aforementioned Situationist International, which was a libertarian Marxist organization (the phrase "libertarian Marxist" is Tom Carson's) formed in 1957 by nearly twenty European filmmakers, painters and writers. Over the course of the next decade, and up until its dissolution in 1972, the SI developed a remarkably total and unfashionably extreme critique of both modern capitalist society and the Stalinist bureaucracies and Western vanguard revolutionary parties that were (and still are) defined as the negations of that society. Both the SI itself and its observers credit the situationists' new methods of agitation with having a significant influence on the May 1968 revolt in France.

The Situationists' principal subject was, like Marx's, economic crisis. In most of the theoretical disputes among Marxists, the central questions have long been: Is there an incorrigible tendency toward periodic crisis in modern capitalism? If so, how does one explain it? Marx himself thought that the rate of profit has an overall tendency to decline, thus precipitating crises that lead to a final revolutionary crisis in which a united proletariat seizes the means of production. Most 20th century Marxists (at least those in the Western countries) have disagreed with this position. They have argued that capitalism is not as fundamentally unstable as Marx thought it was, or that capitalism's instability can be corrected by adjusting the balance between profits and wages. Going against the grain (and back towards Marx, even as they went forward into the future), the Situationists were convinced of capitalism's structural tendency to periodically erupt into crisis. In a July 1965 "Address to the Revolutionaries of Algeria and of All Countries," the SI accurately predicted that capitalist society was being rejected in its entirety by a "new" (newly emerged) revolutionary proletariat.

What distinguished by the Situationists from Marx was the former's attitude toward culture. While Marx was alive, indeed, as late as World War I, culture (and its wellspring, the avant garde) had been defined as the activities in which one could seek and actually find escape from the alienation and fragmentation produced by the capitalist mode of production. Indeed, Marx himself seemed to fear that the working class would deplete or exhaust its revolutionary energies in the pursuit of culture and the physical pleasures of everyday life. But with the perfection of the technologies by which Mankind dominated nature, capitalism was forced (or finally freed to) find an outlet in the consumption, as well as in the production, of commodities. As a result of the capitalist colonialization of both work and leisure, the whole context in which culture has been defined has shifted and changed. Leisure is no longer a privilege, but a duty; leisure has become as unsatisfying ("alienating") as the work it was intended to offset or compensate for. Revolutionary activity is no longer limited to the political or economic spheres, but is compelled to attack capitalism from the vantage point of culture.

In a remarkably arrogant and prescient essay included in a 1963 edition of their journal, the Situationists stated that, by virtue of their new conception of culture, "we are obviously in a good position to discover, a few years ahead of other people, all of the possible gimmicks of the present extreme cultural decomposition. Since they are useful only in our enemies' spectacle, we merely make a few notes on them and file them away. After some time, many of them are indeed discovered independently, by someone or other and ostentatiously launched on the market." At a certain level, this is precisely what happened during the "punk explosion" of 1975-1977. Technically speaking, Malcolm McLaren, manager of the Sex Pistols and reputedly their connection to the Situationists, was the first "someone or other" to ostentatiously launch on the market a version of the Situationists' claim that disaffected young hooligans had abundant revolutionary potential. However, it was the Go4 who tried to transmit – in the context of danceable rock 'n' roll – a version of the SI itself, and thereby test the Situationists' revolutionary potential a full decade after May 1968.

In a letter to Greil Marcus, dated 1980, Jon King remarked that "where I think that Situationism [sic] was good was in the development of its revolutionary tactic: 'reinvesting' the cultural past. Situationism conspicuously used popular imagery in order to subvert it – to make the familiar strange, rather than rejecting the familiar out of hand. The tactic was good, worth ripping off, as in the *Entertainment!* cover, or the original 'Damaged Goods' sleeve." It would appear that the SI's influence on the Go4 was even more extensive than this: vaguely and sometimes explicitly situationist themes appear in or are expressed by the band's manic state behavior, their lyrics and, perhaps most importantly, their brittle, jarring sound, which is like the violence of hooligans transposed on to the level of cultural critique. Fortunately, reliable translations of the situationist Guy Debord's *The Society of the Spectacle* (1967), Raoul Vaneigem's *The Revolution of Everyday Life* (also 1967) and the SI's journal (1958-1969) have recently become available for purchase in the United States. It can only be after reading and absorbing these texts that we will be able to understand the Gang of Four's appropriation and use of the style of the Situationists, the reasons for the band's unfortunate and premature demise, and what it all has to tell us about the usefulness of the Situationists' ideas and tactics in the 1980s.

NOT BORED! #3, May 1984

Radio Noriega, or the Many Moods of Manny

Down in Panama, outside the Vatican embassy, the U.S. Southern Command – armed to the teeth and encircling the whole compound – is licking its chops.

Manuel Noriega is inside. United States forces have heard that he is superstitious, that he wears red underpants to ward off evil demons. And so, to irritate and intimidate him (and to enjoy themselves in the process), the Americans set up their "boom boxes" or the Latin American equivalent, and blast the Vatican embassy with some good ol' kickass American rock 'n' roll – Guns 'n' Roses' "Welcome to the Jungle" is the first song to come roaring through the speakers.

But soon a strange disagreement arises between Tipper Gore's Parents Music Recording Center (PMRC) and the U.S. Southern Command concerning which rock'n'roll songs are appropriate for such a military operation, especially one being watched on TV by millions of impressionable American teenagers. The Army wants the most devilish music available, of course, and is ready to follow "Welcome to the Jungle" with songs by The Birthday Party, Pussy Galore, Sonic Youth and the Rolling Stones (an extremely scratched copy of *Beggar's Banquet*). But the PMRC is afraid that America's youth will "get the wrong idea" if more suitable songs are not blasted at Manny Noriega and relayed to the rest of the world.

Compromises are made: the very best of the pop music world – U2, the Alarm, Motley Crue, Winger, the B52s, INXS, John Cougar Mellencamp, ex-Sex Pistol Steve Jones, Love and Rockets, the Cure, the Replacements, the Dead Milkmen and Madonna – come forward to offer their services, and are deemed acceptable by both the PMRC and the U.S. Southern Command. (It is furthermore agreed that the Beatles' "Revolution" will be played at this and all future military operations of a similar nature.)

Suddenly someone smart gets the idea that in the future – say, when the U.S. army invades Colombia in search of someone high up in the evil Medeillen drug cartel – patriotic bands such as these should play, "live and in person," right in the middle of the theater of operations. Why waste time and energy with records, tapes and CDs? Wouldn't it be much better to have the bands themselves to put their asses on the line for democracy and a zero-tolerance, drug-free world? It would be an even bigger spectacle than Live Aid!! Look, the Pentagon says to the pop musicians, American journalists and cameramen put their asses on the line all over the world – in Korea, in Vietnam, in Nicaragua, in El Salvador, and in Panama – so we don't see any reason why you lot can't start doing the same.

For the Colombian operation, there is a huge outpouring of support from the rock'n'roll world, especially those parts of it that have publicly announced their problems with cocaine. An all-star lineup is assembled. The first day of "Operation Jericho" is New Year's Day, 1990. The fighting is heavy in the areas surrounding the stage. Pro-drug devil worshipers – falsely labeled anti-American militants – are being rounded up and executed by firing squads as the bands are doing their soundchecks. The mood is positively electric! Ex-Mossad member and security consultant to Manuel Noriega Michael Harari is at the soundboard. Current reports claim that the body count is acceptable, with enemy losses far exceeding our own.

Insisting that they need not be protected by American anti-aircraft guns

Musicians

("We're not afraid of anyone!"), the brave members of U2 take the stage. Bono Vox and his band are not more than a few bars into "New Year's Day," their opening song, when a volley is fired in the direction of the stage. Bono is blown to bits on international television. The stage is collapsing under the feet of the surviving members of the band; there is smoke and screaming and utter chaos. Then the picture goes blank. All channels hastily go to a commercial for Pepsi Cola. The rest of the concert is canceled, but no one can say anything about it because of national security concerns. That night, video clips of U2 performing "New Year's Day" and getting blown to bloody bits is shown over and over again on nightly news broadcasts all over the world. Expressions of grief are deeply heart-felt, and quick to be made.

A recording – a rap record called "Bono Go Boom" – is subsequently issued by a label in Washington, D.C. Though the song, which is full of samples of Bono's last words, is intended as a tribute, it is widely perceived as a cynical attempt to make money. In response to "Bono Go Boom," the surviving members of U2 organize and produce an official tribute to Bono called *An Official Tribute to Bono*. Featured on the tribute are New Kids on the Block (performing "In the Name of Love"), Patti Smith ("Gloria"), Frank Sinatra ("Where the Streets have No Name"), Debbie Gibson ("I Will Follow"), Poison ("Angel of Harlem"), Willie Nelson ("With or Without You"), Love and Rockets ("Desire"), and Michael Jackson himself ("Sunday Bloody Sunday"). The record wins a Grammy. The videocassette of the recording of the tribute album sells two million copies. Paramount Pictures readies itself to film *The Bono Vox Story,* with Lee Atwater in the starring role.

NOT BORED! #16, December 1989

Simulating Sinead

On 3 October 1992, the Irish rock singer Sinead O'Connor was the musical guest on *Saturday Night Live*. For her first song, Sinead performed the title track from her most recent album, *Am I Not Your Girl?* with a full backing band. For her second, she went with "War," a song by Bob Marley that had once been banned for its apparent advocacy of violence. In a very risky move, musically speaking, Sinead performed the song *a capella*. Dressed all in white, surrounded by candles and (as usual) shaven-headed, she was a riveting sight. With NBC-TV's cameras focused in-tight on her, Sinead ended her "War" by crying for another one to begin. "Fight the real enemy!" she called, and, out of nowhere, produced a copy of a photograph of Pope John Paul II, which she ripped into pieces. There was stunned silence, and then the station went to a commercial.

Musicians

The NBC switchboard was immediately inundated by complaints (supposedly 4,484 in all) called in by outraged viewers. Denunciations of Sinead's "blasphemy" poured forth from all kinds of religious figures and celebrities, including Frank Sinatra, who was quoted as saying he wanted to "punch" the singer "right in the mouth." NBC was supposedly fined $2.5 million dollars by the Federal Communications Commission (FCC), which had never before fined the network for content aired on *Saturday Night Live.*

In the meantime, Sinead herself said nothing about what she'd done or why she'd done it. (Simply changing one of Marley's lines so that it referred to "sexual abuse" instead of "racial injustice," as Sinead had done in mid-song, hadn't been sufficient explanation and so the press was filled with lurid denunciations of her.) When she returned to the United States on 16 October 1992 to perform at a birthday concert for Bob Dylan at Madison Square Garden in New York, Sinead was greeted by a weird mixture of cheers and boos. Despite the severely divided response to her presence, she once again sang an *a cappella* version of "War." Once she was done, she staggered offstage, where she was comforted by Kris Kristofferson. Shortly thereafter, Sinead O'Connor permanently retired from the pop entertainment industry.

Eventually, Sinead O'Connor made her peace with the Pope. On 22 September 1997, in an interview with the Italian weekly newspaper *Vita,* she asked the Holy Father to forgive her. She claimed that her attack on the photo had been "a ridiculous act, the gesture of a girl rebel," which she did "because I was in rebellion against the faith, but I was still within the faith." Quoting St. Augustine, she went on to add, "Anger is the first step towards courage." Another courageous step Sinead took in the late 1990s was to join the congregation of the controversial Irish Bishop Michael Cox, who eventually ordained Sinead as a priest. Lacking a sense of humor, the Vatican has refused to recognize Sinead's membership in the priesthood, which the Pope considers "bizarre." This is a case of the pot calling the kettle black, but the Pope is right: Sinead's story *is* a bizarre one.

And NBC? In the informative and relatively even-handed biography of the singer that airs on VH1 as part of the cable TV station's on-going *Behind the Music* series, it's said that, "even to this day," NBC refuses to allow the photo-ripping scene to be re-broadcast by anyone. VH1 itself had to settle with a blurry shot of Sinead in mid-rip that was published by one of New York's tabloid newspapers. You can catch a glimpse, but you can't *actually see* what Sinead did that night in 1992: you can only hear about it, thanks to the Vatican's clout and NBC's cowardice.

This would seem a good point to talk about censorship. But it isn't – not yet.

The Comedy Channel shows back episodes of *Saturday Night Live* several times a day. In early August 2001, I happened to see the episode in which Sinead O'Connor is the musical guest. Everything goes as it should – dressed all in white, Sinead performs "War" *a capella* as her second number – until the end of the song. There is no war cry, no identification of "the real enemy." Sinead doesn't hold up a picture of the Pope, but a picture of a cute little black boy, instead. And then the song is over, and Sinead stands, smiling, holding the picture behind her back, as the crowd applauds and cheers.

It took a while for it to sink in that NBC hadn't simply blacked out or removed the photo-ripping scene. Instead, NBC had gone beyond mere censorship and had replaced the Pope-ripping sequence with another one (the song as it was performed in rehearsal). Why would anyone want to block or cut out Sinead's impassioned plea for the children? In times of war, don't we tend to forget about the children, especially the cute little black ones? Nice bullshit, but it wasn't Sinead's.

Like the authors of textbooks on Soviet history, who had to keep changing the past so that it would conform with Stalin's latest purges, NBC has created its own Sinead O'Connor and is now passing her off as the original.

NOT BORED! #33, September 2001

Unanswered questions about "Rough Music"

Charivari is one of the many names (which vary from country to country and region to region) for an ancient and widely diffused act of popular justice, which occurred everywhere in similar, if not identical forms. Such forms are also used as ritual punishments in the cyclical masked feasts and their extreme offshoots, the traditional children's begging rituals; one may therefore immediately draw upon these for an interpretation for charivari-like phenomena. A closer analysis shows that what at first sight seemed to simply be *rough* and wild acts of harassment are in truth well-defined traditional customs and legal forms, by means of which, from time immemorial, the ban and proscription were carried out. – Karl Meuli, *Gesammelte Schriften* (1975), quoted in Giorgio Agamben, *State of Exception,* emphasis added.

A highly evocative phrase, "rough music" doesn't sound difficult to figure out. It must refer to a kind of music, right? – a form of music that is noisy, raucous, impolite, crude, coarse, unrefined, unpolished or harsh to the ear. Rough music must be another name for certain forms of American popular music (the blues, gospel, free jazz, rock 'n' roll in all its forms, etc. etc.), right? Maybe it doesn't need to be either American or "popular" to be rough music, which might refer to *musique concrete* or electronic music made in England, continental Europe or

Asia. Maybe rough music has nothing to do with style, genre or instrumentation, but instead refers to the recording process, to the stage at which a particular piece of music has been developed in the studio. Musicians and sound engineers speak of "rough takes" of songs and "rough mixes" of albums, don't they?

Significantly, rough music – at least as the term is used in folklore, ethnography, dictionaries of regional dialects and social histories of England in the 18th and 19th centuries – has nothing to do with music at all. According to E. P. Thompson, who published a landmark essay in 1972 called "'Rough Music': *Le Charivari anglais*," and went on to include a whole chapter on the subject in *Customs in Common*, his 1993 companion to the landmark volume, *The Making of the English Working Class*, rough music is a generic term for a wide variety of popular rituals in which an embarrassing punishment (we might call it "naming and shaming") is meted out in public to an individual, couple or group of people who have offended the community as a whole. Coined in the late 17th century, the phrase is the British equivalent of the French *charivari*, the Italian *scampanate* and the German *haberfeld-treiben, thierjagen* and *katzenmusik*. In 18th and 19th century America, performances of rough music were called "shivarees" and sometimes included tar-and-feathering or riding someone out of town on a rail or pole.

British performances of rough music were, at times, quite elaborate. Thompson notes that the ritual "might include the riding of the victim (or a proxy) upon a pole or a donkey; masking and dancing; elaborate recitatives; rough [sic] mime or street drama upon a cart or platform; the miming of a ritual hunt; or (frequently) the parading and burning of effigies; or, indeed, various combinations of all these." But "beneath all the elaborations of ritual," Thompson writes, "certain basic properties can be found: raucous, ear-shattering noise, unpitying laughter, and the mimicking of obscenities." Elsewhere in his chapter on the subject, Thompson defines rough music as "noise, lampoons, [and] obscenities," "noisy, masked demonstrations with effigies and obscene verses," and "noise and ridicule." To generate the noise, all kinds of instruments (musical and otherwise) were used: pots and pans, marrowbones and cleavers, tongs, tambourines, kits, crouds, humstrums, chains, ram's horns, empty or stone-filled kettles, whistles, rattles, bells, guns and, of course, the human voice, which can be used to yell, scream, howl, grunt, hiss, boo, chant, etc. etc.

And so, we are confronted with a fascinating paradox: performances of rough music involved or were centered upon *noise*, not noisy or discordant music. As Thompson notes, British performances of rough music didn't involve the tuning, harmonization or even coordination of the instruments in the band, and the performers didn't desire their ritualized gathering to be entertaining or amusing. They were instead trying to make such an unsettling noise that the people to whom it was directed would do whatever was necessary – pay a stiff fine or move out of town immediately – to make the rough band stop playing and go away. (Thompson notes that some instances of rough music involved as many as nine nocturnal performances in front of the home of the intended victims.)

But why continue to refer to something as "music" when it is in fact noise, which is the opposite, negation or total absence of music? Why not call it "rough theater" instead? Isn't theater a better approximation of ritual than music? Note well that this paradox isn't the result of bad translations or cultural differences. One of the German equivalents (*Katzenmusik,* or cat music) also specifically refers to music. Unfortunately, Thompson himself wasn't struck by this paradox, and gave it no attention. He was interested in politics, not music, and so he focused on rough music as an instance of "social self-control," as a custom "in which justice is not wholly delegated or bureau-criticised, but enacted by and within the community."

As a result, Thompson left the musicians among his readers with at least two unanswered questions.

1) What is the relationship between what Thompson calls the "conscious antiphony" of rough music and the self-conscious beauty of the classical symphony? Despite the fact that both were products of the 18th and 19th centuries, rough music and the classical symphony were very, very different from each other. Unlike the classical orchestra, the "rough band" made extensive use of both tuned and untuned percussion instruments, and so bore a certain similarity to bands of African drummers and other musical groups from "primitive" or "rough" cultures. Unlike the classical orchestra, the rough band had no conductor or leader, no specialization of roles, and no internal hierarchy. It didn't play or interpret an already composed song or score: it improvised, collectively, under its own direction, as it went, in the manner of a situationist symphony. And, unlike the classical orchestra, which merely appeared and sounded very "respectable," the "anarchic" band of roving musicians had the force of morality (the judgment of the community) behind its performances.

2) What is the relationship between rough music's use of deliberate noise and the deliberate noise made by a variety of contemporary musicians, including avant-garde composers such as John Cage, jazz musicians such as Sun Ra, and rock musicians such as Lou Reed? Unlike the performers of rough music, who presumably had no fans or musical admirers at all, these contemporary musicians *attract* people, not repel them, by playing (recording and releasing) unlistenable noise. Some of this modern noise is made by all-percussion bands (see, for example, Public Image Ltd's album, *The Flowers of Romance,* released in 1980). Can we attribute this apparent reversal to the possibility that there is no longer a social stigma attached to noise? Or to the simple fact that – with the possible exception of the English punk band the Sex Pistols, which set after the Queen on a boat during Jubilee Week in 1977 – bands of contemporary noise musicians generally do not camp out in front of houses occupied by people the community has judged to be in the wrong?

At issue in these questions is the value or utility of harmony. In the classical symphony, harmony and the dramatic resolution of tension are the most important musical concerns. But in both traditional rough music and modern-day noise, tension is created but never resolved or dissipated, and harmony is replaced by (a)rhythmic repetition. Indeed, the very desirability and naturalness of harmony is gleefully trashed. And so, to the extent that music itself is a metaphor for, model of and ideological force within society as a whole – in other words, to the extent that the political order depends upon music to provide a natural analogy for a "social harmony" that is in fact totally artificial and constantly called into question – both traditional rough music and modern-day noise are deeply subversive. They show that society without harmony is in fact possible.

It seems that, with the possible exception of John Cage,[1] contemporary noise musicians are aware of the political significance of their work and see themselves as working in open opposition to the criminal justice system. They do not use their noise to publicize and moralize about the petty crimes committed by other members of the community, but to expose and denounce those who commit the more serious crime of claiming to speak for the whole community, while actually speaking for themselves alone. Perhaps this is the case because most contemporary noise musicians have learned all-too-well from personal experience that, as a result of the completely irrelevant fact(s) that they are either African-American and/or involved in experimentation with illegal drugs, the criminal justice system has already identified them as suspected criminals (rowdies, ruffians or "rough types"). See, for example, Clifford Odets' classic Broadway play from the mid-1950s entitled *Sweet Smell of Success,* which draws upon the efforts of Harry Anslinger's Federal Bureau of Narcotics (predecessor to the Drug Enforcement Administration) to round up thousands of American jazz musicians who smoked marijuana. In response to such targeting, some of these "roughed-up" musicians gave their noise an overtly oppositional dimension, or have emphasized those elements in it that were already oppositional. And so we have "rough music by and for rough people," a growing awareness of the subversive powers of noise.

Ironically, the practioners of traditional rough music saw themselves as supplementing or filling in for the criminal justice system, not condemning and opposing it. For example, Andrew Marvell's 18th century pamphlet *Last Instructions to a Painter* defines rough music as "a Punishment invented first to awe / Masculine wives, transgressing Nature's Law / Where the brawny Female disobeys, / And beats the Husband till for peace he prays; / No concern'd *Jury* for him Damage finds / No partial *Justice* her Behavior binds; / But the just Street does the [...] House invade" (emphasis in original). Thompson goes to great lengths to show that performances of rough music didn't always enforce patriarchal or puritan sexual mores, and were sometimes used to punish police informers, dishonest traders, strike-breakers and landlords who had illegally evicted his or her tenants. But, despite the noise they made, all of the practitioners of traditional rough

---

[1] Questioned after a talk on "anarchy" at the University of Buffalo in the late 1980s, Cage claimed that his lecture was not an embrace of anarchist politics.

Musicians

music were fulfilling an essentially conservative social function: i.e., preserving the boundary or "harmony" between what the community judged to be tolerable and intolerable socially.

NOT BORED! #33, September 2001

Gang of Four: No Surrender

The original line-up of Gang of Four – guitarist Andy Gill, drummer Hugo Burnham, bass guitarist Dave Allen and singer Jon King – was together for four very productive years (1977 to 1981), during which the band released four albums (two of them great) and a handful of great EPs and singles. In May 1984, after the successive departures of Allen (formed the band Shriekback) and Burnham (went on to play with ABC, Nona Hendryx and Public Image Ltd.), Gang of Four broke up, a fact that wasn't widely announced, known or lamented at the time.[1]

In 1990, EMI/Warner Bros. released *A Brief History of the 20th Century,* a padded-out compilation[2] that included songs from all four of the band's records, even *Hard,* its last and worst. But listeners weren't able to follow-up on what they'd heard: the original albums were out of print, and the band itself didn't have a recording contract. Polygram Records stepped in and convinced King and Gill to re-form the band and record new material. In 1991, with other musicians replacing Allen and Burnham, the Gang of Four released *Mall* and went out on tour to support it. In 1995, the band released *Shrinkwrapped* (Castle Records), once again with other musicians replacing Allen and Burnham. To support the new record and the re-issue of *Entertainment!* by American Recordings/Infinite Zero, the band went out on tour once again.

I've seen Gang of Four perform three times: in 1981, at a small club in Ann Arbor, Michigan; in 1991, in Buffalo, New York, opening for Public Enemy; and in 1997, at the Limelight in New York City. At the Limelight, the band didn't play anything from *Mall* or *Shrinkwrapped,* which was unfortunate, because both were good albums. Instead, the band played nothing but its old material, and did so with vehemence. It was exhilarating to listen to and experience: King and Gill weren't *resorting* to their "hits"; they were reclaiming them (from commercial oblivion), asserting them (the songs' continued richness and relevance), defending them (against dilution or plagiarism by other bands), and celebrating them (their existence in both the past and the present, which means in the future, too).

Ten years (!) after the release of *Shrinkwrapped,* a new Gang of Four record has been released. At first, *Return the Gift* (V2, 2005) appears to be yet another compilation of songs from 1977-1981 – that is to say, a rip-off. Only 14 songs long, it is much shorter than either *A Brief History,* which included 20 songs, or

100 Flowers Bloom, a 40-song compilation released by Rhino/WEA in 1998. But *Return the Gift* is not a new compilation of old recordings: it's a collection of new recordings of old songs by the band's original line-up (King, Gill, Allen and Burnham).

Return the Gift is an extension of the remarkable project begun onstage in 1999 (the reclamation and celebration of the original recordings by the Gang of Four) into the recording studio. A project aiming to "return the gift"[3] – the gift of those great old songs – from the live stage (back) to the recording studio. But the new recordings are also an intensification of this project: return the gift from the middle-aged men who today play the songs (back) to the young men who wrote and recorded them more than 25 years ago. (There's a mumbling voice in the new "Anthrax" that speaks of the archaeology of trying to find out "who these people were.")

Of course, recording studios have changed a lot since 1981. There is no doubt – it is an established or "natural" fact – that recording technology has dramatically improved over the course of the last 25 years. But what of the particular members of the Gang of Four? Have they, too, "improved"? It's difficult to say: technological development is mostly a quantitative thing (how much, how fast), while artistic development is mostly if not exclusively qualitative (how good). The individual members of Gang of Four might well have become better musicians, but this would not necessarily mean that they'd become a better band. (The original Gang of Four was nothing if not a real band, whose music contained no solos or, if you prefer, nothing but solos by each of the players and thus the group itself. Furthermore, better individual musicianship, if taken to the extremes of laziness, self-indulgence or competitiveness, can sometimes distract from, diminish or even destroy the quality of the music being performed.)

And so *Return the Gift* is a very risky, if not impossible (doomed) adventure into largely unknown territory (who else in rock 'n' roll has done this?). To make the adventure a success, it isn't enough to be able to play – to pick up and carry the weight of – the old songs, which were in many cases quite heavy (I mean emotionally charged: the guilty pleasures of the final heedless rush in "Damaged Goods," the confused confidence in "Natural's Not In It," the terror and dread in "He'd Send in the Army," the sense of displacement and flatness in "We Live As We Dream, Alone," et al.). No, to make this work the band must play their old songs *better* than they were originally played. But is it in fact possible to play these songs any better than they were originally played? It may not be. And so it is precisely the merit of this unique collection that it even attempts to try, that is to say, tries to do the impossible.

By and large, *Return the Gift* lives up to its impossible ambitions. The song selection is pretty good. To have been even better, *Return the Gift* would have replaced "Capital" (musically uninteresting) and "What We All Want" (it's been re-recorded before) with "5.45," "It's Her Factory," "Cheeseburger," "Outside the trains don't run on time," and/or even the apparently forgotten classic "Armalite

Rifle." Only one song is an embarrassing failure. Unfortunately that one song ("We Live As We Dream, Alone," from *Songs of the Free*) is one of the band's very best and yet least known songs. Its new version lacks the very thing that made the original version so great, and that is used to enrich and re-energize the new versions of "Why Theory?" "Anthrax" and "He'd Send in the Army": Andy Gill's flat, matter-of-fact, baritone speaking-voice. In its place, Gill *sings* the words of "We Live As We Dream, Alone" in a wavering tenor and ends up sounding like a bad imitation of Iggy Pop imitating David Bowie. The other bad news (not as bad but almost) is that the new versions of "Ether" and "Damaged Goods," which are also among the band's very best songs, aren't as good as the original versions: the former lacks the original's anguish and dread, and the latter lacks the original's drive, especially at the end, when it counts.

I reckon that the new version of "To Hell with Poverty" is just as good as the original version, which means it's pretty damn good (it was never among my favorites). But it's a great song with which to begin *Return the Gift*. "In this land right now / Some are insane and they are in charge" – this was true in 1981, the first year of Ronald Reagan's terrifying reign, and it still is true today, at the height of George W. Bush's murderous rule. As a matter of fact, some of the same lunatics (Dick Cheney and Donald Rumsfeld) are still in charge! Similar moments of shocking recognition – *it's still 1981!* – occur in "Anthrax," "He'd Send in the Army," "I Love a Man in Uniform," and especially "Ether" ("to get to the root of the problem / fly the flag on foreign soil," "There may be oil," and "each day more deaths").

Now for the good news: more than half of the 14 new performances are better than the original versions. In "Anthrax," "Natural's Not In It," "Not Great Men," "Anthrax," "He'd Send in the Army" and "At Home He's a Tourist," Andy Gill's fire-breathing guitar parts are brighter, and Allen & Burnham's rhythms shifts are more physical, more muscular, than they ever were. The drums, especially, sound better than they did back in 1981. In the new, definitive versions of "Paralyzed," "Natural's Not In It," "He'd Send in the Army," "Why Theory?" "At Home He's A Tourist," and "I Love a Man in Uniform," the vocals – the singing voices and the speaking voices, what they are saying and the tones they are taking in their various back-and-forth exchanges – are much better projected and recorded, and thus are easier to hear, follow and understand.

But the most improved, and thus the most noteworthy song on *Return the Gift* – a kind of compensation for the destruction of "We Live As We Dream, Alone" – is "I Love a Man in Uniform." Originally released on *Songs of the Free* (1982), "I Love a Man in Uniform" was a minor hit on dance-floors and college radio stations. I never liked the song, despite its clear mockery of the militarism of Thatcher and Reagan, and I was somewhat embarrassed by its modest success. The groove laid down by drummer Hugo Burnham and new bassist Sara Lee was stiff, the guitar playing was domesticated, and Sara's background vocals were weak, which completely undermined the song's gimmick: the woman's mocking exclamation, "Oh, man, you must be joking."

In the new version, there's no gimmick. Perhaps there doesn't need to be when you've got Dave Allen on bass guitar instead of Sara Lee: the rhythm section is so strong and self-confident that Andy Gill can play his guitar freely and thus give the song space to come to life. When the narrator, a determined and confused little prick ("to have ambition was my ambition"), says that his "woman" needed "protection" and *that's* why he joined the armed forces, or when he boasts that the time he spent with his girl was time well-spent, it isn't a woman's voice who says "Oh, man you must be joking," but a man's.

It's as if time has gone by. The little prick isn't boasting that he's just enlisted, his woman wisecracking at his side, his buddies laughing at him. He's already enlisted, and he's now in basic training or actually in combat. When he swaggers and makes his ridiculous boasts, the wisecrack comes from one of his buddies, not in a girly falsetto, but in a "straight" male voice. His woman, all of the women, are back at home. There's no reason to pretend that what she says matters. There's no irony, either. When "Oh, man you must be joking" is first thrown at him, he starts saying, a little too soon, "*She* needed to be protected," he sounds defensive. There's no time for jokes. There's no time for punchlines. Orders have been requested, orders have been given, shots have been fired. No casualties reported as yet.

(Thanks to Hugo Burnham)

[1] See "Gang of Four Surrender!" *NOT BORED!* #3, May 1984.
[2] The compilation's liner notes were written by Greil Marcus, who'd first written about the Gang of Four in *New West* in 1979. His 1990 liner notes – reprinted in *In the Fascist Bathroom: Punk in Pop Music, 1977-1992* – are easily the best essay ever written about the band's music:

> The Gang of Four acted out, and out into records, a picture of an individual who had discovered that ordinary life – the gestures of affection and resentment one made every day, the catchphrases one spoke every day as if one had invented them – is in fact sold and bought as grease for shopping and silence, for the accumulation of capital and passivity. The person who has made this remarkable discovery begins to re-examine his or her life, and it begins to look different: 'Natural's Not In It.' History – 'Not Great Men.' A woman in the home: 'It's Her factory.'
>
> Life looks different, but it doesn't change. The Gang of Four pursued their subject's discoveries not as if they might lead to some grand general strike [...] but as if, once recognized, those discoveries would remain trapped in the prison of familiarity. Playing everyman on stage, Jon King was never free. He was an explosion of doubt. He

dramatized a glimpse of liberation, but simultaneously the wish the conform, to be at home in the only home available, no matter how false.

[...] The Gang of Four offered no anthems, no tunes of right and wrong. They were interested in constructing a drama in which each listener found his or her place as a new historical subject, set free from all certainties, all forms of common sense and obvious conclusions, set free in a convulsion you can hear in so many of the numbers on this disc, perhaps most fiercely in 'Return the Gift.'

My point is that, though there were no anthems, there was a *theme,* and that theme was the military or, if you prefer, the militarization of society. "Armalite Rifle," "Anthrax," "Guns Before Butter," "Outside the Trains Don't Run on Time," "He'd Send in the Army," "I Love a Man in Uniform" – here the individual pictured by the Gang of Four is active in two different social worlds: the ordinary life of civilians (workers, housewives, consumers), or the ordinary life of *soldiers.* This theme is dramatized in the music itself, in the Gang of Four "sound," no matter what the lyrics are about, in its martial tone, its discipline, precision and rigid postures. On stage, the musician who acted out the soldier's discoveries wasn't Jon King, but Andy Gill. He, too, was never free. But, in contrast to King (the disabused corporate executive), Gill acted like a prisoner of war forced to sing and play his guitar at the point of a gun. He dramatized a glimpse of confinement, but also the wish to escape, to be somewhere, anywhere else.

[3] The phrase "Return the Gift" comes from the title of a great song from *Entertainment!* (Greil Marcus: "Return the gift, the song is shouting; give it back before it's too late!") But this song does *not* appear on *Return the Gift,* the album that bears its name. The phrase stirs many associations, among them *potlatch,* which, among certain tribes of Native Americans, is a form of competition, conquest or social control in which spectacular self-sacrifices are exchanged as gifts.

NOT BORED! #38, October 2006

Taking a Bite of Os Mutantes

"To have known rock as something relatively contemptible during the decisive years of our intellectual growth and, on the other hand, to have had bossa nova as the soundtrack of our rebellion signifies for Brazilians of my generation the right to imagine an ambitious intervention in the future of the world, a right that immediately begins

Musicians

to be lived as a duty." – Caetano Veloso (born 1942), *Tropical Truth: A Story of Music and Revolution in Brazil.*[1]

Of course I can understand why you would think that the Brazilian rock band Os Mutantes ("The Mutants")[2] should be political, that is to say, politically radical. (We want *everything* to be politically radical, don't we?) The band's core consisted of three "politically alienated teenagers"[3] – Arnaldo Baptista (born in 1948), his younger brother, Sergio (1951), and Arnaldo's childhood sweetheart, Rita Lee Jones (1947) – all of whom came from Pompeia, a relatively well-off neighborhood in Sao Paolo, the richest and least typical of Brazilian regions. They formed their band just two years after the ouster of the country's Leftist President, Joao Goulart, and his replacement by Brazil's military forces, which first installed Humberto de Alencar Castello Branco (1964 to 1967), Artur da Costa e Silva (1967-1969), and then Emilio Garrastazu Medici (1969-1974) as president.

Os Mutantes actively participated in *Tropicalia* (sometimes called *Tropicalismo*), which was both a form of total art[4] – using elements drawn from gallery installations, the cinema, theatre, poetry and music in an "anthrophagic" manner[5] – and a syncretic style of music that anthrophagically drew upon and mixed together elements from bossa nova, Bahian folk, Portuguese *fado*, Afro-Cuban dance music and Anglo-American rock 'n' roll. The first musical manifestation of *Tropicalia* was the 1968 album entitled *Tropicalia, ou Panis et Circenses,* which included recordings by Gilberto Gil, Caetano Veloso, Tom Ze, Nara Leao, Gal Costa and Os Mutantes. That same year, Os Mutantes – fleshed out by their older brother, Claudio Cesar, who played drums and created electronic sound-effects using homemade devices – released their self-titled debut album, which included mutated versions of three songs from *Panis et Circenses* ("Batmakumba," "Bread and Circuses," and "Baby").

Before I go on, I know you'll want me to make precise what I mean by "mutated." With the exception of "Baby," which was simply transformed into a pop song by the use of slightly distorted electric guitars and bluesy organ parts, I mean that these songs were hijacked and corrupted: in a word, *detourned.* The best example is "Batmakumba" (*macumba* is the Brazilian equivalent of Haitian "voodoo"). In its original version,[6] "Batmakumba" is, shall we say, a sketch or a description of a magic spell. But in the Os Mutantes' version, which is dominated – pushed off-center, nearly ruined – by an incredibly distorted guitar playing percussive, spluttering notes, the listener feels that the demon is actually coming to life, rising and dancing.

The military reacted quickly and decisively, not just to *Tropicalia,* but to everything potentially subversive or allegedly pro-Communist: in December 1968, it imposed "Institutional Act #5," which abolished *habeas corpus,* closed Congress, and sharply curtailed freedom of speech. The following year, the leaders of the *Tropicalia* movement – Gilberto Gil and Caetano Veloso – were arrested and imprisoned, and then ordered out of the country. Like these two men, the members of Os Mutantes were highly controversial, and not just among the military. According to Rita Lee, their performances were greeted by "a mix of surprise, indignation, excitement . . . and tomatoes!" Not only did the members of the group dress "like [space] aliens, Don Quixote, Sancho Panza and Dulcinea, [a] pregnant bride, toreros, indians, [and] beggars," but each performance also included "an intentional 'offense against authority.'" The music itself was considered threatening because "at the time it was a kind of sacrilege performing MPB [Brazilian Popular Music] using *any* electronic instruments."[7] The use of electric guitars, in particular, opened the groups' members up to denunciations from Leftist nationalists that they were pro-American. In the words of the poet Augusto de Campos, writing in 1968: "Most people have not understood that rock has undergone a transformation in its Brazilian translation and is not, at its best, simply an imitation of imported rock."[8]

And yet Os Mutantes were not suppressed. In 1969, they were allowed to release their second album, entitled *Mutantes* and recorded in late 1968. Indeed, they continued to release an album every year until 1972/1973, when Rita Lee left to pursue her solo career (begun in 1970) and then Arnaldo Baptista dropped out due to psychological problems brought upon by excessive use of LSD.[9] Unfortunately, these problems began to surface as early as 1971, and – to the precise extent that Arnaldo began to hog the spotlight – the last two Os Mutantes records (*Jardim Eletrico,* 1971, and *Mutantes e Seus Cometas no Pais do Baurets,* 1972), as well as Rita Lee's second solo album (*Hoje e o primeiro dia do resto da sua vida,* 1972), are much less enjoyable than the group's first three.

Why weren't Os Mutantes suppressed? Unlike the other members of the *Tropicalia* movement, who were folk musicians, they were rock 'n' rollers. Their second album (a bit weak, to tell the truth) only contained one song ("Dios mil e um") that was in or like the *Tropicalia* style. Their great third album, *A Divina Comedia ou Ando Meio Desligado,* contained none at all. Os Mutantes' strongest similarities ("influences") were vocal groups like Peter Paul and Mary, and the Mamas and the Poppas; guitar-driven psychedelic bands like Pink Floyd and the Jimi Hendrix Experience; "orchestral" pop bands like the Beatles and the Beach Boys; and French and Italian non-rock pop singers from the early 1960s.

Furthermore, unlike Gilberto Gil, the members of Os Mutantes were not Bahian or dark-skinned; unlike Gil and Caetano Veloso, they did not participate in political marches and demonstrations, nor they did write overtly political songs.[10] Interviewed in 1997, Sergio Dias said, "I believe our image of being clean and young helped us to get away with it." At least in the early days, Os Mutantes' innocent look wasn't simply an image. In the words of Veloso, "they looked like three angels"; they possessed "nuance and delicacy"; they mixed together "anarchy and decorum" and "freedom and puritanism." All this was lost when Arnaldo began to upstage Rita.

Finally, Os Mutantes were not suppressed because they knew how to *sell out.* In 1968, they made a series of "wacky" TV commercials for Shell Oil: not only did they compose a jingle and allow snatches of their songs to be used, but they also dressed up (as legionnaires, the crew from *Don Quixote,* the pregnant bride, her boyfriend and her outraged father, cowboys and Indians, and American surfers) and acted in them. Furthermore, the slogan of this series of ads – *Algo Mais Em Sua Vida* (Something more for your life) – echoes or inspired their love song "Algo Mais," which appears on *Mutantes.* But easily the worst aspect of these perhaps very profitable, certainly highly calculated and now very embarrassing decisions was the self-justification that the bossa nova composer Nelson Motta provided for the second album's liner notes: "He who lives in a consumer society has two alternatives: either participate or be devoured by it. There is no escape from these options. The jingle by Os Mutantes, which I simply refer to as 'music,' is better, infinitely better, than the majority of the songs that are in the public squares and bus stops."[11] I do not find this argument at all convincing. Would it not be, uh, rather interesting to see the consumer society try to devour anthrophagic mutants? I'm sure you know the difference: musicians sell their music because it has use-value to their listeners; while sell-outs sell *their image* (the music being secondary) because this image has exchange-value for corporations. And I know the irony isn't lost on you: *none* of the musicians who have championed Os Mutantes' music over the years – Kurt Cobain, Beck, David Byrne, Arto Lindsay and the members of Stereolab, among others – are sell-outs.

But radical politics isn't everything. Few of the musicians who have refused to sell out have made music as exciting and fun as Os Mutantes'. In their very best songs – "A Minha Menina," "Bat Macumba," and "Trem Fantasma" from their first album; "Dois mil e um" from their second album; and "Ando Meio Desligado," "Quem Tem Medo de Brincar de Amor" and "Jogo da Calcada" from their third – Os Mutantes are melodic and up-tempo, exuberant and charming. You love where they are but you can also see where they are going. The future is bright. More than anything else, Os Mutantes are *seductive.* Just look at the slight, knowing smile that plays on Rita Lee's lips as she sings "Quem tem Medo de Brincar de Amor" in front of a group of strangely quiet, thoughtful and slightly embarrassed college students in 1969.[12] Is that not a vision of Eve's smile when she first offered Adam a bite of the apple?

[1] Written in Portuguese and published in 1997, this book was translated into English by Isabel de Sena and published by Knopf in 2002.
[2] The name was taken from the Portuguese translation (*O Imperio dos Mutantes*) of Stefan Wul's science-fiction novel *La Mort Vivant,* originally published in French in 1958.
[3] Interview with Rita Lee conducted in 1997 (by Carlos Colado?) and posted by Luaka Bop Records, which released the *Everything is Possible!* compilation in 1999.
[4] It appears that the word "Tropicalia" was first used in April 1967 as the title for an art installation by Helio Oiticia (1937-1980).

[5] See Oswald de Andrade's *Manifesto Antropofago* ("Cannibal Manifesto"), from 1928.
[6] Gilberto Gil, *The Early Years* (2004).
[7] Interview conducted in 1997 (by Carlos Colado?) with Rita Lee and posted by Luaka Bop Records.
[8] Quoted in Caetano Veloso, *Tropical Truth: A Story of Music and Revolution in Brazil* (2003).
[9] Sergio Dias continued to record under the name Os Mutantes until 1978. Minus Rita Lee, who refused to participate, the group reformed in 2006 and has toured England and the United States.
[10] See our translations of their lyrics: they mostly wrote songs about love and lost innocence. While it is true that they occasionally recorded overtly political songs by other artists – notably "Chao de Estrelas" (by Silvio Caldas and Orestes Barbosa) – they did so in a burlesque fashion, as if to draw mustaches on them.
[11] This translation comes from the Omplatten CD reissue.
[12] Do a search on You Tube for the song's title. There are two versions: one with OK video and bad sound, the other with bad video and OK sound. Play them both!

NOT BORED! #39, September 2007

Pete Townshend Gets His Wish

"If it's a good riff, people are going to listen to it," even in a commercial, said Jason Fine, senior editor at *Rolling Stone* magazine. "It doesn't particularly bother me or steal the song's meaning from me. I know a lot of people do feel that way, but that's become an outdated way of thinking." – *New York Times,* 6 November 2002.

As far as I know, this shit started in 1986, when Michael Jackson allowed the Nike Corporation to abuse the Beatles' song "Revolution" in one of its TV commercials. I'm sure that plenty of great rock 'n' roll songs had been licensed for commercial use before 1986, but Nike's use of "Revolution" was a watershed event, and not only because its composer, John Lennon, had died six years previously and no doubt would have been violently opposed to the idea had he been alive to hear it. (Neither Paul McCartney nor Yoko Ono were able to do anything to stop Jackson, because he'd successfully outbid them both to acquire the rights to all of the Beatles' songs.) The commercialization of "Revolution" was a watershed event because the song itself was so obviously ill-suited for use in a commercial.

Written in 1968 and originally released as a single, "Revolution" was a serious, impassioned and controversial discussion of the dangers of social revolution, which was a very real prospect at the time. Unsatisfied with the way the apparently anti-revolutionary song was originally received, Lennon later re-recorded it for the so-called The White Album as "Revolution #1," which changed the guarded "no" of the original ("don't you know you can count me out") to a furtive "yes" ("count me in"). The White Album also included Lennon's "Revolution #9," which was a 9-minute-long collage of tape recordings in the style of avant-garde composer Karlheinz Stockhausen, and not a proper song. Lennon's point in recording *three* totally different "Revolutions" in a single year was clear: social revolution can't be treated lightly, definitively or with impunity, for it is both unpredictable and certain to spin "back" and overthrow the position of everyone, even or especially that of the revolutionary.

But the people at Nike, the staff at its advertising agency and Michael Jackson all thought that the Beatles' "Revolution" (the first one) would make a great element in a "revolutionary" TV commercial for a "revolutionary" product. No doubt they thought or managed to convince themselves that they weren't prostituting or raping the song by using it to sell something as banal as sneakers, but that they were in fact cleverly adapting the song to changed circumstances and were thus showing it the highest form of respect. Unfortunately for these dialecticians, the subtleties of Nike's "Revolution" commercial were lost on millions of Beatle fans, who were virtually unanimous in their hatred of it. Stung by the experience, Michael Jackson has in the years since then been very conservative in his decisions concerning the commercial exploitation of the Beatles' songbook. One also notes that the use of well-known rock 'n' roll songs in TV commercials – though a constant feature of the last 15 years – has come in waves, with lulls or breaks in between, as if the advertisers and/or the songs' copyright owners are quite aware that consumers will only tolerate so much commercialization of the music they love before they rebel or at least stop buying the products that use rock music in their advertising campaigns.

And yet the fucking things won't go away. Just when you think that you've seen it all – the Rolling Stones' "(I Can't Get No) Satisfaction" used to sell Snickers candy bars, Lou Reed astride a Honda motorbike, and William S. Burroughs as a salesman for Nike – you turn on the TV and come upon a fresh butchery so gruesome that you wouldn't have thought it possible: Bob Marley's "Get Up, Stand Up" used to sell Timberland boots; the Buzzcocks' "What do I get?" used to sell cars (the Buzzcocks?!); not one but two songs from The Who's *Who's Next* ("Baba O'Riley" and "Bargain") used to sell cars; David Bowie's "Changes" used to publicize Microsoft; Iggy Pop's "Lust for Life" used to sell Heineken beer; Devo's "It's a Beautiful World" used to celebrate Target's superstores and "Whip It" used to sell Pringles potato chips (yes, I saw it, it *really* aired!); Credence Clearwater Revival's "Fortunate Son" (no longer owned by its author, John Fogerty) used to sell Wrangler jeans to flag-waving Americans, etc. etc.

Musicians

   Don't these marketing and advertising people *listen to the words* of these songs, most of which concern serious issues, not banalities? Don't they realize that the words are all-too-frequently saying *the exact opposite* of what the commercial is saying? They *must* realize, because on several occasions they have been careful to remove a key word or even an entire line: "Don't want to be a richer man" dropped from Bowie's "Changes"; "It ain't me, I ain't no senator's son" excised from CCR's "Fortunate Son"; "It's a beautiful world for *you*, not me" removed from Devo's "Beautiful World," etc. etc. These aren't bloodless cuts; on the contrary, they tear into these songs' very hearts. Without their ironic or confrontational lines, which almost always form their respective centers, these songs are either corpses or cripples. Blasted out of the TV set every 10 minutes, dead or alive, they invite us to join the dance macabre.

   What about the musicians themselves? Not all of them are dead. Some of them even own the rights to their songs! Why aren't they hiring lawyers and suing? Why are they allowing their songs to be butchered? The obvious answer is money. If you are Devo or the Buzzcocks, both of which broke up in the 1980s, or Credence Clearwater Revival, who broke up in the 1970s, these deals may be the only way they are going to make any money at all from their back catalogue of recordings. If you are Lou Reed or Iggy Pop, both of whom are still active recording artists but have never had (and aren't ever likely to have) a #1 hit single, these deals may be the only way you are ever going to make any serious money in show business. And so these musicians probably figure, "Might as well get it now while I still can. Everyone else is." But money or, rather, greed cannot account for all of what's going on. There must be other factors at work as well. What Michael Jackson did to "Revolution" 15 years ago, today people are doing to their own songs!

   It'll help if we focus on a couple of examples. Take David Bowie: it doesn't surprise me that he's acting like a greedy, cynical bastard these days. (Use the cover of *Aladdin Sane* to sell Absolut vodka?! Turn "Watch That Man" into an ad for The Gap?! Sure! Where do I sign?) It was obvious that Bowie was never attached or committed to the various personae, singing styles, lyrical concerns and musical forms that he'd pick up, use for a while and then dispose of. It was all a put-on for him. And so there's no sting, no resentment, no anger, when Bowie sells something he's got to whomever wants to buy it (as long as the price is right).

   But Pete Townshend's zeal for commercializing his songs is a real shock. His music didn't change from album to album. As he stated in "Long Live Rock," a single from 1973, he was going to continue to play loud, hard rock'n'roll, even if others claimed that "rock is dead." (Indeed, it wasn't until 1978 and the advent of punk that he finally wrote a song that admitted "The Music Must Change.") Townshend's commitment to the music was strong and fast, and it inspired a great many people, David Bowie among them.

   Townshend's probably got quite a lot of money from his days with the Who. Maybe he needs a little extra money now and again. Or maybe he *isn't* rich after all and needs more money than we might think. In any event, because he *is* Pete Townshend (i.e., a man with a well-deserved and long-standing reputation for hard work, honesty and sticking to his guns), you'd think that he'd be cool about it if he ever needed to resort to selling his songs to advertisers. Unlike Bowie, he wouldn't sell any of the songs that he knew or imagined to be dear to his millions of fans, and he wouldn't allow any of the songs that he sold to be trivialized or butchered. But Townshend hasn't been cool about selling out. In fact, he's been quite a dick about it.

Townshend allowed "Baba O'Riley" to be turned into a commercial for a sports utility vehicle. The opening track on 1971's *Who's Next,* "Baba O'Riley" used to be a very serious song that denounced the Woodstock concert as a "teenage wasteland," paid musical tribute to an avant-garde composer (Terry Riley), and based the chords of its glittering synthesizer part (B alternating with A) on the holy name of Baba (as in Mehr Baba, Townshend's spiritual guide at the time). To make matters worse, Townshend allowed *two* songs on *Who's Next* – "Baba O'Riley" and "Bargain," the song that immediately follows "Baba" on Side One – to be turned into car commercials. (Good God! Is "Going Mobile" next, that is, once the troublesome line "I don't care about pollution" has been removed?) Finally, Townshend allowed "Bargain" – a fierce song about a man absolutely desperate for the love of a woman – to be butchered in a uniquely horrible fashion.

The conceit of this spot for Nissan Xterra is that the voice-over announcer answers the singer as if the two were engaged in a conversation. But the announcer doesn't agree with the singer, as you might expect (it's a well-known song by a very popular band, after all). Instead, the announcer flatly contradicts what the singer is saying. "I'd pay any price just to have you," the singer says, only to be told by the announcer "You *don't* have to pay any price." By the end of this weird debate, the announcer has utterly trounced the singer, of course (after all, this *is* a commercial for the great *bargains* you can get at your local Nissan dealer). But the singer's defeat is a very strange thing to have happen in a commercial that is apparently based upon the premise that people have good feelings (and not scorn or ridicule) for the Who's music and so will buy something associated with it.

And so, maybe I was wrong about Townshend: maybe he isn't the man I thought he was. Maybe he's always been a greedy, cynical bastard. Or maybe he's changed and has only recently become a greedy, cynical bastard. But neither greed nor cynicism (nor bastardy) fully explains how someone could sign off on and profit from atrocities such as the "Baba O'Riley" and "Bargain" TV spots. Both common sense and personal experience indicate that only someone who hates himself and consequently has no respect whatsoever for the value or quality of the songs he's written – only a musician who has nothing but contempt or hostility for his fans and admirers – could do such things. "Fuck! Why should anyone else care about what happens to these songs if *I* don't care?" Townshend might well have said to himself when he signed the contracts. "After all, *I'm* the one who wrote them, aren't I? And if I say 'Baba O'Riley' is a piece of shit, then it's a piece of shit, end of story."

If Townshend did indeed say something like this to himself, then we propose the following should be his obituary: Pete Townshend, who proclaimed "Hope I die before I get old" when he started out as a young man, got his wish, but with a twist: he did indeed die before he got old, but didn't realize it and continued to go about his business as if nothing had happened.

NOT BORED! #34, July 2002

On-line notice dated 21 November 2002: Townshend has also licensed the use of the theme from the 1969 Who album *Tommy* for use in a TV commercial for Claritin, an allergy medicine; the 1979 Who song "Who Are You?" for use by TNN, a cable TV station; and the 1982 solo-album hit "Let my Love Open the Door" for use by NBC-TV.

13 September 2003: Townshend has licensed the 1966 Who song "Happy Jack" for use in a TV commercial for Hummer, a truck invented by the US military and now sold commercially.

17 November 2003: Townshend has licensed the classic 1971 song "Won't Get Fooled Again" for use in a TV commercial for MSNBC news program *Hardball with Chris Matthews*.

18 July 2004: Townshend has refused to let Michael Moore use "Won't Get Fooled Again" in his movie *Fahrenheit 911*.

20 April 2005: in the last few months, Townshend has licensed "I Can't Explain" (1965) to the PGA Tour/ABC Sports, "I Can See For Miles" (1965) to Silverstar Headlights, "Pinball Wizard" (1969) to Saab, "Going Mobile" (1971) to CBS-TV in New York City, "Who are you?" to *CSI: Las Vegas,* and "Let My Love Open the Door" (1982) to JC Penny.

8 September 2008: Townshend has licensed "Join Together" (1972) to Nissan.

19 January 2009: Townshend has licensed "My Generation" (1965) to Pepsi.

A Monumental Bad Joke or, Lou Reed laughs all the way to the bank

What does it take to make famously stone-faced rocker Lou Reed crack a smile? Playing the blues for the first time, says Wim Wenders, director of "The Soul of a Man," the first installment in Martin Scorsese seven-film series on the blues which premiered Friday at the Cannes Film Festival. Reed joined Beck, Bonnie Raitt and Nick Cave in interpreting the songs of Mississippi blues legend Skip James. "For Lou, it was so much fun, I am proud to announce he actually laughed," Wenders quipped. "And we have it on tape – no photographer has ever captured him smiling on film." – *New York Daily News,* 25 May 2003.

In other words, Lou Reed is a completely depraved pervert and pathetic death dwarf and everything else you want to think he is. On top of that he's a liar, a wasted talent, an artist continually in flux, and a huckster selling pounds of his own flesh. A panderer . . . . Lou Reed is the guy that gave dignity and poetry and rock 'n' roll to smack, speed, homosexuality, sadomasochism, murder, misogyny, stumblebum passivity, and suicide, and then proceeded to belie all his achievements and return to the mire by turning the whole thing into a monumental bad joke with himself as the woozily insistent Henny Youngman in the center ring, mumbling punch lines that kept losing their punch. – Lester Bangs, "Let Us Now Praise Famous Death Dwarves, or How I Slugged it Out with Lou Reed and Stayed Awake," 1975.

The first time I heard/saw the TV commercial for Nissan Xterra in which a few seconds of the (in)famous Velvet Underground song "Heroin" is used in the soundtrack, *I couldn't believe my fucking ears.* Of course I knew that Lou Reed had done TV commercials before, but he'd only used bullshit Bowie songs like "Take a Walk on the Wild Side" or songs like "Perfect Day," which, though good, aren't well-known and certainly aren't among the best songs ever recorded by the Velvets or Lou himself. But *this* was something totally different, i.e., a real fucking outrage. I was angry for hours after I saw the ad a second time, and confirmed that, yes indeed, it includes a few seconds of the shimmering opening moments of "Heroin."

An unforgettable track on the Velvets' classic first album, recorded in 1966 but not released until the following year, "Heroin" is easily the band's best (and best-known) song, and certainly one of the greatest rock 'n' roll songs ever recorded. As Lester Bangs once noted, "Heroin" is both a glowing, even loving evocation of the drug's euphoric effects and an utterly convincing statement of the reasons for not getting addicted. Eight minutes long, dreamy and yet very noisy in places, "Heroin" could never get (never got) radio airplay in the 1960s or 1970s. Fuck! It probably couldn't even get played on the air *today,* or not without causing a storm of controversies and repercussions.

Musicians

And yet "Heroin" was also Lou Reed's plaything, something he'd just as soon travesty as treat with respect. One of the reasons this famous "Death Dwarf" (a very apposite phrase taken from the writings of William S. Burroughs) was attacked by Lester Bangs was the fact that, in the mid-1970s, Lou Reed – disappointed and bitter that he'd never been given the airplay, respect and financial rewards he deserved – used to pretend to shoot-up during live performances of the song, thereby turning it into a bad joke. *Imagine what Lester would say if he knew about Lou's Nissan Xterra ad!* But, alas, Mr. Bangs, he's dead (accidental in 1982) and no doubt spinning in his grave so fast he's generating white light/white heat.

Fuck playing the blues. No, Lou Reed's idea of a joke is turning "Heroin" – no, not only "Heroin," but also everything that it affirmed, everything that it made possible, everything that wouldn't have been risked or dared to be thought, said or sung if "Heroin" hadn't been released, at a time when most drug-conscious bands were singing superficial songs about softer drugs (for example, the Beatles' ludicrous "Lucy in the Sky with Diamonds") – Lou's idea of a joke is turning it all into a fucking car commercial (and get this!) by the same company for which Pete Townshend recently prostituted himself.

"It's not the song, it's two chords," Reed says. "You really think it's funny when something's banned for so long and they want two chords for whatever." – *Newsday,* 6 June 2003.

No doubt only the completely cynical, the thoroughly corrupt and the Devil himself will be able to join Lou Reed in the full appreciation of the humor of what he's done with "Heroin." At the very least, this precedent, if it is allowed to stand, will permit the very same people (the record company execs, broadcasters and retailers) who once denigrated, rejected and conspired against rough rock 'n' roll (Velvets, Stooges, MC5, the Who) – supposedly because they couldn't sell it on the mass market – to turn around, 35 years later, and make millions by selling an outright betrayal (a "sanitized" version) of it on TV. Note well that the Nissan ad in question doesn't even come close to suggesting that the heavenly pleasures and mortal dangers of owning and driving an Xterra rival or exceed those of shooting smack, even though that's *precisely* what the ad is saying or, rather, *would be* saying if it included the song's words, and not just its opening instrumental passage.

Hey, Lou! I got one for ya. When Nissan is done with it, why dontcha lease "Heroin" to a pharmaceutical company that sells a synthetic opium-based (and very addicting!) prescription painkiller like Oxycontin? Not funny? Not funny enough? OK, OK, you're a hard man to please, but I gotta 'nother one for ya. Why dontcha sell "Venus in Furs" to a company that still makes real fur coats, despite all the PETA protests? Ha ha ha. The possibilities are endless, Lou. Everything is permitted; nothing is true.

NOT BORED! #35, July 2003

Musicians

When the Cure is Worse than the Disease

What's being sold here [in the Budweiser radio commercials that use the music of Squeeze and the Dave Edmunds Band] is not name or personality but style. The familiar but chart-poor groups are not announced, and that anonymity provides an aural itch that you scratch when you remember the product with which the style is associated. The spots take the language of a performer and reduce it to two or three constituent elements; the result is that the performer's language – made of incipient clichés that, by means of a confrontation with a specific occasion of performance, are sometimes dissolved into an efflorescence that transcends cliché and extends language – is now reified into a single cliché hard enough to dominate any mere occasion. From now on, this is all the performer will have to say. His performance will communicate in terms of how well it approximates the reification of the commercial, not necessarily because the commercial will have been more widely or intensely heard than any other work by the performer (though it probably will have been), but because the commercial will have completed – in fact, realized – the performer's career. When one hears an old Squeeze or Dave Edmunds record, it will sound like an attempt to formulate a cliché – to produce a style so recognizable and narrow that it can be marketed as an object, as a thing – which is what the record will have been.

Greil Marcus has changed his mind since he wrote these words, back in 1987, when his "Real Life Top Ten" column was published in *The Village Voice*. He now says, "I think all songs should go up on this block [...] It's a way of finding out if songs that carry people with them, songs that seem tied to a particular time and place, can survive a radical recontextualization, or if that recontectualization dissolves them" (see "Bob Dylan After the 1994 Congressional Elections," in *Double Trouble: Bill Clinton and Elvis Presley in a Land of No Alternatives*, published in 2000). But this essay isn't going to be an examination of Greil Marcus' change of mind or the increasing timidity of his politics. No, this is going to be *yet another* denunciation of the on-going and relentless use of rock 'n' roll songs in TV and radio commercials, a subject we have taken up twice before, in essays about Pete Townshend and Lou Reed.

Much of what Marcus once said about the Budweiser ads can be applied to the anonymous use of "Pictures of You" (a song by the familiar but chart-poor British band The Cure) in a TV ad for Hewlett-Packard printers. But the reification of style in this instance is *much* worse. Unlike Squeeze or Dave Edmunds, the Cure

Musicians

never made "happy" music. All of their songs were dark and brooding, perfect confirmations of Lester Bangs' assertion that "the whole reason pop music was invented in the first place was to vent sick emotions in a deceptively lulling form" (see "On the Merits of Sexual Repression," reprinted in *Mainlines, Blood Feasts, and Bad Taste,* published in 2003).

Released on the 1989 album *Disintegration,* "Pictures of You" is a typical piece of Cure-shit: a "sick" and maudlin tearjerker narrated by someone whose lover has committed suicide ("And you finally found all your courage / To let it all go"). But you couldn't possibly realize any of this from the small part of the song (the chorus, of course) that's used in the commercial:

> I've been looking so long at these pictures of you
> That I almost believe that they're real
> I've been living so long with my pictures of you
> That I almost believe that the pictures are
> All I can do

And so this is *a doubly sanitized* version of the song. Not only has it been cleansed by the removal of all traces of the death and decay of the lover's body, but it has also been rendered sane by the suppression of all hints that its narrator is morbidly depressed. Sure, there's still fragmentation (the full-color pictures of some happy family that are seen pouring out of the Hewitt-Packard printer are separate and distinct from each other), but it's not the result of anger or destruction ("If only I'd thought of the right words / I wouldn't be breaking apart / All my pictures of you"). What was once a messy disintegration has become a series of clean separations.

Unfortunately, that's not all. The last line ("All I can do") is not in the original version of the song. Either it was taken from an alternative mix or was created specially for use in the commercial. The original line was "All I can feel." And so this is *real sickness,* a sickness in the soul of society itself: the narrator no longer feels, no longer feels anything at all; he simply does, he simply takes pictures. Not only are his pictures more "real" than his dead lover, they are more real than he himself is.

NOT BORED! #36, July 2004

The Greatest TV Commercial Ever Made

I *hate it* when rock 'n' roll songs are used as soundbites or soundtracks in TV commercials. And you know why? *I hate TV commercials,* all of them, even the "good ones," the funny ones. I hate *all* commercials, whether they're on TV, radio, the Internet, the Silver Screen, roadside billboards or clothes. In a capitalist economic system such as "ours," there's only affirmation, and no possibility of negation, in all commercial discourse. Think of MTV, source of the pernicious trend of using classic rock music in TV commercials: for almost 25 years it has broadcast *nothing but commercials.* In the November 1983 issue of *Artforum,* Greil Marcus maintained that,

> Within a commodity economy, negation can be packaged and sold as a commodity glamorizing commodities that aggressively affirm. There can be no negation on MTV, not even that of terrorism (if terrorism can be a negation, which is dubious). Were terrorists to take over the MTV transmitter, line the video jockeys up against the studio wall, and shoot them, viewers would rightly wonder what new group was being promoted.

And so, on several occasions, I (good Greil Marcusian that I am) have vehemently denounced the use of the music of Pete Townshend, Lou Reed and the Cure in various TV commercials, most of which have been for cars. I also hate cars, especially Sports Utility Vehicles.

But don't get me wrong, Gentle Reader. I *do* have a sense of humor and I can't/don't get worked up into a frenzy – indeed, I'm far more likely to burst out laughing – when I see such stunners as Devo's "Whip It" used to sell Swiffer cleaning-spray to strangely energetic housewifes or placed in the mouth of *a singing cow* in an ad for Gateway computers; or the Turtles' "Happy Together" used to promote the new steak-and-shrimp combo at the local chainstore restaurant; or etc etc. There's been *dozens* of comical monstrosities like these over the years. I know, I know: "They are *so* stupid that you just *can't* take them seriously; and, if you *do* take them seriously, it will be *you* who looks like a fool." Besides which, who knows? Maybe Devo *really has been* putting subliminal messages of rebellion into their you've-*got*-to-be-kidding appearances in TV commercials!

With all that in mind, and to keep things "fair and balanced" *a la* Fox News, I now give you an example of a TV commercial with a classic rock song as its sound-bite/soundtrack that I happen to think is good, great, even THE GREATEST TV COMMERCIAL EVER MADE. And why's that? Because this particular TV spot, which is a rousing exhortation to buy a Cadillac SUV, is 1) a commercial for Cadillac, which as every American knows is THE GREATEST CAR COMPANY IN THE WORLD, 2) a commercial for an SUV, which is of course THE GREATEST AMERICAN CAR EVER MADE, and 3) a commercial that has as its gimmick/schtick a song by Led Zeppelin, THE GREATEST ROCK 'N' ROLL BAND EVER, even though they were Brits and thus not real Americans.

Now it's true that the Led Zeppelin song used in this all-time great TV commercial – "Rock and Roll," on *Led Zeppelin IV,* released in 1971 – *isn't* THE GREATEST SONG THEY EVER RECORDED, which as every true Led Zep fan knows is "Stairway to Heaven." But nothing's perfect, right? – well, nothing except for the new Cadillac SUV, that is!

Led Zeppelin were THE GREATEST BAND EVER because they set the mold by reversing everybody's expectations: instead of getting better over the years, their music got worse. Their first album, boldly entitled *Led Zeppelin I* (1969) was their best, and their last, *In Through the Out Door* (1979) was their worst. Their decline took place during or immediately after the 1969-1971 period, during which they released three albums in a row – *Led Zeppelin II*, *Led Zeppelin III* and *Untitled* (commonly called *Led Zeppelin IV*) – the very titles of which suggest that a formula or brand was being perfected and capitalized upon ("milked dry") as fast as possible.

Ironically, this branding wasn't good for the band's musical development. Singer Robert Plant and bassist John Paul Jones *stopped trying,* did competent but uninspiring work, coasted through, and let the band be driven/dominated by the cranked-up playing of guitarist Jimmy Page and drummer John Bonham. But Page quickly concentrated on his growing expertise as a producer of recordings at the expense of his guitar-playing, and Bonham was, after all, only the drummer (but let it be remembered that he, too, could give the concert-goers "Moby Dick," a 30-minute-long solo of his own!). And so Led Zeppelin became a lazy dinosaur, a Sloth Behemoth. Perhaps it was the cold expertise of their radio-friendly sound production that kept its rotten core (sexist "cockrock" posturing and racist rip-offs, clichés and put-downs) from stinking the place up.

"Rock and Roll," which is credited to Bonham/Jones/Page/Plant, is a perfect example of why Led Zeppelin was a big fat disappointment. It opens with a sizzling, up-tempo rip-off of the drummer's intro to Little Richard's "You Keep A-Knocking (But You Can't Come In)," and then, powered by two interlocking guitar parts, drives right into an up-tempo, 12-bar blues. Though Plant's vocals are typically lazy and noncommittal, Page's smoldering guitar-playing picks up the slack (there's an extended guitar solo, of course), which keeps the driving momentum going, but does nothing to increase it. The typically self-absorbed lyrics are full of evasions, begged questions, and cynical comparisons to the rock 'n' roll of the 1950s.

> It's been a long time since I rock and rolled,
> It's been a long time since I did The Stroll.
> Ooh, let me get it back, let me get it back,
> Let me get it back, baby, where I come from.
> It's been a long time, been a long time,
> Been a long lonely, lonely, lonely, lonely, lonely time. (Yes it has.)
>
> It's been a long time since the Book of Love,

> I can't count the tears of a life with no love.
> Carry me back, carry me back,
> Carry me back, baby, where I come from.
> It's been a long time, been a long time,
> Been a long lonely, lonely, lonely, lonely, lonely time.
>
> Seems so long since we walked in the moonlight,
> Making vows that just can't work right.
> Open your arms, opens your arms,
> Open your arms, baby, let my love come running in.
> It's been a long time, been a long time,
> Been a long lonely, lonely, lonely, lonely, lonely time.
>
> Yeah, hey! (repeat)
> O yeah, o yeah.
> It's been a long been a long time,
> Been a long lonely, lonely, lonely, lonely, lonely time.

And then . . . *the song just ends* or, rather, Bonham begins the short, triplet-heavy, momentum-killing and utterly pointless drum solo that prematurely signals the end of the song. When the song finally *does* clatter to an end, the sound is metallic and the tone detached and cold. It's all been nothing but a con, an empty affirmation of nothing.

But if you take this bullshit con-job (it's *already* a car commercial), edit it properly (just the "exciting part," the song's beginning), and then put what remains in a slick TV commercial for an SUV, the song is perfect. It now has something to affirm: power. Power steering and power rock: the perfect combination! Dude! Can't you just *see* yourself driving one of those monsters, listening to 'Rock and roll' as you drive roughshod over the face of the whole planet? You'd still be lonely, lonely, lonely, lonely, lonely, but at least you'd have yer SUV, right?

NOT BORED! #36, July 2004

Kurt Cobain's Zombie Identity

Fourteen years after his suicide at the age of 27, Kurt Cobain is still a joke that America keeps telling itself. The joke goes something like this: there was once this scrawny kid from some nowhere town a hundred miles outside of Seattle who wanted to be a rock star, who worked really hard at being a rock star, and when he finally succeeded and got everything he always wanted (a hit record, money and fame), he found he couldn't handle it and he killed himself! And you know what? He used a gun to blow his brains out, even though in one of his songs – a really sincere one, right? – he kept saying "And I swear that I don't have a gun"! He *swears* he doesn't have a gun! *Swears to God!!!*

In the last week, a new joke has been added to the old one: not only does Kurt Cobain want his life back, he also wants money and credit cards and a mansion! It started on 5 March 2008, when Cobain's widow, Courtney Love – a joke in her own right – revealed that the Los Angeles Police Department was finally taking seriously her claim that thieves had stolen Kurt's identity (his social security number) and were using it to get credit cards (188 of them) and buy lots of neat stuff, including a $3 million mansion in New Brunswick, New Jersey. Apparently these thieves have stolen over $36 million from the Cobain estate, which was created to benefit Courtney and Kurt's only child, Frances Bean, who is now 15 years old. To make matters worse, or funnier, depending on your perspective, Courtney claims that she became aware of the identity theft and reported it to the police back in 2003, but "nobody believed me," because she had been, in her own words, "cuckoo, bananas." As if she is nothing but sober and sane these days! As if she herself has not stolen musical ideas from Kurt and the rights to his songs from his fellow band mates!

"I would like to know how [this could happen]" Courtney now says. And then, abruptly switching from the theft of her husband's identity to his apparent return from the dead, she joked, "He should probably get his ass back home if that is the case."

It didn't take long for the other jokes to start. "Kurt Bought a House Last Year," said *The Sun* on 7 March 2008. "Kurt Cobain Back From The Dead," announced the celebrity-baiting blogger Perez Hilton on 8 March. "Kurt Cobain Lives An Hour Away From Me, Apparently," stated a blogger who writes for *Cinema Blend* on 9 March. "Kurt Cobain is alive and well" and "Kurt Cobain Going to Rutgers, Apparently," proclaimed *The Philadelphia Weekly* on 10 March 2008. "Kurt Cobain Still Living – and Spending – Like a Rock Star," announced a blogger writing for seattlest.com on 11 March. And, last but certainly not least, laaaadies and gentlemen, "Kurt's Zombie Identity Stolen. . . by Thieves," heckled a blogger writing for something called hecklerspray.com on 12 March.

Surely there will be people who find none of this funny, sad, shameful or even interesting, because they don't give a shit about Kurt Cobain, Courtney Love or either one of their rock bands, Nirvana and Hole, respectively. "Yeah, it's a shame he killed himself so young, but what do I care? I never liked his music. . . ." As Greil Marcus wrote in an essay originally published in *Rolling Stone* in 1994 and later reprinted in *Double Trouble: Bill Clinton and Elvis Presley in a Land of No Alternatives* (2000),

> Driving for six hours from Kansas City to Fayetteville on Sunday, April 10, the day after the story [of the suicide] was front page all

over the country, there wasn't any Kurt Cobain. Radio is now so demographically segmented its formats are absolutely resistant to events in the world at large [...] On Your Favorite Oldies, Best of the '70s, Lite Rock, not to mention 24-Hour News, talk radio, Adult Contemporary, country, or hip hop stations, Kurt Cobain didn't die, and neither was he ever born.

The only ones who know or care that Kurt Donald Cobain was born on 20 February 1967 and committed suicide on 5 April 1994 are "the kids," the "punk rock kids," in bloom every May, who fork over $50 million each year for Nirvana CDs, making Kurt Cobain the highest-grossing dead rock star in the world. In death, or complete nonexistence, he even makes more money than another joke America loves to tell itself: the one about Elvis Presley.

There are, of course, significant differences (as well as similarities) between Kurt Cobain and Elvis Presley. They both abused drugs, though Elvis favored prescription medications and hated street drugs like heroin; and they both died "shameful deaths," shameful because they disobeyed the law of the spectacle that says, "Die young and leave a beautiful corpse." One died fat and the other died anorexic. And, yes, it makes a difference: "fat" symbolizes the world before 1961, before the conviction and hanging of Eichmann, and before *Judgment at Nuremberg*; "anorexic" symbolizes the world *after that*, if such a thing is possible (Theodor Adorno: "Writing poetry after Auschwitz is barbaric").

With Bill Clinton still alive and in the news (he's running for First Gentleman), and with the incredible popularity and likely nomination of Democratic presidential candidate Barack Obama, America doesn't need Elvis Presley to remind it once again of its failed promises and potential to unite white and black, rich and poor, urban and rural. No, what America needs today – what America needed fourteen years ago and still needs in 2008 – is someone who can dramatize what almost everyone is either feeling or perpetrating upon others: humiliation, abjection, guilt and shame.

In another essay reprinted in *Double Trouble,* Greil Marcus notes that, though "it might be months [...] before you begin to catch what's being said in Nirvana's songs," "what the music says by itself" is "the feeling of humiliation, disintegration, of defeat by some shapeless malevolence." (As we will see, though that malevolence is indeed shapeless, it can still be named.) In still another essay reprinted in *Double Trouble,* Greil notes that "the drama played out in Cobain's performance" (the one captured in the video compilation *Live! Tonight! Sold Out!!*) "was a drama of abjection and abasement, of worthlessness and redundancy, a drama of surplus population, be it that of a solitary nobody who nobody liked or a generation the economy didn't need and the culture didn't want." As southern white trash, Elvis Presley was certainly familiar with these conditions, but his music did not intentionally dramatize social or personal exclusion. Elvis Presley's music was about unity, pride, over-coming, and especially dignity. But Kurt

Cobain knew nothing or wanted nothing of these things. The theme of shame runs through all of Nirvana's lyrics, starting with the first two songs on the band's first album, *Bleach* ("Blew" and "Floyd the Barber"). Shame also features prominently in Kurt's private journals, which were published in 2002 under the name *Journals*.

Though the members of Nirvana clearly thought that it was one of their best songs (it was placed first on the demo tape that the band submitted to Touch & Go Records in 1988), "Floyd the Barber" is not given its due, perhaps because the scene it dramatizes is so outlandish.

> Bell on door clanks, come on in
> Floyd observes my hairy chin
> Sit down chair, don't be afraid
> Steamed hot towel on my face
>
> I was shaved (repeat 3X)
>
> Barney ties me to the chair
> I can't see, I'm really scared
> Floyd breathes hard, I hear a zip
> Pee-pee pressed against my lips
>
> I was shamed (repeat 3X)
>
> I sense others in the room
> Opie, Aunt Bea, I presume
> They take turns in cut me up
> I died smothered in Andy's butt
>
> I was shamed (repeat 3X)

Once you begin exploring the strangeness of this story, you find you can't exhaust it. Everything is mixed together and indistinct. Is this a joke (a calculated and imaginary outrage, thought up by an adult with a perverse sense of humor) or is this a serious allegation (an evocation of one of the ways a child might describe the outrages that were perpetrated on him by real adults)? Is this a private matter (a shameful secret that no one knows) or a public scandal (a parody of the innocence of the characters on a well-known TV show from the '50s and '60s)? But perhaps the strangest, the most ambiguous aspect is this: is the death reported in the last lines metaphorical or real? Is a part of the narrator (his "innocence") dead or is the narrator himself dead (a walking corpse)? Note well how the song ends, with the drums continuing on their own for a bit, as if not yet realizing that everyone else has stopped playing.

In his book *Remnants of Auschwitz: The Witness and the Archive* (1999), the

Italian philosopher Giorgio Agamben notes that "there is certainly nothing shameful in a human being who suffers on account of sexual violence," because it is the abuser, and not the victim, who is or should be full of shame for his other actions (this is precisely what the narrator of Kurt's song "Polly" is struggling to understand). "But if he [the victim] takes pleasure in his suffering violence, if he is moved by his passivity [...] only then can one speak of shame" (Agamben, page 110).

And so perhaps the ambiguity or indistinctness of the themes in "Floyd the Barber" dramatizes Kurt's painful awareness that 1) he found himself excited (either at the time or retrospectively) by the abuse he once suffered or 2) he is excited by the repulsive scenario that he has imagined. Either way, the fantasy of Floyd's Barbershop of Horrors is ultimately unsatisfying. In the first, his mind ("No rape / physical distance desired now") and his body ("Yes feels good / involuntary physical excitation") remain at odds; and in the second, the unification of his desires comes too late (the era of *The Andy Griffith Show* is over, killed off by "1961," thank god). And so a cycle – sometimes soothing cycle, mostly vicious – is set in motion. Kurt is a sincere, out-spoken and brave anti-rape crusader in the rock music business. "Don't rape" is at the top of a list of six commandments that Kurt draws up on page 114 of his journals, and the plain and simple plea "Don't fuck your children" was the last line in Kurt's liner notes for the Nirvana album *Nevermind* (1991), which he sketched out on page 165 of the journals. But Kurt Cobain was also a young man who was abused, angry, sexually frustrated and depressed enough to fantasize about threatening to rape his enemies: "please don't fuck with my freedom or Im gonna have to Rape, torture & mutilate your family," he writes on 129 of the journals, speaking to the right-wing Republicans who have been in power ever since 1980, except for the first two years of the Clinton Presidency. Inevitably, this split or cycling back and forth dominates Kurt's poetry: "My lyrics are a big pile of contradictions. theyre split down the middle between very sincere opinions and feelings that I have and sarcastic and hopefully humorous rebuttles towards cliché – bohemian ideals that have been exhausted for years" (*Journals*, 46). The cycle goes through moments of self-loathing ("Stain," "I Hate Myself and Want to Die"), self-confidence ("About a Girl," "Love Buzz"), and self-parody ("On A Plain," "Dumb").

Speculations about "Floyd the Barber" are rendered even more problematic by Kurt's self-conscious, art-school declaration in his journals that, "when I say I in a song, that doesnt necessarily mean that person is me and it doesnt mean im just a storyteller, it means whoever or whatever you want because everyone has their own definition of specific words and when your dealing in the context of music you cant expect words to have the same meaning as in everyday use of vocabulary because I consider music art and [...] I feel this society somewhere has lost its sense of what art is, Art is expression" (page 120; see also discussions of linguistic "shifters" in John Keats' letter to John Woodhouse dated 27 October 1818: "As to the poetical Character [...] it is not itself – it has no self – it is everything and nothing – It has no character"; in Ingeborg Bachman's *Frankfurt Lectures*: "An 'I' without guarantees! What is the 'I', what could it be?"; in Arthur Rimbaud's letter to P. Demeny: "for 'I' is another"; in Emile Benveniste's *Problems in General Linguistics*: "What then is the reality to which *I* or *you* refers? It is solely to a 'reality of discourse,' and this is a very strange thing. *I* cannot be defined except in terms of 'locution' [...] *I* signifies 'the person who is uttering the present instance of the discourse containing *I*'"; etc. etc.)

Let me be plain. "Floyd the Barber," "Polly" (both the electric and the acoustic versions), "Negative Creep," the infamous "Rape Me": these songs (and others) by Nirvana resonate with people because of their own private experiences with sexual violence. And precisely because so many children and adults in America are the victims of sexual violence, Nirvana's music is popular with (emotionally gripping for) a lot of people, not everyone, but certainly enough to be significant. They find this music both cathartic and depressing, while other people find it just depressing.

But the presence of the theme of struggling against sexual humiliation doesn't fully explain the full intensity or duration of Nirvana's appeal, nor does it exhaust the sources of shame thematized and dramatized in the band's music. In his journals, Kurt describes himself as feeling "guilty for being a white, American male" (page 109). Such men do more than rape women and children of both genders: they also harass and degrade homosexuals, and lynch black men. But the sources or causes of Kurt's shame go even deeper than that. In his sketch for a possible record sleeve ("Floyd the Barber" is listed as the first song), he writes "I'm Ashamed to be a Human" (page 85; note that the words "I'm" and "a" are crossed out but are still legible). And why? Because humans not only rape, torture and mutilate each other, but also other species, plants and animals, even the whole fucking planet.

Here we begin to get a sense of the awesome dimensions and depth of Kurt's shame. In the words of his journals, he is "pregnant with shame" (268). But neither the words nor the music of "Floyd the Barber" fully express it; it can only be adequately or fully expressed by gestures of inexpressibility, that is to say, by the hollowing out of words. "I'll start this song off without any words," he sings at the very beginning of "On A Plain." But Nirvana was not an instrumental band, nor did they record a single instrumental track. ("Tourette's" is the exemplary song here: the words are reduced to almost nothing and the voice is freed to play like any other instrument. Like Iggy Pop in the Stooges' "LA Blues," Kurt sounds like a ranting, wordless maniac, a feral child or a wild animal.) Words quite obviously remain in Nirvana's music, but they are twisted, bent and sometimes broken by groans, screams, cries and shouts. In his journals, Kurt writes,

> I don't have the time to translate what I understand in the form of conversation. I had exhausted most conversation at age nine. I only feel with grunts screams and tones with hand gestures and my body.

Musicians

> Im deaf in spirit [...] I cant speak, I cannot feel. Maybe someday I'll turn myself into Helen Keller by puncturing my ears with a knife, then cutting my voice box out. (pages 124 and 125)

What's left after the ears and voice box are gone? Nothing but "hand gestures and my body," that is to say, the movements and physical presence of the body. As he says in another journal entry, "I make up words – that Arent *ever* heard" (page 201, emphasis added). We can only feel what Kurt is feeling by literally feeling him and, from a distance, seeing him move around and make gestures. We can only be impossibly close to and/or far away from him: "with the lights out, it's less dangerous" to be in such intimate proximity.

But even this is too much: Kurt doesn't want – or can't bear – to be seen. "Whoever experiences shame is overcome by his own being subject to vision," Agamben writes in his book on Auschwitz (page 107). And so, when the mass media eventually focuses its cruel spotlights on Kurt's private life and reveals him to be (in his own words) "a notoriously fucked up heroine addict, alcoholic, self destructive, yet overly sensitive, frail, meek, fragile, compassionate, soft spoken, narcoleptic, NEUROTIC, little piss ant who at any time is going to O.D., jump off a roof and wig out, blow my head off or all three at once because I CANT HANDLE THE SUCCESS! OH THE SUCCESS! THE GUILT! THE GUILT! OH, I FEEL SO INCREDIBLY GUILTY! GUILTY for abandoning our true comrades. the ones who are devoted" (text entitled "OH THE GUILT," signed by "KurDT disclaimer-boy," page 195 of the journals), his response is to demand (ironically?) that the media "Rape Me." The ambiguity or indistinction here is shameful: if rape is something perpetrated on an unwilling person, what can "rape" mean if the victim is literally and explicitly asking for it? "I'm not the only one," Kurt insists over and over in "Rape Me." Not the only one whom the media has raped, or not the only one who sarcastically declares he wants to be raped?

It is in "OH THE GUILT" that Kurt denies he is a heroin addict and explains that he is simply someone who has periodically used heroin to treat a longstanding, irregularly occurring and life-threatening stomach disorder that completely mystifies all of the doctors he has gone to see. Only heroin relieves the terrible pain he experiences and suppresses his hunger, which he could not satisfy in any event, for fear of further irritating his inflamed stomach. Towards the end of "OH THE GUILT" he prays:

> Please lord! To hell with hit records, let me have my very own unexplainable, rare, stomach disease named after me. The title of our next double concept album could be called "COBAINS DISEASE." A rock opera all about vomiting gastric juices, being a borderline anorexic-Auschwitz-grunge-boy. And with this epic, an accompanying ENDOSCOPE rock video.

Auschwitz?! Is the terrible and terribly misunderstood specter of Auschwitz (the Nazi death camps) evoked here in the casual manner in which Kurt's journal refers to the "Nuremberg's rallies" (page 102) held in America in the aftermath of its supposed victory in the Gulf War? No, it appears that Kurt is trying to speak as honestly as possible about his condition. "There were many times that I found myself literally incapacitated in bed for weeks vomiting and starving [...] I was literally starving to death" (pages 207 and 208 of the journals).

Agamben reminds us that "Auschwitz" does not simply refer to the horrible spectacle of naked bodies stacked like cordwood. Human beings (millions of them) were not murdered without first being turned into something else, that is, millions of sub- or non-human beings. And not just sub- or non-human at the level of such abstractions as "civilian," "citizen," "German," or "Aryan" (the realm of politics and the *polis*) but also at the concrete level of the human body (the realm of naked or bare life). This is Agamben on "the decisive function of the camps in the system of Nazi biopolitics":

> [The camps] are not merely the place of death and extermination; they are also, and above all, the site of the production of the *Muselmann*, the final biopolitical substance to be isolated in the biological continuum. Beyond the *Muselmann* lies only the gas chamber. (page 85)

Der Muselmann (literally "the Muslim") was the word – the argot – by which other prisoners or at least the German-speaking prisoners in the camps named the unspeakable person – the "staggering corpse," one of the "mummy-men, the living dead" (Agamben, 41) – who had been starved into a state of such advanced malnutrition that he or she was "giving up and was given up [on] by his comrades" (Amery, quoted in Agamben, 41). In the words of Ryn and Klodzinski,

> No one felt compassion for the Muslim, and no one felt sympathy for him either. The other inmates, who continually feared for their lives, *did not judge him worthy of being looked at.* For the prisoners who collaborated, the Muslims [*Muselmanner*] were a source of anger and worry; for the SS, they were merely useless garbage. Every group thought only about eliminating them, each in its own way. (Quoted in Agamben, 43, emphasis added)

Despite the fact that the production of *Muselmanner* (or the transformation of healthy and sane human beings into *Muselmanner*) was the decisive function of the camps, the latter have largely remained elusive, not only to understanding, but to perception, too. The very indirectness of the word "Muslim" is telling in this regard: it designates a Semite but not a Jew; a Jew who is no longer Jewish. The irony is ferocious: "the Jews knew that they would not die at Auschwitz as Jews"

(Agamben, 45), even though they were consigned to Auschwitz precisely because they were Jewish. "Muslim" also carries the stigma or shame of a foreign language: not Hebrew, Yiddish or even German, which were the dominant languages in the camps, but Arabic, and so radically other. (The "otherness" of "the Muslim" has been a constant theme in democratic-spectacular nations ever since 1945 and reached a fever pitch in the aftermath of September 11th, 2001.)

One hears from survivors of the camps that the *Muselmanner* grimaced, moved very slowly and did not protest; mostly they were silent. Though there are plenty of photographs from 1945 of piles of naked corpses, in and out of pits, there are no pictures of the *Muselmanner*. Nor any paintings. Agamben writes:

> Aldo Carpi, professor of painting at the Academy of Brera, was deported to Gusen in February 1944, where he remained until May 1945. He managed to survive because the SS began to commission paintings and drawings from him once they discovered his profession. Carpi [...] wanted to paint the actual scenes and figures from the camp. But his commissioners had absolutely no interest in such things; indeed, they did not even tolerate the [very] sight of them. "No one wants camp scenes and figures," Capri notes in his diary, "no one wants to see the *Muselmann*" (page 50).

The *Muselmann* had to be invisible, not simply because individual SS officers found them offensive, disgusting, worthless or simply uninteresting, but because Nazi biopolitics was a *spectacular* politics: the spectacle of absolute power. It required a kind of blind spot or "black hole" for it to shine, to blind its spectators. Wolfgang Sofsky writes in *The Order of Terror: The Concentration Camp*:

> The *Muselmann* embodies the anthropological meaning of absolute power in an especially radical form. Power abrogates itself in the act of killing. The death of the other puts an end to the social relationship. But by starving the other, it gains time. It erects a third realm, a limbo between life and death. Like the pile of corpses, the *Muselmanner* document the total triumph of power over the human being. Although still nominally alive, they are nameless hulks. In the configuration of their infirmity, as in organized mass murder, the regime realizes its quintessential self. (quoted in Agamben, pages 47-48)

In the realization of absolute power as "its quintessential self" (the society of the concentrated spectacle), language is confiscated: the *Muselmanner* were without "proper" language. In *Survival in Auschwitz,* Primo Levi remembers a child dubbed Hurbinek.

Hurbinek was a nobody, a child of death, a child of Auschwitz. He looked about three years old, no one knew anything of him, he could not speak and had no name; that curious name, Hurbinek, had been given to him by us, perhaps by one of the women who had interpreted with those syllables one of the inarticulate sounds that the baby let out now and again. He was paralyzed from the waist down, with atrophied legs, as thin as sticks; but his eyes, lost in his triangular and wasted face, flashed terribly alive, full of demand, assertion, of the will to break loose, to shatter the tomb of his dumbness. The speech he lacked, which no one had bothered to teach him, the need of speech charged his stare with explosive urgency (quoted in Agamben, page 37).

Agamben recounts that "Now at a certain point Hurbinek begins to repeat a word over and over again, a word that no one in the camp can understand and that Levi doubtfully transcribes as *mass-klo* or *matisko* [...] Despite the presence of all the languages of Europe in the camp, Hurbinek's word remains obstinately secret" (page 38). Levi reports, "Hurbinek died in the first days of March 1945, free but not redeemed. Nothing remains of him: he bears witness through these words of mine" (*ibid.*). Levi survived, not by collaborating with the SS (painting nice pictures), but by collaborating with Hurbinek: Levi had to survive the camps so that he could bear witness, testify, to Hurbinek's existence, experiences and death. Like the *Muselmanner,* Hurbinek was a "complete witness" to Auschwitz, to the truth of Auschwitz, while survivors such Levi could only ever be partial or indirect witnesses. They did not directly witness the atrocity itself; they witnessed those who did. In a certain way, they were "witness[es] to a missing testimony" (Agamben, 34). In fact, some never testified, never even talked about the subject again.

Despite the apparent nobility, dignity or exoticism of being a witness, of living to tell the tale – despite the cult of the survivor (see Greil Marcus' discussion of the bleak state of rock music in the middle of the 1970s in *Lipstick Traces: A Secret History of the Twentieth Century*) – Primo Levi noted in *The Awakening* that shame was a powerful feeling among the prisoners who weren't *Muselmanner.*

> It was that shame we knew so well, the shame that drowned us after the [completely arbitrary] selection [of who was to die that day], and every time we had to watch, or submit to, some outrage: the shame the Germans did not know, that the just man experiences at another man's crime, at the fact that such a crime should exist, that it should have been introduced irrevocably into the world of things that exist, and that his will for good should have proved too weak or null, and should not have [been] availed in defense (quoted in Agamben, page 88).

Twenty years later, in *The Drowned and the Saved,* Levi returned to those who survived the camps, and found that their shame had not ceased, and indeed that shame was now their dominant sentiment. Indeed, there was a lot to be ashamed of: secretly wanting the *Muselmanner* to be eliminated while they were still "alive"; entering and dwelling in what Levi calls the ethical "gray zone" in which prisoners collaborated with their torturers in order to survive, especially in the *Sonderkommando*. "And certainly the intimacy that one experiences before one's own unknown murderer is the most extreme intimacy, an intimacy that can as such provoke shame" (Agamben, 104). Even the very fact of surviving, when others – many, many others – did not, was perceived as shameful. But the survivors weren't the only ones who were ashamed, or who *should have been*: the Nazis who perpetrated these crimes against humanity (but had no shame or did not know shame), and all those who failed to stop the Nazis from perpetrating them. In *Means Without End*, published a few years before *Remnants of Auschwitz*. Agamben writes: "Primo Levi has shown [...] that there is today [1995] a 'shame of being human,' a shame that in some way or other has tainted every human being. This was – and still is – the shame of the camps, the shame of the fact that what should not happen did happen" (page 132).

Who then was Kurt Cobain? He was a kind of *Muselmann*; he was little Hurbinek if he survived the camps, grew up and became a punk rock musician. This is not a mere pleasantry: it explains a lot, starting with why Kurt Cobain sometimes called himself "Kurdt." He was clearly likening himself to the Kurds, a stateless people who were attacked or abandoned by all sides in the Iran-Iraq war from 1980-1988. The fate of the Kurds remains an urgent matter, twenty years later. (As I write these words, the Turkish military has entered Iraq, a sovereign nation, and is slaughtering Kurdish militants and terrorists at will). One is right to associate the Kurds closely with the Bosnians, Gypsies, Armenians, Palestinians, Basques, Jews of the Diaspora, and other peoples without a state. All of them – unlike the country of Kuwait, which is a state without a people – can "be oppressed and exterminated with impunity, so as to make it clear that the destiny of a people can only be state identity and that the concept of *people* makes sense only if recodified within the concept of citizenship" (Agamben, *Means Without End*, pages 67-68). There is an awful irony here: it was by diverting Kurt Cobain's "state identity" (his social security number) that thieves were able to rob his estate.

The image of Kurt-as-Hurbinek also sheds an interesting light, not on each and every one of Nirvana's songs – I'm with Kurt when he says "mistrust All systematizers" in his journals (page 184) – but on certain ones, especially "Paper Cuts," which contains some of Kurt's most gut-wrenching vocals.

> At feeding time
> She pushed food through the door
> And I crawl towards the crack of light
> Sometimes I can't find my way
> Newspapers spread around

Musicians

Soaking all that they can
A cleaning is due again
A good hosing down

The lady whom I feel maternal love for
Cannot look me in the eyes
But I see hers and they are blue
And they cock and twist and masturbate!

I said so (repeat 3X)
Nirvana (repeat 6X)

Black windows of paint
I scratched with my nails
I see others just like me
Why do they not try to escape?
They bring out the older ones
They point at my way
They come with flashing lights
And take my family away
And very later I have learned

To accept some friends of ridicule
My whole existence is for your amusement
And that is why I'm here with you!
To take you with me, you're right

Nirvana (repeat 8X)

Almost all of the central themes I have identified are here: food and starvation ("food through the door"); spectacle and darkness ("flashing lights" and "black windows"); shame ("Cannot look me in the eyes") and shameful words and shameful sex ("cock and twist and masturbate"); and even enjoyable shame ("To accept some friends of ridicule"). But the key detail is the indistinctness of the location. Is it a prison or a concentration camp? A detention camp? Maybe a refugee camp. The basement of someone's house? A mother's womb? Whatever it is – and it must be unbearable because the mood and sound the music is as heavy, dark and brutal as these musicians could make it – this place has a name: Nirvana.

The other side or the contrary of "Paper Cuts" (the positive side of Nirvana) is the band's best and best-known song: "Smells Like Teen Spirit" (1991). Though the title doesn't appear as one of the song's lines, it opens the song's space: the space of shame. Among teenagers, *all* smells are potentially embarrassing or shameful, but especially those associated with the body's "private parts" (armpits and crotch). Though he didn't know it when he wrote the song – Kurt got the phrase "smells like teens spirit" from a female punk musician who'd known Kurt's ex-girlfriend and who'd spray painted the phrase "Kurt smells like teen spirit" in his room to remind him that he still smelled like his ex, because she wore "Teen Spirit" deodorant – "Teen Spirit" was the name of a very recently launched deodorant targeted at "spirited" teens. In his innocence, Kurt had thought that "Kurt smells like teen spirit" meant that he was a rebel, that he had the "scent" of a rebel. In any event, his song was a spirited rejection of shame: a refusal to be ashamed, in particular by a certain "dirty word" ("Oh no, I know a dirty word"). But this word did not refer to the human body or one of its allegedly "shameful" parts or bodily functions. Thanks to the close association in Kurt's journals of the song's lyrics with the phrase "revolutionary debris litters the floor of Wall Street" (page 146), and the idea that – because "This is the first generation that has brought musical unity between them and their Parents. Today There is no generation gap" (page 162) – "Revolution is no longer an embarrassment" (page 137), we know that *revolution* is the "dirty word" in question. The song's celebrated ending ("A denial! A denial! A denial!") is Kurt's way of showing he is not afraid to call for REVOLUTION aloud, in public.

To conclude: perhaps the most important thing that Kurt-as-Hurbinek provides us with is a clue as to why Nirvana's music was, is, and always will be so gripping to so many people. Not counting the Sex Pistols' brutal, shameful "Belsen Was a Gas" (1977), Nirvana's music was the first to catch up to and express the truth of Auschwitz: Auschwitz isn't in the past; it isn't limited to Nazi Germany; it is here, today, and it is everywhere. That is to say, the production of *Muselmanner* is still going on. Kurt certainly knew it when he saw it.

> Ethnic cleansing is going on right now in the inner cities of the United States. Blacks, Hispanics and others are being exterminated before they can reach the fifth grade. The Right wing republicans Are responsible for releasing crack and Aids in our inner cities. Their logic is better to kill living breathing, freethinking humans rather than unknowing unstimulated, growing cells, encased in A lukewarm chamber. (*Journals*, page 273)

And so I say to you, America, that Kurt Cobain wasn't brought back from the dead by identity thieves. He came back because he *wanted* to; because he knew it was time to take his revenge; because you, America, you deserve to burn; you *will* burn. Remember Kurt's song "Frances Farmer Will Have Her Revenge on Seattle"? "She'll come back as fire / Burn all the liars / A blanket of ash on the ground."

What's happened since 5 April 1994? No, that's too easy. Everyone knows that November 1994 (the mid-term Congressional elections, which were swept by reactionary Republicans) began the six-year-long period in which President Bill

Clinton was publicly shamed. Then what's happened since 2003? A *second* war against the people of Iraq; the use of sex to bring about intense shame at Abu Ghraib; the use of water-boarding as a means of interrogating Muslims in secret detention centers; and the construction and operation of "Camp Delta" (otherwise known by its location in Guantanamo Bay, Cuba), America's very own concentration camp. What happened in 2006 during the mid-term Congressional elections? The voters of America spoke: they wanted an end to all this, immediately, and they voted for Democratic politicians, who quickly, utterly and ignominiously failed to end anything. The war goes on; torture is "not illegal" and can be practiced with impunity by our forces; Guantanamo Bay remains open. Today,[2] America's shame is *a hundred times* what it had been just a few years ago. How could America allow that which happened, but which never should have happened, to *happen again*? And how could it, of all nations, be the one who has perpetrated the crime? The only possible answer is that America is no longer "America." "America" is dead. Think of the TV interview with the policeman in *Night of the Living Dead* (1968): like any walking corpse or zombie, America may not give up, but it will go up real easy.

NOT BORED! #40, May 2008

---

[2] And even today, in 2011, spite election of Barack Obama, the anti-war candidate, in November 2008.

Part VI:

Miscellaneous

Miscellaneous
The 41 Curses, Crises and Conspiracies of Everyday Life

RETROFUTURISM, 1992
The German critic Walter Benjamin envisioned a book composed entirely of assembled quotations from other authors.

GREIL MARCUS, 1989
In December 1957, Guy-Ernest Debord . . . produced a book he called *Memoires*. He didn't write it. He cut scores of paragraphs, sentences, phrases, or sometimes single words out of books, magazines, and newspapers [...]. At first the book seemed entirely a conceit – precious. In fact it told a very specific story, and carried an affirmation that it was the only story worth telling.

RAOUL VANEIGEM, 1967
People who talk about revolution and class struggle without referring explicitly to everyday life, without understanding what is subversive about love and positive in the refusal of constraint, have corpses in their mouths.

GANG OF FOUR, 1981
I need a cheeseburger to go!

GUY DEBORD, 1961
To study everyday life would be a completely absurd undertaking, unable to grasp anything of its object, if this study was not explicitly for the purpose of transforming everyday life. The lecture, the exposition of certain intellectual considerations to an audience . . . itself forms a part of the everyday life to be criticized [...] It is thus desirable to demonstrate, by the slight alteration of the usual procedures, that everyday life is right here. These words are being communicated by way of a tape recorder, not, of course, in order to illustrate the integration of technology into this everyday life [that exists] on the margin of the technological world, but in order to seize the simplest opportunity to break with the appearance of pseudo-collaboration, of artificial dialogue, established between the lecturer "in person" and his spectators.

ROBERT SHEA & ROBERT ANTON WILSON, 1975
Certain dissident elements keep complaining that people don't get a chance to participate in decisions made by their government. Yet, at a time like this, when the whole nation has an opportunity to hear the Attorney General, the ratings are not always as good as they should be. So let's do everything we can to build up those ratings tonight, and let the whole world know that this is still a democracy.

Miscellaneous

STEPHEN E. AMBROSE, 1992
So many important people and powerful agencies wanted to murder President John F. Kennedy in November 1963 that they all but had to draw straws to see who got the first shot at him. According to Jim Marr's book *Crossfire: The Plot That Killed Kennedy* – one of the primary sources for Oliver Stone's movie *J.F.K.* – Kennedy was killed as a result of a conspiracy. "Who done it?" Mr. Marrs asks. "A consensus of powerful men in the leadership of U.S. military, banking, Government, intelligence and organized crime circles ordered their faithful agents to manipulate Mafia-Cuban-[Central Intelligence] Agency pawns to kill the chief." This conspiracy has been hidden from the public by the greatest cover-up of them all, the Warren Commission.

GUY DEBORD, 1992
"The conspiracy theory of history" was in the nineteenth century a reactionary and ridiculous belief, at a time when so many powerful social movements were stirring up the masses.

STEPHEN E. AMBROSE, 1992
That millions of Americans have read these books or seen Mr. Stone's movie may tell us more about the attitude people have toward their Government and their educational experiences than it does about the Kennedy assassination. They believe that government is a conspiracy and that the history they were taught in school is all lie and myth.

ROBERT SHEA & ROBERT ANTON WILSON, 1975
He reckoned most of his countrymen as total mental basket cases and fondly believed that he was exploiting their folly when he told them a vast Illuminist conspiracy controlled the money supply and interest rates [...] That there was an element of truth in these bizarre notions never crossed his mind. In short, [he] was as alienated from the pulse, the poetry, and the profundity of American emotion as a New York intellectual.

GUY DEBORD, 1989
A combination of circumstances has marked almost everything I've done with a certain conspiratorial allure.

VARIOUS FRENCH NEWSPAPERS, 1970-1972
The police of Europe keep track of them. Elusive and underground, conspirators in the tradition, [the Situationist International] refuse[s] all legalities and conformisms, even socialist ones. The Situationist International has its base in Copenhagen and . . . is controlled by the security and espionage police of East Germany [...] Their general headquarters is secret but I think it is somewhere in

London. They are not students, but what are known as situationists; they travel everywhere and exploit the discontent of students.

RAOUL VANEIGEM, 1962
Just as God constituted the reference point of past unitary society, we [situationists] are preparing to create the central reference point for a unitary society now possible.

ANTONIN ARTAUD, 1927
I regret living in a world where sorcerers and soothsayers must live in hiding, and where in any case there are so few genuine soothsayers . . . as far as I'm concerned, I find it astounding that fortune-tellers, tarot-readers, wizards, sorcerers, necromancers and other REINCARNATED ONES have for so long been relegated to the role of mere characters in fables and novels, and that, through one of the most superficial aspects of modern thinking, naïveté is defined as having faith in charlatans. I believe whole-heartedly in charlatans, bonesetters, visionaries, sorcerers and chiromancers, because all these things have being, because, for me, there are no limits, no fixed form to appearances.

HENRI LEFEBVRE, 1947
Oh, women with strange faces, portraits and poems with weird imagery, peculiar objects – all you prove is that there is no more "feminine mystery," that mystery has disappeared from our world, that it has degenerated into something public, that it is a game, an art-form, that it has lost its ancient glamour founded on terror and wild hope, that it has become mere journalism, mere advertizing, mere fashion, a music-hall turn, an exhibit . . .

ROLAND BARTHES, 1958
. . . [a] Spectacle.

THE MEKONS, 1991
He is a sorcerer / Before your eyes cast a spell / Out of control. . . . / He's a bourgeois sorcerer / In a million factories department stores and mills and banks / Dark powers walk in broad daylight / Social forces driven in dreadful directions / Whole populations conjured out of the ground / Ooh! The abyss is close to home.

KARL MARX, 1867
A commodity appears at first sight an extremely obvious, trivial thing. But its analysis brings out that it is a very strange thing, abounding in metaphysical subtleties and theological niceties. In so far as it is a use-value, there is nothing mysterious about it – whether we regard it as something whose natural properties enable it to satisfy human wants, or as something which only acquires such properties as the outcome of human labor. It is absolutely clear that, by his activity,

man changes the forms of the materials of nature in such a way as to make them useful to him. The form of wood, for instance, is altered if a table is made out of it. Nevertheless the table continues to be wood, an ordinary, sensuous thing. But as soon as it emerges as a commodity, it changes into a thing which transcends sensuousness. It not only stands with its feet on the ground, but, in relation to all other commodities, it stands on its head, and evolves out of its wooden brain grotesque ideas, far more wonderful than if it were to begin dancing of its own free will.

GREIL MARCUS, 1984
Pure poetry – and the mystical echoes were no accident. Marx's allusion was to the Spiritualists, who in his time clasped hands around tables in Boston, Paris, Prague, and St. Petersburg, waiting for the spirits of departed loved ones to set their hands knocking on wood, to make the tables dance. The Spiritualists had nothing to do with commodities, but the commodity had everything to do with magic.

HENRI LEFEBVRE, 1947
Everything – life, science, both the ideal and the idea of love, not to mention that arch-sorcerer of the Western world, money – conspires to instill in the sensitive, lucid, cultivated young man with a gift for "belles-lettres" a feeling of unease and dissatisfaction which can only be assuaged by something strange, bizarre or extraordinary [...] Thus philosophy has joined forces with literature in this great conspiracy against man's everyday life. Even in our so-called "modern" poets' and metaphysicians' most polished verbal and technical games we can find the elements of a certain criticism of everyday life, but in an indirect form, and always based upon the confusion between the real in human terms and the real in capitalist terms.

THE GRAND MASONIC LODGE OF THE STATE OF NEW YORK, 1943
[In speaking of Masonry as] a world by itself, with a life of its own . . . the word "life" itself [is not] a misnomer. To the casual observer Freemasonry might appear to be a kind of artificial thing, like the wearing of a fancy dress at a costume ball, something with no roots deep in experience, a luxury rather than a necessity [...] An experienced Freemason, however, knows that Masonry is a way of life, a mode of living, which moves in him and helps to shape his life all of the time, whether inside of Lodge or not.

BROTHER S. JAY KAUFMAN (32d-DEGREE), 1919
[The power of the Scottish Rite] amounts to a group of self-inspections looking to a specific daily conduct. And for Average Men always. For that matter, are we not all average men? [...] [In conclusion] may we repeat what we said a year ago – that Masonry is as near Utopia as anything we know. That to bring about a consideration, by so many men, of finer living is a force for world progress in an

every-day way which the world must encourage.

ADAM WEISHAUPT, 1776
And what is this general object [of the Order of the Illuminati]? THE HAPPINESS OF THE HUMAN RACE. Is it not distressing to a generous mind, after contemplating what human nature is capable of, to see how little we enjoy? When we look at this goodly world, and see that every man may be happy, but that the happiness of one depends on the conduct of another; when we see the wicked so powerful and the good so weak; and that it is in vain to strive singly and alone, against the general current of vice and oppression; the wish naturally arises in the mind, that it were possible to form a durable combination of the most worthy persons, who should work together in removing the obstacles to human happiness [...] Would not such an association be a blessing to the world? . . . The slightest observation shows that nothing will so much contribute to increase the zeal of the members as secret union. We see with what keenness and zeal the frivolous business of Freemasonry is conducted, by persons knit together by the secrecy of their union. It is needless to enquire into the causes of this zeal which secrecy produces. It is a universal fact, confirmed by the history of every age.

GUY DEBORD, 1988
Secrecy dominates this world, and first and foremost as the secret of domination. According to the spectacle, secrecy would only be a necessary exception to the rule of freely available, abundant information [...] No one sees secrecy in its inaccessible purity and its functional universality. Everyone accepts that there are inevitably little areas of secrecy reserved for specialists; as regards things in general, many believe they are in on the secret [...] Their only role is to make domination more respectable, never to make it comprehensible. They are the privilege of front-row spectators who are stupid enough to believe they can understand something, not by making use of what is hidden from them, but by believing what is revealed!

ADAM WEISHAUPT, 1778
We have to struggle with pedantry, with intolerance, with divines and statesmen, and above all, princes and priests are in our way. Men are unfit as they are, and must be formed, each class must be the school of trial for the next [...] Every person shall be made a spy on another and on all around him. Nothing can escape our sight; by these means we shall readily discover who is contented, and who will receive with relish the peculiar state-doctrines and religious opinions that are laid before them; and, at last, the truly worthy alone will be admitted to a participation in the whole maxims and political constitution of the Order.

NESTA WEBSTER, 1921
Amongst the whole correspondence which passed between Weishaupt and his

adepts laid bare by the Government of Bavaria, we find no word of sympathy with the poor or suffering, no hint of social reform, nothing but a desire either for domination, for world power, or sheer love of destruction, and throughout all the insatiable spirit of intrigue. For this purpose every method was held to be justifiable, since the fundamental doctrine of the sect was that "the end sanctifies the means."

ADAM WEISHAUPT, 1781
If in order to destroy all Christianity, all religion, we have pretended to have the sole true religion, remember that the end justifies the means, and that the wise ought to take all the means to do good which the wicked take to do evil.

KENNETH MACKENZIE, 1877
Had the Order [of the Illuminati] been allowed free scope, much good would have resulted, as the members were, as a rule, men of the strictest morality and humanity, and the ideas they sought to instill were those which would have found universal acceptance in our own times.

GUY DEBORD, 1988
The ubiquitous growth of secret societies and networks of influence answers the imperative demand of the new conditions for profitable management of economic affairs, at a time when the state holds a hegemonic role in the direction of production and when demand for all commodities depends strictly on the centralization achieved by spectacular information/promotion, to which forms of distribution must also adapt. It is therefore only a natural product of the centralization of capital, production and distribution. Whatever does not grow must disappear; and no business can grow without adopting the values, techniques and methods of today's industry, spectacle and state. In the final analysis it is the particular form of development chosen by the economy of our epoch which dictates the widespread creation of new personal bonds of dependency and protection.

HENRI LEFEBVRE, 1947
To understand this properly, we need to think about what is happening around us, within us, each and every day. We live on familiar terms with the people in our own family, our own milieu, our own class. This constant impression of familiarity makes us think that we know them, that their outlines are defined for us, and that they see themselves as having those same outlines [...] But the familiar is not necessarily the known [...] Familiarity, what is familiar, conceals human beings and makes them difficult to know by giving them a mask we can recognize, a mask that is merely the lack of something. And yet familiarity . . . is by no means an illusion. It is real, and is part of reality. Masks cling to our faces, to our skin; flesh and blood have become masks.

Miscellaneous

RAOUL VANEIGEM, 1962
There is a place where you create yourself and a time in which you play yourself. The space of everyday life, that of one's true realization, is encircled by every form of conditioning. The narrow space of our true realization defines us, yet we define ourselves in the time of the spectacle. Or, put another way: our consciousness is no longer consciousness of myth and of particular-being-in-myth, but rather consciousness of the spectacle and of particular-role-in-the-spectacle.

HENRI LEFEBVRE, 1947
If there were no roles to play, and thus no familiarity, how could the cultural element or ethical element which should modify and humanize our emotions and our passions be introduced into life? The one involves the other. A role is not a role. It is social life, an inherent part of it. What is faked in one sense is what is the essential, the most precious, the human, in another.

GUY DEBORD, 1988
The highest ambition of the integrated spectacle is still to turn secret agents into revolutionaries, and revolutionaries into secret agents.

NEAL WILGUS, 1978
One of the most ironic and revealing things about Carr's version of Illuminoid history is that if you take such thinking far enough to the right you'll find far leftwingers coming to meet you on common ground: it's a conspiracy! And indeed it *is* a conspiracy, an unending secret war between rich and poor, haves and have-nots, ins and outs.

LT. COL. GORDON MOHR, 1990
Today, the natural organization of labor, which has been founded on mutual need between capital and labor and which has been traditional in all periods of recorded history, has been upset. Now the worker is proclaimed to be equal in all respects with his employer, while he is exempted from the duties and responsibilities of the employer. The result has been a senseless "class struggle" which has all but destroyed American industry and which was designed to do just that.

NEAL WILGUS, 1978
Dan Smoot, Gary Allen and Phoebe Courtney may seem ludicrous in their attack on the Council of Foreign Relations as the brains of the conspiracy, yet what they're saying is essentially the same as scholarly leftwingers such as C. Wright Mills and other trackers of [...] the Military-Industrial Complex.

GARY ALLEN, 1971
The Nixon "Game Plan" is infinitely more clever and dangerous than those of his

predecessors because it masquerades as being the opposite of what it is.

NEAL WILGUS, 1978
The argument is not whether there's a conspiracy –

GARY ALLEN, 1978
The ultimate advantage the creditor has over the king or president is that, if the ruler gets out of line, the banker can finance his enemy or rival. Therefore […] it is wise to have an enemy or rival waiting in the wings [...]. If the King doesn't have an enemy, you must create one [...]. The key to control over governments has always been [the international bankers'] control of money.

NEAL WILGUS, 1978
– but what to do about it.

GIORGIO DE CHIRICO, 1929
And then revolts break out as storms break out in the burning summer sky. Resolute and savage men, led by the kind of bearded colossus like an ancient god, wrested beams from the workshops and hurled them like catapults against the armour-plated palace doors. The most cautious had made their get-away; others than fallen under the first blows and these were precisely the people who had never wanted to believe in the revolt, maintaining that these rumors had no foundation and were started by greedy bankers who aimed to cause a fall in prices and then speculate afterwards on the rise which would follow the denial of the alarming rumors. These were the same people who always ended their optimistic speeches by phrases such as: Our people have too much good sense.

NOT BORED! #21, July 1992
Performed "live" (by lip-syncing along to a tape recording of these quotations read aloud) in Berkeley, CA, May 1992; Providence, RI, May 1992; and Cincinnati, OH, November 2008

United Auto Workers on Strike

Though the United Auto Workers union is emphasizing certain aspects of the strike – nationalism and xenophobia can be exploited to get the rank-and-file agitated enough to strike and to march under Amerikkkan flags – they do not tell the whole, or the real story, from what I can tell.

The real story is how the strike originated: with the stampers, whose jobs are not being exported to places like Mexico. (Stampers make the car bodies; stamping facilities must be near the assembly plants, which remain in the States; it is the small parts that are increasingly manufactured outside the USA and shipped to the assembly plants because labor exploitation in places like Mexico is still allowed to be completely brutal.)

The stampers' story is this: stamping is an incredibly debilitating job. The noise is deafening; the vibrations are intense; the possibility of injury or death is always there; retirement has to come early. Back when General Motors was in its heyday, the stampers had been required to produce a daily quota: so many stamps per eight-hour-work day. Because eight-hours days were literally killing the workers, they unofficially banded together and agreed to double their output, get the quota done in half the time, and then leave early, go home, a bar or a library. (This is incipient socialism, folks: workers organizing unofficially amongst themselves to get the job done better, more efficiently, and more safely than under capitalist conditions. Cf. Cornelius Castoriadis, *Collected Social and Political Writings*). Eventually, this new unofficial organization of production became a union demand, and was "officially permitted" after-the-fact by management, who had no choice. No manager or scab is ever going to step in during a strike and run the stampers themselves.

Management – after nearly running General Motors into the ground in the 1970s and 1980s – is now demanding that the workers pay for these mistakes and for the CEO's multi-million dollar salaries. (All this talk about keeping GM competitive in the global economy is pure horseshit. GM management and the UAW are simply trying to keep capitalist production itself "competitive" on a planet that is ready to dispense with the whole stinking system.)

In particular, the "lazy" stampers – imagine, only working four hours a day! what an outrage! – have been asked to work "a full day" for their money; they have been asked to work eight hours a day at double speed – not the old speed – thereby doubling the workers' "productivity" (profitability of their exploitation), without having to pay them anymore money, or only slightly more. The stampers said "FUCK NO" and walked off. The other strikers – who have their own "local grievances" – walked out in sympathy. Today, 90 percent of GM plants are down.

22 June 1998
NOT BORED! #29, July 1998

The Violence in Seattle

OK: we've heard what *you*, the professionals (the professional newspaper writers, television commentators, politicians and leftist activists) think about the violence in Seattle this past week.

Apparently a diverse group – indeed, the leftist activists among your ranks would have it believed that they are not part of and are actually opposed to the politics of the mainstream writers, commentators and politicians – you have nevertheless reached consensus, which you are now repeating on every occasion and on all channels, as if there could be no disagreement: the violence in Seattle was perpetrated by protesters; the violence was regrettable, counter-productive, stupid and ineffective; the violence was caused by a small "isolated" group of protesters, upon whom you have poured insults, calumnies and contempt; the protesters who self-righteously denounced and tried to detain "the violent anarchists" were courageous and brave, even heroes; and the police should have reserved their armored personnel carriers, three-foot-long solid-oak clubs, pepper spray, tear gas, and rubber bullets for the violent protesters, and let the non-violent protesters alone.

OK: we've heard what you've said; *now shut the fuck up, if only for a second, and let other voices be heard.*

We, like the rioters in Seattle, are sick and tired of your monopolization of communication when it comes to the pressing issues of the day. Despite what you tell us, we know that you do not speak for us and your opinions do not represent what we think. This is especially true for the professional leftist activists who actually defended Starbucks and Niketown against attack, and now feel no shame in proudly reporting this ignominious fact to whomever will listen. These activists, some of whom have in the past actually pretended to protest against Starbucks and Nike, have nevertheless, at the most basic level, always defended them. But now these phony revolutionaries have visibly become what they essentially always were. The hypocrisy of the professional newspaper writers, television commentators, and politicians – as well as their eager collaboration with the police and special services – are well known; we intend to make the hypocrisy and collaboration of the anti-violence leftists *infamous*.

But, first and foremost, we must declare our unconditional support for the anarchists, who live in or came to Seattle armed with a well-thought out form of protest that is different from and intended as an explicit alternative to those forms of protest practiced by the conventional leftist groups (rallies, marches, demonstrations, sit-ins, die-ins, street theater and "festival"). The anarchists – an organic community able to take organized, collective and militant action against their real enemies – formed themselves into black blocs (so named for the black clothes and masks the anarchists wore) and systematically attacked unoccupied corporate chain stores such as McDonalds, the Gap, Nike, Nordstrom, Levi, and Disney, as well as the notoriously corrupt Bank of America. That is to say, the anarchists – unsatisfied with protesting indirectly against an abstraction – directly attacked the physical manifestations in real space of the global economy to which the World Trade Organization is committed to furthering, not people or "mom and pop" stores.

Adherents to non-violent protest methods have always preached in the most self-righteous of tones against the strategy of targeting corporate property. We feel that their alleged "morality" is actually an uncritical acceptance of the essence of corporate ideology, which elevates fictional corporate entities to the status of human beings, violently imposes an identity between these two categories of "persons," and thus demands "equal protection" under the law for both. Because corporations only serve the interests of certain individuals, the inevitable result of this "equal protection for all" is actually double-protection for corporate "persons" and no protection for real ones. The destruction of corporate property is the positive affirmation of autonomous human society and its right to be in control of its institutions, rather than be controlled by them.

But, this time, in Seattle, the allegedly moral non-violent protesters did more than preach to the unconverted: they actually acted like cops until the real cops came and took over. Using their numerical advantage, the non-violent protesters surrounded, denounced, un-masked, beat up and actually turned over to the police the practitioners of violent protest. In doing so, the "moral majority" among the anti-WTO protesters not only helped the police and the National Guard do their dirty work, but they also assisted in the larger and more long-term effort to criminalize radical political philosophies that is taking place all over this country and through-out the rest of the world. Ironically, the "moral majority" was compensated for its counter-revolutionary efforts with indiscriminate and unprovoked beatings, gassings, shootings and arrests.

It is both appalling and quite telling that none of the professionals who have denounced the controlled violence of the anarchists – neither the mainstream commentators and politicians nor the leftist activists – have denounced the unrestrained violence against people (not property) committed in Seattle by the police forces and the National Guard. According to several eyewitness reports, the police tear-gassed "shoppers and people getting dinner, as well as protesters," and that they did so both in downtown Seattle and in the neighborhoods outside the city limits "where the regular people live." In the words of eye-witness Jim Desyllas, a reporter from Portland, Oregon,

> If you were alive, the police gassed you. People got gassed for coming out of restaurants and bars and coffee shops. People coming back from work, kids, women, everyone. People would go out of their houses to see what was happening because these tear gas guns sound like a cannon – and they would get gassed. A block away there was a Texaco gas station – [the riot police] threw tear gas at gas pumps, believe it or not – they were like vandals. They gassed a bus. I saw it with my own eyes. A bus. The driver, the riders, the people just abandoned it.

According to Desyllas, "this was not, as Pres. Clinton claims, a peaceful protest marred by the actions of violent protesters. This was a massive, strong but peaceful demonstration which was attacked repeatedly by the police with the express purpose of provoking a violent response to provide photo opportunities for the

Miscellaneous

Western media" and thus "discredit the movement against the WTO because they couldn't dilute it." Desyllas believes that, "This whole thing, this police attack, this was US foreign policy, not some action decided by some bureaucrat in Seattle. This was the State Department." Eye-witness Damon Krane agrees: "By repeatedly attacking and torturing non-violent protesters, the Seattle police sought to incite a riot and finally succeeded to a small degree."

Thus, the anarchists did not precipitate the vicious crackdown, as all the professionals are alleging; rather, the anarchists knew it was coming and acted accordingly. That is to say, they refused in advance to let the outcome of the inevitable struggle for the streets of Seattle be yet another one-sided victory for the forces of order. Though you wouldn't know it from the reports of the professionals, the crack-down had the effect of radicalizing a great many people, that is, bringing people around the anarchist position, not putting them off from it. Jim Desyllas reports that, "because they were gassing everybody, the local people got mad too and they joined the 100 who had been herded out of the city. So soon there were 500 including the neighborhood people, and all very angry. Then people set up barricades."

For as long as they lasted, those barricades kept out both vicious police squads and "morally superior" leftists. For as long as we last, let us not forget the clear division that the barricades made between those who are truly opposed to this society and those who are not.

Wall poster 2-5 December 1999
NOT BORED! #32, January 2000

Rebuilding the World Trade Center: A New Garden of Eden

"The radical act of the terrorists opens a space for us to think radically as well," Michael Sorkin, director of the Graduate Program in Urban Design at City College, writing in a special issue of the Sunday magazine section of *The New York Times* that was published on 11 November 2001.

Though this may be hard for some to believe, especially in these sentimental times, the so-called Twin Towers at the World Trade Center were *hated* by many New Yorkers, who before September 11, 2001 would have been happy if the goddamned things had never been built and after September 11th are glad that they're gone. An entire neighborhood was emptied out and destroyed to make way for them. *Them* – not just one spectacular tower, but two. And this in a city that is known for singularities and differences, not repetitions and resemblances! Those weirdly self-referential monoliths completely blocked the sunlight from getting through; they blocked the view of the sun setting over New Jersey. Their reflective, steel-belted surfaces played havoc with radio and TV broadcasts, which meant that broadcasters were forced to move their transmitters (they had little choice but to put the transmitters atop one of the towers). Unlike the modestly tall buildings at Rockefeller Center, which are surrounded by an "extroverted" or open space through which pedestrian traffic can move freely, the freakishly tall Twin Towers were surrounded by a blank, abstract space that was "introverted" and closed off. Fully *twice* the size of the buildings around them, the towers were in fact so excessively large that the only place one could escape them and see New York City's famous skyline without distraction was on top of one of them!

Built for an enormous amount of money between 1966 and 1970 by the Port Authority of the State of New York, the Twin Towers were intended to house in one complex a great many foreign financial institutions and to provide everything that their managers, employees and clients might need (hotels, restaurants, shops, movie theaters, etc. etc). Despite the novelty of being the tallest buildings in the world – a distinction that only lasted until 1976, when the Sears Tower was built in Chicago – the Twin Towers were always money-losers as rental properties and required huge subsidies (tens of millions of dollars a year) from the State of New York to remain solvent. Because all of the windows in both towers were sealed up tight, and because neither tower was equipped to take advantage of its unique potential to generate power using the wind or solar energy, the WTC complex was ludicrously costly to heat and light. Furthermore, visiting businessmen and businesswomen *weren't* satisfied to remain within the WTC's purportedly self-sufficient universe, and wished to venture (and shop and do business) outside of it. In the 1980s, advances in information and telecommunication technologies decentralized the financial markets, which in turn "rolled back" the necessity for foreign institutions to be in close physical proximity to each other, Wall Street and the rest of lower Manhattan, which is precisely what the gigantic size and centralized location of the Twin Towers were intended to provide.

In New York City, obsolete buildings are infrequently saved, whatever their historical or architectural interest. Most often, they are simply torn down and replaced. The *only* thing that saved the Twin Towers from demolition was the fact that they were filled with asbestos, which would be released into the air if the buildings were destroyed by controlled explosions. In 2000, the Port Authority calculated that it would cost $1 billion – i.e., much more money than the Port Authority could afford to spend – to remove the asbestos before the buildings were destroyed. And so the Port Authority was stuck with the Twin Towers, that is, until 26 April 2001, when it found a consortium of business interests (Westfield America, led by Larry Silverstein, the owner of the building at 7 World Trade Center) that was willing to lease the property. Supposed to last for 99 years, the $3.2 billion lease mandated that the Port Authority continue to pay taxes on the property. "This is a dream come true," Silverstein said at the 23 July 2001 celebration of the lease's signing. "We will be in control of a prized asset, and we will seek to develop its potential, raising it to new heights."

And so, quite paradoxically, the mass-murdering hijackers who destroyed the Twin Towers by flying fully-fueled passenger airplanes into them did Westfield America an immense favor. Even though Westfield America would obviously have preferred that both the planes and the buildings were unoccupied (save for the hijackers themselves) at the time that the former were used to destroy the latter, the terrorists got rid of the towers quickly, efficiently – the towers fell *down* instead of *over* – and in such a way that Westfield America didn't have to pay for any of it, including the asbestos, which was "removed" from the site by the wind, the rain and the lungs of the search-and-rescue teams employed by the City of New York in the months after the buildings exploded, collapsed and gave off thick clouds of toxic dust.

There has been a lot of speculation about the facts that both towers collapsed and were utterly destroyed by the airplanes. If there *is* any "conspiracy" here, it certainly includes then-NYC-Mayor Rudolph Giuliani's orders to speedily removal and bury in a landfill of all of the structural steel members found at the site. (The normal practice at such sites is to *preserve* these members, because they may contain important and otherwise impossible to find clues as to the cause of the building's collapse and the methods by which such collapses might be prevented in future.) Giuliani's motivation for this highly unusual and very suspicious action was simply to prevent fire investigators from proving that the collapse of 7 World Trade Center – which *wasn't* struck by one of the planes – was in fact caused by the explosion of the fuel tank that Giuliani ordered installed in the building so that his prized "Emergency Command Center" on the 23rd floor could function, even in the event of a "disaster" that might cause the building's electricity to be cut off. According to a report published in *The New York Times* on 20 December 2001,

> Fire Department officials warned the city and the Port Authority of New York and New Jersey in 1998 and 1999 that a giant diesel fuel tank for the mayor's $13 million command bunker in 7 World Trade Center, a 47-story high-rise that burned and collapsed on Sept. 11, posed a hazard and was not consistent with city fire codes [...] Although the city made some design changes to address the concerns – moving a fuel pipe that would have run from the tank up an elevator shaft, for example – it left the tank in place. But the Fire Department repeatedly warned that a tank in that position could spread fumes throughout the building if it leaked, or, if it caught fire, could produce what one Fire Department memorandum called "disaster."

And so, not only did Giuliani deliberately violate the city's fire codes, but he also destroyed evidence of his crime. "Person of the Year"? No way! "Criminal of the

Year"? Quite possibly.

* * *

The site of the disaster is the size of 16 football fields. What should be done with it, once it has been "cleaned up" (if clean-up is indeed possible)? In the words of Museum of Modern Art curator Terence Riley, quoted in the magazine section of the 11 November 2001 issue of *The New York Times,*

> The analogy of the Chicago fire is important. What happened there is that a lot of wood structures burned down. And in their place, of course, wood structures were not put up. The city became a sort of testing ground, the laboratory for the development of the [steel-framed] American skyscraper. So let's imagine that New York can become a laboratory right now – a laboratory of what?

Some have called for the site to become a laboratory for the testing of New York City's ability to recover from the attack and/or refusal to be intimidated by it: they want to re-build the Twin Towers or at least another World Trade Center worthy of the name. Others have proposed making the site a laboratory for the testing of New York City's ability to mourn and honor the people who were killed: and so they want to build some kind of a memorial. Some think a monument should be at the center of this memorial; others think that there should be no monument at all, just open, green space, perhaps a park of some kind.[1]

Re-build the Tower(s) of Babel? No, that would be callous and hubristic. Consecrate a memorial? No, it would inevitably turn the mourners who visited it into spectators. In any event, we already spend too much time contemplating the past and the loss of our innocence.

The New York Psychogeographical Association sees only one viable option: turn the site into a huge community garden that would be open to the public twenty-four hours a day and year-round. All kinds of flowers, fruits and vegetables would be cultivated. The fresh produce could be divided among the gardeners, sold to pay for expenses and/or donated to soup kitchens. Unlike memorials or parks, which do not change after their creation, gardens are living, growing things. A garden at the old WTC would provide a unique opportunity for mourners, tourists and city residents – some of whom who might never have cultivated a garden – to roll up their sleeves and get to work, pulling up weeds, planting seeds, doing anything that might need to be done. There would be no contemplation, nor separation from the land: just collective action towards a common goal. Not only would such a garden be good for the bodies and spirits of the people who visit and/or work it, but it would also be good for the ecology of Manhattan. The birds

---

[1] Today, almost 10 years later, nothing has been built.

would return and sing once again.

There's only one person for the job of Head Gardener, and that's Adam Purple, the creator and principal cultivator of The Garden of Eden. Located in Manhattan's Lower East Side, Eden was begun on abandoned city-owned lots in 1973 and continued to grow and expand (in concentric circles) as the neighborhood deteriorated further. In 1986, the garden was seized and bulldozed. With typical cynicism, the City built a retirement home in its place.

Unlike every other community garden ever cultivated in New York City, Eden was circular in shape. At its center was a large doubled or "squared" Yin-and-Yang symbol. According to Adam, the City of New York *had* to destroy Eden eventually, and not because it allegedly needed the land on which the garden was growing (it didn't), but because the concentric energy emanating from its vortex was disturbing Manhattan's entire rectilinear grid system. Though it may sound as if he's reaching for an explanation, surely Adam's got a point. The grid system is so pervasive and so engrained in the minds and habits of New Yorkers that it is rarely questioned, indeed, rarely even thought about, except during the most extraordinary circumstances. And so, even though there were a lot of other factors involved in the decision to seize and destroy Eden, its distinctive shape somehow implicated or unsettled the grid system, which evidently could allow no challenge to its rigid organization of the city's space.

Today, 15 years after Eden's destruction, the pendulum has swung to the other side. It is the grid system – or, rather, its ultimate expression (the sky-high stack of boxes known as the World Trade Center) – that has been attacked and damaged. Rather than trying to save it, we should deliver a knock-out blow and get rid of the grid system permanently. And there could be no better way – no way that could be more poetically just – than by replacing the destroyed Twin Towers with a new Garden of Eden.

Published on-line 30 November 2001
Revised 6 January 2002
NOT BORED! #34, July 2002

The Relevance of Antonio Negri to the Anti-Globalization Movement

A few days before the G8 Summit took place in Genoa, Italy, a clever editor at *The New York Times* thought that the protests against the summit would provide a great opportunity to run a feature story about Michael Hardt and Antonio (Toni) Negri. A kind of "odd couple" – Hardt is young and American, and Negri is older, Italian and currently in jail for offenses supposedly committed in the 1970s – the two professors are the authors of *Empire,* a recently published book about globalization. The writer for the *Times* latched on to the following quote from the book, which no doubt seemed perfectly suited for the occasion.

> We see seeds of that future already in the sea of faces that stretches from the streets of Seattle to those of Genoa. One of the most remarkable characteristics of these movements is their diversity: trade unionists together with ecologists together with priests and communists. We are beginning to see emerge a multitude that is not defined by any single identity, but can discover commonality in its multiplicity.

Seattle and Genoa, America and Italy, Hardt and Negri. *Bellisimo!*

Let's review what everyone knows or claims to know about Toni Negri (forget about Michael Hardt, sorry). A writer, professor at the University of Padua and Marxist political activist, Negri was arrested on 7 April 1979 and, like over 5,000 other people involved in the Autonomist Workers movement, was accused of "armed insurrection against the powers of the State." To support this absurd and overly broad accusation, Negri's accusers portrayed him as the secret leader of the Red Brigades, the terrorist group that reputedly kidnapped and assassinated Aldo Moro, President of the Christian Democratic Party. After a four-year-long battle, which he waged from a jail cell, Negri was acquitted of all charges and released. When the Italian Chamber of Deputies subsequently voted to send him back to prison, he fled to France, where he lived, taught and prospered as a writer, theorist and author. *In absentia,* Negri was convicted of re-instated charges under still in-effect emergency laws that allow convictions solely based upon the testimony of accused persons who have "repented" their crimes and turned State's evidence. In 1997, in the hope that his action would bring an end to the decades-old deadlock – more than 150 activists were still serving sentences in Italian prisons and another 180 activists were still living in self-imposed exile – Negri returned to Italy and turned himself in. Granted no leniency whatsoever, he was sentenced to more than 13 years in prison, a sentence he began serving on 1 July 1997.

What's missing from the usual biographies of Toni Negri is the charge that it took him far too long to come to the now commonly accepted conclusions that 1) the terrorist campaign inaugurated by the bombing of the Piazza Fontana in Milano on 12 December 1969 wasn't the work of either the far-left (the anarchists) or the far-right (the fascists), but the Italian secret services; and 2) this campaign – now called "the strategy of tension" – wasn't undertaken to destabilize or topple the government, but to provide a pretext for its most reactionary elements to strengthen themselves against an increasingly strong and effective working class movement. The situationists came to these conclusions as early as 19 December 1969, when the Italian section of the Situationist International published the extraordinary tract "Is the Reichstag Burning?" In the following years, as State-sponsored terrorism against targets in Italy became more common and more obvious, Sanguinetti returned to the subject a couple of times: first in *The True Report on the Last Chance to Save Capitalism in Italy* (published in July 1975 and reprinted many times afterwards), and then again in *On Terrorism and the State*, which was published in Italy in 1979 and in France in 1980. Relentlessly persecuted by the Italian government for his writings, Sanguinetti was vindicated in 1982, when the so-called P2 scandal brought to light documents that irrefutably proved that the Italian government had indeed been employing "the strategy of tension" since the end of the 1960s and through-out the 1970s.

But Sanguinetti was a lone voice and easily marginalized. Everyone else – Toni Negri included – preferred to believe what the State and the media told them about "terrorism": that the bombings and assassinations were perpetrated by left-wing extremist groups, and that the Italian State, though it might occasionally infiltrate and provoke such groups, wasn't directly involved in or responsible for their targets and operations. Most importantly, Negri and the rest preferred to believe that, if an ultra-Leftist group such as the Red Brigades was indeed engaging in acts of terrorism, it was committing a grave "tactical error" or making a terrible mistake, despite its good intentions and revolutionary militancy. Even the Aldo Moro affair (1978) didn't lead Negri to question his basic assumptions about the Red Brigades: i.e., that the group really existed, and that it was simply misguided in its use of violence.

Negri's refusal to entertain the theses enunciated by Sanguinetti came back to haunt him. "Right then!" the Italian government said in the aftermath of the Aldo Moro affair; "if *you* are in a position to evaluate the 'errors' and 'mistakes' of the Red Brigades, whose existence you recognize, then *you* must be their mastermind, the brains behind their operations." Ridiculous, but good enough for the original 7 April 1979 arrest.

In the preface to the French edition of *On Terrorism and the State,* Sanguinetti marveled at the fact that, even after his arrest, Negri continued to believe that the Red Brigades actually existed, and wasn't really a clandestine group of State-sponsored terrorists.

> For instance, not one of these great reasoners on the question of terrorism has formulated this most simple and reasonable of questions: If the ghostly Red Brigades [RBs] were, as is said, a spontaneous grouping of subversives, and if Negri and Piperno were, as is made out, the heads of the RBs, then why should these artful RBs allow their leaders – who, however, declare that they are not leaders of the RBs – to be imprisoned without ever seeking their exoneration, even if such an effort was only in order to reclaim them for the revolution? If, on the other hand, Negri and Piperno are not the heads of the RBs, and are not even among the ranks of its militants, then these facts should give all the more reason for the hypothetical

subversives of the RBs to help get these men publicly cleared of all charges against them. And this for three good reasons: so as not to let leaders be wrongly attributed to them without protest; so as not to be accused of letting innocent people be condemned in their place; and finally, because the RBs are protected by anonymity and therefore have no fear of clearing those currently accused. Since, on the contrary, none of this has happened, it must be concluded that the real heads of the RBs have the same desire as our State to make it widely believed that Negri and Piperno are in fact the RBs' leaders. This new convergence of interests between the State and the RBs has nothing fortuitous or extraordinary about it, and can only bemuse the stupid, who do not perceive that the RBs *are the State,* that is to say, one of its multiple armed appendages.

Neither we, nor Sanguinetti, propose that Toni Negri was an agent of the Italian State. Instead, we ascribe his incredible difficulty in recognizing the truth about the Red Brigades to stubbornness and stupidity. And he remains a stubborn and stupid man to this day. Note well his vision of "trade unionists together with ecologists together with priests and communists." *Communists?!* Yes, Negri continues to describe himself as a communist, even though communism has been thoroughly discredited, especially in Italy. But the plain fact of the matter is that the mass demonstrations against globalization (such as those at Seattle and Genoa) were effective precisely because they had *nothing whatsoever* to do with the usual communist horseshit: political parties, splinter groups, "scientific" theories, charismatic leaders and cults of personality, etc. etc. If people like Toni Negri and organizations such as the World Workers Party are full of praise for the "young people," it is because these cynical hacks are absolutely desperate to keep up and not be left behind. Quite obviously, we should not look to a Communist or a book written by one for genuine insight into today's anti-globalization movement.

But there's more to it than that. There is the danger that, today, we – the various groups and individuals involved in the burgeoning anti-globalization movement – might make mistakes very similar to those Toni Negri made back in the 1970s. In particular, we have to be very careful not to dismiss the claims of those who report that, during the protests against the G8 Summit in Genoa, certain – several, but not all – "Black Bloc" groupings were not made up of anarchists, but either Italian police officers or fascist gangs that the Italian police had recruited for the occasion. (It has also been claimed that the Italian police force itself was filled out by recruits from fascist gangs.) These phony Black Bloc groupings were seen getting out of police vehicles before conducting violent rampages in which they attacked peaceful demonstrators as well as private property, and were seen returning to these same vehicles when they were done. It's been reported that the members of these phony Black Blocs were overheard speaking German, not Italian, and that they conducted their rampages with impressive efficiency and coordination. Not surprisingly, the Italian police used the "rogue" actions of the phony Black Blocs as justification for bringing in reinforcements and beating up and arresting everyone in sight – everyone, that is, except for the members of the phony Black Blocs.

It is alarming that, in response to these reports, some anarchists and Black Bloc members have become defensive and indignant. On the pages of the IMC network and in a variety of anarchist list-servs, they have ridiculed the truthfulness of these reports and have contemptuously dismissed their authors as "obvious" police spies and propagandists who are simply trying to create divisions within the larger anti-globalization movement. As a counter-argument, these anarchists have simply taken to repeating the obvious truth that "real" Black Blocs would *never* do the things described in the reports. But the issue here *isn't* what real Black Blocs do or don't do, nor is it what real Black Blocs do when they have been infiltrated or provoked by the police. The issue doesn't concern real Black Blocs at all! It concerns instead the reappearance of State-sponsored terrorism in Italy: e.g., the replacement of the Red Brigades with "the Black Bloc" (not the various haphazard Black Bloc groupings, mind you, but *The* Black Bloc, as if it were a single, very organized transnational organization of professional agitators).

Genoa certainly wasn't the first time that the police dressed themselves up in black, went to a mass demonstration against globalization, pretended to be anarchists spoiling for a fight, and provoked a violent "crack-down" on peaceful demonstrators. A similar incident occurred in Barcelona just a few months ago. Because Black Bloc groupings are relatively easy to fake – all the police or the fascists need are black clothes, things to disguise their faces and a few props – we can expect that such incidents will become more and more frequent. Already there is talk on the IMC network about the need for "the Black Bloc" to re-evaluate its tactics in light of the shooting death of Carlo Giuliani. Here people come very close to making the same mistake that Toni Negri made in the 1970s: our attention should be on the State and its secret services; if we presume to evaluate the mistakes or errors of "the Black Bloc," we might (more) easily be framed as its masterminds.

Posted to the New York Independent Media Center on 31 July 2001
NOT BORED! #33, September 2001

Comments on "The Relevance of Antonio Negri to the Anti-Globalization Movement"

As the Belgium government held the final EU meeting of their six-month Presidency, cops were out on the streets of having a good old ruck with protesters at the summit of Laeken. Undercover cops, dressed in black, were seen directing protesters to smash up the Palace and attack shops, only this time the international black bloc were having none of it. Instead of following their instructions protesters surrounded the 15 cops and herded them into a corner and held them there until riot cops had to rescue their mates. – *SchNEWS*, Issue 336, Winter Solstice 2001, paraphrasing Indymedia's coverage of protests on 14 December 2001.

Even months after de anarho-demo in Brussels I cannot stop thinking about what happened. Trying to not be influenced by other opinions I can write only what I saw with my eyes. The march of the anarchists was really great (around 5000 people) there was no any sign of violence or something like that. In a moment the cops blocked a square in the centrum of the city and all the people were caught in a mousetrap. Then the organisators desided to turn bach to Midi Station. Then I noticed a group of 10-15 guys in black and masks comming from a strange direction where the cordon of the cops was placed. A few minutes later they attacked with stones a single cop from the trafic police. The strange was that they gave him a time to escape !?! A bit later when cops reinforcements arrived the same guys in blach started to trow stones and 2 or 3 fire bombs. I never have trew Molotov coctail but for me it is logical that if somebody wants to do it he is going to trow it against the target (the police car) directly. That was obviously NOT in that case. The fire bomb was trowen up _vertical and it fell maybe 5 meter before the police car while the distance between th! e guy who trew it and the car was not more than 20-25 m. Strange, a? Later the same guys in black attacked some marrocians and even chased them further - the reason was obviously not friendly... So, the conclugion I can take is that [...] there were people specialy trained for that kind of action and they did there job pretty well doing a provocation without hurting any cop. – Posted to a-infos-en@ainfos.ca on 19 February 2002.

We here at *NOT BORED!* received a large number of responses to our essay "The Relevance of Antonio Negri to the Anti-Globalization Movement," in part because it was re-printed by a popular anarchist website as well as posted to a couple of sites associated with the Independent Media Center, for which the essay was originally written. Most of these responses were highly critical. The essay was taken to task for basing all of its positions on a handful of old and obscure situationist pamphlets, for discouraging people from reading Negri & Hardt's book *Empire*, and for conflating Negri's "communism" with the "Communism" of the Italian Communist Party, among other things.

Miscellaneous

All of these criticisms have merit; but it is also true that none of them address the main point of our essay, which doesn't concern Antonio Negri so much as his relevance to certain events that allegedly took place at the huge protests outside the 20-23 July 2001 summit of the leaders of the so-called G8 (Great Eight) Nations in Genoa, Italy – in particular, the widely reported incidences in which anarchist "Black Bloc" formations were either infiltrated or completely faked by police provocateurs. We argued that, in the same way Toni Negri personally suffered because in the 1970s he was slow (for a long time he refused) to recognize the possibility that the "revolutionaries" in the Red Brigades group had been infiltrated or even replaced by government spies and provocateurs, those of us who are active in the anti-globalization movement might also suffer if *we* are slow to believe the reports of fake Black Blocs in Genoa. If we refuse to believe these reports – and too many anarchists have indeed refused to believe them – we, like Negri, might be positioned by unscrupulous police officers or district attorneys as the Black Bloc's theoreticians or leaders, precisely because we've spent our time criticizing the "mistakes" of "well-intentioned" people like ourselves, instead of denouncing the incredible lengths to which the State will go to justify and protect itself. When you've been arrested and imprisoned on false charges – as Negri was in 1979 and then again in 1997 – it hardly matters if you are a "communist" or a "Communist." In either case, you're still in jail, as Negri still is.

As we noted one month after our essay on Negri's relevance was written, there are other recent instances in which a government or one of its "secret services" has perpetrated a despicable act of violence, blamed it on people who have already been vilified, and then used it to justify and provide the pretext for a pre-planned attack against them. As we noted on 3 September 2001, the former Chief of the Genoan Police Department, who resigned in the aftermath of the G8 protests, admitted that approximately 600 neo-nazis from both Germany and Italy were in fact allowed to enter the city and "participate" in the protests, even though the Italian government knew full well that both the presence and the behavior of these people would be disruptive. But *disrupting the protests* – either by allowing the protesters to be attacked by brutal goons or by blaming the protesters for violence perpetrated by brutal goons – was precisely what the police and the pro-globalization politicians intended to do. (This ex-Chief of Police appears to have made no reference to the allegations that some or all of these neo-nazis were dressed like and pretended to be "black bloc" anarchists once they entered Genoa.)

Had it not been for the 11 September 2001 attacks on the Pentagon and the World Trade Center, we would have been content to continue to attach similar footnotes to the original essay, if and when they were needed; we wouldn't have undertaken to write a second essay or make supplementary comments such as these. But these attacks or, rather, the nature of the United States government's response to them, necessitates such an undertaking.

In the aftermath of the attacks, during the beginning of America's self-righteous "war on terrorism," there is no longer *an analogy* one *might* draw between the Red Brigades of the 1970s and the Black Bloc(s) of today: there is now *a direct connection.* On 16 December 2001, the Australian news magazine *The Age* reported that,

> US Attorney General John Ashcroft wrapped up a tour of European capitals today with a pledge of closer cooperation between Italy and the United States on intelligence sharing in the fight against terrorism.
>
> Ashcroft held talks with Italy's Interior Minister Claudio Scajola, at which they decided to revive a bilateral commission as a vehicle for the heightened cooperation.
>
> The US official was completing a tour which included meetings with his counterparts in London, Berlin and Madrid on developing cooperation on extraditing terrorist suspects arrested since the September 11 attacks on America [...]
>
> Ashcroft is keen to establish a clear modus operandi with European countries because between them they hold dozens of suspects linked to terrorist suspect Osama bin Laden and his Al-Qaeda network, blamed for the September 11 attacks.
>
> Washington is determined to bring bin Laden and his associates to justice [...]
>
> He [Ashcroft] said Scajola "clearly understands and recognises that terrorism is international and that the threat to liberty and freedom, and order, and government is international."
>
> The US official said Washington could learn from Italy, which "has known of terrorism in ways that the United States has never experienced" - an apparent reference to bombings by left-wing extremist groups like the Red Brigades in the 1970s and 1980s.
>
> Scajola, who is responsible for Italy's anti-terrorist police [and for the actions of the *carabinieri* in Genoa during the G8 Summit], said: "Italy stands side by side, shoulder to shoulder with the US, in the spirit of solidarity with the US people."

Unlike the writer of this story, we're not sure Ashcroft was in fact referring to the Red Brigades when he spoke of terrorist attacks "that the United States has never experienced." As a matter of fact, there *were* groups like the Red Brigades or, rather, there were left-wing extremist groups (the Weather Underground and the Symbionese Liberation Army, among them) that conducted bombing campaigns in the 1970s that were intended to terrorize the American government. Perhaps Ashcroft intended instead to refer to such uniquely Italian manifestations of terrorism as the 1981 assassination of Pope John Paul or the 1993 bombing of the Uffizi Art Gallery (commonly attributed to the Mafia). Both events are truly without parallel in American history. . . . More than likely, Ashcroft was referring to the "terrorism" of the anti-globalization protesters at the G8 Summit in Genoa, which was supposedly so severe that the *carabinieri* had no choice but to kill one of them, a 20-year-old man named Carlos Giuliani. While there have been several large and violent anti-globalization protests in the United States, none of them has resulted in a fatality. And so it's possible that our reporter has Ashcroft referring to the Red Brigades when the Attorney General was actually referring to violent anti-globalization protesters.

The significant thing about this "mistake" is the fact that it may not be a mistake at all: it might be a helpful hint from either the reporter or his/her editor as to what's more likely to rally public opinion against the anti-globalization movement. The public won't believe there's a connection between the anti-globalization movement and Al Qaeda, that is, unless you insert *the fiction of the Red Brigades* between them. You've got to compare Al Qaedea to the Red Brigades (not as they really were, but as they've been portrayed), and then compare the Red Brigades with the anti-globalization movement, before you can make a connection between the anti-globalization movement and Al Qaeda. Otherwise, the lie is too transparent to work.

And so, once again, it is clear to us that the anti-globalization movement must re-familiarize itself with the Red Brigades and, by extension, with the sad case of Antonio Negri. The movement must learn that Negri, whatever the merits of his books, made a crucial and foreseeable mistake about the Red Brigades back in the 1970s, and that contemporary anti-globalization protesters are at risk of making the same sort of mistake today where fake Black Blocs are concerned. To avoid Negri's fate, we must not automatically assume that unusual or suspicious Black Bloc formations and other possible "false flag" operations are in fact carried out by well-intentioned comrades who are weak on revolutionary theory, inexperienced or prone to making mistakes. We must not attack the integrity or credibility of those who bring back reports of Black Blocs that have behaved as if they were made up of police officers or neo-Nazi thugs; and we must commit ourselves to investigating such reports and then, if and when we are satisfied that they are accurate, to publicizing their contents.

Furthermore, the anti-globalization movement must be prepared to say (must have the *facts* to back up the assertions) that, just like the operatives in Osama Bin Laden's Al Qaeda network, the members of the Red Brigades were once on very close terms with the CIA, and that the CIA used both groups as weapons in its "cold war" against global communism.

Written 17 December 2001
NOT BORED! #34, July 2002

On-line notice dated 20 March 2002: today, a group of terrorists calling themselves "The Red Brigades" – supposedly "the same" Red Brigades that was active in Italy in the 1970s, back in action after 20 years' of silence – took credit for the

Miscellaneous

assassination in Bologna of one Marco Biagi, a university professor who, on behalf of Berlusconi's government, was preparing to repeal key measures of Italy's landmark 1970 labor relations law.

On the Flaws in Michel Foucault's *Discipline and Punish*

The flaws in *Discipline and Punish,* which was published in France in 1974, derive from the fact that its author clearly sees Guy Debord's *The Society of the Spectacle,* published in France in 1967, as competition, that is, as a work that must be discredited, rather than commented upon, supplemented or corrected. Given the nature of the French intellectual scene, perhaps this aspect of competition was inevitable. In any event, unlike Guy Debord, who always mentioned by name those he was criticizing or dismissing, Michel Foucault doesn't mention Debord by name in *Discipline and Punish*; instead, he attempts to appropriate and alter the meaning of what Debord called "the spectacle."

For Foucault, the spectacle is identical to "the spectacle of the scaffold" (that is, public execution in the 18th century); and so "the disappearance of public executions marks therefore the decline of the spectacle." The telescoping of "the spectacle of the scaffold" into "the spectacle" takes place again and again in *Discipline and Punish.* To cite just one example: "the modern rituals of execution attest to this double process: the disappearance of the spectacle and the elimination of pain." According to Foucault, modern social relations are "the exact reverse of the spectacle." He insists that "our society is not one of spectacle, but of surveillance," even though both terms foreground the visible and need not be mutually exclusive. For Foucault, "the power of spectacle" declined and disappeared with the replacement of emperors and kings by "disciplines" and "machines." He insists that "We are much less Greeks than we believe. We are neither in the amphitheatre, nor on the stage, but in the panoptic machine, invested by its effects of power, which we bring to ourselves since we are part of its mechanism."

As many of our readers will already know, the panopticon was originally a circular prison designed by Jeremy Bentham in the early 19th century. Its distinctive feature was a centrally located watcher's booth, from which a warden could see into each and every cell. It is significant that Foucault says that, prior to his own work,

> panopticism has received little attention. It is regarded as not much more than a bizarre little utopia, a perverse dream [...] There were many reasons why it received little praise; the most obvious is that the

discourses to which it gave rise rarely acquired, except in the academic classifications, the status of sciences; but the real reason is no doubt that the power that it operates and which it augments is a direct, physical power that men exercise upon one another. An inglorious culmination had an origin that could only be grudgingly acknowledged.

And so, by discovering and popularizing the relevance of panopticism to modern society, Foucault hopes to displace Debord and his presumably over-rated or over-exposed theory of the spectacle.

But, unlike Debord, Foucault isn't really committed to his buzzword. Note well that Foucault doesn't trace Bentham's panopticon to its "inglorious culmination" in George Orwell's famous novel *Nineteen Eighty-Four,* which unaccountably goes completely without mention in *Discipline and Punish.* Nor does Foucault mention the fact that, though they were frequently built in the 1830s, panoptical prisons weren't often built thereafter, despite their alleged utility. Ironically, it is Foucault himself who provides the reasons for the rejection of panoptical prisons. On the one hand, the position of the centralized watcher can easily be abused: "[I]t does not matter what motive animates him: the curiosity of the indiscreet, the malice of a child, the thirst for knowledge of a philosopher who wishes to visit this museum of human nature, or the perversity of those who take pleasure in spying and punishing." On the other hand, the other employees in the panopticon might object to their working conditions, and thus cause "labor problems." Foucault again:

> In this central tower, the director may spy on all the employees that he has under his orders: nurses, doctors, foremen, teachers, wardens; he will be able to judge them continuously, alter their behavior, impose upon them the methods he thinks best; and it will even be possible to observe the director himself. An inspector arriving unexpectedly at the center of the Panopticon will be able to judge at a glance, without anything being concealed from him, how the entire establishment is functioning.

Combine the two – a malicious child or a sadistic scopophiliac watching over and controlling a staff of well-educated professionals – and you have a system that just won't work.

Even if these problems could be solved, both Bentham and Foucault make serious, even fatal mistakes in their calculations concerning the effectiveness of surveillance. According to Foucault, "the major effect of the Panopticon" is "to induce in the inmate a state of conscious and permanent visibility that assures the automatic functioning of power," which can be accomplished by arranging things so that "the surveillance is permanent in its effects, even if it is discontinuous in its action; that the perfection of power should lead to render its actual exercise unnecessary; that this architectural apparatus should be a machine for creating and sustaining a power relation independent of the person who exercises it; in short, that the inmates should be caught up in a power situation of which they are themselves the bearers." Foucault goes on to say,

> In view of this, Bentham laid down the principle that power should be visible and unverifiable. Visible: the inmates will constantly have before his eyes the tall outline of the central tower from which he is spied upon. Unverifiable: the inmate must never know whether he is being looked at at any one moment; but he must be sure that he may always be so.

As I pointed out in an essay on poker for the Surveillance Camera Players,[2] some – enough – of the people who know or suspect that they might be watched constantly *do not* become anxious, *do not* voluntarily curtail or cease their criminal behavior, *do not* get "caught up" in the "power situation." Instead, undeterred, they treat this situation like it was a game, a game of poker: they suspect the other player (the watcher) is bluffing and/or they engage in bluffs of their own. They constantly experiment: Can I get away with it? When did I get away with it? Can I get away with it again? And, if no one is watching, they will try to get away with it all the time. Furthermore, even if they *are* in fact being watched all the time, some will become "players," that is, will perform for the watchers, and thus demonstrate the facts that being watched isn't enough and that, if "Big Brother" truly wants to be a tyrant, he won't be able to do it easily, cheaply or automatically; he will have to exert force; he will have to get his hands dirty, even bloody.

But who really knows how the watcher will play his hand, once he's been confronted? Will he respond like a child, a philosopher or a sadist? No one knows, and this is the ultimate weakness of the panopticon. If it should turn out that the Great Wizard, "the man behind the curtain," is exposed as a fraud or coward, the damage done to the "perfection" of the machine-illusion would be irreparable. No one would ever be afraid of him again.

NOT BORED! #37, May 2005

---

[2] "Deterrence as poker game," *We Know You Are Watching: Surveillance Camera Players* (New York: Factory School, 2006), pp. 229-230.

Miscellaneous
A Critique of Neo-Anarchism

A strategic analysis of the problem

The last 13 years have seen "anarchism" sprout everywhere. So many books are written about it, so many talks and speeches and conferences are given about it – one might think that the State is actually tottering and about to fall! But of course, the State *isn't* tottering (at least not for these reasons) and anarchism, rather than being everywhere, is actually nowhere. What remains is watered-down Maoism and concentrated Leftism. Have doubts? Just look at A.N.S.W.E.R., the International Action Center, and all the other "Communist" front groups, which completely dominate this country's pathetic anti-war movement, as well as many of the pro-immigration and anti-police brutality groups, the release-Mumia groups, et al.

Note well that many neo-anarchists are completely fixated on the anarchists and anarchist movements of the *early* twentieth century – endless and empty recollections of Sacco and Vanzetti, the glory days of the Spanish Civil War, etc – and know *absolutely nothing* about any of the revolutionary events of the mid- and late-Twentieth Century. Note well the complete stupefaction when someone mentions the events that took place in East Berlin (1953), Budapest (1956), Belgium (1962), Paris (1968), Lisbon (1974), Bologna (1977), Gdansk (1980) etc. All the neo-anarchists know about is Spain and Seattle, Seattle and Spain. (Sometimes they also know about Argentina and Venezuela, but their interest is either Zapatista chic or barely disguised admiration for Leninism.)

In the USA, the Left was never fully de-Stalinized (much like the old East Germany); it never really dealt with its roots in and continuing attachment to Social Democracy and "Communism." And so the neo-anarchists of today are actually Leftists who have simply learned that it is "not cool" to be Marxists and so describe themselves as "anti-authoritarians" instead. But the leopard dies with its spots and the neo-anarchists' underlying Leftism shines through in their unshakeable preoccupation with commodities, corporations and globalization, and their marginalization of the State and its much more significant crimes (concentration camps, secret prison-systems, extraordinary renditions and the systematic use of torture, et al.) Unlike the revolutionary anarchists of Spain, the neo-anarchists and other Leftists of today are also completely blind to the role that *religion* plays in the State's domination of this planet.

If neo-anarchists are against the war in Iraq, they shout "No blood for oil!" as if oil – the commodity, the oil companies, etc – account for all of Bush/Cheney's motivations for going to war. The idea that the war was fought to strengthen the American presidency to the point of totalitarianism completely escapes them. Note as well the neo-anarchists' complete lack of interest in finding out the truth about the various events that are cynically lumped together under the rubric of "September 11th." Like all Leftists, they are content to dismiss the 911 Truth Movement as "conspiracy theorists" and "wingnuts." Why? It speaks directly of the State and its secret/security services, which are beyond the narrow focus of commodity-obsessed former Marxists.

This is why we are so relentlessly hostile to people who are stupid enough to lump "Situationism" (and its slogans) in with Leftism and/or with the art world, whether it is with institutional art or street art. The Situationist International was one of the very few groups in the world that was anti-capitalist *and* anti-Communist. Despite what the contributors, editors and/or publishers involved in, say, *Realizing the Impossible: Art against Authority* (AK Press 2007), the situationist movement was *not* an "art movement." The situationists were – especially after 1962, and even more so during and after 1968 – a revolutionary organization that hated artists and Leftists as much as they hated capitalists and Stalinists.

Some practical observations

As we pushed and defended our right to critique the pseudo-Situationists, neo-anarchists and Leftists who either contributed to the *Realizing the Impossible* book, published it or agreed to be part of a panel that would discuss it – we confined our comments to a single thread on the website of the New York City Independent Media Center – something striking happened. *All* of the comments claimed 1) that the Situationist International was a marginal group, no longer worthy of attention, 2) that the events that are remembered and praised by situationists are also marginal and not worth any attention, and/or 3) that we personally are marginal and not worthy of any attention. And yet these people did *not* ignore this thread and move on to something else, as one would fully expect from the dismissive attitudes (and ridiculously ignorant opinions) that they expressed. Quite the contrary, they kept returning to it and posting what they claimed were "comments."

It is very significant that literally *none* of these "comments" – and there were several dozen of them in total – responded to or even acknowledged the existence of our "strategic critique" of neo-anarchism. Instead, there was a stream of increasingly virulent personal attacks on us. As if to prove Guy Debord right when he wrote the following in 1978 –

> Passions that are forced to remain faraway are generally malevolent. The contemporary spectator appears to perpetually watch for the fleeting occasion to make his opinion known on a great variety of things he knows nothing about, but in every case he only expresses his dominant emotions: omniform envy, ambition without means and pretension without illusion. Because these are the traits that massively

express a system of production that cannot dream of making consumers more successfully than it makes merchandise. This desperate mediocrity regularly hastens to say anything at all with authority, so as to resemble the authorities, who also say anything at all. This mediocrity systematically forgets the obvious, dogmatizes from the rumors that it has itself invented and blindly talks nonsense about its own falsifications.

— the maliciousness, bad faith and self-righteousness of these anonymous comments (which broke all the rules established by the Independent Media Center, if not the laws against *libel,* as well) were really quite spectacular. Though we had attacked ignorant neo-anarchists *in general,* not as individual people (we certainly did not mention any individual's name), we were attacked personally, and by name, by people who chose to remain anonymous. Such is the mindset of the neo-anarchists: push them too hard on the intellectual or theoretical levels, and they become truly vicious on the *personal* level. Their resemblance to Communists is striking.

It is *the way* that they throw mud that is truly significant: though they claim to be courageous and "moral" – and they are certainly very moralizing – they will not identify themselves, they will not speak in their own names, they will act like a gang of thugs. They believe they have "safety in numbers" and act as if their numbers are safe. We are convinced that *any* specific individual who dares to speak out against them will be attacked in this same fashion, though the content and tone of the calumnies might be different from, perhaps less gruesome than, the ones that have been hurled against us. "You are not constructive, you are negative, you undermine our solidarity, you give comfort to our enemies," etc. Raoul Vaneigem was right: it is *the individual as such* that is shameful to the neo-anarchists, Leftists and other "collectivists," even or especially those who speak of the rights of individuals. When an individual criticizes them, they try to shame that individual any way they can, so that the individual in question will feel humiliated and go away. And so attack the neo-anarchists, we say, but do not underestimate their intellectual dishonesty or taste personal vendetta.

11-15 April 2007
NOT BORED! #39, September 2007

Proposals for Revolutionizing the Advertising Industry

Except when it comes to selling its own services to potential clients, advertising is not the direct sale of products, services or other commodities. Advertising only encourages, induces or motivates potential consumers to buy certain commodities. And so the English word "advertising" is very similar to the French word *publicitaire,* that is to say, publicity: advertising *publicizes* the existence, availability and desirability of certain commodities; it informs *the public* of these facts.[1]

But in capitalist society, what *isn't* an inducement to buy and consume? To the extent that separation exists everywhere, everything is an inducement to partake of the "participation," "sense of belonging," "integration" and "community" promised (if not actually delivered) by the advertized commodity. And so "advertising" only designates a particular instance (the most obvious instance) of something that is practiced quite generally and by many different disciplines.

For the moment, let us stay with the narrow conception of advertising. But here, too, it is almost everywhere or, rather, in and on almost everything. Formerly restricted to posters, "ads" now appear in and on every medium of expression: newspapers and magazines; billboards and signs; radio and TV broadcasts; films and videos; the Internet in all of its forms; clothes and shoes; even bodies (tattoos). But this "invasion" of advertising into almost everything – undeniable and important though it is – doesn't tell us everything that we need to know. Today, all media (the various forms of one-way "communication") are created and exist to give the ads a place to do their work, and not the reverse. The media could easily exist without any programming or content (cf. MTV, which is nothing but commercials), but the media could not exist without ads (the costs are too high and there are no sources of sufficiently large funds). Advertising doesn't just invade: it occupies and takes control through a kind of economic censorship. If the programming gets out of line, the sponsors will walk out, thus causing the program itself to be canceled due to lack of funds.

But advertising itself is a commodity and it only exists to make sure that other commodities are purchased. Thus, advertising "works" in the service of the market, that is to say, in the service of an economic system that is based upon the production and consumption of commodities. What gets produced (and thus advertised and hopefully consumed) is not determined by the real needs of the ultimate consumers: it is determined by what will make a profit for the producers. Indeed, from the producers' point of view, it doesn't matter what gets produced, as long as it sells or, rather, as long as one of the producers' many products sells enough to make a profit. Strictly speaking, those products need not be consumable: they need only be purchased. How much of a profit is "enough"? At least enough to ensure that the producers – the system of production-for-profit – can continue to operate.

And so, advertising is basically conservative: it works to conserve the system that produces commodities for profit. But within this narrow confine, advertising must be and must remain persuasive (novel, interesting, entertaining, stimulating, etc. etc.). To be and remain persuasive, advertising must be creative, that is to say, it must constantly come up with new ideas. But, as everyone who has ever worked in the industry knows, advertising is only creative within the relatively narrow confines set for it by the clients, who not only have their own ideas (their history and their habits), but who measure everything against actual sales that are generated. And since purchases are made by consumers, advertising ultimately must follow their tastes and preferences. Advertising can occasionally push consumers, but it must be careful not to push too far nor generate a backlash. Thus, in addition to being conservative, advertising is literally reactionary: it persuades consumers by *reacting* to what they are doing or, rather, to what they have done in the very recent past. Furthermore, if advertising has invaded, occupied and exerted control over areas supposedly outside of its narrow field – entertainment, news and religion (thereby creating such new fields as infotainment, tabloid news and TV evangelism) – it has done so because those fields had already been evacuated or hollowed out by other forces (centralization, monopolization and/or corruption).

And yet, despite all this, advertising sees itself as "revolutionary," as some kind of leader or vanguard in the culture as a whole. Are not the ads the best part of TV? Aren't the new ads the best part of the Super Bowl? This is why the process of getting new business is so dispiriting: it's the moment when, forced to sell its own bullshit instead of someone else's, advertising is forced to realize the truth about itself. It isn't the best part of anything.

To be really revolutionary, advertising must cease to content itself with working upon representations of reality and the psychology or ideology of the consumer, and must start to work directly upon reality and the consumer's physical body. It must not only turn consumers *towards* certain commodities, but it must also turn consumers *away* from others. In short, advertising must model itself on the real revolutionaries in this society that forbids real revolution: the CIA, the military, the police, and the technocrats of genetic modification.

The CIA doesn't just kill people: it engages in several different types of propaganda ("white propaganda" spreads stories that are favorable to the CIA's clients, while "black propaganda" spreads stories that are unfavorable to rival clients). Experts in the field of *commercial propaganda,* advertising agencies should train and deploy their own hit squads, which will destabilize or even neutralize both rival ad agencies and the makers of rival commodities.

The military doesn't just kill people: it attempts to "shock and awe," to overwhelm its adversaries with such a massive and lethal first strike that they decide it would be best to surrender as quickly as possible. Experts in the field of *shocking consumers* (TV viewers, mostly) and filling them with awe concerning the incredible power of the commodity, ad agencies should train and deploy whole armies, which will attack and occupy the territories in which both rival agencies and the makers of rival commodities have their headquarters and/or get their recruits and raw materials.

Miscellaneous

The police do not simply arrest people who have committed criminal acts: they infiltrate non-violent organizations and provoke their members into committing violent actions; they plant weapons on people they have murdered and lie about both of these crimes; etc. Experts in the field of *lying and cynical self-justification*, ad agencies should train and deploy their own cops, who will provide legal cover for anything that supports the status quo in the name of subverting it.

The technocrats who genetically modify or clone foodstuffs, animals and (soon) human beings do not respond to consumer demand, nor do they subject their pure research to any oversight whatsoever: they do whatever their corporate sponsors pay them to do, even if it means "playing God." Experts in *extreme creativity*, ad agencies should also employ teams of genetic engineers, who will literally create human beings who will demand whatever they are programmed to demand.

No one in advertising should be troubled by these modest proposals. By imitating the pornographers ("sex sells") and terrorists ("disrupt the conventional way of thinking to come up with new ideas"), the industry has already taken its first steps towards its dark side. But these have been but baby steps along a road that will surely separate the men from the boys. Onwards!

[1] There are other meanings in play: "advertising" (*advertisen* or *avertir*) also suggests "to notify" and "to warn"; "to advert" (*advertere*) means "to turn towards," and is connected to "adverse," that is, *to turn away* from something that fails to promote one's interests or welfare.

NOT BORED! #40, May 2008

Embarrassing text about Guy Dauve is censored

Just a few hours after it was posted to http://libcom.org, an allegedly "libertarian communist" website, our translation of a text about Gilles Dauve's father, Guy Dauve, was removed; and, without warning or rational explanation, we ourselves were summarily banned for "pointless smearing and being a general obnoxious arsehole." LibCom is completely alone in their belief that the text we translated should be censored: Infoshop saw no problem with posting it; Anarchist News was OK with it, too. And that's because, in translation or in the original French, the text is a legitimate, significant and valuable piece of reporting. If LibCom rushed to suppress it, the problem lies with LibCom, and not with the text.

In the words of Ultra-151: "This text from Bill Brown is interesting as not just an exemplary tale of how spookdom works in practise & where it recruits its' functionaries from, but also in the comments, of the dubious integrity of the 'libertarian' community Libcom." And, in the words of Lawrence, a reader of Infoshop News, the fact "that LibCom banned BNB and disappeared this essay speaks poorly of the intellectual courage of the administrators of LibCom."

Note well that, now that the *messenger* has been killed, these alleged "libertarian communists" now feel themselves at liberty to discuss the *contents* of his message amongst themselves. In the awkward words of "jweidner," "Please keep the discussion to verified, legitimately sourced and preferably english information." Ah, yes: anything that is written in or translated from the language in which Dauve himself writes is not "preferable" because it cannot be "verified" or considered "legitimately sourced" by people who do not know French and must rely upon *translators* to read his writings! And so, when the French version of Wikipedia says, "*Ne en 1947, il est le fils de Guy Dauve (commissaire des Renseignements Generaux),*" while the English version says nothing at all about Guy Dauve, this can only mean . . . *what*? That the former is lying or engaging in a "smear" campaign? is the French Wikipedia, unlike its honorable English counterpart, engaging in what "jweidner" calls "vicious anti-Dauve hysteria and vitriol"? No, of course, not. But in the xenophobic (or at least Francophobic) world of these "libertarian communists," logic and rationality aren't in great supply. For example: Bone-stupid "Steven" can pass for smart among these befuddled people when he realizes that "It would be good if [Gilles Dauve] could just comment himself, because it can be difficult to tell exactly what someone means by their writing," especially when "their writing" is *only available to you in translation*!

In the aforementioned discussion, one encounters the following:

> "Steven," the site administrator who likes to pretend he is evenhanded and yet banned us without due cause from his electronic sandbox, concedes that "The role played by Dauve's father in allegedly helping break the communist movement in France during and after World War II is very interesting."
>
> "jweidner," the worst of the *ad hominen* attackers against the messenger himself, admits that "[Gilles Dauve] often seems a bit glib about taboo type stuff."
>
> "revol68" allows that "in a few of Dauve's texts I think he runs too far in his 'anti moralism' and I can see how it could possibly fit with, if not an actual apologism, perhaps a kind of dismissal of the issue [pedophilia] as being little more than a side concern of bourgeois morality. Likewise I think his comments about the Holocaust in 'Fascism and Anti Fascism' are too glib and don't address the specific mechanisms of the Holocaust that make it stand out from other genocides."
>
> "Jef Costello" declares that "I think that this [remark by Gilles Dauve] is extremely close to the defences of paedophilia which we are

all too accustomed to seeing within anarchist circles and given the nature of the writing it's hardly surprising that I gave up at around this point." Furthermore, "I'm not convinced that [Dauve's text] uses the example of the child in a very sensible or relevant way" and "On the whole I think the problem with this text is that it flirts with these ideas and uses them in what seems to me to [be] a cheap lunge for shock value. I pretty much agree with revol and jweidner on that."

Not content with just one thread to discuss the matter amongst themselves, these "libertarian communists" have created a second page in which to express themselves without undue distractions.

"Vlad336" concedes that "hardly anyone knows anything about [Gilles Dauve's] background," allows that "I suppose it wouldn't be too hard to actually check," and insists that "pro-paed bullshit was published in LB, undoubtedly with Dauve's permission" and that "the issue of Dauve's paed apologism is real enough to merit some discussion."

Someone who hides behind the moniker "treeofjudas" was able to discover, all by himself, that "Pierre Guillaume, owner of the Old Mole, who was, in fact, a supporter of gas chamber negationists, at least according to this Zionist Holocaust-botherer text I've got."

A "Felix Frost" is smart enough to realize that "Dauve's connections with Guillaume and other ultra-leftists turned negationists are the main reason for these attacks against him."

"Jef Costello" realizes – too late, alas! – that "Some person started making mental claims about Dauve's Dad and Holocaust denial but in doing so brought to light an actual proper issue with Dauve's nonce apologism."

On-line notice dated 25 December 2009

Subsequent developments

27 December 2009

During the night, the privilege of being a member of the LibCom "community" was restored to us. But members of the general public, or even other members of this "community," would be hard pressed to find the bland announcement of this restoration, because it – "*admin: BNBs temporary ban has ended*" – was buried, if not hidden, at the bottom of a post by someone named "lumpnboy" (not within a proper post by the LibCom administrators) and posted to the thread concerning Guy Dauve's dodgy text "The X-Filers" (not in a new thread, nor in either of the two discussions threads that were started in response to our comments about Dauve, nor in an older, long-forgotten thread that various members of the LibCom community resuscitated with the sole intent of ridiculing our work and insulting us). These injuries were certainly made worse by the preposterous notion that the ban upon us was "temporary." This ban was *illegitimate* from the start, and so any attempt to distinguish it from a "permanent" ban cannot be taken seriously.

We note with disgust that this restoration of our privileges, like our banning, was delivered without any explanations or apologies. The manner in which we were privately informed of this restoration was just as insulting, inadequate and cowardly: a simple email from a robot indicating that "Your account at libcom.org has been activated," as if we'd just created this account, and had not been in possession of it for almost an entire year.

What are we supposed to do with such access? And access to a website that is both administrated and for the most part visited by cowards, Francophobes, arrogant know-nothings, bullies, and character assassins? We know full well the type of trap that has been set for us. If we attempt to answer any or all of the dozens of ridiculous comments, calumnies or complaints that have been made about us during our "temporary" absence from the LibCom "community," we will be quickly re-convicted of being an "obnoxious arsehole" and, once again without any warning or rational explanation, we will be "permanently" banned.

But these, of course, are minor matters compared with LibCom's unconscionable removal of our translation of Didier Daeninckx's text about Guy Dauve, which is still censored. This remains unacceptable, and is the worst possible indictment of these "libertarian communists" that we could imagine. Of course, we will never again participate in LibCom, and we will continue to publicize their scandalous behavior, even if apologies are made and this censored text is restored.

30 December 2009

The responses to this "affair" from people who speak French fluently are beginning to come in. Dimitri from Hors-d'Oeuvre (Montreal) says:

> As for the polemic with libcom.org, we do not have sufficient information to follow the affair and take a position upon it. Nevertheless, after reading [what you've written], the censorship appears to be idiotic and counter-productive, and this is why we support the initiatives that you have undertaken so as to denounce the managers of that site. (29 Dec 09, our translation)

Afanasius Jerry from AAARGH (L'Association des Anciens Amateurs de Recits de Guerre et d'Holocaustes) says (30 Dec 09, in English):

> BILL "NOTBORED" and Daeninkxxx are tow big unctuous heaps of shit.
> Please circulate.
>
> aaa

It would appear that "tow" is a typo, and that "two" was the intended word.

6-7 January 2010

Another discussion of this affair has begun at a blog called Anti-German Translation, which has also added a wealth of information on the subject.

25 June 2010

Even though it is now *six months later*, these "libertarian communists" at LibCom have found it necessary to create a third discussion thread concerning their censorship of the translated text about Guy Dauve (still in force) and their decision to "temporarily ban" me.

21 July 2010

I take some comfort in the fact that some people who contribute to LibCom, whether as a result of my efforts or not (it doesn't matter), are beginning to ask good questions about Gilles Dauve.

26 July 2010

Inevitably – it only took seven months – someone who posts to LibCom (a fellow named Peter) has managed to say a few truthful and germane words about Gilles Dauve: "His father was definitely a cop and not just an ordinary plod on the beat but one involved in surveillance/repression of the left. Hence Dauve's use of a pseudonym in his early writings." Fortunately for Peter, he has not been banned ("temporarily" or "permanently") by any of LibCom's misadministrators, nor has he been subjected to any personal attacks, calumnies, etc. from the peanut gallery.

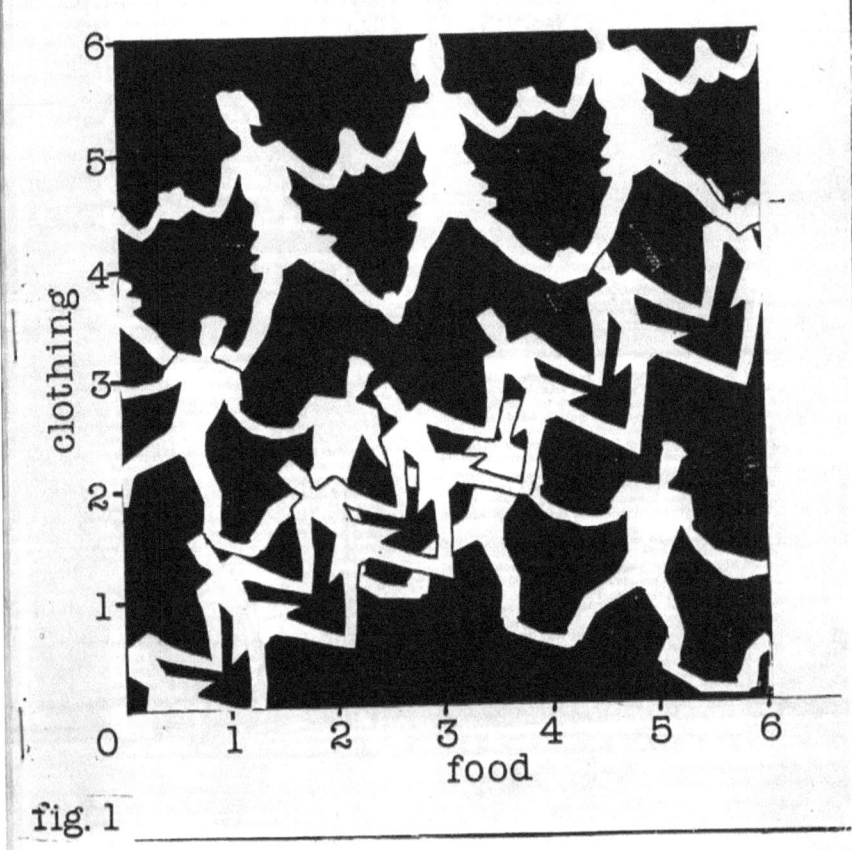

Collaboration with Ellen McCarthy
Cover, *NOT BORED!* #1, July 1983.

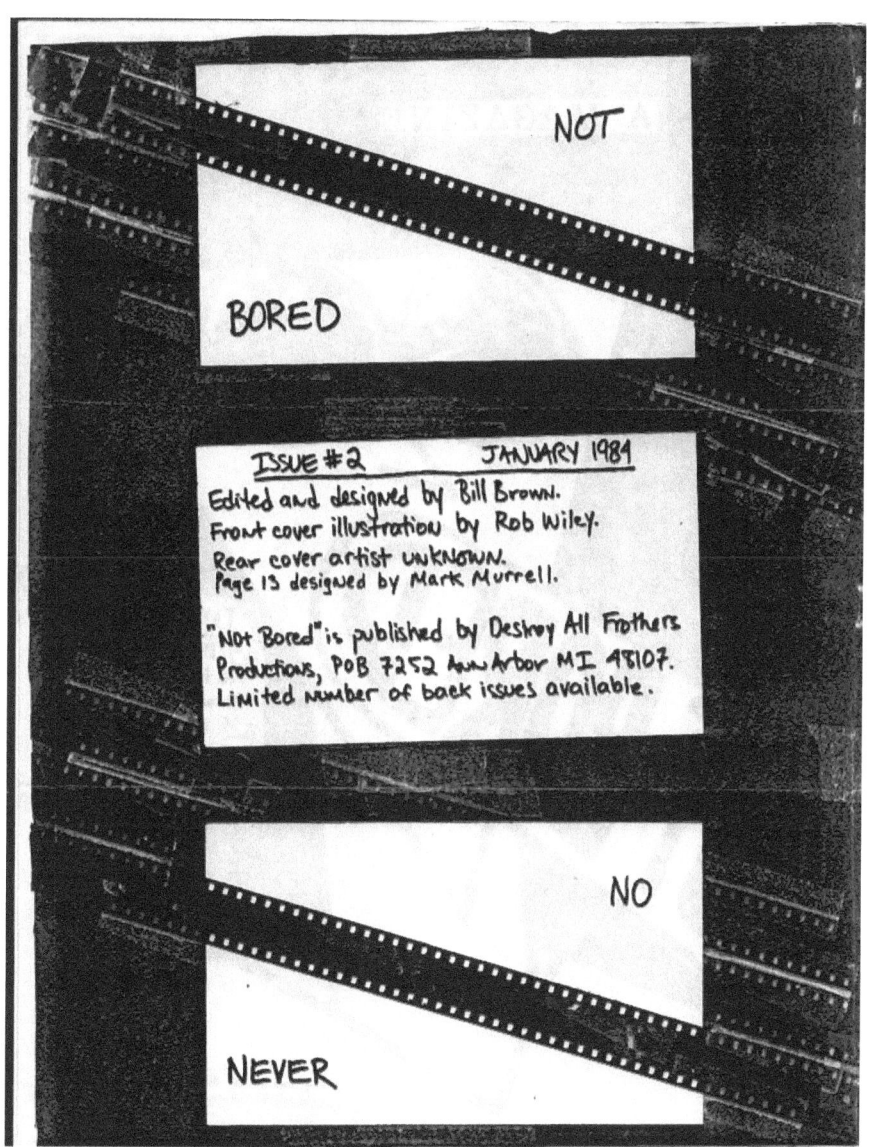

NOT BORED! #2, January 1984.

Text paraphrased from Deleuze & Guattari
Cover, *NOT BORED!* #11, January 1987.

things have advanced this far. It, namely the "methods and goals" of those tactical moves, are a solution to the problem posed to the enemies of class society by the process of endo-colonialization, which makes it seem that the class system (rigorously restricted to the model of int*e*rnational imperialism) is being abolished, even though it is actually qualitatively intensifying it in the form of an intr*a*national imperialism, i.e. the spectacle. The tactical move of "The Graffiti Scandal" had and could still be having the effect of negating the difference or differance between the "e" in "international" and the "a" in "intranational," provided that we understand the "national" to be both a text (what is inscribed on the walls) and a social institution (what the walls form part of).

And yet the methods and goals of those tactical moves create (another) problem, for me, the writer and publisher of the "What's Happening?" section, in particular. Without jeopardizing my job (graduate student) it is impossible for me to keep up with the accelerating pace of the "scandal." Actions need to be taken that I---not <u>can</u> <u>not</u>, but---<u>will</u> <u>not</u> take. Since these actions are the very stuff of the section that dominates the rest of <u>NOT BORED!</u>, my decision not to pull the rope any tighter affects the status of the magazine itself. This does not mean that I'll <u>never</u> undertake these or any other actions; thus is <u>NOT BORED!</u> suspended, <u>up</u> <u>there</u>, hanging by a thread of autiobiography. Cut it down, if you must, but be prepared to paste it to a paper bag that you will wear over your head to parties. All tomorrow's parties.

Photo originally for weekly column in *Ann Arbor News*
(not used)
NOT BORED! Appendix to #13, Vol. I, January 1988.

I'm not really sure why I keep publishing this magazine that I call *NOT BORED!* Nobody that I care about reads it: ----- doesn't read it, or at least doesn't respond to it anymore; ------ doesn't read it, even though she used to contribute to it, and ----- doesn't read it, even though she is the closest person in the world to me. Some people do, of course, read it, but I'm not sure that it makes any difference to most of them. And so it is to a handful of people, scattered across America, to whom I address myself in this issue. Please respond: I've reached a stage in my life at which I'm confused, more so than ever, and

Back cover, *NOT BORED!* Appendix to #13, Vol. II, May 1988.

Badge says, "Sheriff of Hong Kong"
Small print says, "The Anslinger is the registered trademarked feature of the Federal Bureau of Narcotics. Copyright 1930."
NOT BORED! #14, February 1989.

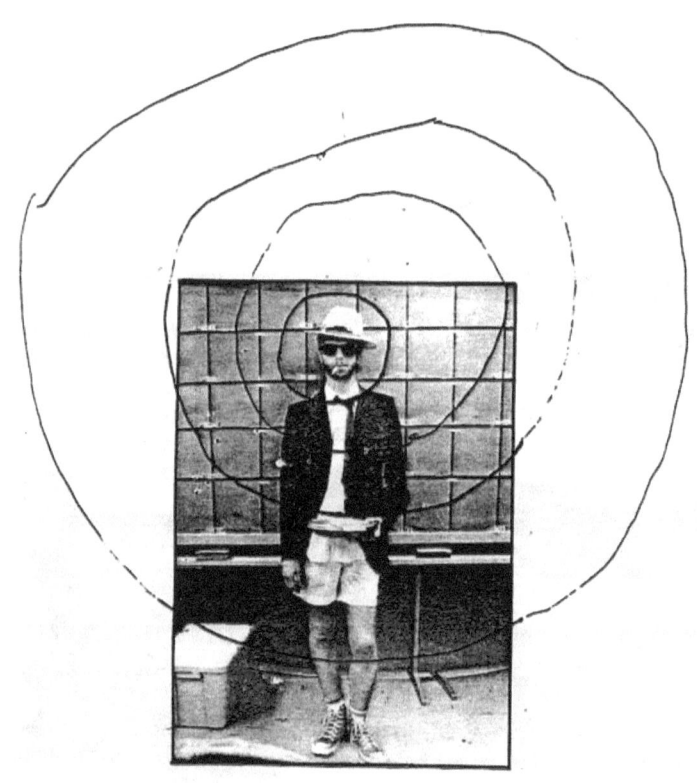

Backlash against the editor-in-chief of *Reach*
NOT BORED! #15, April 1989.

NOT BORED! #16, December 1989.

Cover, *NOT BORED!* #17, July 1990.

```
live evil devil lived
live evil lived devil
lived devil evil live
lived evil devil live
devil lived evil live
devil live lived evil
lived live devil evil
devil evil lived live
live lived devil evil
evil lived devil live
evil devil lived live
live devil lived evil
lived live evil devil
lived evil live devil
devil evil live lived
devil live evil lived

devil live evil lived
devil evil live lived
lived evil live devil
lived live evil devil
live devil lived evil
evil devil lived live
evil lived devil live
live lived devil evil
evil devil live lived
live lived evil devil
live devil evil lived
evil live devil lived
evil lived live devil
evil live lived devil
lived devil live evil
devil lived live evil
```

NOT BORED! #23, January 1995.

Unpublished, circa 1998.

Alice B. Toklas and Gertrude Stein, 1944
NOT BORED! #31, June 1999.

Prisoners in S. Korea celebrate democracy
Cover, *NOT BORED!* #33, September 2001.

Prisoners in S. Korea celebrate democracy
Back cover, *NOT BORED!* #33, September 2001.

First, the original was altered . . .
NOT BORED! #35, July 2003.

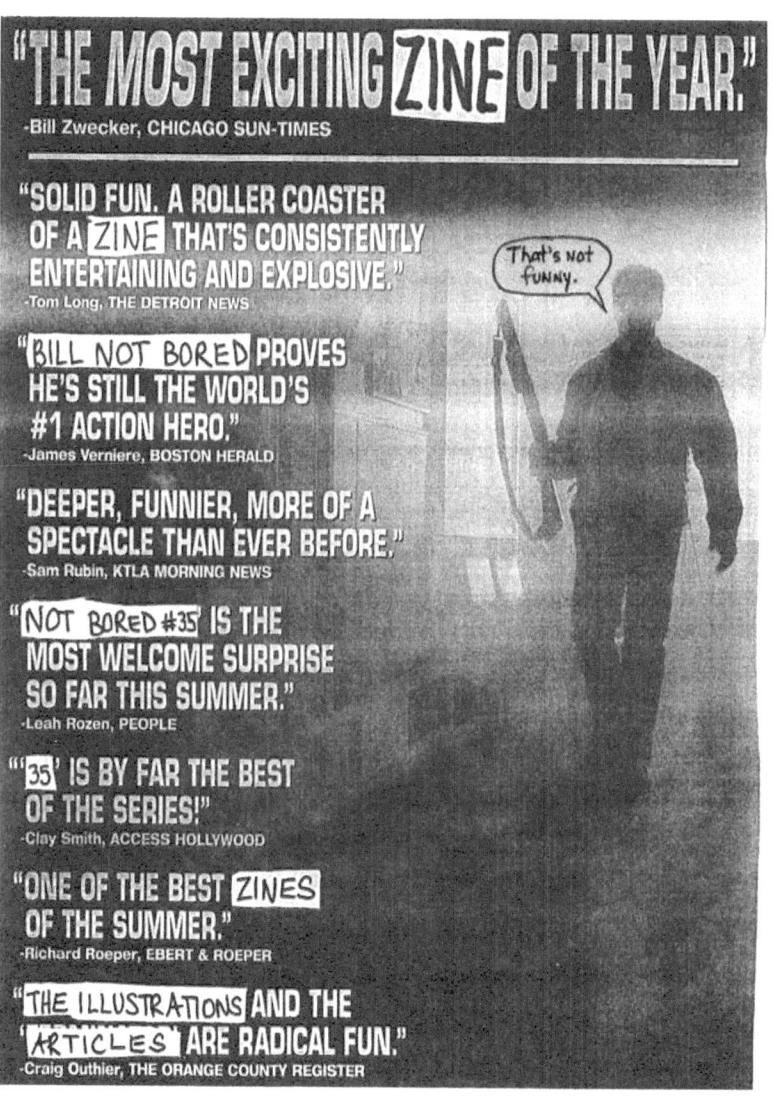

... then, the altered version was photocopied
NOT BORED! #35, July 2003.

WHEN THE RULE OF LAW BECOMES THE LAW OF RULES

Original caption says, "GOTCHA! Police nab the clueless perp, who picked one of the most heavily patrolled areas in town to break the law."
NOT BORED! #36, July 2004.

NOT BORED! #36, July 2004.

POSTCARDS FROM HELL

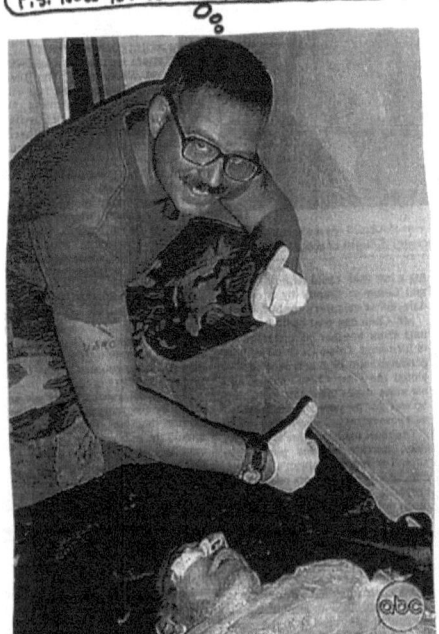

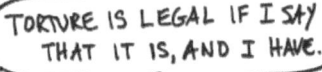

NOT BORED! #36, July 2004.

Index

Agamben, Giorgio, 165, 447-450, 456, 465, 477, 509, 535-536, 539-542
Advertising, 184-185, 575-578
Anarchism, 6, 148-149, 170-171, 259, 344-348, 403-406, 414, 443, 561-570
Ann Arbor, Michigan, iii, iv, 1
Antliff, Alan, 403-406
Artaud, Antonin, 548
At Dusk, 136-140, 147, 153
Attali, Jacques, 296-304, 357
Autonomedia, 70, 78n, 268
Bangs, Lester, i, 406-408, 492, 498, 526, 527, 529
Barthes, Roland, i, 199 , 254, 366, 548
Bataille, Georges, 174, 195, 222-225, 297, 354-355, 397-402, 477
Baudet, Jean-Pierre, vi, 199, 208-209, 491
Baudrillard, Jean, 177, 301, 398, 456, 489
Black, Bob, 74-80, 100-101, 114-119
Blanchard, Daniel, 156-157, 255-256
Bowie, David, i, ii, 500-502, 523, 526
Bracken, Len, 100-101, 261-263, 274-280
Brethren of the Free Spirit, 225-228, 234-238
Buffalo, New York, iii, 4-27, 83-89
Burroughs, William, 28, 136, 330, 347, 406, 407, 423, 431, 495, 522, 527
Bush, George H., 411
Bush, George W., 106, 112, 410-411, 444-450, 515, 573
Cage, John, 302, 429, 511, 512
Camatte, Jacques, 245-247
Canjuers, Pierre, 156-157, 255-256
Castoriadis, Cornelius, 156, 248-258, 304-312, 336, 363-374, 399, 554
Cincinnati, Ohio, vi, vii, 114-119
Clark, T.J., 102-113, 133, 150, 216, 219-225, 259, 262, 329-363, 368, 372
Clausewitz, Carl von, 166, 169, 170, 171, 172, 179, 197-201
Cobain, Kurt, 408-409, 520, 532-545
Cohn, Norman, 98-99, 235, 312-318
Cure, the, 506, 528-529
Curtis, David Ames, vi, 251, 252, 305, 308, 363
Cutler, Chris, 230-235
Dauve, Guy, 578-582
Debord, Alice, 70-71, 91-93, 197, 208, 211-215, 489-491
Debord, Guy, iii, vi, 70-7380, 83, 83-95, 100-101, 102-113, 121-122, 128, 131-133, 134, 138-140, 141-142, 147-148, 150, 155-160, 160-168, 172-186, 191, 193, 195, 197-201, 201-206, 206-210, 211-215, 216, 220-221, 229, 240, 248-258, 261-

583

263, 274-275, 278, 283-284, 281-296, 299, 315-316, 319-329, 330, 357, 363-374, 393-397, 398, 400, 418-420, 426-427, 431, 433-436, 443, 444-445, 450, 452-453, 456, 471-472, 477, 489-491, 546, 547, 550, 551, 552, 570-572, 574-575
Deleuze, Gilles, 22, 203, 205, 323, 336, 352, 384, 423, 456, 477, 485-486, 488
Devo, 522, 523, 530
Dufrene, Francois, 397
Dylan, Bob, 92, 407, 414, 418-424, 430, 492, 497, 508
Feederz, the, 79, 122, 127-131, 141
Ferm, Elizabeth Bryne, 437-443
Foster, Hal, 108-113
Foucault, Michel, 167, 177, 366, 398, 448, 456, 460, 477, 489, 570-572
Freemasonry, 99, 549-550
Freud, Sigmund, 22, 102, 246, 335, 350-355
Galloway, Alex, 199, 200, 201-206
Gang of Four, 60, 141, 502-505, 513-517, 546
Ginsberg, Allen, 423
Grain elevators, vi, 44, 45-46, 221n
Gray, Christopher, 133, 150, 153, 216, 461
Giuliani, Rudolph, 34-35, 51, 52, 559-560
Guillaume, Pierre, 155-160, 252, 365
Guattari, Felix, 22, 132, 323, 485-486
Heatwave, 133-136
Hampton, Howard, 225-226
Hitler, Adolph, 63, 315, 363, 380, 385, 392, 399
Home, Stewart, 95-99, 490
Israel, 199-201, 392, 473-488
Jappe, Anselm, 112, 171-172, 372, 373-374
Jorn, Asger, 161, 167, 285-286, 337-339
Kaczinski, Theodore (see Unabomber, the)
Knabb, Ken, 74, 92, 100, 137, 138, 163-164, 166, 195, 208, 209, 216, 258-261, 433-434, 461-464
Korda, Chris, 245
Labadie Collection, vii, 118-119
Led Zeppelin, 529-531
Lefebvre, Henri, 101, 110-111, 123, 128, 144, 159-160, 216, 228-233, 254, 256, 258, 262, 263, 286, 289-290, 293-294, 295, 301, 318-329, 334, 336, 400, 443, 451-461, 477, 479-480, 548, 549, 551, 552
Marcus, Greil, i, iii, iv, 95-99, 101, 221, 225-228, 235, 262, 264-265, 312-313, 407, 408-409, 418-424, 490, 491-499, 505, 516-517, 528, 530, 533-534, 541, 546, 549
Martos, Jean-Francois, vi, 165, 166, 167, 169, 208-209, 212
Marx, Karl, 65, 107, 112, 123-124, 129, 139, 166, 170, 171, 180, 315-316, 320, 367-371, 377, 414, 452-453, 548

Maximum Rock'N'Roll, 120-131
McDonough, Thomas, 111, 145, 258-261, 286-287, 433-436, 489
McLaren, Malcolm, 264, 265, 505
Mekons, the, 548
Mension, Jean-Michel, 393-395
Money, 340-344, 361
Morrison, Van, 491-499
MTV, 1, 500, 576
Nader, Ralph, 44,
Nairn, Tom, 266-274
Negri, Antonio, 132, 191-192, 205, 561-570
Neo-anarchists, 164, 194, 573-575
New York City, v, vi, 28-43, 43-47, 47-48, 50-53, 53-57, 70-71, 81, 89, 491-492, 557-561
New York Psychogeographical Association, vi, 49, 53-57, 58-69, 560
Nicholson-Smith, Donald, 106, 112, 113, 133, 150, 165, 167-168, 195, 202, 203, 209, 216, 219, 259, 262, 319, 322, 414
Nietzsche, Frederick, 319, 323
Nike, 28, 521-522, 555
Noriega, Manuel, 187, 505-506
Obama, Barack, 413n, 534, 545n
O'Connor, Sinead, 507-509
Ondine, 2
Os Mutantes, 517-521
Palestine, 473-488
Perelman, Michael, 374-381
Picasso, Pablo, i, 355-363
Presley, Elvis, ii, 230, 414, 420, 421, 422, 534
Processed World, 74-80, 115
Providence, Rhode Island, v
Purple, Adam, 561
Pynchon, Thomas, 382-393
Quattrocchi, Angelo, 266-274
Radcliffe, Charles, 133-136, 150
Reclaim the Streets, 67
Reed, lou, 522, 525-527
Reich, Wilhelm, 414
Reid, Jamie, 153, 264-266, 461
Retort, 102-113, 164
Riesel, Rene, 171, 250, 262, 268
Rodman, Dennis, 244-247
Rolling Stones, the, ii, 302-303, 414, 420, 493, 506, 522
Rumney, Ralph, 395-397

Sadler, Simon, 281-296
Sanborn, Keith, 80-83, 83-95, 142, 209
Sanguinetti, Gianfranco, 74, 83-95, 105-113, 165, 167, 204-205, 274-280, 299-304, 328, 432, 563
Seattle, 554-557, 573
Semiotext(e), 78, 209, 275-276, 489-491
September 11th, 104-113, 164-165, 189-190, 411, 446, 448, 557-561, 567, 574
Sex Pistols, the, iii, iv, 120, 126, 141, 153, 185, 264-266, 407, 420, 502, 505, 511, 544
Shell, Marc, 196, 227-228, 235
Situationist International, iii, iv, 74, 79-80, 80-83, 95-99, 102-113, 120-218, 219-221, 235, 248-258, 258-261, 261, 264, 266-274, 274, 281-296, 298-299, 304, 311, 312-313, 319, 333, 364-367, 393-397, 399-400, 414, 418-419, 427, 433-436, 452-453, 461-464, 469-470, 489-491, 504-505, 562, 574
Smith, Adam, 375-381
Socialisme ou Barbarie (see Castoriadis, Cornelius)
Spanish Revolution, 1, 346, 414, 573
Spencer, Wayne, 215-218
Squatting, 28-43
Surveillance Camera Players, vi, 572n
Taibo, Paco Ignacio, 414-418
Townshend, Peter, 521-525, 527
Thompson, E.P., 510-513
Unabomber, the, 46, 238-244
Unabomber for President, 43-47, 245
United Auto Workers, 553-554
Vaneigem, Raoul, iii, 80, 111, 122, 142, 147, 153, 160, 161-162, 164-165, 167, 168, 195, 196, 216, 219-220, 234-238, 249-251, 262, 286, 292, 313, 315, 365, 434, 440, 460, 464-472, 546, 548, 552, 575
Vienet, Rene, 80-83, 93-95, 113, 147, 262, 367, 434
Virilio, Paul, 111, 410-413, 424-431, 431-433, 455, 456
Warhol, Andy, 2, 428
Wark, McKenzie, 165, 206, 489-491
Weishaupt, Adam, 550, 551
Weizman, Eyal, 200, 473-488
Williamsburg, Brooklyn, vi, 53-57, 58-69
Wolfe, Tom, i, ii
Wolman, Gil, 80-83, 101, 262, 397
Workers' councils, 146, 156, 181-182, 192, 216, 248-258, 304, 364, 366
World Trade Center, 47, 108, 189-190, 557-561
World Trade Organization, 554-557
Yuppies Go Home, vi, 59-69
Zerzan, John, 72-73

Bill Brown is also the author of *We Know You Are Watching: Surveillance Camera Players, 1996-2006* (Factory School Books, 2006), *American Colossus: the Grain Elevator, 1843-1943* (Colossal Books, 2009) and *You Should've Heard Just What I Seen: Collected Newspaper Articles 1981-1984* (Colossal Books, 2010). Photo 2010 by Karen Fogarty.

www.ingramcontent.com/pod-product-compliance
Lightning Source LLC
Chambersburg PA
CBHW030327240426
43661CB00052B/1556